Lecture Notes in Computer Science 10869

Commenced Publication in 1973
Founding and Former Series Editors:
Gerhard Goos, Juris Hartmanis, and Jan van Leeuwen

More information about this series at http://www.springer.com/series/7407

María del Mar Gallardo · Pedro Merino (Eds.)

Model Checking Software

25th International Symposium, SPIN 2018
Malaga, Spain, June 20–22, 2018
Proceedings

 Springer

Editors
María del Mar Gallardo
University of Málaga
Málaga
Spain

Pedro Merino
University of Málaga
Málaga
Spain

ISSN 0302-9743   ISSN 1611-3349   (electronic)
Lecture Notes in Computer Science
ISBN 978-3-319-94110-3   ISBN 978-3-319-94111-0   (eBook)
https://doi.org/10.1007/978-3-319-94111-0

Library of Congress Control Number: 2018947326

LNCS Sublibrary: SL1 – Theoretical Computer Science and General Issues

Printed on acid-free paper

This Springer imprint is published by the registered company Springer International Publishing AG
part of Springer Nature
The registered company address is: Gewerbestrasse 11, 6330 Cham, Switzerland

Preface

This volume contains the proceedings of the 25th International Symposium on Model Checking Software, SPIN 2018, held in Málaga, Spain, June 20–22, 2018. SPIN is a well-recognized periodic event started in 1995 around the model checking tool SPIN. Since 1995, the event has evolved and has been consolidated as a reference symposium in the area of formal methods related to model checking. The previous edition of the SPIN symposium took place in Santa Barbara (USA) with a record number of submissions and participants.

The SPIN 2018 edition requested regular papers, short papers, and tool demos in the following areas: formal verification techniques for automated analysis of software; formal analysis for modeling languages, such as UML/state charts; formal specification languages, temporal logic, design-by-contract; model checking, automated theorem proving, including SAT and SMT; verifying compilers; abstraction and symbolic execution techniques; static analysis and abstract interpretation; combination of verification techniques; modular and compositional verification techniques; verification of timed and probabilistic systems; automated testing using advanced analysis techniques; combination of static and dynamic analyses; derivation of specifications, test cases, or other useful material via formal analysis; case studies of interesting systems or with interesting results; engineering and implementation of software verification and analysis tools; benchmark and comparative studies for formal verification and analysis tools; formal methods education and training; and insightful surveys or historical accounts on topics of relevance to the symposium.

The symposium attracted 28 submissions, although two of them were rejected by the chairs because they were not within the scope of the symposium. Each of the remaining submissions was carefully reviewed by three Program Committee (PC) members. The selection process included further online discussion open to all PC members. Only the papers with positive global score were considered for acceptance. In addition, within these papers, only those with no objections from the PC members were accepted. As a result, 16 papers were selected for presentation at the symposium and publication in Springer's proceedings. The program consisted of 14 regular papers, one short paper, and a demo-tool paper.

In addition to the accepted papers, the symposium included one invited tutorial by Irina Mariuca Asavoae and Markus Roggenbach entitled "Software Model Checking for Mobile Security, Collusion Detection in K," and three invited talks: "Efficient Runtime Verification of First-Order Temporal Properties" by Klaus Havelund and Doron Peled, "Applying Formal Methods to Advanced Embedded Controllers" by Rémi Delmas, and "Program Verification with Separation Logic" by Radu Iosif.

We would like to thank all the authors that submitted papers, the Steering Committee, the PC, the additional reviewers, the invited speakers, the participants, and the local organizers for making SPIN 2018 a successful event. We also thank all the sponsors that provided logistics and financial support to make the symposium possible.

May 2018

María del Mar Gallardo
Pedro Merino

Organization

Steering Committee

Dragan Bosnacki (Chair)	Eindhoven University of Technology, The Netherlands
Susanne Graf	Verimag, France
Gerard Holzmann	Nimble Research, USA
Stefan Leue	University of Konstanz, Germany
Neha Rungta	Amazon Web Services, USA
Jaco Van de Pol	University of Twente, The Netherlands
Willem Visser	Stellenbosch University, South Africa

Program Committee

María Alpuente	Technical University of Valencia, Spain
Irina Mariuca Asavoae	Inria, France
Dragan Bosnacki	Eindhoven University of Technology, The Netherlands
Rance Cleaveland	University of Maryland, USA
Stefan Edelkamp	King's College London, UK
Hakan Erdogmus	Carnegie Mellon, USA
María del Mar Gallardo (Chair)	University of Málaga, Spain
Stefania Gnesi	CNR, Italy
Patrice Godefroid	Microsoft Research, USA
Klaus Havelund	NASA/Caltech Jet Propulsion Laboratory, USA
Gerard Holzmann	Nimble Research, USA
Radu Iosif	Verimag, France
Frédéric Lang	Inria, France
Kim Larsen	Aalborg University, Denmark
Stefan Leue	University of Konstanz, Germany
Alberto Lluch Lafuente	Technical University of Denmark, Denmark
Pedro Merino (Chair)	University of Málaga, Spain
Alice Miller	University of Glasgow, UK
Corina Pasareanu	CMU/NASA Ames, USA
Charles Pecheur	Université catholique de Louvain, Belgium
Doron Peled	Bar-Ilan University, Israel
Neha Rungta	Amazon Web Services, USA
Antti Valmari	University of Jyvskyl, Finland
Jaco Van de Pol	University of Twente, The Netherlands
Willem Visser	Stellenbosch University, South Africa
Farn Wang	National Taiwan University, Taiwan

Additional Reviewers

Peter Aldous
Mihail Asavoae
Giovanni Bacci
Georgiana Caltais
Laura Carnevali
Alessandro Fantechi
Grigory Fedyukovich
Martin Koelbl
Florian Lorber
Eric Mercer
Marco Muniz
Julia Sapiña
Andrea Vandin

Organizing Committee

Carlos Canal	University of Málaga, Spain
María del Mar Gallardo	University of Málaga, Spain
Pedro Merino	University of Málaga, Spain
Laura Panizo	University of Málaga, Spain

Sponsors

UNIVERSIDAD DE MÁLAGA

E.T.S. INGENIERÍA
INFORMÁTICA

ANR

Swansea
University
Prifysgol
Abertawe

ONERA
THE FRENCH AEROSPACE LAB

GISUM

MORSE

Abstracts of Invited Papers

Software Model Checking for Mobile Security – Collusion Detection in $\mathbb{K}$

Irina Măriuca Asăvoae[1], Hoang Nga Nguyen[2],
and Markus Roggenbach[1]

[1] Swansea University, UK
{I.M.Asavoae,M.Roggenbach}@swansea.ac.uk
[2] Coventry University, UK
Hoang.Nguyen@coventry.ac.uk

Abstract. Mobile devices pose a particular security risk because they hold personal details and have capabilities potentially exploitable for eavesdropping. The Android operating system is designed with a number of built-in security features such as application sandboxing and permission-based access control. Unfortunately, these restrictions can be bypassed, without the user noticing, by colluding apps whose combined permissions allow them to carry out attacks that neither app is able to execute by itself. In this paper, we develop a software model-checking approach within the $\mathbb{K}$-framework that is capable to detect collusion. This involves giving an abstract, formal semantics to Android applications and proving that the applied abstraction principles lead to a finite state space.

Efficient Runtime Verification of First-Order Temporal Properties

Klaus Havelund[1] and Doron Peled[2]

[1] Jet Propulsion Laboratory, California Institute of Technology, USA
[2] Department of Computer Science, Bar Ilan University, Israel

Abstract. Runtime verification allows monitoring the execution of a system against a temporal property, raising an alarm if the property is violated. In this paper we present a theory and system for runtime verification of a first-order past time linear temporal logic. The first-order nature of the logic allows a monitor to reason about events with data elements. While runtime verification of propositional temporal logic requires only a fixed amount of memory, the first-order variant has to deal with a number of data values potentially growing unbounded in the length of the execution trace. This requires special compactness considerations in order to allow checking very long executions. In previous work we presented an efficient use of BDDs for such first-order runtime verification, implemented in the tool DEJAVU. We first summarize this previous work. Subsequently, we look at the new problem of dynamically identifying when data observed in the past are no longer needed, allowing to reclaim the data elements used to represent them. We also study the problem of adding relations over data values. Finally, we present parts of the implementation, including a new concept of user defined property macros.

The research performed by the first author was carried out at Jet Propulsion Laboratory, California Institute of Technology, under a contract with the National Aeronautics and Space Administration. The research performed by the second author was partially funded by Israeli Science Foundation grant 2239/15: "Runtime Measuring and Checking of Cyber Physical Systems".

A Sample of Formal Verification Research for Embedded Control Software at ONERA

Rémi Delmas, Thomas Loquen, and Pierre Roux

ONERA Centre de Toulouse, 2 av. Édouard Belin, 31055 Toulouse, France
{Rémi Delmas,Thomas Loquen,Pierre Roux}@onera.fr

Abstract. This talk presents a sample of research work conducted by the French Aerospace Lab (ONERA) on tailoring and applying formal methods to advanced embedded controllers, at various phases of the development and verification process, illustrated by industrial projects and collaborations. A first line of work[1], carried out in partnership with Airbus, Dassault and LAAS-CNRS, aims at going beyond simulation for validating advanced hybrid control laws, by leveraging bounded reachability analysis and robustness analysis from the early design phases. This requires to bridge the representation gap existing between hybrid dataflow formalisms used to model control laws (e.g. Simulink, Scade-Hybrid,...), and the automata-based formalisms used by most hybrid model-checkers (e.g. SpaceEx, Flow*, dReach,...) and robustness analysis frameworks. We discuss the steps taken to handle the complexity and size of typical industrial models. A second line of work[1], carried out jointly with academic lab LRI (Paris-Sud, INRIA) and technology provider OcamlPro, addresses the sound combination of SMT-solvers and potentially unsound convex optimization engines to allow proving complex polynomial invariants on advanced control laws implementations. Such implementations are usually obtained by automatic time-discretization and code generation from a hybrid dataflow model. The proposed approach shows a notable performance improvement on controllers of interest with respect to earlier approaches based on interval arithmetic or purely symbolic methods such as cylindrical algebraic decomposition or virtual substitutions. Last, we present research conducted[2] in partnership with Liebherr Aerospace Toulouse and technology provider Systerel on leveraging model-checking techniques for unit-level test case generation for an air management system, taking into account the industrial setting and qualification constraints, following DO-178C and D0-333 guidelines.

Keywords: Hybrid dataflow models · Hybrid automata · Reachability analysis · SMT solvers · Convex optimization · SAT solvers · Test case generation

---

[1] with funding from the French Civil Aviation Authority (DGAC) through the SEFA-IKKY program.

[2] with funding from the CIFRE program of the National Technological Research Agency (ANRT) and the RAPID program of the French Government Defense Procurement and Technology Agency (DGA) (project SATRUCT).

Program Verification with Separation Logic

Radu Iosif

CNRS/VERIMAG/Université Grenoble Alpes, Grenoble, France
Radu.Iosif@univ-grenoble-alpes.fr

Abstract. Separation Logic is a framework for the development of modular program analyses for sequential, inter-procedural and concurrent programs. The first part of the paper introduces Separation Logic first from a historical, then from a program verification perspective. Because program verification eventually boils down to deciding logical queries such as the validity of verification conditions, the second part is dedicated to a survey of decision procedures for Separation Logic, that stem from either SMT, proof theory or automata theory. Incidentally we address issues related to decidability and computational complexity of such problems, in order to expose certain sources of intractability.

Contents

Tutorial and Invited Papers

Software Model Checking for Mobile Security – Collusion Detection in $\mathbb{K}$

Irina Mǎriuca Asǎvoae[1], Hoang Nga Nguyen[2], and Markus Roggenbach[1(✉)]

[1] Swansea University, Swansea, UK
{I.M.Asavoae,M.Roggenbach}@swansea.ac.uk
[2] Coventry University, Coventry, UK
Hoang.Nguyen@coventry.ac.uk

Abstract. Mobile devices pose a particular security risk because they hold personal details and have capabilities potentially exploitable for eavesdropping. The Android operating system is designed with a number of built-in security features such as application sandboxing and permission-based access control. Unfortunately, these restrictions can be bypassed, without the user noticing, by colluding apps whose combined permissions allow them to carry out attacks that neither app is able to execute by itself. In this paper, we develop a software model-checking approach within the $\mathbb{K}$ framework that is capable to detect collusion. This involves giving an abstract, formal semantics to Android applications and proving that the applied abstraction principles lead to a finite state space.

Keywords: Mobile-security · Android · Model-checking · $\mathbb{K}$-framework

1 Introduction

Mobile devices, such as smartphones and tablets are pervasive in modern everyday life. The number of smartphones in use is predicted to grow from 2.6 billion in 2016 to 6.1 billion in 2020 [24]. One reason for this fast adoption is the extensive ecosystem of apps which enable a wide range of functions. Consequently, smartphones hold a great deal of personal information (e.g., photos, financial data, credentials, messages, location history, health data) making them appealing targets for criminals who often employ malicious apps to steal sensitive information [23], extort users [20], or misuse the device services for their own purposes [29].

The Android operating system is designed with a number of built-in security features such as application sandboxing and permission-based access control. Unfortunately, these restrictions can be bypassed, without the user noticing, by colluding apps whose combined permissions allow them to carry out attacks that neither app is able to execute by itself. The possibility of app collusion was first described by Schlegel et al. in 2011 [34]. In 2016, Blasco et al. were the first to report on a discovery of collusion in the wild [11,12].

© Springer International Publishing AG, part of Springer Nature 2018
M. M. Gallardo and P. Merino (Eds.): SPIN 2018, LNCS 10869, pp. 3–25, 2018.
https://doi.org/10.1007/978-3-319-94111-0_1

Attackers have a better chance of evading detection in both pre-deployment and after-deployment scenarios by using app collusion where the malicious activity is split across multiple apps and coordinated through inter-app communications. This kind of attack is possible because sandboxed systems, such as Android, are designed to prevent threats from individual apps. However, they do not restrict or monitor inter-app communications, and therefore they would fail to protect from multiple apps cooperating in order to achieve a malicious goal. Most malware analysis systems, such as antivirus software for smartphones, also check apps individually only.

Within the ACID project[1], we have investigated the phenomenon of collusion with different approaches, including static analysis, machine learning, and software model-checking [5]. It soon became clear that an effective collusion-discovery tool must include methods to isolate potential sets which require further examination. Here, we developed two different filtering methods: a rule based one [11], and one based on machine learning [19]. These filters, however, developed for a first, fast screening, report many false positives. In this paper, we report on a means for further investigation of sets identified by these filters. Objectives included (1) to reduce the number of false positives and (2) to provide evidence of collusion. In particular the second objective was important. Professional malware systems such as the one from our industrial partner McAfee are under permanent scrutiny: they are in constant legal battle to prove their claims that certain software is actually malware.

To perform such program reasoning, we could choose between methods like model checking, static analysis and dynamic analysis: all of these can be used to find program bugs, however are complementary in the way they handle the program(s) under investigation and the properties to verify. On the one hand, model checking and static analysis work with abstract models, without executing the program, while dynamic analysis directly executes the original program. In this sense, dynamic analysis discovers only real bugs, whereas both model checking and static analysis are sensitive to false bug reports. On the other hand, model checking and static analysis are more general techniques than dynamic analysis (which handles one path at a time) as they use abstract program models to (potentially) represent all the program executions. Model checking and static analysis mitigate precision and computation time using different strategies to handle abstractions. Model checking computes the run-time states of the program and could use, for example, local abstractions to verify its properties. Static analysis works on abstract programs which approximate the original program behaviors (i.e., using convenient abstract domains and abstract semantics). In general, model checking is more precise than static analysis, while being the more expensive approach.

In this paper, we use the $\mathbb{K}$ framework [33] to give an abstract semantics to Android applications and demonstrate for the subset of non-recursive Android programs that our abstraction works and can effectively distinguish between

---

[1] http://acidproject.org.uk.

collusion/non-collusion using a model-checking approach. Our discussion of collusion and model checking for collusion builds upon our prior publications [5,7,8].

Related Work. As detecting malware in single apps is well developed, it suggests itself to tackle collusion by merging apps into a single one [22]. There are also dynamic approaches. For instance, TrustDroid [14] classifies apps into logical domains (w.r.t. their data). Later, at run-time, any app communication between different domains is forbidden. In contrast, we analyse sets of apps by exhaustively unfolding their executions while looking for colluding patterns.

Static approaches to detecting collusion are closest to our work. The tool Epicc [28] reduces the collusion detection to an interprocedural data-flow environment problem that connects *sources* to *sinks* (e.g., sensitive data reads and message passing) but does not address app communication. The app communication pattern is analysed by a subsequent tool, IC3 [26], which employs a multi-valued constant propagation solver to produce an accurate string analysis for Intent evaluation (an intent is a special Android data structure that can be shared between different apps). The FUSE tool [30] integrates state-of-the-art pointer analysis of individual apps into building a multi-app information flow graph on which collusion can be detected. The tool FlowDroid [4] uses taint analysis to find connections between source and sink. The app inter-component communication pattern is subsequently analysed using a composite constant propagation technique [27]. We propose a similar approach, namely to track (sensitive) information flow and to detect app communication, but using model checking that gives a witness trace in case of collusion detection. From the proof effort perspective, we mention CompCert [21] that uses the Coq theorem prover to validate a C compiler.

The $\mathbb{K}$ framework was proposed in [33] as a formalism to facilitate the design and analysis of programming languages. A number of languages have already been defined in $\mathbb{K}$, including C [18] and Java [13], facilitating their program analysis. We contribute to the pool of $\mathbb{K}$-defined real languages by giving formal semantics to Android byte code. The $\mathbb{K}$ framework facilitates program analysis and verification from two angles: (1) using a Maude back-end [16] to access the existing infrastructure of the Maude system [15] and (2) building specialized tools over formal language definitions, e.g., a deductive verifier, which is generic in the language definition, based on matching logic [32]. Security properties in the $\mathbb{K}$ framework are explored by K-taint [3] with taint analysis. We use the Maude back-end for model checking the $\mathbb{K}$ specification of Android apps. To avoid the scalability issues of model checking, we specify in $\mathbb{K}$ an abstract semantics for Android apps and employ $\mathbb{K}$ to perform *abstract model checking* on Android apps for collusion.

2   Android Application and Smali

Android applications are packaged in *apk* files. Each consists of resources (e.g., image and sound files), binary code in *dex* files and a manifest (named *Android-Manifest.xml*) for essential information. The binary code is machine-readable and can be executed by Dalvik Virtual Machine (DVM) prior to Android 5.0 or Android Runtime (ART) since Android 4.4. They can be converted into human-readable format, *Smali*, by disassemblers such as *baksmali*. Note, that Smali code has a different semantics than Java bytecode, as Smali is executed on a register based machine, while Java bytecode operates on a stack based architecture. For the rest of this paper, we shall refer to the binary code as Smali code. Smali, similar to Java, is an Object-Oriented Programming (OOP) language. Here, we assume Smali programs to be correctly typed, as they are in general produced by a compiler rather than written manually.

The Smali code of an Android application consists of a set of classes. Essentially, each class is defined as a collection of fields and methods. A field is a variable defined by a name, a type and optionally an initial value. A method is a sequence of *bytecodes*, which will be referred to as Smali instructions hereinafter. Fields and methods can either be static or not. Static fields and methods belong to the class. In other words, all instances of the class share the same copy. Conversely, each instance has a distinct copy of non-static fields and methods.

Fields are identified by names and types. Types in Smali code are either primitive and reference. Primitive types are: V (void, only for return types), Z (boolean), B (byte), S (short), C (char), I (int, 32-bit), J (long, 64-bit), F (float, 32-bit) and D (double, 64-bit). References types are classes and arrays. Class types start with "L" while array types with "[". For example, the class *java.lang.Object* is written in Smali code as "Ljava/lang/Object"; an one-dimensional array of 32-bit integers as "[I".

Methods are identified by names, parameter types and a return type. In contrast to Java, methods in Smali are register-based. Each method is associated with a number of registers which also serve as temporal variables when executed. The number of registers is declared first in the method body by a directive .register n or .local n where n is an integer. If the former is used, then the method has n registers in total; otherwise, it has $n + m$ where m is the number of parameters. If a method has n registers, they are named $v0, \ldots, v(n - 1)$. If it has m parameters ($m \leq n$), the last m registers, i.e. $v(n - m), \ldots, v(n - 1)$, can also be referred to as $p0, \ldots, p(m - 1)$. When calling a method, values of its parameters are copied into these last registers. The method body is a sequence of Smali instructions. They can be grouped into four categories: *invoke-return* for calling and ending methods; *control* for un/conditional jumps; *read-write* for accessing/modifying values stored in registers and memory (fields of instances); and *arithmetic* for arithmetic calculation. Further detail of these instructions can be found on [2]. Android comes with a Platform API which provides a set of predefined classes. Calls to API [1] can be made by invoke instructions. For example, to broadcast an intent (an abstract data structure holding descriptions, usually, of actions to be performed; hence, it can be used to exchange data between applications), an application invokes the API method *sendBroadCast(Intent)* defined in the class *Context*.

The potential entry points of an Android Application are defined by classes inheriting from the following ones: *Activity*, *Service*, *BroadcastReceiver* and

ContentProvider from Android API. To become actual entry points, they must be explicitly declared in the manifest so that they can be instantiated and executed by either DVM or ART. Once instantiated, they are called App components. An activity component is an entry point that provides an interface between the application and users. For example, when a user clicks on the application icon, an activity component corresponding to the declaration in the manifest will be activated. A service component is an entry point to execute the application in the background. A broadcast receiver component is for processing events that are broadcast system-wide. Finally, a content provider component of an application serves requests for accessing and modifying its data from the applications it belongs to as well as other applications.

3   Collusion

ISO 27005 defines a threat as "A potential cause of an incident, that may result in harm of systems and organisations." For mobile devices, the range of such threats includes [35]:

- Information theft: without user consent information is sent outside the device boundaries;
- Money theft: e.g., when – without user consent – an app makes money through sensitive API calls (e.g. SMS); and
- Service or resource misuse: for example – without user consent – a device is remotely controlled.

The Android OS runs apps in sandboxes, trying to keep them separate from each other. However, at the same time Android provides communication channels between apps. These can be documented ones (overt channels), or undocumented ones (covert channels). An example of an overt channel would be a broadcast intent; an example of a covert channel would be volume manipulation (the volume is readable by all apps) in order to pass a message in a special code.

Broadly speaking, app collusion is when, in performing a threat, several apps are working together, i.e., they exchange information which they could not obtain on their own. Technically, we consider a threat to be a sequence of actions. Here, actions are operations provided by the Android API (such as record audio, access file, write file, send data, etc.).

Definition 1 (Collusion). *A threat is realised by collusion if it is distributed over several apps, i.e., there is a set S consisting of at least two apps such that:*

- *each app in S contributes to the execution of at least one action of the threat,*
- *and each app in S communicates with at least one other app in S.*

Example 1 (Information theft collusion). This can be illustrated with a contact app (having no Internet access) that reads the contacts database, passes the data to a weather app (having no access to the contact database), which then sends the data outside the device boundaries. For stealth purposes, the communication between the apps is performed without any visibility to the user, e.g., through a broadcast intent. Such examples can easily be realised, see, e.g., the B.Sc. dissertation by Dicker [17].

Example 2 (App Collaboration). A similar situation to Example 1 is given by a picture app (having no Internet access), the user chooses a picture to be sent via email, the picture is passed over an overt Android channel to an email app, the email app (having no access to the picture database) sends the picture outside the device boundaries. For user-friendliness, the communication between the apps is performed without visibility to the user, e.g., through a shared file. This would be considered as collaboration, and not as collusion.

These two examples show that the distinction between collusion and collaboration actually lies in the notion of intention. The pattern in the sequence of actions is the same: one app reads information that Android protects with a permission, this information is passed to a different app, which then sends it outside the device boundaries (note that sending information off the device requires a permission in Android). In the case of the weather app, one can argue that the intent is malicious (as one might expect a weather app to have no need to deal with contact data in the first place); in the case of sending the email, one would expect the intent to be documented and visible to the user.

In this paper, we aim to analyse sequences of actions for patterns, thus leave out of our definition all aspects relating to psychology, sociology, documentation etc. Consequently, we speak about collusion potential.

For the rest of the paper, we will focus on the threat of information theft only. In this context, it is useful to introduce the concept of 'secret information'. Here, we take the pragmatic view that a secret is any information that Android protects with a permission.

Definition 2 (Collusion potential for information theft). *A set consisting of at least two apps has collusion potential for information theft, if*

- *there is an app reading a secret,*
- *there is communication among the apps on this secret such that*
- *another app sends data on this secret outside the device boundaries.*

An app set with collusion potential would then require further, possibly manual analysis, involving taking into account further information such as the distribution methods, documentation, transparency to the user, in order to distinguish between collusion and collaboration. The possible automation of such analysis with the help of machine learning techniques is discussed in [6].

4   K Framework

The $\mathbb{K}$ framework [31,33] proposes a methodology for the design and analysis of programming languages; the framework comes with a rewriting-based specification language and tool support for parsing, interpreting, model-checking and deductive formal verification. The $\mathbb{K}$ framework adheres to the principle that programming languages ought to have a formal syntax and semantics definition; and that all their execution and verification tools should be derived from a single, formal definition of this language. Consequently, the ideal work-flow in the $\mathbb{K}$ framework starts with a formal and executable language syntax and semantics, given as a $\mathbb{K}$ specification, which then is tested on program examples in order to gain confidence in the language definition. Here, the $\mathbb{K}$ framework proposes model checking, via its compilation into Maude programs (i.e., using the existing reachability tool and LTL Maude model checker) or deductive verification using the matching logic prover - a first-order logic for reasoning with patterns and pattern matching on program structures.

A $\mathbb{K}$ specification consists of *configurations*, *computations*, and *rules*, using a specialised notation to write semantic entities, i.e., $\mathbb{K}$-cells. For example, the $\mathbb{K}$-cell representing the set of program variables as a mapping from identifiers *Id* to values *Val* is given by $\langle Id \mapsto Val \rangle_{\mathsf{vars}}$. In the case of Android apps in their Smali format, the program states essentially consist of the instructions of the current method, method registers mapped to values, and the methods' call-stack. The configurations in $\mathbb{K}$ are labeled and nested $\mathbb{K}$-cells, used to represent the program state structure. In other words, a programming language configuration is the set of all semantic entities which are necessary to represent the program states.

The rules in $\mathbb{K}$ are of two types: computational and structural. Computational rules represent transitions in a program execution and are specified as configuration updates. Structural rules provide internal changes of the program state such that the configuration form can enable the application of computational rules. The computations in $\mathbb{K}$ are configuration updates based on the $\mathbb{K}$ rules; hence a computation represents an execution of the $\mathbb{K}$ specification. Figure 1 depicts all the executions of a $\mathbb{K}$ specification, i.e., its associated transition system. Note that inside the blue boxes we have various forms of the program configuration (cfg[pgm]), potentially transformed by the blue arrows depicting structural rules. The red arrows represent transitions between two boxes, which are achieved by the computational rules applied on the normal forms, e.g., $t_1 \ldots t_n$, of the configuration in the box of origin. For example, the computational rule may be regarded as triggering the execution of an instruction while the structural rules prepare the configuration for the execution of the next instruction. More specifically, a computational rule triggers the execution of an instruction that adds the values of two registers/variables and deposits the result into a third one while a structural rule computes the addition of the two

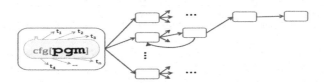

Fig. 1. Transition system produced by a $\mathbb{K}$ specification. (Color figure online)

values. In the rest of the paper we present the configuration, computations, and rules related to our Android $\mathbb{K}$ specification.

5   Concrete Semantics

In this Section, we sketch a first model, a 'concrete semantics', of Android in $\mathbb{K}$. Based upon this concrete semantics, we will then, in Sects. 6 and 7, develop our abstract semantics, which will be suitable for model checking for security.

5.1   Instrumentation Principles

In order to enable the concrete semantics to discover information theft, we apply a number of instrumentation principles:

Instrumentation Principle 1
We mark registers and objects by a Boolean flag that indicates if they are holding sensitive information.

Instrumentation Principle 2
We keep track of the names of those apps which contribute to the generation of the data held in a register or in an object.

For selected instructions, Examples 8 and 9 in Sect. 6 will demonstrate of how we realise these principles.

The Instrumentation Principles 1 and 2 allow us to discover collusion potential for information theft in an easy way. Whenever data is sent outside the device boundaries, we check if this data

- is sensitive and
- was produced with help from an app with a name different from the name of the app which is sending the data;

whenever both of these conditions are true, we have discovered an execution of several apps which leads to potential information theft.

In order to enable the concrete semantics to provide counter example traces leading to information theft, we apply a further instrumentation principles:

Instrumentation Principle 3
For each app, keep track of the instructions that have been carried out.

Section 8 will present an example of such a trace.

5.2 Configurations

Applying the above three instrumentation principles, we capture Android concrete configurations using the cell mechanism of $\mathbb{K}$ as depicted in Fig. 2 in the $\mathbb{K}$ typical notation.

Each configuration contains a number of sandbox cells – one cell for each app belonging to a set of apps which one suspects of collusion. Each sandbox specifies the state of one app. It has a number of sub-cells: appname (string), activities (a list of *activity* class names declared in the manifest) and memory. Additionally, it also hosts zero or more class and thread cells.

A class cell specifies a class by the following sub-cells: classname, super (the name of the super class), interfaces (a list of interfaces that this class implements), fields (a list of fields optionally with initialised values) and zero or more method cells. Each method models a method of the class by three more sub-cells:

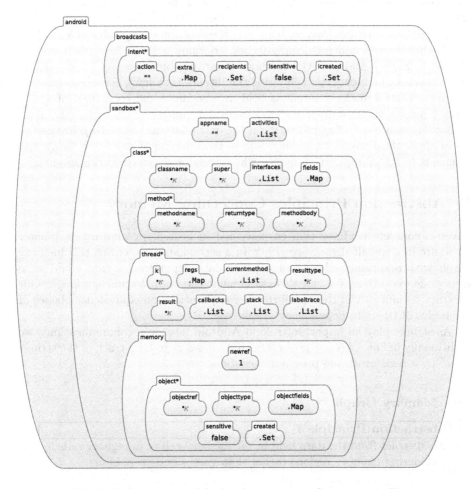

Fig. 2. Cell structure of Android concrete configurations in $\mathbb{K}$.

methodname (the signature of the method including name and parameter types), returntype and methodbody (list of instructions of the method).

A thread cell models a currently running thread by the following sub-cells: k (the remaining instructions to be executed), regs (content of registers), currentmethod (the complete instructions of the method that is currently executed in this thread; i.e., the instructions in k are a suffix of this instructions), result (holding the return value of a method running within this thread), callbacks (a queue of callback function to be called within this thread), stack (for saving the context of currently pending methods), and labeltrace (a record of which labels have been passed during the running of this thread, implementing Instrumentation Principle 3). The regs cell maps registers to a values.

A memory cell contains class objects that have been instantiated so far. It has an auxiliary cell, newref, to hold the reference for an object to be created next, and a number of object cells. Each contains five sub-cells: objectref, objecttype (its class name), objectfields (mapping from non-static fields to their values), sensitive (to indicate if any value stored in objectfields is sensitive) and created (a set of application names that contribute to the creation of any value objectfields).

Furthermore, a concrete configuration contains a single broadcasts cell. It is used to model Android API methods regarding broadcasting intents across applications. The broadcasts cell holds the intents that have been broadcast by the apps. Each broadcast intent is held in a separate cell comprised of action (action name), extra (a mapping from extra data names (strings) to extra data (strings)), isensitive (a flag indicating if the extra data are sensitive), icreated (a set of application names who contribute to the creation of any extra data), and recipients (a set of application names who have already received this intent).

6 Abstraction Principles Concerning Memory

Given a concrete configuration as described in Sect. 5, we capture its pointer structure in a so-called *memory graph*. In a second step, we enrich this memory graph with additional edges that capture data dependencies that could arise from code execution. We call this enrichment the *data dependency graph*. Our abstract semantics will then perform its computations on equivalence classes of the nodes of the data dependency graph.

As strings play an important role in Android inter app communications, we additionally define a *history projection* that allows us to keep track of the strings 'seen' by a register during program execution.

6.1 Memory Graph

Abstraction Principle 1
We abstract from the data held in the memory cell or in register cells by considering memory regions rather than values and/or pointers.

Definition 3 (Memory graph, memory region). *Given the memory cell and all thread cells that belong to one sandbox S of a concrete configuration represented in $\mathbb{K}$, we define its* memory graph *to be the directed graph $G_S = (V, E)$, where*

- *the set of nodes V comprises of*
  - *all object references to be found in the* **memory** *cell, and of*
  - *all registers in the* **regs** *cell, the* **result** *cell, and all registers of the methods in the* **stack** *cell from each of the* **thread** *cells; and where*
- *there is an edge from a node v to a node w*
  - *if v is a register and w is an object reference with $v = (w, \_\_, \_\_, \_\_)$, i.e., register cell v points to the object with reference w, or*
  - *if v and w are both object references, and the object cell whose cell* **objectref** *is v has a cell* **objectfields** *with $\langle \dots, \dots \mapsto w, \dots \rangle$*objectfields*, i.e., the object with reference v contains an object field that points to the object with reference w.*

A memory region *is a connected component in the un-directed graph underlying the memory graph.*

Memory regions form a partition of the set of nodes of the memory graph. Note that our definition of a memory region provides an over-approximation of the actual pointer structure, as we are ignoring the direction of the edges.

```
method onChange (Secret)
registers 3
code
1:    if-eqz r3,
2:    const-string r1, "GPS"
3:    iput r1, r3, myF
4:    const-string r1, "steal"
5:    invoke {r3} getInfoSecret
6:    move-result r2
7:    invoke {r1, r2} sendBroadcast
8:    branch
9:    return-void
endmethod
```

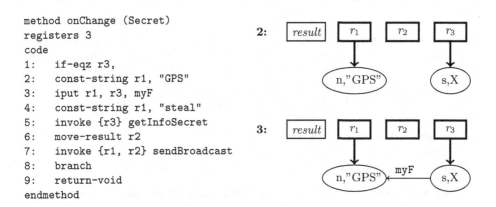

Fig. 3. A sample program in Smali and some of its memory graphs.

Example 3. Consider the Smali method **onChange** in Fig. 3. The same Figure shows possible memory graphs concerning it. There is one *result* cell in the thread that executes it. The method has three registers r_1, r_2, and r_3. After executing line 1 and 2 of the code, register r_1 contains a pointer to a string object containing the string "GPS" and register r_3 contains a pointer to an object containing a secret "X", i.e., we have four memory regions, where we can choose, e.g., *result*, r_1, r_2, and r_3 as representatives. In the graph, we depict the sensitivity of data with "n" for non-sensitive and "s" for sensitive. Execution of line 3 leads to an edge from the object on the right to the object on the left, as myF is set to point to this object (iput assigns to the field myF in the object referenced in register r3 the reference found in register r1), i.e., we have now three memory regions, where we can choose, e.g., *result*, r_1, and r_2 as representatives.

6.2 Data Dependency Graph

Abstraction Principle 2
We abstract from computations by considering data dependencies rather than concrete values.

In order to undertake a further abstraction, for each instruction we perform a *data dependency* analysis among the arguments and result involved. We illustrate such an analysis first on the example of arithmetic binary operators *binop* in Smali, these include, e.g., the commands add, sub, mul.

Example 4 (Data dependency analysis of "binop r_1, r_2, r_3"). The meaning of these instructions is given by $r_1 := r_2 \, binop \, r_3$. After a *binop* instruction, the value of register r_1 depends on the values of the registers r_2 and r_3.

A slightly more involved situation is given when we move the result of a method call, which in Smali is stored in the special result register, into a normal register r.

Example 5 (Data dependency analysis of "move-result r"). The meaning of this instruction is given by $r := result$. After a *move-result* instruction, the value of register r depends on the values in the registers of the last method invocation. Assuming that this call was $invoke\{r_1, r_2, ..., r_n\}m$ for an unimplemented method m, the value of r depends on the values of the registers $r_1, r_2, ..., r_n$ – i.e., we make a worst case assumption in order to be on the 'safe' side. The term 'unimplemented' means that we have no representation of this method in our $\mathbb{K}$ framework for Android. This can happen, e.g., when an app calls a method from a library for which we decide to leave it our from our analysis.

Definition 4 (Data dependency graph, data dependency region). *A data dependency graph is a memory graph enriched by data dependency edges. A data dependency region is a connected component in the un-directed graph underlying the data dependency graph.*

Data dependency regions form a partition of the set of nodes of the data dependency graph. Like in the definition of memory regions, in our definition of data dependency regions we over-approximate the actual information. For instance, in the case of the method invocation, we make a worst case assumption. Another reason of over-approximation is that, again, when forming the equivalence classes we ignore the direction of the edges.

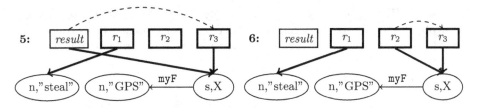

Fig. 4. Some data dependency graphs for the program in Fig. 3.

Example 6. Continuing Example 5, we consider some data dependency graphs for the Smali program of Fig. 3. After invoking the method `getInfoSecret` in line 5, the *result* cell depends on register r_3 – indicated by the dashed arrow. On the implementation level, we realise such dependencies as edges in the memory graph, thus, the edge from *result* to the object that is referenced by r_3. I.e., we have three data dependency regions, where we can choose, e.g., *result*, r_1, and r_2 as representatives. After moving the result into register r_2, r_2 inherits the data dependency of the *result* cell and the *result* cell is cleared of all data dependencies, i.e., we have three data dependency regions, where we can choose, e.g., *result*, r_1 and r_2 as representatives.

6.3 History Projection

Projection Principle
We enrich data dependency regions by a set of strings in order to keep track of 'values of interest'.

We add a history projection component to the data dependency regions so that we can detect Android communication channels for intents. For example, when sending the broadcast intent in the method `OnChange`, see Fig. 3, the communication channel carries the name "steal", given through the string object to which register r_1 points – see the data dependency graph after executing line 6 in Fig. 4. An app that wants to receive this information, needs to 'listen' on broadcast channel "steal", i.e., in collusion analysis we need to have these strings available in order to see which senders and receivers match. For space reasons, we simplified the parameters of the broadcast method invocation in line 7.

Definition 5 (History projection). *We annotate each data dependency region of a data dependency graph with a set of strings, which we call the* history projection *of this region.*

The history projection of a region adds further information and thus makes the two previous abstractions finer grained. Like with data dependencies, each Smali instruction needs to be analysed in order to obtain the rules for history projection. The guiding principle is that the history projection collects all strings that have 'appeared' in the history of a region.

Example 7 (History projection of "const-string r, s"). This instruction creates a new object containing the string s, and lets register r point to this object. In the data dependency graph, this instruction creates a new region consisting of the register r and the string object only. We annotate this region with the one element set $\{s\}$ as its history projection.

We use the values collected in the history projection to perform an over-approximation of app communication. In our example program in Fig. 3, we say that the broadcast intent can use any of the strings that register r_1 has in its history projection. We treat receiving a broadcast in a similar way. I.e., we form the intersection between the history projections of the registers involved: if the intersection is empty, the apps do not communicate, otherwise they do. For better results, one could utilize a composite constant propagation technique as discussed in, e.g., [27].

6.4   Sample Instructions in Abstract Semantics

With the two above abstraction principles, history projection, and the first two instrumentation principles of sensitivity updates and app-name updates as discussed in Sect. 5 on concrete semantics, we can give an abstract semantics in $\mathbb{K}$ for nearly all Smali instructions. However, instructions that deal with the control flow that enable loops and recursive procedure calls, will require the application of further abstraction principles – see Sect. 7, which discusses loops.

Here, we give two concrete semantic rules. Registers in the abstract semantics hold enriched data dependency regions *ddr*, i.e., a symbolic name of the region, a boolean flag *sen* which is true if the region might contain sensitive information, a history projection h, and a set *apps* containing the names of applications that might have influenced the region.

Example 8 (Abstract semantics of of "binop A, B, C"). Let $(ddr_x, h_x, sen_x, apps_x)$ be the contents of registers x, $x \in \{A, B, C\}$ before execution of *binop*. Execution of *binop* creates a new region name *new* and updates all three registers A, B and C to the same values, namely to

- $ddr'_x = new$,
- $h'_x = h_B \cup h_C$,
- $sen'_x = sen_B \vee sen_C$, and
- $apps'_x = apps_B \cup apps_C$

for $x \in \{A, B, C\}$, i.e., *binop* creates a new region subsuming the regions to which the operands B and C were belonging. The new region considers again a worst case scenario by taking the union of the history projects and the app sets, and the logical or for sensitivity. Furthermore, all registers belonging to regions ddr_B and ddr_C need to be updated to the new region.

Note that the instruction $invoke\{r_1, r_2, ..., r_n\}m$ in the abstract semantics behaves in a similar manner to Example 8, namely, the result cell is treated similarly to register A, while the method parameters $r_1, r_2, ..., r_n$ are treated in a similar way to registers B and C.

Example 9 (Abstract semantics of "move-result r"). Assume that this instruction is executed by an app with name n. Let $(ddr_{res}, h_{res}, sen_{res}, apps_{res})$ be the contents of the result cell before execution of *move-result*. Execution of *move-result* updates the result cell and register r as follows:

$$- ddr'_{res} = .K$$

- $ddr'_r = ddr_{res}$
- $h'_r = h_{res}$,
- $sen'_r = sen_{res}$, and
- $apps'_r = apps_{res}$;

i.e., the result cell is marked as empty with the special value $.K$ and register r simply holds all values that were held before in the result cell.

6.5   A Theoretical Result on These Abstractions

We conclude by giving an upper bound to the abstract state space:

Theorem 1 (Abstract state space). *When applying these two abstractions as well as instrumentation for sensitivity and app names, the upper bound for the size of the abstract state space is double exponential in the number of registers of methods either active or on the stacks in the thread cells.*

Proof (Sketch): History projection picks up constants from the program during execution, there are only finitely many constants in the program. Sensitivity is a Boolean value. The data dependency graph forms a partition of the finitely many available registers. There are double exponentially many partitions possible.

Note that the abstract state space grows and shrinks during the execution of an app, depending on how many threads it has, the number of active registers, and the size of the stacks in these threads.

7   Selected Abstraction Principles Concerning Execution

In this Section we focus on guiding abstract execution by model checking principles. In $\mathbb{K}$ we use the search engine, which exhaustively executes the semantics until it either reaches a colluding state or all executions were unfolded without a collusion found. However, during the process of unfolding all possible executions of the semantics, the search engine does not use any model checking techniques. Hence, we have to insert model checking principles into the abstract semantics that, in the context of a finite state space, make program executions finite.

We apply these abstraction principles when defining the abstract semantics of backward jumps, in the case of loops, and method invocation, in the case of recursive calls. Here we present the case of backward jumps only. To recursive calls, one can apply similar principles through utilising a call stack.

```
method onReceive (Context, Intent)
registers 3
code
1:    invoke {r3} getExtras
2:    move-result r1
3:    whileloop
4:    if-eqz r1, exitloop
5:    iget r3, r2, next
6:    iget r2, r1, next
7:    iget r1, r3, next
8:    jump whileloop
9:    exitloop
10: invoke {r3} publish
11: return void
endmethod
```

Fig. 5. A Smali method with a while loop.

Example 10 (Execution of loops). Consider the onReceive method shown in Fig. 5. The method onReceive is activated whenever a message fitting the Intent parameter of the method arrives in the system. The onReceive method extracts the details of the received message (by invocation of the getExtras API method in line 1) and deposits these details in the local register r1. Lines 3–8 describe a loop, where line 3 is the label whileloop marking the beginning of the loop. Line 4 contains the loop condition, i.e., when the register r1 contains the null reference, the loop execution stops and the computation continues from the exitloop label in line 9. The loop body passes information in a round-robin from r2 to r3 (in line 5), from r1 to r2 (in line 6), and r3 to r1 (in line 7). Note that we assume that the information passed is available via the field next of the objects referenced by the registers r1, r2, r3. Finally, in line 10 the information referenced by the register r3 is sent outside the device via the invocation of the publish method.

Figure 6 depicts the data dependency graphs of some of its executions and a representation of the broadcast cell. The condition in line 4 of onReceive can evaluate either to true or false: in case it is false, we enter the loop, i.e., we continue execution in line 5; in case it is true, we leave the loop, i.e., we continue execution in line 9. The left column of Fig. 6 shows the data dependency graphs when in the execution of onReceive the condition is always false. The right column shows the data dependency graphs for never entering the loop, for exiting the loop after one iteration, and for exiting the loop after two iterations.

Our example is artificial in the sense that 'normally' one would not expect a field next in the objects in the API classes Context and Intent (referenced in the beginning of the method by the registers r2 and r3, respectively). However, it is 'typical' in the sense that intents are usually read using loop constructs. For brevity, we decided to skip the 'typical' lines before the loop that prepare registers r2 and r3 to contain objects with a next field, i.e., lists.

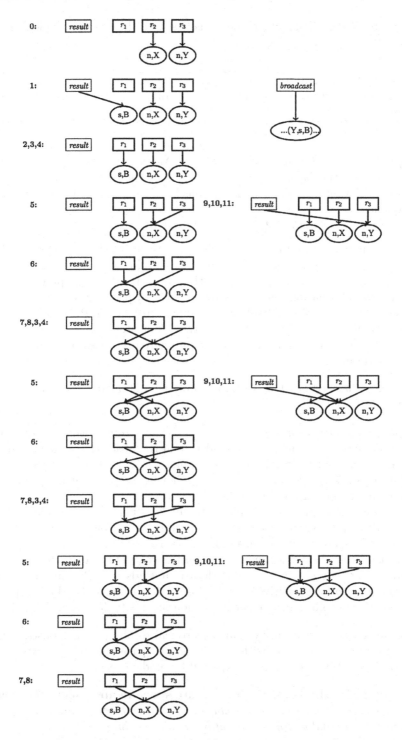

Fig. 6. Abstract loop execution using `onReceive` code.

Our Abstraction Principle for Loops is based on the lasso principle in model checking [10]:

Abstraction Principle for Loops
Stop loop execution at a backward jump point when abstract states are repeated.

Example 11 (Repetition of abstract states). We observe the register contents when executing the backward jump in line 8 of the method `onReceive`, c.f. Fig. 5. The relevant data dependency graphs are shown in Fig. 6. Here we obtain the sequence

$$13_n \mid 2_s \longrightarrow 13_s \mid 2_n \longrightarrow 13_n \mid 2_s,$$

where the numbers stand for registers, the vertical bar divides partitions, and the indices n and s stands of non-sensitive and sensitive, resp, i.e., $13_n \mid 2_s$ says that r_1 and r_3 belong to the same partition of the data dependency graph which holds non-sensitive information, while register r_2 forms a partition of its own which holds sensitive information. Applying the above Abstraction Principle for Loops means that execution is stopped at the third loop iteration since all abstract states that can occur within this loop have already been passed through during the first two iterations.

We have analysed our loop example applying a standard approach of static analysis [25]:

Example 12 (Comparison with static analysis). By comparison, an execution using static analysis principles is bound to join the abstract states collected at the level of backward jumps. In our example, where we start the the loop in the abstract state $1_s \mid 2_n \mid 3_n$, we have the following sequence at the level of the backward jump: $13_s \mid 2_s \longrightarrow 13_s \mid 2_s$.

We observe that in this example static analysis performs a smaller number of loop iterations than our model checking approach. However, this comes at the price of less precision. For example, as seen in Fig. 6, registers 1 and 2 are never sensitive at the same time. If later in the computation this fact becomes important (e.g., for passing sensitive data that leads to collusion) then static analysis reports a false positive for collusion while our model checking approach safely reports no-collusion. Further discussion on this topic can be found in [9].

We conclude this Section by some theoretical results that demonstrate that our abstractions provide us with a finite state space that – at least from a theoretical point of view – can be explored by model-checking.

Theorem 2 (Methods have a finite state space in abstract). *The number of partitions of the registers of a method enriched with sensitivity information, app information, and history information, is always finite.*

Proof: This result holds as a method always has only finitely many registers, sensitivity is a Boolean value, the app sets considered are always finite, and the number of string constants in a program is finite as well.

Corollary 1 (Loops are finite in abstract). *Application of the Abstraction Principle for Loops leads to finite loop executions.*

Corollary 2 (Abstract state space is finite). *The abstractions together result in a finite state space for the abstract semantics, which can be investigated via model-checking.*

Proof (Sketch): We are considering non-recursive apps only. Thanks to Corollary 1, we have only executions of finite length in abstract. A finite execution has only finitely many branches, can start only finitely many threads, and leads to finite stacks only. Thus, by Theorem 1, the abstract state space is finite.

8   First Experimental Results

We demonstrate how collusion is detected using our concrete and our abstract semantics on two Android applications, called LocSender and LocReceiver. Together, these two apps jointly carry out an "information theft". They consist of about 100 lines of Java code/3000 lines of Smali code each. Originally written to explore if collusion was actually possible (there is no APK of the Soundcomber example), here they serve as a first test if our model checking approach works.

LocSender obtains the location of the Android device and communicates it using a broadcast intent. LocReceiver constantly waits for such a broadcast. On receiving such message, it extracts the location information and finally sends it to the Internet as an HTTP request. We have two variants of LocReceiver: one contains a while loop pre-processing the HTTP request while the other does not. Additionally, we create two further versions of each LocReceiver variant where collusion is broken by (1) not sending the HTTP request at the end, (2) altering the name of the intent that it waits for – named LocReceiver1 and LocReceiver2, respectively. Furthermore, we (3) create a LocSender1 which sends a non-sensitive piece of information rather than the location. In total, we will have eight experiments where the two firsts have a collusion while the six lasts do not[2]. Figure 7 summarises the experimental results. When collusion is detected, our implementation provides an output to trace the execution of both colluding apps. For example, the abstract implementation yields the following traces for the first experiment from Fig. 7:

LocSender: "0" -> "68" -> "70" -> "71" -> "73" -> "75" -> "77"
   -> "79" -> "81" -> "83" -> "85" -> "86" -> "88" -> "cond_54".

---

[2] All experiments are carried out on a Macbook Pro with an Intel i7 2.2 GHz quad-core processor and 16 GB of memory.

App1	App2	Loop	Collusion	Concrete		Abstract	
				Runtime	Detected	Runtime	Detected
LocSender	LocReceiver		✓	55s	✓	30s	✓
LocSender	LocReceiver	✓	✓	time-out		33s	✓
LocSender	LocReceiver1			1m13s		31.984s	
LocSender	LocReceiver1	✓		time-out		34s	
LocSender	LocReceiver2			53s		32s	
LocSender	LocReceiver2	✓		time-out		33s	
LocSender1	LocReceiver			1m11s		32s	
LocSender1	LocReceiver	✓		time-out		34s	

Fig. 7. Experimental result.

LocReceiver: "0" -> "44" -> "46" -> "48" -> "0" -> "69" -> "71"
-> "72" -> "74" -> "75" -> "77" -> "goto_14" -> "78" -> "79"
-> "goto_14" -> "cond_23" -> "84" -> "85" -> "86" -> "87" ->
"89" -> "try_start_44" -> "90" -> "91" -> "92" -> "93" ->
"try_end_69" -> "100" -> "goto_69" -> "49" -> "52" -> "53"
-> "56" -> "57" -> "58".

In these traces, labels in Smali code are recorded as they were traversed during the colluded execution. Therefore, it can be used to evidence collusion in the Smali code.

Evaluation: Our experiments indicate that our approach works correctly: if there is collusion it is either detected or has a timeout, if there is no collusion then none is detected. In case of detection, we obtain a trace providing evidence of a run leading to information theft. The experiments further demonstrate the need for an abstract semantics, beyond the obvious argument of speed: e.g., in case of a loop where the number of iterations depends on an environmental parameter that can't be determined, the concrete semantics yields a time out, while the abstract semantics still is able to produce a result. Model checking with the abstract semantics is about twice as fast as with the concrete semantics. At least for such small examples, our approach appears to be feasible.

9   Summary and Future Work

In this paper, we have presented a model-checking approach that is capable to discover the threat of app-collusion. To this end, we gave a formal definition of collusion and briefly discussed that it is often a challenge to distinguish between benign and malicious behavior. Formal methods alone are not capable to distinguish between malign collusion and benign collaboration as they need a reference point, a definition of what a program's behavior should be. As such reference points are lacking in the context of mobile apps, the classification that a certain behavior is malicious remains in the end a decision to be made by humans.

Towards model-checking for collusion potential, we presented an abstract semantics of Smali within the $\mathbb{K}$ framework. As a theoretical result we proved that our abstractions lead to a finite state space (for non-recursive apps). On the practical side, we demonstrated that our abstract semantics can effectively detect collusion potential for information theft. Together with our other work within the ACID project, this results in a tool chain for dealing with app collusion:

- First, one isolates sets of apps with high collusion risk – this can be done with some filter mechanism, e.g., the rule based one [11] or the machine learning based one [19].
- These app sets then need to be investigated further, where it is essential to provide evidence for collusion potential – this is, where our model-checking approach from this paper comes into play.
- Finally, there needs to be a decision if the combined effort of the apps is collusion or collaboration – as discussed above, this needs to be carried out manually, in the future possibly supported by machine learning [6].

In terms of future work for our approach, we plan to work out the formal details of how to treat recursion and, in particular, expand our work on information theft to other forms of collusion by developing further instrumentation principles. Furthermore, we want to address the question of scalability, in particular of how to solve the combinatorial explosion of n colluding apps with BigData search methods.

For the topic in general, one should note that app collusion is not restricted to Android OS. In principle, it is also a vulnerability of other mobile platforms as well as cloud environments. In the context of the Internet of Things (IoT), malware experts see collusion between devices as 'threat of the future': with increasingly more powerful analysis methods to protect devices against attacks performed by a single program only, criminals might be forced to move to collusion attacks, though these are technically more involved.

Yet another perspective is that model-checking might develop into a third, established technique for malware discovery and analysis, besides static analysis and dynamic analysis.

Acknowledgments. We would like to thank our colleagues and friends Magne Haveraaen, Alexander Knapp, and Bernd-Holger Schlingloff who commented on early drafts and helped us shape this paper; a special thanks goes to Erwin R. Catesbeijana (Jr.) for pointing out that not all inter app communication leads to collusion.

References

1. Android API reference. https://developer.android.com/reference/classes. Accessed 01 May 2018
2. Android bytecode. https://source.android.com/devices/tech/dalvik/dalvik-bytecode. Accessed 01 May 2018
3. Alam, M.I., Halder, R., Goswami, H., Pinto, J.S.: K-taint: an executable rewriting logic semantics for taint analysis in the k-framework. In: ENASE, pp. 359–366. SciTePress (2018)

4. Arzt, S., Rasthofer, S., Fritz, C., Bodden, E., Bartel, A., Klein, J., Traon, Y.L., Octeau, D., McDaniel, P.: FlowDroid: precise context, flow, field, object-sensitive and lifecycle-aware taint analysis for android apps. In: PLDI 2014, p. 29. ACM (2014)

5. Asavoae, I.M., Blasco, J., Chen, T.M., Kalutarage, H.K., Muttik, I., Nguyen, H.N., Roggenbach, M., Shaikh, S.A.: Detecting malicious collusion between mobile software applications: the Android^{TM} case. In: Carrascosa, I.P., Kalutarage, H.K., Huang, Y. (eds.) Data Analytics and Decision Support for Cybersecurity. Springer, Cham (2017). https://doi.org/10.1007/978-3-319-59439-2_3

6. Asavoae, I.M., Blasco, J., Chen, T.M., Kalutarage, H.K., Muttik, I., Nguyen, H.N., Roggenbach, M., Shaikh, S.A.: Distinguishing between malicious app collusion and benign app collaboration: a machine learning approach. Virus Bulletin (2018)

7. Asavoae, I.M., Nguyen, H.N., Roggenbach, M., Shaikh, S.A.: Utilising $\mathbb{K}$ semantics for collusion detection in Android applications. In: ter Beek, M.H., Gnesi, S., Knapp, A. (eds.) FMICS-AVoCS 2016, pp. 142–149 (2016)

8. Asavoae, I.M., Nguyen, H.N., Roggenbach, M., Shaikh, S.A.: Software model checking: a promising approach to verify mobile app security. CoRR abs/1706.04741 (2017). http://arxiv.org/abs/1706.04741

9. Beyer, D., Gulwani, S., Schmidt, D.: Combining model checking and data-flow analysis. In: Clarke, E.M., Henzinger, T.A., Veith, H. (eds.) Handbook on Model Checking. Springer, Cham (2018). https://doi.org/10.1007/978-3-319-10575-8_16

10. Biere, A., Cimatti, A., Clarke, E., Zhu, Y.: Symbolic model checking without BDDs. In: Cleaveland, W.R. (ed.) TACAS 1999. LNCS, vol. 1579, pp. 193–207. Springer, Heidelberg (1999). https://doi.org/10.1007/3-540-49059-0_14

11. Blasco, J., Chen, T.M., Muttik, I., Roggenbach, M.: Detection of app collusion potential using logic programming. J. Netw. Comput. Appl. **105**, 88–104 (2018). https://doi.org/10.1016/j.jnca.2017.12.008

12. Blasco, J., Muttik, I., Roggenbach, M.: Wild android collusions (2016). https://www.virusbulletin.com/conference/vb2016/

13. Bogdănaş, D., Roşu, G.: K-Java: a complete semantics of Java. In: POPL 2015. ACM (2015)

14. Bugiel, S., Davi, L., Dmitrienko, A., Heuser, S., Sadeghi, A.R., Shastry, B.: Practical and lightweight domain isolation on Android. In: SPSM 2011. ACM (2011)

15. Clavel, M., Durán, F., Eker, S., Lincoln, P., Martí-Oliet, N., Meseguer, J., Talcott, C.: All About Maude - A High-Performance Logical Framework. LNCS, vol. 4350. Springer, Heidelberg (2007). https://doi.org/10.1007/978-3-540-71999-1

16. Şerbănuţă, T.F., Roşu, G.: K-Maude: a rewriting based tool for semantics of programming languages. In: Ölveczky, P.C. (ed.) WRLA 2010. LNCS, vol. 6381, pp. 104–122. Springer, Heidelberg (2010). https://doi.org/10.1007/978-3-642-16310-4_8

17. Dicker, C.: Android security: delusion to collusion. B.Sc. dissertation, Swansea University (2015)

18. Hathhorn, C., Ellison, C., Roşu, G.: Defining the undefinedness of C. In: PLDI 2015. ACM (2015)

19. Kalutarage, H.K., Nguyen, H.N., Shaikh, S.A.: Towards a threat assessment framework for apps collusion. Telecommun. Syst. **66**(3), 417–430 (2017). https://doi.org/10.1007/s11235-017-0296-1

20. Kovacs, E.: Malware abuses Android accessibility feature to steal data (2015). http://www.securityweek.com/malware-abuses-android-accessibility-feature-steal-data

21. Leroy, X.: Formal verification of a realistic compiler. Commun. ACM **52**(7), 107–115 (2009)
22. Li, L., Bartel, A., Bissyandé, T.F., Klein, J., Le Traon, Y.: ApkCombiner: combining multiple android apps to support inter-app analysis. In: Federrath, H., Gollmann, D. (eds.) SEC 2015. IAICT, vol. 455, pp. 513–527. Springer, Cham (2015). https://doi.org/10.1007/978-3-319-18467-8_34
23. Lipovsky, R.: ESET analyzes first Android file-encrypting, TOR-enabled ransomware (2014). http://www.welivesecurity.com/2014/06/04/simplocker/
24. Lunden, I.: 6.1B Smartphone Users Globally By 2020, Overtaking Basic Fixed Phone Subscriptions. http://techcrunch.com/2015/06/02/6-1b-smartphone-users-globally-by-2020-overtaking-basic-fixed-phone-subscriptions/#.pkatr9: RPIH. Accessed 10 Nov 2015
25. Nielson, F., Nielson, H.R., Hankin, C.: Principles of Program Analysis. Springer, Heidelberg (1999). https://doi.org/10.1007/978-3-662-03811-6
26. Octeau, D., Luchaup, D., Dering, M., Jha, S., McDaniel, P.: Composite constant propagation: application to Android inter-component communication analysis. In: ICSE 2015. IEEE Computer Society (2015)
27. Octeau, D., Luchaup, D., Jha, S., McDaniel, P.D.: Composite constant propagation and its application to Android program analysis. IEEE Trans. Softw. Eng. **42**(11), 999–1014 (2016)
28. Octeau, D., McDaniel, P., Jha, S., Bartel, A., Bodden, E., Klein, J., Traon, Y.L.: Effective inter-component communication mapping in Android: an essential step towards holistic security analysis. In: Security Symposium. USENIX Association (2013)
29. Page, C.: MKero: Android malware secretly subscribes victims to premium SMS services (2015). http://www.theinquirer.net/inquirer/news/2425201/mkero-android-malware-secretly-subscribes-victims-to-premium-sms-services
30. Ravitch, T., Creswick, E.R., Tomb, A., Foltzer, A., Elliott, T., Casburn, L.: Multi-app security analysis with FUSE: statically detecting Android app collusion. In: ACSAC 2014. ACM (2014)
31. Roşu, G.: From rewriting logic, to programming language semantics, to program verification. In: Martí-Oliet, N., Ölveczky, P.C., Talcott, C. (eds.) Logic, Rewriting, and Concurrency. LNCS, vol. 9200, pp. 598–616. Springer, Cham (2015). https://doi.org/10.1007/978-3-319-23165-5_28
32. Roşu, G.: Matching logic. In: RTA 2015. LIPIcs, vol. 36, pp. 5–21. SchlossDagstuhl–Leibniz-Zentrum fuer Informatik, July 2015
33. Roşu, G., Şerbănuţă, T.F.: An overview of the K semantic framework. J. Logic Algebraic Program. **79**(6), 397–434 (2010)
34. Schlegel, R., Zhang, K., Zhou, X.y., Intwala, M., Kapadia, A., Wang, X.: Soundcomber: a stealthy and context-aware sound Trojan for smartphones. In: NDSS, vol. 11, pp. 17–33 (2011)
35. Suarez-Tangil, G., Tapiador, J.E., Peris-Lopez, P., Ribagorda, A.: Evolution, detection and analysis of malware for smart devices. IEEE Commun. Surv. Tutor. **16**(2), 961–987 (2014)

Efficient Runtime Verification
of First-Order Temporal Properties

Klaus Havelund[1]([⊠]) and Doron Peled[2]([⊠])

[1] Jet Propulsion Laboratory, California Institute of Technology, Pasadena, USA
klaus.havelund@jpl.nasa.gov
[2] Department of Computer Science, Bar Ilan University, Ramat Gan, Israel
doron.peled@gmail.com

Abstract. Runtime verification allows monitoring the execution of a system against a temporal property, raising an alarm if the property is violated. In this paper we present a theory and system for runtime verification of a first-order past time linear temporal logic. The first-order nature of the logic allows a monitor to reason about events with data elements. While runtime verification of propositional temporal logic requires only a fixed amount of memory, the first-order variant has to deal with a number of data values potentially growing unbounded in the length of the execution trace. This requires special compactness considerations in order to allow checking very long executions. In previous work we presented an efficient use of BDDs for such first-order runtime verification, implemented in the tool DEJAVU. We first summarize this previous work. Subsequently, we look at the new problem of dynamically identifying when data observed in the past are no longer needed, allowing to reclaim the data elements used to represent them. We also study the problem of adding relations over data values. Finally, we present parts of the implementation, including a new concept of user defined property macros.

1 Introduction

Runtime verification (RV) is used to check the execution of a system against a temporal property, expressed, e.g., in Linear Temporal Logic (LTL), alarming when it is violated, so that aversive action can be taken. To inspect an execution, the monitored system is instrumented to report on occurrences of events. The monitor performs incremental computation, updating its internal memory. It is important that this operation is efficient in terms of time and space, in order to be able to keep up with rapid occurrence of events in very long executions.

The research performed by the first author was carried out at Jet Propulsion Laboratory, California Institute of Technology, under a contract with the National Aeronautics and Space Administration. The research performed by the second author was partially funded by Israeli Science Foundation grant 2239/15: "Runtime Measuring and Checking of Cyber Physical Systems".

M. M. Gallardo and P. Merino (Eds.): SPIN 2018, LNCS 10869, pp. 26–47, 2018.
https://doi.org/10.1007/978-3-319-94111-0_2

Even if monitoring is performed offline, i.e. on log files, performance is an issue when logs are large. For each consumed event, a monitor has to decide whether the property is violated based on the finite part of the execution trace that it has viewed so far. Thus, the checked properties are often limited to *safety* properties [24]. For a safety property, any violating execution has a prefix that cannot be completed into an execution that satisfies it [2]. Hence, by definition, safety properties are those that are finitely refutable. In LTL, safety properties are those that can be written in the form $\Box\varphi$ (for *always* φ), where φ uses past operators: $\ominus$ for *previous-time* and $\mathcal{S}$ for *since* [25]. While it is sufficient to find one prefix that violates φ to deduce that $\Box\varphi$ does not hold, RV often keeps monitoring the system and reporting on further prefixes that fail to satisfy φ. We shall henceforth not prefix properties with $\Box$.

Two central challenges in RV are to increase the expressiveness of the properties that can be monitored, and to improve the efficiency of monitoring. Unfortunately, there is often a tradeoff between these goals. Therefore, the combined goal is to achieve a good balance that would allow checking the property we want to monitor with a reasonable efficiency. While propositional LTL is useful for describing some properties, in many cases we want to monitor executions with events that contain data values that need to be related to each other. Such properties can be expressed e.g., using first-order temporal logic or parametric automata. As monitoring may be done without assuming a bound on the length of the execution or the cardinality of the data elements, remembering an unbounded amount of elements may be unavoidable. Consider the property that asserts that each file that is closed was opened before. This can be expressed in a first-order temporal logic as follows (where $\mathbf{P}\ \varphi$ means: *sometime in the past* φ):

$$\forall f\,(close(f) \longrightarrow \mathbf{P}\ open(f)) \tag{1}$$

If we do not remember for this property *all* the files that were opened, then we will not be able to check when a file is closed whether it was opened before. This calls, in the first place, for using an algorithm and data structure where memory growth is often quite moderate, allowing to check large executions. In previous work [18] we presented an algorithm based on the use of BDDs, and its implementation in the DEJAVU runtime verification tool. In this paper we go a step further in increasing efficiency (and hence the magnitude of executions that can be monitored) by presenting an approach for detecting when data elements that were seen so far do not affect the rest of the execution and can be discarded, also referred to as *dynamic data reclamation*. As mentioned, the temporal formula (1) forces a monitor to store information about all the files that were ever opened so that it can check that no file is closed without being opened. Consider now a more refined specification, requiring that a file can be closed only if (in the previous step) it was opened before, and has not been closed since:

$$\forall f\,(close(f) \longrightarrow \ominus(\neg close(f)\,\mathcal{S}\,open(f))) \tag{2}$$

We can observe that if a file was opened and subsequently closed, then if it is closed again before opening, the property would be invalidated just as in the case where it was not opened at all. This means that we can "forget" that a file was opened when it is closed without affecting our ability to monitor the formula. Assume that at any time during the execution there are no more than N files opened simultaneously. Then, in the approach to be presented here, we need space for only N file names for monitoring the property. This is in contrast to our original algorithm, where space for all new file names must be allocated.

The contributions of the paper are the following. We present an elegant algorithm, and its implementation in DEJAVU for dynamically reclaiming data elements that can not affect the value of the property anymore. Our solution is based on using a non-trivial combination of BDD operations to automatically detect values that are not further needed for the rest of the monitoring. Note that the approach does not involve static analysis of formulas. We furthermore introduce relations between variables (such as $x > y$) and a distinction between two forms of quantification: quantification over infinite domains and, as a new concept in DEJAVU, quantification over values *seen* in the trace.

The remaining part of the paper is organized as follows. Section 2 presents the syntax and semantics of the logic, while Sect. 3 presents the BDD-based algorithm. Section 4 introduces the new dynamic data reclaiming algorithm. Section 5 introduces relations and the new forms of quantification over seen values. Section 6 outlines the implementation. Section 7 presents an evaluation of the dynamic data reclamation implementation. Section 8 describes related work, and finally Sect. 9 concludes the paper.

2   Syntax and Semantics

In this section we present briefly the syntax and semantics of the logic used by the DEJAVU tool. Assume a finite set of domains $D_1, D_2, \ldots$. Assume further that the domains are infinite, e.g., they can be the integers or strings[1]. Let V be a finite set of *variables*, with typical instances x, y, z. An *assignment* over a set of variables W maps each variable $x \in W$ to a value from its associated domain $domain(x)$. For example $[x \rightarrow 5, y \rightarrow$ "abc"] maps x to 5 and y to "abc". Let T a set of *predicate names* with typical instances p, q, r. Each predicate name p is associated with some domain $domain(p)$. A predicate is constructed from a predicate name, and a variable or a constant of the same type. Thus, if the predicate name p and the variable x are associated with the domain of strings, we have predicates like $p(\text{"gaga"}), p(\text{"baba"})$ and $p(x)$. Predicates over constants are called *ground predicates*. An *event* is a finite set of ground predicates. (Some restrictions may be applied by the implementation, e.g., DEJAVU allows only a single ground predicate in an event.) For example, if $T = \{p, q, r\}$, then $\{p(\text{"xyzzy"}), q(3)\}$ is a possible event. An *execution* $\sigma = s_1 s_2 \ldots$ is a finite sequence of events.

For runtime verification, a property φ is interpreted on prefixes of a monitored sequence. We check whether φ holds for every such prefix, hence, conceptually, check whether $\Box\varphi$ holds, where $\Box$ is the "always in the future" linear temporal

---

[1] For dealing with finite domains see [18].

logic operator. The formulas of the core logic, referred to as QTL (Quantified Temporal Logic) are defined by the following grammar. For simplicity of the presentation, we define here the logic with unary predicates, but this is not due to any principle limitation, and, in fact, our implementation supports predicates with multiple arguments.

$$\varphi ::= true \mid p(a) \mid p(x) \mid (\varphi \wedge \varphi) \mid \neg\varphi \mid (\varphi \, \mathcal{S} \, \varphi) \mid \ominus \varphi \mid \exists x \, \varphi$$

The formula $p(a)$, where a is a constant in $domain(p)$, means that the ground predicate $p(a)$ occurs in the most recent event. The formula $p(x)$, for a variable $x \in V$, holds with a binding of x to the value a if a ground predicate $p(a)$ appears in the most recent event. The formula $(\varphi_1 \, \mathcal{S} \, \varphi_2)$ means that φ_2 held in the past (possibly now) and since then φ_1 has been true. The property $\ominus \varphi$ means that φ was true in the previous event. We can also define the following additional operators: $false = \neg true$, $(\varphi \vee \psi) = \neg(\neg\varphi \wedge \neg\psi)$, $(\varphi \longrightarrow \psi) = (\neg\varphi \vee \psi)$, $\mathbf{P} \, \varphi = (true \, \mathcal{S} \, \varphi)$ (previously φ), $\mathbf{H} \, \varphi = \neg\mathbf{P} \, \neg\varphi$ (historically φ, or φ always in the past), and $\forall x \, \varphi = \neg\exists x \neg\varphi$. The operator $[\varphi, \psi)$, borrowed from [23], has the same meaning as $(\neg\psi \, \mathcal{S} \, \varphi)$, but reads more naturally as an interval.

Let $free(\varphi)$ be the set of free (i.e., unquantified) variables of a subformula φ. Then $(\gamma, \sigma, i) \models \varphi$, where γ is an assignment over $free(\varphi)$, and $i \geq 1$, if φ holds for the prefix $s_1 s_2 \ldots s_i$ of the execution σ with the assignment γ. We denote by $\gamma|_{free(\varphi)}$ the restriction (projection) of an assignment γ to the free variables appearing in φ and by ϵ the empty assignment. The semantics of QTL can be defined as follows.

- $(\epsilon, \sigma, i) \models true$.
- $(\epsilon, \sigma, i) \models p(a)$ if $p(a) \in \sigma[i]$.
- $([x \mapsto a], \sigma, i) \models p(x)$ if $p(a) \in \sigma[i]$.
- $(\gamma, \sigma, i) \models (\varphi \wedge \psi)$ if $(\gamma|_{free(\varphi)}, \sigma, i) \models \varphi$ and $(\gamma|_{free(\psi)}, \sigma, i) \models \psi$.
- $(\gamma, \sigma, i) \models \neg\varphi$ if not $(\gamma, \sigma, i) \models \varphi$.
- $(\gamma, \sigma, i) \models (\varphi \mathcal{S} \psi)$ if $(\gamma|_{free(\psi)}, \sigma, i) \models \psi$ or the following hold: $i > 1$, $(\gamma|_{free(\varphi)}, \sigma, i) \models \varphi$, and $(\gamma, \sigma, i - 1) \models (\varphi \mathcal{S} \psi)$.
- $(\gamma, \sigma, i) \models \ominus\varphi$ if $i > 1$ and $(\gamma, \sigma, i - 1) \models \varphi$.
- $(\gamma, \sigma, i) \models \exists x \, \varphi$ if there exists $a \in domain(x)$ such that[2] $(\gamma [x \mapsto a], \sigma, i) \models \varphi$.

Set Semantics. It helps to present the BDD-based algorithm by first refining the semantics of the logic in terms of sets of assignments satisfying a formula. Let $I[\varphi, \sigma, i]$ be the semantic function, defined below, that returns a set of assignments such that $\gamma \in I[\varphi, \sigma, i]$ iff $(\gamma, \sigma, i) \models \varphi$. The empty set of assignments $\emptyset$ behaves as the Boolean constant 0 and the singleton set that contains an assignment over an empty set of variables $\{\epsilon\}$ behaves as the Boolean constant 1. We define the union and intersection operators on sets of assignments, even if they are defined over non identical sets of variables. In this case, the assignments are extended over the union of the variables. Thus intersection between two sets of assignments A_1 and A_2 is defined like database "join" operator; i.e., it consists

---

[2] $\gamma [x \mapsto a]$ is the overriding of γ with the binding $[x \mapsto a]$.

of the assignments whose projection on the *common* variables agrees with an assignment in A_1 and with an assignment in A_2. Union is defined as the dual operator of intersection. Let A be a set of assignments over the set of variables W; we denote by $hide(A, x)$ (for "hiding" the variable x) the set of assignments obtained from A after removing from each assignment the mapping from x to a value. In particular, if A is a set of assignments over only the variable x, then $hide(A, x)$ is $\{\epsilon\}$ when A is nonempty, and $\emptyset$ otherwise. $A_{free(\varphi)}$ is the set of all possible assignments of values to the variables that appear free in φ. We add a 0 position for each sequence σ (which starts with s_1), where I returns the empty set for each formula. The assignment-set semantics of QTL is shown in the following. For all occurrences of i, it is assumed that $i > 0$.

- $I[\varphi, \sigma, 0] = \emptyset$.
- $I[true, \sigma, i] = \{\epsilon\}$.
- $I[p(a), \sigma, i] = $ if $p(a) \in \sigma[i]$ then $\{\epsilon\}$ else $\emptyset$.
- $I[p(x), \sigma, i] = \{[x \mapsto a] | p(a) \in \sigma[i]\}$.
- $I[(\varphi \wedge \psi), \sigma, i] = I[\varphi, \sigma, i] \bigcap I[\psi, \sigma, i]$.
- $I[\neg\varphi, \sigma, i] = A_{free(\varphi)} \setminus I[\varphi, \sigma, i]$.
- $I[(\varphi \mathcal{S} \psi), \sigma, i] = I[\psi, \sigma, i] \bigcup (I[\varphi, \sigma, i] \bigcap I[(\varphi\mathcal{S}\psi), \sigma, i - 1])$.
- $I[\ominus\varphi, \sigma, i] = I[\varphi, \sigma, i - 1]$.
- $I[\exists x\ \varphi, \sigma, i] = hide(I[\varphi, \sigma, i], x)$.

As before, the interpretation for the rest of the operators can be obtained from the above using the connections between the operators.

3 An Efficient Algorithm Using BDDs

We describe here briefly an algorithm for monitoring first order past time LTL properties, first presented in [18] and implemented as the first version of the tool DEJAVU.

We shall represent a set of assignments as an Ordered Binary Decision Diagram (OBDD, although we write simply BDD) [10]. A BDD is a compact representation for a Boolean valued function of type $\mathbb{B}^k \rightarrow \mathbb{B}$ for some $k > 0$ (where $\mathbb{B}$ is the Boolean domain $\{0, 1\}$), as a directed acyclic graph (DAG). A BDD is essentially a compact representation of a Boolean tree, where compaction glues together isomorphic subtrees. Each non-leaf node is labeled with one of the Boolean variables $b_0, \ldots, b_{k-1}$. A non-leaf node b_i is the source of two arrows leading to other nodes. A dotted-line arrow represents that b_i has the Boolean value 0, while a thick-line arrow represents that it has the value 1. The nodes in the DAG have the same order along all paths from the root. However, some of the nodes may be absent along some paths, when the result of the Boolean function does not depend on the value of the corresponding Boolean variable. Each path leads to a leaf node that is marked by either a 0 or a 1, representing the Boolean value returned by the function for the Boolean values on the path. Figure 1 contains five BDDs (a)–(e), over three Boolean variables b_0, b_1, and b_2 (referred to by their subscripts 0, 1, and 2), as explained below.

Mapping Data to BDDs. Assume that we see $p(\text{"ab"}), p(\text{"de"}), p(\text{"af"})$ and $q(\text{"fg"})$ in subsequent states in a trace, where p and q are predicates over the domain of strings. When a value associated with a variable appears for the first time in the current event (in a ground predicate), we add it to the set of values of that domain that were seen. We assign to each new value an *enumeration*, represented as a binary number, and use a hash table to point from the value to its enumeration.

Consistent with the DEJAVU implementation, the least significant bit in an enumeration is denoted in this figure (and in the rest of this paper) by BDD variable with index 0, and the most significant bit by BDD variable with index $n - 1$, where n is the number of bits. Using e.g. a three-bit enumeration $b_2 b_1 b_0$, the first encountered value "ab" can be represented as the bit string 000, "de" as 001, "af" as 010 and "fg" as 011. A BDD for a subset of these values returns a 1 for each bit string representing an enumeration of a value in the set, and 0 otherwise. E.g. a BDD representing the set $\{\text{"de"}, \text{"af"}\}$ (2nd and 3rd values) returns 1 for 001 and 010. This is the Boolean function $\neg b_2 \wedge (b_1 \leftrightarrow \neg b_0)$. Figure 1 shows the BDDs for each of these values as well as the BDD for the set containing the values "de" and "af".

When representing a set of assignments for e.g. two variables x and y with k bits each, we will have Boolean variables $x_0, \ldots, x_{k-1}, , y_0, \ldots y_{k-1}$. A BDD will return a 1 for each bit string representing the concatenation of enumerations that correspond to the represented assignments, and 0 otherwise. For example, to represent the assignments $[x \mapsto \text{"de"}, y \mapsto \text{"af"}]$, where "de" is enumerated as 001 and "af" with 010, the BDD will return a 1 for 001010.

The BDD-based Algorithm. Given some ground predicate $p(a)$ observed in the execution matching with $p(x)$ in the monitored property, let **lookup**(x, a) be the enumeration of a. If this is a's first occurrence, then it will be assigned a new enumeration. Otherwise, **lookup** returns the enumeration that a received before. We can use a counter, for each variable x, counting the number of different values appearing so far for x. When a new value appears, this counter is incremented, and the value is converted to a Boolean representation. Enumerations that were not yet used represent the values not seen yet. In the next section we introduce data reclaiming, which allows reusing enumerations for values that no longer affect the checked property. This involves a more complicated enumeration mechanism.

The function **build**(x, A) returns a BDD that represents the set of assignments where x is mapped to (the enumeration of) v for $v \in A$. This BDD is independent of the values assigned to any variable other than x, i.e., they can have any value. For example, assume that we use three Boolean variables (bits) x_0, x_1 and x_2 for representing enumerations over x (with x_0 being the least significant bit), and assume that $A = \{a, b\}$, **lookup**$(x, a) = 011$, and **lookup**$(x, b) = 001$. Then **build**(x, A) is a BDD representation of the Boolean function $x_0 \wedge \neg x_2$.

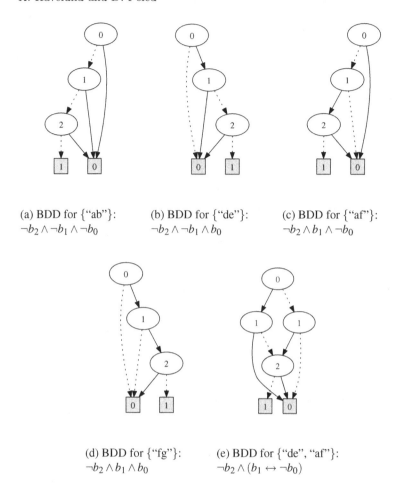

(a) BDD for {"ab"}:
$\neg b_2 \wedge \neg b_1 \wedge \neg b_0$

(b) BDD for {"de"}:
$\neg b_2 \wedge \neg b_1 \wedge b_0$

(c) BDD for {"af"}:
$\neg b_2 \wedge b_1 \wedge \neg b_0$

(d) BDD for {"fg"}:
$\neg b_2 \wedge b_1 \wedge b_0$

(e) BDD for {"de", "af"}:
$\neg b_2 \wedge (b_1 \leftrightarrow \neg b_0)$

Fig. 1. BDDs for the trace: $p(\text{"ab"}).p(\text{"de"}).p(\text{"af"}).q(\text{"fg"})$

Intersection and union of sets of assignments are translated simply to conjunction and disjunction of their BDD representation, respectively, and complementation becomes negation. We will denote the Boolean BDD operators as **and**, **or** and **not**. To implement the existential (universal, respectively) operators, we use the BDD existential (universal, respectively) operators over the Boolean variables that represent (the enumerations of) the values of x. Thus, if B_φ is the BDD representing the assignments satisfying φ in the current state of the monitor, then **exists**$(\langle x_0, \ldots, x_{k-1} \rangle, B_\varphi)$ is the BDD that represents the assignments satisfying $\exists x \varphi$ in the current state. Finally, BDD($\bot$) and BDD($\top$) are the BDDs that return always 0 or 1, respectively.

The algorithm, shown below, operates on two vectors (arrays) of values indexed by subformulas (as in [20]): pre for the state before that event, and now for the current state (after the last seen event).

1. Initially, for each subformula φ, $\mathsf{now}(\varphi) := \mathrm{BDD}(\bot)$.
2. Observe a new event (as a set of ground predicates) s as input.
3. Let $\mathsf{pre} := \mathsf{now}$.
4. Make the following updates for each subformula. If φ is a subformula of ψ then $\mathsf{now}(\varphi)$ is updated before $\mathsf{now}(\psi)$.
    - $\mathsf{now}(true) := \mathrm{BDD}(\top)$.
    - $\mathsf{now}(p(a)) := $ if $p(a) \in s$ then $\mathrm{BDD}(\top)$ else $\mathrm{BDD}(\bot)$.
    - $\mathsf{now}(p(x)) := \mathbf{build}(x, A)$ where $A = \{a | p(a) \in s\}$.
    - $\mathsf{now}((\varphi \wedge \psi)) := \mathbf{and}(\mathsf{now}(\varphi), \mathsf{now}(\psi))$.
    - $\mathsf{now}(\neg\varphi) := \mathbf{not}(\mathsf{now}(\varphi))$.
    - $\mathsf{now}((\varphi \ \mathcal{S} \ \psi)) := \mathbf{or}(\mathsf{now}(\psi), \mathbf{and}(\mathsf{now}(\varphi), \mathsf{pre}((\varphi\mathcal{S}\psi))))$.
    - $\mathsf{now}(\ominus \varphi) := \mathsf{pre}(\varphi)$.
    - $\mathsf{now}(\exists x \ \varphi) := \mathbf{exists}(\langle x_0, \ldots, x_{k-1}\rangle, \mathsf{now}(\varphi))$.
5. Goto step 2.

An important property of the algorithm is that, at any point during monitoring, enumerations that are not used in the pre and now BDDs represent all values that have *not* been seen so far in the input. This can be proved by induction on the size of temporal formulas and the length of the input sequence. We specifically identify one enumeration to represent all values not seen yet, namely the largest possible enumeration, given the number of bits we use, $11 \ldots 11$. We let $\mathrm{BDD}(11 \ldots 11)$ denote the BDD that returns 1 exactly for this value. This trick allows us to use a finite representation and quantify existentially and universally over *all* values in infinite domains.

Dynamic Expansion of the BDDs. We can sometimes define the number k of Boolean variables per domain to be a large enough such that we anticipate no more than $2^k - 1$ different values. However, if the number of bits used for representing enumerations becomes insufficient, we can dynamically expand it during RV [18]. As explained above, the enumeration $11 \ldots 11$ of length k represents for every variable "all the values not seen so far in the input sequence". Consider the following two cases:

- When the added (most significant) bit has the value 0, the enumeration still represents the same value. Thus, the updated BDD needs to return the same values that the original BDD returned without the additional 0.
- When the added bit has the value 1, we obtain enumerations for values that were not seen so far in the input. Thus, the updated BDD needs to return the same values that the original BDD gave to $11 \ldots 11$.

An increase in one bit allows doubling the number of enumerations, hence, this, relatively expensive operation does not need to take place frequently (if at all). We demonstrate the expansion of the enumerations by a single bit on formulas with three variables, x, y and z, represented using three BDD bits each, i.e., x_0, x_1, x_2, y_0, y_1, y_2, z_0, z_1, z_2. We want to add a new most significant bit y_{new} for representing y. Let B be the BDD before the expansion. The case where the value of y_{new} is 0 is the same as for a single variable. For the case where y_{new} is 1, the new BDD needs to represent a function that behaves like B when all the y bits are set to 1. Denote this by $B[y_0 \setminus 1, y_1 \setminus 1, y_2 \setminus 1]$. This function returns the same Boolean values independent of any value of the y bits, but it depends on the other bits, representing the x and z variables. Thus, to expand the BDD, we generate a new one as follows:

$$((B \wedge \neg y_{new}) \vee (B[y_0 \setminus 1, y_1 \setminus 1, y_2 \setminus 1] \wedge y_{new}))$$

Expanding the number of bits allowed for enumerations, when needed, has the disadvantage that memory can grow unbounded. The next section suggests a method for identifying enumerations of values that can no longer affect the checked property, and therefore can be reclaimed.

4   Dynamic Data Reclamation

In the previous section, we described an algorithm that implements runtime verification with data, based on a BDD representation. The algorithm generates a new enumeration for each value that appears in the input and uses a hash table to map from a value to its enumeration. It is possible that the set of enumerations for some variable eventually exceeds the number of bits allocated for the BDD. In this case, the BDD can be expanded dynamically, as shown in the previous section. However, this can be very costly, and we may eventually run out of memory. In this section we study the possibility of reusing enumerations of data values, when this does not affect the decision whether the property holds or not. When a value a is *reclaimed*, its enumeration e can be reused for representing another value that appears later in the execution.

We saw in the introduction an example of a property where values that already occurred cannot be reclaimed (1), and a similar property, where there are values that are not useful any more from some point in the execution (2). Consider a more complicated example:

$$\forall z \, (r(z) \rightarrow \exists y \, (q(y) \mathcal{S} p(z))) \tag{3}$$

It asserts that when a ground predicate $r(a)$ appears with some value a, then there should be at least one value b for which $q(b)$ appeared ever since the most recent appearance of $p(a)$ (an appearance of $p(a)$ is required). Consider an execution σ with some prefix ρ that does not contain $r(a)$ since the most recent appearance of $p(a)$. Furthermore, no ground predicate $q(b)$ commonly appears since the last occurrence of $p(a)$. In this case, when $r(a)$ later occurs in σ, the property (3) will be violated. This is indistinguishable from the case where $p(a)$ never occurred. Thus, after seeing ρ, we can "forget" the value a.

Recall that upon the occurrence of a new event, the basic algorithm uses the BDD $\mathsf{pre}(\psi)$, for any subformula ψ, representing assignments satisfying this subformula calculated based on the sequence monitored so far. Since these BDDs sufficiently summarize the information that will be used about the execution monitored so far, reclaiming data can be performed fully automatic, without user guidance or static formula analysis, solely based on the information the BDDs contain.

We are seeking a condition for reclaiming values of a variable x. Let A be a set of assignments over some variables that includes x. Denote by $A[x = a]$ the set of assignments from A in which the value of x is a. We say that the values a and b are *analogous* for variable x in A, if $hide(A[x = a], x) = hide(A[x = b], x)$. This means that a and b, as values of the variable x, are related to all other values in A in the same way. A value can be reclaimed if it is analogous to the values not seen yet, in all the assignments represented in $\mathsf{pre}(\psi)$, for each subformula ψ.

As the pre BDDs use enumerations to represent values, we find the enumerations that can be reclaimed and then, their corresponding values are removed from the hash table, and these enumerations can later be reused to represent new values. Recall that the enumeration $11 \ldots 11$ represents all the values that were *not* seen so far, as explained in Sect. 3. Thus, we can check whether a value a for x is analogous to the values not seen so far for x by performing the checks between the enumeration of a and the enumeration $11 \ldots 11$ on the pre BDDs. In fact, we do not have to perform the checks enumeration by enumeration, but use a BDD expression that constructs a BDD representing (returning 1 for) all enumerations that can be reclaimed for a variable x.

To simplify the presentation and prevent using many indexes, assume that a subformula ψ has three free variables, x, y and z, each with k bits, i.e., $x_0, \ldots, x_{k-1}, y_0, \ldots, y_{k-1}$ and $z_0, \ldots, z_{k-1}$. The following expression returns a BDD representing all the enumerations of x values that are analogous to $11 \ldots 11$ in $\mathsf{pre}(\psi)$.

$$I_{\psi,x} = \forall y_0 \ldots \forall y_{k-1} \forall z_0 \ldots \forall z_{k-1} (\mathsf{pre}(\psi)[x_0 \setminus 1, \ldots x_{k-1} \setminus 1] \leftrightarrow \mathsf{pre}(\psi))$$

The available enumerations for the variable x are represented then by the conjunction of $I_{\psi,x}$ over all subformulas ψ of the specification φ. (Note that this will also include enumerations that are not used, as they are also analogous to $11 \ldots 11$ in all subformulas.)

To take advantage of reclaimed enumerations, we cannot generate them in successive order using a counter anymore. Thus we need to keep a set of available enumerations. This can be represented using a BDD. Let $avail(x)$ be the BDD that represents the enumerations (given as a Binary encoding $x_0, \ldots, x_{k-1}$) that are available for values of x. Initially at the start of monitoring, we set $avail(x) := \neg BDD(11 \ldots 11)$. Let $sub(\varphi)$ be the set of subformulas of the property φ. When the number of available enumerations becomes short, and we want to perform data reclamation, we calculate $I_{\psi,x}$ for all the subformulas $\psi \in sub(\varphi)$ that contain x as a free variable, and set:

$$avail(x) := (\bigwedge_{\psi \in sub(\varphi), x \in free(\psi)} I_{\psi,x}) \wedge \neg BDD(11 \ldots 11)$$

This updates $avail(x)$ to denote all available enumerations, including reclaimed enumerations. When we need a new enumeration, we just pick some enumeration

e that satisfies $avail(x)$. Let $BDD(e)$ denote a BDD that represents only the enumeration e. To remove that enumeration from $avail(x)$, We update $avail(x)$ as follows:

$$avail(x) := avail(x) \land \neg BDD(e)$$

The formula $I_{\psi,x}$ includes multiple quantifications (over the bits used to represent the free variables other than x). Therefore, it may not be efficient to reclaim enumerations too frequently. We can reclaim enumerations either periodically or when $avail(x)$ becomes empty or close to empty. Data reclaiming may sometimes be time consuming and also result in expanding the BDD. This is based on the observation that a BDD representing just the Binary enumerations from 1 to n is much more compact than a BDD representing some n random enumerations. On the other hand, as we observe in the evaluation section, the ability to use less Boolean variables for enumerations due to reclaiming data may require less memory and time.

As the BDD-based algorithm detects an enumeration e that can be reclaimed, we need to identify the related data value a and update the hash table, so that a will not point to e. In particular, we need to be able to find the data that is represented by a given enumeration. To do that, one can use a *trie* [11]: in our case this will be a trie with at most two edges from each node, marked with either 0 or 1. Traversing the trie from its root node on edges labeled according to the enumeration e reaches a node that contains the value a that is enumerated as e. Traversing and updating the trie is linear per each enumeration. The current implementation, however, uses the simpler straightforward strategy of walking though all values and removing those which point to reclaimed enumerations.

5   Relations and Quantification over Seen Values

Quantification over Seen Values. The QTL logic allows assertions over infinite domains (for handling finite domains, see [18]). The quantification defined in Sect. 2 is over all possible domain values, whether they appeared already in the monitored sequence or not. It is sometimes more natural to quantify only over values that already appeared in events. Consider the property that asserts that there exists a session s, such that any user u that has ever logged into any session (s') so far, is currently logged into this session s and not logged out yet. This can be expressed in the following slightly inconvenient manner:

$$\exists s \forall u((\exists s' \, \mathbf{P} \, login(u, s')) \rightarrow (\neg logout(u, s) \, \mathcal{S} \, login(u, s))) \tag{4}$$

One may be tempted to use the following shorter formula with the naive intent that we quantify over all users u seen in the trace so far:

$$\exists s \forall u(\neg logout(u, s) \, \mathcal{S} \, login(u, s)) \tag{5}$$

Unfortunately, this formula does not have the intended semantics because it asserts that *all potential users* have not logged out since they logged into s. For an unbounded domain, this property can never hold, since at any time, only a finite number of users could have been observed to log in. Property (5) can, however, be corrected to conveniently quantify only over values u that were seen so far in the monitored sequence. We extend the logic QTL with the bounded quantifiers $\tilde{\exists}$ and $\tilde{\forall}$, quantifying over only seen values, hence we can now express property (4) as:

$$\tilde{\exists}s\tilde{\forall}u(\neg logout(u,s) \, \mathcal{S} \, login(u,s)) \tag{6}$$

The new kind of quantifiers do not extend the expressive power of the logic, as one can always use the form of property (4) to limit the quantification to seen values. However, it allows writing shorter formulas, and is also supported by an efficient implementation.

In order to implement the quantifiers $\tilde{\exists}$ and $\tilde{\forall}$, we keep, for each variable x that is quantified in this way, a BDD $seen(x)$. $seen(x)$ is initialized to the empty BDD (BDD($\bot$)). Upon seeing an event with a new value a for x, we update $seen(x)$ such that for the BDD bits representing the new enumeration e for a it will also return 1. That is, $seen(x) := \mathbf{or}(seen(x), BDD(e))$. We augment our algorithm with $\mathsf{now}(\tilde{\exists}x\,\varphi) := \mathbf{exists}(\langle x_0, \ldots, x_{k-1}\rangle, \mathbf{and}(seen(x), \mathsf{now}(\varphi)))$. For implementing $\tilde{\forall}x$, note that $\tilde{\forall}x\,\varphi = \neg\tilde{\exists}x\,\neg\varphi$.

Arithmetic Relations. Another extension of the QTL logic is the ability to use arithmetic relations. This allows comparing between values that occurred, as in the following property:

$$\forall x\,(p(x) \rightarrow \exists y \ominus (\mathbf{P}\,q(y) \wedge x > y)) \tag{7}$$

It asserts that if $p(x)$ is seen with some value of x, then there exists a smaller value y such that $q(y)$ was seen in the past. In order to implement this comparison along the same lines of the set semantics BDD-based solution, we can represent a BDD $\mathsf{now}(x > y)$ over the enumerations of the variables x and y. Suppose that x and y are represented using the BDD bits $x_0, \ldots, x_{k-1}, y_0, \ldots y_{k-1}$. Then, $\mathsf{now}(x > y)$ returns a 1 when $x_0, \ldots, x_{k-1}$ represents the enumeration for some seen value a, and $y_0, \ldots, y_{k-1}$ represents the enumeration of some seen value b, where $b > a$.

The BDD $\mathsf{now}(x > y)$ is updated incrementally, when a new value for x or for y is seen. For property (7), that would be an occurrence of an event that contains a ground predicate of the form $p(a)$ or $q(b)$. Suppose that a is a new value for the variable x. We build at this point a temporary BDD $B_{a>x}$ that represents the set of assignments $\{[x \mapsto a, y \mapsto b] \mid b \in seen(y) \wedge a > b\}$. Then we set $\mathsf{now}(x > y) := \mathbf{or}(\mathsf{pre}(x > y), B_{a>y})$.

Property (7) guarantees (due to the subformula $\mathbf{P}\,q(y)$) that the values compared using $x > y$ were already seen. The following property, however, appears more ambiguous since the domain of y is not completely clear:

$$\forall x\,(p(x) \rightarrow \exists y\,x > y) \tag{8}$$

For example, assuming standard mathematical reasoning, if y ranges over the integers, then this property should always hold; if y ranges over the naturals, then this should hold if x is bigger than 0, although some definitions of the naturals do not contain 0, in which case this should hold if x is bigger than 1. To solve ambiguity, we chose an alternative implementation; we analyze the formulas, and if a relation contains an occurrence of a variable x in the scope of a quantification $\forall x$ or $\exists x$, we change the quantification into $\tilde{\forall} x$ or $\tilde{\exists} x$, respectively.

6   Implementation

Basic Algorithm. DEJAVU is implemented in SCALA. The current version, which supports data reclamation, is an augmentation of the tool previously described in [18]. DEJAVU takes as input a specification file containing one or more properties, and generates a self-contained SCALA program (a text file) - the monitor. This program (which first must be compiled) takes as input the trace file and analyzes it. The tool uses the following libraries: SCALA's parser combinator library for parsing [28], the Apache Commons CSV (Comma Separated Value format) parser for parsing log files [4], and the JavaBDD library for BDD manipulations [21]. We shall illustrate the monitor generation using an example. Consider the property CLOSE in Fig. 4, which corresponds to property 1 on page 2, but in the input format for the tool. The property-specific part[3] of the generated monitor, shown in Fig. 2 (left), relies on an enumeration of the subformulas, shown in Fig. 2 (right). Specifically, two arrays are declared,

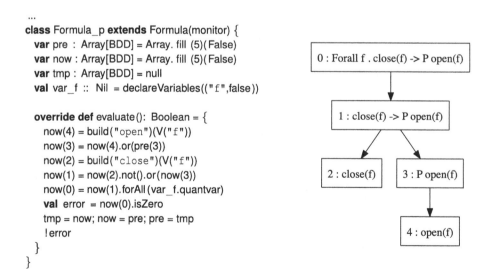

Fig. 2. Monitor (left) and subformula enumeration (right) for property CLOSE

---

[3] An additional 530 lines of property independent boilerplate code is generated.

indexed by subformula indexes: pre for the previous state and now for the current state. For each observed event, the function evaluate() computes the now array from highest to lowest index, and returns true (property is satisfied in this position of the trace) iff now(0) is not *false*, i.e., not BDD($\bot$). At composite subformula nodes, BDD operators are applied. For example for subformula 3, the new value is now(4).or(pre(3)), which is the interpretation of the formula P open(f) corresponding to the law: $\mathbf{P}\,\varphi = (\varphi \vee \ominus \mathbf{P}\,\varphi)$. As can be seen, for each new event, the evaluation of a formula results in the computation of a BDD for each subformula. It turns out that this process, linear in the size of the formula, is rather efficient.

Dynamic Memory Reclamation. The implementation of dynamic data reclamation is illustrated with the code snippets in Fig. 3. The method build(...)(...):BDD (lines 1–3) is called in Fig. 2 (left) for subformulas 2 and 4. It in turn calls the method getBddOf(v: Any):BDD (line 2) on the Variable object (the class of which is defined on lines 5–34) denoted by the variable name 'name' (looked up in varMap), and with the value v occurring in the current event. This method (lines 6–17) returns the BDD corresponding to the newly observed value v. In case the value has previously been encountered (line 7–9), the previously allocated BDD is returned. Otherwise (line 10), if the variable avail of available BDDs is False (none available), the data reclamation is activated (explained below). An Out Of Memory error is thrown in case there still are no available BDDs (line 11). Otherwise (line 12), we select an available BDD from avail using JavaBDD's SAT solver (satOne() which when called on a BDD returns some bit enumeration for which the BDD returns 1). The selected BDD (result) is then "removed" from the avail BDD (line 13), and the hash table from values to the BDDs that represent them is finally updated (line 14). Note that the hash table maps each data value directly to a BDD representing its enumeration. The method reclaimData() (lines 19–26) starts with an avail BDD allowing any assignment different from $11\ldots11$ (line 20), and then refines it by repeatedly (line 22) computing formula $I_{\psi,x}$ from Sect. 4 for each temporal subformula (the method getFreeBDDOf(...):BDD computes $I_{\psi,x}$.), and and-ing the result to avail (line 23), corresponding to down-selecting with set intersection. The method removeReclaimedData() (lines 36–42) finally removes those values that map to a BDD that is included in avail. The test bdd.imp(avail).isOne (line 31) is the logic formulation of "the BDD avail contains the BDD bdd".

Relations and Quantification over Seen Values. Relations and quantification over seen values are implemented in a straight forward manner as explained in Sect. 5. We shall explain here just the concrete syntax chosen for relations and quantifiers. Relations are written exactly as in Sect. 5, e.g. y < x. It is also possible to compare variables to constants, as in z < 10. Concerning the two forms of quantifiers (quantification over infinite domains and quantification over seen values) we use **Exists** (for $\exists$) and **Forall** (for $\forall$) to quantify over infinite domains, and **exists** (for $\tilde{\exists}$) and **forall** (for $\tilde{\forall}$) to quantify over seen values. For

```
1    def build(name: String)(patterns: Pattern*): BDD = {
2        ... varMap(name).getBDDOf(v) ...
3    }
4
5    class Variable(name: String) {
6      def getBDDOf(v: Any): BDD = {
7        if (bdds.contains(v)) {
8          bdds(v)
9        } else {
10           if (avail.isZero) reclaimData()
11           if (avail.isZero) error()
12           val result = avail.satOne(...)
13           avail = avail.and(result.not())
14           bdds = bdds + (v → result)
15           result
16         }
17       }
18
19       def reclaimData(): Unit = {
20         avail = allOnes.not
21         for (i ← indicesOfTemporalOps) {
22           val bdd_i = getFreeBDDOf(name, pre(i))
23           avail = avail.and(bdd_i)
24         }
25         removeReclaimedData()
26       }
27
28       def removeReclaimedData(): Unit = {
29         for (v ← bdds.keySet) {
30           val bdd = bdds(v)
31           if (bdd.imp(avail).isOne) bdds = bdds − v
32         }
33       }
34     }
35
36     def getFreeBDDOf(varName: String, formula: BDD): BDD = {
37       val variable = varMap(varName)
38       val formulaWithOnes = formula.restrict(variable.allOnes)
39       var result = formulaWithOnes.biimp(formula)
40       for (quantVar ← otherQuantVars(varName)) result = result.forAll(quantVar)
41       result
42     }
```

Fig. 3. Implementation of dynamic data reclamation

example, property (6) in Sect. 5, reading $\exists s \tilde{\forall} u (\neg logout(u, s) \, \mathcal{S} \, login(u, s))$ (*there exists a session s such that any user u that has ever logged into a session so far, is currently logged into session s - and not logged out yet*), is expressed as follows in DEJAVU's concrete syntax: **Exists** s . **forall** u . !logout(u,s) **S** login (u,s).

7   Evaluation of Dynamic Data Reclamation

In this section we evaluate the implementation of DEJAVU's dynamic data recla-mation algorithm. We specifically evaluate the four temporal properties shown in Fig. 4, written in DEJAVU's input notation, on different sizes and shapes of traces (auto-generated specifically for stress testing the algorithm), while vary-ing the number of bits allocated to represent variables in BDDs. The properties come in two variants: those that do not trigger data reclamation and therefore cause accumulation of data in the monitor, and those (who's names have suffix 'DR') that do trigger data reclamation, and therefore save memory. The first two properties model variants of the requirement that a file can only be closed if has been opened. Property CLOSE corresponds to formula (1), and will not trig-ger data reclamation as explained previously. Property CLOSEDR corresponds to formula (2) and will trigger data reclamation. The next two properties model variants of the requirement that a file cannot be opened if it has already been opened. Property OPEN states that if a file is opened then either (in the previ-ous step) it must have been closed in the past and not opened since, or it must not have been opened at all in the past. This latter disjunct causes the formula not to trigger data reclamation, essentially for the same reason as for CLOSE. Finally, property OPENDR states this more elegantly by requiring that if a file was opened in the past, and not closed since then, it cannot be opened. This property will trigger data reclamation.

// A file can only be closed if has been opened:
prop close   : **Forall** f . close (f) → **P** open(f)
prop closeDR : **Forall** f . close (f) → @ (! close (f) **S** open(f))

// A file cannot be opened if it has already been opened:
prop open   : **Forall** f . open(f) → @ (((! open(f) **S** close (f))) | ! **P** open(f))
prop openDR : **Forall** f . @ (! close (f) **S** open(f)) → ! open(f)

Fig. 4. Four evaluation properties

Table 1 shows the result of the evaluation, which was performed on a Mac OS X 10.10.5 (Yosemite) operating system with a 2.8 GHz Intel Core i7, and 16 GB of memory. The properties were evaluated on traces of sizes spanning from (approximately) 2 million to 3 million events, with approximately 1–1.5 million files opened in each log (see table for exact numbers). Traces have the following general form: initially O files, where O ranges from 0 to 50,000, are opened in order to accumulate a large amount of data stored in the monitor. This is followed by a repetitive pattern of closing C files and opening C **new** files. This pattern is repeated R times. The shape of each log is shown in the table as $O:C:R$. For example, for Log 1 we have that: $O:C:R = 50,000 : 1,000 : 1,000$.

For each combination of property and log file, we experimented with different number of bits used to represent observed file values in the traces: 21, 20, 16,

Table 1. Evaluation. For each property, the performance against each log is shown. For each log, its size in number of events, and number of files opened are shown. Furthermore the pattern of the log is shown as three numbers $O : C : R$ where O is the number of events opened initially, C is the number of close events and new open events in each iteration, and R indicates how many times the C pattern is repeated. For each experiment is shown how many bits (followed by a 'b') per variable, how many seconds ('s') the trace analysis took, and whether there was an out of memory (**OOM**) or whether the presented data reclamation was invoked (**dr**).

Property	Log 1	Log 2	Log 3	Log 4
	2,052,003 events 1,051,000 files 50,000:1,000:1,000	3,007,003 events 1,504,000 files 1,000:500:3,000	2,400,009 events 1,200,006 files 6:5:200,000	2,000,004 events 1,000,001 files 1:1:1,000,000
CLOSE	21b : 10.2s 20b : 12.5s **OOM**	21b : 14.3s 20b : 12.5s **OOM**	21b : 10.6s 20b : 12.8s **OOM**	20b : 9.5s 2b : 0.6s **OOM**
CLOSEDR	20b : 13.3s **dr** 15b : 14.8s **dr**	21b : 17.0s 20b : 21.2s **dr** 10b : 10.6s **dr**	21b : 12.5s 20b : 14.0s **dr** 10b : 7.6s **dr** 3b : 5.4s **dr**	20b : 9.0s 2b : 4.7s **dr**
OPEN	21b : 15.2s 20b : 17.5s **OOM**	21b : 25.3s 20b : 18.9s **OOM**	21b : 17.1s 20b : 17.7s **OOM**	20b : 11.7s 2b : 0.6s **OOM**
OPENDR	20b : 15.2s **dr** 16b : 16.1s **dr**	20b : 27.4s **dr** 10b : 10.6s **dr**	20b : 13.8s **dr** 10b : 8.2s **dr** 3b : 5.5s **dr**	20b : 9.1s 2b : 5.6s **dr**

15, 10, 3, and 2 bits, corresponding to the ability to store respectively 2097151, 1048575, 65535, 32767, 1023, 7, and 3 different values for each variable (having subtracted the $11 \ldots 11$ pattern reserved for representing "all other values"). The following abbreviations are used: **OOM** = Out of Memory (the number of bits allocated for a variable are not sufficient), and **dr** = data reclamation according to the algorithm presented in this paper has occurred. Typically when data reclamation occurs, approximately 1–1.5 million data values are reclaimed.

Table 1 demonstrates that properties CLOSE and OPEN run out of memory (bits) if the allocated number of bits is not large enough to capture all opened files. For these properties, 21 bits are enough, while 20 bits are insufficient in most cases. On the other hand, the properties CLOSEDR and OPENDR can be monitored on all logs without **OOM** errors, by invoking the data reclamation, and without substantial differences in elapsed trace analysis time. In fact, we observe for these latter two properties, that as we reduce the number of bits, and thereby force the data reclamation to occur more often, the lower are the elapsed trace analysis times. As a side remark, for logs with an initially large amount of file openings, specifically logs 1 and 2, a certain minimum amount of bits are required to store these files. E.g. we cannot go below 15 bits for the CLOSEDR property on log 1. In contrast, we can go down to 2 bits for log 4 for the same property, even though logs 1 and 4 have approximately the same length

and the same number of files being opened. In summary, for certain data reclamation friendly properties, data reclamation can allow monitoring of traces that
would otherwise not be monitorable. In addition, data reclamation combined
with reducing the number of bits representing variables seems to reduce execution time, a surprisingly positive result. We had in fact expected the opposite
result.

It is well known that efficiency on BDD-based techniques are sensitive to the
ordering of variables in the BDDs. Currently, as already indicated, the variable
corresponding to the least significant bit always occurs first (at the top), and the
variable corresponding to the most significant bit appears last (at the bottom),
in the BDD. One may consider alternative orderings, either determined statically
from the formula or dynamically as monitoring progresses. We have not explored
such alternatives at the time of writing. Another factor potentially influencing
efficiency may be the structure of monitored data. Consider e.g. the monitoring of
data structures in a program, such as *sets*, *lists*, or, generally, *objects* in an object-
oriented programming language. It is here important to stress that the shape of
data monitored is not reflected in the BDDs themselves, but only concerns the
mapping from data to BDDs using a hash table, which indeed supports complex
data keys. However, as we have only experimented with offline log file analysis,
we have not explored this online monitoring problem.

Macros. A new addition to DEJAVU is the possibility to define data parameterized macros representing subformulas, which can be called in properties, without
having any performance consequences for the evaluation. Macros are expanded
at the call site. Macros can call macros in a nested manner, supporting a compositional way of building more complex properties. Figure 5 illustrates the use
of macros to define the properties from Fig. 4, and should be self explanatory.
Also, events can be declared up front in order to ensure that properties refer to
the correct events, and with the correct number of arguments (not shown here).

```
pred isOpen(f) = ! close (f) S open(f)
pred isClosed (f) = !open(f) S close (f)
pred wasOpened(f) = P open(f)

// A file can only be closed if has been opened:
prop close    : Forall f .  close (f)  → wasOpened(f)
prop closeDR : Forall f .  close (f)  → @ isOpen(f)

// A file cannot be opened if it has already been opened:
prop open     : Forall f .  open(f)  → @ (isClosed(f) | ! wasOpened(f))
prop openDR : Forall f .  @ isOpen(f)  → ! open(f)
```

Fig. 5. our evaluation properties using macros

8 Related Work

There are several systems that allow monitoring temporal properties with data. The systems closest to our presentation, in monitoring first-order temporal logic, are MONPOLY [8] and LTL^{FO} [9]. As in the current work, MONPOLY monitors first-order temporal properties. In fact, it also has the additional capabilities of asserting and checking properties that involve progress of time and a limited capability of reasoning about the future. The main difference between our system and MONPOLY is in the way in which data are represented and manipulated. MONPOLY exists in two versions. The first one models unbounded sets of values using regular expressions (see, e.g., [22] for a simple representation of sets of values). This version allows unrestricted complementation of sets of data values. Another version of MONPOLY, which is several orders of magnitude faster according to [8], is based on storing finite sets of assignments, and applying database operators to these. In that implementation complementation, and some of the uses of logical and modal operators is restricted, due to the explicit finite set-representation used. This has as consequence that not all formulas are monitorable, see [19] for details. The BDD representation in DEJAVU provides full expressiveness, allowing for any arbitrary combination of Boolean operators, including negation, temporal operators, and quantifiers, and with a fully compositional interpretation of formulas. In [18] we compared DEJAVU to this latter version of MONPOLY and showed performance advantages of DEJAVU.

LTL^{FO} [9] supports first-order future time LTL, where quantification is restricted to those elements that appear in the current position of the trace. The monitoring algorithm is based on spawning automata. Monitoring first-order specifications has also been explored in the database community [12] in the context of so-called temporal triggers, which are first-order temporal logic specifications that are evaluated w.r.t. a sequence of database updates.

An important volume of work on data centric runtime verification is the set of systems based on trace slicing. Trace slicing is based on the idea of mapping variable bindings to propositional automata relevant for those particular bindings. This results in very efficient monitoring algorithms, although with limitations w.r.t. expressiveness. Systems based on trace slicing include TRACEMATCHES [1], MOP [26], and QEA [27]. QEA is an attempt to increase the expressiveness of the trace slicing approach. It is based on automata, as is the ORHCIDS system [15]. Other systems include BEEPBEEP [16] and TRACECONTRACT [6], which are based on future time temporal logic using formula rewriting. Very different kinds of specification formalisms can be found in systems such as EAGLE [5], RULER [7], LOGFIRE [17] and LOLA [3]. The system MMT [14] represents sets of assignments as constraints solved with an SMT solver. An encoding of enumerations of values as BDDs appears in [29], where BDDs are used to represent large relations in order to efficiently perform program analysis expressed as Datalog programs. However, that work does not deal with unbounded domains.

Concerning reclamation of data values no longer needed in a monitor we are aware of the following alternative approaches. MONPOLY is interesting since it is part of the monitoring algorithm to get rid of such unnecessary values, and as such data reclamation is not an orthogonal concept. This is possible due to the explicit representation of sets of assignments. However, as already mentioned, the explicit representation has as consequence that some formulas are not monitorable. In LARVA [13] it is up to the user to indicate that an entire monitor can be garbage collected by using acceptance states: when the monitor enters such an acceptance state it can be discarded, and released for normal garbage collection. In systems such as RULER [7], LOGFIRE [17] and TRACECONTRACT [6], monitor states get garbage collected the normal way when data structures are no longer needed. The last variant occurs in MOP [26], where monitored data values can be structured objects in the monitored program (such as a set, a list, an iterator). When such a monitored object is no longer used in the monitored program, a garbage collector would normally collect it. However, if the monitor keeps a reference to it, this is not possible. To circumvent this, MOP monitors use JAVA's so-called *weak references* to refer to objects in the monitored program. An object referenced only by weak references is considered to be garbage by the garbage collector. Hence the object is garbage collected when nothing or only monitors refer to it.

9   Conclusion

We described a BDD-based runtime verification algorithm for checking the execution of a system against a first-order past time temporal logic property. The propositional version of such a logic is independent of the length of the prefix seen so far. The first-order version may need to represent an amount of values that can grow linearly with the number of data values observed so far. The challenge is to provide a compact representation that will grow slowly and can be updated quickly with each incremental calculation that is performed per each new monitored event, even for very long executions.

We used a BDD representation of sets of assignments for the variables that appear in the monitored property. While the size of such BDDs can grow linearly with the number of represented values, it is often much more compact, and the BDD functions of a standard BDD package are optimized for speed. Our representation allows assigning a large number of bits for representing the encoding of values, so that even extremely long executions can be monitorable. However, a lower number of bits is still preferable to a larger number of bits. We presented an algorithm and its implementation for dynamically reclaiming data no longer used, as a function of all current subformula BDDs, representing sets of assignments. That is, the specification is not statically analyzed to achieve this reclamation. Experiments demonstrated that even frequent activation of data reclamation is not necessarily costly, and in fact in combination with a lower number of bits needed can reduce the trace analysis time compared to using more bits and no data reclamation.

We also presented support for numerical relations between variables and constants, and a new form of quantification over values seen in the trace. Future work includes support for functions applied to data values seen in the trace, and real-time constraints. Other future work includes comparison with slicing-based algorithms, as found in e.g. MOP [26] and QEA [27], which are very efficient, however at the price of some limited expressiveness.

References

1. Allan, C., Avgustinov, P., Christensen, A.S., Hendren, L.J., Kuzins, S., Lhotak, O., de Moor, O., Sereni, D., Sittampalam, G., Tibble, J.: Adding trace matching with free variables to AspectJ. In: OOPSLA 2005, pp. 345–364. IEEE (2005)
2. Alpern, B., Schneider, F.B.: Recognizing safety and liveness. Distrib. Comput. **2**(3), 117–126 (1987)
3. D'Angelo, B., Sankaranarayanan, S., Sánchez, C., Robinson, W., Finkbeiner, B., Sipma, H.B., Mehrotra, S., Manna, Z.: LOLA: runtime monitoring of synchronous systems. In: TIME 2005, pp. 166–174 (2005)
4. Apache Commons CSV parser. https://commons.apache.org/proper/commons-csv
5. Barringer, H., Goldberg, A., Havelund, K., Sen, K.: Rule-based runtime verification. In: Steffen, B., Levi, G. (eds.) VMCAI 2004. LNCS, vol. 2937, pp. 44–57. Springer, Heidelberg (2004). https://doi.org/10.1007/978-3-540-24622-0_5
6. Barringer, H., Havelund, K.: TraceContract: a Scala DSL for trace analysis. In: Butler, M., Schulte, W. (eds.) FM 2011. LNCS, vol. 6664, pp. 57–72. Springer, Heidelberg (2011). https://doi.org/10.1007/978-3-642-21437-0_7
7. Barringer, H., Rydeheard, D., Havelund, K.: Rule systems for run-time monitoring: from Eagle to RuleR. In: Sokolsky, O., Taşıran, S. (eds.) RV 2007. LNCS, vol. 4839, pp. 111–125. Springer, Heidelberg (2007). https://doi.org/10.1007/978-3-540-77395-5_10
8. Basin, D.A., Klaedtke, F., Müller, S., Zalinescu, E.: Monitoring metric first-order temporal properties. J. ACM **62**(2), 45 (2015)
9. Bauer, A., Küster, J.-C., Vegliach, G.: From propositional to first-order monitoring. In: Legay, A., Bensalem, S. (eds.) RV 2013. LNCS, vol. 8174, pp. 59–75. Springer, Heidelberg (2013). https://doi.org/10.1007/978-3-642-40787-1_4
10. Bryant, R.E.: Symbolic boolean manipulation with ordered binary-decision diagrams. ACM Comput. Surv. **24**(3), 293–318 (1992)
11. Cormen, Th.H., Leiserson, C.E., Rivest, R.L.: Introduction to Algorithms. The MIT Press and McGraw-Hill Book Company (1989)
12. Chomicki, J.: Efficient checking of temporal integrity constraints using bounded history encoding. ACM Trans. Database Syst. **20**(2), 149–186 (1995)
13. Colombo, C., Pace, G.J., Schneider, G.: LARVA - safer monitoring of real-time Java programs (tool paper), 7th IEEE International Conference on Software Engineering and Formal Methods (SEFM), Hanoi, Vietnam, pp. 33–37. IEEE Computer Society (2009)
14. Decker, N., Leucker, M., Thoma, D.: Monitoring modulo theories. J. Softw. Tools Technol. Transf. **18**(2), 205–225 (2016)
15. Goubault-Larrecq, J., Olivain, J.: A smell of ORCHIDS. In: Leucker, M. (ed.) RV 2008. LNCS, vol. 5289, pp. 1–20. Springer, Heidelberg (2008). https://doi.org/10.1007/978-3-540-89247-2_1
16. Hallé, S., Villemaire, R.: Runtime enforcement of web service message contracts with data. IEEE Trans. Serv. Comput. **5**(2), 192–206 (2012)
17. Havelund, K.: Rule-based runtime verification revisited. J. Softw. Tools Technol. Transf. **17**(2), 143–170 (2015)

18. Havelund, K., Peled, D., Ulus, D.: First-order temporal logic monitoring with BDDs. In: FMCAD 2017, pp. 116–123. IEEE (2017)
19. Havelund, K., Reger, G., Thoma, D., Zălinescu, E.: Monitoring events that carry data. In: Bartocci, E., Falcone, Y. (eds.) Lectures on Runtime Verification. LNCS, vol. 10457, pp. 61–102. Springer, Cham (2018). https://doi.org/10.1007/978-3-319-75632-5_3
20. Havelund, K., Roşu, G.: Synthesizing monitors for safety properties. In: Katoen, J.-P., Stevens, P. (eds.) TACAS 2002. LNCS, vol. 2280, pp. 342–356. Springer, Heidelberg (2002). https://doi.org/10.1007/3-540-46002-0_24
21. JavaBDD. http://javabdd.sourceforge.net
22. Henriksen, J.G., Jensen, J., Jørgensen, M., Klarlund, N., Paige, R., Rauhe, T., Sandholm, A.: Mona: monadic second-order logic in practice. In: Brinksma, E., Cleaveland, W.R., Larsen, K.G., Margaria, T., Steffen, B. (eds.) TACAS 1995. LNCS, vol. 1019, pp. 89–110. Springer, Heidelberg (1995). https://doi.org/10.1007/3-540-60630-0_5
23. Kim, M., Kannan, S., Lee, I., Sokolsky, O.: Java-MaC: a run-time assurance tool for Java. In: Proceedings of the 1st International Workshop on Runtime Verification (RV 2001). ENTCS, vol. 55(2). Elsevier (2001)
24. Lamport, L.: Proving the correctness of multiprocess programs. IEEE Trans. Softw. Eng. 3(2), 125–143 (1977)
25. Manna, Z., Pnueli, A.: Completing the temporal picture. Theor. Comput. Sci. 83, 91–130 (1991)
26. Meredith, P.O., Jin, D., Griffith, D., Chen, F., Rosu, G.: An overview of the MOP runtime verification framework. J. Softw. Tools Technol. Transf. 14, 249–289 (2012)
27. Reger, G., Cruz, H.C., Rydeheard, D.: MarQ: monitoring at runtime with QEA. In: Baier, C., Tinelli, C. (eds.) TACAS 2015. LNCS, vol. 9035, pp. 596–610. Springer, Heidelberg (2015). https://doi.org/10.1007/978-3-662-46681-0_55
28. Scala Parser Combinators. https://github.com/scala/scala-parser-combinators
29. Whaley, J., Avots, D., Carbin, M., Lam, M.S.: Using Datalog with binary decision diagrams for program analysis. In: Yi, K. (ed.) APLAS 2005. LNCS, vol. 3780, pp. 97–118. Springer, Heidelberg (2005). https://doi.org/10.1007/11575467_8

Program Verification with Separation Logic

Radu Iosif[✉]

CNRS/VERIMAG/Université Grenoble Alpes, Grenoble, France
`Radu.Iosif@univ-grenoble-alpes.fr`

Abstract. Separation Logic is a framework for the development of modular program analyses for sequential, inter-procedural and concurrent programs. The first part of the paper introduces Separation Logic first from a historical, then from a program verification perspective. Because program verification eventually boils down to deciding logical queries such as the validity of verification conditions, the second part is dedicated to a survey of decision procedures for Separation Logic, that stem from either SMT, proof theory or automata theory. Incidentally we address issues related to decidability and computational complexity of such problems, in order to expose certain sources of intractability.

1 How It All Started

Separation Logic [Rey02] is nowadays a major paradigm in designing scalable modular verification methods for programs with dynamic memory and destructive pointer updates, which is something that most programs written using imperative languages tend to use. The basic idea that enabled the success, both in academia and in industry, is the embedding of a notion of *resource* within the syntax and proof system of the logic, before it's now widely accepted semantics was even defined.

Resources are understood as items, having finite volume, that can be split (separated) among individuals. Since volumes are finite, splitting reduces the resources in a measurable way and cannot be done *ad infinitum*. The story of how resources and separation ended up in logic can be traced back to Girard's *Linear Logic* [Gir87], the first one to restrict the proof rules of *weakening* and *contraction* in natural deduction:

$$\frac{\Gamma \vdash \psi}{\Gamma, \varphi \vdash \psi} \ (W) \qquad \frac{\Gamma, \varphi, \varphi \vdash \psi}{\Gamma, \varphi \vdash \psi} \ (C)$$

With them, the sequents $\Gamma, \varphi \vdash \psi$ and $\Gamma, \varphi, \varphi \vdash \psi$ can be deduced one from another, but without them, they become unrelated. Removing the (W) and (C) rules leads to two distinct conjunction connectives, illustrated below by their introduction rules:

$$\frac{\Gamma \vdash \varphi \quad \Gamma \vdash \psi}{\Gamma \vdash \varphi \wedge \psi} \ (\wedge I) \qquad \frac{\Gamma \vdash \varphi \quad \Delta \vdash \psi}{\Gamma, \Delta \vdash \varphi * \psi} \ (*I)$$

While $\wedge$ is the classical conjunction, for which (W) and (C) apply, $*$ is a new *separating* conjunction, for which they don't [OP99].

© Springer International Publishing AG, part of Springer Nature 2018
M. M. Gallardo and P. Merino (Eds.): SPIN 2018, LNCS 10869, pp. 48–62, 2018.
https://doi.org/10.1007/978-3-319-94111-0_3

In natural deduction, conjunction and implication are intertwined, the following introduction rule being regarded as the definition of the implication:

$$\frac{\Gamma, \varphi \vdash \psi}{\Gamma \vdash \varphi \to \psi} \, (\to I)$$

The connection is given by the fact that the comma on a sequent's antecedent is interpreted as conjunction. However, if now we have two conjunctions, we must distinguish them in the antecedents, and moreover, we obtain two implications:

$$\frac{\Gamma; \varphi \vdash \psi}{\Gamma \vdash \varphi \to \psi} \, (\to I) \qquad \frac{\Gamma, \varphi \vdash \psi}{\Gamma \vdash \varphi \twoheadrightarrow \psi} \, (\twoheadrightarrow I)$$

We use semicolumn and comma for the classical and separating conjunctions, while $\to$ and $\twoheadrightarrow$ denote the classical and separating implications, respectively. Antecedents are no more viewed as sets but as trees (bunches) with leaves labeled by propositions and internal nodes labeled with semicolumns or commas. Furthermore, $(\twoheadrightarrow I)$ leads to consumption of antecedent nodes and cannot be applied indefinitely. This is where resources became part of the logic, before any semantics was attributed to it.

2   Heaps as Resources

Since the most expensive resource of a computer is the memory, it is only natural to define the semantics of the logic (initially called BI, for *Bunched Implications*) with memory as the resource. There are several memory models and the one on the lowest level views memory as an array of bounded values indexed by addresses.

However, the model which became widespread is the one allowing to reason about the shape (topology) of recursive data structures. In this model, the memory (heap) is viewed as a graph, where nodes represent cells and edges represent pointers between cells, and there is no comparison between cells, other than equality.

This new logic, called *Separation Logic* (SL), is equipped with equality and two atomic propositions, emp for the empty heap and $x \mapsto (y_1, \ldots, y_k)$ meaning that x is the only allocated memory address and there are exactly k pointers from x to $y_1, \ldots, y_k$, respectively. From now on, k is a strictly positive parameter of the logic and SL^k denotes the set of formulae generated by the grammar below:

$$\varphi := \bot \mid \top \mid \mathrm{emp} \mid x \approx y \mid x \mapsto (y_1, \ldots, y_k) \mid \varphi \wedge \varphi \mid \neg \varphi \mid \varphi * \varphi \mid \varphi \twoheadrightarrow \varphi \mid \exists x . \varphi$$

SL^k formulae are interpreted over SL-*structures* $I = (\mathfrak{U}, \mathfrak{s}, \mathfrak{h})$, where $\mathfrak{U}$ is a countable set, called the *universe*, the elements of which are called *locations*, $\mathfrak{s} : \mathrm{Var} \rightharpoonup \mathfrak{U}$ is a mapping of variables to locations, called a *store* and $\mathfrak{h} : \mathfrak{U} \rightharpoonup_{fin} \mathfrak{U}^k$ is a finite partial mapping of locations to k-tuples of locations, called a *heap*. We denote by $\mathrm{dom}(\mathfrak{h})$ the domain of the heap $\mathfrak{h}$. A cell $\ell \in \mathfrak{U}$ is *allocated* in I if $\ell \in \mathrm{dom}(\mathfrak{h})$ and *dangling* otherwise.

The notion of separable resources is now embedded in the semantics of SL. Two heaps $\mathfrak{h}_1$ and $\mathfrak{h}_2$ are *disjoint* if and only if $\text{dom}(\mathfrak{h}_1) \cap \text{dom}(\mathfrak{h}_2) = \emptyset$, in which case $\mathfrak{h}_1 \uplus \mathfrak{h}_2$ denotes their union ($\uplus$ is undefined for non-disjoint heaps). A heap $\mathfrak{h}$ is a *subheap* of $\mathfrak{h}'$ if and only if $\mathfrak{h}' = \mathfrak{h} \uplus \mathfrak{h}''$, for some heap $\mathfrak{h}''$. The relation $(\mathfrak{U}, \mathfrak{s}, \mathfrak{h}) \models \varphi$ is defined inductively below:

$$
\begin{aligned}
(\mathfrak{U}, \mathfrak{s}, \mathfrak{h}) &\models \text{emp} & &\Leftrightarrow \mathfrak{h} = \emptyset \\
(\mathfrak{U}, \mathfrak{s}, \mathfrak{h}) &\models x \mapsto (y_1, \ldots, y_k) & &\Leftrightarrow \mathfrak{h} = \{\langle \mathfrak{s}(x), (\mathfrak{s}(y_1), \ldots, \mathfrak{s}(y_k)) \rangle\} \\
(\mathfrak{U}, \mathfrak{s}, \mathfrak{h}) &\models \varphi_1 * \varphi_2 & &\Leftrightarrow \text{there exist disjoint heaps } h_1, h_2 \text{ such that } h = h_1 \uplus h_2 \\
& & & \quad \text{and } (\mathfrak{U}, \mathfrak{s}, \mathfrak{h}_i) \models \varphi_i, \text{ for } i = 1, 2 \\
(\mathfrak{U}, \mathfrak{s}, \mathfrak{h}) &\models \varphi_1 \mathbin{-\!\!*} \varphi_2 & &\Leftrightarrow \text{for all heaps } \mathfrak{h}' \text{ disjoint from } \mathfrak{h} \text{ such that } (\mathfrak{U}, \mathfrak{s}, \mathfrak{h}') \models \varphi_1, \\
& & & \quad \text{we have } (\mathfrak{U}, \mathfrak{s}, \mathfrak{h}' \uplus \mathfrak{h}) \models \varphi_2
\end{aligned}
$$

The semantics of equality, boolean and first-order connectives is the usual one and thus omitted. The question is now what can be expressed in SL and what kind of reasoning[1] could be carried out?

First, one defines a single (finite) heap structure up to equality on dangling cells. This is done considering the following fragment of *symbolic heaps*:

$$
\Pi := x \approx y \mid x \neq y \mid \Pi_1 \wedge \Pi_2
$$
$$
\Sigma := \text{emp} \mid x \mapsto (y_1, \ldots, y_k) \mid \Sigma_1 * \Sigma_2
$$

The Π formulae are called *pure* as they do not depend on the heap. The Σ formulae are called *spatial*. A symbolic heap is a conjunction $\Sigma \wedge \Pi$, defining a finite set of heaps.

For instance, $x \mapsto (y_1, y_2) * y_1 \mapsto (x, y_2) \wedge y_1 \neq y_2$ defines cyclic heaps of length two, in which x and y_1 are distinct, x points to y_1, y_1 points to x and both point to y_2. Further, y_2 is distinct from y_1, but could be aliased with x. Observe that $x \mapsto (y_1, y_2) * y_1 \mapsto (x, y_2) \wedge x \approx y_1$ is unsatisfiable, because $x \mapsto (y_1, y_2)$ and $y_1 \mapsto (x, y_2)$ define separated singleton heaps, in which $x \approx y_1$ is not possible.

However, being able to define just bounded heaps is not satisfactory, because one needs to represent potentially infinite sets of structures of unbounded size, such as the ones generated during the execution of a program. Since most imperative programmers are used to working with recursive data structures, a natural requirement is using SL to define the usual recursive datatypes, such as singly- and doubly-linked lists, trees, etc. It turns out that this requires *inductive definitions*. For instance, the following inductive definitions describe an acyclic and a possibly cyclic list segment, respectively:

$$
\begin{aligned}
\widehat{\text{ls}}(x, y) &\leftarrow \text{emp} \wedge x \approx y \ \vee\ \neg(x \approx y) \wedge \exists z \,.\, x \mapsto z * \widehat{\text{ls}}(z, y) & &\text{acyclic list segment from } x \text{ to } y \\
\text{ls}(x, y) &\leftarrow \text{emp} \wedge x \approx y \ \vee\ \exists u \,.\, x \mapsto u * \text{ls}(u, y) & &\text{list segment from } x \text{ to } y
\end{aligned}
$$

Intuitively, an acyclic list segment is either empty, in which case the head and the tail coincide [$\text{emp} \wedge x \approx y$], or contains at least one element which is disjoint from the

---

[1] We use the term "reasoning" in general, not necessarily push-button automated decision.

rest of the list segment. Observe that $x \mapsto z$ and $\widehat{ls}(z,y)$ hold over disjoint parts of the heap, which ensures that the definition unfolds producing distinct cells. The constraint $\neg(x \approx y)$, in the inductive definition of $\widehat{ls}$, captures the fact that the tail of the list segment is distinct from every allocated cell in the list segment, which ensures the acyclicity condition. Since this constraint is omitted from the definition of the second (possibly cyclic) list segment $ls(x,y)$, its tail y is allowed to point inside the set of allocated cells.

As usual, the semantics of inductive definitions is given by the least fixed point of a monotone function between sets of finite SL-structures. To avoid clutter, we omit this definition, but point out that the reasons why symbolic heaps define monotone functions are that (i) $*$'s do not occur negated, and (ii) $-*$'s are not used.

In fact, one may wonder, at this point, why only $*$'s are used for specification of data structures and what is the rôle of $-*$ in reasoning about programs? The answer is given in the next section.

3   Program Verification

Program verification means providing a proof for the following problem: given a program P and a set of states Ψ, is there an execution of P ending in a state from Ψ? More concretely, Ψ can be a set of "bad" states in which the program ends after attempting to dereference an unallocated pointer variable, or after leaking memory. A program proof consist in annotating the program with assertions that (i) must hold each time the control reaches an assertion site, such that (ii) the set Ψ is excluded from the reachable states of P.

Ensuring the point (i) requires proving the validity of a certain number of Hoare triples of the form $\{\phi\}$ C $\{\psi\}$, each of which amounts to proving the validity of an entailment $\phi \Rightarrow \widetilde{\mathrm{pre}}(C,\psi)$, or equivalently, $\widetilde{\mathrm{post}}(C,\phi) \Rightarrow \psi$, where $\widetilde{\mathrm{pre}}$ and $\widetilde{\mathrm{post}}$ are the weakest precondition and the strongest postcondition predicate transformers. Such entailments are called *verification conditions*.

In the seminal papers of Ishtiaq and O'Hearn [IO01] and Reynolds [Rey02], SL was assigned the purpose of an assertion logic in a Hoare-like logic used for writing correctness proofs of pointer-manipulating programs. This turn from proof theory [OP99] to program proofs removes a long-standing thorn from the side of Hoare logicians, namely that the substitution-based assignment rule $\{\phi[E/x]\}$ x $= E$ $\{\phi\}$ [Hoa69] is no longer valid in the presence of pointers and aliasing.

The other problems, originally identified in the seminal works of Floyd [Flo67] and Hoare [Hoa69] are how to accomodate program proofs with procedure calls and concurrency. Surprisingly, the $*$ connective provides very elegant solutions to these problems as well, enabling the effective transfer of this theory from academia to industry.

In general, writing Hoare-style proofs requires lots of human insight, essentially for (i) infering appropriate loop invariants, and (ii) solving the verification conditions obtained from the pre- or postcondition calculus that captures the semantics of a straight-line program. With SL as an assertion language, automation is possible but currently at (what we believe are) the early stages.

For instance, the problem (i) can be tackled using abstract interpretation [CC79], but the (logical) abstract domains currently used are based on the hardcoded $ls(x,y)$

predicate, making use of specific properties of heaps with a single pointer field, that are composed of lists, and which can be captured by finitary abstractions [BBH+06]. An extension to nested lists (doubly-linked lists of … of doubly-linked lists) has been since developed in the SPACEINVADER tool [BCC+07] and later shipped to industry in the INFER tool [CD11].

Alternatives to invariant inference using fixed point computations are also possible. These methods use the expressive power of the higher-order inductive definitions of SL and attempt to define inductive predicates that precisely define loop invariants, using only a single symbolic execution pass through the loop [LGQC14]. The difficulty of the verification problem is then shipped to the decision procedure that solves the verification condition thus obtained (ii). This is probably the real problem standing in front of the researchers that aim at developing a fully push-button program verification method for real-life programs, based on SL. We shall survey this issue at large in Sect. 4

3.1 While Programs

Perhaps the longest lasting impression after reading Ishtiaq and O'Hearn's paper [IO01] is that a sound and complete weakest precondition calculus for programs with pointers and destructive updates has finally been found. But let us first recall the problem with Hoare's substitution-based assignment rule. Consider the triple

$$\{(y.data = 2 \wedge x = y)[1/x.data]\} \; x.data := 1 \; \{y.data = 2 \wedge x = y\}$$

which is the same as $\{y.data = 2 \wedge x = y\} \; x.data := 1 \; \{y.data = 2 \wedge x = y\}$ because the substitution has no effect on the precondition. The triple is clearly invalid, because the assignment x.data := 1 makes the assertion x.data = 2 false.

The solution provided by SL is of great simplicity and elegance. Since pointer updates alter a small part of the heap, we can "remove" this part using $*$ and "replace" it with an updated heap, using $-\!\!*$, while requiring that the postcondition hold afterwards:

$$\{\exists x \exists y \, . \, u \mapsto (x, y) * ((u \mapsto (v, y)) -\!\!* \phi)\} \; u.1 := v \; \{\phi\}$$

where u.1 := v denotes the assignment of the first selector of the cell referred to by u to v. We have a similar weakest precondition for memory allocation, where we adopt the more structured object-oriented constructor cons(v, w) instead of C's malloc(n):

$$\{\forall x. \, (x \mapsto (v, w)) -\!\!* \phi[x/u]\} \; u := cons(v, w) \; \{\phi\}$$

Observe that this calculus produces preconditions that mix $*$ and $-\!\!*$ with quantifiers. Very early, this hindered the automation of program proofs, because at the time, there was no "*automatic theorem prover which can deal with the form of these assertions (which use quantification and the separating implication)*" [BCO05]. This issue, together with a rather coarse undecidability result for quantified SL formulae [CYO01] made researchers almost entirely forget about the existence of $-\!\!*$ and of the weakest precondition calculus, for more than a decade. During this time, program verifiers used (and still do) incomplete, overapproximating, postcondition calculi on (inductive definitions on top of) $*$-based symbolic heaps. In the light of recent results concerning decision procedures for the base assertion SL language, we believe this difficulties can be overcome. A detailed presentation of these results is given in Sect. 4.1.

Before going further, an interesting observation can be made. The weakest precondition of a straight-line program, in which more than one such statement occurs in a sequence, would be a formula in which first-order quantifiers occur within the scope of a separating connective. This could potentially be problematic for automated reasoning because, unlike first order logic, SL formulae do not have a prenex form: $\phi * \forall x . \psi(x) \not\equiv \forall x . \phi * \psi(x)$ and $\phi \mathbin{-\!\!*} \exists x . \psi(x) \not\equiv \exists x . \phi \mathbin{-\!\!*} \psi(x)$. However, the following notion of *precise formulae* comes to rescue in this case [OYR04]:

Definition 1. *A* SL *formula* ϕ *is precise if and only if, for all* SL*-structures* $I = (\mathfrak{U}, \mathfrak{s}, \mathfrak{h})$ *there exists at most one subheap* $\mathfrak{h}'$ *of* $\mathfrak{h}$ *such that* $(\mathfrak{U}, \mathfrak{s}, \mathfrak{h}') \models \phi$.

If ϕ is precise, we recover the equivalences $\phi * \forall x . \psi(x) \equiv \forall x . \phi * \psi(x)$ and $\phi \mathbin{-\!\!*} \exists x . \psi(x) \equiv \exists x . \phi \mathbin{-\!\!*} \psi(x)$. Moreover, since formulae such as $x \mapsto (y, z)$ are precise, one can hoist the first-order quantifiers and write any precondition in prenex form. As we shall see (Sect. 4.1) prenexisation of formulae is an important step towards the decidability of the base assertion language.

3.2   Local Reasoning and Modularity

Being able to provide easy-to-write specifications of recursive data structures (lists, trees, etc.) as well as concise weakest preconditions of pointer updates, were the first salient features of SL. With separating conjunction $*$ as the main connective, a principle of *local reasoning* has emerged:

> *To understand how a program works, it should be possible for reasoning and specification to be confined to the cells that the program actually accesses. The value of any other cell will automatically remain unchanged* [ORY01].

The rôle of the separating conjunction in local reasoning requires little explanation. If a set of program states is specified as $\varphi * \psi$, and the update occurs only in the φ part, then we are sure that ψ is not affected by the update and can be copied from pre- to postcondition as it is. This is formalized by the following *frame rule*:

$$\frac{\{\varphi\}\, P\, \{\phi\}}{\{\varphi * \psi\}\, P\, \{\phi * \psi\}} \quad \mathsf{modifies}(\mathsf{P}) \cap \mathsf{var}(\psi) = \emptyset$$

where $\mathsf{modifies}(\mathsf{P})$ is the set of variables whose value is changed by the program P, defined recursively on the syntactic structure of P.

The frame rule allows to break a program proof into small pieces that can be specified locally. However, locality should not be confounded with *modularity*, which is the key to scalability of program verification technique. Indeed, most large, industrial-size programs are built from a large number of small *components*, such as functions (procedures) or threads, in a concurrent setting.

By a *modular program verification* we understand a method capable of inferring specifications of any given program component in isolation, independently on the context in which the other components interact with the component's environment. Then the local specifications are combined into a global one, using the frame rule or a variant thereof. Observe that this is not to be mixed up with program verification algorithms that store and reuse analysis results.

An example of modular program verification with SL is the compositional shape analysis based on the inference of *footprints* [CDOY07]. These are summaries specified as pairs of pre-/postconditions, that guarantee absence of implicit memory faults, such as null pointer dereferences or memory leaks. The important point is that footprints can be inferred directly from the program, without user-supplied pre- or postconditions.

Combining component footprints into a global verification condition is the other ingredient of a modular verification technique. Since footprints are generated without knowledge of their context, sometimes their combination requires some "adjustment". To understand this point, consider an interprocedural analysis in which a function $foo(x,y)$ is invoked at a call site. The summary of the function, inferred by footprint analysis, is say $ls(x,z) * ls(y,nil)$, using the previously defined inductive predicates (Sect. 2). Informally, this sais that there is a list segment from x to z and disjointly a nil-ending list starting with y. Assume further that $x \mapsto z$ is the assertion at the call site. Clearly $x \mapsto z$ does not entail $ls(x,z) * ls(y,nil)$, in which case a classical interprocedural analysis would give up.

However, an SL-based interprocedural analysis uses the frame rule for function calls and may reason in the following way: find a frame ϕ such that $x \mapsto z * \phi \Rightarrow ls(x,z) * ls(y,nil)$. In this case, a possible answer (frame) is $\phi = ls(y,nil)$. If the current precondition of the caller of $foo(x,y)$ is φ, we percolate the frame all the way up to the caller and modify its precondition to $\varphi * \phi$, as local reasoning allows us to do. This method is implemented by the INFER analyzer and is used, on an industrial scale, at Facebook [CD11].

This style of modular verification introduces *abductive reasoning* as a way to perform frame inference. In classical logic, the abduction problem is: given an assumption ϕ and a goal ψ, find a missing assumption X such that $\phi \wedge X \Rightarrow \psi$. Typically, we aim at finding the weakest such assumption, which belongs, moreover, to a given language (a disjunction of conjunctive assertions pertaining to a restricted set). If we drop the latter requirement, about the allowed form of X, we obtain the weakest solution $X = \phi \rightarrow \psi$.

Abductive reasoning in SL follows a very similar pattern. An abduction problem is: given assertions ϕ and ψ, find an assertion X such that $\phi * X \Rightarrow \psi$. Similar to the classical case, the weakest solution, in this case is ... $X = \phi -\!* \psi$! So the long-forgotten magic wand comes back to program analysis, this time by way of abduction. However, since decision procedures for SL still have a hard time in dealing with $-\!*$, they use underapproximations of the weakest solutions, that are mostly good enough for the purposes of the proof [CDOY11].

4 Decision Procedures

As mentioned in the introduction of Sect. 3, the job of a verifier is turning a program verification problem into a (finite) number of logical entailments of the form $\phi \Rightarrow \psi$, called verification conditions. In this section, we survey how one can establish the validity of such entailments, provided that ϕ and ψ are SL formulae.

If the fragment of SL to which ϕ and ψ belong is closed under negation, the entailment $\phi \Rightarrow \psi$ is valid if and only if the formula $\phi \wedge \neg \psi$ is unsatisfiable. Usually negation is part of basic SL assertions, that do not use inductive definitions. These are mostly discussed in Sect. 4.1. In this case, we reduce the entailment to a satisfiability problem, that ultimately, can be solved using SMT technology.

If the logic in which ϕ and ψ are written does not have negation, which is typically the case of inductive definitions built on top of symbolic heaps, we deal with entailments directly, either by proof-theoretic (we search for a sequent calculus proof of the entailment) or automata-theoretic (we reduce to the inclusion between the languages of two automata) arguments. The pros and cons of each approach are discussed in Sect. 4.2.

4.1 Basic Logic

Let us consider the language SL^k given in Sect. 2. For $k \geq 2$, undecidability of this logic occurs even if separating connectives are almost not used at all. If one encodes an uninterpreted binary relation $R(x,y)$ as $\exists z \, . \, z \mapsto (x,y) * \top$, undecidability occurs as a simple consequence of Trakhtenbrot's result for finite satisfiability of first-order logic [BGG97]. If $k = 1$, the logic is still undecidable, but the fragment of SL^1 without $-\!*$ becomes decidable, with a nonelementary recursive complexity lower bound [BDL12].

On the other hand, the quantifier-free fragment of SL^k is PSPACE-complete, for any $k \geq 1$ [CYO01]. The crux of this proof is a small model property of quantifier-free SL^k. If a formula ϕ in this language has a model $(\mathfrak{U}, \mathfrak{s}, \mathfrak{h})$ then it has a model where $\|\mathfrak{h}\| = O(\mathrm{size}(\phi))$. This also provides effective algorithms for the satisfiability problem. It is possible, for instance, to encode the quantifier-free SL^k formula in first-order logic with bitvectors and use existing SMT technology for the latter [CGH05], or directly using a DPLL(T)-style algorithm that attempts to build a model of bounded size and learns from backtracking [RISK16].

The quantifier-free fragment of SL^k is also important in understanding the expressiveness of SL, relative to that of classical first- and second-order logics. This point addresses a more fundamental question, relative to the presence of the separating connectives $*$ and $-\!*$: is it possible to reason about resources and separation in first-order logic, or does one need quantified relations, as the heap semantics of SL^k suggests?

It turns out that, surprisingly, the entire *prenex fragment* of SL^k can be embedded into uninterpreted first-order logic. This is the set of formulae $Q_1 x_1 \ldots Q_n x_n \, . \, \phi$, where ϕ is quantifier-free. First, we consider a small set of patterns, called *test formulae*, that use $*$ and $-\!*$ in very restricted ways:

Definition 2. *The following patterns are called* test formulae*:*

$$x \hookrightarrow (y_1, \ldots, y_k) \stackrel{\mathrm{def}}{=} x \mapsto (y_1, \ldots, y_k) * \top \qquad |U| \geq n \stackrel{\mathrm{def}}{=} \neg(\top -\!* \neg(|h| \geq n)), \, n \in \mathbb{N}$$

$$\mathrm{alloc}(x) \stackrel{\mathrm{def}}{=} x \mapsto \underbrace{(x, \ldots, x)}_{k \text{ times}} -\!* \bot \qquad |h| \geq |U| - n \stackrel{\mathrm{def}}{=} |h| \geq n+1 -\!* \bot, n \in \mathbb{N}$$

$$|h| \geq n \stackrel{\mathrm{def}}{=} \begin{cases} |h| \geq n-1 * \neg\mathrm{emp}, & \text{if } n > 0 \\ \top, & \text{if } n = 0 \\ \bot, & \text{if } n = \infty \end{cases}$$

and $x \approx y$, where $x, y \in \mathsf{Var}$, $\mathbf{y} \in \mathsf{Var}^k$ and $n \in \mathbb{N}_\infty$ is a positive integer or ∞.

Observe first that $-\!\!\ast$ is instrumental in defining allocation without the use of existential quantifiers, as in $\mathsf{alloc}(x) \stackrel{\text{def}}{=} \exists y_1 \ldots \exists y_n . x \mapsto (y_1, \ldots, y_k) \ast \top$. Second, it can express cardinality constraints relative to the size of the universe $|U| \geq n$ and $|h| \geq |U| - n$, assuming that it is finite.

In contrast with the majority of the literature on Separation Logic, here the universe of *available* memory locations (besides the ones occurring in the heap, which is finite) is not automatically assumed to be infinite. In particular, the finite universe hypothesis is useful when dealing with bounded memory issues, for instance checking that the execution of the program satisfies its postcondition, provided that there are sufficiently many available memory cells. Having different interpretations of the universe is also motivated by a recent integration of SL^k within the DPLL(T)-based SMT solver CVC4 [RISK16, RIS17], in which the SL theory is parameterized by the theory of locations, just like the theories of arrays and sets are parameterized by theories of values.

A first nice result is that any quantifier-free SL^k formula is equivalent to a boolean combination of test formulae [EIP18b]. Then we can define an equivalence-preserving translation of the quantifier-free fragment of SL^k into FO. Let $\eth$ be a unary predicate symbol and let $\mathfrak{f}_i$ (for $i = 1, \ldots, k$) be unary function symbols. We define the following transformation from quantified boolean combinations of test formulae into first order formulae:

$$\Theta(x \approx y) \stackrel{\text{def}}{=} x \approx y$$
$$\Theta(x \hookrightarrow (y_1, \ldots, y_k)) \stackrel{\text{def}}{=} \eth(x) \wedge \bigwedge_{i=1}^{k} y_i \approx \mathfrak{f}_i(x)$$
$$\Theta(\mathsf{alloc}(x)) \stackrel{\text{def}}{=} \eth(x)$$
$$\Theta(\neg\phi) \stackrel{\text{def}}{=} \neg\Theta(\phi)$$
$$\Theta(\phi_1 \bullet \phi_2) \stackrel{\text{def}}{=} \Theta(\phi_1) \bullet \Theta(\phi_2) \qquad \text{if } \bullet \in \{\wedge, \vee, \rightarrow, \leftrightarrow\}$$
$$\Theta(Qx . \phi) \stackrel{\text{def}}{=} Qx . \Theta(\phi) \qquad \text{if } Q \in \{\exists, \forall\}$$
$$\Theta(|U| \geq n) \stackrel{\text{def}}{=} \exists x_1, \ldots, x_n . \mathsf{distinct}(x_1, \ldots, x_n)$$
$$\Theta(|h| \geq n) \stackrel{\text{def}}{=} \exists x_1, \ldots, x_n . \mathsf{distinct}(x_1, \ldots, x_n) \wedge \bigwedge_{i=1}^{n} \eth(x_i)$$
$$\Theta(|h| \geq |U| - n) \stackrel{\text{def}}{=} \exists x_1, \ldots, x_n \forall y . \bigwedge_{i=1}^{n} y \not\approx x_i \rightarrow \eth(y)$$

As a result of this translation, any formula of the prenex fragment of SL^k is equivalent to a first-order formula that uses one monadic predicate and k monadic function symbols. Thus, we obtain the decidability of the prenex fragment of SL^1 as a consequence of the decidability of first-order logic with one monadic function symbol and any number of monadic predicate symbols [BGG97]. Moreover, for $k \geq 2$, undecidability occurs even for the quantifier prefix of the form $\exists^* \forall^*$, if universally quantified variables occur under the scope of $-\!\!\ast$. However, if this is not the case, $\exists^* \forall^*$ fragment of SL^k becomes PSPACE-complete [EIP18b].

Interestingly, if $k = 1$ again, the $\exists^* \forall^*$ fragment is PSPACE-complete independently of how $-\!\!\ast$ is used [EIP18a]. This result points out the difference between the prenex fragment of SL^1 and SL^1 with unrestricted use of quantifiers, which is undecidable: in fact, the full second-order logic can be embedded within it [BDL12]. For program verification, the good news is that, as discussed in Sect. 3, the prenex fragment is closed under weakest preconditions, making it possible to verify straight-line programs obtained by loop unfolding, à la Bounded Model Checking.

4.2 Inductive Definitions

Let us now turn to the definition of recursive data structures using inductive definitions in SL^k. As a first remark, the base assertion language is usually that of symbolic heaps $\Sigma \wedge \Pi$, where Σ is either emp or a finite $*$-conjunction and Π is either $\top$ or a nonempty conjunction of equalities and disequalities between variables. A system of inductive definitions is a set of rules of the form $p(\mathbf{x}_0) \leftarrow \Sigma \wedge \Pi * p_1(\mathbf{x}_1) * \ldots p_n(\mathbf{x}_n)$, where w.l.o.g. $\mathbf{x}_0, \ldots, \mathbf{x}_n$ are pairwise disjoint sets of variables and $var(\Sigma \wedge \Pi) \subseteq \bigcup_{i=0}^{n} \mathbf{x}_i$. The examples below show the inductive definitions of a doubly-linked list $dll(hd, p, tl, n)$ and of a tree with linked leaves $tll(root, ll, lr)$, respectively:

$$dll(hd, p, tl, n) \leftarrow hd \mapsto (n, p) \wedge hd = tl$$
$$dll(hd, p, tl, n) \leftarrow \exists x . hd \mapsto (x, p) * dll(x, hd, tl, n)$$

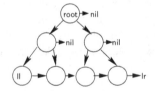

$$tll(root, ll, lr) \leftarrow root \mapsto (nil, nil, lr) \wedge root = ll$$
$$tll(root, ll, lr) \leftarrow \exists l \exists r \exists z . root \mapsto (l, r, nil) * tll(l, ll, z) * tll(r, z, lr)$$

A solution of an inductive predicate system is a mapping of predicates to sets of SL-structures and the semantics of a predicate p, denoted $[\![p]\!]$ corresponds to the set of structures assigned to it by the least solution of the system. The *entailment problem* is given a system and two predicates p and q, does $[\![p]\!] \subseteq [\![q]\!]$ hold? In general, this problem is undecidable [AGH+14, IRV14].

Automata-Based Techniques. As usual, we bypass undecidability by defining a number of easy-to-check restrictions on the system of predicates:

- *Progress*: each rule allocates exactly one node, called the root of the rule. This condition makes our technical life easier, and can be lifted in many cases — rules with more than one allocation can be split by introducing new predicates.
- *Connectivity*: for each inductive rule of the form $\Sigma * p_1(\mathbf{x}_1) * \ldots * p_n(\mathbf{x}_n) \wedge \Pi$, there exists at least one edge between the root of the rule and the root of each rule of p_i, for all $i \in [1, n]$. This restriction prevents the encoding of context-free languages in SL, which requires disconnected rules, leading to undecidability.

– *Establishment*: all existentially quantified variables in a recursive rule are eventually allocated. This restriction is not required for the satisfiability problem, but it is essential for entailment.

The fragment of SL obtained by applying the above, rather natural, restrictions, is denoted SL_{btw} in the following. The proof of decidability for entailments in SL_{btw} relies on three main ingredients:

1. for each predicate p in the system, all heaps from the least solution $[\![p]\!]$ are represented by graphs, whose *treewidth is bounded* by a linear function in the size of the system.
2. we define, for each predicate p, a formula Φ_p in *monadic second-order logic* (MSO) of graphs whose models are exactly the graphs encoding the heaps from the least solution $[\![p]\!]$.
3. the entailment problem $[\![p]\!] \subseteq [\![q]\!]$ is reduced to the satisfiability of an MSO formula $\Phi_p \wedge \neg\Phi_q$. Since all models of p (thus of Φ_p) have bounded treewidth, this problem is decidable, by Courcelle's Theorem [Cou90].

This approach suggests that a direct encoding of the least solution of a system of inductive definitions is possible, using tree automata. That is, for each predicate p, we define a tree automaton A_p that recognizes the set of structures from $[\![p]\!]$, and the entailment problem $[\![p]\!] \subseteq [\![q]\!]$ reduces to a language inclusion problem between tree automata $\mathcal{L}(A_p) \subseteq \mathcal{L}(A_q)$.

However, there are instances of the entailment problem that cannot be directly solved by language inclusion between tree automata, due to the following *polymorphic representation problem*: the same set of states can be defined by two different inductive predicates, and the tree automata mirroring their definitions will report that the entailment does not hold. For example, doubly-linked lists can also be defined in reverse:

$$\mathsf{dll}_{rev}(\mathsf{hd},\mathsf{n},\mathsf{tl},\mathsf{p}) \equiv \mathsf{hd} \mapsto (\mathsf{p},\mathsf{n}) \wedge \mathsf{hd} = \mathsf{tl} \vee \exists x \,.\, \mathsf{tl} \mapsto (x,\mathsf{n}) * \mathsf{dll}_{rev}(\mathsf{hd},\mathsf{tl},x,\mathsf{p})$$

A partial solution is to build tree automata only for a restriction of SL_{btw}, called the *local fragment* (SL_{loc}). The structures that are models of predicates defined in this fragment have the following nice property: whenever the same structure is encoded by two different spanning trees, the two trees are related by a *rotation* relation, which changes the root to an arbitrary internal node, and the orientation of the edges from the path to the root to that node. We can thus check $[\![p]\!] \subseteq [\![q]\!]$ in this fragment by checking the inclusion between A_p and A_q^{rot}, where A_q^{rot} is automaton recognizing the closure of the language of A_q under rotation. Moreover, since the rotation closure of a tree automaton is possible in polynomial (quadratic) time, the entailment problem for SL_{loc} can be shown to be EXPTIME-complete [IRV14]. It is still an open question, whether this tight complexity bound applies to the entire SL_{btw} logic.

Proof-Based Techniques. An experimental evaluation of SL inductive entailment solvers, carried out during the SL-COMP 2014 solver competition [SC14], shows the strengths and weaknesses of automata-based versus proof-based solvers. On one hand, automata-based solvers can cope with polymorphic representations in a much better way than proof-based solvers, which require complex cut rules, whose completeness is far from being understood [CJT15].

On the other hand, proof-based solvers are more flexible in dealing with extensions of the base theory (symbolic heaps), such as arbitrary equalities and disequalities or even (limited forms of) data constraints. Moreover, they can easily interact with SMT solvers and discharge proof obligations belonging to the base logic. However, as the example below shows, this requires quantifiers.

Consider a fragment of the inductive proof showing that any acyclic list segment is also a list segment, given below:

$$\dfrac{\dfrac{\widehat{\mathsf{ls}}(z,y) \vdash \mathsf{ls}(z,y)}{\neg(x \approx y) \wedge x \mapsto z * \widehat{\mathsf{ls}}(z,y) \vdash \exists u \,.\, x \mapsto u * \mathsf{ls}(u,y) \vee \mathsf{emp} \wedge x \approx y}}{\widehat{\mathsf{ls}}(x,y) \vdash \mathsf{ls}(x,y)} \qquad \dfrac{\neg(x \approx y) \wedge x \mapsto z \models \exists u \,.\, x \mapsto u}{\text{by instantiation } u \leftarrow z}$$

The bottom inference rule introduces one of the two cases produced by unfolding the inductive definitions on both sides of the sequent[2]. The second inference rule is a reduction of the sequent obtained by unfolding, to a sequent matching the initial one (by renaming z to x), and allows to close this branch of the proof by an inductive argument, based on the principle of infinite descent [BDP11].

The simplification applied by the second inference above relies on the validity of the entailment $\neg(x \approx y) \wedge x \mapsto z \models \exists u \,.\, x \mapsto u$, which reduces to the (un)satisfiability of the formula $\neg(x \approx y) \wedge x \mapsto z \wedge \forall u \,.\, \neg x \mapsto u$. The latter falls into the prenex fragment, defined by the $\exists^*\forall^*$ quantifier prefix, and can be proved unsatisfiable using the instantiation of the universally quantified variable u with the existentially quantified variable z (or a corresponding Skolem constant). In other words, this formula is unsatisfiable because the universal quantified subformula asks that no memory cell is pointed to by x, which is contradicted by $x \mapsto z$. The instantiation of u that violates the universal condition is $u \leftarrow z$, which is carried over in the rest of the proof.

This example shows the need for a tight interaction between the decision procedures for the (quantified) base logic SL^k and the entailment provers for systems of inductive definitions built on top of it. An implementation of an inductive prover that uses SMT technology to simplify sequents is INDUCTOR [Ser17], which uses CVC4 [BCD+11] for the reduction step. Just like the CYCLIST prover [BGP12] before, INDUCTOR is based on the principle of infinite descent [BDP11].

Future plans for INDUCTOR involve adding cut rules that would allow dealing with polymorphic representations of recursive data structures in a proof-theoretic fashion, as well as dealing with theories of the data within memory cells.

5   Conclusions

This paper surveys Separation Logic, a logical framework used to design modular and local analyses for programs that manipulate pointers and dynamically allocated mem-

---

[2] The second case $\mathsf{emp} \wedge x \approx y \vdash \exists u \,.\, x \mapsto u * \mathsf{ls}(u,y) \vee \mathsf{emp} \wedge x \approx y$ is trivial and omitted for clarity.

ory cells. The essence of the logic is a notion of separable resource, which is embedded in the syntax and the proof system of the logic, before its nowadays widely accepted semantics was adopted. Program verifiers based on Separation Logic use local reasoning to model the updates in a compact way, by distinguishing the parts of the heap modified from the ones that are unchanged. The price to be paid for this expressivity is the difficulty of providing push-button decision procedures for it. However, recent advances show precisely what are the theoretical limits of decidability and how one can accomodate interesting program verification problems within them.

References

[AGH+14] Antonopoulos, T., Gorogiannis, N., Haase, C., Kanovich, M.I., Ouaknine, J.: Foundations for decision problems in separation logic with general inductive predicates. In: Muscholl, A. (ed.) FoSSaCS 2014. LNCS, vol. 8412, pp. 411–425. Springer, Heidelberg (2014). https://doi.org/10.1007/978-3-642-54830-7_27

[BBH+06] Bouajjani, A., Bozga, M., Habermehl, P., Iosif, R., Moro, P., Vojnar, T.: Programs with lists are counter automata. In: Ball, T., Jones, R.B. (eds.) CAV 2006. LNCS, vol. 4144, pp. 517–531. Springer, Heidelberg (2006). https://doi.org/10.1007/11817963_47

[BCC+07] Berdine, J., Calcagno, C., Cook, B., Distefano, D., O'Hearn, P.W., Wies, T., Yang, H.: Shape analysis for composite data structures. In: Damm, W., Hermanns, H. (eds.) CAV 2007. LNCS, vol. 4590, pp. 178–192. Springer, Heidelberg (2007). https://doi.org/10.1007/978-3-540-73368-3_22

[BCD+11] Barrett, C., Conway, C.L., Deters, M., Hadarean, L., Jovanović, D., King, T., Reynolds, A., Tinelli, C.: CVC4. In: Gopalakrishnan, G., Qadeer, S. (eds.) CAV 2011. LNCS, vol. 6806, pp. 171–177. Springer, Heidelberg (2011). https://doi.org/10.1007/978-3-642-22110-1_14

[BCO05] Berdine, J., Calcagno, C., O'Hearn, P.W.: Symbolic execution with separation logic. In: Yi, K. (ed.) APLAS 2005. LNCS, vol. 3780, pp. 52–68. Springer, Heidelberg (2005). https://doi.org/10.1007/11575467_5

[BDL12] Brochenin, R., Demri, S., Lozes, E.: On the almighty wand. Inf. Comput. **211**, 106–137 (2012)

[BDP11] Brotherston, J., Distefano, D., Petersen, R.L.: Automated cyclic entailment proofs in separation logic. In: Bjørner, N., Sofronie-Stokkermans, V. (eds.) CADE 2011. LNCS (LNAI), vol. 6803, pp. 131–146. Springer, Heidelberg (2011). https://doi.org/10.1007/978-3-642-22438-6_12

[BGG97] Börger, E., Grädel, E., Gurevich, Y.: The Classical Decision Problem. Perspectives in Mathematical Logic. Springer, Heidelberg (1997)

[BGP12] Brotherston, J., Gorogiannis, N., Petersen, R.L.: A generic cyclic theorem prover. In: Jhala, R., Igarashi, A. (eds.) APLAS 2012. LNCS, vol. 7705, pp. 350–367. Springer, Heidelberg (2012). https://doi.org/10.1007/978-3-642-35182-2_25

[CC79] Cousot, P., Cousot, R.: Systematic design of program analysis frameworks. In: POPL, pp. 269–282. ACM (1979)

[CD11] Calcagno, C., Distefano, D.: Infer: an automatic program verifier for memory safety of C programs. In: Bobaru, M., Havelund, K., Holzmann, G.J., Joshi, R. (eds.) NFM 2011. LNCS, vol. 6617, pp. 459–465. Springer, Heidelberg (2011). https://doi.org/10.1007/978-3-642-20398-5_33

[CDOY07] Calcagno, C., Distefano, D., O'Hearn, P.W., Yang, H.: Footprint analysis: a shape analysis that discovers preconditions. In: Nielson, H.R., Filé, G. (eds.) SAS 2007. LNCS, vol. 4634, pp. 402–418. Springer, Heidelberg (2007). https://doi.org/10.1007/978-3-540-74061-2_25

[CDOY11] Calcagno, C., Distefano, D., O'Hearn, P.W., Yang, H.: Compositional shape analysis by means of bi-abduction. J. ACM 58(6), 26:1–26:66 (2011)

[CGH05] Calcagno, C., Gardner, P., Hague, M.: From separation logic to first-order logic. In: Sassone, V. (ed.) FoSSaCS 2005. LNCS, vol. 3441, pp. 395–409. Springer, Heidelberg (2005). https://doi.org/10.1007/978-3-540-31982-5_25

[CJT15] Chu, D.-H., Jaffar, J., Trinh, M.-T.: Automatic induction proofs of data-structures in imperative programs. In: Proceedings of the 36th ACM SIGPLAN Conference on Programming Language Design and Implementation, Portland, OR, USA, 15–17 June 2015, pp. 457–466. ACM, New York (2015)

[Cou90] Courcelle, B.: The monadic second-order logic of graphs. i. recognizable sets of finite graphs. Inf. Comput. 85(1), 12–75 (1990)

[CYO01] Calcagno, C., Yang, H., O'Hearn, P.W.: Computability and complexity results for a spatial assertion language for data structures. In: Hariharan, R., Vinay, V., Mukund, M. (eds.) FSTTCS 2001. LNCS, vol. 2245, pp. 108–119. Springer, Heidelberg (2001). https://doi.org/10.1007/3-540-45294-X_10

[EIP18a] Echenim, M., Iosif, R., Peltier, N.: The complexity of prenex separation logic with one selector. CoRR, abs/1804.03556 (2018)

[EIP18b] Echenim, M., Iosif, R., Peltier, N.: On the expressive completeness of bernays-schönfinkel-ramsey separation logic. CoRR, abs/1802.00195 (2018)

[Flo67] Floyd, R.W.: Assigning meanings to programs. In: Proceedings of Symposia in Applied Mathematics, vol. 19, pp. 19–32 (1967)

[Gir87] Girard, J.-Y.: Linear logic. Theor. Comput. Sci. 50(1), 1–101 (1987)

[Hoa69] Hoare, C.A.R.: An axiomatic basis for computer programming. Commun. ACM 12(10), 576–580 (1969)

[IO01] Ishtiaq, S.S., O'Hearn, P.W.: Bi as an assertion language for mutable data structures. In: ACM SIGPLAN Notices, vol. 36, pp. 14–26 (2001)

[IRV14] Iosif, R., Rogalewicz, A., Vojnar, T.: Deciding entailments in inductive separation logic with tree automata. In: Cassez, F., Raskin, J.-F. (eds.) ATVA 2014. LNCS, vol. 8837, pp. 201–218. Springer, Cham (2014). https://doi.org/10.1007/978-3-319-11936-6_15

[LGQC14] Le, Q.L., Gherghina, C., Qin, S., Chin, W.-N.: Shape analysis via second-order bi-abduction. In: Biere, A., Bloem, R. (eds.) CAV 2014. LNCS, vol. 8559, pp. 52–68. Springer, Cham (2014). https://doi.org/10.1007/978-3-319-08867-9_4

[OP99] O'Hearn, P.W., Pym, D.J.: The logic of bunched implications. Bull. Symb. Log. 5(2), 215–244 (1999)

[ORY01] O'Hearn, P.W., Reynolds, J.C., Yang, H.: Local reasoning about programs that alter data structures. In: Fribourg, L. (ed.) CSL 2001. LNCS, vol. 2142, pp. 1–19. Springer, Heidelberg (2001). https://doi.org/10.1007/3-540-44802-0_1

[OYR04] O'Hearn, P.W., Yang, H., Reynolds, J.C.: Separation and information hiding. SIGPLAN Not. 39(1), 268–280 (2004)

[Rey02] Reynolds, J.C.: Separation logic: a logic for shared mutable data structures. In: Proceedings of the 17th Annual IEEE Symposium on Logic in Computer Science, LICS 2002, pp. 55–74. IEEE Computer Society (2002)

[RIS17] Reynolds, A., Iosif, R., Serban, C.: Reasoning in the bernays-schönfinkel-ramsey fragment of separation logic. In: Bouajjani, A., Monniaux, D. (eds.) VMCAI 2017. LNCS, vol. 10145, pp. 462–482. Springer, Cham (2017). https://doi.org/10.1007/978-3-319-52234-0_25

[RISK16] Reynolds, A., Iosif, R., Serban, C., King, T.: A decision procedure for separation logic in SMT. In: Artho, C., Legay, A., Peled, D. (eds.) ATVA 2016. LNCS, vol. 9938, pp. 244–261. Springer, Cham (2016). https://doi.org/10.1007/978-3-319-46520-3_16

[SC14] Sighireanu, M., Cok, D.: Report on sl-comp 2014. J. Satisfiability Boolean Model. Comput. **1** (2014)

[Ser17] Serban, C.: Inductor: an entailment checker for inductive systems (2017). https://github.com/cristina-serban/inductor

Regular Papers

Petri Net Reductions for Counting Markings

Bernard Berthomieu, Didier Le Botlan$^{(\boxtimes)}$, and Silvano Dal Zilio

LAAS-CNRS, Université de Toulouse, CNRS, INSA, Toulouse, France
{bernard,dlebotla,dalzilio}@laas.fr

Abstract. We propose a method to count the number of reachable markings of a Petri net without having to enumerate these first. The method relies on a structural reduction system that reduces the number of places and transitions of the net in such a way that we can faithfully compute the number of reachable markings of the original net from the reduced net and the reduction history. The method has been implemented and computing experiments show that reductions are effective on a large benchmark of models.

1 Introduction

Structural reductions are an important class of optimization techniques for the analysis of Petri Nets (PN for short). The idea is to use a series of reduction rules that decrease the size of a net while preserving some given behavioral properties. These reductions are then applied iteratively until an irreducible PN is reached on which the desired properties are checked directly. This approach, pioneered by Berthelot [2,3], has been used to reduce the complexity of several problems, such as checking for boundedness of a net, for liveness analysis, for checking reachability properties [10] or for LTL model checking [5].

In this paper, we enrich the notion of structural reduction by keeping track of the relation between the markings of an (initial) Petri net, N_1, and its reduced (final) version, N_2. We use reductions of the form (N_1, Q, N_2), where Q is a system of linear equations that relates the (markings of) places in N_1 and N_2. The reductions are tailored so that the state space of N_1 (its set of reachable markings) can be reconstructed from that of N_2 and equations Q. In particular, when N_1 is totally reduced (N_2 is then the empty net), the state space of N_1 corresponds with the set of non-negative integer solutions to Q. Then Q acts as a symbolic representation for sets of markings, in much the same way one can use decision diagrams or SAT-based techniques.

In practice, reductions often lead to an irreducible non-empty residual net. In this case, we can still benefit from an hybrid representation combining the state space of the residual net (expressed, for instance, using a decision diagram) and the symbolic representation provided by linear equations. This approach can provide a very compact representation of the state space of a net. Therefore it is suitable for checking *reachability properties*, that is whether some reachable

© Springer International Publishing AG, part of Springer Nature 2018
M. M. Gallardo and P. Merino (Eds.): SPIN 2018, LNCS 10869, pp. 65–84, 2018.
https://doi.org/10.1007/978-3-319-94111-0_4

marking satisfies a given set of linear constraints. However, checking reachability properties could benefit of more aggressive reductions since it is not generally required there that the full state space is available (see e.g. [10]).   At the opposite, we focus on computing a (symbolic) representation of the full state space. A positive outcome of our choice is that we can derive a method to count the number of reachable markings of a net without having to enumerate them first.

Computing the cardinality of the reachability set has several applications. For instance, it is a straightforward way to assess the correctness of tools—all tools should obviously find the same results on the same models. This is the reason why this problem was chosen as the first category of examination in the recurring Model-Checking Contest (MCC) [6,7]. We have implemented our approach in the framework of the TINA toolbox [4] and used it on the large set of examples provided by the MCC (see Sect. 7). Our results are very encouraging, with numerous instances of models where our performances are several orders of magnitude better than what is observed with the best available tools.

Outline. We first define the notations used in the paper then describe the reduction system underlying our approach, in Sect. 3. After illustrating the approach on a full example, in Sect. 4, we prove in Sect. 5 that the equations associated with reductions allow one to reconstruct the state space of the initial net from that of the reduced one. Section 6 discusses how to count markings from our representation of a state space while Sect. 7 details our experimental results. We conclude with a discussion on related works and possible future directions.

2   Petri Nets

Some familiarity with Petri nets is assumed from the reader. We recall some basic terminology. Throughout the text, comparison $(=, \geq)$ and arithmetic operations $(-, +)$ are extended pointwise to functions.

A marked *Petri net* is a tuple $N = (P, T, \mathbf{Pre}, \mathbf{Post}, m_0)$ in which P, T are disjoint finite sets, called the *places* and *transitions*, $\mathbf{Pre}, \mathbf{Post} : T \rightarrow (P \rightarrow \mathbb{N})$ are the *pre* and *post condition* functions, and $m_0 : P \rightarrow \mathbb{N}$ is the *initial marking*.

Figure 1 gives an example of Petri net, taken from [18], using a graphical syntax: places are pictured as circles, transitions as squares, there is an arc from place p to transition t if $\mathbf{Pre}(t)(p) > 0$, and one from transition t to place p if $\mathbf{Post}(t)(p) > 0$. The arcs are weighted by the values of the corresponding pre or post conditions (default weight is 1). The initial marking of the net associates integer 1 to place p_0 and 0 to all others.

A *marking* $m : P \rightarrow \mathbb{N}$ maps a number of *tokens* to every place. A transition t in T is said *enabled* at m if $m \geq \mathbf{Pre}(t)$. If enabled at m, transition t may *fire* yielding a marking $m' = m - \mathbf{Pre}(t) + \mathbf{Post}(t)$. This is written $m \xrightarrow{t} m'$, or simply $m \rightarrow m'$ when only markings are of interest. Intuitively, places hold integers and together encode the state (or marking) of a net; transitions define state changes.

The *reachability set*, or *state space*, of N is the set of markings $\mathcal{R}(N) = \{ m \mid m_0 \xrightarrow{*} m \}$, where $\xrightarrow{*}$ is the reflexive and transitive closure of $\rightarrow$.

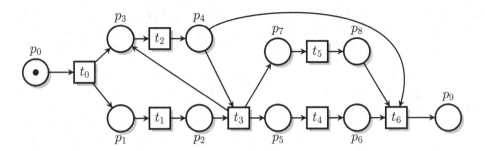

Fig. 1. An example Petri net

A *firing sequence* σ over T is a sequence $t_1, \ldots, t_n$ of transitions in T such that there are some markings $m_1 \ldots, m_{n+1}$ with $m_1 \xrightarrow{t_1} m_2 \wedge \ldots \wedge m_n \xrightarrow{t_n} m_{n+1}$. This can be written $m_1 \xrightarrow{\sigma} m_{n+1}$. Its *displacement*, or *marking change*, is $\Delta(\sigma) = \Sigma_{i=1}^n (\mathbf{Post}(t_i) - \mathbf{Pre}(t_i))$, where $\Delta : P \to \mathbb{Z}$, and its *hurdle* $H(\sigma)$ is the smallest marking (pointwise) from which the sequence is firable.

Displacements (or marking changes) and hurdles are discussed in [8], where the existence and uniqueness of hurdles is proved. As an illustration, the displacement of sequence $t_2 t_5 t_3$ in the net Fig. 1 is $\{(p_2, -1), (p_5, 1), (p_9, 1)\}$ (and 0 for all other places, implicitly), its hurdle is $\{(p_2, 1), (p_3, 1), (p_7, 1)\}$.

The *postset* of a transition t is $t^\bullet = \{p \mid \mathbf{Post}(t)(p) > 0\}$, its *preset* is $^\bullet t = \{p \mid \mathbf{Pre}(t)(p) > 0\}$. Symmetrically for places, $p^\bullet = \{t \mid \mathbf{Pre}(t)(p) > 0\}$ and $^\bullet p = \{t \mid \mathbf{Post}(t)(p) > 0\}$.

A net is *ordinary* if all its arcs have weight one; for all transition t in T, and place p in P, we have $\mathbf{Pre}(t)(p) \leq 1$ and $\mathbf{Post}(t)(p) \leq 1$. Otherwise it is said *generalized*.

A net N is *bounded* if there is an (integer) bound b such that $m(p) \leq b$ for all $m \in \mathcal{R}(N)$ and $p \in P$. The net is said *safe* when the bound is 1. All nets considered in this paper are assumed bounded.

The net in Fig. 1 is ordinary and safe. Its state space holds 14 markings.

3   The Reduction System

We describe our set of reduction rules using three main categories. For each category, we give a property that can be used to recover the state space of a net, after reduction, from that of the reduced net.

3.1   Removal of Redundant Transitions

A transition is redundant when its effects can always be achieved by firing instead an alternative sequence of transitions. Our definition of redundant transitions slightly strengthens that of *bypass* transitions in [15]. It is not fully structural either, but makes it easier to identify special cases structurally.

Definition 1 (Redundant transition). *Given a net* $(P, T, \mathbf{Pre}, \mathbf{Post}, m_0)$, *a transition t in T is* redundant *if there is a firing sequence σ over $T \setminus \{t\}$ such that $\Delta(t) = \Delta(\sigma)$ and $H(t) \geq H(\sigma)$.* ∎

There are special cases that do not require to explore combinations of transitions. This includes *identity* transitions, such that $\Delta(t) = 0$, and *duplicate* transitions, such that for some other transition t' and integer k, $\Delta(t) = k.\Delta(t')$. Finding redundant transitions using Definition 1 can be convenient too, provided the candidate σ are restricted (e.g. in length). Figure 2(left) shows some examples of redundant transitions. Clearly, removing a redundant transition from a net does not change its state space.

Theorem 1. *If net N' is the result of removing some redundant transition in net N then $\mathcal{R}(N) = \mathcal{R}(N')$*

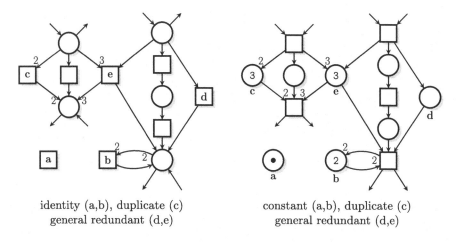

identity (a,b), duplicate (c)   constant (a,b), duplicate (c)
general redundant (d,e)   general redundant (d,e)

Fig. 2. Some examples of redundant transitions (left) and places (right)

3.2   Removal of Redundant Places

A place is redundant if it never restricts the firing of its output transitions. Removing redundant places from a net preserves its language of firing sequences [3]. We wish to avoid enumerating marking for detecting such places, and further be able to recover the marking of a redundant place from those of the other places. For these reasons, our definition of redundant places is a slightly strengthened version of that of *structurally redundant* places in [3] (last clause is an equation).

Definition 2 (redundant place). *Given a net* $(P, T, \mathbf{Pre}, \mathbf{Post}, m_0)$, *a place p in P is* redundant *if there is some set of places I from $P \setminus \{p\}$, some valuation $v : (I \cup \{p\}) \to (\mathbb{N} - \{0\})$, and some constant $b \in \mathbb{N}$ such that, for any $t \in T$:*

1. *The weighted initial marking of p is not smaller than that of I:*
   $b = v(p).m_0(p) - \Sigma_{q \in I} v(q).m_0(q)$
2. *To fire t, the difference between its weighted precondition on p and that on I may not be larger than b:* $v(p).\mathbf{Pre}(t)(p) - \Sigma_{q \in I} v(q).\mathbf{Pre}(t)(q) \leq b$
3. *When t fires, the weighted growth of the marking of p is equal to that of I:*
   $v(p).(\mathbf{Post}(t)(p) - \mathbf{Pre}(t)(p)) = \Sigma_{q \in I} v(q).(\mathbf{Post}(t)(q) - \mathbf{Pre}(t)(q))$ ∎

This definition can be rephrased as an integer linear programming problem [17], convenient in practice for computing redundant places in reasonably sized nets (say when $|P| \leq 50$). Like with redundant transitions, there are special cases that lead to easily identifiable redundant places. These are *constant places*—those for which set I in the definition is empty—and *duplicated* places, when set I is a singleton. Figure 2(right) gives some examples of such places.

From Definition 2, we can show that the marking of a redundant place p can always be computed from the markings of the places in I and the valuation function v. Indeed, for any marking m in $\mathcal{R}(N)$, we have $v(p).m(p) = \Sigma_{q \in I} v(q).m(q) + b$, where the constant b derives from the initial marking m_0. Hence we have a relation $k_p.m(p) = \rho_p(m)$, where $k_p = v(p)$ and ρ_p is some linear expression on the places of the net.

Theorem 2. *If N' is the result of removing some redundant place p from net N, then there is an integer constant $k \in \mathbb{N}^*$, and a linear expression ρ, such that, for all marking m: $m \cup \{(p, (1/k).\rho(m))\} \in \mathcal{R}(N) \Leftrightarrow m \in \mathcal{R}(N')$.*

3.3   Place Agglomerations

Conversely to the rules considered so far, place agglomerations do not preserve the number of markings of the nets they are applied to. They constitute the cornerstone of our reduction system; the purpose of the previous rules is merely to simplify the net so that agglomeration rules can be applied. We start by introducing a convenient notation.

Definition 3 (Sum of places). *A place a is the sum of places p and q, written $a = p \boxplus q$, if: $m_0(a) = m_0(p) + m_0(q)$ and, for all transition t, $\mathbf{Pre}(t)(a) = \mathbf{Pre}(t)(p) + \mathbf{Pre}(t)(q)$ and $\mathbf{Post}(t)(a) = \mathbf{Post}(t)(p) + \mathbf{Post}(t)(q)$.*   ∎

Clearly, operation $\boxplus$ is commutative and associative. We consider two categories of *place agglomeration* rules; each one consisting in the simplification of a sum of places. Examples are shown in Fig. 3.

Definition 4 (Chain agglomeration). *Given a net $(P, T, \mathbf{Pre}, \mathbf{Post}, m_0)$, a pair of places p, q in P can be chain agglomerated if there is some $t \in T$ such that: $\bullet t = \{p\}$; $t^\bullet = \{q\}$; $\mathbf{Pre}(t)(p) = \mathbf{Post}(t)(q) = 1$; $\bullet q = \{t\}$; and $m_0(q) = 0$. Their agglomeration consists of replacing places p and q by a place a equal to their sum: $a = p \boxplus q$.*   ∎

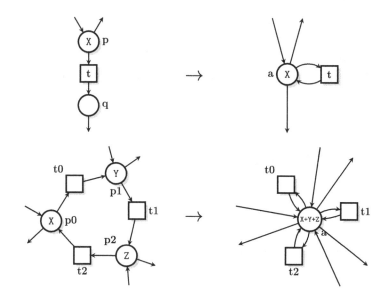

Fig. 3. Agglomeration examples: chain (top), loop (for $n = 3$, bottom)

Definition 5 (Loop agglomeration). *A sequence of n places $(\pi_i)_{i=0}^{n-1}$ can be* loop agglomerated *if the following condition is met:*

$$(\forall i < n)(\exists t \in T)(\mathbf{Pre}(t) = \{(\pi_i, 1)\} \wedge \mathbf{Post}(t) = \{(\pi_{(i+1)(mod\ n)}, 1)\}).$$

Their agglomeration consists of replacing places $\pi_0, \ldots, \pi_{n-1}$ by a single place, a*, defined as their sum: $a = \boxplus_{i=0}^{n-1} \pi_i$.* ∎

Clearly, whenever some place a of a net obeys $a = p \boxplus q$ for some places p and q of the same net, then place a is redundant in the sense of Definition 2. The effects of agglomerations on markings are stated by Theorem 3.

Theorem 3. *Let N and N' be the nets before and after agglomeration of some set of places A as place a. Then for all markings m over $(P \setminus A)$ and m' over A we have: $(m \cup m') \in \mathcal{R}(N) \Leftrightarrow m \cup \{(a, \Sigma_{p \in A} m'(p))\} \in \mathcal{R}(N')$.*

Proof. Assume N is a net with set of places P. Let us first consider the case of the chain agglomeration rule in Fig. 3(top). We have to prove that for all marking m of $P \setminus \{p, q\}$ and for all values x, y in $\mathbb{N}$:

$$m \cup \{(p, x), (q, y)\} \in \mathcal{R}(N) \Leftrightarrow m \cup \{(a, x + y)\} \in \mathcal{R}(N')$$

Left to Right (L): Let N^+ be net N with place $a = p \boxplus q$ added. Clearly, a is redundant in N^+, with $v(a) = v(p) = v(q) = 1$. So N and N^+ admit the same firing sequences, and for any $m \in \mathcal{R}(N^+)$, we have $m(a) = m(p) + m(q)$. Next, removing places p and q from N^+ (the result is net N') can only relax firing constraints, hence any σ firable in N^+ (and thus in N) is also firable in N', which implies the goal.

Right to Left (R): we use two intermediate properties ($\forall m, x, u, v$ implicit). We write $m \sim m'$ when m and m' agree on all places except p, q and a, and $m \approx m'$ when $m \sim m' \wedge m(p) = m'(a) \wedge m(q) = 0$.
Property (1): $m \cup \{(a, x)\} \in \mathcal{R}(N') \Rightarrow m \cup \{(p, x), (q, 0)\} \in \mathcal{R}(N)$.

Since $\Delta(t) = 0$, any marking reachable in N' is reachable by a sequence not containing t, call these sequences t-free. Property (1) follows from a simpler relation, namely (Z): *whenever* $m \approx m'$ ($m \in \mathcal{R}(N)$, $m' \in \mathcal{R}(N')$) *and* $m' \xrightarrow{\delta} w'$, ($\delta$ t-free), *then there is a sequence* ω *such that* $m \xrightarrow{\omega} w$ *and* $w \approx w'$.

Any t-free sequence firable in N' but not in N can be written $\sigma.t'.\gamma$, where σ is firable in N and transition t' is not firable in N after σ. Let w, w' be the markings reached by σ in N and N', respectively. Since σ is firable in N, we have $w \approx w'$, by (L) and the fact that σ is t-free (only t can put tokens in q). That t' is not firable at w but firable at w' is only possible if t' is some output transition of a since $w \sim w'$ and the preconditions of all other transitions of N' than a are identical in N and N'. That is, t' must be an output transition of either or both p or q in N. If t' has no precondition on q in N, then it ought to be firable at w in N since $w(p) = w'(a)$. So t' must have a precondition on q; we have $w(q) \not\geq \mathbf{Pre}(t')(q)$ in N and $w'(a) \geq \mathbf{Pre}'(t')(a)$ in N'. Therefore, we can fire transition t n times from w in N, where $n = \mathbf{Pre}(t')(q)$, since $w'(a) = w(p)$ and t' is enabled at w', and this leads to a marking enabling t'. Further, firing t' at that marking leaves place q in N empty since only transition t may put tokens in q. Then the proof of Property (1) follows from (Z) and the fact that Definition 4 ensures $m_0 \approx m'_0$.

Property (2): if $m \cup \{(p, x), (q, 0)\} \in \mathcal{R}(N)$ and $(u + v = x)$ then $m \cup \{(p, u), (q, v)\} \in \mathcal{R}(N)$.

Obvious from Definition 4: the tokens in place p can be moved one by one into place q by firing t in sequence v times.

Combining Property (1) and (2) is enough to prove (R), which completes the proof for chain agglomerations. The proof for loop agglomerations is similar. $\square$

3.4 The Reduction System

The three categories of rules introduced in the previous sections constitute the core of our reduction system. Our implementation actually adds to those a few special purpose rules. We mention three examples of such rules here, because they play a significant role in the experimental results of Sect. 7, but without technical details. These rules are useful on nets generated from high level descriptions, that often exhibit translation artifacts like dead transitions or source places.

The first extra rule is the *dead transition removal* rule. It is sometimes possible to determine statically that some transitions of a net are never firable. A fairly general rule for identifying statically dead transitions is proposed in [5]. Removal of statically dead transitions from a net has no effects on its state space.

A second rule allows us to remove a transition t from a net N when t is the sole transition enabled in the initial marking and t is firable only once. Then, instead of counting the markings reachable from the initial marking of the net, we count those reachable from the output marking of t in N and add 1. Removing such transitions often yields structurally simpler nets.

Our last example is an instance of simple rules that can be used to do away with very basic (sub-)nets, containing only a single place. This is the case, for instance, of the source-sink nets defined below. These rules are useful if we want to fully reduce a net. We say that a net is *totally reduced* when its set of places and transitions are empty ($P = T = \emptyset$).

Definition 6 (Source-sink pair). *A pair (p,t) in net N is a* source-sink pair *if* $^\bullet p = \emptyset$, $p^\bullet = \{t\}$, $\mathbf{Pre}(t) = \{(p, 1)\}$ *and* $\mathbf{Post}(t) = \emptyset$.   ■

Theorem 4 (Source-sink pairs). *If N' is the result of removing a source-sink pair (p,t) in net N then $(\forall z \leq m_0(p))(\forall m)(m \cup \{(p, z)\} \in \mathcal{R}(N) \Leftrightarrow m \in \mathcal{R}(N'))$.*

Omitting for the sake of clarity the first two extra rules mentioned above, our final reduction system resumes to removal of redundant transitions (referred to as the T rule) and of redundant places (R rule), agglomeration of places (A rules) and removal of source-sink pairs (L rule).

Rules T have no effects on markings. For the other three rules, the effect on the markings can be captured by an equation or an inequality. These have shape $v_p.m(p) = \sum_{q \neq p} v_q.m(q) + b$ for redundant places, where b is a constant, shape $m(a) = \Sigma_{p \in A} m(p)$ for agglomerations, and shape $m(p) \leq k$ for source-sink pairs, where k is some constant. In all these equations, the terms $m(q)$ are marking variables; variable $m(q)$ is associated with the marking of place q. For readability, we will often use the name of the place instead of its associated marking variable. For instance, the marking equation $2.m(p) = 3.m(q) + 4$, resulting from a (R) rule, would be simply written $2.p = 3.q + 4$.

We show in Sect. 5 that the state space of a net can be reconstructed from that of its reduced net and the set of (in)equalities collected when a rule is applied. Before considering this result, we illustrate the effects of reductions on a full example.

4   An Illustrative Example — HouseConstruction

We take as example a model provided in the *Model Checking Contest* (MCC, http://mcc.lip6.fr), a recurring competition of model-checking tools [6]. This model is a variation of a Petri net model found in [14], which is itself derived from the PERT chart of the construction of a house found in [11]. The model found in the MCC collection, reproduced in Fig. 4, differs from that of [14] in that it omits time constraints and a final sink place. In addition, the net represents the house construction process for a number of houses simultaneously rather than a single one. The number of houses being built is represented by the marking of place p_1 of the net (10 in the net represented in Fig. 4).

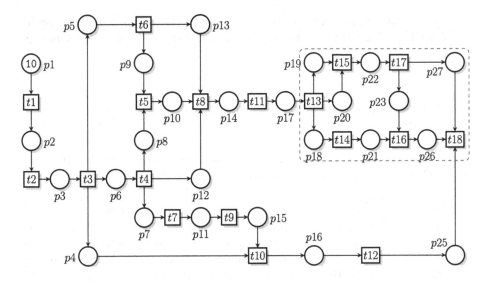

Fig. 4. HouseConstruction-10 example net.

We list in Fig. 5 a possible reduction sequence for our example net, one for each line. To save space, we have omitted the removal of redundant transitions. For each reduction, we give an indication of its kind (R, A, ...), the marking equation witnessing the reduction, and a short description. The first reduction, for instance, says that place p_{19} is removed, being a duplicate of place p_{20}. At the second step, places $p11$ and $p7$ are agglomerated as place $a1$, a "fresh" place not found in the net yet.

```
R |- p19 = p20        p19 duplicate      R |- p4 = p6 + a7      p4 redundant
A |- a1 = p11 + p7     agglomeration      A |- a9 = a2 + p10     agglomeration
A |- a2 = p17 + p14    agglomeration      A |- a10 = a6 + a7     agglomeration
A |- a3 = p2 + p1      agglomeration      A |- a11 = p23 + a5    agglomeration
A |- a4 = p21 + p18    agglomeration      A |- a12 = p9 + p5     agglomeration
A |- a5 = p22 + p20    agglomeration      A |- a13 = a11 + p26   agglomeration
A |- a6 = p25 + p16    agglomeration      A |- a14 = a13 + a9    agglomeration
A |- a7 = p15 + a1     agglomeration      R |- a12 = p6 + p8     a12 redundant
A |- a8 = p3 + a3      agglomeration      R |- a10 = a14 + p8    a10 redundant
R |- p12 = p10 + p8    p12 redundant      A |- a15 = a14 + p8    agglomeration
R |- p13 = p10 + p9    p13 redundant      A |- a16 = p6 + a8     agglomeration
R |- a4 = a5 + p23     a4 redundant       A |- a17 = a15 + a16   agglomeration
R |- p27 = p23 + p26   p27 redundant      L |- a17 <= 10         a17 source
```

Fig. 5. Reduction traces for net HouseConstruction-10

Each reduction is associated with an equation or inequality linking the markings of the net before and after application of a rule. The system of inequalities gathered is shown below, with agglomeration places a_i eliminated. We show in the next section that the set of solutions of this system, taken as markings, is exactly the set of reachable markings of the net.

$$p19 = p20 \qquad\qquad p4 = p6 + p15 + p11 + p7$$
$$p12 = p10 + p8 \qquad\qquad p9 + p5 = p6 + p8$$
$$p13 = p10 + p9 \qquad\qquad p21 + p18 = p22 + p20 + p23$$
$$p27 = p23 + p26$$
$$p25 + p16 + p15 + p11 + p7 = p26 + p23 + p22 + p20 + p17 + p14 + p10 + p8$$
$$p26 + p23 + p22 + p20 + p17 + p14 + p10 + p8 + p6 + p3 + p2 + p1 \le 10$$

This example is totally reduced using the sequence of reductions listed. And we have found other examples of totally reducible net in the MCC benchmarks. In the general case, our reduction system is not complete; some nets may be only partially reduced, or not at all. When a net is only partially reducible, the inequalities, together with an explicit or logic-based symbolic description of the reachability set of the residual net, yield a hybrid representation of the state space of the initial net. Such hybrid representations are still suitable for model checking reachability properties or counting markings.

Order of Application of Reduction Rules. Our reduction system does not constrain the order in which reductions are applied. Our tool attempts to apply them in an order that minimizes reduction costs.

The rules can be classified into "local" rules, detecting some structural patterns on the net and transforming them, like removal of duplicate transitions or places, or chain agglomerations, and "non-local" rules, like removal of redundant places in the general case (using integer programming). Our implementation defers the application of the non-local rules until no more local rule can be applied. This decreases the cost of non-local reductions as they are applied to smaller nets.

Another issue is the confluence of the rules. Our reduction system is not confluent: different reduction sequences for the same net could yield different residual nets. This follows from the fact that agglomeration rules do not preserve in general the *ordinary* character of the net (that all arcs have weight 1), while agglomeration rules require that the candidate places are connected by arcs of weight 1 to the same transition.

An example net exhibiting the problem is shown in Fig. 6(a). Agglomeration of places $p3$ and $p4$ in this net, followed by removal of identity transitions, yields the net in Fig. 6(b). Place $a1$ in the reduced net is the result of agglomerating $p3$ and $p4$; this is witnessed by equation $a1 = p3+p4$. Note that the arcs connecting place $a1$ to transitions $t0$ and $t1$ both have weight 2.

Next, place $p2$ in the reduced net is a duplicate of place $a1$, according to the definitions of Sect. 3.2, the corresponding equation is $2.p2 = a1$. But, from the same equation, $a1$ is a duplicate of $p2$ as well. But removing $p2$ or $a1$ have differents effects:

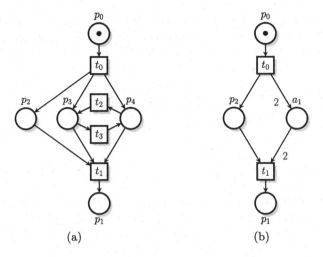

(a)   (b)

Fig. 6. Non confluence example

- If $a1$ is removed, then we can fully reduce the net by the following sequence of reductions:

  ```
  A |- a2 = p1 + p2   agglomeration
  A |- a3 = a2 + p0   agglomeration
  R |- a3 = 1         constant place
  ```

- If $p2$ is removed instead, then the resulting net cannot be reduced further: places $p0$, $a1$ and $p1$ cannot be agglomerated because of the presence of arcs with weight larger than 1.

Confluence of the system could be easily obtained by restricting the agglomeration rules so that no arcs with weight larger than 1 could be produced. But it is more effective to favour the expressiveness of our reduction rules.

5   Correctness of Markings Reconstruction

We prove that we can reconstruct the markings of an (initial) net, before application of a rule, from that of the reduced net. This property ensues from the definition of a *net-abstraction* relation, defined below.

We start by defining some notations useful in our proofs. We use $\mathcal{U}, \mathcal{V}, \ldots$ for finite sets of non-negative integer variables. We use Q, Q' for systems of linear equations (and inequalities) and the notation $\mathbf{V}(Q)$ for the set of variables occurring in Q. The system obtained by concatenating the relations in Q_1 and Q_2 is denoted $(Q_1; Q_2)$ and the "empty system" is denoted $\emptyset$.

A valuation e of $\mathbb{N}^{\mathcal{V}}$ is a solution of Q, with $\mathcal{V} = \mathbf{V}(Q)$, if all the relations in Q are (trivially) valid when replacing all variables x in $\mathcal{V}$ by their value $e(x)$. We denote $\langle Q \rangle$ the subset of $\mathbb{N}^{\mathbf{V}(Q)}$ consisting in all the solutions of Q.

If $E \subseteq \mathbb{N}^{\mathcal{V}}$ then $E \downarrow \mathcal{U}$ is the projection of E over variables $\mathcal{U}$, that is the subset of $\mathbb{N}^{\mathcal{U}}$ obtained from E by restricting the domain of its elements to $\mathcal{U}$. conversely, we use $E \uparrow \mathcal{U}$ to denote the lifting of E to $\mathcal{U}$, that is the largest subset E' of $\mathbb{N}^{\mathcal{U}}$ such that $E' \downarrow \mathcal{V} = E$.

Definition 7 (Net-abstraction). *A triple* (N_1, Q, N_2) *is a* net-abstraction, *or simply an* abstraction, *if* N_1, N_2 *are nets with respective sets of places* P_1, P_2 *(we may have* $P_1 \cap P_2 \neq \emptyset$*),* Q *is a linear system of equations, and:*

$$\mathcal{R}(N_1) = ((\mathcal{R}(N_2) \uparrow \mathcal{V}) \cap (\langle Q \rangle \uparrow \mathcal{V})) \downarrow P_1 \qquad where \ \mathcal{V} = \mathbf{V}(Q) \cup P_1 \cup P_2 \ .$$

Intuitively, N_2 is an abstraction of N_1 (through Q) if, from every reachable marking $m \in \mathcal{R}(N_2)$, the markings obtained from solutions of Q—restricted to those solutions such that $x = m(x)$ for all "place variable" x in P_2—are always reachable in N_1. The definition also entails that all the markings in $\mathcal{R}(N_1)$ can be obtained this way.

Theorem 5 (Net-abstractions from reductions). *For any nets* N, N_1, N_2:

1. $(N, \emptyset, N)$ *is an abstraction;*
2. *If* (N_1, Q, N_2) *is an abstraction then* (N_1, Q', N_3) *is an abstraction if either:*
   (T) $Q' = Q$ *and* N_3 *is obtained from* N_2 *by removing a redundant transition (see Sect. 3.1);*
   (R) $Q' = (Q; k.p = l)$ *and* N_3 *is obtained from* N_2 *by removing a redundant place* p *and* $k.p = l$ *is the associated marking equation (see Sect. 3.2);*
   (A) $Q' = (Q; a = \Sigma_{p \in A}(p))$, *where* $a \notin \mathbf{V}(Q)$ *and* N_3 *is obtained from* N_2 *by agglomerating the places in* A *as a new place,* a *(see Sect. 3.3);*
   (L) $Q' = (Q; p \leq k)$ *and* N_3 *is obtained from* N_2 *by removal of a source-sink pair* (p, t) *with* $m_0(p) = k$ *(see Sect. 3.4).*

Proof. Property (1) is obvious from Definition 7. Property (2) is proved by case analysis. First, let $\mathcal{V} = \mathbf{V}(Q) \cup P_1 \cup P_2$ and $\mathcal{U} = \mathcal{V} \cup P_3$ and notice that for all candidate (N_1, Q', N_3) we have $\mathbf{V}(Q') \cup P_1 \cup P_3 = \mathcal{U}$. Then, in each case, we know $(H) : \mathcal{R}(N_1) = (\mathcal{R}(N_2) \uparrow \mathcal{V} \cap \langle Q \rangle \uparrow \mathcal{V}) \downarrow P_1$ and we must prove $(G) : \mathcal{R}(N_1) = (\mathcal{R}(N_3) \uparrow \mathcal{U} \cap \langle Q' \rangle \uparrow \mathcal{U}) \downarrow P_1$.

Case (T) : $Q' = Q$. By Theorem 1, we have $P_3 = P_2$, hence $\mathcal{V} = \mathcal{U}$, and $\mathcal{R}(N_3) = \mathcal{R}(N_2)$. Replacing $\mathcal{R}(N_2)$ by $\mathcal{R}(N_3)$ and $\mathcal{V}$ by $\mathcal{U}$ in (H) yields (G).

Case (R) : By Theorem 2 we have : $\mathcal{R}(N_2) = \mathcal{R}(N_3) \uparrow P_2 \cap \langle k.p = l \rangle \uparrow P_2$. replacing $\mathcal{R}(N_2)$ by this value in (H) yields $\mathcal{R}(N_1) = ((\mathcal{R}(N_3) \uparrow P_2 \cap \langle k.p = l \rangle \uparrow P_2) \uparrow \mathcal{V} \cap \langle Q \rangle \uparrow \mathcal{V}) \downarrow P_1$. Since $P_2 \subseteq \mathcal{V}$, we may safely lift to $\mathcal{V}$ instead of P_2, so: $\mathcal{R}(N_1) = (\mathcal{R}(N_3) \uparrow \mathcal{V} \cap \langle k.p = l \rangle \uparrow \mathcal{V} \cap \langle Q \rangle \uparrow \mathcal{V}) \downarrow P_1$. Which is equivalent to: $\mathcal{R}(N_1) = (\mathcal{R}(N_3) \uparrow \mathcal{V} \cap \langle Q; k.p = l \rangle \uparrow \mathcal{V}) \downarrow P_1$, and equal to (G) since $P_3 \subseteq \mathcal{V}$ and $Q' = (Q; k.p = l)$.

Case (A): Let S_p denotes the value $\Sigma_{p \in A}(p)$. By Theorem 3 we have: $\mathcal{R}(N_2) = (\mathcal{R}(N_3) \uparrow (P_2 \cup P_3) \cap \langle a = S_p \rangle \uparrow (P_2 \cup P_3)) \downarrow P_2$. Replacing $\mathcal{R}(N_2)$ by this value in (H) yields: $\mathcal{R}(N_1) = (((\mathcal{R}(N_3) \uparrow (P_2 \cup P_3) \cap \langle a = S_p \rangle \uparrow (P_2 \cup P_3)) \downarrow P_2) \uparrow$ $\mathcal{V} \cap \langle Q \rangle \uparrow \mathcal{V}) \downarrow P_1$. Instead of $\mathcal{V}$, we may lift to $\mathcal{U}$ since $\mathcal{U} = \mathcal{V} \cup \{a\}$, $a \notin \mathbf{V}(Q)$ and $a \notin P_1$, so: $\mathcal{R}(N_1) = (((\mathcal{R}(N_3) \uparrow (P_2 \cup P_3) \cap \langle a = S_p \rangle \uparrow (P_2 \cup P_3)) \downarrow P_2) \uparrow$ $\mathcal{U} \cap \langle Q \rangle \uparrow \mathcal{U}) \downarrow P_1$. Projection on P_2 may be omitted since $P_2 \cup P_3 = P_2 \cup \{a\}$ and $a \notin \mathbf{V}(Q)$, leading to:

$\mathcal{R}(N_1) = ((\mathcal{R}(N_3) \uparrow (P_2 \cup P_3) \cap \langle a = S_p \rangle \uparrow (P_2 \cup P_3)) \uparrow \mathcal{U} \cap \langle Q \rangle \uparrow \mathcal{U}) \downarrow P_1$.
Since $P_2 \cup P_3 \subseteq \mathcal{U}$, this is equivalent to: $\mathcal{R}(N_1) = (\mathcal{R}(N_3) \uparrow \mathcal{U} \cap \langle a = S_p \rangle \uparrow$ $\mathcal{U} \cap \langle Q \rangle \uparrow \mathcal{U}) \downarrow P_1$. Grouping equations yields: $\mathcal{R}(N_1) = (\mathcal{R}(N_3) \uparrow \mathcal{U} \cap \langle Q; a =$ $S_p \rangle \uparrow \mathcal{U}) \downarrow P_1$, which is equal to (G) since $Q' = (Q; a = S_p)$.

case (L): The proof is similar to that of case (R) and is based on the relation $\mathcal{R}(N_2) = \mathcal{R}(N_3) \uparrow P_2 \cap \langle p \leq k \rangle \uparrow P_2$, obtained from Theorem 4.   □

Theorem 5 states the correctness of our reduction systems, since we can compose reductions sequentially and always obtain a net-abstraction. In particular, if a net N is fully reducible, then we can derive a system of linear equations Q such that $(N, Q, \emptyset)$ is a net-abstraction. In this case the reachable markings of N are exactly the solutions of Q, projected on the places of N. If the reduced net, say N_r, is not empty then each marking $m \in \mathcal{R}(N_r)$ represents a set of markings $\langle Q \rangle_m \subset \mathcal{R}(N)$: the solution set of Q in which the places of the residual net are constrained as in m, and then projected on the places of N. Moreover the family of sets $\{ \langle Q \rangle_m \mid m \in \mathcal{R}(N_r) \}$ is a partition of $\mathcal{R}(N)$.

6   Counting Markings

We consider the problem of counting the markings of a net N from the set of markings of the residual net N_r and the (collected) system of linear equations Q. For totally reduced nets, counting the markings of N resumes to that of counting the number of solutions in non negative integer variables of system Q. For partially reduced nets, a similar process must be iterated over all markings m reachable in N_r (a better implementation will be discussed shortly).

Available Methods. Counting the number of integer solutions of a linear system of equations (inequalities can always be represented by equations by the addition of slack variables) is an active area of research.

A method is proposed in [1], implemented in the tool Azove, for the particular case where variables take their values in $\{0, 1\}$. The method consists of building a Binary Decision Diagram for each equation, using Shannon expansion, and then to compute their conjunction (this is done with a specially tailored algorithm). The number of paths of the BDD gives the expected result. Our experiments with Azove show that, although the tool can be fast, its performances on larger system heavily depend on the ordering chosen for the BDD variables, a typical drawback of decision diagram based techniques. In any case, its usage in our context would be limited to safe nets.

For the general case, the current state of the art can be found in the work of De Loera et al. [12,13] on counting lattice points in convex polytopes. Their approach is implemented in a tool called LaTTe; it relies on algebraic and geometric methods; namely the use of rational functions and the decomposition of cones into unimodular cones. Our experiments with LaTTe show that it can be conveniently used on systems with, say, less than 50 variables. For instance, LaTTe is strikingly fast (less than 1s) at counting the number of solutions of the system computed in Sect. 4. Moreover, its running time does not generally depend on the constants found in the system. As a consequence, computing the reachability count for 10 or, say, 10^{12} houses takes exactly the same time.

An Ad-hoc Method. Though our experiments with LaTTe suffice to show that these approaches are practicable, we implemented our own counting method. Its main benefits over LaTTe, important for practical purposes, are that it can handle systems with many variables (say thousands), though it can be slower than LaTTe on small systems. Another reason for finding an alternative to LaTTe is that it provides no builtin support for parameterized systems, that is in the situation where we need to count the solutions of many instances of the same linear system differing only by some constants.

Our solution takes advantage of the stratified structure of the systems obtained from reductions, and it relies on combinatorial rather than geometric methods. While we cannot describe this tool in full details, we illustrate our approach and the techniques involved on a simple example.

Consider the system of equations obtained from the PN corresponding to the dashed zone of Fig. 4. This net consists of places in the range p_{18}–p_{27} and is reduced by our system to a single place, a_{13}. The subset of marking equations related to this subnet is:

$$
\begin{array}{ll}
R \vdash p_{19} = p_{20} & R \vdash p_{27} = p_{23} + p_{26} \\
A \vdash a_4 = p_{21} + p_{18} & A \vdash a_{11} = p_{23} + a_5 \\
A \vdash a_5 = p_{22} + p_{20} & A \vdash a_{13} = a_{11} + p_{26} \\
R \vdash a_4 = a_5 + p_{23} &
\end{array}
\qquad (Q)
$$

Assume place a_{13} is marked with n tokens. Then, by Theorem 5, the number of markings of the original net corresponding with marking $a_{13} = n$ in the reduced net is the number of non-negative integer solutions to system $(Q, a_{13} = n)$. Let us define the function $A_{13} : \mathbb{N} \longrightarrow \mathbb{N}$ that computes that number.

We first simplify system (Q). Note that no agglomeration is involved in the redundancy (R) equations for p_{19} and p_{27}, so these equations have no effects on the marking count and can be omitted. After elimination of variable a_5 and some rewriting, we obtain the simplified system (Q'):

$$
\begin{array}{ll}
A \vdash a_4 = p_{21} + p_{18} & R \vdash a_4 = a_{11} \\
A \vdash a_{11} = p_{23} + p_{22} + p_{20} & A \vdash a_{13} = a_{11} + p_{26}
\end{array}
\qquad (Q')
$$

Let $((k))(x)$ denote the expression $\binom{x+k-1}{k-1}$, which denotes the number of ways to put x tokens into k slots. The first equation is $a_4 = p_{21} + p_{18}$. If $a_4 = x$, its number of solutions is $((2))(x) = x + 1$. The second equation is $a_{11} = p_{23} + p_{22} + p_{20}$. If $a_{11} = x$, its number of solutions is $((3))(x) = \frac{(x+2)(x+1)}{2}$.

Now consider the system consisting of the first two equations and the redundancy equation $a_4 = a_{11}$. If $a_{11} = x$, its number of solutions is $((2))(x) \times ((3))(x)$ (the variables in both equations being disjoint). Finally, by noticing that a_{11} can take any value between 0 and n, we get:

$$A_{13}(n) = \sum_{a_{11}=0}^{n} ((2))(a_{11}) \times ((3))(a_{11})$$

This expression is actually a polynomial, namely $\frac{1}{8}n^4 + \frac{11}{12}n^3 + \frac{19}{8}n^2 + \frac{31}{12}n + 1$. By applying the same method to the whole net of Fig. 4, we obtain an expression involving six summations, which can be reduced to the following 18th-degree polynomial in the variable X denoting the number of tokens in place p_1.

$$\frac{11}{19401132441600}X^{18} + \frac{1}{16582164480}X^{17} + \frac{2491}{836911595520}X^{16} + \frac{1409}{15567552000}X^{15}$$
$$+ \frac{3972503}{2092278988800}X^{14} + \frac{161351}{5535129600}X^{13} + \frac{32745953}{96566722560}X^{12} + \frac{68229017}{22353408000}X^{11}$$
$$+ \frac{629730473}{29262643200}X^{10} + \frac{83284643}{696729600}X^9 + \frac{3063053849}{5852528640}X^8 + \frac{74566847}{41472000}X^7$$
$$+ \frac{1505970381239}{313841848320}X^6 + \frac{32809178977}{3353011200}X^5 + \frac{259109541797}{17435658240}X^4 + \frac{41924892461}{2594592000}X^3$$
$$+ \frac{4496167537}{381180800}X^2 + \frac{62925293}{12252240}X^1 + 1$$

In the general case of partially reduced nets, the computed polynomial is a multivariate polynomial with at most as many variables as places remaining in the residual net. When that number of variables is too large, the computation of the final polynomial is out of reach, and we only make use of the intermediate algebraic term.

7   Computing Experiments

We integrated our reduction system and counting method with a state space generation tool, *tedd*, in the framework of our *TINA* toolbox for analysis of Petri nets [4] (www.laas.fr/tina). Tool *tedd* makes use of symbolic exploration and stores markings in a Set Decision Diagram [19]. For counting markings in presence of agglomerations, one has the choice between using the external tool LaTTe or using our native counting method discussed in Sect. 6.

Benchmarks. Our benchmark is constituted of the full collection of Petri nets used in the Model Checking Contest [6,9]. It includes 627 nets, organized into 82 classes (simply called models). Each class includes several nets (called instances) that typically differ by their initial marking or by the number of components constituting the net. The size of the nets vary widely, from 9 to 50 000 places, 7 to 200 000 transitions, and 20 to 1 000 000 arcs. Most nets are ordinary (arcs have weight 1) but a significant number are generalized nets. Overall, the collection provides a large number of PN with various structural and behavioral characteristics, covering a large variety of use cases.

Reduction Ratio and Prevalence. Our first results are about how well the reductions perform. We provide two different reduction strategies: `compact`, that applies all reductions described in Sect. 3, and `clean`, that only applies removal of redundant places and transitions. The reduction ratios on number of places (number of places before and after reduction) for all the MCC instances are shown in Fig. 7, sorted in descending order. We overlay the results for our two reduction strategies (the lower, in light color, for `clean` and the upper, in dark, for `compact`). We see that the impact of strategy `clean` alone is minor compared to `compact`. Globally, Fig. 7 shows that reductions have a significant impact on about half the models, with a very high impact on about a quarter of them. In particular, there is a surprisingly high number of models that are totally reducible by our approach (about 19% of the models are fully reducible).

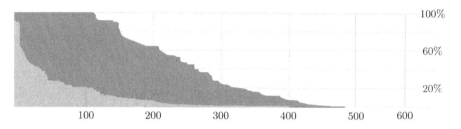

Fig. 7. Distribution of reduction ratios (place count) over the 627 PN instances. (Color figure online)

Computing Time of Reductions. Many of the reduction rules implemented have a cost polynomial in the size of the net. The rule removing redundant places in the general case is more complex as it requires to solve an integer programming problem. For this reason we limit its application to nets with less than 50 places. With this restriction, reductions are computed in a few seconds in most cases, and in about 3 min for the largest nets. The restriction is necessary but, because of it, we do not reduce some nets that would be fully reducible otherwise.

Impact on the Marking Count Problem. In our benchmark, there are 169 models, out of 627, for which no tool was ever able to compute a marking count. With our method, we could count the markings of at least 14 of them.

If we concentrate on *tractable nets*—instances managed by at least one tool in the MCC 2017—our approach yields generally large improvements on the time taken to count markings; sometimes orders of magnitude faster. Table 1(top) lists the CPU time (in seconds) for counting the markings on a selection of fully reducible instances. We give the best time obtained by a tool during the last MCC (third column) and compare it with the time obtained with *tedd*, using two different ways of counting solutions (first with our own, native, method then with LaTTe). We also give the resulting speed-up. These times also include parsing and applying reductions. An absent value (−) means that it cannot be computed in less than 1 h with 16 Gb of storage.

Table 1. Computation times (in seconds) and speed-up for counting markings on some totally (top) and partially (bottom) reduced nets

Net instance	Size		MCC (best)	*tedd* native	*tedd* LaTTe	Speed up
	♯ places	♯ states				
BART-050	11 822	1.88e118	2 800	346	-	8
BART-060	14 132	8.50e141	-	496	-	∞
DLCround-13a	463	2.40e17	9	0.33	-	27
FlexibleBarrier-22a	267	5.52e23	5	0.25	-	20
NeighborGrid-d4n3m2c23	81	2.70e65	330	0.21	44	1571
NeighborGrid-d5n4m1t35	1 024	2.85e614	-	340	-	∞
Referendum-1000	3 001	1.32e477	29	12	-	2
RobotManipulation-00050	15	8.53e12	94	0.1	0.17	940
RobotManipulation-10000	15	2.83e33	-	102	0.17	∞
Diffusion2D-50N050	2 500	4.22e105	1 900	5.84	-	325
Diffusion2D-50N150	2 500	2.67e36	-	5.86	-	∞
DLCshifumi-6a	3 568	4.50e160	950	6.54	-	145
Kanban-1000	16	1.42e30	240	0.11	0.24	2182
HouseConstruction-100	26	1.58e24	630	0.4	0.85	1575
HouseConstruction-500	26	2.67e36	-	30	0.85	∞
Airplane-4000	28 019	2.18e12	2520	102	-	25
AutoFlight-48a	1127	1.61e51	19	3.57	-	5
DES-60b	519	8.35e22	2300	364	-	6
Peterson-4	480	6.30e8	470	35.5	-	13
Peterson-5	834	1.37e11	-	1200	-	∞

Concerning partially reducible nets, the improvements are less spectacular in general though still significant. Counting markings in this case is more expensive than for totally reduced nets. But, more importantly, we have to build in that case a representation of the state space of the residual net, which is typically much more expensive than counting markings. Furthermore, if using symbolic methods for that purpose, several other parameters come into play that may impact the results, like the choice of an order on decision diagram variables or the particular kind of diagrams used. Nevertheless, improvements are clearly visible on a number of example models; some speedups are shown in Table 1(bottom). Also, to minimize such side issues, instead of comparing *tedd* with compact reductions with the best tool performing at the MCC, we compared it with *tedd* without reductions or with the weaker clean strategy. In that case, compact reductions are almost always effective at reducing computing times.

Finally, there are also a few cases where applying reductions lower performances, typically when the reduction ratio is very small. For such quasi-irreducible nets, the time spent computing reductions is obviously wasted.

8   Related Work and Conclusion

Our work relies on well understood structural reduction methods, adapted here for the purpose of abstracting the state space of a net. This is done by representing the effects of reductions by a system of linear equations. To the best of our knowledge, reductions have never been used for that purpose before.

Linear algebraic techniques are widely used in Petri net theory but, again, not with our exact goals. It is well known, for instance, that the state space of a net is included in the solution set of its so-called "state equation", or from a basis of marking invariants. But these solutions, though exact in the special case of live marked graphs, yield approximations that are too coarse. Other works take advantage of marking invariants obtained from semiflows on places, but typically for optimizing the representation of markings in explicit or symbolic enumeration methods rather than for helping their enumeration, see e.g. [16,20]. Finally, these methods are only remotely related to our.

Another set of related work concerns symbolic methods based on the use of decision diagrams. Indeed they can be used to compute the state space size. In such methods, markings are computed symbolically and represented by the paths of some directed acyclic graph, which can be counted efficiently. Crucial for the applicability of these methods is determining a "good" variable ordering for decision diagram variables, one that maximizes sharing among the paths. Unfortunately, finding a convenient variable ordering may be an issue, and some models are inherently without sharing. For example, the best symbolic tools participating to the MCC can solve our illustrative example only for $p_1 \leq 100$, at a high cost, while we compute the result in a fraction of a second for virtually any possible initial marking of p_1.

Finally, though not aimed at counting markings nor relying on reductions, the work reported in [18] is certainly the closest to our. It defines a method for decomposing the state space of a net into the product of "independent sets of submarkings". The ideas discussed in the paper resemble what we achieved with agglomeration. In fact, the running example in [18], reproduced here in Fig. 1, is a fully reducible net in our approach. But no effective methods are proposed to compute decompositions.

Concluding Remarks. We propose a new symbolic approach for representing the state space of a PN relying on systems of linear equations. Our results show that the method is almost always effective at reducing computing times and memory consumption for counting markings. Even more interesting is that our methods can be used together with traditional explicit and symbolic enumeration methods, as well as with other abstraction techniques like symmetry reductions for example. They can also help for other problems, like reachability analysis.

There are many opportunities for further research. For the close future, we are investigating richer sets of reductions for counting markings and application of the method to count not only the markings, but also the number of transitions of the reachability graph. Model-checking of linear reachability properties is another obvious prospective application of our methods. On the long term, a question to be investigated is how to obtain efficiently fully equational descriptions of the state spaces of bounded Petri nets.

References

1. Behle, M., Eisenbrand, F.: 0/1 vertex and facet enumeration with BDDs. In: 9th Workshop on Algorithm Engineering and Experiments. SIAM (2007)
2. Berthelot, G.: Checking properties of nets using transformations. In: Rozenberg, G. (ed.) APN 1985. LNCS, vol. 222, pp. 19–40. Springer, Heidelberg (1986). https://doi.org/10.1007/BFb0016204
3. Berthelot, G.: Transformations and decompositions of nets. In: Brauer, W., Reisig, W., Rozenberg, G. (eds.) ACPN 1986. LNCS, vol. 254, pp. 359–376. Springer, Heidelberg (1987). https://doi.org/10.1007/978-3-540-47919-2_13
4. Berthomieu, B., Ribet, P.-O., Vernadat, F.: The tool TINA-construction of abstract state spaces for Petri nets and Time Petri nets. Int. J. Prod. Res. **42**(14), 2741–2756 (2004)
5. Esparza, J., Schröter, C.: Net reductions for LTL model-checking. In: Margaria, T., Melham, T. (eds.) CHARME 2001. LNCS, vol. 2144, pp. 310–324. Springer, Heidelberg (2001). https://doi.org/10.1007/3-540-44798-9_25
6. Kordon, F., et al.: Complete Results for the 2017 Edition of the Model Checking Contest, June 2017. http://mcc.lip6.fr/
7. Kordon, F., Garavel, H., Hillah, L.M., Paviot-Adet, E., Jezequel, L., Rodríguez, C., Hulin-Hubard, F.: MCC'2015-the fifth model checking contest. In: Koutny M., Desel J., Kleijn J. (eds.) Transactions on Petri Nets and Other Models of Concurrency XI. LNCS, vol 9930, pp. 262–273. Springer, Heidelberg (2016)
8. Hack, M.: Decidability questions for Petri Nets. Ph.D. thesis, Massachusetts Institute of Technology (1976)
9. Hillah, L.M., Kordon, F.: Petri nets repository: a tool to benchmark and debug petri net tools. In: van der Aalst, W., Best, E. (eds.) PETRI NETS 2017. LNCS, vol. 10258, pp. 125–135. Springer, Cham (2017). https://doi.org/10.1007/978-3-319-57861-3_9
10. Jensen, J.F., Nielsen, T., Oestergaard, L.K., Srba, J.: TAPAAL and reachability analysis of P/T nets. In: Koutny, M., Desel, J., Kleijn, J. (eds.) Transactions on Petri Nets and Other Models of Concurrency XI. LNCS, vol. 9930, pp. 307–318. Springer, Heidelberg (2016). https://doi.org/10.1007/978-3-662-53401-4_16
11. Levy, F.K., Thompson, G.L., Wiest, J.D.: Introduction to the Critical-Path Method. Industrial Scheduling. Prentice-Hall, Englewood Cliffs (1963)
12. De Loera, J.A., Hemmecke, R., Köppe, M.: Algebraic and Geometric Ideas in the Theory of Discrete Optimization. SIAM, Philadelphia (2013)
13. De Loera, J.A., Hemmecke, R., Tauzer, J., Yoshida, R.: Effective lattice point counting in rational convex polytopes. J. Symbolic Comput. **38**(4), 1273–1302 (2004)
14. Peterson, J.L.: Petri Net Theory and the Modeling of Systems. Prentice Hall PTR, Upper Saddle River (1981)

15. Recalde, L., Teruel, E., Silva, M.: Improving the decision power of rank theorems. In: 1997 IEEE International Conference on Systems, Man, and Cybernetics. Computational Cybernetics and Simulation, vol. 4, pp. 3768–3773 (1997)

16. Schmidt, K.: Using petri net invariants in state space construction. In: Garavel, H., Hatcliff, J. (eds.) TACAS 2003. LNCS, vol. 2619, pp. 473–488. Springer, Heidelberg (2003). https://doi.org/10.1007/3-540-36577-X_35

17. Silva, M., Terue, E., Colom, J.M.: Linear algebraic and linear programming techniques for the analysis of place/transition net systems. In: Reisig, W., Rozenberg, G. (eds.) ACPN 1996. LNCS, vol. 1491, pp. 309–373. Springer, Heidelberg (1998). https://doi.org/10.1007/3-540-65306-6_19

18. Stahl, C.: Decomposing petri net state spaces. In: 18th German Workshop on Algorithms and Tools for Petri Nets (AWPN 2011), Hagen, Germany, September 2011

19. Thierry-Mieg, Y., Poitrenaud, D., Hamez, A., Kordon, F.: Hierarchical set decision diagrams and regular models. In: Kowalewski, S., Philippou, A. (eds.) TACAS 2009. LNCS, vol. 5505, pp. 1–15. Springer, Heidelberg (2009). https://doi.org/10.1007/978-3-642-00768-2_1

20. Wolf, K.: Generating petri net state spaces. In: Kleijn, J., Yakovlev, A. (eds.) ICATPN 2007. LNCS, vol. 4546, pp. 29–42. Springer, Heidelberg (2007). https://doi.org/10.1007/978-3-540-73094-1_5

Improving Generalization in Software IC3

Tim Lange[1][(✉)], Frederick Prinz[1], Martin R. Neuhäußer[2], Thomas Noll[1], and Joost-Pieter Katoen[1]

[1] RWTH Aachen University, Aachen, Germany
{tim.lange,noll,katoen}@cs.rwth-aachen.de
[2] Siemens AG, Munich, Germany
martin.neuhaeusser@siemens.com

Abstract. Generalization is a key feature to support state-space abstraction in IC3-based algorithms for software model checking, such as Tree-IC3 or IC3CFA. This paper introduces several improvements that range from efficient caching of generalizations over variable reductions to syntax-oriented generalization. Our techniques are generic in that they are independent of the underlying theory, and some of them are even applicable to IC3 in general. Their evaluation on multiple benchmarks, including a significant subset of the SV-COMP 2017 benchmarks, yields promising results.

1 Introduction

IC3 [3] is one of the most prominent state-of-the-art model-checking algorithms designed for bit-level verification of hardware systems, represented as finite-state transition systems. The IC3 algorithm tries to prove the correctness of an invariant property by iteratively deriving overapproximations of the reachable state space until a fixpoint is reached. Its impressive impact on the model-checking community and its superior performance base on two important aspects: In contrast to most other (bounded) model-checking algorithms, IC3 does not rely on unrolling the transition relation, but instead generates clauses that are inductive relative to stepwise reachability information. In addition, IC3 applies aggressive abstraction to the explored state space, so-called generalization.

An adaptation of IC3 to software model checking, called IC3CFA, was presented in [14]. In IC3CFA, the control-flow of a program is represented as control-flow automaton (CFA) while the data space is handled symbolically. This explicit structure can further guide the reachability analysis of IC3 when dealing with software. While IC3CFA was originally developed in the context of Programmable Logic Controller code verification, it is successfully applied to the verification of C programs, too, as shown in Sect. 4.

As the author of the original IC3 algorithm [3] states, "one of the key components of IC3 is inductive generalization" [12]. Even though IC3 is sound and complete without generalization, by explicitly enumerating models in a finite state space, it largely depends on its ability to abstract from specific states in

© Springer International Publishing AG, part of Springer Nature 2018
M. M. Gallardo and P. Merino (Eds.): SPIN 2018, LNCS 10869, pp. 85–102, 2018.
https://doi.org/10.1007/978-3-319-94111-0_5

order to scale to huge state spaces. While the original procedure of literal elimination on the Boolean skeleton can be applied to IC3 in the first-order setting [5], generalization in IC3CFA still offers a large potential for improvements.

Our contributions are five small and elegant modifications of the generalization procedure of IC3CFA that improve the overall performance of IC3CFA by up to two orders of magnitude for certain benchmarks and allow us to verify ten instances more than using IC3-style generalization, with a verification time that is in total 10% lower. In addition, our improvements are general in the sense that the presented algorithms are independent of the underlying SMT theory and support existing generalization methods, such as unsatisfiable cores [3], obligation ordering [11] and interpolation [2].

Related Work. Another approach to software model checking with IC3 is Tree-IC3 [5], which iteratively derives a tree-like structure given in terms of an abstract reachability tree (ART) and computes abstractions of candidate counterexamples. However, generalization is not discussed in [5]. [19] presents an algorithm to apply IC3 to software model checking using the theory of quantifier-free bitvector formulas, thereby lifting standard IC3 from one-dimensional to multi-dimensional Boolean variables. Due to this restriction to bit vectors, the algorithm is highly theory-aware and cannot be applied to other theories such as unbounded integers. It utilizes the standard generalization of IC3. [13] also addresses IC3-style software model checking, but focuses on pushdown automata and general Horn clauses, as well as linear real arithmetic. [2] utilizes the ideas of IC3 to enhance a predicate abstraction/refinement-based analysis of infinite-state systems by using counterexamples to induction to guide the refinement process of the predicates. In [6], the authors use the Tree-IC3 algorithm [5] and combine it with implicit predicate abstraction. By abstracting the exact transition relation, they are able to verify a software system in terms of a purely abstract state space by executing a Boolean IC3 algorithm, using only the basic generalization of IC3.

Overview. In the remainder we provide basic concepts for IC3CFA generalization in Sect. 2, present our contributions to the generalization procedure in Sect. 3, and show their evaluation in Sect. 4. We conclude with a short summary and outlook in Sect. 5. Proofs are provided in the appendix.

2   Preliminaries

To abstract from different input languages and to maintain a small set of commands, we use a guarded command language (GCL) for loop-free code.

Definition 1 (GCL commands). *The syntax of the Guarded Command Language (GCL) is defined as*

$$\mathcal{C} ::= \textit{Assume } b \mid x := a \mid \mathcal{C}_1; \mathcal{C}_2 \mid \mathcal{C}_1 \square \mathcal{C}_2,$$

where x is a variable and

$$a ::= z \mid x \mid a_1 \diamond a_2$$
$$b ::= true \mid false \mid a_1 \circ a_2 \mid b_1 \wedge b_2$$

with $z \in \mathbb{Z}$, $\diamond \in \{+, -, *, /, \%\}$, *and* $\circ \in \{=, \neq, \leq, \geq, <, >\}$.

For our modifications to the generalization algorithm, we disallow disjunction and negation in Boolean expressions of `Assume` commands. We can compensate this restriction by nondeterministic branching using the □ operator and pushing negations into relational expressions, which are closed under negation. While this may seem overly restrictive, it is necessary to enable some of our improvements, in particular those presented in Sect. 3.1. GCL only supports loop-free code. To manipulate control flow we use a control-flow automaton [14]:

Definition 2 (Control-flow automaton). *A control-flow automaton (CFA) is a tuple* $A = (L, G, \ell_0, \ell_E)$ *of locations* $L = \{\ell_0, \ldots, \ell_n\}$, *edges* $G \subseteq L \times GCL \times L$, *initial location* $\ell_0 \in L$ *and error location* $\ell_E \in L$.

Furthermore we use the GCL command C of edge $e = (l, C, l') \in G$ to define the quantifier-free first-order term T_e of e, i.e. the term representing the semantics of C, transforming unprimed current states φ to primed successor states φ' by replacing every variable x in φ by x'. Given a subset V of variables in CFA edges, a *cube* $c \in Cube$ over V is defined as a conjunction of *literals*, each literal being a variable or its negation in the propositional case and a theory atom or its negation in the quantifier-free first-order case. The negation of a cube, i.e. a disjunction of literals, is called a *clause*. A *frame* $F \in Frame$ is defined as a conjunction of clauses. For simplicity, we will refer to cubes and frames as sets of implicitly conjoined literals and clauses, respectively. To facilitate this reasoning, we will distinguish between two different, converse perspectives: Given two cubes c_1 and c_2, then $c_1 \subseteq c_2$ holds if the set of literals of c_1 is a subset of the literals of c_2. However, if we think of a cube as a symbolic representation of states, then c_1 represents more states than c_2. To take this converse perspective into account, we introduce the partial order $\sqsubseteq$:

Definition 3. *Given two cubes* c_1 *and* c_2, *let* $c_2 \sqsubseteq c_1$ *iff* $c_1 \subseteq c_2$.

Similar to the definition of relative inductivity [3], [14] defines relative inductivity for single edges of a CFA as follows:

Definition 4 (Edge-relative inductivity [14]). *Assuming frame* F *and cube* c *at location* ℓ', *we define inductivity of* c *edge-relative to* F *along edge* $e = (\ell, C, \ell')$ *with transition formula* T_e *(based on semantics of* C*) by*

$$F \wedge T_e \Rightarrow \neg c', \qquad\qquad if\ \ell \neq \ell' \qquad\qquad (1)$$
$$F \wedge \neg c \wedge T_e \Rightarrow \neg c', \qquad\qquad if\ \ell = \ell'. \qquad\qquad (2)$$

We define the predicate $relInd_e(F, c)$ *to hold iff* c *is inductive edge-relative to* F *along* e.

While this holds for IC3CFA without generalization, (2) cannot be applied in the presence of generalization any more, as stated by the following lemma.

Lemma 1. *Given two distinct edges* $e_1 = (\ell_1, \mathcal{C}_1, \ell')$ *and* $e_2 = (\ell_2, \mathcal{C}_2, \ell')$ *with* $\ell_1 \neq \ell_2$, *two frames* F_1 *and* F_2 *and two respective cubes* g_1, g_2, *generalization does not necessarily preserve* (2):

$$(F_1 \wedge T_{e_1} \Rightarrow \neg g_1') \wedge (F_2 \wedge \neg g_2 \wedge T_{e_2} \Rightarrow \neg g_2')$$
$$\nRightarrow \quad ((F_1 \wedge T_{e_1}) \vee (F_2 \wedge \neg (g_1 \wedge g_2) \wedge T_{e_2})) \Rightarrow \neg (g_1' \wedge g_2')$$

As a result of Lemma 1, we will only use (1) for all inductivity queries in the remainder. Like [3], we verify validity of (1) by checking whether

$$F \wedge T_{\ell_1 \to \ell_2} \wedge c'$$

is unsatisfiable.

Analogously to a Boolean generalization of IC3 [3], we can define a generalization that preserves edge-relative inductivity.

Definition 5 (Edge-relative inductive generalization). *We call a function* $gen : Frame \times Cube \times GCL \to Cube$ *an edge-relative inductive generalization for edge* e *if the following holds for every cube* c *and every frame* F:

1. $gen(F, c, e) \subseteq c$
2. $relInd_e(F, c) \Rightarrow relInd_e(F, gen(F, c, e))$.

Note that 1. and 2. together imply that

$$gen(F, c, e) \Leftrightarrow relInd_e(F, c)$$

IC3

Let $S = (X, I, T)$ be a transition system over a finite set X of Boolean variables, and $I(X)$ and $T(X, X')$ two propositional formulas describing the initial condition over variables in X, and the transition relation over X and next-state primed successors X', respectively. Given a propositional formula $P(X)$, we want to verify that P is an S-invariant, i.e. that every state in S that is reachable from a state in I satisfies P. Sometimes also an inverted formulation is used like in [8] where $\neg P$ states are *bad states* and we want to show that no bad state is reachable from any of the initial states. The main idea of the IC3 algorithm [3] is to show that P is *inductive*, i.e. that $I \Rightarrow P$ and $P \wedge T \Rightarrow P'$ hold, which entails that P is an S-invariant. However, the reverse implication does generally not apply. Therefore the goal of IC3 is to produce a so-called *inductive strengthening* F of P, s.t. $F \wedge P$ is inductive. In contrast to its predecessor FSIS [4], IC3 constructs F *incrementally*. This incremental construction is based on a dynamic sequence of *frames* $F_0, \ldots, F_k$ for which

$$I \Rightarrow F_0 \tag{3}$$
$$F_i \Rightarrow F_{i+1}, \qquad \text{for } 0 \leq i < k \tag{4}$$
$$F_i \Rightarrow P, \qquad \text{for } 0 \leq i \leq k \tag{5}$$
$$F_i \wedge T \Rightarrow F_{i+1}', \qquad \text{for } 0 \leq i < k \tag{6}$$

has to hold in order to produce an inductive invariant. Note that k is a dynamic bound that will be extended by IC3 on demand. Due to the usage of a satisfiability (SAT) solver, [3] uses the implication $F \Rightarrow F'$ to compare frames. This semantic check covers the syntactic check whether $F \sqsubseteq F'$. The algorithm starts with initial checks for 0- and 1-step reachable states in $\neg P$ and afterwards initializes the first frame F_0 to I. The rest of the algorithm can be divided into an inner and an outer loop, sometimes referred to as *blocking* and *propagation* phases.

The outer loop iterates over the maximal frame index k, looking for states in F_k that can reach $\neg P$, so-called *counterexamples to induction* (CTI). If such a CTI exists, it is analyzed in the inner loop, the blocking phase. If no such CTI exists, IC3 tries to propagate clauses learned in frame F_i forward to F_{i+1}, for $0 \leq i < k$. In the end it checks for termination, which is given if $F_i = F_{i+1}$ for some $0 \leq i < k$.

The blocking phase decides whether a CTI is reachable from I or not. For this purpose, it maintains a set of pairs of frame index and symbolic states in form of a cube, called *proof obligations*. From this set it picks a pair (i, c) with smallest frame index i. For (i, c), IC3 checks whether $\neg c$ is inductive relative to F_{i-1}. If it is, we can block c in frames F_j for $0 \leq j \leq i + 1$. But rather than just adding $\neg c$, IC3 tries to obtain a clause $cl \subseteq \neg c$ excluding more states. This *generalization* of $\neg c$ is added to the frames. If $\neg c$ is not inductive relative to F_{i-1}, this means that there exists an F_{i-1}-predecessor p reaching c. IC3 therefore adds $(i-1, p)$ as proof obligation. The blocking phase terminates at obligation $(0, p)$, in which case there exists a counterexample path, or when for every proof obligation (i, c) it holds that $i > k$, i.e. every predecessor of the CTI is relative inductive.

IC3CFA [14] adapts IC3 to software model checking, based on the idea to exploit the structure of the CFA of a program to guide the search of IC3. For this purpose we have to split the frame at index i, i.e. F_i into a set of frames, one for each location ℓ, i.e. $F_{(i,\ell)}$. [14] proposes an algorithm similar to the original IC3: It starts searching for CTIs by computing states in every predecessor location of the error location ℓ_E (representing all *bad states*) using *weakest preconditions*. Those states at their respective index and location are stored as proof obligations. As long as the obligation queue is non-empty, the algorithm picks an obligation with minimal index and checks whether the obligation is inductive edge-relative to the location-specific predecessor frame on every incoming edge. If the inductivity check succeeds, the cube is generalized and blocked by adding it to the frame matrix at the respective index and location. If the check does not succeed, a predecessor is computed and added to the obligation queue. If at some point the initial location ℓ_0 is reached, a counterexample can be reported. If, on the other hand, the obligation queue becomes empty, the strengthening of frames up to bound k is complete and termination is checked. The termination condition verifies that for some i, at every location the frame with index i is equal to the frame with index $i + 1$. If this condition is not met, the algorithm proceeds by increasing its bound to $k + 1$. In [14] it is shown that the original IC3CFA algorithm, without any generalization, already outperforms some other IC3 algorithms for software, such as Tree-IC3 and the trivial lifting to IC3SMT [5].

3   Generalization

This section presents five improvements to the IC3CFA algorithm that pave the way towards a powerful, efficient generalization. Since IC3CFA as published in [14] does not include generalization, we must first take a look at how a generalization for a location can be computed while using the positive effects of only considering individual edges. In Lemma 1 and Definition 5, we have shown how inductivity and generalization work on a single CFA edge. Given some ℓ' with predecessor locations $\ell_1, \ldots, \ell_n$, we can compute edge-relative generalizations $g_1, \ldots, g_n$ and merge them to a generalization to be blocked at ℓ' by constructing the cube g that contains all literals appearing in each g_i ($1 \leq i \leq n$). Using this merge to lift the syntactic generalization based on dropping literals will be referred to as *IC3-style generalization* in the remainder.

As mentioned before, IC3 uses the model generated by the SAT solver as a set of predecessor states of a non-inductive state set for further backward search. If such a cube c, or more precisely its negation, is shown to be inductive relative to a frame F, it is generalized to a subcube g that is still inductive relative to F. While this method is complete for Boolean IC3, its application to IC3 for software, such as Tree-IC3 [5] or IC3CFA [14], has two main consequences that will be driving forces behind the contributions of this section: (1) there may exist infinitely many predecessor states, so model enumeration is not complete, and (2) the generalization should ideally be theory-unaware to support its use with different backend theories. While this may seem counter-intuitive, since theory-aware implementations may be more performant, the independence from any theory allows a modular, flexible approach to backend theories that enables us to solve many more problem domains. For example, a generalization that uses Linear Real Arithmetic (LRA) is only able to solve a limited number of problems, whereas we can switch from LRA to Floating Point (FP) depending on whether we need bit-precise arithmetic, including overflows, or not. Note that in contrast to IC3, IC3CFA does not use the global transition relation but only single transitions between control-flow locations.

3.1   Predecessor Computation

A solution to (1) is presented in [5,14]: The computation of the weakest precondition (WP) yields an exact pre-image and thus provides a suitable way to extract predecessor states. While various definitions of WPs can be found in the literature [9,15], the most commonly used is the *demonic* version [7]. For non-deterministic choices this variant only covers states that reach a state in the postcondition under *all* possible executions. However, in safety verification we are not only interested in those states that *must* lead to a failure, but also in states that *may* lead to a failure under certain conditions, which corresponds to the *angelic* interpretation of weakest preconditions. In contrast to [5], [14] splits the semantics of an edge into GCL commands and SMT expressions. By applying standard GCL predicate transformer semantics [7] and rewriting the SMT expressions, our angelic WP computation does *not introduce quantifiers* and thus there is no need to eliminate those. Based on the four types of GCL commands (Definition 1), the angelic WP is defined according to the following rules:

$$wp(\texttt{Assume}\ b, \varphi) = \varphi \wedge b$$
$$wp(x := a, \varphi) = \varphi[x \mapsto a]$$
$$wp(\mathcal{C}_1; \mathcal{C}_2, \varphi) = wp(\mathcal{C}_1, wp(\mathcal{C}_2, \varphi))$$
$$wp(\mathcal{C}_1 \square \mathcal{C}_2, \varphi) = wp(\mathcal{C}_1, \varphi) \vee wp(\mathcal{C}_2, \varphi).$$

where $\varphi[x \mapsto a]$ equals φ with all free occurrences of x replaced by a. When applying this WP to a state set represented symbolically, it yields a first-order term whose structure is highly dependent on the structure of the transition. However, this ambiguity exacerbates the structured processing of proof obligations and generalization. In our experiments we found that a restricted representation like cubes, which are used in [3], offers two-fold advantages: The simpler data structures improve the performance of our implementation while at the same time the generalization is able to drop more literals. To employ the cube structure of [3], we can translate the results of WP computations into disjunctive normal form (DNF), resulting in a number of cubes that can potentially lead into the target states. While this translation has exponential worst-case runtime, our experiments have revealed an overall beneficial effect.

After closer inspection of the decomposition of the WP into DNF, we found that we can organize the conversion to DNF as a translation on the GCL structure. We call this operation *split*, as it splits a single choice command into a set of parallel commands that can be represented as parallel edges in the CFA.

Definition 6 (Split). *The function* $spl : GCL \to 2^{GCL}$ *is given by:*

$$spl(\mathcal{C}) = \begin{cases} spl(\mathcal{C}_1) \cup spl(\mathcal{C}_2) & if\ \mathcal{C} = (\mathcal{C}_1 \square \mathcal{C}_2) \\ \{c_1; c_2 \mid \forall i \in \{1, 2\}.\ c_i \in spl(\mathcal{C}_i)\} & if\ \mathcal{C} = (\mathcal{C}_1; \mathcal{C}_2) \\ \{\mathcal{C}\} & otherwise. \end{cases}$$

Applying the function *spl* to the commands along edges in G yields a refined set of control-flow edges

$$G' = \{(\ell, \mathcal{C}', \ell') \mid (\ell, \mathcal{C}, \ell') \in G, \mathcal{C}' \in spl(\mathcal{C})\}.$$

Intuitively, an edge $e = (\ell, \mathcal{C}, \ell') \in G$ labeled with $\mathcal{C}$ including a choice, is split into multiple edges between the same locations. Each new edge contains no choice command any more, such that it models a deterministic, sequential behaviour. This in turn means that the result of a WP computation of a cube with respect to a split edge is now guaranteed to be a cube again.

Theorem 1. *For any GCL command* $\mathcal{C}$ *and cube* c:

$$dnf(wp(\mathcal{C}, c)) = \bigvee \{wp(\mathcal{C}', c) \mid \mathcal{C}' \in spl(\mathcal{C})\}$$

where $dnf(\varphi)$ *converts the given quantifier-free first-order formula* φ *into DNF.*

To prove the correctness of Theorem 1, we use the following auxiliary lemma:

Lemma 2. *For each GCL command C without $\square$ and cube c: $dnf(wp(C,c)) = wp(C,c)$, where $dnf(\varphi)$ converts the quantifier-free first-order formula φ into DNF.*

Proof. Note that the GCL command C contains no choice. We prove the lemma by structural induction over C without the choice case.

$C = (\texttt{Assume } b)$:	$C = (x := a)$:	$C = (C_1; C_2)$:
$dnf(wp(\texttt{Assume } b, c))$	$dnf(wp(x := a, c))$	$dnf(wp(C_1; C_2, c))$
$= dnf(c \wedge b)$	$= dnf(c[x \mapsto a])$	$= dnf(wp(C_1, wp(C_2, c)))$
$= c \wedge b$	$= c[x \mapsto a]$	$= wp(C_1, wp(C_2, c))$
$= wp(\texttt{Assume } b, c)$	$= wp(x := a, c)$	$= wp(C_1; C_2, c)$

Proof (Theorem 1).

$$dnf(wp(C, c))$$
$$= dnf(\bigvee\{wp(C', c) \mid C' \in split(C)\})$$
$$= \bigvee\{dnf(wp(C', c)) \mid C' \in split(C)\}$$
$$= \bigvee\{wp(C', c) \mid C' \in split(C)\} \qquad \text{(Lemma 2)}$$

Using the *spl* function, we can split the WP transformer into a number of transformers that directly yield cubes, rather than arbitrarily structured formulas. The disjunction of those partial WPs is equal to the DNF of the original WP, as shown in Theorem 1. While this additional split operation is not beneficial on its own, it enables a subsequent optimization that has the potential to statically derive a generalization of good quality without any SMT calls.

3.2   Predecessor Cubes

This approach computes the generalization of a given cube c based on a syntactic check of the predecessor frame. If the predecessor frame $F_{(i-1,\ell)}$ contains a clause $\neg \bar{c}$ which blocks at least $wp(C, c)$, i.e. $\bar{c} \subseteq wp(C, c)$ with respect to edge $e = (\ell, C, \ell') \in G$, then the cube c is inductive edge-relative to $F_{(i-1,\ell)}$ w.r.t. e. This static test can be applied to every inductivity check of IC3CFA, not only to those used in generalization.

Lemma 3. *Let (L, G, ℓ_0, ℓ_E) be a CFA with edge $e = (\ell, C, \ell') \in G$, and cube c to be blocked at $\ell' \in L$ and index i. For frame $F_{(i-1,\ell)}$:*

$$\left(\exists \bar{c} \in Cube. \ \left(\neg \bar{c} \in F_{(i-1,\ell)}\right) \wedge \left(\bar{c} \subseteq wp(C, c)\right)\right)$$
$$\implies relInd_e(F_{(i-1,\ell)}, c).$$

Proof.

$$\exists \bar{c} \in Cube. \ \neg\bar{c} \in F_{(i-1,\ell)} \wedge \bar{c} \subseteq wp(\mathcal{C}, c)$$
$$\Rightarrow \quad \exists \bar{c} \in Cube. \ unsat(F_{(i-1,\ell)} \wedge \bar{c}) \wedge \bar{c} \subseteq wp(\mathcal{C}, c)$$
$$\Rightarrow \quad unsat(F_{(i-1,\ell)} \wedge wp(\mathcal{C}, c))$$
$$\Rightarrow \quad relIndWP_e(F_{(i-1,\ell)}, c) \qquad\qquad\qquad \text{(Definition 7)}$$
$$\Leftrightarrow \quad relInd_e(F_{(i-1,\ell)}, c) \qquad\qquad\qquad\quad \text{(Lemma 3)}$$

Given such a predecessor cube $\bar{c}$, we can also derive the generalization $g \subseteq c$ of the original cube c.

Lemma 4. *Let $\mathcal{C}$ be a choice-free GCL command. Given two cubes c_1, c_2, it holds that*

$$wp(\mathcal{C}, c_1 \wedge c_2) \iff wp(\mathcal{C}, c_1) \wedge wp(\mathcal{C}, c_2).$$

Proof. We prove Lemma 4 by structural induction over GCL command $\mathcal{C}$ without choice.

$\mathcal{C} = $ Assume b:	$\mathcal{C} = x := a$:
$wp(\text{Assume } b, c_1 \wedge c_2)$	$wp(x := a, c_1 \wedge c_2)$
$= (c_1 \wedge c_2) \wedge b$	$= (c_1 \wedge c_2)[x \mapsto a]$
$= (c_1 \wedge b) \wedge (c_2 \wedge b)$	$= c_1[x \mapsto a] \wedge c_2[x \mapsto a]$
$= wp(\text{Assume } b, c_1) \wedge wp(\text{Assume } b, c_2)$	$= wp(x := a, c_1) \wedge wp(x := a, c_2)$

$\mathcal{C} = \mathcal{C}_1; \mathcal{C}_2$:

$wp(\mathcal{C}_1; \mathcal{C}_2, c_1 \wedge c_2)$
$= wp(\mathcal{C}_1, wp(\mathcal{C}_2, c_1 \wedge c_2))$
$= wp(\mathcal{C}_1, wp(\mathcal{C}_2, c_1) \wedge wp(\mathcal{C}_2, c_2))$
$= wp(\mathcal{C}_1, wp(\mathcal{C}_2, c_1)) \wedge wp(\mathcal{C}_1, wp(\mathcal{C}_2, c_2))$
$= wp(\mathcal{C}_1; \mathcal{C}_2, c_1) \wedge wp(\mathcal{C}_1; \mathcal{C}_2, c_2)$

Given that wp distributes over conjunction for choice-free GCL commands, we can decompose cube c into its literals $l_1, \dots, l_n$ and construct the wp for each $l_i, i \in \{1, \dots, n\}$ individually. The result of $wp(\mathcal{C}, c)$, a conjunction of n WPs of the literals l_i, is $w = w_1 \wedge \cdots \wedge w_n$. If we now encounter a predecessor cube $\bar{c} \subseteq w$, we map each $w_i \in \bar{c}$ back to its original literal $l_i \in c$ and obtain a new cube $g = \{l_i \mid w_i \in \bar{c}, w_i = wp(\mathcal{C}, l_i)\}$. Since our approach obviously satisfies monotonicity for choice-free GCL commands that do not contain disjunctions according to Definition 1, it holds that

$$\bar{c} \subseteq w \implies g \subseteq c.$$

Furthermore, since $\neg wp(\mathcal{C}, l_i) \in F_{(i-1,\ell)}$ for each $l_i \in g$, g is inductive relative to $F_{(i-1,\ell)}$ and thus g is a valid generalization for c. Note that semantically g is a strongest postcondition of $\bar{c}$, but differs in the syntactic structure.

Theorem 2. *Let* (L, G, ℓ_0, ℓ_E) *be a CFA with edge* $e = (\ell, \mathcal{C}, \ell') \in G$, *and cube* c *be blocked at* $\ell' \in L$ *and index* i. *For frame* $F_{(i-1,\ell)}$ *and cube* g:

$$\left(\forall \mathcal{C}' \in spl(\mathcal{C}).\neg wp(\mathcal{C}', g) \in F_{(i-1,\ell)} \land wp(\mathcal{C}', g) \subseteq wp(\mathcal{C}', c)\right)$$
$$\implies gen(F_{(i,\ell')}, c, e) = g.$$

Proof. Let $\widehat{c}$ be a cube and $\mathcal{C}$ be a GCL command without a choice

$$\neg wp(\mathcal{C}, \widehat{c}) \in F_{(i-1,\ell)} \land wp(\mathcal{C}, \widehat{c}) \subseteq wp(\mathcal{C}, c)$$
$$\Rightarrow \quad relInd_e(F_{(i-1,\ell)}, \widehat{c}) \land wp(\mathcal{C}, \widehat{c}) \subseteq wp(\mathcal{C}, c) \qquad \text{(Lemma 3)}$$
$$\Rightarrow \quad relInd_e(F_{(i-1,\ell)}, \widehat{c}) \land \widehat{c} \subseteq c \qquad \text{(Monotonicity)}$$
$$\Rightarrow \quad gen(F_{(i,\ell')}, c, e) = \widehat{c} \qquad \text{(Definition 5)}$$

We execute the static check for predecessor cubes, as given in Lemma 3, in the generalization of IC3CFA whenever deriving a generalization from the methods proposed in Sects. 3.4 and 3.6 fails. If we find a predecessor cube, we can immediately use that to construct a generalization and skip the generalization phase entirely.

3.3   WP Inductivity

Like the original IC3 algorithm, IC3CFA makes heavy use of the underlying solver, such that small optimizations in its usage can have significant effect on the overall performance. As we compute exact pre-images by taking weakest preconditions in each step anyway, we may replace the transition part of the relative inductivity check (cf. implication (1) in Definition 4) by the simpler test whether the frame and the WP share common states. Since the resulting formula only reasons about unprimed variables, we reduce the number of variables in the SMT query by half in best case, and also decrease the size of the formula in general. However, since the inductivity check happens before the WP construction, we never know whether we can actually reuse the constructed WP afterwards. To avoid unnecessary overhead we introduce an additional step: Given a failed inductivity query, IC3CFA constructs the WP and decomposes it into a set of cubes. However, not all cubes from the set of WP cubes may be of interest. In fact, the likelihood that some of the cubes are already excluded by the respective frame is very high. Here we can use the modified inductivity check to filter those cubes that are actually causing the failed inductivity. An experimental evaluation is given in Sect. 4.

Definition 7 (WP-based inductivity). *Let* (L, G, ℓ_0, ℓ_E) *be a CFA with edge* $e = (\ell, \mathcal{C}, \ell') \in G$ *and* $i \in \mathbb{N}, i \geq 1$. *Given the frame* $F_{(i-1,\ell)}$ *and a cube* c, *we define the predicate* $relIndWP_e(F_{(i-1,\ell)}, c)$ *by*

$$relIndWP_e(F_{(i-1,\ell)}, c) \Leftrightarrow unsat(F_{(i-1,\ell)} \land wp(\mathcal{C}, c)).$$

Cube c *is inductive relative to frame* $F_{(i-1,\ell)}$ *and edge* e *iff* $relIndWP_e(F_{(i-1,\ell)}, c)$ *holds. In the following we will also refer to* $relIndWP$ *as* $relInd$.

The correctness of WP-based relative inductivity is given by:

Theorem 3. *Let* (L, G, ℓ_0, ℓ_E) *be a CFA with edge* $e = (\ell, \mathcal{C}, \ell') \in G$ *and* $i \in \mathbb{N}, i \geq 1$. *For every frame* $F_{(i-1,\ell)}$ *and cube* c:

$$relIndWP_e(F_{(i-1,\ell)}, c) \quad \Leftrightarrow \quad relInd_e(F_{(i-1,\ell)}, c).$$

Proof.

$$relIndWP_e(F_{(i-1,\ell)}, c)$$
$$\Leftrightarrow \quad unsat(F_{(i-1,\ell)} \wedge wp(\mathcal{C}, c)) \qquad \text{(Definition 7)}$$
$$\Leftrightarrow \quad unsat(F_{(i-1,\ell)} \wedge T_e \wedge c') \qquad \text{(WP)}$$
$$\Leftrightarrow \quad relInd_e(F_{(i-1,\ell)}, c) \qquad \text{(Definition 4)}$$

3.4 Caching of Generalization Context

For IC3 software model checking algorithms that determine predecessor cubes using weakest preconditions, cubes and thus generalizations often reappear, but so far they are always recomputed. This approach of recomputing generalizations again and again is obviously not very efficient, as has been shown in other areas, such as SMT calls [18]. While we also use caching of SMT calls, we aim to store the information that is obtained during a generalization of a cube in order to reuse this information in subsequent generalizations. In contrast to caching only SMT calls, this enables us to reuse not only exact generalization attempts, but also slightly different ones. To do so, not only do we need to store the generalization g, we also have to store all other aspects of the used inductivity query: the cube c that the generalization was derived from as well as the frame F and the edge e relative to which it was determined. We call this set of information the *context* of the generalization or simply *generalization context*.

Definition 8 (Generalization context). *The generalization context* GC_i *of a CFA* (L, G, ℓ_0, ℓ_E) *at index* i *is a set of quadruples*

$$GC_i \subseteq Cube \times G \times Frame \times Cube$$

where

$$(c, e, F, g) \in GC_i \text{ with } e = (\ell, \mathcal{C}, \ell')$$
$$\implies \left(\exists j \leq i. \; gen(F_{(j,\ell')}, c, e) = g \text{ and } F = F_{(j-1,\ell)} \right).$$

Following Definition 8, each generalization g of a cube c at index j and edge e relative to frame F is stored as one generalization context (c, e, F, g) available in all sets GC_i ($i \geq j$). In our implementation we use a least-recently-used cache for this purpose such that generalizations that are older and less likely to reappear are replaced.

3.5 Upper Bounds from Generalization Context

Given a cube c to be generalized along edge $e \in G$, our aim is to derive a generalization based on previous generalizations of c along e (if any) relative to frame F. Due to the monotonically growing behaviour of frames in IC3, a generalization of a fixed cube c along fixed edge e with only a shrinked frame $F \sqsubseteq F'$ will yield a result that contains *at most* the literals of the previous attempt. In other words, by excluding states from a frame, the set of states unreachable from that frame can only grow but never shrink. Therefore the old generalization gives an *upper bound* on the literals of the new generalization.

Theorem 4. *Let (L, G, ℓ_0, ℓ_E) be a CFA with edge $e = (\ell, \mathcal{C}, \ell') \in G$ and c a cube to be generalized at index $i \geq 1$ and location ℓ'. Given the frame $F_{(i-1,\ell)}$, it holds that*

$$\big((c, e, F, g) \in GC_i \wedge F_{(i-1,\ell)} \sqsubseteq F\big) \implies g = gen(F_{(i,\ell')}, c, e).$$

Proof.

$$
\begin{aligned}
& (c, e, F, g) \in GC_i \wedge F_{(i-1,\ell)} \sqsubseteq F \\
\Rightarrow\ & \exists j \leq i.\ gen(F_{(j,\ell')}, c, e) = g \\
& \wedge F = F_{(j-1,\ell)} \wedge F_{(i-1,\ell)} \sqsubseteq F & \text{(Definition 8)} \\
\Leftrightarrow\ & relInd_e(F_{(j-1,\ell)}, g) \wedge F = F_{(j-1,\ell)} \wedge F_{(i-1,\ell)} \sqsubseteq F & \text{(Definition 5)} \\
\Rightarrow\ & relInd_e(F_{(i-1,\ell)}, g) \\
\Rightarrow\ & gen(F_{(i,\ell')}, c, e) = g & \text{(Definition 5)}
\end{aligned}
$$

So far, we might reuse a generalization g based on the generalization context (c, e, F, g) if we encounter the exact same cube c along e again, but relative to a shrinked frame $F' \sqsubseteq F$. We extend the use of generalization contexts to cover those cases when we encounter a similar cube $\hat{c}$. More precisely, $\hat{c}$ has to be a superset of the previous generalization g with respect to the literals, i.e. $g \subseteq \hat{c}$. If this is the case and the frame condition $F_{(i-1,\ell)} \sqsubseteq F$ also holds, then we also get g as generalization of $\hat{c}$. As a result, we avoid even more computations. Corollary 1 shows the effect of the improved upper bounds.

Corollary 1. *Let (L, G, ℓ_0, ℓ_E) be a CFA with edge $e = (\ell, \mathcal{C}, \ell') \in G$, and $\hat{c}$ a cube to be·generalized at index i and location ℓ'. Given the frame $F_{(i-1,\ell)}$, it holds that*

$$
\begin{aligned}
& \big((c, e, F, g) \in GC_i\big) \wedge \big(F_{(i-1,\ell)} \sqsubseteq F\big) \wedge (g \subseteq \hat{c}) \\
\implies\ & gen(F_{(i,\ell')}, \hat{c}, e) = g.
\end{aligned}
$$

While this caching of generalizations may seem counter-intuitive for SAT-based IC3, it drastically improves the performance of certain types of IC3 for software verification: Due to the pseudo-random choice of predecessor cubes based on the SAT model, lazily resetting the SAT solver and re-generalizing cubes prevents IC3 from investigating bad paths too deeply [10]. However, if we swap the model-based predecessor extraction for WP-based predecessors, the computed cubes will be deterministic in every iteration, making resets and re-generalizations less useful while caching becomes more effective.

3.6   Lower Bounds from Generalization Context

Generalization contexts are used to derive a generalization based on previous computations. More precisely, if there exists a matching generalization context gc, then it will yield all literals that will *at most* be contained in the new generalization, i.e. an upper bound on the literals of the generalization. In this section we use generalization contexts to determine all literals that will *at least* be contained in the generalization, i.e. lower bounds on the literals.

Let (c, e, F, g) be a generalization context. For this previous generalization, c has been generalized to the cube $g \subseteq c$, thus it follows that all proper subsets $\widehat{g} \subset g$ are not inductive relative to F. If we later encounter c with a larger frame F', i.e. $F \sqsubseteq F'$, every cube larger than g will not be inductive relative to F'. However, there might be a state f that is part of F', but not part of F, i.e. $f \models F' \land \neg F$, such that f enables a transition to a g-state. Thus, the resulting generalization $\bar{g}$ will be somewhere between g and c, i.e. $g \subseteq \bar{g} \subseteq c$, making g a lower bound[1] of the literals of the new generalization. Theorem 5 shows the correctness of necessary literals based on the generalization context.

Theorem 5. *Let* (L, G, ℓ_0, ℓ_E) *be a CFA with* $e = (\ell, C, \ell') \in G$, *and* c *a cube to be generalized at* ℓ'. *It holds for* $i \geq 1$:

$$((c, e, F, g) \in GC_i) \land (F \sqsubseteq F_{(i-1,\ell)}) \land (\widehat{g} \subset g)$$
$$\implies gen(F_{(i,\ell')}, c, e) \neq \widehat{g}$$
$$\implies g \subseteq gen(F_{(i,\ell')}, c, e) \subseteq c.$$

Proof.

$$(c, e, F, g) \in GC_i \land F_{(i-1,\ell)} \sqsubseteq F \land \widehat{g} \subset g$$
$$\Rightarrow \exists j \leq i.\ gen(F_{(j,\ell')}, c, e) = g$$
$$\qquad \land F = F_{(j-1,\ell)} \land F_{(i-1,\ell)} \sqsubseteq F \land \widehat{g} \subset g \qquad \text{(Definition 8)}$$
$$\Rightarrow \exists j \leq i.\ gen(F_{(j,\ell')}, c, e) \neq \widehat{g}$$
$$\qquad \land F = F_{(j-1,\ell)}) \land F_{(i-1,\ell)} \sqsubseteq F$$
$$\Leftrightarrow \neg relInd_e(F_{(j-1,\ell)}, \widehat{g}) \qquad \text{(Definition 5)}$$
$$\Rightarrow \neg relInd_e(F_{(i-1,\ell)}, \widehat{g})$$
$$\Rightarrow gen(F_{(i,\ell')}, c, e) \neq \widehat{g} \qquad \text{(Definition 5)}$$

---

[1] Note that g is a lower bound but not necessarily the greatest one, as states in $F' \land \neg F$ may have a transition into g.

Using the generalization context we have shown that we can store old generalization results and their corresponding context *to give both an upper and a lower bound for the new generalization*. This means that for a cube c to be generalized, cube g with $g \subseteq c$ as upper bound and cube g' with $g' \subseteq g \subseteq c$ as lower bound, we effectively only have to check whether we can drop the literals of $g \backslash g'$ from c.

4   Evaluation

We implemented our optimizations to IC3CFA on top of an existing proprietary model checker with bit-precise analysis. The input C file is processed by the CIL Parser [16] and translated into an intermediate language. We apply static minimizations, construct the CFA, apply Large-Block Encoding [1] and execute IC3CFA. All results are obtained using Z3 4.6.1.

To evaluate the performance of our proposed improvements, we use a benchmark set consisting of 99 benchmarks from [5] and 254 SV-COMP 2017 benchmarks [17] from the *ReachSafety* category with the subcategories: *ReachSafety-BitVectors*, *ReachSafety-ControlFlow* and *ReachSafety-Loops*. Note that in some subsets of these categories, all files contain constructs, e.g. function pointers, that our parser and bit-precise memory model do not support. We therefore excluded the subsets *ntdrivers* and *ssh* and evaluated our contributions on the remaining 353 instances. All our results are obtained on an Intel Xeon CPU E5-2670 v3 @ 2.30 GHz with a timeout of 1800 s and a memory limit of 3 GB, using one core per instance, executed in Benchexec 1.16.

We evaluate the improvements of each optimization using scatter plots with logarithmic axes (see Fig. 1), where every mark below/right of the diagonal indicates that the given optimization pays off, with points on the dashed line indicating a variation of one order of magnitude. To evaluate the isolated effect of each modification, we ran a *Baseline* configuration with every optimization disabled and separate configurations *Pre-Cubes*[2] and *WP Inductivity* where we enable just the specific modification. Due to the close relation between our proposed methods for using generalization contexts as upper and lower bounds, we evaluate these in a stepwise fashion: *Baseline* disables lower and upper bounds from generalization contexts; *Upper Bounds* enables upper bounds, while lower bounds are disabled; *All Bounds* enables upper and lower bounds, thus evaluating the isolated effect of lower bounds when compared to *Upper Bounds* and evaluating the overall effect of generalization contexts when compared to *Baseline*. To further compare the overall effect of all contributions the *All* configuration has all proposed optimizations enabled. To evaluate the performance of our new IC3CFA implementation with generalization and the presented modifications against the version presented in [14], we add the *No Generalization* configuration.

---

[2] Note that, as mentioned in Sect. 3.1, we apply *split* only in combination with the search for predecessor cubes and thus also evaluate their effect together.

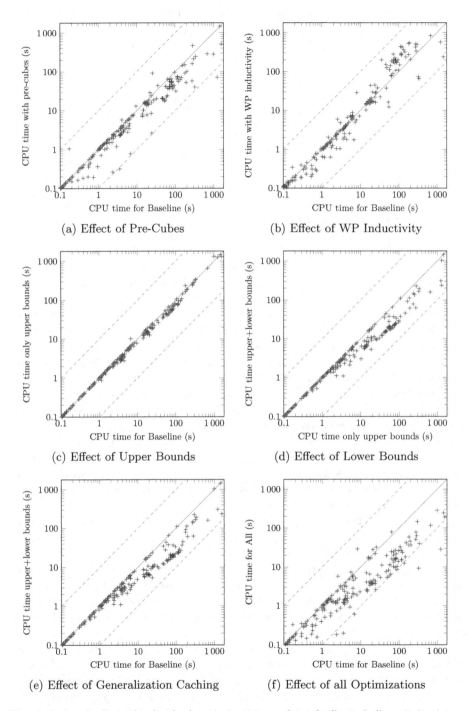

(a) Effect of Pre-Cubes

(b) Effect of WP Inductivity

(c) Effect of Upper Bounds

(d) Effect of Lower Bounds

(e) Effect of Generalization Caching

(f) Effect of all Optimizations

Fig. 1. Isolated effect of individual optimizations and total effect of all optimizations

Configuration	# Solved	Time(s)
Baseline	234	12340
Pre-Cubes	238	9992
WP Inductivity	236	11925
Upper Bounds	234	11571
Upper+Lower Bounds	242	11913
All	**244**	11160
No Generalization	161	6075

Fig. 2. Summary of all configurations

Considering the configuration *Pre-Cubes*, the scatter plot (Fig. 1a) shows a strong positive impact of enabling the extraction of a generalization based on subcubes in the predecessor frame. While a very small number of instances exhibit negative performance with enabled *Pre-Cubes*, multiple benchmarks are found near the dashed line, indicating a verification time that is one order of magnitude faster with *Pre-Cubes* enabled, with the most notable case resulting in a verification time of 1200 s without and 72 s with *Pre-Cubes*. We conclude that the proposed method is highly favorable and improves the verification time of IC3CFA dramatically. Figure 2 shows that IC3CFA with *Pre-Cubes* is able to solve four more instances than without.

The proposed WP inductivity (Fig. 1b) yields a more ambivalent result. We achieve a speedup for almost all small instances with runtime up to 10 s. For instances between 10 and 100 s runtime, we see an indeterminate situation with results equally spread to both sides. For larger/harder benchmarks, enabling *WP-Inductivity* clearly yields a worse runtime than *Baseline*. Interestingly, Fig. 2 reveals that *WP-Inductivity* can solve two more instances than *Baseline*.

As mentioned, our proposed caching of generalization contexts enables multiple optimizations, allowing us to identify literals that can be dropped, as well as literals that cannot be dropped. Due to the strong connection, we evaluate the performance in a three-fold way:

We start with the effect of upper bounds (Fig. 1c), i.e. we store generalization contexts, but only use them to identify literals that can be removed, and compare the results to *Baseline*. Except for three outliers, *Upper Bounds* shows a small improvement in performance for all benchmarks. As shown in Fig. 2, the number of solved instances is identical to *Baseline* and the total verification time improves slightly. We conclude that the overhead of managing and searching the cache entries almost outweighs the saved solver calls if we use generalization contexts for upper bounds only.

Next, we evaluate the effect of lower bounds (Fig. 1d) by comparing the results of the *Upper Bounds* configuration with one where upper and lower bounds are activated, i.e. we use cached generalization contexts to identify which literals can be dropped and which cannot. In contrast to upper bounds, *also* enabling lower bounds enables a massive performance improvement with all instances being solved faster than without lower bounds.

Finally, we evaluate the performance of generalization caching, i.e. the total effect of upper and lower bounds against *Baseline* (Fig. 1e). We can see that no instance is being solved slower with generalization caching than without and some instances can be solved almost one order of magnitude faster. In particular the few instances that perform worse with just upper bounds are being compensated by the massive improvement that lower bounds yield.

To evaluate the overall effect of all contributions, we compare a configuration with all improvements activated (*All*) against *Baseline*. Figure 1f shows the large potential that our improvements to the generalization procedure of IC3CFA yield. The few instances with negligible deterioration are all simpler instances that are executed in less than 100 s. On the other hand, the majority of instances benefit heavily from our generalization with multiple instances performing about one order of magnitude better. For the most noticeable instance, the runtime is reduced from 1200 s to only 28 s, a gain of almost two orders of magnitude. Enabling all optimizations, we are able to solve 10 more out of all 353 benchmark instances.

5   Conclusion

In this paper we presented a number of simple and easy to implement improvements of the generalization procedure in IC3CFA software model checking. As evaluated in Sect. 4, these straight-forward improvements offer performance improvements of up to two orders of magnitude and enable 10 more benchmarks to be solved. In addition, we are able to solve 35% more benchmarks than the original IC3CFA algorithm [14]. According to our experiments, the amendments of predecessor cubes and generalization contexts turned out to be the most beneficial. Predecessor cubes that extract a generalization based on an occurrence of a sub-cube in the previous frame are tailored towards software IC3 with weakest preconditions and can also be applied to other IC3 software model checkers that use weakest preconditions, like Tree-IC3. Our small and elegant amendment of generalization contexts is simple in the sense that it caches generalizations and the context in which they appeared to give upper as well as lower bounds for the current generalization and therefore drastically reduce the number of literals that are tested for dropping. It is also general in the sense that it can be applied to any IC3 algorithm as it operates on the elementary data structures *cube* and *frame*, which are identical in IC3CFA thanks to our DNF-based decomposition, and IC3 algorithms for word- and bit-level verification [2,3,6,8,11] that operate on cubes and clauses.

References

1. Beyer, D., Cimatti, A., Griggio, A., Keremoglu, M.E., Sebastiani, R.: Software model checking via large-block encoding. In: FMCAD, pp. 25–32. IEEE (2009)
2. Birgmeier, J., Bradley, A.R., Weissenbacher, G.: Counterexample to induction-guided abstraction-refinement (CTIGAR). In: Biere, A., Bloem, R. (eds.) CAV 2014. LNCS, vol. 8559, pp. 831–848. Springer, Cham (2014). https://doi.org/10.1007/978-3-319-08867-9_55
3. Bradley, A.R.: SAT-based model checking without unrolling. In: Jhala, R., Schmidt, D. (eds.) VMCAI 2011. LNCS, vol. 6538, pp. 70–87. Springer, Heidelberg (2011). https://doi.org/10.1007/978-3-642-18275-4_7
4. Bradley, A.R., Manna, Z.: Checking safety by inductive generalization of counterexamples to induction. In: FMCAD, pp. 173–180. IEEE (2007)
5. Cimatti, A., Griggio, A.: Software model checking via IC3. In: Madhusudan, P., Seshia, S.A. (eds.) CAV 2012. LNCS, vol. 7358, pp. 277–293. Springer, Heidelberg (2012). https://doi.org/10.1007/978-3-642-31424-7_23
6. Cimatti, A., Griggio, A., Mover, S., Tonetta, S.: Infinite-state invariant checking with IC3 and predicate abstraction. Form. Methods Syst. Des. **49**(3), 190–218 (2016)
7. Dijkstra, E.W.: A Discipline of Programming. Prentice-Hall, Englewood Cliffs (1976)
8. Eén, N., Mishchenko, A., Brayton, R.K.: Efficient implementation of property directed reachability. In: FMCAD, pp. 125–134. FMCAD Inc. (2011)
9. Flanagan, C., Saxe, J.B.: Avoiding exponential explosion: generating compact verification conditions. In: POPL, pp. 193–205. ACM (2001)
10. Griggio, A., Roveri, M.: Comparing different variants of the IC3 algorithm for hardware model checking. IEEE Trans. CAD Integr. Circuits Syst. **35**(6), 1026–1039 (2016)
11. Gurfinkel, A., Ivrii, A.: Pushing to the top. In: FMCAD, pp. 65–72. IEEE (2015)
12. Hassan, Z., Bradley, A.R., Somenzi, F.: Better generalization in IC3. In: FMCAD, pp. 157–164. IEEE (2013)
13. Hoder, K., Bjørner, N.: Generalized property directed reachability. In: Cimatti, A., Sebastiani, R. (eds.) SAT 2012. LNCS, vol. 7317, pp. 157–171. Springer, Heidelberg (2012). https://doi.org/10.1007/978-3-642-31612-8_13
14. Lange, T., Neuhäußer, M.R., Noll, T.: IC3 software model checking on control flow automata. In: FMCAD, pp. 97–104. IEEE (2015)
15. Leino, K.R.M.: Efficient weakest preconditions. Inf. Process. Lett. **93**(6), 281–288 (2005)
16. Necula, G.C., McPeak, S., Rahul, S.P., Weimer, W.: CIL: intermediate language and tools for analysis and transformation of C programs. In: Horspool, R.N. (ed.) CC 2002. LNCS, vol. 2304, pp. 213–228. Springer, Heidelberg (2002). https://doi.org/10.1007/3-540-45937-5_16
17. Competition on software verification (SV-COMP). https://sv-comp.sosy-lab.org/2017/. Accessed 23 Jan 2017
18. Visser, W., Geldenhuys, J., Dwyer, M.B.: Green: reducing, reusing and recycling constraints in program analysis. In: SIGSOFT FSE, p. 58. ACM (2012)
19. Welp, T., Kuehlmann, A.: QF BV model checking with property directed reachability. In: DATE, pp. 791–796. EDA Consortium (2013)

Star-Topology Decoupling in SPIN

Daniel Gnad[1(✉)], Patrick Dubbert[1], Alberto Lluch Lafuente[2],
and Jörg Hoffmann[1]

[1] Saarland Informatics Campus, Saarland University, Saarbrücken, Germany
{gnad,hoffmann}@cs.uni-saarland.de, patrick@dexpot.de
[2] Technical University of Denmark, Kongens Lyngby, Denmark
albl@dtu.dk

Abstract. Star-topology decoupling is a state space search method
recently introduced in AI Planning. It decomposes the input model into
components whose interaction structure has a star shape. The decoupled
search algorithm enumerates transition paths only for the center component, maintaining the leaf-component state space separately for each leaf.
This is a form of partial-order reduction, avoiding interleavings across
leaf components. It can, and often does, have exponential advantages
over stubborn set pruning and unfolding. AI Planning relates closely to
model checking of safety properties, so the question arises whether decoupled search can be successful in model checking as well. We introduce
a first implementation of star-topology decoupling in SPIN, where the
center maintains global variables while the leaves maintain local ones.
Preliminary results on several case studies attest to the potential of the
approach.

1 Introduction

AI Planning develops algorithms that, given an initial state s_0 (an assignment to
a vector of state variables), a goal formula G, and a set A of actions (transition
rules), find an action sequence that transforms s_0 into a state s s.t. $s \models G$. In
other words, AI Planning addresses reachability checking in compactly described
transition systems. This relates closely to model checking of safety properties,
a well-known connection (e.g. [3,6,27–29]) that has been exploited to transfer
techniques. In the context of the SPIN model checker [24], AI Planning heuristic search methods have been adapted to SPIN [9,10], and compilations from
Promela to AI Planning languages have been designed [8].

Here we adapt a new method from AI Planning, *star-topology decoupling*
[14,15], to model checking. Contrary to other methods developed in AI, which
typically aim at finding solution paths quickly, the major strength of star-
topology decoupling lies in proving unreachability: in a model checking setting,
verifying correctness of safety properties. We provide a first implementation in
SPIN, and initial empirical results.

Star-topology decoupling decomposes the input problem into components
identified by a partition of state variables. Two components *interact* if there is

© Springer International Publishing AG, part of Springer Nature 2018
M. M. Gallardo and P. Merino (Eds.): SPIN 2018, LNCS 10869, pp. 103–114, 2018.
https://doi.org/10.1007/978-3-319-94111-0_6

an action reading or updating state variables from both of them. Star-topology decoupling chooses components whose interactions take a star shape, where there is a *center* component to which all interactions are incident. All other components are then referred to as *leaves*. Given such a topology, the leaves depend only indirectly on each other, via the center. The *decoupled search* algorithm exploits this through a two-level search, where only the center is considered at the primary level, while each leaf is considered separately at the secondary level. Multiplication of states across leaf components is avoided.

Star-topology decoupling relates to partial-order reduction (e.g. [12,19,32, 34,37]), in that it avoids interleavings of leaf paths. It can be viewed as a variant of unfolding, exploiting star shapes by organizing the unfolding in terms of transition paths over the center, which ensures by design that there are no cross-leaf conflicts. Star-topology decoupling can have exponential advantages over other partial-order reduction methods. Consider the following excerpt of Gnad and Hoffmann's [15] results (Fig. 1):

Benchmark	#	Exp	SSS	Unf	STD	Exp	SSS	Unf	STD
Elevators	100	21	17	3	**41**	1,941.8	1,941.5	543.3	**36.3**
Logistics	63	12	12	11	**27**	1,121.2	1,121.2	118.4	**12.1**
Miconic	150	50	45	30	**145**	154.6	152.3	143.1	**.7**
NoMystery	40	11	11	7	**40**	266.2	248.8	101.3	**3.9**
TPP	30	5	5	4	**11**	192.5	192.5	12.4	**.2**
Woodworking	100	11	20	**22**	16	109,174.4	199.9	**1.2**	4,274.2
$\sum$ (over all)	1144	202	196	123	**435**				

Fig. 1. Left: #state spaces successfully exhausted in 30 min/4 GB memory. Right: State-space representation size (#integer variables, in thousands, used in the final representation). Exp: explicit-state search without enhancements. SSS: strong stubborn sets (as per [39]). Unf: unfolding (using Cunf [34] given the presence of read arcs). STD: star-topology decoupling.

Here we observe that, in automata networks such as described in Promela, decoupled search can be applied by viewing "local" transitions, affecting only a single process P, as being part of a leaf component P; while viewing non-local transitions, affecting more than one process, as being part of the center component. In the simplest case, where processes communicate only via global variables, this takes the global variables as the center and takes the local variables of each process as a leaf. But also more general forms of communication, via channels, can be viewed in this way. The decoupled search then explores non-local transitions at the primary level, and local transitions at the secondary level. We supply initial empirical evidence suggesting that this form of decomposition can be useful in the verification of safety properties.

2   Star-Topology Decoupling

We first describe star-topology decoupling in the context of AI Planning where it was invented. We give a brief outline and refer to Gnad and Hoffmann [15] for details. In Sect. 2.2, we prove correctness of star-topology decoupling for reachability checking. Finally, we show complementarity to previous state-space reduction methods.

2.1   Decoupling in AI Planning

An AI Planning *task* is a tuple (V, A, s_0, G). V is a finite set of *state variables* v, each with a finite domain D_v. A *state* s is an assignment to V and s_0 is the *initial state*. The goal G is a partial assignment to V, interpreted as a conjunctive formula where $s \models (v, d)$ iff $s(v) = d$. A is a set of *actions*, each action a associated with two partial assignments to V namely the *precondition pre[a]* and *effect eff[a]*. An action is *applicable* to s if $s \models pre[a]$. If so, the outcome state of applying a in s, denoted $s[\![a]\!]$, is defined by $s[\![a]\!](v) = eff[a](v)$ where $eff[a]$ is defined, and $s[\![a]\!](v) = s(v)$ where not. The applicability and outcome $s[\![\pi]\!]$ of an action sequence π is defined accordingly. The planning problem is to decide whether there exists π such that $s_0[\![\pi]\!] \models G$.

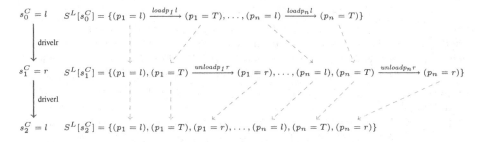

Fig. 2. The decoupled state space of our transportation example, one decoupled state per row. Center states and transitions are highlighted in blue. Transitions $a \xrightarrow{l} b$ within a leaf state set are used to illustrate that a new leaf state b becomes reachable via leaf action l. Dashed lines indicate leaf states that remain reachable in the successor decoupled state (i.e., are compatible with a^C).

As an example, simple yet enough to show exponential separations from previous methods, say that $V = \{t, p_1, \ldots, p_n\}$ where t encodes the position of a truck on a map with two locations l, r; and each p_i encodes the position of a package. We have $D_t = \{l, r\}$ and $D_{p_i} = \{l, r, T\}$ where T stands for being in the truck. In s_0, all variables have value l. The goal is to bring all packages to r, i.e., $G = \{(p_1, r), \ldots, (p_n, r)\}$. The actions drive, e.g. *drivelr* with precondition $\{(t, l)\}$ and effect $\{(t, r)\}$; or load a package, e.g. *loadp$_1$l* with precondition

$\{(t,l),(p_1,l)\}$ and effect $\{(p_1,T)\}$; or unload a package, e.g. $unload\,p_1\,r$ with precondition $\{(t,r),(p_1,T)\}$ and effect $\{(p_1,r)\}$. The decoupled state space of the example, which we define next, is illustrated in Fig. 2.

Let $P = \{P_1, P_2, \dots\}$ be a partitioning of V, i.e. $\biguplus_{P_i \in P} P_i = V$. Consider the undirected graph with vertices P and an arc (P_1, P_2) for $P_1 \neq P_2$ if there exists $a \in A$ s.t. the set V_a of variables touched by a (defined in either $pre[a]$ or $eff[a]$) intersects both P_1 and P_2. We say that P is a *star-topology decomposition* if there exists a unique $C \in P$ s.t. all arcs in the graph are incident to C. In that case, C is the *center* and all other $L \in P$ are *leaves*. In the example, $P = \{\{t\}, \{p_1\}, \dots, \{p_n\}\}$ is a star-topology decomposition with center $C = \{t\}$ and leaves $L_i = \{p_i\}$.

Refer to value assignments to C as *center states* s^C, and to value assignments to a leaf L as *leaf states* s^L. These are the atomic composites of the search graph built by decoupled search. The search starts with the center state $s_0^C := s_0|_C$. It then augments s_0^C with a full exploration of leaf states reachable given s_0^C: it iteratively applies all *leaf actions* a^L, affecting only some L, where $s_0^C \models pre[a^L]|_C$. Denote the set of all s^L reached this way by $S^L[s_0^C]$. Then s_0^C together with $S^L[s_0^C]$ forms a *decoupled state*. In the example, $s_0^C = \{(t,l)\}$ and $S^L[s_0^C] = \{(p_i, l), (p_i, T) \mid 1 \leq i \leq n\}$. Observe that, given the star-topology decomposition, the leaves do not interact with each other, so any combination of leaf states $s^{L_1}, \dots, s^{L_n} \in S^L[s_0^C]$ is jointly reachable. Intuitively, fixing the center, the leaves – which interact only via the center – become independent.

Given a decoupled state $(s^C, S^L[s^C])$, the successor center states r^C are those reached from s^C by some *center action* a^C, affecting C, that is applicable: $s^C \models pre[a^C]|_C$, and for every leaf L there exists $s^L \in S^L[s^C]$ s.t. $s^L \models pre[a^C]|_L$. Each such r^C reached by a^C is added to the search graph. Then r^C is augmented into a decoupled state by (1) selecting from $S^L[s^C]$ the subset $S^L[s^C, a^C]$ of leaf states compatible with a^C, and (2) setting $S^L[r^C]$ to be all leaf states reachable from r^C and $S^L[s^C, a^C]$.

The goal G is reached if, for some decoupled state $(s^C, S^L[s^C])$ in the search graph, $s^C \models G|_C$ and for every leaf L there exists $s^L \in S^L[s^C]$ s.t. $s^L \models G|_L$.

In the example, the only successor center state of $(s_0^C, S^L[s_0^C])$ is $s_1^C = \{(t,r)\}$ reached by the center action $a^C = drive\,l\,r$. We get $S^L[s_1^C] = \{(p_i, l), (p_i, T), (p_i, r) \mid 1 \leq i \leq n\}$, because (1) all $s^L \in S^L[s_0^C]$ are compatible with $drive\,l\,r$, and (2) given s_1^C we can unload each package at r. Thus the goal is reached in the decoupled state $(s_1^C, S^L[s_1^C])$. The complete *decoupled state space* $\mathcal{S}^{\mathcal{F}}$ of the task contains a third decoupled state $(s_2^C, S^L[s_2^C])$ that results from applying $drive\,r\,l$ in $(s_1^C, S^L[s_1^C])$.

2.2 Correctness of Decoupling for Reachability Analysis

Given the star-topology decomposition, any decoupled state $(s^C, S^L[s^C])$ represents exactly the states s reachable in the original task using the same center-action sequence π^C that led to $(s^C, S^L[s^C])$. Those s are exactly the ones where $s|_C = s^C$ and, for every leaf L, $s|_L \in S^L[s^C]$. In particular, the goal is reachable in decoupled search iff it is reachable in the original task. When the goal is reached in $(s^C, S^L[s^C])$, a solution can be extracted by backchaining from the leaf states $G|_L \in S^L[s^C]$. Duplicate decoupled states can be pruned, so exploring the set of reachable decoupled states in any order leads to a finite decoupled search space $\mathcal{S}^{\mathcal{F}}$. In consequence, star-topology decoupling guarantees correctness for reachability checking. The claim of Theorem 1 follows directly from previous results of Gnad and Hoffmann [15].

Theorem 1. *Star-topology decoupling captures reachability exactly, i.e., a state s is reachable in a task iff there exists a decoupled state in $\mathcal{S}^{\mathcal{F}}$ in which s is represented. A path to s can be extracted in time linear in $|\mathcal{S}^{\mathcal{F}}|$. Checking if a conjunctive property c is reachable in $\mathcal{S}^{\mathcal{F}}$ is linear in the number of decoupled states.*

Proof (sketch). Every decoupled state $(s^C, S^L[s^C])$ captures exactly those states that are reachable via the center-action subsequence π^C that led to $(s^C, S^L[s^C])$. Thus, all states reachable in the task are represented by a decoupled states in $\mathcal{S}^{\mathcal{F}}$. A path to an s in $(s^C, S^L[s^C])$ can efficiently be obtained by augmenting π^C with leaf action sequences for each leaf component by backchaining from the leaf states that compose s. Reachability of a conjunctive property c in a decoupled state is done by checking, for each partition P separately, if the projection of c onto P is reached. □

2.3   Complementarity from Other Methods

Several other methods relate to star-topology decoupling in that they can also lead to exponential reductions in search effort. Decoupling can still be exponentially more efficient, as our transportation example shows:

There are exactly three reachable decoupled states: the initial state $(s_0^C, S^L[s_0^C])$, its successor $(s_1^C, S^L[s_1^C])$ from *drivelr*, plus the only successor of $(s_1^C, S^L[s_1^C])$, reached via *driverl* (which differs from $(s_0^C, S^L[s_0^C])$ because (p_i, r) is reached for each p_i).

The separation into partial component states may be reminiscent of abstraction methods, which over-approximate the set of reachable states given one such component (e.g. [4,7,22,23]). Star-topology decoupling is very different, partitioning the variables to avoid enumerating combinations of independent leaf component assignments. Given this particular structure, star-topology decoupling captures reachability exactly.

The search space under strong stubborn set (SSS) pruning has size exponential in the number of packages. This is because an SSS on the initial state must include a *loadp$_i$l* action to make progress to the goal, must include *drivelr* as that interferes with *loadp$_i$l*, and must then include all other *loadp$_j$l* actions as these interfere with *drivelr*. So all subsets of packages that may be loaded at l are enumerated.

In unfolding, the non-consumed preconditions of load actions on the truck position induce read arcs. Both ways of encoding these (consuming and producing the truck position, or place replication) result in an unfolding enumerating all subsets of loaded packages. In contextual Petri nets that support read arcs natively [2], the same explosion arises in the enumeration of "event histories".

Symmetry breaking (e.g. [5,11,13,33,35]) is complementary to star-topology decoupling, simply because the leaf partitions do not need to be symmetric. In our example, where the leaves *are* symmetric, even perfect symmetry breaking keeps track of the number of packages at every location, enumerating all possible combinations.

3 Implementation in SPIN

We implemented star-topology decoupling in the most recent version of SPIN (6.4.7). We focus on reachability properties only (more general properties are a topic for future work). Our current implementation is preliminary in that it does not handle the full Promela language accepted by SPIN itself. We specify the handled fragment below. Let us first describe the star-topology decomposition and the modified search algorithms.

In Promela models, a star-topology decomposition arises directly from the formulation as interacting processes. Each process becomes a leaf component on its own; but anything that affects more than a single process is grouped into the center component. Concretely, each of the statements st in a process type $\_t$ corresponds to either a local transition, affecting only local variables or advancing the process location; or a global transition, namely a channel operation, a statement that affects a global variable, or a run command invoking a new process. Then the instantiations of $\_t$ can be made leaf processes if $\_t$ contains at least one local transition. All remaining processes, global variables, as well as channels, together form the center component. This partitioning ensures that every interaction across processes involves the center component. Center and leaf states are defined as assignments to the respective parts of the model, and center (resp. leaf) transitions are ones that affect the center (resp. only that leaf). The annotation of statements to become leaf or center transitions is done fully automatic.

Our implementation of decoupled search is minimally intrusive. We keep SPIN's current state *now* to store the center state s^C. Alongside *now*, we maintain a data structure storing the associated set $S^L[s^C]$ of reached leaf states. The decoupled search algorithm is then adopted as follows. The primary search only branches over center transitions, i.e., center processes and center transitions in leaf processes. We loop over $S^L[s^C]$ to determine the center transitions enabled by the reached leaf states. A center transition t^C applied to a decoupled state $(s^C, S^L[s^C])$ can have updates on leaf processes, so we need to compute the set $S^L[s^C, t^C]$ as before, and apply the leaf updates of t^C to the states in that set. Afterwards, $S^L[s^C, t^C]$ is augmented by all reachable leaf states to obtain the successor decoupled state $(r^C, S^L[r^C])$. We perform duplicate checking over decoupled states, testing the center states first to save runtime.

The remaining issue with our implementation is SPIN's parsing process. Due to the generation of model-specific code, the distinction between local (leaf) and global (center) transitions cannot be identified anymore within the verifier itself, but must be identified at Promela level. SPIN's parsing process must be extended to identify the leaf-vs-center information, and to communicate that to the verifier. Currently, our implementation supports this for *assignments*, *conditions*, basic control constructs (`do...od`, `if...fi`), all unary and binary *operators*, channel operations (*send/receive*, both synchronous and buffered), and `run` commands. We do not yet support `timeout`, `unless`, and channel *polling* statements (`empty/full/...`), nor the process constraints `priority` and `provided`, nor more complex constructs like `c-code` and `inline`. For `atomic` and `d_step` sequences, we handle basic compounds of statements, series of conditions, assignments, and channel operations, but not more complex control flows.

Regarding the relation to other search methods used in SPIN, partial-order reduction is orthogonal, and potentially exponentially worse, as we have already shown in the planning context. The same is true of *statement merging*, which can only reduce the number of states local to a process, merging statements that only touch local variables. It cannot merge statements that have conditions on global variables, and thus cannot tackle the exponential search space size in our transportation example. Similar arguments apply to reduction methods based on τ-*confluence* (e.g. [20,21]). Note also that leaf transitions, while local to a process, may be relevant to the property being checked (e.g. be part of a conjunctive reachability property as in planning).

4 Experiments

We performed experiments on several case studies, selected to suit the Promela fragment we can currently handle, and selected to showcase the potential of star-topology decoupling. We emphasize that the experiments are preliminary and we do not wish to make broad claims regarding their significance. Our implementation and all models used in the below are available at https://bitbucket.org/dagnad/decoupled-spin-public.

We run the scalable variant of Peterson's Mutex algorithm from Lynch [31], an elevator control model developed by Armin Biere and used as benchmark in several papers (e.g. [9,10]), the X.509 protocol from Jøsang [26], and a client-server communication protocol. The latter is a toy example we created for the purpose of this study, as a simple pattern to highlight the kind of structure relevant to star-topology decoupling. The model consists of a server process handling requests from a scalable number of client processes. Communication is via two channels. In star-topology decoupling all processes become leaf components, and the technique is beneficial if there is local content within each client. To show this, we experiment with two variants, EmptyC where the clients do nothing other than communicating with the server, and NonEmptyC where each client increments a local variable from 0 to 1. For illustrative purposes, we also include the transportation planning example described earlier. Modeling this in Promela is straightforward. We scale the number of packages from 1 to 50.

Model		SPIN -M -POR				SPIN				Star-topology decoupling (STD)			
		Time	Mem	#S	D	Time	Mem	#S	D	Time	Mem	#S	D
Peterson	3	0.04	0.13	33434	6924	**0**	0.13	2999	615	**0**	0.13	274	120
	4	19	1.14	8886434	1703147	0.53	0.21	533083	165342	**0.1**	**0.13**	6698	1615
	5	-	-	-	-	124	10.08	76620358	25309679	**4.16**	**0.27**	153548	27392
	6	-	-	-	-	-	-	-	-	157	4.79	3503908	473228
Elevator	3	0.23	0.14	99057	4609	0.12	**0.13**	78284	4950	**0.06**	**0.13**	7081	590
	4	3.15	0.19	685169	29487	1.49	0.17	498676	30239	**0.42**	**0.16**	37095	1643
	5	15.5	0.44	3620470	28638	5.02	0.33	2354211	27634	**2.38**	**0.26**	115077	1630
	6	95.7	1.86	18813600	30818	26.7	1.13	10868993	29712	**7.35**	**0.65**	359163	1728
	7	676	10.31	97574250	32998	153	5.56	49636481	31790	**25.5**	**2.08**	1119285	1826
	8	-	-	-	-	782	26.62	224704000	33868	**95.5**	**7.51**	3483243	1924
	9	-	-	-	-	-	-	-	-	360	27	10825893	2022
X.509		1.58	0.18	403311	91	**0**	**0.13**	3054	57	**0**	**0.13**	1090	35
Client-	6	0.72	0.15	141312	16235	**0.08**	**0.13**	32296	6830	0.15	0.14	13128	755
Server-	7	4.84	0.21	745472	63236	**0.42**	**0.15**	143741	27442	0.74	0.19	51037	1607
EmptyC	8	31.3	0.59	3801088	263835	**2.05**	**0.24**	507967	104759	3.3	0.42	192464	3297
	9	199	2.83	18874368	1062399	**8.53**	**0.44**	2206702	370926	14.6	1.36	708597	6274
	10	1160	12.38	91750400	4252067	**35**	**1.66**	8140911	1277049	63.2	5.34	2558800	13414
	11	-	-	-	-	**149**	**4.45**	29856762	4335070	256	21.11	9093557	28150
	12	-	-	-	-	**609**	**21.06**	109424300	14937082	-	-	-	-
Client-	5	2.69	0.18	450560	65354	0.05	0.13	23614	6209	**0.04**	**0.13**	3245	324
Server-	6	30.2	0.73	4816896	518833	0.33	0.15	132210	32645	**0.21**	**0.15**	13128	755
NonEmptyC	7	416	7.6	49545216	4256969	2.12	0.27	708019	172048	**1.04**	**0.21**	51037	1607
	8	-	-	-	-	14	0.74	3813278	882008	**4.86**	**0.53**	192464	3297
	9	-	-	-	-	83.8	3.79	19384754	4254923	**20.4**	**1.87**	708597	6274
	10	-	-	-	-	480	22.14	95568530	19967819	**87.1**	**7.57**	2558800	13414
	11	-	-	-	-	-	-	-	-	369	30.39	9093557	28150
Transport-	4	0.22	0.13	112735	329	**0**	0.13	31018	311	**0**	0.13	18	8
Planning	5	3.85	0.19	1240092	978	0.36	0.14	237249	892	**0**	**0.13**	21	9
	6	47.8	0.95	13641019	2923	3.14	0.24	1815310	2698	**0**	**0.13**	24	10
	7	728	12.8	150051220	8756	29	1.07	13954478	6404	**0**	**0.13**	27	11
	8	-	-	-	-	269	8.03	107967020	19740	**0**	**0.13**	30	12
	50	-	-	-	-	-	-	-	-	**0.01**	**0.13**	156	54

Fig. 3. Performance of SPIN with default options (SPIN), disabling statement merging (-M) and partial-order reduction (-POR), and with star-topology decoupling (STD). We show runtime (in seconds) and memory consumption (in GB), as well as the number of stored states (#S), and the maximum search depth (D) reported by SPIN. Best runtime/memory is highlighted in **bold face**.

We compare our decoupled-search SPIN (STD) to SPIN 6.4.7 with standard settings, providing no additional command line options (SPIN), and to a configuration disabling statement merging (-M) and partial-order reduction (-POR). All configurations exhaust the entire state space, using the verifier options -A -E. Restricting ourselves to safety properties, we removed any *never claims* from the models. We use runtime (memory) limits of 60 min (32 GB). Figure 3 shows the results, scaling each case study until all configurations run out of memory (indicated by a "-").

STD works very well in Peterson, significantly reducing memory consumption and runtime. To a lesser extent, STD also has advantages in Elevator and X.509. In Client-Server, as expected STD is beneficial only if there is local content in the clients. In the transportation case study adopted from planning, STD excels. This is not a relevant observation in model checking per se, but points to the power star-topology decoupling may in principle have over previous search methods in SPIN.

The number of decoupled states is consistently smaller than the number of states in SPIN (and, e.g., by 2 orders of magnitude in Peterson). Where the reduction is relatively small, it is outweighed by the runtime overhead of handling decoupled states. Regarding the search depth, keep in mind that the maximum depth of STD is that of the *center transitions* only. The depth bound can, thus, in general be kept significantly smaller for STD, leading to a reduced memory consumption for the search stack.

5 Conclusion

Star-topology decoupling is a novel approach to reduce state space size in checking reachability properties. Our implementation in SPIN is still preliminary, but exhibits encouraging performance on some case studies. As work in the planning domain has already shown, star-topology decoupling is orthogonal to, and may have exponential advantages over, partial-order reduction, symmetry breaking, symbolic representations, and heuristic search. It can also be fruitfully combined with all of these [15–18].

We believe that the technique's application to model checking is promising, and we hope that our preliminary study will have an impact in this direction. Foremost, more realistic case studies are required. Client-server architectures, and concurrent programs under weak memory constraints (e.g. [1,25,30,36]), carry promise insofar as such models might exhibit relevant local structure to be exploited in leaf components: client/process parts that may read the server/shared memory state, and that may have indirect effects thereupon, but that do not update it directly.

An important research challenge is the extension to liveness properties. This can be approached by encoding the property that is to be checked as a finite automaton that is added to the center component. We can then perform a lasso search in the decoupled state space. This should work similar as in explicit state search, yet potentially leads to more interaction between center and leaves, which has a negative influence on the performance of star-topology decoupling. Further research topics include the combination with other search techniques like (lossy) state compression, and application to other model checking frameworks.

Acknowledgments. Daniel Gnad was partially supported by the German Research Foundation (DFG), as part of project grant HO 2169/6-1, "Star-Topology Decoupled State Space Search".

References

1. Abd Alrahman, Y., Andric, M., Beggiato, A., Lafuente, A.L.: Can we efficiently check concurrent programs under relaxed memory models in maude? In: Escobar, S. (ed.) WRLA 2014. LNCS, vol. 8663, pp. 21–41. Springer, Cham (2014). https://doi.org/10.1007/978-3-319-12904-4_2
2. Baldan, P., Bruni, A., Corradini, A., König, B., Rodríguez, C., Schwoon, S.: Efficient unfolding of contextual Petri nets. Theoret. Comput. Sci. **449**, 2–22 (2012)

3. Cimatti, A., Pistore, M., Roveri, M., Traverso, P.: Weak, strong, and strong cyclic planning via symbolic model checking. Artif. Intell. **147**(1–2), 35–84 (2003)
4. Culberson, J.C., Schaeffer, J.: Pattern databases. Comput. Intell. **14**(3), 318–334 (1998)
5. Domshlak, C., Katz, M., Shleyfman, A.: Enhanced symmetry breaking in cost-optimal planning as forward search. In: Bonet, B., McCluskey, L., Silva, J.R., Williams, B. (eds.) Proceedings of the 22nd International Conference on Automated Planning and Scheduling (ICAPS 2012). AAAI Press (2012)
6. Dräger, K., Finkbeiner, B., Podelski, A.: Directed model checking with distance-preserving abstractions. In: Valmari [38], pp. 19–34
7. Edelkamp, S.: Planning with pattern databases. In: Cesta, A., Borrajo, D. (eds.) Proceedings of the 6th European Conference on Planning (ECP 2001), pp. 13–24. Springer (2001). https://www.aaai.org/ocs/index.php/ECP/ECP01/paper/view/7280
8. Edelkamp, S.: Promela planning. In: Ball, T., Rajamani, S.K. (eds.) SPIN 2003. LNCS, vol. 2648, pp. 197–213. Springer, Heidelberg (2003). https://doi.org/10.1007/3-540-44829-2_13
9. Edelkamp, S., Lafuente, A.L., Leue, S.: Directed explicit model checking with HSF-SPIN. In: Dwyer, M. (ed.) SPIN 2001. LNCS, vol. 2057, pp. 57–79. Springer, Heidelberg (2001). https://doi.org/10.1007/3-540-45139-0_5
10. Edelkamp, S., Lluch-Lafuente, A., Leue, S.: Directed explicit-state model checking in the validation of communication protocols. Int. J. Softw. Tools Technol. Transf. **5**(2–3), 247–267 (2004)
11. Emerson, E.A., Sistla, A.P.: Symmetry and model-checking. Formal Methods Syst. Des. **9**(1/2), 105–131 (1996)
12. Esparza, J., Römer, S., Vogler, W.: An improvement of Mcmillan's unfolding algorithm. Formal Methods Syst. Des. **20**(3), 285–310 (2002)
13. Fox, M., Long, D.: The detection and exploitation of symmetry in planning problems. In: Pollack, M. (ed.) Proceedings of the 16th International Joint Conference on Artificial Intelligence (IJCAI 1999), pp. 956–961. Morgan Kaufmann, Stockholm, Sweden, August 1999
14. Gnad, D., Hoffmann, J.: Beating LM-cut with h^{max} (sometimes): Fork-decoupled state space search. In: Brafman, R., Domshlak, C., Haslum, P., Zilberstein, S. (eds.) Proceedings of the 25th International Conference on Automated Planning and Scheduling (ICAPS 2015). pp. 88–96. AAAI Press (2015)
15. Gnad, D., Hoffmann, J.: Star-topology decoupled state space search. Artif. Intell. **257**, 24–60 (2018)
16. Gnad, D., Torralba, Á., Hoffmann, J.: Symbolic leaf representation in decoupled search. In: Fukunaga, A., Kishimoto, A. (eds.) Proceedings of the 10th Annual Symposium on Combinatorial Search (SOCS 2017). AAAI Press (2017)
17. Gnad, D., Torralba, Á., Shleyfman, A., Hoffmann, J.: Symmetry breaking in star-topology decoupled search. In: Proceedings of the 27th International Conference on Automated Planning and Scheduling (ICAPS 2017). AAAI Press (2017)
18. Gnad, D., Wehrle, M., Hoffmann, J.: Decoupled strong stubborn sets. In: Kambhampati, S. (ed.) Proceedings of the 25th International Joint Conference on Artificial Intelligence (IJCAI 2016), pp. 3110–3116. AAAI Press/IJCAI (2016)
19. Godefroid, P. (ed.): Partial-Order Methods for the Verification of Concurrent Systems: An Approach to the State-Explosion Problem. Lecture Notes in Computer Science, vol. 1032. Springer, Heidelberg (1996). https://doi.org/10.1007/3-540-60761-7

20. Groote, J.F., van de Pol, J.: State space reduction using partial τ-confluence. In: Nielsen, M., Rovan, B. (eds.) MFCS 2000. LNCS, vol. 1893, pp. 383–393. Springer, Heidelberg (2000). https://doi.org/10.1007/3-540-44612-5_34
21. Groote, J.F., Sellink, M.P.A.: Confluence for process verification. In: Lee, I., Smolka, S.A. (eds.) CONCUR 1995. LNCS, vol. 962, pp. 204–218. Springer, Heidelberg (1995). https://doi.org/10.1007/3-540-60218-6_15
22. Haslum, P., Botea, A., Helmert, M., Bonet, B., Koenig, S.: Domain-independent construction of pattern database heuristics for cost-optimal planning. In: Howe, A., Holte, R.C. (eds.) Proceedings of the 22nd National Conference of the American Association for Artificial Intelligence (AAAI 2007), pp. 1007–1012. AAAI Press, Vancouver, BC, Canada, July 2007
23. Helmert, M., Haslum, P., Hoffmann, J., Nissim, R.: Merge and shrink abstraction: a method for generating lower bounds in factored state spaces. J. Assoc. Comput. Mach. **61**(3) (2014)
24. Holzmann, G.: The Spin Model Checker - Primer and Reference Manual. Addison-Wesley, Reading (2004)
25. Jonsson, B.: State-space exploration for concurrent algorithms under weak memory orderings. SIGARCH Comput. Architect. News **36**(5), 65–71 (2008)
26. Jøsang, A.: Security protocol verification using spin. In: The First SPIN Workshop, Montreal, Quebec, Canada (1995)
27. Kupferschmid, S., Hoffmann, J., Dierks, H., Behrmann, G.: Adapting an AI planning heuristic for directed model checking. In: Valmari [38], pp. 35–52
28. Kupferschmid, S., Dräger, K., Hoffmann, J., Finkbeiner, B., Dierks, H., Podelski, A., Behrmann, G.: UPPAAL/DMC – abstraction-based heuristics for directed model checking. In: Grumberg, O., Huth, M. (eds.) TACAS 2007. LNCS, vol. 4424, pp. 679–682. Springer, Heidelberg (2007). https://doi.org/10.1007/978-3-540-71209-1_52
29. Kupferschmid, S., Hoffmann, J., Larsen, K.G.: Fast directed model checking via Russian doll abstraction. In: Ramakrishnan, C.R., Rehof, J. (eds.) TACAS 2008. LNCS, vol. 4963, pp. 203–217. Springer, Heidelberg (2008). https://doi.org/10.1007/978-3-540-78800-3_15
30. Linden, A., Wolper, P.: A verification-based approach to memory fence insertion in PSO memory systems. In: Piterman, N., Smolka, S.A. (eds.) TACAS 2013. LNCS, vol. 7795, pp. 339–353. Springer, Heidelberg (2013). https://doi.org/10.1007/978-3-642-36742-7_24
31. Lynch, N.A.: Distributed Algorithms. Morgan Kaufmann, San Francisco (1996)
32. McMillan, K.L.: Using unfoldings to avoid the state explosion problem in the verification of asynchronous circuits. In: von Bochmann, G., Probst, D.K. (eds.) CAV 1992. LNCS, vol. 663, pp. 164–177. Springer, Heidelberg (1993). https://doi.org/10.1007/3-540-56496-9_14
33. Rintanen, J.: Symmetry reduction for SAT representations of transition systems. In: Giunchiglia, E., Muscettola, N., Nau, D. (eds.) Proceedings of the 13th International Conference on Automated Planning and Scheduling (ICAPS 2003), pp. 32–41. Morgan Kaufmann, Trento, Italy (2003)
34. Rodríguez, C., Schwoon, S.: Cunf: a tool for unfolding and verifying petri nets with read arcs. In: Van Hung, D., Ogawa, M. (eds.) ATVA 2013. LNCS, vol. 8172, pp. 492–495. Springer, Cham (2013). https://doi.org/10.1007/978-3-319-02444-8_42
35. Starke, P.: Reachability analysis of petri nets using symmetries. J. Math. Model. Simul. Syst. Anal. **8**(4/5), 293–304 (1991)

36. Travkin, O., Mütze, A., Wehrheim, H.: SPIN as a linearizability checker under weak memory models. In: Bertacco, V., Legay, A. (eds.) HVC 2013. LNCS, vol. 8244, pp. 311–326. Springer, Cham (2013). https://doi.org/10.1007/978-3-319-03077-7_21
37. Valmari, A.: A stubborn attack on state explosion. Form. Methods Syst. Des. **1**(4), 297–322 (1992)
38. Valmari, A. (ed.): SPIN 2006. LNCS, vol. 3925, pp. 19–34. Springer, Heidelberg (2006). https://doi.org/10.1007/11691617_2
39. Wehrle, M., Helmert, M.: Efficient stubborn sets: generalized algorithms and selection strategies. In: Chien, S., Do, M., Fern, A., Ruml, W. (eds.) Proceedings of the 24th International Conference on Automated Planning and Scheduling (ICAPS 2014). AAAI Press (2014)

Joint Forces for Memory Safety Checking

Marek Chalupa[✉], Jan Strejček, and Martina Vitovská

Masaryk University, Brno, Czech Republic
{xchalup4,strejcek,xvitovs1}@fi.muni.cz

Abstract. The paper describes a successful approach to checking computer programs for standard memory handling errors like invalid pointer dereference or memory leaking. The approach is based on four well-known techniques, namely pointer analysis, instrumentation, static program slicing, and symbolic execution. We present a particular very efficient combination of these techniques, which has been implemented in the tool SYMBIOTIC and won by a large margin the *MemSafety* category of SV-COMP 2018. We explain the approach and provide a detailed analysis of effects of particular components.

1 Introduction

A popular application of formal methods in software development is to check whether a given program contains some common defects like assertion violations, deadlocks, race conditions, or memory handling errors. In this paper, we focus on the last mentioned group consisting of the following types of errors:

- invalid dereference (e.g. `null` pointer dereference, use-after-free)
- invalid deallocation (e.g. double free)
- memory leak

We present the approach to memory safety checking of sequential C programs implemented in SYMBIOTIC [7], the winner of the *MemSafety* category of SV-COMP 2018. The official competition graph in Fig. 1 shows that SYMBIOTIC (represented by the rightmost line) won by a considerable margin. One can also see that the tool is impressively fast: it would win even with its own time limit lowered to 1 s for each benchmark (the competition time limit was 900 s).

In general, our approach to memory safety checking combines static data-flow analysis with compile-time instrumentation. Static data-flow analyses for memory safety checking [11,14,35] proved to be fast and efficient. However, they typically work with under- or over-approximation and thus tend to produce false alarms or miss some errors. Instrumentation, usually used for runtime monitoring, extends the program with code that tracks the memory allocated by the program and that checks correctness of memory accesses and absence of memory leaks. If a check fails, the instrumented program reaches an error location.

The research is supported by The Czech Science Foundation, grant GA18-02177S.

M. M. Gallardo and P. Merino (Eds.): SPIN 2018, LNCS 10869, pp. 115–132, 2018.
https://doi.org/10.1007/978-3-319-94111-0_7

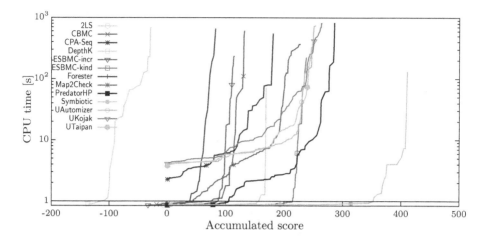

Fig. 1. The quantile plot taken from https://sv-comp.sosy-lab.org/2018/results/ representing the results of SV-COMP 2018 in the category *MemSafety*. For each tool, the plot shows what accumulated score would the tool achieve if the time limit for checking a single benchmark is set to a given time. The scoring schema assigns 1 point for every detected error provided that the tool generates an error witness which is confirmed by an independent witness checker, 1 point for the verification of a safe program (and 1 additional point if a correctness witness is generated and confirmed), and a high penalty (−16 or −32 points) for an incorrect answer. Further, the overall score is weighted by the size of subcategories. Precise description can be found at: https://sv-comp.sosy-lab.org/2018/rules.php

We combine both approaches along with static program slicing to get a reduced instrumented program that contains a reachable error location if and only if the original program contained a memory safety error. Reachability analysis is then performed to reveal possible errors in manipulation with the memory. This is the most expensive step of our approach.

The basic schema of our approach is depicted in Fig. 2. First, the program is instrumented. The instrumentation process has been augmented such that it reduces the amount of inserted code with the help of a data-flow analysis, namely an extended form of pointer analysis. We reduce the inserted code by the following three improvements:

(I1) We do not insert a check before a pointer dereference if the pointer analysis guarantees that the operation is safe. For example, when the pointer analysis says that a given pointer always refers to the beginning of a global variable and a dereference via this pointer does not use more bytes than the size of the global variable, we know that the dereference is safe and we do not insert any check before it.

(I2) If the pointer analysis cannot guarantee safety of a pointer dereference, but it says that the pointer refers into a memory block of a fixed known size, we insert a simpler check that the dereference is within the bounds of the block.

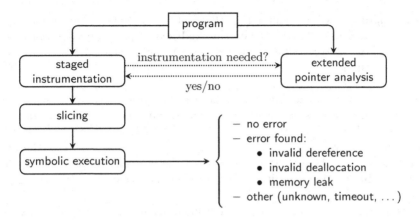

Fig. 2. The schema of our approach.

(I3) We track only information about memory blocks that can be potentially used by some of the inserted checks.

Note that interconnecting the instrumentation with a pointer analysis is not completely straightforward. Since typical pointer analyses do not care whether a memory block was freed or its lifetime has ended, a pointer analysis could mark some parts of programs as safe even when they are not (e.g. dereferencing a freed memory). For this reason, we needed to extend pointer analysis such that it takes into account information about freeing heap-allocated memory and the lifetime of local variables. Due to (I3), we perform the instrumentation in two stages. During the first stage we insert checks and remember which memory blocks are relevant for these checks. The second stage inserts the code tracking information about the relevant blocks.

After instrumentation, the program is statically sliced in order to remove the parts that are irrelevant for the reachability of inserted error locations. Finally, we use symbolic execution to perform the reachability analysis.

Our instrumentation extends the program with real working code, not just with calls to undefined functions that are to be interpreted inside a verifier tool. The advantage of instrumenting the whole machinery for checking memory safety into the analyzed program (instead of inserting calls to place-holder functions interpreted by a verifier or instead of monitoring the memory inside the tool) is that the program is extended in tool-independent manner and any tool (working with the same program representation) can be used to perform the reachability analysis. Moreover, the instrumented program can be even compiled and run (provided the original program was executable). The disadvantage is that the reachability analysis tools that have problems with precise handling of complicated heap-allocated data structures may struggle with handling the inserted functions since these typically use structures like search trees for tracking the state of memory blocks.

The approach is implemented in the tool SYMBIOTIC, which builds upon the LLVM framework [22,24]. Hence the analyzed C program is compiled into LLVM before the instrumentation starts. LLVM is an intermediate representation language on the level of instructions that is suitable for verification for its simplicity. Examples contained in this paper are also in LLVM, which is slightly simplified to improve readability. For the needs of presentation, we explain few of the LLVM instructions: `alloca` instruction allocates memory on the stack and returns its address, `load` reads a value from the address given as its operand, `store` writes a given value to the memory on the address given as the other operand. Finally, `call` instruction is used to call a given function. When there is any other instruction used in the paper, its semantics is described in relevant places in the text.

This paper focuses mainly on the instrumentation part, as we use a standard static program slicing based on dependency graphs [12] and a standard symbolic execution [20]. The rest of the paper is organized as follows. Section 2 describes the basic version of code instrumentation for checking memory safety that does not use any auxiliary analysis. Section 3 introduces the extended pointer analysis and explains the instrumentation improvements (I1)–(I3). Section 4 is devoted to the implementation of our approach in SYMBIOTIC. Section 5 presents experimental results comparing SYMBIOTIC with state-of-the-art tools for memory safety checking and illustrating the contribution of instrumentation improvements and program slicing to the overall performance. Related work is discussed in Sect. 6.

2   Basic Instrumentation

To check memory safety, our basic instrumentation inserts a code that tracks all allocated memory blocks (including global and stack variables) and checks all memory accesses at run-time. Similarly as Jones and Kelly [19], for every allocated block of memory we maintain a record with its address and size. The records are stored in three lists:

- *StackList* for blocks allocated on the stack
- *HeapList* for blocks allocated on the heap
- *GlobalsList* for global variables

Additionally, we maintain *DeallocatedList* for blocks on the heap that were already deallocated. This list can be safely omitted as it serves only to provide more precise error descriptions. For example, the information in this list enables us to distinguish double free from generic invalid deallocation, or use-after-free from vague invalid dereference error.

To maintain the three lists, after each allocation we call one of the functions `remember_stack`(*addr*, *size*) or `remember_heap`(*addr*, *size*) or `remember_global`(*addr*, *size*). Before every deallocation, we call function `handle_free`(*addr*) that checks that *addr* points to the beginning of a memory block allocated on the heap and removes the corresponding record from

```
1. %p = alloca i32*                      %p = alloca i32*
   call remember_stack(%p, 8)            call remember_stack(%p, 8)
   call check_pointer(%p, 8)
2. store null to %p                       store null to %p
3. %addr = call malloc(20)                %addr = call malloc(20)
   call remember_heap(%addr, 20)         call remember_heap(%addr, 20)
   call check_pointer(%p, 8)
4. store %addr to %p                       store %addr to %p
   call handle_free(%addr)               call handle_free(%addr)
5. call free(%addr);                       call free(%addr);
   check_pointer(%p, 8)
6. %tmp = load %p                          %tmp = load %p
   check_pointer(%tmp, 4)                check_pointer(%tmp, 4)
7. store i32 1 to %tmp                     store i32 1 to %tmp
```

Fig. 3. Instrumentation of a code with an invalid pointer dereference on line 7. The code on the left is instrumented by the basic instrumentation while the code on the right is instrumented using the improvement (I1) described in Sect. 3. We assume that the width of a pointer is 8 bytes and the width of an integer (in LLVM denoted as the type i32) is 4 bytes.

HeapList. Since local variables on the stack are destroyed when a function finishes, we call function destroy_stack() to remove relevant records from *StackList* right before returning from a function. Further, before every instruction loading or storing n bytes from/to the address *addr* we call function check_pointer($addr, n$) to check that the memory operation is safe. Finally, we insert check_leaks() at the end of main function to check that *HeapList* is empty.

During runtime, there can be situations when a pointer is incorrectly shifted to a different valid object in memory (e.g. when two arrays are allocated on the stack one next to the other, a pointer may overflow from the first one to the second one). In this case, the checking function finds a record for the object pointed to by the pointer and it does not raise any error even though the pointer points outside of its base object. To overcome this problem, some approaches instrument also every pointer arithmetic operation [9,19,31]. We do not instrument pointer arithmetic as we do not execute the code but pass it to a verification tool that keeps strict distinction between objects in memory. Therefore, a pointer derived from an object cannot overflow to a different object.

An example of a basic instrumentation is provided in Fig. 3 (left). Allocations on lines 1 and 3 are instrumented with calls to remember_stack and remember_heap, respectively. The address of the memory allocated by the call to malloc is stored to %p on line 4. This memory is then freed and handle_free is called in reaction to this event. The call of check_pointer before line 7 reveals use-after-free error as the value of %p loaded on line 6 is the address of the memory allocated on line 3 and freed on line 5.

3   Instrumentation Improvements

All suggested instrumentation improvements rely on an extended pointer analysis. Hence, we first recall the standard pointer analysis and describe its extension.

3.1   Extended Pointer Analysis

Roughly speaking, a standard pointer analysis computes for each pointer variable its *points-to set* containing all *memory locations* the variable may point to. Here a memory location is an abstraction of a concrete object located in memory during runtime. A frequent choice used also by our analysis is to abstract these objects by instructions allocating them. For example, the object allocated on line 3 in Fig. 3 is represented by memory location 3:malloc(20) referring to the function call that allocates the memory and its line number. Note that one memory location can represent more objects, for example when the allocation is within a program loop. Besides the memory locations, points-to sets can also contain two special elements: null if the pointer's value may be null, and unknown if the analysis fails to establish information about any referenced memory location.

The precision of pointer analysis can be tuned in several directions. We focus on *flow-sensitivity* and *field-sensitivity*. A pointer analysis is called *flow-sensitive* [16] if it takes into consideration the flow of data in the program and computes specific points-to information for every control location in the program. On the contrary, *flow-insensitive* analyses ignore the execution order of instructions and compute summary information about a pointer that holds at any control location in the program. For instance, in Fig. 3 a flow-insensitive analysis would tell us that %tmp may point either to null or to the memory location 3:malloc(20) due to the assignments on lines 2 and 4. The flow-sensitive analysis can tell us that %tmp may point only to 3:malloc(20). In the context of standard programming languages, one has to specify a control location when asking a flow-sensitive pointer analysis for the points-to set of some pointer variable. When working with LLVM, we do not do that as LLVM programs are in the SSA form [8] where every program variable is assigned at a single program location only. A pointer analysis is called *field-sensitive* if it differentiates between individual elements of arrays and structures. We achieve field-sensitivity by refining information in points-to sets with offsets (e.g. p points to memory location A at offset 4).

Standard pointer analyses ignore information whether a memory block was freed or whether the lifetime of a local variable has ended because of the end of its scope. Even though such events do not change pointer values, they are crucial if we want to use pointer analysis to optimize the instrumentation process. Consider the dereference on line 7 in Fig. 3. Usual flow- and field-sensitive pointer analysis tells us that the pointer %tmp points to the location 3:malloc(20) at offset 0 and thus writing 4 bytes to that memory seems to be safe. However, it is not as this memory has been already freed on line 5.

There exist sophisticated forms of pointer analysis that can model the heap and the stack and provide information about deallocation and ceased lifetime of memory objects (e.g. shape analysis [16,29]), but these are too expensive for our use case. Instead, we extended a simple flow- and field-sensitive Andersen's style [1] pointer analysis so that it can track whether a pointer variable can possibly point to an invalidated memory (i.e. a memory that was freed or its lifetime ended). In such a case, it includes invalidated in its points-to set. The extension is straightforward. Whenever the pointer analysis passes the end of a function, we traverse the points-to information and to all pointers that may point to a local object we add the invalidated element. Similarly, when free is called, we add invalidated element to the points-to set of pointers that may point to the freed object.

More formally, the extended pointer analysis assigns to every pointer variable p the corresponding points-to set

$$ptset(p) \subseteq (Mem \times Offset) \cup \{\texttt{null}, \texttt{unknown}, \texttt{invalidated}\},$$

where Mem is the set of memory locations and $Offset = \mathbb{N}_0 \cup \{?\}$ is the set of non-negative integers extended with a special element '?' denoting an unknown offset. In the following, we assume that the information computed by the pointer analysis is *sound*, i.e. every address that can be assigned to a pointer variable p during runtime has a corresponding element in $ptset(p)$ (where unknown pointer covers any address).

(I1) Reduce the Number of Checks

The extended pointer analysis can often guarantee that each possible memory dereference performed by a particular instruction is safe. Let us assume that an instruction reads or writes n bytes from/to the memory pointed by a pointer variable p. The extended pointer analysis guarantees its safety if $ptset(p)$ contains neither null nor unknown nor invalidated, and for every $(A, offset) \in ptset(p)$ it holds that every object represented by memory location A contains at least $offset + n$ bytes. Formally, the access is safe if

- $ptset(p) \cap \{\texttt{unknown}, \texttt{null}, \texttt{invalidated}\} = \emptyset$ and
- for each $(A, offset) \in ptset(p)$ it holds that $offset \neq ?$ and $offset + n \leq size(A)$,

where $size(A)$ denotes the minimum size of the memory objects represented by A if it is known at compile time, otherwise it denotes 0 (and thus the condition does not hold as $n \geq 1$).

Before instrumenting a memory access with a check, we query the extended pointer analysis. If the analysis says that the memory access is safe, the check is not inserted. For example, in Fig. 3 the dereferences of the variable %p on lines 2, 4, and 6 are safe and thus need not be instrumented with a check. However, we insert a check before line 7 because the analysis says that %tmp may point to an invalidated memory. Figure 3 (right) provides the example code instrumented using the improvement (I1).

```
1. %array = alloca [10 x i32]
   call remember_stack(%array, 10*4)
2. %m = call input()
3. %tmp = getelementptr %array, %m
   call check_bounds(%tmp, 4, %array, 0, 40)
4. store 1 to %tmp
```

Fig. 4. Instrumentation of a code using the simpler, constant-time check. Recall that we assume that the width of an integer (i32) is 4 bytes.

(I2) Simplify Checks When Possible

The function check_pointer($addr, n$) used by our instrumentation approach to check validity of memory accesses is not cheap. It searches the lists of records (*StackList*, *HeapList*, and *GlobalsList*) for the one that represents the memory block where $addr$ points to. Hence, it has a linear complexity with respect to the number of records in the lists. Here we present an improvement that can sometimes replace this check with a simpler, constant-time check.

Let us assume that there is an instruction accessing n bytes at the memory pointed by a pointer variable p_1 and such that the extended pointer analysis cannot guarantee its safety. Further, assume that the value of p_1 has been computed as a pointer p_0 shifted by some number of bytes. Instead of a possibly expensive call check_pointer(p_1, n), we can insert a simpler check if we know the size of the memory block referred by p_0 and where precisely p_0 points into the object (i.e. its offset). Formally, we insert the simpler check before a potentially unsafe dereference of p_1 if

- $ptset(p_0) \cap \{\text{unknown}, \text{null}, \text{invalidated}\} = \emptyset$ and
- there exist $size_0 > 0$ and $offset_0 \neq ?$ such that, for each $(A, offset) \in ptset(p_0)$, it holds that $size(A) = size_0$ and $offset = offset_0$.

Indeed, in this case we can compute the actual offset of p_1 as $offset_1 = offset_0 + (p_1 - p_0)$ and we know the size of the object that p_1 points into. The dereference is safe iff all the accessed bytes are within the bounds of the memory object, i.e. $0 \leq offset_1$ and $offset_1 + n \leq size_0$. This constant-time check is implemented by the function check_bounds($p_1, n, p_0, offset_0, size_0$).

Figure 4 provides an example where the simpler check is applied before the last instruction. In this example, an array of ten integers is allocated on line 1. The instruction %tmp = getelementptr %array, %m on line 3 returns the address of the m-th element of the array, i.e. the address %array increased by $4m$ bytes. Line 4 stores integer 1 on this address. The extended pointer analysis cannot determine the offset of this address as it depends on the user input. However, it can determine that %array points to the beginning (i.e. at offset 0) of the block of the size 40. Hence, the call to check_bounds is inserted instead of the usual check_pointer.

(I3) Extension with Staged Instrumentation

Although the previous two instrumentation improvements eliminate or simplify checks of dereference safety, the approach still tracks all memory allocations. However, it is sufficient to track only memory blocks that are relevant for some check. For example, the code in Fig. 3 (right) remembers records for both allocations on lines 1 and 3, but no record corresponding to the allocation on line 1 is ever used: handle_free(%addr) searches only *HeapList* and the extended pointer analysis tells us that the pointer checked by check_pointer(%tmp, 4) can never point to the location 1:alloca i32*. Hence, the call to remember_stack inserted after line 1 can be safely omitted. Note that we always track all allocations on heap as they are relevant for the memory leaks checking.

In order to insert only relevant calls to remember_stack and remember_global functions, we perform the instrumentation in two stages.

1. In the first stage, checks are inserted as described before. Additionally, for every inserted check_pointer call, we remember its first argument, i.e. the pointer variable. In the first stage, we also insert all calls to remember_heap, handle_free, and destroy_stack.
2. The second stage inserts calls to remember_stack and remember_global. For every memory location A corresponding to a global variable or some allocation on the stack, we check whether any pointer variable remembered in the first stage can point into the memory location A. Formally, we check that there exists some remembered pointer p such that $(A, \text{\textit{offset}}) \in \text{\textit{ptset}}(p)$ for some *offset*, or unknown $\in \text{\textit{ptset}}(p)$. We insert the call to remember_stack or remember_global only if the answer is positive. Further, we insert the call to check_leaks at the end of main function only if some call to remember_heap was inserted in the first stage.

Note that in the first stage we do not remember arguments of check_bounds introduced by (I2) as this function does not search the lists of records.

In Figs. 3 (right) and 4, the presented staged instrumentation would not insert any call to remember_stack.

In general, inserting fewer calls to functions that create records has a positive effect on the speed of reachability analysis since *StackList* and *GlobalsList* are shorter. All the described extensions together can significantly reduce the amount of inserted code. This has also a positive effect on the portion of code possibly removed by program slicing before the reachability analysis.

4   Implementation

The described approach was implemented in SYMBIOTIC [7]. The tool consists of three main parts, namely *instrumentation module*, *slicing module* and the external state-of-the-art open-source symbolic executor KLEE [5]. Moreover, the instrumentation and slicing modules rely on our library called dg that provides dependence graph construction and various pointer analyses including the extended pointer analysis described in Sect. 3.

Instead of implementing a single-purpose instrumentation for memory safety checking, we developed a configurable instrumentation module [34]. The instrumentation process is controlled by a configuration file provided by the user. A configuration can specify an arbitrary number of instrumentation stages, each defined by a set of instrumentation rules. Every rule describes which instructions should be matched and how to instrument them. At the moment, the instrumentation can insert only `call` instructions as it is sufficient for most use-cases. An instrumentation rule can trigger an additional action like setting a flag or remembering values or variables used by the matched instructions. Further, a rule can be guarded by conditions of several kinds. A condition can claim that

- a given flag has a particular value,
- a given value or a variable has been already remembered (or not),
- an external plugin returns a particular answer on a given query constructed with parts of matched instructions.

A rule with conditions is applied only if all conditions are satisfied. For example, in memory safety checking we use the extended pointer analysis as a plugin in order to instrument only dereferences that are not safe due to (I1).

Besides a configuration, the user has to also provide definitions of functions whose calls are inserted into the program. For checking memory safety, these functions are written in C and translated to LLVM. After a successful instrumentation, these functions are linked to the instrumented code.

We implemented a static backward slicing algorithm based on dependence graphs [12] as we have not found any suitable program slicer for LLVM bitcode. The algorithm has been extended to a simple form of inter-procedural slicing, where dependence graphs for procedures are connected by inter-procedural edges and the slice is obtained by one backward search instead of using the traditional two-pass algorithm introduced in [18].

SYMBIOTIC applies code optimizations provided by the LLVM framework after instrumentation and again after slicing. Finally, KLEE is executed on the sliced and optimized code to check for reachability of the inserted error locations.

The tool SYMBIOTIC and its components are licensed under the MIT and Apache-2.0 open-source licenses and can be found at:

https://github.com/staticafi/symbiotic

KLEE is licensed under the University of Illinois license.

5   Experimental Evaluation

The section is divided into two parts. First, we compare several setups of the described approach in order to show which ingredients are essential for good performance. The second part provides a closer comparison of SYMBIOTIC with the other two winning tools in the *MemSafety* category of SV-COMP 2018.

Table 1. For each instrumentation configuration, the table shows the total numbers of inserted calls of check_pointer, check_bounds, and rememeber* functions. Further, it shows the total numbers of instructions in instrumented benchmarks (as sent to KLEE) with and without slicing, together with their ratio in the column *relative size*. Finally, the table shows the numbers of solved benchmarks with and without slicing.

	Inserted calls			Number of instruct.			Solved benchmarks			
	check_pointer	check_bounds	remember*	w/o slicing	with slicing	relative size	w/o slicing		with slicing	
							safe	unsafe	safe	unsafe
Basic	32333	0	10511	575k	343k	60%	116	132	118	131
(I1)	4930	0	10511	538k	303k	56%	119	132	125	132
(I1) + (I2)	4750	180	10511	538k	301k	56%	119	132	126	132
(I1) + (I3)	4930	0	830	478k	174k	36%	130	132	180	132
(I1) + (I2) + (I3)	4750	180	792	478k	171k	36%	132	132	181	132

5.1 Contribution of Instrumentation Improvements and Slicing

We evaluated 10 setups of the approach presented in this paper. More precisely, we consider five different configurations of instrumentation referred as *basic*, *(I1)*, *(I1)+(I2)*, *(I1)+(I3)*, and *(I1)+(I2)+(I3)*, each with and without slicing. The *basic* instrumentation is the one described in Sect. 2 and the other four configurations employ the corresponding improvements presented in Sect. 3. We do not consider other configurations as they are clearly inferior.

For the evaluation, we use 390 memory safety benchmarks from SV-COMP 2018[1], namely 326 benchmark from the *MemSafety* category and another 64 benchmarks of the subcategory *TerminCrafted*, which was not included in the official competition this year. The benchmark set consists of 140 unsafe and 250 safe benchmarks. The unsafe benchmarks contain exactly one error according to the official SV-COMP rules. All experiments were performed on machines with *Intel(R) Core(TM) i7-3770* CPU running at 3.40 GHz. The CPU time limit for each benchmark was set to 300 s and the memory limit was 6 GB. We used the utility *Benchexec* [4] for reliable measurement of consumed resources.

The results are presented in Table 1 and Fig. 5. The numbers of inserted calls in the table show that the extended pointer analysis itself can guarantee safety of approximately 85% of all dereferences. In other words, (I1) reduces the number of inserted checks to 15%. Further, (I2) can replace a relatively small part of these checks by simpler ones. The improvement (I3) reduces the number of inserted memory-tracking calls to around 8% in both configurations *(I1)+(I3)* and *(I1)+(I2)+(I3)*.

The numbers of instructions show that (I3) not only reduces the instrumented program size, but also substantially improves efficiency of program slicing. Altogether, all instrumentation improvements and slicing reduce the total size of programs to 30% comparing to the basic instrumentation without slicing.

Obviously, the most important information is the numbers of solved benchmarks. We can see that all setups detected 132 unsafe benchmarks except the

---

[1] https://github.com/sosy-lab/sv-benchmarks/, revision tag svcomp2018.

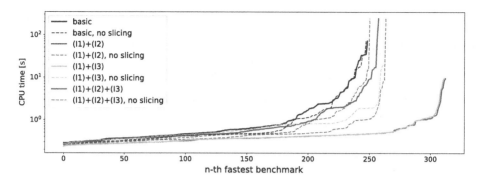

Fig. 5. Quantile plot of running times of the considered setups (excluding timeouts and errors). The plot depicts the number of benchmarks (x-axis) that the tool is able to solve in the given configuration with the given time limit (y-axis) for one benchmark. We omitted the lines for *(I1)* with and without slicing as they almost perfectly overlap with the corresponding lines for *(I1)+(I2)*.

basic configuration with slicing, where the slicing procedure did not finish for one benchmark within the time limit. As the considered benchmark set contains only 140 unsafe benchmarks, this confirms the generic observation that for verification tools, finding a bug is usually easy. The situation is different for safe benchmarks. All considered setups verified between 116 and 132 safe benchmarks except *(I1)+(I3)* with slicing and *(I1)+(I2)+(I3)* with slicing, which verified 180 and 181 benchmarks, respectively. This performance gap is also well illustrated by Fig. 5. The lines clearly show that even though the instrumentation improvements help on their own, it is the combination of (I1), (I3) *and* program slicing that helps considerably. The effect of (I2) is rather negligible.

5.2   Comparison of Symbiotic, PredatorHP, and UKojak

Now we take a closer look at the performance of the top three tools in *Mem-Safety* category of SV-COMP 2018, namely SYMBIOTIC, PREDATORHP [17], and UKOJAK [28]. What we present and interpret are the official data of this category available on the competition website https://sv-comp.sosy-lab.org/2018/. Note that SV-COMP 2018 used 900 s timeout and memory limit of 15 GB per benchmark.

Table 2 shows the numbers of solved safe and unsafe benchmarks in each subcategory and total time needed to solve these benchmarks. None of the tools reported any incorrect answer. SYMBIOTIC was able to solve the most benchmarks (almost 80%) in very short time compared to the other two tools. Moreover, all unsafe benchmarks solved by PREDATORHP and UKOJAK were also solved by SYMBIOTIC. PREDATORHP is better in solving safe instances of *Heap* and *LinkedLists* subcategories. Let us note that while SYMBIOTIC and UKO-JAK are general purpose verification tools, PREDATORHP is a highly specialized tool for shape analysis of C programs operating with pointers and linked lists.

Table 2. Numbers of bechmarks solved by the three considered tools in each subcategory of *MemSafety*. The last row shows total CPU time spent on all solved benchmarks.

subcategory	number of benchmarks	SYMBIOTIC		PREDATORHP		UKOJAK	
		solved	safe / unsafe	solved	safe / unsafe	solved	safe / unsafe
Arrays	69	**62**	44 / 18	7	0 / 7	44	27 / 17
Heap	180	145	55 / 90	**148**	66 / 82	51	26 / 25
LinkedLists	51	27	3 / 24	**43**	19 / 24	4	0 / 4
Other	26	**26**	23 / 3	18	16 / 2	23	23 / 0
total	326	**260**	125 / 135	216	101 / 115	122	76 / 46
CPU time [s]		**310**		2100		11000	

In particular, it uses an abstraction allowing to represent unbounded heap-allocated structures, which is something at least SYMBIOTIC cannot handle.

Scatter plots in Fig. 6 provide another comparison of the tools. On the left, one can immediately see that running times of UKOJAK are much longer than these of SYMBIOTIC for nearly all benchmarks. The fact that UKOJAK is written in Java and starting up the Java Virtual Machine takes time can explain a fixed delay, but not the entire speed difference. Moreover, there are 141 benchmarks solved by SYMBIOTIC and unsolved by UKOJAK, compared to only 3 benchmarks where the situation is the other way around. In many of these cases, UKOJAK gave up or crashed even before time limit.

The plot on the right shows that PREDATORHP outperforms SYMBIOTIC on simple benchmarks solved by both tools within one second. Further, there are 34 benchmarks where SYMBIOTIC timed out but which were successfully solved by PREDATORHP. On the other hand, SYMBIOTIC decided 78 benchmarks that were not decided by PREDATORHP. For most of these benchmarks, PREDATORHP gave up very quickly as its static analysis is unable to decide. Moreover, many benchmarks were solved by SYMBIOTIC within a second whereas PREDATORHP computed much longer. To sum up, it seems that the benefits of SYMBIOTIC and PREDATORHP are complementary to a large extent.

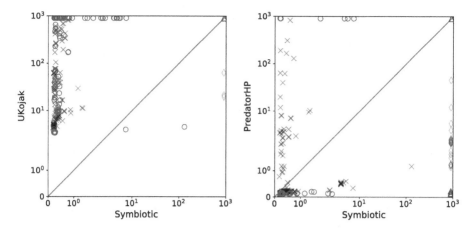

Fig. 6. Scatter plots comparing SYMBIOTIC with UKOJAK (left) and with PREDA-TORHP (right) by their running times (in seconds) on individual benchmarks. The symbols × represent benchmarks solved by both tools, ○ are benchmarks solved by SYMBIOTIC but not by the other tool, ◇ are benchmarks solved by the other tool but not by SYMBIOTIC, and △ are benchmarks that were solved by neither of the tools.

6 Related Work

There is plenty of papers on runtime instrumentation for detecting memory errors, but very little that optimize this process for the context of software verification. Nevertheless, the basic principles and ideas are shared no matter whether the instrumented code is executed or passed to a verification tool. Therefore, we give an overview of tools that perform *compile-time* instrumentation although they do not verify but rather monitor the code. Further, an overview of tools for verification of memory safety is also provided.

6.1 Runtime Monitoring Tools

Our instrumentation process is similar to the one of Kelly and Jones [19] or derived approaches like [9,31]. The difference is that we do not need to instrument also every pointer arithmetic (as explained in Sect. 2) and we use simple singly-linked lists instead of splay trees to store records about allocated memory.

A different approach than remembering state of the memory in records is taken by Tag-Protector [32]. This tool keeps records and a mapping of memory blocks to these records only during the instrumentation process (the resulting program does not maintain any lookup table or list of records) and insert ghost variables into the program to keep information needed for checking correctness of memory accesses (e.g. size and base addresses of objects). These variables are copied along with associated pointers. We believe a similar technique could be used to speed up our approach.

AddressSanitizer [33] is a very popular plugin for compile-time instrumentation available in modern compilers. It uses shadow memory to keep track of the program's state and it is highly optimized for direct execution.

To the extent of our knowledge, none of the above-mentioned approaches use static analysis to reduce the number or the runtime cost of inserted instructions.

CCured [27] is a source-to-source translator for C programming language that transforms programs to be memory safe and uses static analysis to reduce the complexity of inserted runtime checks. Static analysis is used to divide pointers into three classes: *safe*, *sequential*, and *wild* pointers, each of them deserving gradually more expansive tracking and checking mechanism. CCured does not use a lookup table but extends the pointer representation to keep also the metadata (the so-called "fat" pointers). The static analysis used by CCured is less precise as it uses unification-based approach opposed to our analysis which is inclusion-based. Therefore, our analysis can prune the inserted checks more aggressively.

NesCheck [26] uses very similar static analysis as CCured to reduce the number of inserted checks, but does not transform the pointer representation while instrumenting. Instead, it keeps metadata about pointer separately in a dense, array-based binary search tree.

SAFECode [10] is an instrumentation system that uses static analyses to reduce the number of runtime checks. In fact, they also suggest to use this reduction in the context of verification. SAFECode does not try to eliminate the tracking of memory blocks as our tool does. However, it employs automatic pool allocation [23] to make lookups of metadata faster.

As far as we known, the idea of using pointer analysis to reduce the fragment of memory that needs to be tracked appeared only in [36]. Even though the high-level concept of this work seems similar to our approach, they focus on runtime protection against exploitation of unchecked user inputs.

6.2 Memory Safety Verification Tools

In the rest of this section, we move from runtime memory safety checkers to verification tools. Instrumentation is common in this context as well, but using static analysis to reduce the number of inserted checks has not caught as much attention as we believe it deserves.

Modern verification tools also support checking memory safety usually through some kind of instrumentation, but the instrumented functions are interpreted directly by the tool (they are not implemented in the program). CPAchecker [3] and UltimateAutomizer [15] insert checks for correctness of memory operations directly into their internal representation. SMACK [6] and Sea-Horn [13] instrument code on LLVM level. SeaHorn uses ghost variables for checking out-of-bound memory accesses via assertions inserted into code, and shadow memory to track other types of errors. SMACK inserts a check before every memory access. Map2Check [30] is a memory bug hunting tool that instruments programs and then uses verification to find possible errors in memory operations. It used bounded model checking as the verification backend, but it has switched to LLVM and KLEE recently [25]. All these tools use no static analysis to reduce inserted checks.

One of few publications that explore possibilities of combination of static analysis and memory safety verification is [2], where authors apply CCured to instrument programs and then verify them using BLAST. The main goal was to eliminate as much inserted checks as possible using model checking.

Finally, CBMC [21] injects checks into its internal code representation. Checking its source code reveals that it uses a kind of lightweight field-insensitive taint analysis to reduce the number of inserted checks.

7   Conclusion

We have presented a technique for checking memory safety properties of programs which is based on a combination of instrumentation with extended pointer analysis, program slicing, and symbolic execution. We describe how the extended pointer analysis can be used to reduce the number of inserted checks and showed that in some cases these checks can be further simplified. We introduced an instrumentation improvement that allows us to dramatically reduce also the number of tracked memory blocks. These instrumentation enhancements combined with program slicing result in much faster analysis of error location reachability that is performed by symbolic execution. We implemented this technique in the tool SYMBIOTIC that has consequently won the *MemSafety* category of Software Verification Competition 2018 and thus proved to be able to compete with state-of-the-art memory safety verification tools.

References

1. Andersen, L.O.: Program Analysis and Specialization for the C Programming Language. Ph.D thesis, DIKU, University of Copenhagen (1994)
2. Beyer, D., Henzinger, T.A., Jhala, R., Majumdar, R.: Checking memory safety with blast. In: Cerioli, M. (ed.) FASE 2005. LNCS, vol. 3442, pp. 2–18. Springer, Heidelberg (2005). https://doi.org/10.1007/978-3-540-31984-9_2
3. Beyer, D., Keremoglu, M.E.: CPAchecker: a tool for configurable software verification. In: Gopalakrishnan, G., Qadeer, S. (eds.) CAV 2011. LNCS, vol. 6806, pp. 184–190. Springer, Heidelberg (2011). https://doi.org/10.1007/978-3-642-22110-1_16
4. Beyer, D., Löwe, S., Wendler, P.: Benchmarking and resource measurement. In: Fischer, B., Geldenhuys, J. (eds.) SPIN 2015. LNCS, vol. 9232, pp. 160–178. Springer, Cham (2015). https://doi.org/10.1007/978-3-319-23404-5_12
5. Cadar, C., Dunbar, D., Engler, D.R.: KLEE: unassisted and automatic generation of high-coverage tests for complex systems programs. In: 8th USENIX Symposium on Operating Systems Design and Implementation, OSDI 2008, 8–10 December 2008, San Diego, California, USA, Proceedings, pp. 209–224. USENIX Association (2008)
6. Carter, M., He, S., Whitaker, J., Rakamarić, Z., Emmi, M.: SMACK software verification toolchain. In: Proceedings of the 38th IEEE/ACM International Conference on Software Engineering (ICSE) Companion, pp. 589–592. ACM (2016)

7. Chalupa, M., Vitovská, M., Strejček, J.: SYMBIOTIC 5: boosted instrumentation. In: Beyer, D., Huisman, M. (eds.) TACAS 2018. LNCS, vol. 10806, pp. 442–446. Springer, Cham (2018). https://doi.org/10.1007/978-3-319-89963-3_29

8. Cytron, R., Ferrante, J., Rosen, B.K., Wegman, M.N., Zadeck, F.K.: An efficient method of computing static single assignment form. In: Conference Record of the Sixteenth Annual ACM Symposium on Principles of Programming Languages, Austin, Texas, USA, 11–13 January 1989, pp. 25–35. ACM (1989)

9. Dhurjati, D., Adve, V.: Backwards-compatible array bounds checking for C with very low overhead. In: Proceedings of the 28th International Conference on Software Engineering, ICSE 2006, pp. 162–171. ACM (2006)

10. Dhurjati, D., Kowshik, S., Adve, V.: SAFECode: enforcing alias analysis for weakly typed languages. In: PLDI 2006: Proceedings of the 2006 ACM SIGPLAN Conference on Programming Language Design and Implementation, pp. 144–157. ACM (2006)

11. Dor, N., Rodeh, M., Sagiv, M.: Detecting memory errors via static pointer analysis (preliminary experience). In: Proceedings of the 1998 ACM SIGPLAN-SIGSOFT Workshop on Program Analysis for Software Tools and Engineering, PASTE 1998, pp. 27–34. ACM (1998)

12. Ferrante, J., Ottenstein, K.J., Warren, J.D.: The program dependence graph and its use in optimization. In: Paul, M., Robinet, B. (eds.) Programming 1984. LNCS, vol. 167, pp. 125–132. Springer, Heidelberg (1984). https://doi.org/10.1007/3-540-12925-1_33

13. Gurfinkel, A., Kahsai, T., Komuravelli, A., Navas, J.A.: The SeaHorn verification framework. In: Kroening, D., Păsăreanu, C.S. (eds.) CAV 2015. LNCS, vol. 9206, pp. 343–361. Springer, Cham (2015). https://doi.org/10.1007/978-3-319-21690-4_20

14. Guyer, S.Z., Lin, C.: Error checking with client-driven pointer analysis. Sci. Comput. Program. 58(1), 83–114 (2005)

15. Heizmann, M., Hoenicke, J., Podelski, A.: Software model checking for people who love automata. In: Sharygina, N., Veith, H. (eds.) CAV 2013. LNCS, vol. 8044, pp. 36–52. Springer, Heidelberg (2013). https://doi.org/10.1007/978-3-642-39799-8_2

16. Hind, M.: Pointer analysis: haven't we solved this problem yet? In: Proceedings of the 2001 ACM SIGPLAN-SIGSOFT Workshop on Program Analysis For Software Tools and Engineering, PASTE 2001, Snowbird, Utah, USA, 18–19 June 2001, pp. 54–61. ACM (2001)

17. Holík, L., Kotoun, M., Peringer, P., Šoková, V., Trtík, M., Vojnar, T.: Predator shape analysis tool suite. In: Bloem, R., Arbel, E. (eds.) HVC 2016. LNCS, vol. 10028, pp. 202–209. Springer, Cham (2016). https://doi.org/10.1007/978-3-319-49052-6_13

18. Horwitz, S., Reps, T.W., Binkley, D.W.: Interprocedural slicing using dependence graphs. ACM Trans. Program. Lang. Syst. 12(1), 26–60 (1990)

19. Jones, R.W.M., Kelly, P.H.J.: Backwards-compatible bounds checking for arrays and pointers in C programs. In: AADEBUG, pp. 13–26 (1997)

20. King, J.C.: Symbolic execution and program testing. Commun. ACM 19(7), 385–394 (1976)

21. Kroening, D., Tautschnig, M.: CBMC – C bounded model checker. In: Ábrahám, E., Havelund, K. (eds.) TACAS 2014. LNCS, vol. 8413, pp. 389–391. Springer, Heidelberg (2014). https://doi.org/10.1007/978-3-642-54862-8_26

22. Lattner, C., Adve, V.: LLVM: a compilation framework for lifelong program analysis & transformation. In: 2nd IEEE / ACM International Symposium on Code Generation and Optimization (CGO 2004), 20–24 March 2004, San Jose, CA, USA, CGO 2004, pp. 75–88. IEEE Computer Society (2004)

23. Lattner, C., Adve, V.: Automatic pool allocation: Improving performance by controlling data structure layout in the heap. SIGPLAN Not. **40**(6), 129–142 (2005)

24. The LLVM compiler infrastructure (2017). http://llvm.org

25. Map2check tool (2018). https://map2check.github.io/

26. Midi, D., Payer, M., Bertino, E.: Memory safety for embedded devices with nesCheck. In: Proceedings of the 2017 ACM on Asia Conference on Computer and Communications Security, ASIA CCS 2017, pp. 127–139. ACM (2017)

27. Necula, G.C., McPeak, S., Weimer, W.: CCured: type-safe retrofitting of legacy code. SIGPLAN Not. **37**(1), 128–139 (2002)

28. Nutz, A., Dietsch, D., Mohamed, M.M., Podelski, A.: ULTIMATE KOJAK with memory safety checks. In: Baier, C., Tinelli, C. (eds.) TACAS 2015. LNCS, vol. 9035, pp. 458–460. Springer, Heidelberg (2015). https://doi.org/10.1007/978-3-662-46681-0_44

29. Rinetzky, N., Sagiv, M.: Interprocedural shape analysis for recursive programs. In: Wilhelm, R. (ed.) CC 2001. LNCS, vol. 2027, pp. 133–149. Springer, Heidelberg (2001). https://doi.org/10.1007/3-540-45306-7_10

30. Rocha, H.O., Barreto, R.S., Cordeiro, L.C.: Hunting memory bugs in C programs with Map2Check. In: Chechik, M., Raskin, J.-F. (eds.) TACAS 2016. LNCS, vol. 9636, pp. 934–937. Springer, Heidelberg (2016). https://doi.org/10.1007/978-3-662-49674-9_64

31. Ruwase, O., Lam, M.S.: A practical dynamic buffer overflow detector. In: Proceedings of the Network and Distributed System Security Symposium, NDSS 2004, San Diego, California, USA, pp. 159–169. The Internet Society (2004)

32. Saeed, A., Ahmadinia, A., Just, M.: Tag-protector: an effective and dynamic detection of out-of-bound memory accesses. In: Proceedings of the Third Workshop on Cryptography and Security in Computing Systems, CS2 2016, pp. 31–36. ACM (2016)

33. Serebryany, K., Bruening, D., Potapenko, A., Vyukov, D.: Addresssanitizer: a fast address sanity checker. In: Proceedings of the 2012 USENIX Conference on Annual Technical Conference, USENIX ATC 2012, pp. 28–28. USENIX Association (2012)

34. Vitovská, M.: Instrumentation of LLVM IR. Master's thesis, Masaryk University, Faculty of Informatics, Brno (2018)

35. Xia, Y., Luo, J., Zhang, M.: Detecting memory access errors with flow-sensitive conditional range analysis. In: Yang, L.T., Zhou, X., Zhao, W., Wu, Z., Zhu, Y., Lin, M. (eds.) ICESS 2005. LNCS, vol. 3820, pp. 320–331. Springer, Heidelberg (2005). https://doi.org/10.1007/11599555_32

36. Yong, S.H., Horwitz, S.: Protecting C programs from attacks via invalid pointer dereferences. In: Proceedings of the 9th European Software Engineering Conference Held Jointly with 11th ACM SIGSOFT International Symposium on Foundations of Software Engineering, ESEC/FSE-11, pp. 307–316. ACM (2003)

Model-Checking HyperLTL for Pushdown Systems

Adrien Pommellet[1]($\boxtimes$) and Tayssir Touili[2]($\boxtimes$)

[1] LIPN and Université Paris-Diderot, Paris, France
`pommellet@irif.fr`
[2] LIPN, CNRS, and Université Paris 13, Villetaneuse, France
`touili@lipn.fr`

Abstract. Temporal logics such as LTL are often used to express safety or correctness properties of programs. However, they cannot model complex formulas known as hyperproperties introducing relations between different execution paths of a same system. In order to do so, the logic *HyperLTL* adds existential and universal quantifications of path variables to LTL. The model-checking problem, that is, determining if a given representation of a program verifies a HyperLTL property, has been shown to be decidable for finite state systems. In this paper, we prove that this result does not hold for Pushdown Systems nor for the subclass of Visibly Pushdown Systems. We therefore introduce an algorithm that over-approximates the model-checking problem with an automata-theoretic approach. We also detail an under-approximation method based on a phase-bounded analysis of Multi-Stack Pushdown Systems. We then show how these approximations can be used to check security policies.

1 Introduction

The analysis of execution traces of programs can be used to prove correctness properties often expressed with the unifying framework of the *linear temporal logic* LTL. However, a LTL formula only quantifies a single execution trace of a system; LTL can't express properties on multiple, simultaneous executions of a program.

These properties on sets of execution traces are known as *hyperproperties*. Many safety and security policies can be expressed as hyperproperties; this is in particular true of information-flow analysis. As an example, the *non-interference* policy states that if two computations share the same public inputs, they should have identical public outputs as well, even if their private inputs differ. This property implies a relation between computations that can't be expressed as a simple LTL formula.

HyperLTL is an extension of LTL introduced by Clarkson et al. in [6] that allows the universal and existential quantifications of multiple *path variables* that range over traces of a system in order to define hyperproperties. As an example, the formula $\forall \pi_1, \forall \pi_2, (a_{\pi_1} \wedge a_{\pi_2}) \Rightarrow X((b_{\pi_1} \wedge b_{\pi_2}) \vee (c_{\pi_1} \wedge c_{\pi_2}))$ means

M. M. Gallardo and P. Merino (Eds.): SPIN 2018, LNCS 10869, pp. 133–152, 2018.
https://doi.org/10.1007/978-3-319-94111-0_8

that, given two path variables π_1 and π_2 in the set $Traces_\omega(S)$ of infinite traces of a system S, if π_1 and π_2 verify the same atomic property a at a given step, then they should both verify either b or c at the next step.

Clarkson et al. have shown that the model-checking problem $S \models \psi$ of Hyper-LTL, that is, knowing if the set of traces of a system S verifies the HyperLTL formula ψ, can be solved when S is a finite state transition system (i.e. equivalent to a finite state automaton). However, simple transition models cannot accurately model programs with infinite recursion and procedure calls. *Pushdown Systems* (PDSs) that can simulate the *call stack* of a program are commonly used instead. The call stack stores information about the active procedures of a program such as return addresses, passed parameters and local variables.

Unfortunately, we show in this paper that the model-checking problem of HyperLTL for PDSs is undecidable: the set of traces of a PDS is a context-free language, and deciding whether the intersection of two context-free languages is empty or not remains an undecidable problem that can be reduced to the model-checking problem by using a HyperLTL formula that synchronizes traces.

On the other hand, determining the emptiness of the intersection of two *visibly context-free languages* is decidable. This class of languages is generated by *Visibly Pushdown Automata* (VPDA), an input-driven subclass of *pushdown automata* (PDA) first introduced by Alur et al. in [1]: at each step of a computation, the next stack operation will be determined by the input letter in Σ read, depending on a partition of the input alphabet. We study the model-checking problem of HyperLTL for *Visibly Pushdown Systems* (VPDSs), and prove that it is also undecidable, as it happens to be a reduction of the emptiness problem for *Two-Stack Visibly Pushdown Automata* (2-VPDA), which has been shown to be undecidable by Carotenuto et al. in [4].

To overcome these undecidability issues, since the emptiness of the intersection of a context-free langage with regular sets is decidable, one idea is to consider the case where only one path variable of the formula ranges over the set of traces $Traces_\omega(\mathcal{P})$ of a PDS or VPDS $\mathcal{P}$, while the other variables range over a regular abstraction $\alpha(Traces_\omega(\mathcal{P}))$. Using an automata-theoretic approach, this idea allows us to over-approximate the model-checking problem of Hyper-LTL formulas that only use universal quantifiers $\forall$ with the exception of at most one path variable: if the HyperLTL formula holds for the over-approximation, it holds for the actual system as well.

On the other hand, under-approximations can be used to discover errors in programs: if a HyperLTL formula does not hold for an under-approximation of the model-checking problem, it does not hold for the actual system as well. We show that the model-checking problem for PDSs of HyperLTL formulas that only use universal quantifiers $\forall$ can be under-approximated by relying on a bounded-phase model-checking of a LTL formula for a *Multi-Stack Pushdown System* (MPDS), where a *phase* is a part of a run during which there is at most one stack that is popped from, as defined by Torre et al. in [16].

Related Work. Clarkson and Schneider introduced *hyperproperties* in [7] to formalize security properties, using second-order logic. Unfortunately, this logic isn't verifiable in the general case.

However, fragments of it can be verified: in [6], Clarkson et al. formalized the temporal logics HyperLTL and HyperCTL*, extending the widespread and flexible framework of linear time and branching time logics to hyperproperties. The model-checking problem of these logics for finite state systems has been shown to be decidable by a reduction to the satisfiability problem for the quantified propositional temporal logic QPTL defined in [15].

Proper model-checking algorithms were then introduced by Finkbeiner et al. in [9]. These algorithms follow the automata-theoretic framework defined by Vardi et al. in [17], and can be used to verify security policies in circuits. However, while circuits can be modelled as finite state systems, actual programs can feature recursive procedure calls and infinite recursion. Hence, a more expressive model such as PDSs is needed.

In [3,8], the forward and backward reachability sets of PDSs have been shown to be regular and effectively computable. As a consequence, the model-checking problem of LTL for PDSs is decidable; an answer can be effectively computed using an automata-theoretic approach. We try to extend this result to HyperLTL.

Multi-Stack Pushdown Systems (MPDSs) are unfortunately Turing powerful. Following the work of Qadeer et al. in [13], La Torre et al. introduced in [16] MPDSs with *bounded phases*: a run is split into a finite number of phases during which there is at most one stack that is popped from. Anil Seth later proved in [14] that the backward reachability set of a multi-stack pushdown system with bounded phases is regular; this result can then be used to solve the model-checking problem of LTL for MPDSs with bounded phases. We rely on a phase-bounded analysis of a MPDS to under-approximate an answer to the model-checking problem of HyperLTL for PDSs.

Paper Outline. In Sect. 2 of this paper, we provide background on *Pushdown Systems* (PDSs) and *Visibly Pushdown Systems* (VPDSs). We define in Sect. 3 the hyper linear time logic *HyperLTL*, and prove that its model-checking problem for PDSs and VPDSs is undecidable. Then, in Sect. 4, we solve the model-checking problem of HyperLTL on constrained sets of traces then find an over-approximation of the model-checking problem for PDSs. In Sect. 5, we use *Multi-Stack Pushdown Systems* (MPDSs) and bounded phase analysis to under-approximate the model-checking problem. Finally, in Sect. 6, we apply the logic HyperLTL to express security properties. Due to a lack of space, detailed proofs of some theorems can be found in the appendix.

2   Pushdown Systems

2.1   The Model

Pushdown systems are a natural model for sequential programs with recursive procedure calls [8].

Definition 1 (Pushdown System). *A Pushdown System (PDS) is a tuple* $\mathcal{P} = (P, \Sigma, \Gamma, \Delta, c_0)$ *where* P *is a finite set of control states,* Σ *a finite input alphabet,* Γ *a finite stack alphabet,* $\Delta \subseteq P \times \Gamma \times \Sigma \times P \times \Gamma^*$ *a finite set of transition rules, and* $c_0 \in P \times \Gamma^*$ *an initial configuration.*

If $d = (p, \gamma, a, p', w) \in \Delta$, we write $d = (p, \gamma) \xrightarrow{a} (p', w)$. We call a the *label* of Σ. We can assume without loss of generality that $\Delta \subseteq P \times \Gamma \times \Sigma \times P \times \Gamma^{\leq 2}$ and that c_0 is of the form $\langle p_0, \bot \rangle$, where $\bot \in \Gamma$ is a special bottom stack symbol shared by every PDS on the stack alphabet Γ and $p_0 \in P$. A *configuration* of $\mathcal{P}$ is a pair $\langle p, w \rangle$ where $p \in P$ is a control state and $w \in \Gamma^*$ a stack content.

For each $a \in \Sigma$, we define a transition relation $\xrightarrow{a}_{\mathcal{P}}$ on configurations as follows: if $(p, \gamma) \xrightarrow{a} (p', w) \in \Delta$, for each $w' \in \Gamma^*$, $\langle p, \gamma w' \rangle \xrightarrow{a}_{\mathcal{P}} \langle p', ww' \rangle$. We then consider the immediate successor relation $\rightarrow_{\mathcal{P}} = \underset{a \in \Sigma}{\cup} \xrightarrow{a}_{\mathcal{P}}$. We may omit the variable $\mathcal{P}$ when only a single PDS is being considered.

A *run* r is a sequence of configurations $r = (c_i)_{i \geq 0}$ such that $\forall i \geq 0$, $c_i \xrightarrow{a_i}_{\mathcal{P}} c_{i+1}$, c_0 being the initial configuration of $\mathcal{P}$. The word $(a_i)_{i \geq 0}$ is then said to be the *trace* of r. Traces and runs may be finite or infinite. Let $Traces_\omega(\mathcal{P})$ (resp. $Traces(\mathcal{P})$) be the set of all infinite (resp. finite) traces of $\mathcal{P}$.

A *Büchi Pushdown Automaton* (BPDA) is a pair $\mathcal{BP} = (\mathcal{P}, F)$, where $\mathcal{P} = (P, \Sigma, \Gamma, \Delta, c_0)$ is a PDS and $F \subseteq P$ a set of final states. An infinite run $r = (c_i)_{i \geq 0}$ of $\mathcal{BP}$ and its matching trace $(a_i)_{i \geq 0}$ are said to be *accepting* if there exists at least one infinitely often occurring state f in r such that $f \in F$. The language $L_\omega(\mathcal{BP})$ accepted by $\mathcal{BP}$ is the set of all accepting traces of $\mathcal{BP}$, and is said to be ω *context-free*.

2.2 Visibly Pushdown Systems

We consider a particular subclass of PDSs introduced by Alur et al. in [1]. Let $\langle \Sigma_c, \Sigma_r, \Sigma_l \rangle$ be a partition of the input alphabet, where Σ_c, Σ_r, and Σ_l stand respectively for the *call*, *return*, and *local* alphabets.

Definition 2 (Visibly Pushdown System). *A Visibly Pushdown System (VPDS) over a partition* $\langle \Sigma_c, \Sigma_r, \Sigma_l \rangle$ *of* Σ *is a PDS* $\mathcal{P} = (P, \Sigma, \Gamma, \Delta, c_0)$ *verifying the following properties:*

- *if* $(p, \gamma_1) \xrightarrow{a} (p', \gamma_2) \in \Delta$*, then* $a \in \Sigma_l$*,* $\gamma_1 = \gamma_2$*, and* $\forall \gamma \in \Gamma$*,* $(p, \gamma) \xrightarrow{a} (p', \gamma) \in \Delta$*;*
- *if* $(p, \gamma) \xrightarrow{a} (p', \varepsilon) \in \Delta$*, then* $a \in \Sigma_r$*;*
- *if* $(p, \gamma_1) \xrightarrow{a} (p', \gamma_2 \gamma_1) \in \Delta$*, then* $a \in \Sigma_c$*, and* $\forall \gamma \in \Gamma$*,* $(p, \gamma) \xrightarrow{a} (p', \gamma_2 \gamma) \in \Delta$*;*

VPDSs are an *input driven* subclass of PDSs: at each step of a computation, the next stack operation will be determined by the input letter in Σ read, depending on which subset of the partition $\langle \Sigma_c, \Sigma_r, \Sigma_l \rangle$ the aforementioned letter belongs to.

Visibly Pushdown Automata accept the class of *visibly pushdown languages*. If a BPDA $\mathcal{BP}$ is visibly pushdown according to a partition of Σ, we say it's a

Büchi Visibly Pushdown Automata (BVPDA). The class of languages accepted by BVPDA is called ω *visibly pushdown languages.*

Unlike context-free languages, the emptiness of the intersection of visibly pushdown languages is a decidable problem and the complement of a visibly pushdown language is a visibly pushdown language that can be computed. The same properties also hold for ω visibly pushdown languages.

3 HyperLTL

3.1 The Logic

Let AP be a finite set of atomic propositions used to express facts about a program; a *path* is an infinite word in $(2^{AP})^\omega = \mathcal{T}$. Let $\mathcal{V}$ be a finite set of *path variables*. The *HyperLTL* logic relates multiple paths by introducing path quantifiers.

Definition 3 (Syntax of HyperLTL). *Unquantified HyperLTL formulas are defined according to the following syntax equation:*

$$\varphi:: = \bot \mid (a, \pi) \in AP \times \mathcal{V} \mid \neg\varphi \mid \varphi \vee \varphi \mid \varphi \wedge \varphi \mid X\,\varphi \mid$$
$$\varphi\,U\,\varphi \mid G\,\varphi \mid F\,\varphi$$

From then on, we write $a_\pi = (a, \pi)$. *HyperLTL formulas are defined according to the following syntax equation:*

$$\psi:: = \exists\pi, \psi \mid \forall\pi, \psi \mid \varphi \text{ such that } \varphi \text{ is a LTL formula.}$$

where $\pi \in \mathcal{V}$ *is a path variable.*

The existential $\exists$ and universal quantifiers $\forall$ are used to define path variables, to which atomic propositions in AP are bound. A HyperLTL formula is said to be *closed* if there is no free variable: each path variable is bound by a path quantifier once.

As an example, the closed formula $\forall\pi_1, \exists\pi_2, \varphi$ means that for all paths π_1, there exists a path π_2 such that the formula φ holds for π_1 and π_2. Simple LTL formulas can be considered as a subclass of closed HyperLTL formulas of the form $\forall\pi, \varphi$ with a single path variable.

Let $\Pi : \mathcal{V} \rightarrow \mathcal{T}$ be a *path assignment function* of $\mathcal{V}$ that matches to each path variable π a path $\Pi(\pi) \in \mathcal{T}$. If $\Pi(\pi) = (t_j)_{j\geq 0}$, for all $i \geq 0$, we define the i-th value of the path $\Pi(\pi)[i] = t_i$ and a suffix assignment function $\Pi[i, \infty]$ such that $\Pi[i, \infty](\pi) = (t_j)_{j\geq i}$.

We first define the semantics of this logic for path assignment functions.

Definition 4 (Semantics of unquantified HyperLTL formulas). *Let φ be an unquantified HyperLTL formula. We define by induction on φ the following semantics on path assignment functions:*

$$\Pi \models a_\pi \Leftrightarrow a \in \Pi(\pi)[0]$$
$$\Pi \models \neg\varphi \Leftrightarrow \Pi \not\models \varphi$$
$$\Pi \models \varphi_1 \vee \varphi_2 \Leftrightarrow (\Pi \models \varphi_1) \vee (\Pi \models \varphi_2)$$
$$\Pi \models \varphi_1 \wedge \varphi_2 \Leftrightarrow (\Pi \models \varphi_1) \wedge (\Pi \models \varphi_2)$$
$$\Pi \models X \varphi \Leftrightarrow \Pi[1, \infty] \models \varphi$$
$$\Pi \models \varphi \ U \ \psi \Leftrightarrow \exists j \geq 0, \Pi[j, \infty] \models \psi \ and \ \forall i \in \{0, \ldots, j-1\}, \Pi[i, \infty] \models \varphi$$
$$\Pi \models G \varphi \Leftrightarrow \forall i \geq 0, \Pi[i, \infty] \models \varphi$$
$$\Pi \models F \varphi \Leftrightarrow \exists i \geq 0, \Pi[i, \infty] \models \varphi$$

$\Pi \models \varphi$ if φ holds for a given assignment of path variables defined according to Π.

Let $T : \mathcal{V} \rightarrow 2^{\mathcal{T}}$ be a *set assignment function* of $\mathcal{V}$ that matches to each path variable $\pi \in \mathcal{V}$ a set of paths $T(\pi) \subseteq \mathcal{T}$. We can now define the semantics of closed HyperLTL formulas for set assignment functions.

Definition 5 (Semantics of closed HyperLTL formulas). *We consider a closed HyperLTL formula* $\psi = \chi_0 \pi_0, \ldots, \chi_n \pi_n, \varphi$, *where each* $\chi_i \in \{\forall, \exists\}$ *is an universal or existential quantifier, and* φ *an unquantified HyperLTL formula using trace variables* $\pi_0, \ldots, \pi_n$.

For a given set assignment function T, *we write that* $T \models \psi$ *if for* $\chi_0 t_0 \in T(\pi_0)$, $\ldots$, $\chi_n t_n \in T(\pi_n)$, *we have* $\Pi \models \varphi$, *where* Π *is the path assignment function such that* $\forall i \in \{0, \ldots, n\}, \Pi(\pi_i) = t_i$.

As an example, if $\psi = \forall \pi_1, \exists \pi_2, \varphi$ is a closed HyperLTL formula and T is a set assignment function of $\mathcal{V}$, then $T \models \psi$ if $\forall t_1 \in T(\pi_1), \exists t_2 \in T(\pi_2)$ such that $\Pi \models \varphi$, where $\Pi(\pi_1) = t_2$ and $\Pi(\pi_2) = t_2$. Intuitively, $T \models \psi$ if, assuming path variables belong to path sets defined according to T, the closed formula ψ holds. From then on, we assume that *every HyperLTL formula considered in this paper is closed*.

3.2   HyperLTL and PDSs

Let $\mathcal{P}$ be a PDS on the input alphabet $\Sigma = 2^{AP}$ and ψ a closed HyperLTL formula. We write that $\mathcal{P} \models \psi$ if and only if $T \models \psi$ where the set assignment function T is such that $\forall \pi \in \mathcal{V}, T(\pi) = Traces_\omega(\mathcal{P})$. Determining whether $\mathcal{P} \models \psi$ for a given PDS $\mathcal{P}$ and a given HyperLTL formula ψ is called the *model-checking* problem of HyperLTL on PDSs. The following theorem holds:

Theorem 1. *The model-checking problem of HyperLTL for PDSs is undecidable.*

The Intuition. We can prove this result by reducing the emptiness of the intersection of two context-free languages, a well-known undecidable problem, to the model-checking problem. Our intuition is to consider two context-free languages $\mathcal{L}_1$ and $\mathcal{L}_2$ on the alphabet Σ. As HyperLTL formulas apply to infinite words, we define two BPDA $\mathcal{BP}_1$ and $\mathcal{BP}_2$ that accept $\mathcal{L}_1 f^\omega$ and $\mathcal{L}_2 f^\omega$ respectively, where $f \notin \Sigma$ is a special ending symbol. We then define a PDS $\mathcal{P}$ that can simulate either $\mathcal{BP}_1$ or $\mathcal{BP}_2$.

We now introduce the formula $\psi = \exists \pi_1, \exists \pi_2, \varphi_{start} \wedge \varphi_{sync} \wedge \varphi_{end}$: φ_{start} expresses that trace variables π_1 and π_2 represent runs of $\mathcal{BP}_1$ and $\mathcal{BP}_2$ respectively, φ_{sync} means that the two traces are equal from their second letter onwards, and φ_{end} implies that the two traces are accepting. Hence, if $\mathcal{P} \models \psi$, then $\mathcal{BP}_1$ and $\mathcal{BP}_2$ share a common accepting run, and $\mathcal{L}_1 \cap \mathcal{L}_2 \neq \emptyset$.

On the other hand, if $\mathcal{L}_1 \cap \mathcal{L}_2 \neq \emptyset$, there is an accepting trace π common to $\mathcal{BP}_1$ and $\mathcal{BP}_2$ and we can define two traces π_1 and π_2 of $\mathcal{P}$ such that the formula $\varphi_{start} \wedge \varphi_{sync} \wedge \varphi_{end}$ holds. Since the emptiness problem is undecidable, so must be the model-checking problem.

Proof of Theorem 1. Let $\mathcal{L}_1$ and $\mathcal{L}_2$ be two context-free languages, and $\mathcal{P}_1 = (P_1, \Sigma \cup \{f\}, \Gamma, \Delta_1, \langle p_0^1, \bot \rangle, F_1)$ and $\mathcal{P}_2 = (P_2, \Sigma \cup \{f\}, \Gamma, \Delta_2, \langle p_0^2, \bot \rangle, F_2)$ two PDA accepting $\mathcal{L}_1$ and $\mathcal{L}_2$ respectively. Without loss of generality, we can consider that $P_1 \cap P_2 = \emptyset$. Let $e_1 \notin P_1$, $e_2 \notin P_2$, and $f \notin \Sigma$.

We define two BPDA $\mathcal{BP}_i = (P_i, 2^{\Sigma \cup \{f\}}, \Gamma, \Delta_i', \langle p_0^i, \bot \rangle, \{e_i\})$ for $i = 1, 2$, where Δ_i' is such that $(e_i, \gamma) \xrightarrow{\{f\}} (e_i, \gamma) \in \Delta_i$ and $(p_f, \gamma) \xrightarrow{\{f\}} (e_i, \gamma) \in \Delta_i$ for all $\gamma \in \Gamma$ and $p_f \in F_i$, and if $(p, \gamma) \xrightarrow{a} (p', w) \in \Delta_i$, then $(p, \gamma) \xrightarrow{\{a\}} (p', w) \in \Delta_i'$. If we consider that $\{a\}$ is equivalent to the label $a \in \Sigma \cup \{f\}$, $\mathcal{BP}_1$ and $\mathcal{BP}_2$ accept $\mathcal{L}_1 f^\omega$ and $\mathcal{L}_2 f^\omega$ respectively. Since HyperLTL formulas apply to infinite words in $2^A P$, for $i = 1, 2$, we have designed a BPDA $\mathcal{BP}_i$ that extends words in $\mathcal{L}_i$ by adding a final dead state e_i from which the automaton can only output an infinite sequence of a special ending symbol f.

We consider the PDS $\mathcal{P} = (\{p_0\} \cup P_1 \cup P_2, \{\{\iota^1\}, \{\iota^2\}\} \cup 2^{\Sigma \cup \{f\}}, \Gamma, \Delta, c_0)$, where $p_0 \notin P_1 \cup P_2$, $\iota^1, \iota^2 \notin \Sigma \cup \{f\}$, $c_0 = \langle p_0, \bot \rangle$, and $\Delta = \{(p_0, \bot) \xrightarrow{\{\iota^1\}} (p_0^1, \bot), (p_0, \bot) \xrightarrow{\{\iota^2\}} (p_0^2, \bot)\} \cup \Delta_1' \cup \Delta_2'$. The PDS $\mathcal{P}$ can simulate either $\mathcal{BP}_1$ or $\mathcal{BP}_2$, depending on whether it applies first a transition labelled by $\{\iota^1\}$ or $\{\iota^2\}$ from the initial configuration c_0.

We introduce the formula $\psi = \exists \pi_1, \exists \pi_2, \varphi_{start} \wedge \varphi_{sync} \wedge \varphi_{end}$ on $AP = \{\iota^1, \iota^2\} \cup \Sigma \cup \{f\}$, where $\varphi_{start} = \iota_{\pi_1}^1 \wedge \iota_{\pi_2}^2$, $\varphi_{sync} = \text{XG} \bigwedge_{a \in AP} (a_{\pi_1} \leftrightarrow a_{\pi_2})$, and $\varphi_{end} = \text{FG} (f_{\pi_1} \wedge f_{\pi_2})$. We suppose that $\mathcal{P} \models \psi$; φ_{start} expresses that trace variables π_1 and π_2 represent runs of $\mathcal{BP}_1$ and $\mathcal{BP}_2$ respectively. φ_{sync} means that the two traces are equal from their second letter onwards. φ_{end} implies that the two traces are accepting runs.

Therefore, if $\mathcal{P} \models \psi$, then $\mathcal{B}_1$ and $\mathcal{B}_2$ share a common accepting run and $\mathcal{L}_1 \cap \mathcal{L}_2 \neq \emptyset$. On the other hand, if $\mathcal{L}_1 \cap \mathcal{L}_2 \neq \emptyset$, there is an accepting run π common to $\mathcal{B}_1$ and $\mathcal{B}_2$, and we can then find two traces π_1 and π_2 of $\mathcal{P}$ such that the formula $\exists \pi_1, \exists \pi_2, \varphi_{start} \wedge \varphi_{sync} \wedge \varphi_{end}$ holds. The emptiness problem is, however, undecidable, and therefore so must be the model-checking problem. $\square$

As a consequence of Theorem 1, determining whether $T \models \psi$ for a generic set assignment function T and a given HyperLTL formula ψ is an undecidable problem.

3.3   HyperLTL and VPDSs

Since the emptiness of the intersection of visibly pushdown languages is decidable, the previous proof does not apply to VPDSs and one might wonder if the model-checking problem of HyperLTL for this particular subclass is decidable. Unfortunately, we can show that this is not the case:

Theorem 2. *The model-checking problem of HyperLTL for VPDSs is undecidable.*

The Intuition. In order to prove this theorem, we will rely on a class of two-stack automata called *2-visibly pushdown automata* (2-VPDA) introduced in [4]. In a 2-VPDA, each stack is input driven, but follows its own partition of Σ. The same input letter may result in different pushdown rules being applied to the first and second stack: as an example, a transition can push a word on the first stack and pop the top letter of the second stack, depending on which partition is used by each stack. Moreover, in a manner similar to VPDA, transitions of 2-VPDA do not depend on the top stack symbols unless they pop them.

It has been shown in [4] that the emptiness problem is undecidable for 2-VPDA. Our intuition is therefore to prove Theorem 2 by reducing the emptiness problem for 2-VPDA to the model-checking problem of HyperLTL for VPDSs. To do so, for a given 2-VPDA $\mathcal{D}$, we define a VPDS $\mathcal{P}$ and a HyperLTL formula ψ on two trace variables such that $\mathcal{P} \models \psi$ if and only if $\mathcal{D}$ has an accepting run.

$\mathcal{P}$ is such that it can simulate either stack of the 2-VPDA. However, both stacks must be synchronized in order to properly represent the whole automaton: the content of one stack can lead to a control state switch that may enable a transition modifying the other stack. The HyperLTL formula ψ determines which trace variable is related to which stack, synchronizes two runs of $\mathcal{P}$ in such a manner that they can be used to define an execution path of $\mathcal{D}$, and ensure that this path is an accepting one.

Introducing 2-Visibly Pushdown Automaton. Let Σ be a finite input alphabet with two partitions $\Sigma = \Sigma_{c_j} \cup \Sigma_{r_j} \cup \Sigma_{l_j}$, $j \in \{1, 2\}$. We then introduce a *2-pushdown alphabet* $\aleph = \langle (\Sigma_{c_1}, \Sigma_{r_1}, \Sigma_{l_1}), (\Sigma_{c_2}, \Sigma_{r_2}, \Sigma_{l_2}) \rangle$ on Σ.

Definition 6 (Carotenuto et al. [4]). *A 2-visibly pushdown automaton (2-VPDA) over $\aleph$ is a tuple $\mathcal{D} = (P, \Sigma, \Gamma, \Delta, c_0, F)$ where P is a finite set of control states, Σ a finite input alphabet, Γ a finite stack alphabet, $\Delta \subseteq (P \times \Gamma \times \Gamma) \times \Sigma \times (P \times \Gamma^* \times \Gamma^*)$ a finite set of transition rules, $c_0 = \langle p_0, \bot, \bot \rangle \in P \times \Gamma \times \Gamma$ an initial configuration, and $F \subseteq P$ a set of final states. Moreover, Δ is such that $\forall d \in \Delta$, and for $i \in \{1, 2\}$:*

- *if d is labelled by a letter in Σ_{c_i}, d pushes a word on the i-th stack regardless of its top stack symbol;*
- *if d is labelled by a letter in Σ_{r_i}, d pops the top letter of the i-th stack;*
- *if d is labelled by a letter in Σ_{l_i}, d does not modify the i-th stack.*

The semantics of 2-VPDA is defined in a manner similar to PDA, and so are configurations, runs, execution paths, languages, and 2-Büchi visibly pushdown automata (2-BVPDA). The following theorem holds:

Theorem 3 (Carotenuto et al. [4]). *The emptiness problem for 2-VPDA is undecidable.*

Proof of Theorem 2. Let $\mathcal{D} = (P, \Sigma, \Gamma, \Delta, \langle p_0, \bot, \bot \rangle, F)$ be a 2-VPDA on an input alphabet Σ according to a partition $\aleph = \langle (\Sigma_{c_1}, \Sigma_{r_1}, \Sigma_{l_1}), (\Sigma_{c_2}, \Sigma_{r_2}, \Sigma_{l_2}) \rangle$. We introduce a 2-BVPDA $\mathcal{BD} = (P, 2^{\Sigma \cup \{f\}}, \Gamma, \Delta', \langle p_0, \bot, \bot \rangle, \{e\})$ such that $(e, \gamma, \gamma') \xrightarrow{\{f\}} (e, \gamma, \gamma') \in \Delta'$ and $(p_f, \gamma, \gamma') \xrightarrow{\{f\}} (e, \gamma, \gamma') \in \Delta'$ for all $\gamma, \gamma' \in \Gamma$ and $p_f \in F$, and if $(p, \gamma, \gamma') \xrightarrow{a} (p', w, w') \in \Delta$, then $(p, \gamma, \gamma') \xrightarrow{\{a\}} (p', w, w') \in \Delta'$ on the input alphabet $\Sigma \cup \{f\}$. Obviously, $\mathcal{BD}$ is visibly if we add the symbol f to Σ_{l_1} and Σ_{l_2} and accepts $\mathcal{L}(\mathcal{D})f^\omega$, assuming the label $\{a\}$ is equivalent to the label $a \in \Sigma \cup \{f\}$.

Let P^1 and P^2 (resp. Δ^1 and Δ^2) be two disjoint copies of P (resp. Δ'). To each $p \in P$ (resp. $d \in \Delta'$), we match its copies $p^1 \in P^1$ and $p^2 \in P^2$ (resp. $d^1 \in \Delta^1$ and $d^2 \in \Delta^2$). We define a PDS $P = (\{\sigma\} \cup P^1 \cup P^2, \{\{\iota^1\}, \{\iota^2\}, \{f\}\} \cup 2^{\Delta^1} \cup 2^{\Delta^2}, \Gamma, \delta, \langle \sigma, \bot, \rangle)$. The set δ is such that, for each transition $d = (p, \gamma_1, \gamma_2) \xrightarrow{a} (p', w_1, w_2) \in \Delta$, $a \neq f$, we add two transitions $(p^1, \gamma_1) \xrightarrow{\{d^1\}} (p'^1, w_1)$ and $(p^2, \gamma_2) \xrightarrow{\{d^2\}} (p'^2, w_2)$ to δ. If $a = f$, we add instead $(p^1, \gamma_1) \xrightarrow{\{f\}} (p'^1, w_1)$ and $(p^2, \gamma_2) \xrightarrow{\{f\}} (p'^2, w_2)$. Transitions in δ are projections of the original transitions of the 2-BVPDA on one of its two stacks; their label depends on the original transition in Δ, unless they are labelled by f. Moreover, $(\sigma, \bot) \xrightarrow{\{\iota_1\}} (p_0^1, \bot)$ and $(\sigma, \bot) \xrightarrow{\{\iota_2\}} (p_0^2, \bot)$ both belong to δ.

$\mathcal{P}$ is such that it can either simulate the first or the second stack of the 2-BVPDA $\mathcal{BD}$, depending on which transition was used first. $\mathcal{P}$ is indeed a VPDS: a suitable partition of its input alphabet can be computed depending on which operation on the i-th stack transitions in Δ perform. As an example, if $d \in \Delta$ pushes a symbol on the first stack and pops from the second, d^1 belongs to the call alphabet and d^2, to the return alphabet.

Given a set of trace variables $\mathcal{V} = \{\pi_1, \pi_2\}$ and a predicate alphabet $AP = \{\iota^1, \iota^2, f\} \cup \Delta^1 \cup \Delta^2$, we then consider an unquantified HyperLTL formula φ of the form $\varphi = \varphi_{start} \wedge \varphi_{sync} \wedge \varphi_{end}$, where φ's sub-formulas are defined as follows:

Initialization Formula: $\varphi_{start} = \iota^1_{\pi_1} \wedge \iota^2_{\pi_2}$; $\Pi \models \varphi_{start}$ if and only if for $i \in \{1, 2\}$, $\Pi[1, \infty](\pi_i)$ is a run that simulates the i-th stack of $\mathcal{BD}$;

Synchronization Formula: $\varphi_{sync} = XG \bigwedge\limits_{d \in \Delta} (d^1_{\pi_1} \Leftrightarrow d^2_{\pi_2})$; $\Pi \models \varphi_{start} \wedge \varphi_{sync}$ if and only if $\Pi[1, \infty](\pi_1)$ and $\Pi[1, \infty](\pi_2)$ can be matched to a common run of the 2-BVPDA $\mathcal{BD}$;

Acceptance Formula: $\varphi_{end} = FG (f_{\pi_1} \wedge f_{\pi_2})$; $\Pi \models \varphi_{start} \wedge \varphi_{sync} \wedge \varphi_{end}$ if and only if $\Pi[1, \infty](\pi_1)$ and $\Pi[1, \infty](\pi_2)$ can be used to define an accepting run of the 2-BVPDA $\mathcal{BD}$.

Therefore, if $\Pi \models \varphi$, we have $\Pi(\pi_i) = (\iota^i, d_1^i, d_2^i \ldots)$ for $i = 1, 2$, and the sequence of transitions $(d_1, d_2, \ldots) \in \Delta^\omega$ defines an accepting run on $\mathcal{BD}$. Therefore, we can solve the model-checking problem $\mathcal{P} \models \exists \pi_1, \exists \pi_2, \varphi$, if and only if we can determine whether $\mathcal{L}(\mathcal{BD})$ is empty or not, hence, $\mathcal{L}(\mathcal{D})$ as well. By here is a contradiction and the former problem is undecidable.   □

4   Model-Checking HyperLTL with Constraints

Theorem 1 proves that the model-checking problem of HyperLTL for PDSs is undecidable. Intuitively, this issue stems from the undecidability of the intersection of context-free languages. However, since the emptiness problem of the intersection of a context-free language with regular sets is decidable, one can think of a way to abstract the set of runs of a PDS for some - but not all - path variables of a HyperLTL formula as a mean of regaining decidability.

As shown in [2,12], runs of a PDS can be over-approximated in a regular fashion. Hence, for a given PDS $\mathcal{P}$, if we consider a regular abstraction of the set of runs $\alpha(Traces_\omega(\mathcal{P}))$, we can change the set assignment function for a path variable π in such a manner that $T(\pi) = \alpha(Traces_\omega(\mathcal{P}))$ instead of $T(\pi) = Traces_\omega(\mathcal{P})$.

For a set assignment function T on a set of path variables $\mathcal{V}$ and a variable $\pi \in \mathcal{V}$, we say that π is context-free w.r.t. to T if $T(\pi) = Traces_\omega(\mathcal{P})$ for a PDS $\mathcal{P}$. We define regular and visibly pushdown variables in a similar manner.

Let $\psi = \chi_0 \pi_0, \ldots, \chi_n \pi_n, \varphi$ be a closed HyperLTL formula on the alphabet AP with $n + 1$ trace variables $\pi_0, \ldots, \pi_n$, where $\chi_0 \ldots, \chi_n \in \{\forall, \exists\}$. In this section, we will present a procedure to determine whether $T \models \psi$ in two cases.

1. If the variable π_0 is context-free w.r.t. T, and all the other variables are regular, then we can determine whether $T \models \psi$ or not. We can then apply this technique in order to over-approximate the model-checking problem if $T(\pi_0) = Traces_\omega(\mathcal{P})$, $T(\pi_j) = \alpha(Traces_\omega(\mathcal{P}))$ for $j = 1 \ldots n$, and $\chi_1, \ldots, \chi_n = \forall$. The last n variables can only be universally quantified. $T \models \psi$ then implies that $\mathcal{P} \models \psi$: indeed, the universal quantifiers on the path variables that range over the abstracted traces are such that, if the formula φ holds for every run in the over-approximation, then it also holds for every run in the actual set of traces. This is an over-approximation of the actual model-checking problem.
2. If there exists a variable π_i such that π_i is visibly context-free w.r.t. T, and all the other variables are regular, then we can determine whether $T \models \psi$ or not. A single path variable at most can be visibly context-free (not necessarily π_0, though), and all the others must be regular. We can then apply this technique in order to over-approximate the model-checking problem if $\mathcal{P}$ is a VPDS, $T(\pi_i) = Traces_\omega(\mathcal{P})$, $T(\pi_j) = \alpha(Traces_\omega(\mathcal{P}))$ and $\chi_j = \forall$ for $j \neq i$. Each path variable with the exception of the visibly context-free one must be universally quantified.

Because of the universal quantifiers on the regular path variables, $T \models \psi$ implies again that $\mathcal{P} \models \psi$. This is another over-approximation of the model-checking problem.

Moreover, these over-approximations are accurate for at least one variable in the trace variable set, as the original, ω context-free (or ω visibly pushdown) set of runs is assigned to this variable instead of an ω regular over-approximation.

4.1   With One Context-Free Variable and n Regular Variables

Let $\mathcal{P}$ be a PDS such that $T(\pi_0) = Traces_\omega(\mathcal{P})$, and $\mathcal{K}_1, \ldots, \mathcal{K}_n$, finite state transition systems (i.e. finite automata without final states) such that for $i = 1, \ldots, n$, $T(\pi_i) = Traces_\omega(\mathcal{K}_i)$.

Theorem 4. *If π_0 is context-free w.r.t. T and the other variables are regular, we can decide whether $T \models \chi_0\pi_0, \ldots, \chi_n\pi_n, \varphi$ or not.*

To do so, we use the following well-known result:

Lemma 1. *Let φ be an LTL formula. There exists a Büchi automaton $\mathcal{B}_\varphi$ on the alphabet 2^{AP} such that $L(\mathcal{B}_\varphi) = \{w \in (2^{AP})^\omega \mid w \models \varphi\}$. We say that $\mathcal{B}_\varphi$ accepts φ.*

An *unquantified* HyperLTL formula with m trace variables $\pi_1, \ldots, \pi_m$ can be considered as a LTL formula on the alphabet $(2^{AP})^m$: given a word w on $(2^{AP})^m$ and $a \in AP$, we say that $w \models a_{\pi_i}$ if $a \in w_i(0)$, where w_i is the i-th component of w. We then apply Lemma 1 and introduce a Büchi automaton $\mathcal{B}_\varphi$ on the alphabet $(2^{AP})^{n+1}$ accepting φ. We denote $\Sigma = 2^{AP}$.

We then compute inductively a sequence of Büchi automata $\mathcal{B}_{n+1}, \ldots, \mathcal{B}_1$ such that:

- $\mathcal{B}_{n+1}$ is equal to the Büchi automaton $\mathcal{B}_\varphi$ on the alphabet Σ^{n+1};
- if the quantifier χ_i is equal to $\exists$ and $\mathcal{B}_{i+1} = (Q, \Sigma^{i+1}, \delta, q_0, F)$ is a Büchi automaton on the alphabet Σ^{i+1}, let $\mathcal{K}_i = (S, \Sigma, \delta', s_0)$ be the finite state transition system generating $T(\pi_i)$; we now define the Büchi automaton $\mathcal{B}_i = (Q \times S, \Sigma^i, \rho, (q_0, s_0), F \times S)$ where the set ρ of transitions is such that if $q \xrightarrow{(a_0,\ldots,a_i)} q' \in \delta$ and $s \xrightarrow{a_i} s' \in \delta'$, then $(q, s) \xrightarrow{(a_0,\ldots,a_{i-1})} (q', s') \in \rho$. Intuitively, the Büchi automaton $\mathcal{B}_i$ represents the formula $\exists \pi_i, \chi_{i+1}\pi_{i+1}, \ldots, \chi_n\pi_n, \varphi$; its input alphabet Σ^i depends on the number of variables that are not quantified yet;
- if the quantifier χ_i is equal to $\forall$, we consider instead the complement $\mathcal{B}'_{i+1}$ of $\mathcal{B}_{i+1}$ and compute its product with $\mathcal{K}_i$ in a similar manner to the previous construction; $\mathcal{B}_i$ is then equal to the complement of this product; intuitively, $\forall \pi, \psi = \neg(\exists \pi, \neg\psi)$.

Having computed $\mathcal{B}_1 = (Q, \Sigma, \delta, q_0, F)$, let $\mathcal{P} = (P, \Sigma, \Gamma, \Delta, \langle p_0, \bot \rangle)$ be the PDS generating $T(\pi_0)$. We assume that $\chi_0 = \exists$. Let $\mathcal{BP} = (P \times$

$Q, \Sigma, \Delta', \langle (p_0, q_0), \bot \rangle, P \times F)$ be a Büchi pushdown automaton, where the set of transitions Δ' is such that if $q \xrightarrow{a} q' \in \delta$ and $(p, \gamma) \xrightarrow{a} (p', w) \in \Delta$, then $((p, q), \gamma) \xrightarrow{a} ((p', q'), w) \in \Delta'$. $\mathcal{BP}$ represents the fully quantified formula $\exists \pi_0, \chi_1 \pi_1, \ldots, \chi_n \pi_n, \varphi$. Obviously, $\mathcal{B}$ is not empty if and only if $T \models \psi$.

If $\chi_0 = \forall$, we consider instead the complement $\mathcal{B}'_1$ of $\mathcal{B}_1$, then define a Büchi pushdown automaton $\mathcal{BP}$ in a similar manner. $\mathcal{B}$ is empty if and only if $T \models \psi$.

It has been proven in [3,8] that the emptiness problem is decidable for Büchi pushdown automata. Hence, given our initial constraints on T and ψ, we can determine whether $T \models \psi$ or not.   □

The Büchi automaton $\mathcal{B}_\varphi$ has $O(2^{|\varphi|})$ states; if we assume that all variables are existentially quantified, the BPDS $\mathcal{BP}$ has $\nu = O(2^{|\varphi|}|\mathcal{P}||\mathcal{K}_1| \ldots |\mathcal{K}_n|)$ states. According to [8], checking the emptiness of $\mathcal{BP}$ can be done in $O(\nu^2 k)$ operations, where k is the number of transitions of $\mathcal{BP}$, hence, in $O(\nu^4 |\Gamma|^2)$.

Complementation of a Büchi Automaton may increase its size exponentially, hence, this technique may incur an exponential blow-up depending on the number of universal quantifiers.

Application. If we consider that π_0 range over $Traces_\omega(\mathcal{P})$ and that $\pi_1, \ldots, \pi_n$ range over a regular abstraction $\alpha(Traces_\omega(\mathcal{P}))$ of the actual set of traces, and we assume that $\chi_1, \ldots, \chi_n = \forall$, we can apply this result to over-approximate the model-checking problem, as detailed earlier in this section.

It is worth noting that the complement of an ω context-free language is not necessarily an ω context-free language. Hence, we can't use the previous procedure to check a HyperLTL formula of the form $\psi = \exists \pi, \forall \pi' \varphi$ where π' is a context-free variable and π is regular. We know, however, that ω visibly pushdown languages are closed under complementation. We therefore consider the case of a single visibly pushdown variable in the following subsection.

4.2 With One Visibly Pushdown Variable and n Regular Variables

Let $\mathcal{P}$ be a VPDS such that $T(\pi_i) = Traces_\omega(\mathcal{P})$, and $(\mathcal{K}_j)_{j \neq i}$ finite state transition systems such that for $j \neq i$, $T(\pi_j) = Traces_\omega(\mathcal{K}_j)$. Unlike the previous case, the visibly context-free variable no longer has to be the first one π_0.

Theorem 5. *If a variable π_i is visibly pushdown w.r.t. T and the other variables are regular, we can decide whether $T \models \chi_0 \pi_0, \ldots, \chi_n \pi_n, \varphi$ or not.*

The proof of this theorem is similar to the proof of Theorem 4. We first build a sequence of Büchi automata $\mathcal{B}_{n+1}, \ldots, \mathcal{B}_{i+1}$ in a similar manner to the proof of Theorem 4, starting from a finite state automaton $\mathcal{B}_{n+1} = \mathcal{B}_\varphi$ on the alphabet Σ^{n+1} representing the unquantified formula φ then computing products with the transition systems $\mathcal{K}_{n+1}, \ldots, \mathcal{K}_{i+1}$ until we end up with a Büchi automaton $\mathcal{B}_{i+1}$ on the alphabet Σ^{i+1}.

Having computed $\mathcal{B}_{i+1} = (Q, \Sigma^{i+1}, \delta, q_0, F)$, let $\mathcal{P} = (P, \Sigma, \Gamma, \Delta, \langle p_0, \bot \rangle)$ be the VPDS generating $T(\pi_i)$. We assume that $\chi_i = \exists$. Let $\mathcal{BP}_i = (P \times Q, \Sigma^{i+1}, \Delta', \langle (p_0, q_0), \bot \rangle, P \times F)$ be a visibly Büchi pushdown automaton, where

Δ' is such that if $q \xrightarrow{(a_0,\ldots,a_{i-1},a)} q' \in \delta$ and $(p,\gamma) \xrightarrow{a} (p',w) \in \Delta$, then $((p,q),\gamma) \xrightarrow{(a_0,\ldots,a_{i-1},a)} ((p',q'),w) \in \Delta'$. $\mathcal{BP}_i$ is indeed a BVPDA on the alphabet Σ^{i+1} as its stack operations only depend on its $i+1$-th variable. If $\chi_i = \forall$, we consider instead the complement $\mathcal{B}'_{i+1}$.

From the i-th variable onwards, we compute a sequence of visibly Büchi pushdown automata $\mathcal{BP}_i,\ldots,\mathcal{BP}_0$ on the alphabets $\Sigma^{i+1},\ldots,\Sigma^1$ respectively. For $i \geq k \geq 1$, if $\mathcal{BP}_k = (P',\Sigma^{k+1},\Delta',\langle p'_0,\bot\rangle,F')$, $\mathcal{K}_i = (S,\Sigma,\delta,s_0)$, and $\chi_k = \exists$, let $\mathcal{BP}_{k-1} = (P'\times S,\Sigma^k,\Delta'',\langle(p'_0,s_0),\bot\rangle,F''\times S)$ be a visibly Büchi pushdown automaton, where the set of transitions Δ'' is such that if $(p,\gamma) \xrightarrow{(a_0,\ldots,a_{k-1},a_i)} (p',w) \in \Delta'$ and $q \xrightarrow{a_{k-1}} q' \in \delta$, then $((p,q),\gamma) \xrightarrow{(a_0,\ldots,a_{k-2},a_i)} ((p',q'),w) \in \Delta''$. The last letter of each tuple always stands for the visibly pushdown path variable π_i: $\mathcal{BP}_{k-1}$ is visibly pushdown as its stack operations only depend on this variable. If $\chi_k = \forall$, we consider the complement $\mathcal{BP}'_k$ of $\mathcal{BP}_k$ instead, which is a visibly pushdown automaton as well.

We can check the emptiness of $\mathcal{BP}_0$. If it is indeed empty, then $T \models \psi$. $\qquad\square$

It has been proven in [1] that the complement of a VPDA incurs an exponential blow-up in terms of states. Hence, the technique shown here is exponential (in terms of time) in the size of $\mathcal{P}$ and φ.

Application. If we consider that π_i range over $Traces_\omega(\mathcal{P})$ and that $\pi_j, j \neq i$ range over a regular abstraction $\alpha(Traces_\omega(\mathcal{P}))$ of the actual set of traces, and we assume that $\chi_j = \forall$ for $j \neq i$, we can apply this result to over-approximate the model-checking problem, as detailed earlier in this section.

5   Model-Checking HyperLTL with Bounded Phases

In this section, we use results on *Multi-Stack Pushdown Automata* to define an under-approximation of the model-checking problem of HyperLTL formulas with universal quantifiers for PDSs.

Multi-stack pushdown systems (MPDSs) are pushdown systems with multiple stacks. Their semantics is defined in a manner similar to PDSs, and so are configurations, traces, runs, *Multi-Stack Pushdown Automata* (MPDA), and the semantics of LTL. MPDA are unfortunately Turing powerful even with only two stacks. Thus, La Torre et al. introduced in [16] a restriction called *phase-bounding*:

Definition 7 (Phases of runs). *A run r of a MPDS $\mathcal{M}$ is said to be k-phased if it can be split in a sequence of k runs $r_1,\ldots,r_k$ of $\mathcal{M}$ (i.e. $r = r_1 \ldots r_k$) such that during the execution of a given run r_i, at most a single stack is popped from.*

For a given integer k, this restriction can be used to define a phase-bounded semantics on MPDSs: only traces matched to runs with at most k phases are considered. It has been proven in [14] that the backward reachability set of MPDSs with bounded phases is regular and can be effectively computed; this property can then be used to show that the following theorem holds:

Theorem 6 (Model-checking with bounded phases [14]**).** *The model-checking problem of LTL for MPDSs with bounded phases is decidable.*

Phase-bounding can be used to under-approximate the set of traces of a MPDS. If a given LTL property φ does not hold for a MPDS $\mathcal{M}$ with a phase-bounding constraint, it does not hold for the MPDS $\mathcal{M}$ w.r.t. the usual semantics as well. We write $\mathcal{M} \models_k \varphi$ if the LTL formula φ holds for traces of $\mathcal{M}$ with at most k phases.

We can use decidability properties of MPDSs with bounded phases to under-approximate the model-checking problem for pushdown systems. Let $\mathcal{P} = (P, \Sigma, \Gamma, \Delta, c_0)$ be a PDS on the input alphabet $\Sigma = 2^{AP}$, and $\psi = \forall \pi_1, \ldots, \forall \pi_n, \varphi$, a HyperLTL formula on n trace variables with only universal quantifiers.

Our intuition is to define a MPDS $\mathcal{M}$ such that each stack represents a path variable of the HyperLTL formula. This MPDS is the product of n copies of $\mathcal{P}$. Because ψ features *universal quantifiers* only, the model-checking problem of the LTL formula φ for $\mathcal{M}$ is then equivalent to the model-checking problem of ψ for $\mathcal{P}$: $\mathcal{M}$ simulates n runs of $\mathcal{P}$ simultaneously, hence, LTL formulas on $\mathcal{M}$ can be used to synchronize these runs. We can therefore use a phase-bounded approximation of the former problem to under-approximate the latter.

We introduce the MPDS $\mathcal{M} = (P^n, \Sigma^n, \Gamma^n, n, \Delta', c_0')$, with an initial configuration $c_0' = \langle (p_0, \ldots, p_0), \bot, \ldots, \bot \rangle \in P^n \times \Gamma^n$ and a set of transitions Δ' defined as follows: $\forall d_1, \ldots, d_n \in \Delta^n$ where $d_i = (p_i, \gamma_i) \xrightarrow{a_i} (p_i', w_i)$ for $i = 1, \ldots, n$, the transition $((p_1, \ldots, p_n), \gamma_1, \ldots, \gamma_n) \xrightarrow{(a_1, \ldots, a_n)} ((p_1', \ldots, p_n'), w_1, \ldots, w_n)$ belongs to Δ'. The following lemma then holds:

Lemma 2. *$\mathcal{M} \models \varphi$ if and only if $\mathcal{P} \models \psi$.*

As a consequence, if $\mathcal{M} \not\models \varphi$, then $\mathcal{P} \not\models \psi$. We can then consider a phase-bounded analysis of $\mathcal{M}$: for a given integer k, if $\mathcal{M} \not\models_k \varphi$, then $\mathcal{M} \not\models \varphi$, hence $\mathcal{P} \not\models \psi$. We can therefore under-approximate the model-checking problem of HyperLTL formulas with universal quantifiers only.

6   Applications to Security Properties

We apply in this section our results to information flow security, and remind how, as shown in [6], security policies can be expressed as HyperLTL formulas. If we model a given program as a PDS or a VPDS $\mathcal{P}$ following the method outlined in [8], we can then either over-approximate or under-approximate an answer to the model-checking problem $\mathcal{P} \models \psi$ of a policy represented by a HyperLTL formula ψ for this program, or even try both if the first method used does not provide a definitive answer to the model-checking problem.

6.1 Observational Determinism

The *strict non-interference* security policy is the following: an attacker should not be able to distinguish two computations from their outputs if they only vary in their secret inputs. Few actual programs meet this requirement, and different versions of this policy have thus been defined.

We partition variables of a program into high and low security variables, and into input and output variables. The *observational determinism* property holds if, assuming two starting configurations have identical low security input variables, their low security output variables will be equal as well and can't be used to guess high security variables. It is a weaker property than the actual strict non-interference.

We model the program as a PDS $\mathcal{P}$ on the input alphabet 2^{AP}, where atomic propositions in AP contain variable values: if a variable x can take a value a, then $(x, a) \in AP$. We can express the observational determinism policy as the following HyperLTL formula:

$$\psi_{OD} = \forall \pi_1, \forall \pi_2, \left(\bigwedge_{a \in LS_i} (a_{\pi_1} \Leftrightarrow a_{\pi_2}) \right) \Rightarrow G \left(\bigwedge_{b \in LS_o} (b_{\pi_1} \Leftrightarrow b_{\pi_2}) \right)$$

where LS_i (resp. LS_o) is the set of low security input (resp. output) variables values. Using our techniques detailed in Sects. 5 and 4.1, we can both under-approximate and over-approximate the model-checking problem $\mathcal{P} \models \psi_{OD}$ that is otherwise undecidable.

A Context-Free Example. Let $AP = \{i, o, h_1, h_2\}$, $LS_i = \{i\}$, $LS_o = \{o\}$, and let $HS_i = \{h_1, h_2\}$ be a set of high security inputs. We suppose we are given a program that can be abstracted by the following PDS $\mathcal{P}$ on the alphabet $\Sigma = 2^{AP}$, the stack alphabet $\Gamma = \{\gamma, \bot\}$, and the set of states $P = \{p_0, p_1, p_2, p_3, p_4\}$, with the following set of transitions, as represented by Fig. 1:

$$(init)\ (p_0, \bot) \xrightarrow{\{i\}} (p_0, \gamma \bot) \quad (\mu_2)\ (p_2, \gamma) \xrightarrow{\{h_1\}} (p_3, \varepsilon)$$
$$(\lambda_1)\ (p_0, \gamma) \xrightarrow{\{h_1\}} (p_1, \gamma\gamma) \quad (\mu_3)\ (p_3, \gamma) \xrightarrow{\{o\}} (p_2, \gamma)$$
$$(\lambda_2)\ (p_0, \gamma) \xrightarrow{\{h_2\}} (p_1, \gamma\gamma) \quad (\nu_1)\ (p_3, \bot) \xrightarrow{\{o\}} (p_4, \bot)$$
$$(\lambda_3)\ (p_1, \gamma) \xrightarrow{\{o\}} (p_0, \gamma) \quad (\nu_2)\ (p_4, \bot) \xrightarrow{\{o\}} (p_4, \bot)$$
$$(\mu_1)\ (p_1, \gamma) \xrightarrow{\{o\}} (p_2, \gamma)$$

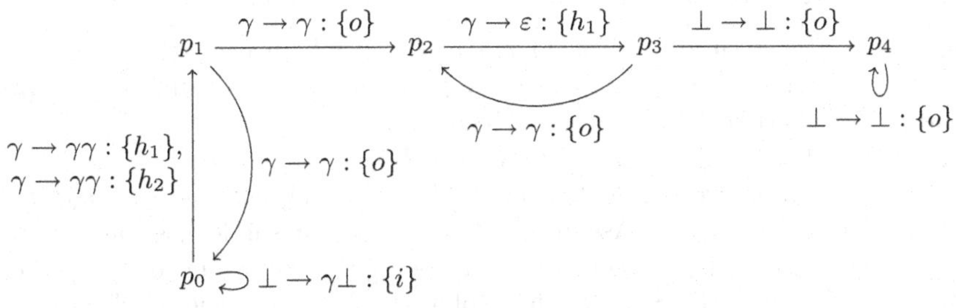

Fig. 1. The PDS $\mathcal{P}$

We would like to check if $P \models \psi_{OD}$, where ψ_{OD} is the observational determinism HyperLTL formula outlined above. Intuitively, it will not hold: two runs always have the same input i but, if they do not push the same number of symbols on the stack, their low-security outputs will differ.

Since transitions of $\mathcal{P}$ are only labelled by singletons, we can write ρ instead of $\{\rho\}$ when describing traces. The set $Traces_{\omega}(\mathcal{P})$ of infinite traces of $\mathcal{P}$ is equal to $\bigcup_{n \in \mathbb{N}} i \cdot ((h_1 + h_2) \cdot o)^n \cdot (h_1 \cdot o)^{n+1} \cdot o^*$: from the bottom symbol $\bot$, rules $(init)$, (λ_1), (λ_2), and (λ_3) push $n+1$ symbols γ on the stack, rules (μ_1), (μ_2), and (μ_3) pop these $(n+1)$ symbols, then rule (ν_2) loop in state p_4 once the bottom of the stack is reached again and rule (ν_1) has been applied. $Traces_{\omega}(\mathcal{P})$ is context-free, hence, we can't model-check the observational determinism policy on $\mathcal{P}$ using the algorithms outlined in [7].

Using the under-approximation technique outlined in Sect. 5, we can show that ψ_{OD} does not hold if we bound the number of phases to 2: we find a counter-example $\pi_1 = i \cdot h_2 \cdot o \cdot h_1 \cdot o \cdot o^*$ and $\pi_2 = i \cdot (h_2 \cdot o)^2 \cdot (h_1 \cdot o)^2 \cdot o^*$. We can therefore reach the conclusion that $\mathcal{P} \not\models \psi_{OD}$; the observational determinism security policy therefore does not hold for the original program.

6.2   Declassification

The strict non-interference security policy is very hard to enforce as many programs must, one way or another, leak secret information during their execution. Thus, we must relax the previously defined security properties.

We introduce instead a *declassification* policy: at a given step, leaking a specific high security variable is allowed, but the observational determinism must otherwise holds. As an example, let's consider a program accepting a password as a high security input in its initial state, whose correctness is then checked during the next execution step. The program's behaviour then depends on the password's correctness. We express this particular declassification policy as the following HyperLTL formula:

$$\psi_D = \forall \pi_1, \forall \pi_2, \left(\left(\bigwedge_{a \in LS_i} (a_{\pi_1} \Leftrightarrow a_{\pi_2}) \right) \wedge X\, (\rho_{\pi_1} \Leftrightarrow \rho_{\pi_2}) \right) \Rightarrow G\, \left(\bigwedge_{b \in LS_o} (b_{\pi_1} \Leftrightarrow b_{\pi_2}) \right)$$

where ρ is a high security atomic proposition specifying that an input password is correct. Again, using our techniques detailed in Sects. 5 and 4.1, we can both under-approximate and over-approximate the model-checking problem $\mathcal{P} \models \psi_D$.

Checking a Password. We consider a program where the user can input a low-security username and a high-security password, then get different outputs depending on whether the password is true or not.

Let $AP = \{u, pw_1, pw_2, pw_3, o, \rho, h_1, h_2\}$, $LS_i = \{u\}$, $LS_o = \{o\}$, let ρ be a variable that is allowed to leak, and let $HS_i = \{pw_1, pw_2, pw_3, h_1, h_2\}$ be a set of high security inputs. Assuming there is only a single username u and three possible passwords pw_1, pw_2, pw_3, pw_3 being the only right answer, we can consider the following PDS $\mathcal{P}$ on the alphabet $\Sigma = 2^{AP}$, the stack alphabet

$\Gamma = \{\gamma, \bot\}$, the set of states $P = \{p_0, p_1, p_2, p_3, p_{true}, p_{false}\}$, with the following set of transitions, as represented by Fig. 2:

$$(init_1) \quad (p_0, \bot) \xrightarrow{\{u, pw_1\}} (p_{false}, \bot) \quad (\mu_1) \quad (p_1, \bot) \xrightarrow{\{o\}} (p_1, \bot)$$

$$(init_2) \quad (p_0, \bot) \xrightarrow{\{u, pw_2\}} (p_{false}, \bot) \quad (\mu_2) \quad (p_2, \gamma) \xrightarrow{\{h_1\}} (p_2, \gamma\gamma)$$

$$(init_3) \quad (p_0, \bot) \xrightarrow{\{u, pw_3\}} (p_{true}, \bot) \quad (\mu_3) \quad (p_2, \gamma) \xrightarrow{\{h_2\}} (p_3, \gamma)$$

$$(pw_{true}) \quad (p_{true}, \bot) \xrightarrow{\{\rho\}} (p_1, \bot) \quad (\mu_4) \quad (p_3, \gamma) \xrightarrow{\{h_2\}} (p_3, \varepsilon)$$

$$(pw_{false}) \quad (p_{false}, \bot) \xrightarrow{\{o\}} (p_2, \gamma\bot) \quad (\mu_2) \quad (p_3, \bot) \xrightarrow{\{h_1\}} (p_3, \bot)$$

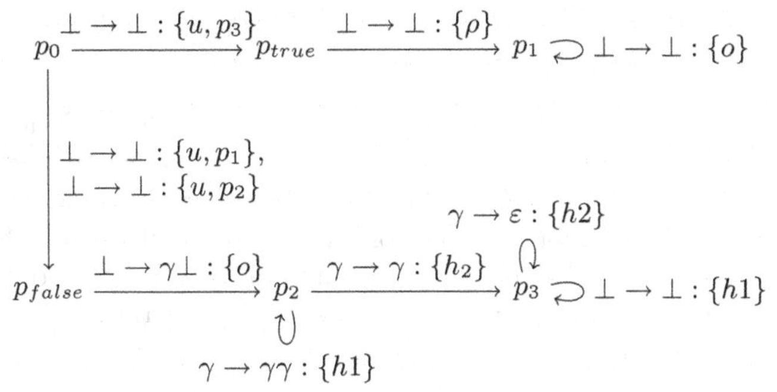

Fig. 2. The PDS $\mathcal{P}$

We would like to check if $P \models \psi_D$, where ψ_D is the declassification HyperLTL formula outlined above. Obviously, if we consider that $\rho \in LS_o$, then observational determinism does not hold: given the same username u, depending on whether the high-security password p_i chosen is right or not, the low-security output will differ. However, intuitively, the declassification policy should hold: given two different input passwords, the PDS will behave in the same manner as long as both are either true or false.

The set $Traces_\omega(\mathcal{P})$ of infinite traces of $\mathcal{P}$ is equal to $(\{u, p_3\} \cdot \{\rho\} \cdot \{o_1\}^*) \cup$ $\bigcup_{n \in \mathbb{N}} ((\{u, p_1\} + \{u, p_2\}) \cdot \{o\} \cdot \{h_1\}^n \cdot \{h_2\}^{n+2} \cdot \{h_1\}^*)$: from the bottom symbol $\bot$, if the right password pw_3 has been input, rules $(init_3)$ and (p_{true}) lead to state p_1 where the PDS loops; otherwise, if the password is wrong, rules $(init_1), (init_2)$ and (p_{false}) push a symbol γ and lead to state p_2, where rule (μ_2) pushes n symbols γ on the stack, then the PDS switches to state p_3 where it pops these $(n + 1)$ symbols with rules (μ_3) and (μ_4) then loops with rule (μ_5) once the bottom of the stack has been reached. $Traces_\omega(\mathcal{P})$ is context-free, hence, we can't model-check the declassification policy on $\mathcal{P}$ using the algorithms outlined in [7].

Using the over-approximation techniques detailed in Sect. 4.1, we can consider the regular abstraction $\alpha(Traces_\omega(\mathcal{P})) = (\{u, p_3\} \cdot \{\rho\} \cdot \{o_1\}^*) \cup ((\{u, p_1\} +$

$\{u, p_2\}) \cdot \emptyset \cdot \{h_1\}^* \cdot \{h_2\}^* \cdot \{h_1\}^*)$ of the actual set of traces. We can then reach the conclusion that $\mathcal{P} \models \psi_D$, since this property holds for the over-approximation as well; the declassification security policy therefore holds for this example.

6.3   Non-inference

Non-inference is a variant of the non-interference security policy. It states that, should all high security input variables be replaced by a dummy input λ, the behaviour of low security variables should not change and cannot therefore be used to guess the values of the aforementioned high security inputs.

We express this property as the following HyperLTL formula:

$$\psi = \forall \pi_1, \exists \pi_2, \, G \, (\bigwedge_{x \in V_i^h} (x, \lambda)_{\pi_2}) \wedge G \, (\bigwedge_{b \in LS} (b_{\pi_1} \Leftrightarrow b_{\pi_2}))$$

where LS stands for the set of all low security variables values, V_i^h for the set of high security input variables, and (x, λ) means that variable x has value λ. We can't rely on the method outlined in Sect. 4.1 because π_2 is existentially quantified, but an over-approximation can nonetheless be found using the method detailed in Sect. 4.2, if we model the program as a VPDS $\mathcal{P}$, choose π_2 as the visibly context-free path variable, and make it so that π_1 ranges over a regular abstraction of the traces.

7   Conclusion and Future Works

In this paper, we study the model-checking problem of hyper properties expressed by the logic HyperLTL for PDSs. We show that it is undecidable, even for the sub-class of visibly pushdown automata. We therefore design an automata-theoretic framework to abstract the model-checking problem given some constraints on the use of universal quantifiers in the HyperLTL formula. We also use phase-bounding constraints on multi-stack pushdown automata to under-approximate the actual answer. Finally, we show some relevant examples of security properties that cannot be expressed with LTL but can be checked using our approximation algorithms on a HyperLTL formula.

An implementation of these algorithms would be a valuable addition to existing model-checking software. We plan to design a new tool that would take as an input either a binary program or a Java program. We could perform in the former case a static analysis of the binary code with the tool Jakstab [11] that allows us to model the program as a control flow graph (CFG). By parsing this CFG, we could design a PDS model of the original code. In the latter case, we could use the PDS generated by the tool JimpleToPDSolver [10]. We could also handle C and C++ programs if we translate them into boolean programs with the tool SATABS [5].

References

1. Alur, R., Madhusudan, P.: Visibly pushdown languages. In: Proceedings of the Thirty-sixth Annual ACM Symposium on Theory of Computing, STOC 2004, pp. 202–211. ACM, New York (2004)
2. Bermudez, M.E., Schimpf, K.M.: Practical arbitrary lookahead LR parsing. J. Comput. Syst. Sci. **41**(2), 230–250 (1990)
3. Bouajjani, A., Esparza, J., Maler, O.: Reachability analysis of pushdown automata: application to model-checking. In: Mazurkiewicz, A., Winkowski, J. (eds.) CONCUR 1997. LNCS, vol. 1243, pp. 135–150. Springer, Heidelberg (1997). https:// doi.org/10.1007/3-540-63141-0_10
4. Carotenuto, D., Murano, A., Peron, A.: 2-visibly pushdown automata. In: Harju, T., Karhumäki, J., Lepistö, A. (eds.) DLT 2007. LNCS, vol. 4588, pp. 132–144. Springer, Heidelberg (2007). https://doi.org/10.1007/978-3-540-73208-2_15
5. Clarke, E., Kroening, D., Sharygina, N., Yorav, K.: SATABS: SAT-based predicate abstraction for ANSI-C. In: Halbwachs, N., Zuck, L.D. (eds.) TACAS 2005. LNCS, vol. 3440, pp. 570–574. Springer, Heidelberg (2005). https://doi.org/10.1007/978-3-540-31980-1_40
6. Clarkson, M.R., Finkbeiner, B., Koleini, M., Micinski, K.K., Rabe, M.N., Sánchez, C.: Temporal logics for hyperproperties. In: Abadi, M., Kremer, S. (eds.) POST 2014. LNCS, vol. 8414, pp. 265–284. Springer, Heidelberg (2014). https://doi.org/10.1007/978-3-642-54792-8_15
7. Clarkson, M.R., Schneider, F.B.: Hyperproperties. J. Comput. Secur. **18**(6), 1157–1210 (2010)
8. Esparza, J., Hansel, D., Rossmanith, P., Schwoon, S.: Efficient algorithms for model checking pushdown systems. In: Emerson, E.A., Sistla, A.P. (eds.) CAV 2000. LNCS, vol. 1855, pp. 232–247. Springer, Heidelberg (2000). https://doi.org/10.1007/10722167_20
9. Finkbeiner, B., Rabe, M.N., Sánchez, C.: Algorithms for model checking Hyper-LTL and HyperCTL*. In: Kroening, D., Păsăreanu, C.S. (eds.) CAV 2015. LNCS, vol. 9206, pp. 30–48. Springer, Cham (2015). https://doi.org/10.1007/978-3-319-21690-4_3
10. Hague, M., Ong, C.-H.L.: Analysing mu-calculus properties of pushdown systems. In: van de Pol, J., Weber, M. (eds.) SPIN 2010. LNCS, vol. 6349, pp. 187–192. Springer, Heidelberg (2010). https://doi.org/10.1007/978-3-642-16164-3_14
11. Kinder, J., Veith, H.: Jakstab: a static analysis platform for binaries. In: Gupta, A., Malik, S. (eds.) CAV 2008. LNCS, vol. 5123, pp. 423–427. Springer, Heidelberg (2008). https://doi.org/10.1007/978-3-540-70545-1_40
12. Pereira, F.C.N., Wright, R.N.: Finite-state approximation of phrase structure grammars. In: Proceedings of the 29th Annual Meeting on Association for Computational Linguistics, ACL 1991, pp. 246–255. Association for Computational Linguistics, Stroudsburg (1991)
13. Qadeer, S., Rehof, J.: Context-bounded model checking of concurrent software. In: Halbwachs, N., Zuck, L.D. (eds.) TACAS 2005. LNCS, vol. 3440, pp. 93–107. Springer, Heidelberg (2005). https://doi.org/10.1007/978-3-540-31980-1_7
14. Seth, A.: Global reachability in bounded phase multi-stack pushdown systems. In: Touili, T., Cook, B., Jackson, P. (eds.) CAV 2010. LNCS, vol. 6174, pp. 615–628. Springer, Heidelberg (2010). https://doi.org/10.1007/978-3-642-14295-6_53
15. Prasad Sistla, A., Vardi, M.Y., Wolper, P.: The complementation problem for Büchi automata with applications to temporal logic. Theoret. Comput. Sci. **49**(2), 217–237 (1987)

16. Torre, S.L., Madhusudan, P., Parlato, G.: A robust class of context-sensitive languages. In: 22nd Annual IEEE Symposium on Logic in Computer Science (LICS 2007), pp. 161–170, July 2007
17. Vardi, M.Y.: An automata-theoretic approach to linear temporal logic. In: Moller, F., Birtwistle, G. (eds.) Logics for Concurrency. LNCS, vol. 1043, pp. 238–266. Springer, Heidelberg (1996). https://doi.org/10.1007/3-540-60915-6_6

A Branching Time Variant of CaRet

Jens Oliver Gutsfeld$^{(\boxtimes)}$, Markus Müller-Olm, and Benedikt Nordhoff

Institut für Informatik, Westfälische Wilhelms-Universität Münster,
Einsteinstraße 62, 48149 Münster, Germany
{jens.gutsfeld,markus.mueller-olm,benedikt.nordhoff}@wwu.de

Abstract. A shortcoming of traditional logics like LTL and CTL on Pushdown Systems is their inability to express specifications about the call-/return-behavior or the stack content. A natural approach to this problem is the logic CaRet. CaRet adds modalities to LTL that allow specifications to navigate over calls and returns of procedures. In this paper, BranchCaRet, a natural CTL-like variant of CaRet is defined that provides existentially and universally quantified CaRet modalities. We prove that BranchCaRet model checking is decidable and EXPTIME-complete by extending a known CTL model checking algorithm for Pushdown Systems based on Alternating Büchi Pushdown Systems.

1 Introduction

In recent years, model checking has been ported from finite state systems to a plethora of other models. One of these model classes are Pushdown Systems (PDSs) which offer a natural abstraction of recursive programs [27]. Unlike finite Kripke structures, they represent a possibly infinite state space and allow us to track procedure calls using a call stack. In the last two decades, the well-known logics LTL and CTL as well as the full modal μ-calculus have been considered for PDSs [9,13,27,29,31]. However, these logics lack the ability to specify properties about the call-/return-behaviour or the stack content. An example property one would like to express is: "Every call has a matching return." The logic CaRet (**Ca**ll and **Ret**urn) [5] provides a solution to this problem. It extends the logic LTL by two types of modalities: abstract modalities and caller modalities. Intuitively, abstract modalities inspect the local behaviour of procedures, while caller modalities inspect the call chain. However, just like LTL, CaRet only defines properties for paths and cannot specify CTL-like requirements such as "There is a path arising from this configuration satisfying ϕ" or "For all paths arising from this configuration, ϕ holds".

In this paper, we propose the novel logic BranchCaRet, a CTL-style variant of CaRet, that combines the ability of CaRet to specify call/return-related properties with the ability of CTL to specify branching time properties. We show that the BranchCaRet model checking problem can be solved by reduction to

This work was partially funded by the DFG under project IFC4MC (MU 1508/2) in the priority program RS³ (SPP 1496).

the emptiness problem of Alternating Büchi Pushdown Systems and prove that it is EXPTIME-complete, like CTL model checking on PDSs [9].

This paper is organised as follows: In Sect. 2, we introduce several well-known classes of automata. In particular, we define Pushdown Systems as our model of systems, Alternating Büchi Pushdown Systems as our main tool of analysis as well as Büchi Pushdown Systems and Multiautomata.

Then, in Sect. 3, we formally introduce the logics BranchCaRet*, CaRet, and BranchCaRet and explain their potential usefulness as well as their relation to each other. In Sect. 4, we show how the BranchCaRet model checking problem can be decided using Alternating Büchi Pushdown Systems (ABPDSs) by extending the model checking algorithm of Song and Touili for CTL [29] to BranchCaRet. Finally, in Sect. 5, we summarise this paper and offer suggestions for future work.

Related Work. The logic CaRet was introduced by Alur et al. [5] for Recursive State Machines and ported to PDSs by Nguyen and Touili [24]. Several extensions of CaRet have later been proposed in the literature. These include past-time operators [10,25], a "Within"-modality [1] and a variant for multithreaded programs [21,22]. The practical usefulness of CaRet model checking for malware detection has been demonstrated by Nguyen and Touili [22,23]. Approaches to pushdown model checking have been conceptually unified by the frameworks of *visibly pushdown languages* [6] and *nested words* [4,7]. A generalisation of the modal μ-calculus called *visibly pushdown μ-calculus* that can express all CaRet properties is given by Alur et al. [3]. We should mention that the translation of CaRet is not direct but works via an encoding of a non-deterministic Büchi Visibly Pushdown Automaton computed from a given CaRet formula. Further logics for visibly pushdown languages were introduced by Bozzelli et al. [11] and Weinert et al. [32].

ABPDSs were introduced by Song and Touili [29] and our approach for the construction of the ABPDS from a BranchCaRet formula is based on their approach for CTL, as mentioned already. Model checking for classical logics such as LTL, CTL and the modal μ-calculus has been studied for some time in the literature [12,16,18]. A general overview of model checking techniques for PDSs can be found in Schwoon's Phd thesis [27].

On a practical level, the tools Moped [19] and PuMoC [28] are available for model checking pushdown systems.

2   Preliminaries

In this section, we introduce Pushdown Systems as our system model class and several language acceptor models. Let AP denote a finite, non-empty set of atomic propositions. A *Pushdown System* [8,29] is a tuple $\mathcal{P} = (P, \Gamma, \Delta, \lambda, I)$ consisting of a finite, non-empty set of control locations P, a finite, non-empty stack alphabet Γ, a transition relation $\Delta \subseteq (P \times \Gamma) \times (P \times \Gamma^*)$, a labelling function $\lambda : P \times \Gamma \to 2^{AP}$, and a non-empty set of initial configurations $I \subseteq P \times \Gamma$. We write $(p, \gamma) \to (p', \omega)$ to denote $((p, \gamma), (p', \omega)) \in \Delta$. By slight abuse of notation, we also write $(p, \gamma) \rightarrow (p', \omega) \in \Delta$. For simplicity, we assume that Δ is total. We say that a rule $(p, \gamma) \rightarrow (p', \omega) \in \Delta$ *pushes* symbols onto the stack if $|\omega| \geq 2$ and *pops* a symbol from the stack if $\omega = \varepsilon$. We also presume the existence of a bottom of stack symbol $\# \in \Gamma$. This symbol may never be pushed or popped and only self-loops (rules of the form $(p, \#) \rightarrow (p, \#)$) are allowed from it. We also require the existence of these self-loops since Δ is total. In the following, we use variants of γ, β and τ to denote symbols of Γ and variants of ω to denote elements of Γ^*. Following a widely used convention, we allow only the following types of rules in Δ: $(p, \gamma) \rightarrow (p', \gamma')$ (Internal actions), $(p, \gamma) \rightarrow (p', \beta\tau)$ (Calls) and $(p, \gamma) \rightarrow (p', \varepsilon)$ (Returns).

A configuration of $\mathcal{P}$ is a tuple $(p, \omega) \in P \times \Gamma^*$ and consists of a control location p and a stack ω. A configuration can be thought of as a snapshot of an execution of $\mathcal{P}$. We say (p, γ) is the *configuration head* of a configuration (p, ω) if $\omega = \gamma\omega'$. We use the same terminology for our other model classes.

The *reachability relation* $\Rightarrow_{\mathcal{P}} \subseteq (P \times \Gamma^+) \times \Delta^* \times (P \times \Gamma^*)$ for a PDS $\mathcal{P}$ is defined as follows: $(p, \omega) \overset{\varepsilon}{\Rightarrow}_{\mathcal{P}} (p, \omega)$, $(p, \gamma\omega) \overset{r_1 w}{\Longrightarrow}_{\mathcal{P}} (p', \omega')$ if $r_1 = (p, \gamma) \rightarrow (p'', \omega'') \in \Delta$ and $(p'', \omega''\omega) \overset{w}{\Rightarrow}_{\mathcal{P}} (p', \omega')$. We sometimes omit the rules and write $(p, \omega) \Rightarrow_{\mathcal{P}} (p', \omega')$ if there is a sequence of rules w such that $(p, \omega) \overset{w}{\Rightarrow}_{\mathcal{P}} (p', \omega')$ for $w \in \Delta^*$. Furthermore, we write $(p, \omega) \overset{+}{\Rightarrow}_{\mathcal{P}} (p', \omega')$ for $(p, \omega) \overset{w}{\Rightarrow}_{\mathcal{P}} (p', \omega')$ with $w \in \Delta^+$. From the reachability relation, we naturally obtain a function Pre^* : $2^{P \times \Gamma^*} \rightarrow 2^{P \times \Gamma^*}$ with $Pre^*(C) = \{(p, \omega) \mid \exists(p', \omega') \in C : (p, \omega) \Rightarrow_{\mathcal{P}} (p', \omega')\}$. The function Pre^* returns the set of configurations from which a given set of configurations is reachable.

We model the executions of Pushdown Systems by Kripke structures. The Kripke structure $\mathcal{K}_P = (Q, Q_0, \kappa, \delta)$ for a PDS $\mathcal{P} = (P, \Gamma, \Delta, \lambda, I)$ consists of the set of states $Q = P \times \Gamma^+$, the set of initial states $Q_0 = \{(p, \gamma\#) \mid (p, \gamma) \in I\}$, the labelling function $\kappa : P \times \Gamma^* \rightarrow 2^{AP}$ with $\kappa(p, \gamma\omega) = \lambda(p, \gamma)$, and the transition relation $\delta = \{(q, q') \in Q \times Q \mid \exists r \in \Delta : q \overset{r}{\Rightarrow}_{\mathcal{P}} q'\}$. A *path* of a Kripke structure is an infinite sequence $\pi = \pi_0\pi_1 \ldots$ such that $\pi_0 \in Q_0$ and $(\pi_i, \pi_{i+1}) \in \delta$ for all i. We write $\pi(i)$ for the configuration π_i. For a configuration $\pi(i) = (p, \omega)$ of a path π of $K_{\mathcal{P}}$, we write $|\pi(i)|$ to denote the size of the stack $|\omega|$. We denote the set of paths of $\mathcal{K}_{\mathcal{P}}$ by $\Pi_{\mathcal{P}}$. Furthermore, we denote by $Ext(\pi, i)$ the set $\{\pi' \in \Pi_{\mathcal{P}} \mid \forall j \leq i : \pi'(j) = \pi(j)\}$ of *possible extensions* of π at index i.

In order to analyse executions of PDSs, we need three types of successor functions: global successors, abstract successors and callers. We define these successor functions following Alur et al. [5]. The function $succ_g : \Pi_{\mathcal{P}} \times \mathbb{N} \rightarrow \mathbb{N}$ defined by $succ_g(\pi, i) = i+1$ is the *global successor function*. The global successor is the next index in the execution. $succ_g$ is a total function as all executions of PDSs are infinite and the configuration at the position $i + 1$ can thus never be undefined. In order to denote that a function is partial, we use the symbol $\rightsquigarrow$. The partial function $succ_a : \Pi_{\mathcal{P}} \times \mathbb{N} \rightsquigarrow \mathbb{N}$ with

$$succ_a(\pi, i) = \begin{cases} inf\,\{j \mid j > i \wedge |\pi(i)| = |\pi(j)|\}, & |\pi(i+1)| \geq |\pi(i)|, \\ undefined, & otherwise \end{cases}$$

is the *abstract successor function*. Unlike the global successor, it behaves differently for different types of configurations. If the configuration at index $i + 1$ is obtained by an internal rule, the abstract successor is equal to the global successor. If the configuration at index $i + 1$ is obtained by a call rule, the abstract successor is the corresponding return (or undefined if that return does not exist). If the global successor of the configuration at index i is a return, the abstract successor is always undefined.

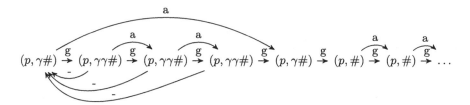

Fig. 1. A sample execution of a PDS $\mathcal{P} = (P, \Gamma\Delta, \lambda, I)$ where $P = \{p\}$, $\Gamma = \{\gamma, \#\}$, $\Delta = \{((p, \gamma), (p, \gamma\gamma)), ((p, \gamma), (p, \gamma)), ((p, \gamma), (p, \varepsilon)), ((p, \#), (p, \#))\}$, $\lambda(p, \gamma) = \lambda(p, \#) = \{\}$, and $I = \{(p, \gamma)\}$.

Finally, for $\pi \in \Pi_\mathcal{P}$ and $i \in \mathbb{N}$, let $M_{\pi,i} = \{j \mid j < i \wedge |\pi(j)| < |\pi(i)|\}$. The partial function $succ_- : \Pi_\mathcal{P} \times \mathbb{N} \rightsquigarrow \mathbb{N}$ defined by

$$succ_-(\pi, i) = \begin{cases} \sup M_{\pi,i}, & M_{\pi,i} \neq \emptyset \\ undefined, & otherwise \end{cases}$$

is the *caller function*. This function assigns to an index i the index of the last pending call before it, if there is one. Figure 1 illustrates the three different kinds of successor functions.

In order to find configurations from which calls without matching returns are possible, we use Büchi Pushdown Systems. A *Büchi Pushdown System* (BPDS) [27] is a tuple $\mathcal{BPS} = (P, \Gamma, \Delta, G)$ consisting of a finite, non-empty set of control locations P, a finite, non-empty stack alphabet Γ, a transition relation $\Delta \subseteq (P \times \Gamma) \times (P \times \Gamma^*)$, and a set of accepting control locations $G \subseteq P$.

The *reachability relation* and the function Pre^* for BPDSs are defined just as for PDSs, and we write $(p, \omega) \overset{w}{\Rightarrow}_{\mathcal{BPS}} (p', \omega')$ and $(p, \omega) \Rightarrow_{\mathcal{BPS}} (p', \omega')$. To avoid ambiguities, we also differentiate between $Pre^*_\mathcal{P}$ and $Pre^*_{\mathcal{BPS}}$.

A *run* $c = (c_0, c_1 \dots)$ of a BPDS $\mathcal{BPS} = (P, \Gamma, \Delta, G)$ is an infinite sequence of configurations with $c_0 = (p, \omega\#)$ and $c_i \overset{r_i}{\Rightarrow}_{\mathcal{BPS}} c_{i+1}$ for transition rules $r_i \in \Delta$. A run is *accepting* if it visits control locations from G infinitely often (Büchi condition). $\mathcal{BPS}$ accepts a configuration $(p, \omega\#)$ if there is an accepting run starting from $(p, \omega\#)$.

For two configurations c and c' of a BPDS $\mathcal{BPS} = (P, \Gamma, \Delta, G)$, we write $c \twoheadrightarrow c'$ to denote $c \Rightarrow_{\mathcal{BPS}} (g, \omega) \overset{+}{\Rightarrow}_{\mathcal{BPS}} c'$ for $g \in G$. Let $(p, \gamma) \in P \times \Gamma$ be a head. We say that (p, γ) is a *repeating head* iff $(p, \gamma) \twoheadrightarrow (p, \gamma\omega)$ for some $\omega \in \Gamma^*$. We denote the set of repeating heads by R.

Two well-known theorems guide our analysis of BPDSs:

Theorem 1 ([27]). *There is an accepting run from $(p, \gamma\omega)$ iff $\omega = \omega''\#$ and $(p, \gamma\omega) \Rightarrow_{BPS} (p', \gamma'\omega')$ for a repeating head (p', γ').*

Theorem 2 ([16]). *The repeating heads of a BPDS $\mathcal{BPS} = (P, \Gamma, \Delta, G)$ can be computed in time $\mathcal{O}(|P|^2 \cdot |\Delta|)$ and space $\mathcal{O}(|P| \cdot |\Delta|)$.*

In conjunction with Theorem 5, these theorems allow us to efficiently compute the configurations accepted by a BPDS.

For model checking our logic, we also need a variant of BPDSs with the ability to branch existentially and universally. This variant is given by Alternating Büchi Pushdown Systems. An *Alternating Büchi Pushdown System* (ABPDS) $\mathcal{BP} = (P, \Gamma, \Delta, F)$ consists of a finite, non-empty set of control locations P, a finite, non-empty stack alphabet Γ, a function $\Delta : (P \times \Gamma) \rightarrow \phi_{P \times \Gamma^*}$ that maps elements of $P \times \Gamma$ to positive boolean formulae over $P \times \Gamma^*$ in disjunctive normal form, and a non-empty set of final states $F \subseteq P$.

For any configuration head (p, γ), the associated formula $\phi = \Delta(p, \gamma)$ has the form $\bigvee_{j=1}^{n} \bigwedge_{i=1}^{m_j} (p_i^j, \omega_i^j)$. We can consider each conjunction as a rule $(p, \gamma) \rightarrow \{(p_1^j, \omega_1^j), \ldots (p_{m_j}^j, \omega_{m_j}^j)\}$ and ϕ as a whole to be the set consisting of the right hand sides of these rules. This allows us to express logical conditions that we want to be true as transition rules and vice versa. We always implicitly assume that there are two control locations $p, p' \in P$ such that $p \in F$ and $p' \notin F$ and for these states, the only possible transition rules are $(p, \gamma) \rightarrow \{(p, \gamma)\}$ and $(p', \gamma) \rightarrow \{(p', \gamma)\}$ for all $\gamma \in \Gamma$. For some fixed $\gamma \in \Gamma$, we use *true* to denote (p, γ) and *false* to denote (p', γ). Furthermore, we mostly provide the transition rules for ABPDSs by enumeration. Whenever we do not provide a transition rule for a head (p, γ), we implicitly assume $\Delta(p, \gamma) = false$ to ensure Δ is defined for all heads. A *run* ρ of an ABPDS $\mathcal{BP}$ is an infinite tree of configurations that has a root node c_0 and if the configurations $c_{i+1}, \ldots, c_k$ are the children of a node $c_i = (p, \gamma\omega)$, then there is a rule $(p, \gamma) \rightarrow \{(p_{i+1}, \omega_{i+1}), \ldots, (p_k, \omega_k)\} \in \Delta$ such that $c_i = (p_{i+1}, \omega_{i+1}\omega), \ldots, c_k = (p_k, \omega_k\omega)$ holds.

A *path* of a run ρ is a sequence $r_0 r_1 \ldots$ of configurations such that $r_0 = c_0$ and r_{i+1} is a child node of r_i. Such a run ρ of $\mathcal{BP}$ is *accepting* if every path of ρ visits control locations in F infinitely often. We say that $\mathcal{BP}$ accepts a configuration (p, ω) iff there is an accepting run from (p, ω). By construction, all runs arising from a configuration with configuration head *true* are always accepting and all runs arising from a configuration with configuration head *false* are not accepting.

The *reachability relation* for an ABPDS $\mathcal{BP} \Rightarrow_{BP} \subseteq (P \times \Gamma) \times 2^{P \times \Gamma^*}$ is given by the following rules: $(p, \omega) \Rightarrow_{BP} \{(p, \omega)\}$ and $(p, \gamma\omega) \Rightarrow_{BP} \{(p_1, \omega_1\omega), \ldots, (p_n, \omega_n\omega)\}$ if $(p, \gamma) \rightarrow \{(p_1, \omega_1), \ldots, (p_n, \omega_n)\} \in \Delta$, $(p, \gamma\omega) \Rightarrow_{BP} \bigcup C_i$ if $(p, \gamma\omega) \Rightarrow_{BP} \{(p_1, \omega_1), \ldots, (p_n, \omega_n)\}$ and $(p_i, \omega_i) \Rightarrow_{BP} C_i$.

For our model checking algorithm, we need to compute the configurations accepted by an ABPDS. This can be done, for instance, by exploiting corresponding constructions for Parity Pushdown Games (PPG). For a PPG, an Alternating Multiautomaton (AMA) can be computed that recognises whether a configuration belongs to the winning region of a given player in time exponential in the number of control locations and the maximum priority of the PPG [20]. Since an ABPDS corresponds to a PPG with maximum priority two and since there is an algorithm that checks whether an AMA accepts a configuration in time polynomial in the size of the AMA [15], we obtain the following:

Theorem 3. *For a configuration c of an ABPDS* $\mathcal{BP}$, *we can determine whether* $\mathcal{BP}$ *accepts c in time exponential in* $|P|$ *and polynomial in all other parameters.*

Finally, we need a class of automata that assists in reachability analysis and the definition of regular valuations. This class is given by Multiautomata. Let $\mathcal{P} = (P, \Gamma, \Delta, \lambda, I)$ be a PDS. A *Multiautomaton (MA)* [8,29] *for* $\mathcal{P}$ is a tuple $\mathcal{A} = (Q, \Gamma, \delta, Q_f)$ such that Q is a finite, non-empty set of states with $P \subseteq Q$, Γ, the input alphabet of $\mathcal{A}$, is the finite, non-empty stack alphabet of $\mathcal{P}$, $\delta \subseteq Q \times \Gamma \times Q$ is a transition relation and $Q_f \subseteq Q$ is a set of final states. We write $q \xrightarrow{\gamma} q'$ to denote $(q, \gamma, q') \in \delta$. $\rightarrow_\delta \subseteq Q \times \Gamma^* \times Q$ is the *reachability relation* for an MA given by the following rules: $q \xrightarrow{\varepsilon}_\delta q$ and $q \xrightarrow{\gamma\omega}_\delta q'$ if $q \xrightarrow{\gamma}_\delta q''$ and $q'' \xrightarrow{\omega}_\delta q'$ for some $q'' \in Q$. We say that an MA $\mathcal{A}$ accepts (p, ω) if $p \xrightarrow{\omega} q'$ for some $q' \in Q_f$. We define the language of $\mathcal{A}$ as

$$L(\mathcal{A}) = \{(p, \omega) \in P \times \Gamma^* \mid \mathcal{A} \text{ accepts } (p, \omega)\}.$$

A set of configurations is called *regular* if there is an MA that recognises it.

It is well-known that MAs are closed under union, intersection and complementation [8].

Theorem 4 ([14]). *For an MA* $\mathcal{A}$ *and a configuration* (p, ω), *it can be determined in time* $\mathcal{O}(|\delta| \cdot |\omega|)$ *whether* $(p, \omega) \in L(\mathcal{A})$ *holds.*

We can now state the following theorem which guides our analysis of possible abstract successors in PDSs:

Theorem 5 ([27]). *Let* $\mathcal{P} = (P, \Gamma, \Delta, \lambda, I)$ *be a PDS and* $\mathcal{A} = (Q, \Gamma, \delta, Q_f)$ *be an MA for* $\mathcal{P}$. *An MA* $\mathcal{A}_{Pre^*} = (Q, \Gamma, \delta', Q_f)$ *with* $L(\mathcal{A}_{Pre^*}) = Pre^*(L(\mathcal{A}))$ *can be computed in time* $\mathcal{O}(|Q|^2 \cdot |\Delta|)$ *and space* $\mathcal{O}((|Q| \cdot |\Delta|) + |\delta|)$.

3   CaRet and BranchCaRet

In this section, we briefly present the well-known logic CaRet and introduce the new logic BranchCaRet. In order to consider both logics in a common framework, we first introduce the novel logic BranchCaRet* that includes both logics as subsets in order to allow for a more concise definition. Intuitively, BranchCaRet* is analogous to CTL* while CaRet and BranchCaRet are analogous to LTL and CTL respectively.

A *BranchCaRet* formula* ϕ is a formula that can be built from the following context-free grammar:

$$\phi := ap \mid \neg\phi \mid \phi \wedge \phi \mid \phi \vee \phi \mid E\phi \mid A\phi \mid \bigcirc^f\phi \mid \bigcirc_W^l\phi \mid \phi\,\mathcal{U}^f\,\phi \mid \phi\,\mathcal{U}_W^a\,\phi \mid \phi\,\mathcal{R}^f\,\phi \mid$$
$$\phi\,\mathcal{R}_W^a\,\phi$$

for $f \in \{g, a, -\}$, $l \in \{a, -\}$ and $ap \in AP$. Since AP is non-empty, we can define $true \equiv ap \vee \neg ap$ and $false \equiv ap \wedge \neg ap$ for a fixed $ap \in AP$. We also define $\Rightarrow$ in the usual way. The semantics of BranchCaRet* is defined as follows. Let $\mathcal{P}$ be a PDS. $\mathcal{P}$ fulfills a formula ϕ (written $P \vDash \phi$) if and only if $\pi \vDash \phi$ for all $\pi \in \Pi_{\mathcal{P}}$ where $\pi \vDash \phi$ is inductively defined by the following rules:

1. $\pi \vDash \phi$ iff $(\pi, 0) \vDash \phi$,
2. $(\pi, i) \vDash ap$ iff $ap \in \kappa(\pi(i))$, $ap \in AP$,
3. $(\pi, i) \vDash \neg\phi$ iff $(\pi, i) \nvDash \phi$,
4. $(\pi, i) \vDash \phi_1 \wedge \phi_2$ iff $(\pi, i) \vDash \phi_1 \wedge (\pi, i) \vDash \phi_2$,
5. $(\pi, i) \vDash \phi_1 \vee \phi_2$ iff $(\pi, i) \vDash \phi_1 \vee (\pi, i) \vDash \phi_2$,
6. $(\pi, i) \vDash \bigcirc^f \phi_1$ iff $\exists k : succ_f(\pi, i) = k \wedge (\pi, k) \vDash \phi_1, f \in \{g, a, -\}$,
7. $(\pi, i) \vDash \bigcirc_W^f \phi_1$ iff $\forall k : succ_f(\pi, i) = k \Rightarrow (\pi, k) \vDash \phi_1, f \in \{a, -\}$,
8. $(\pi, i) \vDash \phi_1 \, \mathcal{U}^f \, \phi_2$ iff $\exists k : (\pi, succ_f^k(\pi, i)) \vDash \phi_2 \wedge$

$$\forall 0 \le l < k : (\pi, succ_f^l(\pi, i)) \vDash \phi_1, f \in \{g, a, -\},$$

9. $(\pi, i) \vDash \phi_1 \, \mathcal{U}_W^a \, \phi_2$ iff $((\pi, i) \vDash \phi_1 \, \mathcal{U}^a \, \phi_2) \vee$

$$(\exists k : succ_a^k(\pi, i) \text{ is undefined} \wedge$$

$$\forall 0 \le l < k : (\pi, succ_a^l(\pi, i)) \vDash \phi_1),$$

10. $(\pi, i) \vDash \phi_1 \, \mathcal{R}^f \, \phi_2$ iff $\forall k : (succ_f^k(\pi, i) \text{ is undefined} \vee$

$$(\pi, succ_f^k(\pi, i)) \vDash (\neg\phi_2)) \Rightarrow$$

$$(\exists n < k : (\pi, succ_f^n(\pi, i)) \vDash \phi_1),$$

11. $(\pi, i) \vDash \phi_1 \, \mathcal{R}_W^a \, \phi_2$ iff $((\pi, i) \vDash \phi_1 \, \mathcal{R}^a \, \phi_2) \vee$

$$(\exists k : succ_a^k(\pi, i) \text{ is undefined} \wedge$$

$$\forall 0 \le l < k : (\pi, succ_a^l(\pi, i)) \vDash \phi_2),$$

12. $(\pi, i) \vDash E\phi_1$ iff $\exists \pi' \in Ext(\pi, i) : (\pi', i) \vDash \phi_1$,
13. $(\pi, i) \vDash A\phi_1$ iff $\forall \pi' \in Ext(\pi, i) : (\pi', i) \vDash \phi_1$.

The BranchCaRet* model checking problem is to check whether $\mathcal{P} \vDash \phi$ for a given PDS $\mathcal{P}$ and a BranchCaRet* formula ϕ. We sometimes need to consider the equivalence of formulae and write $\phi \equiv \phi'$ for two BranchCaRet* formulae iff for any $\mathcal{P}$ and any $\pi \in \Pi_{\mathcal{P}}$, $\pi \vDash \phi \iff \pi \vDash \phi'$.

The modalities $\bigcirc^g$, $\mathcal{U}^g$ and $\mathcal{R}^g$ are just the usual LTL modalities, i.e. they navigate over sequences of global successors. On the other hand, the modalities $\bigcirc^a$, $\mathcal{U}^a$ and $\mathcal{R}^a$ navigate over abstract successors and the modalities $\bigcirc^-$, $\mathcal{U}^-$ and $\mathcal{R}^-$ navigate over callers.

The modalities $\bigcirc_W^f$, $\mathcal{R}_W^f$ and $\mathcal{U}_W^f$ are called *weak modalities*. For a formula $\bigcirc_W^f \phi$ involving the weak successor modality, it is required that either the respective successor fulfill ϕ or be undefined. Formulae with a weak Until-Operator, i.e. $\phi_1 \, \mathcal{U}_W^f \, \phi_2$, are fulfilled if either ϕ_2 holds at some point in the respective sequence or the respective successor is undefined at some point, and in both cases, all configurations before that point in the sequence fulfill ϕ_1. The weak Release-operator is defined analogously. Notice that the weak modalities can be derived from the normal modalities and we only introduce them for the purpose of constructing formulae in Negation Normal Form (NNF). The term *weak* is used only for modalities which also allow undefined successors in this paper and not for constructs such as the well-known weak Until from the literature that allows ϕ_1 to hold forever.

For caller modalities, the existential and universal variant have the same semantics because there is only one caller path anyway. We therefore consider only existential caller modalities in the following.

From the basic modalities, we can derive other well-known modalities such as $F^f \phi = true \, U^f \, \phi$ (*Future*) or $G^f \phi = \neg(true \, U^f \, \neg\phi)$ (*Generally*). Furthermore, we can define $\phi_1 \, \mathcal{U}_W^- \, \phi_2 = \phi_1 \, \mathcal{U}^- \, (\phi_2 \vee (\phi_1 \wedge \bigcirc_W^- false))$ and $\phi_1 \, \mathcal{R}_W^- \, \phi_2 = (\phi_1 \vee \bigcirc_W^- false) \, \mathcal{R}^- \, \phi_2$. Therefore, we did not include the modalities $\mathcal{U}_W^-$ and $\mathcal{R}_W^-$ in the syntax or semantics of BranchCaRet*.

The logic *CaRet* is the set of BranchCaRet* formulae which do not contain any quantifiers. For instance, formula $\bigcirc^a(\phi_1 \, U^- \, \phi_2)$ is a CaRet formula, while $\bigcirc^a(E \bigcirc^g \psi)$ is not because CaRet does not allow for quantifiers. CaRet was originally introduced in [5] for the model of Recursive State Machines (RSMs). However, it is well-known that the dynamic behaviour of RSMs can be represented by PDSs [2] and, indeed, CaRet has recently been ported to PDSs explicitly [24]. We therefore restrict our analysis to PDSs.

CaRet can be considered an extension of LTL with modalities for navigating over sequences of abstract successors and callers instead of only global successors (as in LTL).

3.1 BranchCaRet

The logic *BranchCaRet* is the set of BranchCaRet* formulae in which quantifiers are only present in front of modalities and all modalities are quantified. As an example, the formula $E\phi_1 U^g(A \bigcirc^a \phi_2)$ is a BranchCaRet formula, while $\bigcirc^a(A \bigcirc^g \phi_1)$ is not because the first modality is not quantified. The difference between CaRet and BranchCaRet is analogous to the difference between LTL and CTL: LTL and CaRet only allow modalities without quantifiers, CTL and BranchCaRet only allow quantified modalities. Therefore, CaRet is a logic that talks about linear properties of paths, while BranchCaRet is a branching-time logic.

Naturally, BranchCaRet can express branching time variants of CaRet properties such as the ones presented in [5]. Furthermore, it can express classical CTL properties in a local manner, i.e. on abstract paths and caller paths. It is well-known, for instance, that pushdown systems can be used for interprocedural dataflow analysis e.g. to identify live variables, very busy expressions or available expressions [3,17,26,27,30]. In BranchCaRet, we can now express specifications for these problems not just for global variables, but also for local variables using abstract modalities. In order to illustrate this, we assume that the variables of a program are divided into global (G) and local (L) variables with $G \cap L = \emptyset$. We call a variable x *live* at a control location u if there exists a path that, after visiting u, encounters a use of x without encountering a definition of x in between.

Now, to check whether a global variable x is live at a designated control location labelled At_u, we can use the specification $EF^g(At_u \wedge E(\neg def_x \, \mathcal{U}^g \, use_x))$, where the atomic proposition def_x is valid just for the control locations where the variable x is defined and use_x for those where it is used. Liveness of a local variable x can now be specified in BranchCaRet very similarly by the formula $EF^g(At_u \wedge E(\neg def_x \, \mathcal{U}^a \, use_x))$. Note that the abstract until modality $\mathcal{U}^a$ ensures that the uses and definitions of x are not confused with uses and definitions of other variables with the same name x, e.g. in recursively called instances of the same procedure. Similarly, recall that an expression e is *very busy* at a control location u if it is evaluated on all paths emerging from u before any of its free variables are redefined. To check whether an expression e that may contain local as well as global variables is very busy at u, we use the formula $AG^g(At_u \Rightarrow A((\bigwedge_{x \in FV(e) \cap G} \neg def_x) \, \mathcal{U}^g \, eval_e) \wedge A((\bigwedge_{x \in FV(e) \cap L} \neg def_x) \, \mathcal{U}^a \, eval_e))$, where $FV(e)$ denotes the free variables of e. Furthermore, we can express stack-related liveness properties in BranchCaRet. An example is the property that the stack can always fully be emptied which can be expressed by the following specification: $AG^g(E \, F^g \, (E \, \bigcirc_W^- \, false)$. Another example is the property that for every call, it is possible to return later. Assuming that control locations from which calls are possible are labelled *call* and no other actions are possible from these control locations, we can describe this property by the formula $AG^g(call \Rightarrow E \, \bigcirc^a \, true)$. In this setting, the same property can be expressed by $AG^g(E \, \bigcirc_W^- \, (E \, \bigcirc^a \, true))$ without the assumption that calls are labelled.

For the relation between CaRet and BranchCaRet, we have the following theorem since we can consider both logics on Kripke structures (treated as PDSs without stack action) only and they then reduce to LTL and CTL respectively:

Theorem 6. *The expressive power of BranchCaRet and CaRet is incomparable.*

4   Model Checking

4.1   Computing Abstract Successors and Loops

In addition to the well-known CTL modalities, BranchCaRet allows us to reference callers and abstract successors. In order to cope with the latter in a model checking procedure, two problems need to be considered. First of all, we have to compute all possible abstract successors for a given configuration. Secondly, we need to find the heads from which a call without a matching return is possible. This is necessary for handling abstract modalities correctly.

The first problem is solved by precomputing the heads of possible abstract successors. It is easy to see that the head of a possible abstract successor depends only on the head of the current configuration. Hence we can reduce the analysis of abstract successors of configurations to the analysis of abstract successors of heads. For this purpose, we introduce the function $PSReturns_H : P \times \Gamma \to 2^{P \times \Gamma}$ defined by

$$PSReturns_H(p, \gamma) = \{(p', \tau) | (p, \gamma) \to (p'', \beta\tau) \wedge (p'', \beta\#) \Rightarrow_P (p', \#)\}.$$

This function associates every head with heads of possible returns.

Theorem 7. *Let $\pi \in \Pi_{\mathcal{P}}$ and $\pi(i) = (p, \gamma\omega)$. There is $\pi' \in Ext(\pi, i)$ such that (π', i) is a call and $succ_a(\pi', i) = k$ and $\pi'(k) = (p', \tau\omega)$ iff $(p', \tau) \in PSReturns_H(p, \gamma)$.*

Theorem 7 implies we solely need $PSReturns_H$ to find the possible heads of returns for a call.

Algorithm 1. An algorithm for computing PSReturns$_H$.

1: Input: A PDS $\mathcal{P} = (P, \Gamma, \Delta, \lambda, I)$
2: Output: The function $PSReturns_H$ as a set
3: $Calls = \{(p, \gamma) \rightarrow (p'', \beta\tau) \in \Delta\}$;
4: **for all** $(p, \gamma) \in P \times \Gamma$ **do**
5:     $PSReturns_H(p, \gamma) = \emptyset$;
6: **while** $Calls \neq \emptyset$ **do**
7:     Choose and remove a rule $(p, \gamma) \rightarrow (p'', \beta\tau)$ from $Calls$;
8:     **for all** $p' \in P$ **do**
9:         **if** $((p'', \beta\#) \in Pre^*(\{(p', \#)\}))$ **then**
10:             $PSReturns_H(p, \gamma) = PSReturns_H(p, \gamma) \cup \{(p', \tau)\}$;
11: return $PSReturns_H$;

From the definition of $PSReturns_H$, we can directly infer a procedure to compute it. This procedure is given by Algorithm 1.

Using Theorems 4 and 5 for the complexity of the computation of Pre^* and the membership check in the MA generated by the Pre^* algorithm, we obtain the following complexity:

Theorem 8. *Algorithm 1 computes $PSReturns_H$ in time $\mathcal{O}(|\Delta|^2 \cdot |P|)$.*

We now turn to the analysis of possibly undefined abstract successors. For a PDS $\mathcal{P} = (P, \Gamma, \Delta, \lambda, I)$, let $PSLoops_H \subseteq P \times \Gamma$ be the set such that $(p, \gamma) \in PSLoops_H$ iff there is $(p, \gamma) \rightarrow (p', \beta\tau) \in \Delta$ and an infinite sequence $c_0 c_1 \ldots$ with $c_0 = (p', \beta\#)$. For each c_i we require a rule $r_i \in \Delta$ such that $c_i \overset{r_i}{\Rightarrow}_{\mathcal{P}} c_{i+1}$ and $|c_i| \geq |c_0|$ must hold for all i. The set $PSLoops_H$ thus characterises the heads from which a call with an undefined abstract successor is possible. The name $PSLoops_H$ for configurations with calls without matching returns is chosen in the spirit of infinite loops in computer programs.

Theorem 9. *Let $\mathcal{P} = (P, \Gamma, \Delta, \lambda, I)$ be a PDS, $\pi \in \Pi_{\mathcal{P}}$ and $\pi(i) = (p, \gamma\omega)$ for $i \in \mathbb{N}$. There is $\pi' \in Ext(\pi, i)$ such that (π', i) is a call and $succ_a(\pi', i)$ is undefined iff $(p, \gamma) \in PSLoops_H$.*

Let $\mathcal{P} = (P, \Gamma, \Delta, \lambda, I)$ be a PDS. Then $\mathcal{BPS}_{\mathcal{P}} = (P', \Gamma, \Delta', G)$ is the associated BPDS with $P' = P \dot{\cup} \{p_{loop}\}$, $\Delta' = (\Delta \setminus \{(p, \#) \rightarrow (p, \#) \mid p \in P\}) \cup \{(p, \#) \rightarrow (p_{loop}, \#) \mid p \in P'\}$ and $G = P$.

Theorem 10. *For any head (p, γ), $(p, \gamma) \in PSLoops_H$ iff there is $(p, \gamma) \rightarrow (p', \beta\tau) \in \Delta$ and there is an accepting run from $(p', \beta\#)$ in $\mathcal{BPS}_{\mathcal{P}}$.*

Algorithm 2. An algorithm for computing $PSLoops_H$.

1: Input: A PDS $\mathcal{P} = (P, \Gamma, \Delta, \lambda, I)$
2: Output: The set $PSLoops_H$
3: $Calls = \{(p, \gamma) \rightarrow (p', \beta\tau) \in \Delta\}$;
4: $PSLoops_H = \emptyset$;
5: Construct $\mathcal{BPS}_\mathcal{P}$;
6: Compute the repeating heads R of $\mathcal{BPS}_\mathcal{P}$;
7: **while** $Calls \neq \emptyset$ **do**
8:     Remove a rule $(p, \gamma) \rightarrow (p', \beta\tau)$ from $Calls$;
9:     **if** $(p', \beta\#) \in Pre^*_{\mathcal{BPS}}(\{(p'', \gamma''\omega) \mid (p'', \gamma'') \in R\})$ **then**
10:         $PSLoops_H = PSLoops_H \cup \{(p, \gamma)\}$;
11: Return $PSLoops_H$;

Algorithm 2 uses the observation from Theorem 10 that $PSLoops_H$ can be computed by analysing accepting runs from heads in $\mathcal{BPS}_\mathcal{P}$. Using Theorems 2, 4 and 5, we obtain the following complexity result:

Theorem 11. *Algorithm 2 computes the set $PSLoops_H$ in time $\mathcal{O}(|\Delta|^2 \cdot |P|^2)$.*

4.2 Configurations with Call Histories

In order to check formulae involving caller modalities, we need to know the last call without a matching return that was made before a configuration. However, there is in general no way to infer this call just from the configuration itself because different calls can lead to the same configuration. In order to solve this problem, we store the caller's head in the stack. For this, we use special stack symbols of the form $(\gamma, (p', \gamma'))$. More concretely, for a call rule $(p, \gamma) \rightarrow (p', \beta\tau)$, we switch to $(p', \beta(\tau, (p, \gamma)))$ instead of $(p', \beta\tau)$. For this purpose, we introduce *configurations with call histories*. Let $\Sigma = (P \times \Gamma)$ be the set of possible caller heads and $\Xi = \Gamma \cup (\Gamma \times \Sigma)$ be the set of stack symbols and stack symbols equipped with caller heads. We call the elements of $P \times \Xi^+$ *configurations with call histories*. In the following, we use variants of ξ for elements of Ξ, variants of σ to denote elements of Σ and variants of Ω to denote elements of Ξ^*. In each configuration with call history, the symbol from Γ is the usual stack symbol as in a normal configuration and the symbol from Ξ denotes the head of the caller.

In order to employ configurations with call histories for model checking, we need a method to construct a configuration with call history from a configuration in a path. The function $Conf$ serves this purpose. Let $\pi \in \Pi_\mathcal{P}, \pi(i) = (p, \gamma_1 \ldots \gamma_n\#)$ and $\pi(succ^m_-(\pi, i)) = (p'_m, \gamma'_m\omega_m)$ for $1 \leq m < n$. Then $Conf : (\Pi_\mathcal{P} \times \mathbb{N}) \rightarrow (P \times \Xi^+)$,

$$Conf(\pi, i) = \begin{cases} (p, \gamma_1(\gamma_2, (p'_1, \gamma'_1)) \ldots (\gamma_n, (p'_{n-1}, \gamma'_{n-1}))\#), & n > 1 \\ (p, \gamma_1\#), & n = 1 \\ (p, \#), & n = 0 \end{cases}$$

is the function that assigns to each (π, i) the corresponding configuration with call history.

Configurations with call histories now enable us to handle caller modalities very easily. Whenever we need to reason about the caller of (π, i) and $Conf(\pi, i) = (p, \gamma(\gamma', (p', \gamma'')) \Omega)$, we can just pop the symbol γ from the stack and afterwards switch to $(p', \gamma'' \Omega)$ to restore the caller.

For the analysis of configurations with call histories, we introduce two types of successor relations. These relations lift the global and the abstract successor to configurations with call histories. The relation $\hookrightarrow_g \subseteq (P \times \Gamma) \times (P \times \Xi^*)$ is the smallest relation for which the following conditions hold:

1. If $(p, \gamma) \to (p', \gamma') \in \Delta$, then $(p, \gamma) \hookrightarrow_g (p', \gamma')$.
2. If $(p, \gamma) \to (p', \varepsilon) \in \Delta$, then $(p, \gamma) \hookrightarrow_g (p', \varepsilon)$.
3. If $(p, \gamma) \to (p', \beta\tau) \in \Delta$, then $(p, \gamma) \hookrightarrow_g (p', \beta(\tau, (p, \gamma)))$.

The relation $\hookrightarrow_g$ lifts the global successor to configurations with call histories. For internal moves, the transition is the same as in Δ. For calls, the control location and top of stack symbol are updated, but additionally, the head of the caller is saved in the second stack symbol. This enables us to reconstruct the caller at any point of time. The relation $\hookrightarrow_a \subseteq (P \times \Gamma) \times (P \times \Xi^*)$ is the smallest relation for which the following conditions hold:

1. If $(p, \gamma) \to (p', \gamma') \in \Delta$, then $(p, \gamma) \hookrightarrow_a (p', \gamma')$.
2. If $(p', \tau) \in PSReturns_H(p, \gamma)$, then $(p, \gamma) \hookrightarrow_a (p', \tau)$.

The relation $\hookrightarrow_a$ lifts the abstract successor to configurations with call histories. If a possible abstract successor is given by an internal move, it works exactly as $\hookrightarrow_g$. On the other hand, if a call from the current configuration is possible and a matching return exists, $\hookrightarrow_a$ can jump directly to that successor.

We now introduce ADF (**A**lways **Def**ined) sets that indicate whether successors of different types are always defined for configurations.

- $ADF_a = \{(p, \gamma\Omega) \mid (p, \gamma) \to (p', \varepsilon) \notin \Delta \land (p, \gamma) \notin PSLoops_H\}$ is the set of configurations with call histories such that $succ_a(\pi, i)$ is always defined iff $Conf(\pi, i) \in ADF_a$.
- $ADF_g = P \times \Xi^+$ is the set of configurations with call histories such that $succ_g(\pi, i)$ is always defined iff $Conf(\pi, i) \in ADF_g$.

Notice that since $succ_g(\pi, i)$ is always defined, we introduce the set ADF_g for mere notational convenience to simplify rules in our ABPDS.

4.3   Negation Normal Form

In order to check whether a formula holds in a given PDS, we need to transform the formula to a special form for the construction of the ABPDS. A BranchCaRet formula is in *Negation Normal Form* (NNF) iff the operator $\neg$ occurs only in front of atomic propositions.

Since the existential quantifier is dual to the universal quantifier and $\bigcirc_W$, $\mathcal{U}_W$ and $\mathcal{R}_W$ are dual to $\bigcirc$, $\mathcal{R}$ and $\mathcal{U}$ respectively, we can drive the negations inwards to obtain a BranchCaRet formula ϕ' in NNF for any BranchCaRet formula ϕ. Hence, we have:

Theorem 12. *For every BranchCaRet formula ϕ, there is an equivalent BranchCaRet formula ϕ' in NNF.*

4.4   An ABPDS for BranchCaRet Model Checking

In this section, we define the ABPDS for a PDS and a formula and show how it can be used for model checking. Our construction extends the construction by Song and Touili for CTL [29]. The construction we use for the global modalities is largely the same as theirs, but we also need to take abstract successors and callers into account. We thus have to add appropriate transitions to possible returns and save the call history on the stack to handle caller modalities. Our construction relies on the closure of a formula. This closure will be used to define the states of our ABPDS: For a BranchCaRet formula ϕ in NNF, the closure $cl(\phi)$ is the smallest set such that

- $\phi \in cl(\phi)$,
- If $\phi_1 \wedge \phi_2 \in cl(\phi)$ or $\phi_1 \vee \phi_2 \in cl(\phi)$, then $\phi_1 \in cl(\phi)$ and $\phi_2 \in cl(\phi)$,
- If $\phi' \equiv Q\ Op\ \psi \in cl(\phi)$, then $\psi \in cl(\phi)$, $Op \in \{\bigcirc^f, \bigcirc_W^l\}$,
- If $Q\ \phi_1\ Op\ \phi_2 \in cl(\phi)$, then $\phi_1 \in cl(\phi)$ and $\phi_2 \in cl(\phi)$, $Op \in \{\mathcal{U}^f, \mathcal{R}^f, \mathcal{U}_W^l, \mathcal{R}_W^l\}$,
- If $\phi' \equiv E\ \phi_1\ Op\ \phi_2 \in cl(\phi)$, then $\phi_1 \in cl(\phi)$, $\phi_2 \in cl(\phi)$ and $E \bigcirc^- \phi' \in cl(\phi)$, $Op \in \{\mathcal{R}^-, \mathcal{U}^-\}$
- If $\phi' \equiv E\ \phi_1\ Op\ \phi_2 \in cl(\phi)$, then $\phi_1 \in cl(\phi)$, $\phi_2 \in cl(\phi)$ and $E \bigcirc_W^- \phi' \in cl(\phi)$, $Op \in \{\mathcal{R}_W^-, \mathcal{U}_W^-\}$

for $f \in \{g, a, -\}$, $l \in \{g, a\}$ and $Q \in \{E, A\}$. For a formula ϕ without caller modalities, the closure is simply the set of subformulae of ϕ. On the other hand, for caller modalities, we also require that the formula itself as well as an appropriate formula involving a caller modality be in the closure. This is necessary because caller modalities are backwards looking. For example, when we encounter a Caller-Until formula $\phi \equiv \phi_1\ \mathcal{U}^-\ \phi_2$ and we see that ϕ_2 does not hold at (π, i), we need to check whether ϕ_1 holds at (π, i) and ϕ holds at the caller of (π, i). We can do this by checking the formula $\phi' \equiv \phi_1 \wedge E \bigcirc^- \phi$, but for this purpose, we need $E \bigcirc^- \phi$ in the closure of ϕ.

Let $\mathcal{P} = (P, \Gamma, \Delta, \lambda, I)$ be a PDS and ϕ be a BranchCaRet formula in NNF. Let further $P' = (P \cup \{p_c\}) \times cl(\phi)$ for a fresh control location p_c. We denote the elements of P' as $[p, \phi]$ and $[p_c, \phi]$ respectively. We define an ABPDS $\mathcal{BP} = (P', \Xi, \Delta', F)$. Let $F \subseteq P'$ be the smallest set such that

1. $[p, ap] \in F$, $ap \in AP$,
2. $[p, \neg ap] \in F$, $ap \in AP$,
3. $[p, E\ \phi_1\ \mathcal{R}^f\ \phi_2] \in F$, $f \in \{g, a\}$,

4. $[p, A\ \phi_1\ \mathcal{R}^f\ \phi_2] \in F$, $f \in \{g, a\}$,
5. $[p, E\ \phi_1\ \mathcal{R}^a_W\ \phi_2] \in F$,
6. $[p, A\ \phi_1\ \mathcal{R}^a_W\ \phi_2] \in F$

iff the respective control locations are members of P'. In order to define the transition rules of Δ, we often use conjunctions of the form $\bigwedge_{i \in I} \phi_i$ and disjunctions of the form $\bigvee_{i \in I} \phi_i$ for an index set I and certain formulae ϕ_i. We adopt the convention that if I is empty, $\bigwedge_{i \in I} \phi_i$ evaluates to *true* and $\bigvee_{i \in I} \phi_i$ evaluates to *false*. Δ' has the following transition rules iff the respective control locations of the form $[p, \phi]$ and $[p_c, \phi]$ are members of P':

1. $([p, \phi], (\gamma, (p, \gamma'))) \rightarrow ([p, \phi], \gamma) \in \Delta'$,
2. $([p, ap], \gamma) \rightarrow ([p, ap], \gamma) \in \Delta', ap \in AP \wedge ap \in \lambda(p, \gamma)$,
3. $([p, \neg ap], \gamma) \rightarrow ([p, \neg ap], \gamma) \in \Delta', ap \in AP \wedge ap \notin \lambda(p, \gamma)$,
4. $([p, \phi_1 \wedge \phi_2], \gamma) \rightarrow ([p, \phi_1], \gamma) \wedge ([p, \phi_2], \gamma) \in \Delta'$,
5. $([p, \phi_1 \vee \phi_2], \gamma) \rightarrow ([p, \phi_1], \gamma) \vee ([p, \phi_2], \gamma) \in \Delta'$,
6. $([p, E \bigcirc^f \phi_1], \gamma) \rightarrow \bigvee_{(p, \gamma) \hookrightarrow_f (p', \Omega)} ([p', \phi_1], \Omega) \in \Delta', f \in \{g, a\}$,
7. $([p, A \bigcirc^f \phi_1], \gamma) \rightarrow \bigwedge_{(p, \gamma) \hookrightarrow_f (p', \Omega)} ([p', \phi_1], \Omega) \in \Delta'$, $f \in \{g, a\} \wedge (p, \gamma) \in ADF_f$,
8. $([p, E \phi_1 \mathcal{U}^f \phi_2], \gamma) \rightarrow ([p, \phi_2], \gamma) \in \Delta', f \in \{g, a\}$,
9. $([p, E \phi_1 \mathcal{U}^f \phi_2], \gamma) \rightarrow \bigvee_{(p, \gamma) \hookrightarrow_f (p', \Omega)} (([p, \phi_1], \gamma) \wedge ([p', E \phi_1 \mathcal{U}^f \phi_2], \Omega)) \in \Delta'$, $f \in \{g, a\}$,
10. $([p, A \phi_1 \mathcal{U}^f \phi_2], \gamma) \rightarrow ([p, \phi_2], \gamma) \in \Delta', f \in \{g, a\}$,
11. $([p, A \phi_1 \mathcal{U}^f \phi_2], \gamma) \rightarrow \bigwedge_{(p, \gamma) \hookrightarrow_f (p', \Omega)} (([p, \phi_1], \gamma) \wedge ([p', A \phi_1 \mathcal{U}^f \phi_2], \Omega)) \in \Delta', (p, \gamma) \in ADF_f$,
12. $([p, E \phi_1 \mathcal{R}^f \phi_2], \gamma) \rightarrow ([p, \phi_2], \gamma) \wedge ([p, \phi_1], \gamma) \in \Delta'$,
13. $([p, E \phi_1 \mathcal{R}^f \phi_2], \gamma) \rightarrow \bigvee_{(p, \gamma) \hookrightarrow_f (p', \Omega)} (([p, \phi_2], \gamma) \wedge ([p', E \phi_1 \mathcal{R}^f \phi_2], \Omega)) \in \Delta', f \in \{g, a\}$,
14. $([p, A \phi_1 \mathcal{R}^f \phi_2], \gamma) \rightarrow ([p, \phi_2], \gamma) \wedge ([p, \phi_1], \gamma) \in \Delta', f \in \{g, a\}$,
15. $([p, A \phi_1 \mathcal{R}^f \phi_2], \gamma) \rightarrow \bigwedge_{(p, \gamma) \hookrightarrow_f (p', \Omega)} (([p, \phi_2], \gamma) \wedge ([p', A \phi_1 \mathcal{R}^f \phi_2], \Omega)) \in \Delta', f \in \{g, a\} \wedge (p, \gamma) \in ADF_f$,
16. $([p, E \bigcirc^a_W \phi_1], \gamma) \rightarrow true \in \Delta', (p, \gamma) \notin ADF_a$,
17. $([p, E \bigcirc^a_W \phi_1], \gamma) \rightarrow \bigvee_{(p, \gamma) \hookrightarrow_a (p', \Omega)} ([p', \phi_1], \Omega) \in \Delta'$,
18. $([p, A \bigcirc^a_W \phi_1], \gamma) \rightarrow \bigwedge_{(p, \gamma) \hookrightarrow_a (p', \Omega)} ([p', \phi_1], \Omega) \in \Delta'$,
19. $([p, E \phi_1 \mathcal{U}^a_W \phi_2], \gamma) \rightarrow ([p, \phi_1], \gamma) \in \Delta', (p, \gamma) \notin ADF_a$,
20. $([p, E\ \phi_1\ \mathcal{U}^a_W\ \phi_2], \gamma) \rightarrow ([p, \phi_2],\ \gamma) \vee \bigvee_{(p, \gamma) \hookrightarrow_a (p', \Omega)} (([p, \phi_1],\ \gamma) \wedge ([p', E \phi_1 \mathcal{U}^f_W \phi_2], \Omega)) \in \Delta'$,
21. $([p, A \phi_1 \mathcal{U}^a_W \phi_2], \gamma) \rightarrow ([p, \phi_2], \gamma) \in \Delta'$,
22. $([p, A \phi_1 \mathcal{U}^a_W \phi_2], \gamma) \rightarrow (([p, \phi_1], \gamma) \wedge \bigwedge_{(p, \gamma) \hookrightarrow_a (p', \Omega)} ([p', A \phi_1 U^a_W \phi_2], \Omega)) \in \Delta'$,
23. $([p, E \phi_1 \mathcal{R}^a_W \phi_2], \gamma) \rightarrow ([p, \phi_2], \gamma) \in \Delta', (p, \gamma) \notin ADF_a$,
24. $([p, E \phi_1 \mathcal{R}^a_W \phi_2], \gamma) \rightarrow (([p, \phi_2], \gamma) \wedge ([p, \phi_1], \gamma)) \vee \bigvee_{(p, \gamma) \hookrightarrow_a (p', \Omega)} (([p, \phi_2], \gamma) \wedge ([p', E \phi_1 \mathcal{R}^a_W \phi_2], \Omega)) \in \Delta'$,
25. $([p, A \phi_1 \mathcal{R}^a_W \phi_2], \gamma) \rightarrow (([p, \phi_2], \gamma) \wedge ([p, \phi_1], \gamma)) \in \Delta'$,

26. $([p, A \phi_1 \mathcal{R}_W^a \phi_2], \gamma) \rightarrow (([p, \phi_2], \gamma) \land \bigwedge_{(p,\gamma) \hookrightarrow_a (p', \Omega)} ([p', A \phi_1 \mathcal{R}_W^a \phi_2], \Omega)) \in \Delta'$,

27. $([p, EM\phi_1], \gamma) \rightarrow ([p_c, EM\phi_1], \varepsilon) \in \Delta', M \in \{\bigcirc^-, \bigcirc_W^-\} \land \gamma \neq \#$,

28. $([p', E \bigcirc_W^- \phi_1], \#) \rightarrow true \in \Delta', p' \in P \cup \{p_c\}$

29. $([p_c, EM\phi_1], (\gamma, (p', \gamma'))) \rightarrow ([p', \phi_1], \gamma') \in \Delta', M \in \{\bigcirc^-, \bigcirc_W^-\}$,

30. $([p, E \phi_1 \mathcal{U}^- \phi_2], \gamma) \rightarrow ([p, \phi_2], \gamma) \lor (([p, \phi_1], \gamma) \land ([p, E \bigcirc^- (E \phi_1 \mathcal{U}^- \phi_2)], \gamma)) \in \Delta'$,

31. $([p, E \phi_1 \mathcal{R}^- \phi_2], \gamma) \rightarrow (([p, \phi_2], \gamma) \land ([p, \phi_1], \gamma)) \lor (([p, \phi_2], \gamma) \land ([p, E \bigcirc^- (E \phi_1 \mathcal{R}^- \phi_2)], \gamma)) \in \Delta'$.

Finally, we need a function that associates executions of our PDS and formulae with configurations of our ABPDS: Let $Conf(\pi, i) = (p, \Omega)$ and ϕ be a BranchCaRet formula in NNF. Then $Assoc : (\Pi_\mathcal{P} \times \mathbb{N}) \times cl(\phi) \rightarrow P' \times \Xi^+$, $Assoc(\pi, i, \phi) = ([p, \phi], \Omega)$ is the function that associates every (π, i) and Branch-CaRet formula ϕ with a configuration of $\mathcal{BP}$. After this formal introduction, we now explain the intuition behind the construction of $\mathcal{BP}$. Our objective is to show that $(\pi, i) \vDash \phi$ iff there is an accepting run from $Assoc(\pi, i, \phi)$.

The control locations P' of $\mathcal{BP}$ are divided into two sets: control locations equipped with formulae $[p, \phi]$ and intermediate states $[p_c, \phi]$. Starting from $Assoc(\pi, i, \phi)$, the configurations of $\mathcal{BP}$ reachable with a single transition rule are of the form $Assoc(\pi', k, \phi')$ for $\pi' \in Ext(\pi, i)$, $\phi' \in cl(\phi)$ and some index k. The only exception are configurations with control locations of the form $[p_c, \phi]$ in their head. These control locations solely are used to restore the caller in case we encounter a caller modality. The transition rules in Δ' are straightforward applications of the semantics of BranchCaRet. We explain these rules and the set F in turn to establish an intuitive basis for the formal correctness proof of our approach. Our rules consist of three general blocks. The first block (rules 1–15) handles (negated) atomic propositions as well as global and abstract modalities. An atomic proposition holds iff the current configuration is labelled with it, so we construct an accepting run via an infinite loop in this case and include no transitions at all otherwise. For successor modalities, we can just check if the formula ϕ_1 holds in the respective successor, while also requiring that the successor be always defined in the universal case. For Until formulae, we always check whether ϕ_2 holds directly or ϕ_1 holds and the Until formula holds again in the respective successor. The Release modality is handled analogously. The only outlier in this block is rule 1. This rule is only applicable after a symbol has been popped from the stack using a rule that does not refer to caller modalities. In this case, when we encounter a symbol that combines a stack symbol and the head of a caller, we can just ignore that caller and place just the stack symbol on the stack. The second block (rules 16–26) handles weak abstract modalities. The rules for these modalities are largely similar to the corresponding rules in the first block, but we also allow the abstract successor to be undefined in the relevant cases. For example, for the existential abstract successor modality, we require that either the abstract successor be undefined (as indicated by the ADF_a set) or fulfill ϕ_2. In both blocks, the control locations for the Release modality are in F because we also need to construct accepting runs in case these are visited infinitely often. In contrast, all other modalities only lead to finitely many steps before either a Release modality or a (negated) atomic proposition is encountered. Therefore, the control locations for these modalities do not need to be included in the set F. The third block (rules 27–31) deals with caller modalities. The caller is handled by popping the current symbol from the stack and switching into the intermediate state p_c. If the current configuration with call history has a caller, this intermediate state will contain a stack symbol of the form $(\gamma, (p', \gamma'))$ and (p, γ') will be the configuration head of the caller. Thus, we can restore the configuration with call history that was present when the call was made then check whether the formula holds in that configuration. If the stack symbol is not of that form, we know there is no caller and can use this information to construct an accepting run for weak caller formulae. The other caller modalities are handled by reduction to the simple caller modality. For caller modalities, we do not need to include the control locations for Release in F because only finitely many steps are possible anyway. We can now state our main theorem for the connection between BranchCaRet model checking and the ABPDS $\mathcal{BP}$.

Theorem 13. *Let ϕ be a BranchCaRet formula in NNF and $\pi \in \Pi_{\mathcal{P}}$. Then $(\pi, i) \vDash \phi$ iff there is an accepting run from $Assoc(\pi, i, \phi)$ in BP.*

Using Algorithms 1 and 2 to compute $PSReturns_H$ and the ADF sets, we can construct $\mathcal{BP}$ in polynomial time. Since there are only at most $|P| \cdot |\Gamma|$ initial configurations and thus only that many variants of $\pi(0)$, we only need to check for $|P| \cdot |\Gamma|$ configurations whether there is an accepting run from the respective configuration to solve the BranchCaRet model checking problem. There are $\mathcal{O}(|P| \cdot |\phi|)$ control locations in $\mathcal{BP}$ and we can therefore use Theorem 3 to obtain that the BranchCaRet model checking problem can be solved in time exponential in $|P|$ and $|\phi|$ and polynomial in $|\Gamma|$ and $|\Delta|$. In conjunction with the fact that CTL model checking is already EXPTIME-hard [9] (even for a fixed size formula), we obtain the following result:

Theorem 14. *BranchCaRet model checking is EXPTIME-complete (even for a fixed size formula).*

This is the same model checking complexity as for CTL. Theorem 14 also shows why it is prudent to consider BranchCaRet separately from the whole BranchCaRet*. For the latter logic, we obtain a lower bound of 2EXPTIME-hardness because this bound already holds for the subset CTL* [9]. Thus, model checking BranchCaRet is generally more efficient. We note that our approach can easily be extended to accommodate regular stack properties as atomic propositions with similar transition rules as in [29].

5   Conclusion

In this paper, we introduced the logic BranchCaRet as a branching time variant of CaRet. We showed how the BranchCaRet model checking problem can be solved via the construction of ABPDSs and checking them for emptiness. We further proved BranchCaRet model checking to be EXPTIME-complete and therefore to have the same asymptotic model checking complexity as CTL.

Future Work. We would like to implement our model checking algorithm in a model checker to analyse its feasibility in case studies. Furthermore, a natural question would be whether and how our model checking approach for Branch-CaRet can be extended to the full logic BranchCaRet* which was only considered as a general framework in this paper. As mentioned in Sect. 1, the visibly pushdown μ-calculus (VP-μ) [3] can express all properties of the logic CaRet. It would be interesting to investigate the relation of VP-μ to BranchCaRet. Finally, we would like to analyse whether our approach can be extended to a branching time version of the logic NWTL and the *Within*-modality introduced by Alur et al. in [1].

References

1. Alur, R., Arenas, M., Barceló, P., Etessami, K., Immerman, N., Libkin, L.: First-order and temporal logics for nested words. Log. Methods Comput. Sci. **4**(4) (2008). https://lmcs.episciences.org/782
2. Alur, R., Benedikt, M., Etessami, K., Godefroid, P., Reps, T.W., Yannakakis, M.: Analysis of recursive state machines. ACM Trans. Program. Lang. Syst. **27**(4), 786–818 (2005)
3. Alur, R., Chaudhuri, S., Madhusudan, P.: A fixpoint calculus for local and global program flows. In: POPL 2006, pp. 153–165 (2006)
4. Alur, R., Chaudhuri, S., Madhusudan, P.: Languages of nested trees. In: Ball, T., Jones, R.B. (eds.) CAV 2006. LNCS, vol. 4144, pp. 329–342. Springer, Heidelberg (2006). https://doi.org/10.1007/11817963_31
5. Alur, R., Etessami, K., Madhusudan, P.: A temporal logic of nested calls and returns. In: Jensen, K., Podelski, A. (eds.) TACAS 2004. LNCS, vol. 2988, pp. 467–481. Springer, Heidelberg (2004). https://doi.org/10.1007/978-3-540-24730-2_35
6. Alur, R., Madhusudan, P.: Visibly pushdown languages. In: STOC 2004, pp. 202–211 (2004)
7. Alur, R., Madhusudan, P.: Adding nesting structure to words. J. ACM **56**(3), 16:1–16:43 (2009)
8. Bouajjani, A., Esparza, J., Maler, O.: Reachability analysis of pushdown automata: application to model-checking. In: Mazurkiewicz, A., Winkowski, J. (eds.) CONCUR 1997. LNCS, vol. 1243, pp. 135–150. Springer, Heidelberg (1997). https://doi.org/10.1007/3-540-63141-0_10
9. Bozzelli, L.: Complexity results on branching-time pushdown model checking. Theor. Comput. Sci. **379**(1–2), 286–297 (2007)
10. Bozzelli, L.: CaRet with forgettable past. Electr. Notes Theor. Comput. Sci. **231**, 343–361 (2009)
11. Bozzelli, L., Sánchez, C.: Visibly linear temporal logic. J. Autom. Reason. **60**(2), 177–220 (2018)
12. Burkart, O., Steffen, B.: Model checking for context-free processes. In: Cleaveland, W.R. (ed.) CONCUR 1992. LNCS, vol. 630, pp. 123–137. Springer, Heidelberg (1992). https://doi.org/10.1007/BFb0084787

13. Burkart, O., Steffen, B.: Model checking the full modal mu-calculus for infinite sequential processes. Theor. Comput. Sci. **221**(1–2), 251–270 (1999)
14. Cachat, T.: Symbolic strategy synthesis for games on pushdown graphs. In: Widmayer, P., Eidenbenz, S., Triguero, F., Morales, R., Conejo, R., Hennessy, M. (eds.) ICALP 2002. LNCS, vol. 2380, pp. 704–715. Springer, Heidelberg (2002). https://doi.org/10.1007/3-540-45465-9_60
15. Cachat, T.: Games on pushdown graphs and extensions. Ph.D. thesis, RWTH Aachen University, Germany (2003)
16. Esparza, J., Hansel, D., Rossmanith, P., Schwoon, S.: Efficient algorithms for model checking pushdown systems. In: Emerson, E.A., Sistla, A.P. (eds.) CAV 2000. LNCS, vol. 1855, pp. 232–247. Springer, Heidelberg (2000). https://doi.org/10.1007/10722167_20
17. Esparza, J., Knoop, J.: An automata-theoretic approach to interprocedural dataflow analysis. In: Thomas, W. (ed.) FoSSaCS 1999. LNCS, vol. 1578, pp. 14–30. Springer, Heidelberg (1999). https://doi.org/10.1007/3-540-49019-1_2
18. Esparza, J., Kucera, A., Schwoon, S.: Model checking LTL with regular valuations for pushdown systems. Inf. Comput. **186**(2), 355–376 (2003)
19. Esparza, J., Schwoon, S.: A BDD-based model checker for recursive programs. In: Berry, G., Comon, H., Finkel, A. (eds.) CAV 2001. LNCS, vol. 2102, pp. 324–336. Springer, Heidelberg (2001). https://doi.org/10.1007/3-540-44585-4_30
20. Hague, M., Ong, C.-H.L.: Winning regions of pushdown parity games: a saturation method. In: Bravetti, M., Zavattaro, G. (eds.) CONCUR 2009. LNCS, vol. 5710, pp. 384–398. Springer, Heidelberg (2009). https://doi.org/10.1007/978-3-642-04081-8_26
21. La Torre, S., Napoli, M.: A temporal logic for multi-threaded programs. In: Baeten, J.C.M., Ball, T., de Boer, F.S. (eds.) TCS 2012. LNCS, vol. 7604, pp. 225–239. Springer, Heidelberg (2012). https://doi.org/10.1007/978-3-642-33475-7_16
22. Nguyen, H., Touili, T.: CARET analysis of multithreaded programs. CoRR abs/1709.09006 (2017)
23. Nguyen, H., Touili, T.: CARET model checking for malware detection. In: SPIN Symposium 2017, pp. 152–161 (2017)
24. Nguyen, H., Touili, T.: CARET model checking for pushdown systems. In: SAC 2017, pp. 1393–1400 (2017)
25. Roşu, G., Chen, F., Ball, T.: Synthesizing monitors for safety properties: this time with calls and returns. In: Leucker, M. (ed.) RV 2008. LNCS, vol. 5289, pp. 51–68. Springer, Heidelberg (2008). https://doi.org/10.1007/978-3-540-89247-2_4
26. Schmidt, D.A.: Data flow analysis is model checking of abstract interpretations. In: POPL 1998, pp. 38–48 (1998)
27. Schwoon, S.: Model checking pushdown systems. Ph.D. thesis, Technical University Munich, Germany (2002)
28. Song, F., Touili, T.: PuMoC: a CTL model-checker for sequential programs. In: ASE 2012, pp. 346–349 (2012)
29. Song, F., Touili, T.: Efficient CTL model-checking for pushdown systems. Theor. Comput. Sci. **549**, 127–145 (2014)
30. Steffen, B.: Data flow analysis as model checking. In: Ito, T., Meyer, A.R. (eds.) TACS 1991. LNCS, vol. 526, pp. 346–364. Springer, Heidelberg (1991). https://doi.org/10.1007/3-540-54415-1_54
31. Walukiewicz, I.: Pushdown processes: games and model-checking. Inf. Comput. **164**(2), 234–263 (2001)
32. Weinert, A., Zimmermann, M.: Visibly linear dynamic logic. In: FSTTCS 2016, 13–15 December 2016, pp. 28:1–28:14 (2016)

Control Strategies for Off-Line Testing
of Timed Systems

Léo Henry$^{(\boxtimes)}$, Thierry Jéron, and Nicolas Markey

Univ. Rennes, Inria & CNRS, Rennes, France
`leo.henry@irisa.fr`

Abstract. Partial observability and controllability are two well-known issues in test-case synthesis for interactive systems. We address the problem of partial control in the synthesis of test cases from timed-automata specifications. Building on the tioco timed testing framework, we extend a previous game interpretation of the test-synthesis problem from the untimed to the timed setting. This extension requires a deep reworking of the models, game interpretation and test-synthesis algorithms. We exhibit strategies of a game that tries to minimize both control losses and distance to the satisfaction of a test purpose, and prove they are winning under some fairness assumptions. This entails that when turning those strategies into test cases, we get properties such as soundness and exhaustiveness of the test synthesis method.

1 Introduction

Real-time interactive systems are systems interacting with their environment and subject to timing constraints. Such systems are encountered in many contexts, in particular in critical applications such as transportation, control of manufacturing systems, etc. Their correctness is then of prime importance, but it is also very challenging due to multiple factors: combination of discrete and continuous behaviours, concurrency aspects in distributed systems, limited observability of behaviours, or partial controllability of systems.

One of the most-used validation techniques in this context is testing, with variations depending on the design phases. Conformance testing is one of those variations, consisting in checking whether a real system correctly implements its specification. Those real systems are considered as black boxes, thereby offering only partial observability, for various reasons (*e.g.* because sensors cannot observe all actions, or because the system is composed of communicating components whose communications cannot be all observed, or again because of intellectual property of peer software). Controllability is another issue when the system makes its own choices upon which the environment, and thus the tester, have a limited control. One of the most-challenging activities in this context is the design of test cases that, when executed on the real system, should produce meaningful information about the conformance of the system at hand with respect to its specification. Formal models and methods are a good candidate to help this test-case synthesis [Tre96].

© Springer International Publishing AG, part of Springer Nature 2018
M. M. Gallardo and P. Merino (Eds.): SPIN 2018, LNCS 10869, pp. 171–189, 2018.
https://doi.org/10.1007/978-3-319-94111-0_10

Timed Automata (TA) [AD94] form a class of model for the specification of timed reactive systems. It consists of automata equipped with real-valued clocks where transitions between locations carry actions, are guarded by constraints on clock values, and can reset clocks. TAs are also equipped with invariants that constrain the sojourn time in locations. TAs are popular in particular because reachability of a location is decidable using symbolic representations of sets of configurations by zones. In the context of testing, it is adequate to refine TAs by explicitly distinguishing (controllable) inputs and (uncontrollable) outputs, giving rise to TAIOs (Timed Automata with Inputs and Outputs). In the following, this model will be used for most testing artifacts, namely specifications, implementations, and test cases. Since completeness of testing is hopeless in practice, it is helpful to rely on test purposes that describe those behaviours that need to be tested because they are subject to errors. In our formal testing framework, an extension of TAIOs called Open TAIOs (or OTAIOs) is used to formally specify those behaviors. OTAIOs play the role of observers of actions and clocks of the specification: they synchronize on actions and clock resets of the specification (called observed clocks), and control their proper clocks. The formal testing framework also requires to formally define conformance as a relation between specifications and their possible implementations. In the timed setting, the classical tioco relation [KT09] states that, after a timed observable trace of the specification, the outputs and delays of the implementation should be specified.

Test-case synthesis from TAs has been extensively studied during the last 20 years (see [COG98, CKL98, SVD01, ENDK02, NS03, BB04, LMN04, KT09], to cite a few). As already mentioned, one of the difficulties is partial observation. In off-line testing, where the test cases are first computed, stored, and later executed on the implementation, the tester should anticipate all specified outputs after a trace. In the untimed framework, this is tackled by determinization of the specification. Unfortunately, this is not feasible for TAIO specifications since determinization is not possible in general [AD94, Fin06]. The solution was then either to perform on-line testing where subset construction is made on the current execution trace, or to restrict to determinizable sub-classes. More recently, some advances were obtained in this context [BJSK12] by the use of an approximate determinization using a game approach [BSJK15] that preserves tioco conformance. Partial observation is also dealt with by [DLL+10] with a variant of the TA model where observations are described by observation predicates composed of a set of locations together with clock constraints. Test cases are then synthesized as winning strategies, if they exist, of a game between the specification and its environment that tries to guide the system to satisfy the test purpose.

The problem of test synthesis is often informally presented as a game between the environment and the system (see *e.g.* [Yan04]). But very few papers effectively take into account the controllability of the system. In the context of testing for timed-automata models [DLLN08b], proposes a game approach where test cases are winning strategies of a reachability game. But this is restricted to deterministic models and controllability is not really taken into account. In fact, like in [DLL+10], the game is abandoned when control is lost, and it is suggested to modify the test purpose in this case. This is mitigated in [DLLN08a] with cooperative strategies, which rely on the cooperation of the system under test to win the game. A more convincing approach to the control problem is the one of [Ram98] in the untimed setting, unfortunately a quite little-known work. The game problem consists in satisfying the test purpose (a simple subsequence), while trying to avoid control losses occurring when outputs offered by the system leave this behaviour. The computed strategy is based on a rank that measures both the distance to the goal and the controls losses.

The current paper adapts the approach proposed in [Ram98] to the timed context using the framework developed in [BJSK12]. Compared to [Ram98], the model of TA is much more complex than transition systems, the test purposes are also much more powerful than simple sub-sequences, thus even if the approach is similar, the game has to be completely revised. Compared to [DLL+10], our model is a bit different since we do not rely on observation predicates, but partial observation comes from internal actions and choices. We do not completely tackle non-determinism since we assume determinizable models at some point. In comparison, [DLL+10] avoids determinizing TAs, relying on the determinization of a finite state model, thanks to a projection on a finite set of observable predicates. Cooperative strategies of [DLLN08a] have similarities with our fairness assumptions, but their models are assumed deterministic. Our approach takes controllability into account in a more complete and practical way with the reachability game and rank-lowering strategies.

The paper is organized as follows. Section 2 introduces basic models: TAs, TAIOs and their open counterparts OTAs, OTAIOs, and then timed game automata (TGA). Section 3 is dedicated to the testing framework with hypothesis on models of testing artifacts, the conformance relation and the construction of the *objective-centered tester* that denotes both non-conformant traces and the goal to reach according to a test purpose. Section 4 constitutes the core of the paper. The test synthesis problem is interpreted as a game on the objective-centered tester. Rank-lowering strategies are proposed as candidate test cases, and a fairness assumption is introduced to make such strategies win. Finally properties of test cases with respect to conformance are proved.

By lack of space, not all proofs could be included. They can be found in [HJM18].

2   Timed Automata and Timed Games

In this section, we introduce our models for timed systems and for concurrent games on these objects, along with some useful notions and operations.

2.1   Timed Automata with Inputs and Outputs

Timed automata (TAs) [AD94] are one of the most widely-used classes of models for reasoning about computer systems subject to real-time constraints.

Timed automata are finite-state automata augmented with real-valued variables (called *clocks*) to constrain the occurrence of transitions along executions. In order to adapt these models to the testing framework, we consider TAs with inputs and outputs (TAIOs), in which the alphabet is split between input, output and internal actions (the latter being used to model partial observation). We present the *open* TAs (and open TAIOs) [BJSK12], which allow the models to observe and synchronize with a set of non-controlled clocks.

Given a finite set of *clocks* X, a *clock valuation* over X is a function $v \colon X \to \mathbb{R}_{\geq 0}$. We note $\overline{0}_X$ (and often omit to mention X when clear from the context) for the valuation assigning 0 to all clocks in X. Let v be a clock valuation, for any $t \in \mathbb{R}_{\geq 0}$, we denote with $v + t$ the valuation mapping each clock $x \in X$ to $v(x) + t$, and for a subset $X' \subseteq X$, we write $v_{[X' \leftarrow 0]}$ for the valuation mapping all clocks in X' to 0, and all clocks in $X \setminus X'$ to their values in v.

A *clock constraint* is a finite conjunction of atomic constraints of the form $x \sim n$ where $x \in X$, $n \in \mathbb{N}$, and $\sim \in \{<, \leq, =, \geq, >\}$. That a valuation v satisfies a clock constraint g, written $v \models g$, is defined in the obvious way. We write $\mathcal{C}(X)$ for the set of clock constraints over X.

Definition 1. *An* open timed automaton *(OTA) is a tuple[1]* $\mathcal{A} = (L^{\mathcal{A}}, l_0^{\mathcal{A}}, \Sigma^{\mathcal{A}}, X_p^{\mathcal{A}} \uplus X_o^{\mathcal{A}}, I^{\mathcal{A}}, E^{\mathcal{A}})$ *where:*

- $L^{\mathcal{A}}$ *is a finite set of* locations, *with* $l_0^{\mathcal{A}} \in L^{\mathcal{A}}$ *the initial location,*
- $\Sigma^{\mathcal{A}}$ *is a finite alphabet,*
- $X^{\mathcal{A}} = X_p^{\mathcal{A}} \uplus X_o^{\mathcal{A}}$ *is a finite set of clocks, partitioned into* proper clocks $X_p^{\mathcal{A}}$ *and* observed clocks $X_o^{\mathcal{A}}$; *only proper clocks may be reset along transitions.*
- $I^{\mathcal{A}} \colon L^{\mathcal{A}} \to \mathcal{C}(X^{\mathcal{A}})$ *assigns invariant constraints to locations.*
- $E^{\mathcal{A}} \subseteq L^{\mathcal{A}} \times \mathcal{C}(X^{\mathcal{A}}) \times \Sigma^{\mathcal{A}} \times 2^{X_p^{\mathcal{A}}} \times L^{\mathcal{A}}$ *is a finite set of transitions. For* $e = (l, g, a, X', l') \in E^{\mathcal{A}}$, *we write* $\mathsf{act}(e) = a$.

An Open Timed Automaton with Inputs and Outputs (OTAIO) is an OTA in which $\Sigma^{\mathcal{A}} = \Sigma_?^{\mathcal{A}} \uplus \Sigma_!^{\mathcal{A}} \uplus \Sigma_\tau^{\mathcal{A}}$ *is the disjoint union of* input actions *in* $\Sigma_?^{\mathcal{A}}$ *(noted* $?a, ?b, ...$), *output actions in* $\Sigma_!^{\mathcal{A}}$ *(noted* $!a, !b, ...$), *and internal actions in* $\Sigma_\tau^{\mathcal{A}}$ *(noted* $\tau_1, \tau_2, ...$) *We write* $\Sigma_{obs} = \Sigma_? \uplus \Sigma_!$ *for the alphabet of* observable *actions. Finally, a* Timed Automaton *(TA) (resp. a* Timed Automaton with Inputs and Outputs *(TAIO)) is an OTA (resp. an OTAIO) with no observed clocks.*

TAIOs will be sufficient to model most objects, but the ability of OTAIOs to observe other clocks will be essential for test purposes (see Sect. 3.1), which need to synchronize with the specification.

Let $\mathcal{A} = (L, l_0, \Sigma, X_p \uplus X_o, I, E)$ be an OTA. Its *semantics* is defined as an infinite-state transition system $\mathcal{T}^{\mathcal{A}} = (S^{\mathcal{A}}, s_0^{\mathcal{A}}, \Gamma^{\mathcal{A}}, \to^{\mathcal{A}})$ where:

- $S^{\mathcal{A}} = \{(l, v) \in L \times \mathbb{R}_{\geq 0}^X \mid v \models I(l)\}$ is the (infinite) set of *configurations*, with initial configuration $s_0^{\mathcal{A}} = (l_0, \overline{0}_X)$.

---

[1] For this and the following definitions, we may omit to mention superscripts when the corresponding automaton is clear from the context.

- $\Gamma^{\mathcal{A}} = \mathbb{R}_{\geq 0} \uplus (E \times 2^{X_o})$ is the set of *transitions labels*.
- $\rightarrow^{\mathcal{A}} \subseteq S^{\mathcal{A}} \times \Gamma^{\mathcal{A}} \times S^{\mathcal{A}}$ is the *transition relation*. It is defined as the union of
    - the set of transitions corresponding to *time elapses*: it contains all triples $((l, v), \delta, (l', v')) \in S^{\mathcal{A}} \times \mathbb{R}_{\geq 0} \times S^{\mathcal{A}}$ for which $l = l'$ and $v' = v + \delta$. By definition of $S^{\mathcal{A}}$, both v and v' satisfy the invariant $I(l)$.
    - the set of transitions corresponding to *discrete moves*: it contains all triples $((l, v), (e, X'_o), (l', v')) \in S^{\mathcal{A}} \times (E \times 2^{X_o}) \times S^{\mathcal{A}}$ such that, writing $e = (m, g, a, X'_p, m')$, it holds $m = l$, $m' = l'$, $v \models g$, and $v' = v_{[X'_p \cup X'_o \leftarrow 0]}$. Again, by definition, $v \models I(l)$ and $v' \models I(l')$.

An OTA has no control over its observed clocks, the intention being to synchronize them later in a product (see Definition 2). Hence, when a discrete transition is taken, any set X'_o of observed clocks may be reset. When dealing with plain TAs, where X_o is empty, we may write $(l, v) \xrightarrow{e} (l', v')$ in place of $(l, v) \xrightarrow{(e, \emptyset)} (l', v')$.

A *partial run* of $\mathcal{A}$ is a (finite or infinite) sequence of transitions in $T^{\mathcal{A}}$ $\rho = ((s_i, \gamma_i, s_{i+1}))_{1 \leq i < n}$, with $n \in \mathbb{N} \cup \{+\infty\}$. We write first$(\rho)$ for s_1 and, when $n \in \mathbb{N}$, last(ρ) for s_n. A *run* is a partial run starting in the initial configuration $s_0^{\mathcal{A}}$. The duration of ρ is dur$(\rho) = \sum_{\gamma_i \in \mathbb{R}_{\geq 0}} \gamma_i$. In the sequel, we only consider TAs in which any infinite run has infinite duration. We note Ex$(\mathcal{A})$ for the set of runs of $\mathcal{A}$ and pEx$(\mathcal{A})$ the subset of partial runs.

State s is *reachable* from state s' when there exists a partial run from s' to s. We write Reach$(\mathcal{A}, S')$ for the set of states that are reachable from some state in S', and Reach$(\mathcal{A})$ for Reach$(\mathcal{A}, \{s_0^{\mathcal{A}}\})$.

The *(partial) sequence* associated with a (partial) run $\rho = ((s_i, \gamma_i, s'_i))_i$ is seq$(\rho) = (\text{proj}(\gamma_i))_i$, where proj$(\gamma) = \gamma$ if $\gamma \in \mathbb{R}_{\geq 0}$, and proj$(\gamma) = (a, X'_p \cup X'_o)$ if $\gamma = ((l, g, a, X'_p, l'), X'_o)$. We write pSeq$(\mathcal{A}) = \text{proj}(\text{pEx}(\mathcal{A}))$ and Seq$(\mathcal{A}) = \text{proj}(\text{Ex}(\mathcal{A}))$ for the sets of (partial) sequences of $\mathcal{A}$. We write $s \xrightarrow{\mu} s'$ when there exists a (partial) finite run ρ such that $\mu = \text{proj}(\rho)$, first$(\rho) = s$ and last$(\rho) = s'$, and write dur(μ) for dur(ρ). We write $s \xrightarrow{\mu}$ when $s \xrightarrow{\mu} s'$ for some s.

If $\mathcal{A}$ is a TAIO, the *trace* of a (partial) sequence corresponds to what can be observed by the environment, namely delays and observable actions. The trace of a sequence is the limit of the following inductive definition, for $\delta_i \in \mathbb{R}_{\geq 0}$, $a \in \Sigma_{obs}$, $\tau \in \Sigma_\tau$, $X' \subseteq X$, and a partial sequence μ:

$$\text{Trace}(\delta_1 ... \delta_k) = \sum_{i=1}^{k} \delta_i \qquad (\text{in particular Trace}(\epsilon) = 0)$$

$$\text{Trace}(\delta_1 ... \delta_k.(\tau, X').\mu) = (\sum_{i=1}^{k} \delta_i) \cdot \text{Trace}(\mu)$$

$$\text{Trace}(\delta_1 ... \delta_k.(a, X').\mu) = (\sum_{i=1}^{k} \delta_i) \cdot a \cdot \text{Trace}(\mu)$$

We note Traces$(\mathcal{A}) = \text{Trace}(\text{Seq}(\mathcal{A}))$ the set of traces corresponding to runs of $\mathcal{A}$ and pTraces$(\mathcal{A})$ the subset of traces corresponding to partial runs. Two OTAIOs are said to be *trace-equivalent* if they have the same sets of traces. We furthermore define, for an OTAIO $\mathcal{A}$, a trace σ and a configuration s:

- $\mathcal{A}$ after $\sigma = \{s \in S \mid \exists \mu \in \text{Seq}(\mathcal{A}), s_0 \xrightarrow{\mu} s \wedge \text{Trace}(\mu) = \sigma\}$ is the set of all configurations that can be reached when σ has been observed from $s_0^{\mathcal{A}}$.

- $\mathsf{enab}(s) = \{e \in E^{\mathcal{A}} \mid s \xrightarrow{e}\}$ is the set of transitions enabled in s.
- $\mathsf{elapse}(s) = \{t \in \mathbb{R}_{\geq 0} \mid \exists \mu \in (\mathbb{R}_{\geq 0} \cup (\Sigma_\tau \times 2^X))^*, s \xrightarrow{\mu} \wedge \mathsf{dur}(\mu) = t\}$ is the set of delays that can be observed from location s without any observation.
- $\mathsf{out}(s) = \{a \in \Sigma_! \mid \exists e \in \mathsf{enab}(s), \mathsf{act}(e) = a\} \cup \mathsf{elapse}(s)$ is the set of possible outputs and delays that can be observed from s. For $S' \subseteq S$, we note $\mathsf{out}(S') = \bigcup_{s \in S'} \mathsf{out}(s)$.
- $\mathsf{in}(s) = \{a \in \Sigma_! \mid \exists e \in \mathsf{enab}(s), \mathsf{act}(e) = a\}$ is the set of possible inputs that can be proposed when arriving in s. For $S' \subseteq S$, we note $\mathsf{in}(S') = \bigcup_{s \in S'} \mathsf{in}(s)$.

We now define some useful sub-classes of OTAIOs. An OTAIO $\mathcal{A}$ is said

- *deterministic* if for all $\sigma \in Traces(\mathcal{A})$, $\mathcal{A}$ after σ is a singleton;
- *determinizable* if there exists a trace-equivalence deterministic OTAIO;
- *complete* if $S = L \times \mathbb{R}_{\geq 0}^X$ (i.e., all invariants are always true) and for any $s \in S$ and any $a \in \Sigma$, it holds $s \xrightarrow{a,X'}$ for some $X' \subseteq X$;
- *input-complete* if for any $s \in \mathsf{Reach}(\mathcal{A})$, $\mathsf{in}(s) = \Sigma_?$;
- *non-blocking* if for any $s \in \mathsf{Reach}(\mathcal{A})$ and any non-negative real t, there is a partial run ρ from s involving no input actions (i.e., $\mathsf{proj}(\rho)$ is a sequence over $\mathbb{R}_{\geq 0} \cup (\Sigma_! \cup \Sigma_\tau) \times 2^X$) and such that $\mathsf{dur}(\rho) = t$;
- *repeatedly observable* if for any $s \in \mathsf{Reach}(\mathcal{A})$, there exists a partial run ρ from s such that $\mathsf{Trace}(\rho) \notin \mathbb{R}_{\geq 0}$.

The product of two OTAIOs extends the classical product of TAs.

Definition 2. *Given two OTAIOs* $\mathcal{A} = (L^{\mathcal{A}}, l_0^{\mathcal{A}}, \Sigma_? \uplus \Sigma_! \uplus \Sigma_\tau, X_p^{\mathcal{A}} \uplus X_o^{\mathcal{A}}, I^{\mathcal{A}}, E^{\mathcal{A}})$ *and* $\mathcal{B} = (L^{\mathcal{B}}, l_0^{\mathcal{B}}, \Sigma_? \uplus \Sigma_! \uplus \Sigma_\tau, X_p^{\mathcal{B}} \uplus X_o^{\mathcal{B}}, I^{\mathcal{B}}, E^{\mathcal{B}})$ *over the same alphabets, their product is the OTAIO* $\mathcal{A} \times \mathcal{B} = (L^{\mathcal{A}} \times L^{\mathcal{B}}, (l_0^{\mathcal{A}}, l_0^{\mathcal{B}}), \Sigma_? \uplus \Sigma_! \uplus \Sigma_\tau, (X_p^{\mathcal{A}} \cup X_p^{\mathcal{B}}) \uplus ((X_o^{\mathcal{A}} \cup X_o^{\mathcal{B}}) \setminus (X_p^{\mathcal{A}} \cup X_p^{\mathcal{B}})), I, E)$ *where* $I: (l_1, l_2) \mapsto I^{\mathcal{A}}(l_1) \wedge I^{\mathcal{B}}(l_2)$ *and* E *is the (smallest) set such that for each* $(l^1, g^1, a, X_p'^1, l'^1) \in E^{\mathcal{A}}$ *and* $(l^2, g^2, a, X_p'^2, l'^2) \in E^{\mathcal{B}}$, E *contains* $((l^1, l^2), g^1 \wedge g^2, a, X_p'^1 \cup X_p'^2, (l'^1, l'^2))$.

The product of two OTAIOs corresponds to the intersection of the sequences of the orginial OTAIOs, *i.e.* $\mathsf{Seq}(\mathcal{A} \times \mathcal{B}) = \mathsf{Seq}(\mathcal{A}) \cap \mathsf{Seq}(\mathcal{B})$ [BSJK15].

2.2   Timed Games

We introduce timed game automata [AMPS98], which we later use to turn the test artifacts into games between the tester (controlling the environment) and the implementation, on an arena constructed from the specification.

Definition 3. *A timed game automaton (TGA) is a timed automaton* $\mathcal{G} = (L, l_0, \Sigma_c \uplus \Sigma_u, X, I, E)$ *where* $\Sigma = \Sigma_c \uplus \Sigma_u$ *is partitioned into actions that are controllable* (Σ_c) *and uncontrollable* (Σ_u) *by the player.*

All the notions of runs and sequences defined previously for TAs are extended to TGAs, with the interpretation of Σ_c as inputs and Σ_u as outputs.

Definition 4. *Let* $\mathcal{G} = (L, l_0, \Sigma_c \uplus \Sigma_u, X, I, E)$ *be a TGA. A* strategy *for the player is a partial function* $f: Ex(\mathcal{G}) \to \mathbb{R}_{\geq 0} \times (\Sigma_c \cup \{\bot\}) \setminus \{(0, \bot)\}$ *such that for any finite run* ρ, *letting* $f(\rho) = (\delta, a)$, $\delta \in elapse(last(\rho))$ *is a possible delay from* $last(\rho)$, *and there is an a-transition available from the resulting configuration (unless* $a = \bot$*).*

Strategies give rise to sets of runs of $\mathcal{G}$, defined as follows:

Definition 5. *Let* $\mathcal{G} = (L, l_0, \Sigma, X, I, E)$ *be a TGA, f be a strategy over $\mathcal{G}$, and s be a configuration. The* set of outcomes *of f from s, noted* $Outcome(s, f)$, *is the smallest subset of partial runs starting from s containing the empty partial run from s (whose last configuration is s), and s.t. for any* $\rho \in Outcome(s, f)$, *letting* $f(\rho) = (\delta, a)$ *and* $last(\rho) = (l, v)$, *we have*

- $\rho \cdot ((l, v), \delta, (l, v+\delta')) \cdot ((l, v+\delta'), e, (l', v')) \in Outcome(s, f)$ *for any* $0 \leq \delta' \leq \delta$ *and* $act(e) \in \Sigma_u$ *such that* $((l, v+\delta'), e, (l', v')) \in pEx(\mathcal{A})$;
- *and*
  - *either* $a = \bot$, *and* $\rho \cdot ((l, v), \delta, (l, v+\delta)) \in Outcome(s, f)$;
  - *or* $a \in \Sigma_c$, *and* $\rho \cdot ((l, v), \delta, (l, v+\delta)) \cdot ((l, v+\delta), e, (l', v')) \in Outcome(s, f)$ *with* $act(e) = a$;

An infinite partial run is in $Outcome(s, f)$ *if infinitely many of its finite prefixes are.*

In this paper, we will be interested in reachability winning conditions (under particular conditions). In the classical setting, the set of winning configurations can be computed iteratively, starting from the target location and computing controllable predecessors in a backward manner. The computation can be performed on regions, so that it terminates (in exponential time) [AMPS98, CDF+05]. We extend this approach to our test-generation framework in Sect. 4.

3   Testing Framework

We now present the testing framework, defining *(i)* the main testing artifacts *i.e.* specifications, implementations, test purposes, and test cases, along with the assumptions on them; *(ii)* a conformance relation relating implementations and specifications. The combination of the test purposes and the specification and the construction of an approximate deterministic tester is afterward explained.

3.1   Test Context

We use TAIOs as models for specifications, implementations and test cases, and OTAIOs for test purposes. This allows to define liberal test purposes, and on a technical side, gives a unity to the manipulated objects.

In order to enforce the occurrence of conclusive verdicts, we equip specifications with *restart transitions*, corresponding to a system shutdown and restart, and assume that from any (reachable) configuration, a restart is always reachable.

Definition 6. *A specification with restarts (or simply specification) on* $(\Sigma_?, \Sigma_!, \Sigma_\tau)$ *is a non-blocking, repeatedly-observable TAIO* $\mathcal{S} = (L^\mathcal{S}, l_0^\mathcal{S}, (\Sigma_? \cup \{\zeta\}) \uplus \Sigma_! \uplus \Sigma_\tau, X_p^\mathcal{S}, I^\mathcal{S}, E^\mathcal{S})$ *where* $\zeta \notin \Sigma_?$ *is the restart action. We let* $\mathsf{Restart}^\mathcal{S} = E^\mathcal{S} \cap (L^\mathcal{S} \times G_{M^\mathcal{S}}(X^\mathcal{S}) \times \{\zeta\} \times \{X_p^\mathcal{S}\} \times \{l_0^\mathcal{S}\})$ *be the set of* ζ*-transitions, and it is assumed that from any reachable configuration, there exists a finite partial execution containing* ζ*, i.e. for any* $s \in \mathsf{Reach}(\mathcal{S})$*, there exists* μ *s.t.* $s \xrightarrow{\mu \cdot \zeta} s_0^\mathcal{S}$.

The non-blocking hypothesis rules out "faulty" specifications having no conformant physically-possible implementation. Repeated-observability will be useful for technical reasons, when analyzing the exhaustiveness property of test cases. Our assumption on ζ-transitions entails:

Proposition 7. *Let* $\mathcal{S}$ *be a specification with restarts. Then* $\mathsf{Reach}(\mathcal{T}_\mathcal{S})$ *is strongly-connected.*

Example 1. Figure 1 is an example of specification for a conveyor belt. After a maximum time of 2 units (depending for example on their weight), packages reach a sorting point where they are automatically sorted between packages to reject and packages to ship. Packages to reject go to waste, while packages to ship are sent to a boarding platform, where an operator can send them to two different destinations. If the operator takes more than 3 units of time to select a destination, the package goes past the boarding platform and restarts the process.

In practice, test purposes are used to describe the intention of test cases, typically behaviours one wants because they must be correct and/or an error is suspected. In our formal testing framework, we describe them with OTAIOs that observe the specification together with accepting locations.

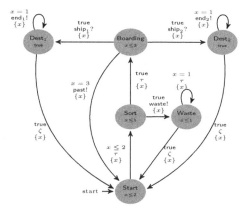

Fig. 1. A conveyor belt specification.

Definition 8. *Given a specification* $\mathcal{S} = (L^\mathcal{S}, l_0^\mathcal{S}, (\Sigma_? \cup \{\zeta\}) \uplus \Sigma_! \uplus \Sigma_\tau, X_p^\mathcal{S}, I^\mathcal{S}, E^\mathcal{S} \uplus \mathsf{Restart})$, *a test purpose for* $\mathcal{S}$ *is a pair* $(\mathcal{TP}, \mathsf{Accept}^{\mathcal{TP}})$ *where* $\mathcal{TP} = (L^{\mathcal{TP}}, l_0^{\mathcal{TP}}, \Sigma_? \cup \{\zeta\} \uplus \Sigma_! \uplus \Sigma_\tau, X_p^{\mathcal{TP}} \uplus X_p^\mathcal{S}, I^{\mathcal{TP}}, E^{\mathcal{TP}})$ *is a complete OTAIO together with a subset* $\mathsf{Accept}^{\mathcal{TP}} \subseteq L^{\mathcal{TP}}$ *of accepting locations, and such that transitions carrying restart actions* ζ *reset all proper clocks and return to the initial state (i.e., for any* ζ*-transition* $(l, g, \zeta, X', l') \in E$*, it must be* $X' = X_p^{\mathcal{TP}}$ *and* $l' = l_0^{\mathcal{TP}}$*).*

In the following, we may simply write $\mathcal{TP}$ in place of $(\mathcal{TP}, \mathsf{Accept}^{\mathcal{TP}})$. We force test purposes to be complete because they should never constrain the runs of the specification they observe, but should only label the accepted behaviours to be tested. Test purposes observe exactly the clocks of the specification in order to synchronize with them, but cannot reset them.

Example 2. Figure 2 is a test purpose for our conveyor-belt example. We want to be sure that it is possible to ship a package to destination 2 in less than 5 time units, while avoiding to go in waste. The Accept set is limited to a location, named Accept. We note oth the set of transitions that reset no clocks, and is enabled for an action other than ζ when no other transition is possible for this action. This set serves to complete the test purpose. The test purpose has a proper clock y.

In practice, conformance testing links a mathematical model, the specification, and a black-box implementation, that is a real-life *physical* object observed by its interactions with the environment. In order to formally reason about conformance, one needs to bridge the gap between the mathematical world and the physical world.

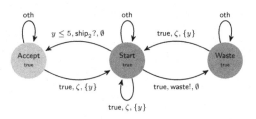

Fig. 2. A test purpose for the conveyor belt.

We then assume that the implementation corresponds to an unknown TAIO.

Definition 9. *Let* $\mathcal{S} = (L^{\mathcal{S}}, l_0^{\mathcal{S}}, (\Sigma_? \cup \{\zeta\}) \uplus \Sigma_! \uplus \Sigma_\tau, X_p^{\mathcal{S}}, I^{\mathcal{S}}, E^{\mathcal{S}} \cup \mathsf{Restart})$ *be a specification TAIO. An* implementation *of* $\mathcal{S}$ *is an input-complete and non-blocking TAIO* $\mathcal{I} = (L^{\mathcal{I}}, l_0^{\mathcal{I}}, (\Sigma_? \cup \{\zeta\}) \uplus \Sigma_! \uplus \Sigma_\tau^{\mathcal{I}}, X_p^{\mathcal{I}}, I^{\mathcal{I}}, E^{\mathcal{I}})$. *We note* $\mathcal{I}(\mathcal{S})$ *the set of possible implementations of* $\mathcal{S}$.

The hypotheses made on implementations are not restrictions, but model real-world contingencies: the environment might always provide any input and the system cannot alter the course of time.

Having defined the necessary objects, it is now possible to introduce the *timed input-output conformance* (tioco) relation [KT09]. Intuitively, it can be understood as "after any specified behaviour, outputs and delays of the implementation should be specified".

Definition 10. *Let* $\mathcal{S}$ *be a specification and* $\mathcal{I} \in \mathcal{I}(\mathcal{S})$. *We say that* $\mathcal{I}$ *conforms to* $\mathcal{S}$ *for tioco, and write* $\mathcal{I}$ *tioco* $\mathcal{S}$ *when:*

$$\forall \sigma \in \mathsf{Traces}(\mathcal{S}), \mathsf{out}(\mathcal{I} \text{ after } \sigma) \subseteq \mathsf{out}(\mathcal{S} \text{ after } \sigma)$$

Note that it is not assumed that restarts are well implemented: if they are not, it is significant only if it induces non-conformant behaviours.

3.2 Combining Specifications and Test Purposes

Now that the main objects are defined, we explain how the behaviours targeted by the test purpose $\mathcal{TP}$ are characterized on the specification $\mathcal{S}$ by the construction of the product OTAIO $\mathcal{P} = \mathcal{S} \times \mathcal{TP}$. Since $\mathcal{S}$ is a TAIO and the observed clocks of $\mathcal{TP}$ are exactly the clocks of $\mathcal{S}$, the product $\mathcal{P}$ is actually a TAIO. Furthermore, since $\mathcal{TP}$ is complete, $\mathsf{Seq}(\mathcal{P}) = \mathsf{Seq}(\mathcal{S})$. This entails that $\mathcal{I}$ tioco $\mathcal{S}$ is equivalent to $\mathcal{I}$ tioco $\mathcal{P}$. Note in particular that ζ of $\mathcal{S}$ synchronize with ζ of $\mathcal{TP}$, which are available everywhere.

By defining accepting locations in the product by $\mathsf{Accept}^{\mathcal{P}} = L^{\mathcal{S}} \times \mathsf{Accept}^{\mathcal{TP}}$, we get that sequences accepted in $\mathcal{P}$ are exactly sequences of $\mathcal{S}$ accepted by $\mathcal{TP}$.

Example 3. Figure 3 represents the product of the conveyor-belt specification of Fig. 1 and the test purpose of Fig. 2. All nodes are named by the first letters of the corresponding states of the specification (first) and of the test purpose. The only accepting location is (D_2, A).

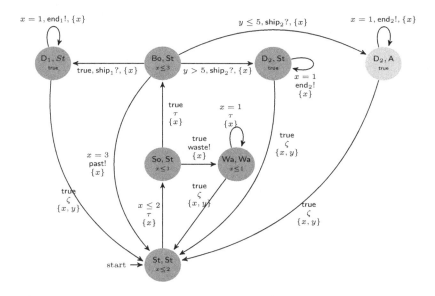

Fig. 3. Product of the conveyor belt specification and the presented test purpose.

We make one final hypothesis: we consider only pairs of specifications $\mathcal{S}$ and test purposes $\mathcal{TP}$ whose product $\mathcal{P}$ can be exactly determinized by the determinization game presented in [BSJK15]. This restriction is necessary for technical reasons: if the determinization is approximated, we cannot ensure that restarts are still reachable in general. Notice that it is satisfied in several classes of automata, such as strongly non-zeno automata, integer-reset automata, or event-recording automata.

Given the product $\mathcal{P} = \mathcal{S} \times \mathcal{TP}$, let $\mathcal{DP}$ be its exact determinization. In this case, $\mathsf{Traces}(\mathcal{DP}) = \mathsf{Traces}(\mathcal{P})$, hence the reachability of ζ transitions is preserved. Moreover the traces leading to $\mathsf{Accept}^{\mathcal{DP}}$ and $\mathsf{Accept}^{\mathcal{P}}$ are the same.

Example 4. The automaton in Fig. 4 is a deterministic approximation of the product presented in Fig. 3. The internal transitions have collapsed, leading to an augmented Start locality.

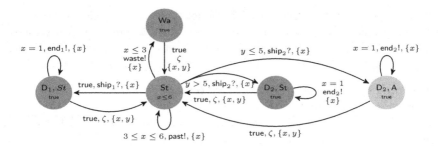

Fig. 4. A deterministic approximation of the product.

3.3 Accounting for Failure

At this stage of the process, we dispose of a deterministic and fully-observable TAIO $\mathcal{DP}$ having exactly the same traces as the original specification, and having a subset of its localities labelled as accepting for the test purpose. From this TAIO, we aim to build a tester, that can be able to monitor the implementation, feeding it with inputs and selecting verdicts from the returned outputs.

$\mathcal{DP}$ models the accepted traces with $\mathsf{Accept}^{\mathcal{DP}}$. In order to also explicitly model faulty behaviours (unspecified outputs after a specified trace), we now complete $\mathcal{DP}$ with respect to its output alphabet, by adding an explicit Fail location. We call this completed TAIO the *objective-centered tester*.

Definition 11. *Given a deterministic TAIO* $\mathcal{DP} = (L^{\mathcal{DP}}, l_0^{\mathcal{DP}}, \Sigma_? \uplus \Sigma_! \uplus \Sigma_\tau, X_p^{\mathcal{DP}}, I^{\mathcal{DP}}, E^{\mathcal{DP}})$, *we construct its objective-centered tester* $\mathcal{OT} = (L^{\mathcal{DP}} \cup \{\mathsf{Fail}\}, l_0^{\mathcal{DP}}, \Sigma_? \uplus \Sigma_! \uplus \Sigma_\tau, X_p^{\mathcal{DP}}, I^{\mathcal{OT}}, E^{\mathcal{OT}})$ *where* $I^{\mathcal{OT}}(l) = \mathbf{true}$. *The set of transitions* $E^{\mathcal{OT}}$ *is defined from* $E^{\mathcal{DP}}$ *by:*

$$E^{\mathcal{OT}} = E^{\mathcal{DP}} \cup \bigcup_{\substack{l \in L^{\mathcal{DP}} \\ a \in \Sigma_!^{\mathcal{DP}}}} \{(l, g, a, \emptyset, \mathsf{Fail}) \mid g \in \overline{G}_{a,l}\}$$

$$\cup \{(\mathsf{Fail}, \mathbf{true}, a, \emptyset, \mathsf{Fail}) \mid a \in \Sigma_!^{\mathcal{DP}}\}$$

where for each a *and* l, $\overline{G}_{a,l}$ *is a set of guards complementing the set of all valuations* v *for which an* a-*transition is available from* (l, v) *(notice that* $\overline{G}_{a,l}$ *generally is non-convex, so that it cannot be represented by a single guard).*

  Verdicts are defined on the configurations of $\mathcal{OT}$ *as follows:*

- $\boldsymbol{Pass} = \bigcup_{l \in \mathsf{Accept}^{\mathcal{DP}}} (\{l\} \times I^{\mathcal{DP}}(l))$,
- $\boldsymbol{Fail} = \{\mathsf{Fail}\} \times \mathbb{R}_{\geq 0} \cup \bigcup_{l \in L^{\mathcal{DP}}} \left(\{l\} \times (\mathbb{R}_{\geq 0}^{X_p} \setminus I^{\mathcal{DP}}(l))\right)$.

Notice that we do not define the usual ***Inconclusive*** verdicts (*i.e.* configurations in which we cannot conclude to non-conformance, nor accept the run with respect to the test purpose) as we will enforce the apparition of ***Pass*** or ***Fail***. ***Pass*** corresponds to behaviours accepted by the test purpose, while ***Fail*** corresponds to non-conformant behaviours. Note that $\mathcal{OT}$ inherits the interesting structural properties of $\mathcal{DP}$. More importantly, ζ is always reachable as long as no verdict has been emitted, and $\mathcal{OT}$ is repeatedly-observable out of ***Fail***.

It remains to say that $\mathcal{OT}$ and $\mathcal{DP}$ model the same behaviours. Obviously, their sets of traces differ, but the traces added in $\mathcal{OT}$ precisely correspond to runs reaching **Fail**. We now define a specific subset of runs, sequences and traces corresponding to traces that are meant to be accepted by the specification.

Definition 12. *A run ρ of an objective-centered tester $\mathcal{OT}$ is said conformant if it does not reach **Fail**. We note $\mathsf{Ex}_{conf}(\mathcal{OT})$ the set of conformant runs of $\mathcal{OT}$, and $\mathsf{Seq}_{conf}(\mathcal{OT})$ (resp. $\mathsf{Traces}_{conf}(\mathcal{OT})$) the corresponding sequences (resp. traces). We note $\mathsf{Ex}_{fail}(\mathcal{OT}) = \mathsf{Ex}(\mathcal{OT}) \setminus \mathsf{Ex}_{conf}(\mathcal{OT})$ and similarly for the sequences and traces.*

The conformant traces are exactly those specified by $\mathcal{DP}$, i.e. $\mathsf{Traces}(\mathcal{DP}) = \mathsf{Traces}_{conf}(\mathcal{OT})$ and correspond to executions tioco-conformant with the specification, while Ex_{fail} are runs where a non-conformance is detected.

4   Translating Objectives into Games

In this section, we interpret objective-centered tester into games between the tester and the implementation and propose strategies that try to avoid control losses. We then introduce a scope in which the tester always has a winning strategy, and discuss the properties of the resulting test cases (*i.e.* game structure and built strategy).

We want to enforce conclusive verdicts when running test cases, i.e. either the implementation does not conform to its specification (**Fail** verdict) or the awaited behaviour appears (**Pass** verdict). We thus say that an execution ρ is winning for the tester if it reaches a **Fail** or **Pass** configuration and note $\mathsf{Win}(\mathcal{G})$ the set of such executions. In the following, we consider the TGA $\mathcal{G}^{\mathcal{OT}} = (L^{\mathcal{OT}}, l_0^{\mathcal{OT}}, \Sigma_?^{\mathcal{OT}} \uplus \Sigma_!^{\mathcal{OT}}, X_p, I^{\mathcal{OT}}, E^{\mathcal{OT}})$ where the controllable actions are the inputs $\Sigma_c = \Sigma_?^{\mathcal{OT}}$ and the uncontrollable actions are the outputs $\Sigma_u = \Sigma_!^{\mathcal{OT}}$.

4.1   Rank-Lowering Strategy

In this part, we restrict our discussion to TGAs where **Pass** configurations are reachable (when seen as plain TAs). Indeed, if none can be reached, and we will discuss the fact that the proposed method can detect this fact, trying to construct a strategy seeking a **Pass** verdict is hopeless. This is a natural restriction, as it only rules out unsatisfiable test purposes.

The tester cannot force the occurrence of a non-conformance (as he does not control outputs and delays), and hence cannot push the system into a **Fail** configuration. A strategy for the tester should thus target the **Pass** set in a partially controllable way, while monitoring **Fail**. For that purpose, we define a hierarchy of configurations, depending on their "distance" to **Pass**. This uses a backward algorithm, for which we define the predecessors of a configuration.

Given a set of configurations $S' \subseteq S$ of $\mathcal{G}^{\mathcal{OT}}$, we define three kinds of predecessors, letting $\overline{V}$ denote the complement of V:

– discrete predecessors by a sub-alphabet $\Sigma' \subseteq \Sigma$:

$$\mathsf{Pred}_{\Sigma'}(S') = \{(l, v) \mid \exists a \in \Sigma',\ \exists (l, a, g, X', l') \in E, v \models g \wedge (l', v_{[X' \leftarrow 0]}) \in S'\}$$

– timed predecessors, while avoiding a set V of configurations:

$$\mathsf{tPred}(S', V) = \{(l, v) \mid \exists \delta \in \mathbb{R}_{\geq 0},\ (l, v+\delta) \in S' \wedge \forall\, 0 \leq \delta' \leq \delta.\ (l, v+\delta') \notin V\}$$

We furthermore note $\mathsf{tPred}(S') = \mathsf{tPred}(S', \emptyset)$.
– final timed predecessors are defined for convenience (see below):

$$\mathsf{ftPred}(S') = \mathsf{tPred}(\boldsymbol{Fail}, \mathsf{Pred}_{\Sigma_u}(\overline{S'})) \cup \overline{\mathsf{tPred}(\mathsf{Pred}_{\Sigma}(\overline{S'}))}$$

The final timed predecessors correspond to situations where the system is 'cornered', having the choice between taking an uncontrollable transition to S' (as no uncontrollable transition to $\overline{S'}$ will be available) or reach $\boldsymbol{Fail}$. Such situations are not considered as control losses, as the system can only take a beneficial transition for the tester (either by going to S' or to $\boldsymbol{Fail}$). Note that tPred and ftPred need not return convex sets, but are efficiently computable using Pred and simple set constructions [CDF+05]. Now, using these notions of predecessors, a hierarchy of configurations based on the 'distance' to $\boldsymbol{Pass}$ is defined.

Definition 13. *The sequence* $(W_i^j)_{j,i}$ *of sets of configurations is defined as:*

– $W_0^0 = \boldsymbol{Pass}$
– $W_{i+1}^j = \pi(W_i^j)$ *with* $\pi(S') = \mathsf{tPred}\left(S' \cup \mathsf{Pred}_{\Sigma_c}(S'), \mathsf{Pred}_{\Sigma_u}(\overline{S'})\right) \cup \mathsf{ftPred}(S')$
– $W_0^{j+1} = \mathsf{tPred}(W_\infty^j \cup \mathsf{Pred}_{\Sigma}(W_\infty^j))$ *with* W_∞^j *the limit[2] of the sequence* $(W_i^j)_i$.

In this hierarchy, j corresponds to the minimal number of *control losses* the tester has to go through (in the worst case) in order to reach $\boldsymbol{Pass}$, and i corresponds to the minimal number of steps before the next control loss (or to $\boldsymbol{Pass}$). The W_0^{j+1} are considered 'control losses' as the implementation might take an output transition leading to an undesirable configuration (higher on the hierarchy). On the other hand, in the construction of W_i^j the tester keep a full control, as it is not possible to reach such bad configuration with an uncontrollable transition. Notice that the sequence (W_i^j) is an increasing sequence of regions, and hence can be computed in time exponential in $X^{\mathcal{OT}}$ and linear in $L^{\mathcal{OT}}$.

We then have the following property:

Proposition 14. *There exists* $i, j \in \mathbb{N}$ *such that* $\mathsf{Reach}(\mathcal{G}^{\mathcal{OT}}) \setminus \boldsymbol{Fail} \subseteq W_i^j$.

As explained above, this property is based on the assumption that the $\boldsymbol{Pass}$ verdict is reachable. Nevertheless, if it is not it will be detected during the hierarchy construction that will converge to a fixpoint not including $s_0^{\mathcal{G}}$. As all the configurations in which we want to define a strategy are covered by the hierarchy, we can use it to define a partial order.

---

[2] The sequence $(W_i^j)_i$ is non-decreasing, and can be computed in terms of clock regions; hence the limit exists and is reached in a finite number of iterations [CDF+05].

Definition 15. *Let $s \in \text{Reach}(\mathcal{G}^{\mathcal{OT}}) \setminus \textbf{Fail}$. The rank of s is:*

$$r(s) = (j_s = \arg\min_{j \in \mathbb{N}}(s \in W^j_\infty), i_s = \arg\min_{i \in \mathbb{N}}(s \in W^{j_s}_i))$$

For $r(s) = (j, i)$; j is the minimal number of control losses before reaching an accepting state, and i is the minimal number of steps in the strategy before the next control loss. We note $s \sqsubseteq s'$ when $r(s) \leq_{\mathbb{N}^2} r(s')$, where $\leq_{\mathbb{N}^2}$ is the lexical order on $\mathbb{N}^2$.

Proposition 16. $\sqsubseteq$ *is a partial order on* $\text{Reach}(\mathcal{G}^{\mathcal{OT}}) \setminus \textbf{Fail}$.

We dispose of a partial order on configurations, with **Pass** being the minimal elements. We use it to define a strategy trying to decrease the rank during the execution. For any $s \in S$, we write $r^-(s)$ for the largest rank such that $r^-(s) <_{\mathbb{N}^2} r(s)$, and $W^-(s)$ for the associated set in $(W^j_i)_{j,i}$. We (partially) order pairs $(\delta, a) \in \mathbb{R}_{\geq 0} \times \Sigma$ according to δ.

Definition 17. *A strategy f for the tester is* rank-lowering *if, for any finite run ρ with $\text{last}(\rho) = s = (l, v)$, it selects the lesser delay satisfying one of the following constraints:*

- *if $s \in \text{tPred}(\text{Pred}_{\Sigma_c}(W^-(s)))$, then $f(\rho) = (\delta, a)$ with $a \in \Sigma_c$ s.t. there exists $e \in E$ with $\text{act}(e) = a$ and $s \xrightarrow{\delta} \xrightarrow{e} t$ with $t \in W^-(s)$, and δ is minimal in the following sense: if $s \xrightarrow{\delta'} \xrightarrow{e'} t'$ with $t' \in W^-(s)$ and $\delta' \leq \delta$, then $v + \delta$ and $v + \delta'$ belong to the same region;*
- *if $s \in \text{tPred}(W^-(s))$, then $f(\rho) = (\delta, \perp)$ such that $s \xrightarrow{\delta} t$ with $t \in W^-(s)$, and δ is minimal in the same sense as above;*
- *otherwise $f(\rho) = (\delta, \perp)$ where δ is maximal in the same sense as above (maximal delay-successor region).*

The two first cases follow the construction of the W^j_i and propose the shortest behaviour leading to W^-. The third case corresponds, either to a configuration of **Pass**, where W^- is undefined, or to a ftPred. Notice that (possibly several) rank-lowering strategies always exist.

Example 5. An example of a rank-lowering strategy on the automaton of Fig. 4 is: in (D_2, A), play $\perp$ (as W^0_0 has been reached); in St, play $(0, \text{ship}_2?)$; in any other state, play $(0, \zeta)$. Note that Fig. 4 has not been completed in a objective-centered tester. This does not impact the strategies, as the transition to the fail states lead to a victory, but are not targeted by the strategies.

It is worth noting that even in a more general setup where the models are not equipped with ζ-transitions, as in [BSJK15], rank-lowering strategies may still be useful: as they are defined on the co-reachable set of Accept, they can still constitute test cases, and the configurations where they are not defined are exactly the configurations corresponding to a **Fail** verdict or to an **Inconclusive** verdict, i.e., no conclusions can be made since an accepting configuration cannot be reached.

4.2 Making Rank-Lowering Strategies Win

A rank-lowering strategy is generally not a winning strategy: it relies on the implementation fairly exploring its different possibilities and not repeatedly avoiding an enabled transition. In this section, fair runs are introduced, and the rank-lowering strategies are shown to be winning in this subset of the runs.

Lemma 18. *If $\mathcal{OT}$ is repeatedly-observable, then for all $\rho = ((s_i, \gamma_i, s_{i+1}))_{i \in \mathbb{N}} \in Ex(\mathcal{G})$ ending with an infinite sequence of delays, we have[3]*

$$\rho \in \mathsf{Ex}_{\mathsf{fail}}(\mathcal{G}) \vee \exists e \in E^{\mathcal{G}}, \ \overset{\infty}{\exists} \ i \in \mathbb{N}, e \in \mathsf{enab}(s_i).$$

This lemma ensures that we cannot end in a situation where no transitions can be taken, forcing the system to delay indefinitely. It will be used with the support of fairness. In order to introduce our notion of fairness, we define the infinite support of a run.

Definition 19. *Let ρ be an infinite run, its* infinite support $\mathsf{Inf}(\rho)$ *is the set of regions appearing infinitely often in ρ.*

$$\mathsf{Inf}((s_i, \gamma_i, s_{i+1})_{i \in \mathbb{N}}) = \{r \mid \overset{\infty}{\exists} \ i \in \mathbb{N}, \ s_i \in r \ \vee$$
$$(\gamma_i \in \mathbb{R}_{\geq 0} \wedge \exists s_i' \in r, \ \exists \delta_i < \gamma_i, \ s_i \overset{\delta_i}{\longrightarrow} s_i')\}$$

The notion of enabled transitions and delay transitions are extended to regions as follows: for a region r, we let $\mathsf{enab}(r) = \mathsf{enab}(s)$ for any s in r, and write $r \overset{t}{\rightarrow} r'$ for all time-successor region r' of r.

Definition 20. *An infinite run ρ in a TGA $\mathcal{G} = (L, l_0, \Sigma_u \uplus \Sigma_c, X, I, E)$ (with timed transitions system $\mathcal{T} = (S, s_0, \Gamma, \rightarrow_{\mathcal{T}}))$ is said to be* fair *when:*

$$\forall e \in E, (\mathsf{act}(e) \in \Sigma_u \Rightarrow (\exists r \in \mathsf{Inf}(\rho), r \overset{e}{\rightarrow} r' \Rightarrow r' \in \mathsf{Inf}(\rho))) \ \wedge$$
$$\forall r \in \mathsf{Inf}(\rho), \exists \gamma \in (\mathsf{enab}(r) \cap \{e \mid \mathsf{act}(e) \in \Sigma_c\}) \cup \{\mathsf{t}\}), r \overset{\gamma}{\rightarrow} r' \wedge r' \in \mathsf{Inf}(\rho)$$

We note $\mathsf{Fair}(\mathcal{G})$ *the set of fair runs of $\mathcal{G}$.*

Fair runs model restrictions on the system runs corresponding to strategies of the system. The first part of the definition assures that any infinitely-enabled action of the implementation will be taken infinitely many times, while the second part ensures that the implementation will infinitely often let the tester play, by ensuring that a delay or controllable action will be performed. It matches the "strong fairness" notion used in model checking. Restricting to fair runs is sufficient to ensure a winning execution when the tester uses a rank-lowering strategy. Intuitively, combined with Lemma 18 and the repeated-observability assumption, it assures that the system will keep providing outputs until a verdict is reached, and allows to show the following property.

---

[3] In this expression, $\overset{\infty}{\exists} \ i \in \mathbb{N}, \ \phi(i)$ means that $\phi(i)$ is true for infinitely many integers.

Proposition 21. *Rank-lowering strategies are winning on* Fair($\mathcal{G}$) *(i.e., all fair outcomes are winning).*

Under the hypothesis of a fair implementation, we thus have identified a test-case generation method, starting from the specification with restarts and the test purpose, and constructing a test case as a winning strategy on the game created from the objective-centered tester. The complexity of this method is exponential in the size of $\mathcal{DP}$. More precisely:

Proposition 22. *Given a deterministic product* $\mathcal{DP}$, $\mathcal{OT}$ *can be linearly computed from* $\mathcal{DP}$, *and the construction of a strategy relies on the construction of the* W_i^j *and is hence exponential in* $X^{\mathcal{DP}}$ *and linear in* $L^{\mathcal{DP}}$.

Note that if $\mathcal{DP}$ is obtained from $\mathcal{P}$ by the game presented in [BSJK15], then $L^{\mathcal{DP}}$ is doubly exponential in the size of $X^{\mathcal{S}} \uplus X^{\mathcal{TP}} \uplus X^{\mathcal{DP}}$ (notice that in the setting of [BSJK15], $X^{\mathcal{DP}}$ is a parameter of the algorithm).

4.3   Properties of the Test Cases

Having constructed strategies for the tester, and identified a scope of implementation behaviours that allows these strategies to enforce a conclusive verdict, we now study the properties obtained by the test generation method presented above. We call *test case* a pair $(\mathcal{G}, f)$ where $\mathcal{G}$ is the game corresponding to the objective-centered tester $\mathcal{OT}$, and f is a rank-lowering strategy on $\mathcal{G}$. We note $\mathcal{TC}(\mathcal{S}, \mathcal{TP})$ the set of possibles test cases generated from a specification $\mathcal{S}$ and a test purpose $\mathcal{TP}$, and $\mathcal{TC}(\mathcal{S})$ the test cases for any test purpose. Recall that it is assumed that the test purposes associated with a specification are restricted to those leading to a determinizable product. *Behaviours* are defined as the possible outcomes of a test case combined with an implementation, and model their parallel composition.

Definition 23. *Given a test case* $(\mathcal{G}, f)$ *and an implementation* $\mathcal{I}$, *their behaviours are the runs* $((s_i, s_i'), (e_i, e_i'), (s_{i+1}, s_{i+1}'))_i$ *such that* $((s_i, e_i, s_{i+1}))_i$ *is an outcome of* $(\mathcal{G}, f)$, $((s_i', e_i', s_{i+1}'))_i$ *is a run of* $\mathcal{I}$, *and for all* i, *either* $e_i = e_i'$ *if* $e_i \in \mathbb{R}_{\geq 0}$ *or* act(e_i) = act(e_i') *otherwise. We write* Behaviour($\mathcal{G}, f, \mathcal{I}$) *for the set of behaviours of the test case* $(\mathcal{G}, f)$ *and of the implementation* $\mathcal{I}$.

We say that an implementation $\mathcal{I}$ fails a test case $(\mathcal{G}, f)$, and note $\mathcal{I}$ fails $(\mathcal{G}, f)$, when there exists a run in Behaviour($\mathcal{G}, f, \mathcal{I}$) that reaches **Fail**. Our method is sound, that is, a conformant implementation cannot be detected as faulty.

Proposition 24. *The test-case generation method is* sound: *for any specification* $\mathcal{S}$, *it holds*

$$\forall \mathcal{I} \in \mathcal{I}(\mathcal{S}), \ \forall (\mathcal{G}, f) \in \mathcal{TC}(\mathcal{S}), \ (\mathcal{I} \ \text{fails} \ (\mathcal{G}, f) \Rightarrow \neg(\mathcal{I} \ \text{tioco} \ \mathcal{S})).$$

The proofs of this property and the following one are based on the exact cor-respondance between **Fail** and the faulty behaviours of $\mathcal{S}$, and use the trace equivalence of the different models ($\mathcal{DP}$, $\mathcal{P}$ and $\mathcal{S}$) to conclude. As they exploit mainly the game structure, fairness is not used.

We define the notion of outputs after a trace in a behaviour, allowing to extend tioco to these objects and to state a strictness property. Intuitively, when a non-conformance appears it should be detected.

Definition 25. *Given a test case* $(\mathcal{G}, f)$ *and an implementation* $\mathcal{I}$, *for a trace* σ:

$$\mathit{out}(\mathit{Behaviour}(\mathcal{G}, f, \mathcal{I}) \text{ after } \sigma) =$$
$$\{a \in \Sigma_! \cup \mathbb{R}_{\geq 0} \mid \exists \rho \in \mathit{Behaviour}(\mathcal{G}, f, \mathcal{I}), \ \mathit{Trace}(\rho) = \sigma \cdot a\}$$

Proposition 26. *The test generation method is* strict*: given a specification* $\mathcal{S}$,

$$\forall \mathcal{I} \in \mathcal{I}(\mathcal{S}), \ \forall (\mathcal{G}, f) \in \mathcal{TC}(\mathcal{S}), \ \neg(\mathit{Behaviour}(\mathcal{G}, f, \mathcal{I}) \text{ tioco } \mathcal{S}) \Rightarrow \mathcal{I} \text{ fails } (\mathcal{G}, f)$$

This method also enjoys a precision property: traces leading the test case to **Pass** are exactly traces conforming to the specification and accepted by the test purpose. The proof of this property uses the exact encoding of the Accept states and the definition of **Pass**. As the previous two, it then propagates the property through the different test artifacts.

Proposition 27. *The test case generation method is* precise*: for any specifica-tion* $\mathcal{S}$ *and test purpose* $\mathcal{TP}$ *it can be stated that*

$$\forall (\mathcal{G}, f) \in \mathcal{TC}(\mathcal{S}, \mathcal{TP}), \forall \sigma \in \mathit{Traces}(\mathit{Outcome}(s_0^{\mathcal{G}}, f)),$$
$$\mathcal{G} \text{ after } \sigma \in \textbf{Pass} \ \Leftrightarrow \ (\sigma \in \mathit{Traces}(\mathcal{S}) \wedge \mathcal{TP} \text{ after } \sigma \cap \mathit{Accept}^{\mathcal{TP}} \neq \emptyset)$$

Lastly, this method is exhaustive in the sense that for any non-conformance, there exist a test case that allows to detect it, under fairness assumption.

Proposition 28. *The test generation method is* exhaustive*: for any exactly determinizable specification* $\mathcal{S}$ *and any implementation* $\mathcal{I} \in \mathcal{I}(\mathcal{S})$ *making fair runs*

$$\neg(\mathcal{I} \text{ tioco } \mathcal{S}) \Rightarrow \exists (\mathcal{G}, f) \in \mathcal{TC}(\mathcal{S}), \mathcal{I} \text{ fails } (\mathcal{G}, f).$$

To demonstrate this property, a test purpose is tailored to detect a given non-conformance, by targeting a related conformant trace.

5   Conclusion

This paper proposes a game approach to the controllability problem for confor-mance testing from timed automata (TA) specifications. It defines a test synthe-sis method that produces test cases whose aim is to maximize their control upon the implementation under test, while detecting non-conformance. Test cases are defined as strategies of a game between the tester and the implementation, based on the distance to the satisfaction of a test purpose, both in terms of number of transitions and potential control losses. Fairness assumptions are used to make those strategies winning and are proved sufficient to obtain the exhaustiveness of the test synthesis method, together with soundness, strictness and precision.

This paper opens numerous directions for future work. First, we intend to tackle partial observation in a more complete and practical way. One direction consists in finding weaker conditions under which approximate determinization [BSJK15] preserves strong connectivity, a condition for the existence of winning strategies. One could also consider a mixture of our model and the model of [DLL+10] whose observer predicates are clearly adequate in some contexts. Quantitative aspects could also better meet practical needs. The distance to the goal could also include the time distance or costs of transitions, in particular to avoid restarts when they induce heavy costs but longer and cheaper paths are possible. The fairness assumption could also be refined. For now it is assumed on both the specification and the implementation. If the implementation does not implement some outputs, a tester could detect it with a bounded fairness assumption [Ram98], adapted to the timed context (after sufficiently many experiments traversing some region all outputs have been observed), thus allowing a stronger conformance relation with egality of output sets. A natural extension could also be to complete the approach in a stochastic view. Finally, we plan to implement the results of this work in an open tool for the analysis of timed automata, experiment on real examples and check the scalability of the method.

References

[AD94]   Alur, R., Dill, D.L.: A theory of timed automata. Theoret. Comput. Sci. **126**(2), 183–235 (1994)

[AMPS98]   Asarin, E., Maler, O., Pnueli, A., Sifakis, J.: Controller synthesis for timed automata. In: Proceedings of the 5th IFAC Conference on System Structure and Control (SSC 1998), pp. 469–474. Elsevier, July 1998

[BB04]   Briones, L.B., Brinksma, E.: A test generation framework for *quiescent* real-time systems. In: Grabowski, J., Nielsen, B. (eds.) FATES 2004. LNCS, vol. 3395, pp. 64–78. Springer, Heidelberg (2005). https://doi.org/10.1007/978-3-540-31848-4_5

[BJSK12]   Bertrand, N., Jéron, T., Stainer, A., Krichen, M.: Off-line test selection with test purposes for non-deterministic timed automata. Log. Methods Comput. Sci. **8**(4) (2012)

[BSJK15]   Bertrand, N., Stainer, A., Jéron, T., Krichen, M.: A game approach to determinize timed automata. Form. Methods Syst. Des. **46**(1), 42–80 (2015)

[CDF+05]   Cassez, F., David, A., Fleury, E., Larsen, K.G., Lime, D.: Efficient on-the-fly algorithms for the analysis of timed games. In: Abadi, M., de Alfaro, L. (eds.) CONCUR 2005. LNCS, vol. 3653, pp. 66–80. Springer, Heidelberg (2005). https://doi.org/10.1007/11539452_9

[CKL98] Castanet, R., Koné, O., Laurençot, P.: On-the-fly test generation for real time protocols. In: Proceedings of the International Conference on Computer Communications and Networks (ICCCN 1998), pp. 378–387. IEEE Comp. Soc. Press, October 1998

[COG98] Cardell-Oliver, R., Glover, T.: A practical and complete algorithm for testing real-time systems. In: Ravn, A.P., Rischel, H. (eds.) FTRTFT 1998. LNCS, vol. 1486, pp. 251–261. Springer, Heidelberg (1998). https://doi.org/10.1007/BFb0055352

[DLL+10] David, A., Larsen, K.G., Li, S., Mikucionis, M., Nielsen, B.: Testing real-time systems under uncertainty. In: Aichernig, B.K., de Boer, F.S., Bonsangue, M.M. (eds.) FMCO 2010. LNCS, vol. 6957, pp. 352–371. Springer, Heidelberg (2011). https://doi.org/10.1007/978-3-642-25271-6_19

[DLLN08a] David, A., Larsen, K.G., Li, S., Nielsen, B.: Cooperative testing of timed systems. In: Proceedings of the 4th Workshop on Model Based Testing (MBT 2008), vol. 220, pp. 79–92 (2008)

[DLLN08b] David, A., Larsen, K.G., Li, S., Nielsen, B.: A game-theoretic approach to real-time system testing. In: Proceedings of the Conference on Design, Automation and Test in Europe (DATE 2008), pp. 486–491, March 2008

[ENDK02] En-Nouaary, A., Dssouli, R., Khendek, F.: Timed Wp-method: testing real-time systems. IEEE Trans. Softw. Eng. 28(11), 1023–1038 (2002)

[Fin06] Finkel, O.: Undecidable problems about timed automata. In: Asarin, E., Bouyer, P. (eds.) FORMATS 2006. LNCS, vol. 4202, pp. 187–199. Springer, Heidelberg (2006). https://doi.org/10.1007/11867340_14

[HJM18] Henry, L., Jéron, T., Markey, N.: Control strategies for off-line testing of timed systems. Technical report 1804.11234, arXiv, April 2018

[KT09] Krichen, M., Tripakis, S.: Conformance testing for real-time systems. Form. Methods Syst. Des. 34(3), 238–304 (2009)

[LMN04] Larsen, K.G., Mikucionis, M., Nielsen, B.: Online testing of real-time systems using UPPAAL. In: Grabowski, J., Nielsen, B. (eds.) FATES 2004. LNCS, vol. 3395, pp. 79–94. Springer, Heidelberg (2005). https://doi.org/10.1007/978-3-540-31848-4_6

[NS03] Nielsen, B., Skou, A.: Automated test generation from timed automata. Int. J. Softw. Tools Technol. Transfer 5(1), 59–77 (2003)

[Ram98] Ramangalahi, S.: Strategies for comformance testing. Research Report 98-010, Max-Planck Institut für Informatik, May 1998

[SVD01] Springintveld, J., Vaandrager, F., D'Argenio, P.R.: Testing timed automata. Theoret. Comput. Sci. 254(1–2), 225–257 (2001)

[Tre96] Tretmans, J.: Conformance testing with labelled transition systems: implementation relations and test generation. Comput. Netw. ISDN Syst. 29(1), 49–79 (1996)

[Yan04] Yannakakis, M.: Testing, optimizaton, and games. In: Díaz, J., Karhumäki, J., Lepistö, A., Sannella, D. (eds.) ICALP 2004. LNCS, vol. 3142, pp. 28–45. Springer, Heidelberg (2004). https://doi.org/10.1007/978-3-540-27836-8_6

An Extension of TRIANGLE Testbed with Model-Based Testing

Laura Panizo$^{(\boxtimes)}$ ⓘ, Almudena Díaz ⓘ, and Bruno García ⓘ

Andalucía Tech, Dept. de Ciencias de la Computación,
Universidad de Málaga, Málaga, Spain
{laurapanizo,almudiaz,bgarcia}@lcc.uma.es

Abstract. Traditional testing methods for mobile apps focus on detecting execution errors. However, the evolution of mobile networks towards 5G will require additional support for app developers to ensure also the performance and user-experience. Manual testing in a number of scenarios is not enough to satisfy the expectations of the apps final users. This paper presents the testing framework developed in the TRIANGLE project (https://www.triangle-project.eu/) that integrates a complete mobile network testbed and a model-based testing approach, which is based on model checking, to automatically evaluate the apps performance in different network scenarios.

Keywords: Model-based testing · Mobile network testbed
Model checking

1 Introduction to Triangle Testing Framework

The TRIANGLE testbed [1] is devoted to the testing and benchmarking of mobile applications and devices. Figure 1 shows an overview of the main functional blocks of the testbed architecture.

The testbed provides a high-level access based on a *web portal* whose main purpose is preparing and running tests, and later reviewing the results. It provides an intuitive interface for the definition and execution of the *testing campaigns*, hiding unnecessary complexity. Testing campaigns are based on the execution of the *test cases* specified in the TRIANGLE project for app testing. A test case defines the configuration of the network scenarios, the app user flow (sequence of actions) that will be used to activate the feature under test, and finally the measurements that have to be collected, which are determined by the Key Performance Indicators (KPIs) associated to the features under test. The network scenarios and the measurement are configured automatically based on the app features, the device or the *high-level scenario* selected by the user. In addition, the user has to provide the app users flows. All these user inputs are processed and transformed into inputs for the different components of the underlying architecture.

This work is funded by the European Union's Horizon 2020 research and innovation programme, grant agreement No 688712 (TRIANGLE project).

ⓒ Springer International Publishing AG, part of Springer Nature 2018
M. M. Gallardo and P. Merino (Eds.): SPIN 2018, LNCS 10869, pp. 190–195, 2018.
https://doi.org/10.1007/978-3-319-94111-0_11

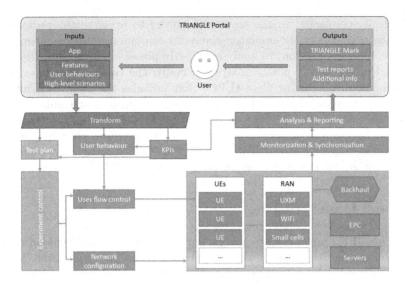

Fig. 1. TRIANGLE testing framework overview

The web portal stores all the campaigns and other user provided data, as well as the results obtained from the testbed, so that test case results are completely traceable to their configuration, and can be repeated if needed.

The *experiment control* module coordinates the configuration and execution of all network components. The configuration of the different network elements is determined by the high-level scenarios, which abstract similar network configurations that are reproduced during the test case execution. The high-level scenarios are translated into the specific configurations that are applied to each network component. In TRIANGLE, we use the Keysight Testing Automation Platform (TAP) [4] to automate the whole process. TAP is a flexible platform that orchestrates the interaction of the testing framework with a number of instruments that interact around the testbed device.

An integral part of testing apps is automating their execution, i.e., simulating the interactions of a user with the app. Quamotion automation tools[1] provide the means to create sequences of user actions, and then replaying them on a testbed device. In addition, the testbed provides an instrumentation library in order to collect measurements related to the internal performance of the app under test. The source code of the app is instrumented with this library to push measurements points into the logcat, the Android logging system, and correlate these points with radio and power measurements.

The Radio Access Network (RAN) is provided by a mobile network emulator that provides test features such as flexible Inter Cell Interference Coordination (eICIC) schemes or IMS/End-to-End VoLTE communications between multiple devices. The mobile devices, where the applications under test are executed,

---

[1] http://quamotion.mobi/Mwc.

are physically connected to the testbed. In order to preserve the radio conditions configured at network emulator, the radio antenna connection is conducted through cables. In addition, to analyse properly power consumption, the device is powered directly by a power analyser. Finally, the testbed also integrates a commercial Evolved Packet Core (EPC) that includes the main elements of a standard core network and local application servers such as streaming or VoIP servers.

The next section presents the model-based testing approach, which is based on model checking, to automatically generate the app user flows to achieve the complete automatisation of the app testing process.

2   Model-Based Testing

The TRIANGLE project defines generic app features, such as download content or playback media files, that are evaluated by the KPIs. In the simplest case, the app developer provides an app user flow that activates the feature under test to compute the KPIs. For instance, if the app under test playbacks live streaming, the app user flow has to start and end the playback. The TRIANGLE testbed integrates model-based testing techniques to support the automatic generation of a set of app user flows.

In [5], we presented a preliminary method to guide the generation of app user flows by means of app user flow requirements. The requirements allow us to produce only the set of app user flows that are useful to compute any given KPI. The approach is based on the exhaustive exploration of an app model and the requirements with the model checker SPIN [3].

The app model is described with a language based on nested state machines [2] that are able to capture the interaction of the user with the app, and the intrinsic behaviour of mobile operating systems. An app state machine is composed of one or more activity state machines, which corresponded to the different activities (screens) in an app. In addition, an activity state machine can contain one or more state machines with states and edges defining the user behaviour. The edges of a state machine represent the user actions, such as tapping a button, that should be executed when traversing the edge. Connection states are used to transit between state machines. These states are represented as unlabelled empty circles with two outgoing transitions, one pointing to a state, and another targeting to a state machine. When a connection state is reached, the execution continues with the initial state of the state machine referenced. When the target state machine finishes, that is, when it reaches an end state, the execution comes back in the returning state. Figure 2 shows a model of Exoplayer app, an Android video player that supports different video codecs. The app is divided into two activities: *SampleChooserActivity*, which shows the list of videos that can be played, and *PlayerActivity*, which shows the playback controls.

In [5], the app user flow requirements were directly described with Promela code and the app model was manually written by the user, which can be tedious and error-prone. In the TRIANGLE testbed, these issues are solved. The app

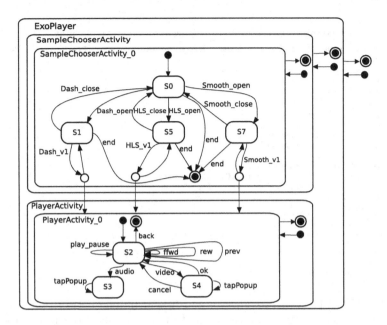

Fig. 2. Exoplayer model with nested state machines

user flow requirements are described in a xml-based language, more intuitive for an app developer, and are automatically transformed into Promela. The requirements define the states that have to be visited (or not) and the events that can be fired. Listing 1.1 shows an example related to the Exoplayer app model. This example defines an invariant that forces only one event play_pause in the complete app user flow. In addition, it also specifies a sequence of events and states that have to be visited (relative order). Any other events or states can be fired and visited if the invariant is still satisfied. Finally, we have defined an approach to automatically extract the app model from the compiled code of the app. Due to space limits, we do not provide details about the automatic model generation.

The app model, manually or automatically extracted, and the requirements are uploaded to the web portal. The model is automatically translated into a Promela specification and the requirements are translated into a *never claim*, which is a special Promela process that guides and prunes the exploration of the app model. Then, the SPIN model checker verifies the app model against the set of requirements, in such a way that counterexamples represent the app user flows satisfying the requirements. During the exploration, we also restrict the minimum and maximum length of the app user flows. Each counterexample is recorded in the format of Quamotion automation tool, in order to automate the app user flow execution on the device. For example, the analysis of the Exoplayer model (see Fig. 2 and Listing 1.1) produces 274 app user flows with 10 user actions at most that can be used to evaluate a given KPI.

Listing 1.1. Example of requirements in XML format

```
1   <appUserFlowRequirement xmlns="appuserflowrequirement" name="DemoPlayer_never_1">
2     <invariants>
3       <event name="play_pause" max="1"/>
4     </invariants>
5     <sequence>
6       <constraint type="simple">
7         <event name="Dash_video_1" min="1" max="1"/>
8       </constraint>
9       <constraint type="simple">
10        <event name="play_pause" min="1" max="1"/>
11      </constraint>
12      <constraint type="simple">
13        <state name="end" view="SampleChooserActivity"
14          statemachine="SampleChooserActivity_0" visit="true"/>
15      </constraint>
16    </sequence>
17  </appUserFlowRequirement>
```

3   Conclusions

The TRIANGLE testbed provides an end-to-end mobile network environment that enables app developers to thoroughly test their applications in real network scenarios, including radio conditions, which are not under the control when running tests in live mobile deployments. So the most important feature of the testbed is that the network scenarios emulate realistic conditions, are totally repeatable and the experiments are reproducible. This ensures the validity of the test results.

So the previous version of the testbed is able to rigorously test the application in numerous combinations of radio and network configurations. The integration of model-based testing techniques pursue this same rigour to generate app use flow to stimulate applications under test in different network scenarios.

In particular, the integration of model-based testing techniques improves the usability and flexibility of the testbed in different ways:

- The testbed automatically produces a pool of app user flows that use the app features in different ways, improving the test coverage.
- App user flows satisfying different requirements are generated with the same app model. If the testbed is extended with new test cases, the app model does not change, and only new requirements have to be defined.
- The automation of app user flow format is transparent for the app developer. Currently, the portal supports app user flows in JSON format, but we plant to migrate to Powershell scripts in the near future due to new functionality integrated in the testbed.

References

1. Cattoni, A.F., Corrales-Madueño, G., Dieudonne, M., Merino, P., Díaz-Zayas, A., Salmerón, A., Carlier, F., Saint-Germain, B., Morris, D., Figueiredo, R., Caffrey, J., Baños, J., Cardenas, C., Roche, N., Moore, A.: An end-to-end testing ecosystem for 5G. In: European Conference on Networks and Communications, EuCNC 2016, Athens, Greece, 27–30 June 2016, pp. 307–312 (2016). https://doi.org/10.1109/EuCNC.2016.7561053
2. Espada, A.R., Gallardo, M.M., Salmerón, A., Merino, P.: Performance analysis of spotify® for android with model-based testing. Mob. Inf. Syst. **2017**, 14 (2017). https://doi.org/10.1155/2017/2012696
3. Holzmann, G.: The SPIN Model Checker: Primer and Reference Manual. Addison-Wesley Professional, Boston (2003)
4. Keysight Technologies: Test Automation Platform Developer's System. http://www.keysight.com/en/pd-2747943-pn-KS8400A/test-automation-platform-developers-system?cc=ES&lc=eng. Accessed Mar 21 2018
5. Panizo, L., Salmerón, A., Gallardo, M.M., Merino, P.: Guided test case generation for mobile apps in the TRIANGLE project: work in progress. In: Proceedings of the 24th International SPIN Symposium on Model Checking of Software, pp. 192–195. ACM (2017). https://doi.org/10.1145/3092282.3092298

Local Data Race Freedom
with Non-multi-copy Atomicity

Tatsuya Abe[(✉)]

STAIR Lab, Chiba Institute of Technology, 2-17-1 Tsudanuma,
Narashino, Chiba 275-0016, Japan
abet@stair.center

Abstract. Data race freedom ensures the sequentially consistent behaviors of concurrent programs under relaxed memory consistency models (MCMs), and reduces the state explosion problem for software model checking with MCMs. However, data race freedom is too strong to include all interesting programs. In this paper, we define small-step operational semantics for relaxed MCMs, define an observable equivalence using the notion of bisimulation, and propose the property of local data race freedom (LDRF), which requires a kind of race freedom locally instead of globally. LDRF includes some interesting programs, such as the independent reads independent writes program, which is well known to exhibit curious behaviors under non-multi-copy atomic MCMs, and some concurrent copying garbage collection algorithms. In this paper, we introduce an optimization method called memory sharing for model checking of LDRF programs, and show that memory sharing optimization mitigates state explosion problems with non-multi-copy atomic MCMs through experiments.

Keywords: Data race freedom · Memory consistency model
Software model checking · State explosion problem
Non-multi-copy atomicity · Observable equivalence · Bisimulation
Independent reads independent writes program
Concurrent copying garbage collection algorithm

1 Introduction

Memory consistency models (MCMs), which specify how multiple threads use shared memory, have become extremely important because modern computer architectures have multiple cores. Their computing performance depends on the MCMs that the architectures adopt.

Saraswat et al. and Owens provided an insightful definition of MCM [19,25]. Saraswat et al. focused on an earlier study of observable equivalences between MCMs and data race freedom (DRF) by Gao and Sarkar [11]. Saraswat et al. defined some relaxed MCMs, and presented the so-called *fundamental property* such that DRF programs have only *observable* and *sequentially consistent (SC)*

© Springer International Publishing AG, part of Springer Nature 2018
M. M. Gallardo and P. Merino (Eds.): SPIN 2018, LNCS 10869, pp. 196–215, 2018.
https://doi.org/10.1007/978-3-319-94111-0_12

behaviors [17] on the relaxed MCMs. Saraswat et al. explained that the fundamental property ensures that most programmers writing DRF programs only have to be concerned about SC executions [25]. Owens considered that the fundamental property is the essence of MCMs and defined MCMs as rules that are designed to guarantee that DRF programs do not have non-SC behaviors [19].

The so-called *state explosion problem* of software model checking of DRF programs with MCMs is mitigated because non-SC behaviors of DRF programs on relaxed MCMs can be observably reduced to SC behaviors. However, DRF is so strong that we cannot expect it for all programs. Software model checking of *data racy* programs with MCMs still suffers from the state explosion problem.

Owens moderated a condition of DRF and presented the notion of *triangular race freedom (TRF)*, which includes the spinlock used in the Linux kernel [19]. Observable behaviors of TRF programs are reduced to SC behaviors on the x86-TSO [20], which is adopted by Intel architectures. However, TRF is a *global* property of a program; that is, *all* threads in the program must uniformly follow the TRF condition. TRF is also strongly specific to x86-TSO, which is stricter than modern MCMs, and cannot reduce behaviors on more relaxed MCMs to SC behaviors.

In this paper, we provide a formulation to define small-step operational semantics for relaxed memory consistency models and an observable equivalence on the semantics using the notion of bisimulation (note that Owens used trace semantics [19]), and propose the novel notion of *local data race freedom (LDRF)*, which claims that *some* threads follow a race free condition, but not all threads follow the condition, unlike DRF and TRF, which require that *all* threads must uniformly follow their conditions. LDRF is a variant of DRF in another direction that is different from the direction of TRF.

LDRF includes *the independent reads independent writes (IRIW) program*, which is well known to have curious behaviors under MCMs with *non-multi-copy atomicity*, which is more relaxed than x86-TSO. Although the IRIW program enjoys TRF, we cannot use the SC reduction for TRF programs on model checking with relaxed MCMs because TRF is specific to x86-TSO and we cannot observe the curious behavior on x86-TSO. Some *concurrent copying garbage collection (CCGC) algorithms* are typical LDRF programs. There exists no load-store race in any period between synchronization points at the garbage collection layer because end-user programmers must write DRF programs in programming languages with MCMs that require DRF, although it may be the case that a collector and mutators share variables because a collector communicates with mutators when collecting objects that have not been used.

In this paper, we also provide an optimization called *memory sharing* for the software model checking of LDRF programs with non-multi-copy atomic MCMs, which do not ensure atomicities among multiple effects (of a store) to multiple threads. We demonstrate the effectiveness of memory sharing optimization by conducting experiments for the IRIW program and some CCGC algorithms.

Related Work. To the best of our knowledge, there exists only the following one literature to propose an extension of DRF by focusing on locality.

Dolan et al. proposed a notion of local data race freedom independently, and showed that data race free portions of programs follow SC behaviors [9]. However, the MCMs in their paper are stricter than those in this paper. Actually, their LDRF do not provide any optimization on relaxed MCMs which allow load buffering and non-multi-copy atomicity.

There exists no relevant literature of an optimization specific to model checking with non-multi-copy atomic MCMs, although there exists a model checker such as Nidhugg [1] which supports the POWER MCM [12].

Owens used trace semantics and showed that x86-TSO behaviors of DRF programs can be reduced to SC behaviors [19]. In the present paper, we provide an alternative formalization of an observable equivalence using the notion of bisimulation, and show that behaviors of LDRF programs with non-multi-copy atomicity can be observably simulated by behaviors on a general machine with memory sharing optimization on a partition of threads.

Partitioning threads is reminiscent of *clustered-based partial order reduction*, which clusters multiple threads that are dependent on each other, and utilizes the independencies between the clusters to improve the efficiency of the partial order reduction [8]. However, the idea looks different from our memory sharing optimization, which makes independent threads on an LDRF program to share a common memory.

Ownership and separation are promising reasoning concepts regarding concurrency in program logic [18]. The author also proposed the notion of *observation invariants* in concurrent program logic [3]. However, this paper studies model checking, and provides no logic.

Outline. The remainder of this paper is organized as follows: In Sect. 2, we present a review of the observable equivalence of DRF programs. In Sect. 3, we introduce a general machine with non-multi-copy atomicity. In Sect. 4, we propose the notion of LDRF together with an optimization called memory sharing for software model checking with non-multi-copy atomic MCMs. In Sect. 5, we provide formal definitions that are introduced in Sects. 2, 3 and 4, and prove the validity of memory sharing under appropriate conditions. In Sect. 6, we explain how to implement memory sharing optimization in model checker VeriDAG that supports non-multi-copy atomic MCMs [2]. In Sect. 7, we present an assessment of the effectiveness of memory sharing using experiments. In Sect. 8, we conclude the paper by identifying future studies.

2   Observable Equivalence of Data Race Free Programs

In this section, we informally explain observable equivalence.

Saraswat et al. and Owens formally proved that non-SC behaviors of DRF and TRF programs, respectively, can be reduced to SC behaviors [19, 25]. This means that non-SC behaviors do not disappear but cannot be observed. Non-SC behaviors exist internally on computer architectures.

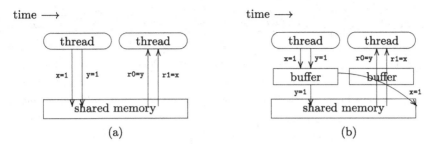

Fig. 1. Different behaviors without/with buffers

We can observe non-SC behavior for a data racy program: (x=1; y=1) ∥ (r0=y; r1=x), where ∥ denotes parallel composition, x and y are shared variables, r0 and r1 are thread-local variables, and all variables are initialized to 0. All six SC executions satisfy r0==1 -> r1==1 when all four instructions are complete. However, there exists a non-SC execution, x=1 (buffered); y=1 (buffered); y=1 (visible); r0=y; r1=x; x=1 (visible) for which r1==1 && r0==0 on modern computer architectures such that each thread might have one buffer that does not preserve the order of stores, as shown in Fig. 1(b); Fig. 1(a) shows SC behavior on computer architecture without a buffer.

Consequently, we cannot ignore relaxed MCMs on modern computer architectures. However, this is not the case for DRF programs. We consider a DRF program (x=1; y=1) ∥ (r0=y'; r1=x'), where x' and y' are shared variables. Although the buffer can delay the effects of the two stores to the shared memory, that can be ignored because the first thread cannot recognize whether the effects of the stores are delayed or the stores are not invoked.

To be precise, we cannot *describe* an assertion that distinguishes which effects are delayed in the assertion language; that is, the expressive power of the assertion language is not strong. We can distinguish them by describing an assertion y==1 -> x==1 if the assertion language enables us to describe arbitrary states on computer architectures. However, it is reasonable to infer that the assertion language does not admit threads to read values of shared variables without loading the shared variables. The observable equivalence of a DRF program is defined as the non-existence of assertions that specify a non-SC behavior of the program, as formally defined in Sect. 5.3.

3   General Machine with Non-multi-copy Atomicity

In this section, we introduce a general machine, which assumes non-multi-copy atomicity [26].

There exist some computer architectures, such as ARMv7 [6] and POWER [12,26], that do not always assume multi-copy atomicity, that is, distinct threads can observe distinct behaviors of threads. We consider *the IRIW program* (r0=y; r1=x) ∥ (r2=x; r3=y) ∥ x=1 ∥ y=1, where r2 and

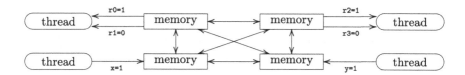

Fig. 2. A curious behavior on computer architectures with non-multi-copy atomicity

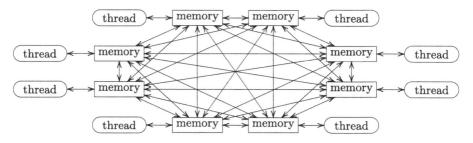

Fig. 3. General machine consisting of eight threads

r3 are thread-local variables. The first and second threads read x and y, respectively, in program order. Therefore, the assertion (r0==1 && r2==1) -> (r1==1 || r3==1) appears to hold when the program ends. However, non-multi-copy atomic MCMs allow distinct threads to observe distinct behaviors of threads. For example, the first observes y=1 and is invoked before x=1 is invoked, whereas the second observes x=1 and is invoked before y=1 is invoked. This is natural for the computer architecture in Fig. 2.

As described in this paper, we consider a *general* machine with non-multi-copy atomicity. Each thread has its own *memory*. Each thread reads a shared variable from its own memory. A store to a memory is reflected to the other memories as shown in Fig. 3.

Every pair of memories is connected directly so that stores are passed through other memories, and buffers are separated to manage reflects of shared variables to memories. A question that arises is why no buffer exists in the general machine. Buffers are unnecessary for representing non-multi-copy atomic MCMs because each memory at each thread works as a buffer. The operational semantics of the general machine is formally defined in Sect. 5.2.

4   Memory Sharing and Local Data Race Freedom

In this section, we propose the notion of *LDRF* and an optimization called *memory sharing* for software model checking with non-multi-copy atomic MCMs.

LDRF is based on a simple concept. To introduce LDRF, we first consider DRF. Figure 4(a) denotes the behavior of a DRF program x=1 || y=1 on computer architecture with buffers. The behavior is often regarded as being reduced to the behavior of computer architecture without a buffer, as shown in Fig. 4(b).

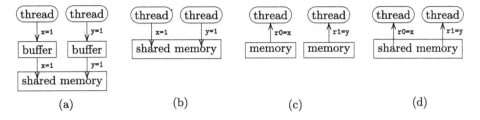

Fig. 4. Behaviors of a DRF program on various architectures

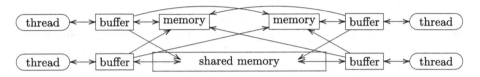

Fig. 5. Machine with memory sharing optimization

However, this can be also regarded such that two buffers are merged and integrated into the shared memory. We consider other threads that load x and y (to r0 and r1, respectively). The loading of x and y from memories, as shown in Fig. 4(c), can be regarded as that from *one shared memory*, as shown in Fig. 4(d), by identifying buffers with memories.

This concept is the origin of the optimization of the general machine for which each thread has its own memory. If *some* threads enjoy load-store race freedom, then the threads can share their memories. Additionally, even if the threads do not enjoy load-load race freedom in a period between synchronization points, if there exists no store in the period on the other threads, then the threads can share their memories. We call that *local data race freedom (LDRF)*. This notion is formally defined in Sect. 5.

The behavior on the architecture shown in Fig. 2 can be observably simulated by behaviors on the machine shown in Fig. 5, which consists of four buffers, two memories, and one shared memory. The stores between writer threads on the general machine are ignored on the machine shown in Fig. 5. It must be the case that the curious behavior of the IRIW program can be observed, as shown in Fig. 6.

It may be considered slightly discouraging that memory sharing optimization cannot reduce behaviors on non-multi-copy atomic MCMs to SC behaviors; that is, memory sharing optimization does not improve model checking with non-multi-copy atomicity to a great degree, whereas SC reduction drastically addresses the state explosion problem; the sequential execution of multiple threads can simulate all parallel executions of multiple threads. However, LDRF includes IRIW programs, and memory sharing optimization mitigates the state explosion problem of model checking for LDRF programs. We demonstrate that memory sharing optimization is effective through experiments in Sect. 7.

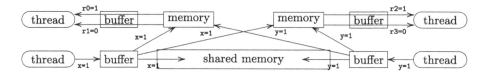

Fig. 6. Reduced behavior for memory sharing optimization

5   Formal Theory

In this section, we present formal definitions of the notions that were introduced informally in Sects. 2, 3 and 4, and prove that memory sharing is valid under appropriate conditions.

5.1   Concurrent Programs

The sets of instructions C^i and sequential programs S^i on thread i are defined as

$$C^i ::= \text{Nop}^i \mid r = \text{MV}^i\, e \mid r = \text{LD}^i\, x \mid x = \text{ST}^i\, e \mid r = \text{CAS}^i\, x\, e\, e$$
$$S^i ::= C^i \mid S^i; C^i,$$

where r denotes thread-local variables, x denotes shared variables, e denotes *thread-local* expressions (e.g., thread-local variables, constant value v, and arithmetic operations), and superscript i represents an identifier of the thread on which the associated statement is executed. In the remainder of this paper, this superscript is omitted when it is readily apparent from the context. The Nop statement represents an ordinary no-effect statement. We distinguish thread-local assignment statements from assignment statements to shared memory. MV denotes ordinary variable substitution. LD and ST denote read and write operations, respectively, for shared variables. CAS denotes *compare-and-swap* in a standard manner.

We adopt compare-and-swap as a primitive to ensure atomicity, whereas Owens adopted *locking* [19]. We adopted this approach because fine-grained synchronization, such as compare-and-swap, is preferred to coarse-grained synchronization, such as locking, on modern many-core computer architectures.

In this section, memory allocation, jump (conditional and loop statements), function call, and thread creation instructions are omitted, for simplicity. Actually, the model checker VeriDAG introduced in Sect. 6 and used at the experiments in Sect. 7 supports them by introducing the notions of the so-called addresses, labels, and basic blocks.

A concurrent program with N threads is defined as

$$P, Q ::= S^0 \parallel S^1 \parallel \cdots \parallel S^{N-1},$$

where $\parallel$ denotes a parallel composition of threads in a standard manner.

We assume that the number of threads is fixed during program execution.

To represent shared buffers and memories, we introduce the notion of partitions of a set of threads. We assume a partition $\{I_{(m)} \mid 0 \leq m < M\}$ of $\{0, \ldots, N-1\}$; that is, there exists M such that $0 \leq M \leq N$, $I_{(m)} \cap I_{(n)} = \varnothing$ for any $0 \leq m \neq n < M$, and $\bigsqcup\{I_{(m)} \mid 0 \leq m < M\} = \{0, \ldots, N-1\}$. An element $I_{(m)}$ of a partition is called a segment.

Threads in a common segment are regarded to share a common memory. For example, the writer threads (whose identifiers are 2 and 3) in the IRIW program (r0=y; r1=x) || (r2=x; r3=y) || x=1 || y=1 can share a common memory as shown in Fig. 6. In the case, the partition of thread identifiers $\{0, 1, 2, 3\}$ is $\{\{0\}, \{1\}, \{2, 3\}\}$.

We define a state. Register ς takes a thread-local variable r and returns value v. Shared memory σ takes a segment $I_{(m)}$ of the partition and shared variable x, and returns value v. Buffer Σ takes a pair of thread identifier and a segment $\langle i, I_{(m)} \rangle$, and returns a *queue set*, where one queue is defined for *each* shared variable. Four methods *method* are defined for a queue set qs. One method $qs.\text{enqueue}(x, v)$ enqueues v at x in qs. Another method $qs.\text{dequeue}(x, v)$ dequeues a value at x in qs, and returns that the value is v. Another method $qs.\text{empty}(x)$ determines that the queue at x in qs is empty. The other method $qs.\text{latest}(x)$ returns the latest value at x in qs without dequeuing any element.

5.2 Operational Semantics

In the following, we assume a partition $\{I_{(m)} \mid 0 \leq m < M\}$ of $\{0, \ldots, N-1\}$, and write a meta-variable I as a segment $I_{(m)}$ of the partition.

For brevity, we write σ^I and $\Sigma^{i,I}$ as $\sigma(I)$ and $\Sigma(\langle i, I \rangle)$, respectively. We use an update operation of function f in a standard manner as follows:

$$f[a := b](c) = \begin{cases} b & \text{if } a = c \\ f(c) & \text{otherwise.} \end{cases}$$

We also write $\sigma[\sigma^I[x := v]]$ as $\sigma[I := \sigma^I[x := v]]$ because it is readily apparent that the update is about I. Similarly, for brevity, we express $\Sigma[\Sigma^{i,I}.method]$ as $\Sigma[\langle i, I \rangle := \Sigma^{i,I}.method]$. We respectively write $\sigma[\{\sigma^I[x := v] \mid I\}]$ and $\Sigma[\{\Sigma^{i,I}.method \mid I\}]$ as $\sigma[\sigma^{I_{(0)}}[x := v]] \cdots [\sigma^{I_{(M-1)}}[x := v]]$ and $\Sigma[\Sigma^{i,I_{(0)}}.method] \cdots [\Sigma^{i,I_{(M-1)}}.method]$.

Furthermore, we introduce an update of shared memory by a shared buffer as

$$\sigma^I[\Sigma^{i,I}](x) = \begin{cases} \Sigma^{i,I}.\text{latest}(x) & \text{if the queue at } x \text{ is not empty} \\ \sigma^I(x) & \text{otherwise.} \end{cases}$$

A *state* is defined as a triple: $\langle \varsigma, \sigma, \Sigma \rangle$. A *configuration* is defined as $\langle P, \langle \varsigma, \sigma, \Sigma \rangle \rangle$. A small-step operational semantics is defined as shown in Fig. 7. Transition $\xrightarrow{c}$ indicates that an instruction is invoked and that a state is updated.

$$\langle r = \mathtt{MV}^i\ e, \langle \varsigma, \sigma, \Sigma \rangle \rangle \xrightarrow{c} \langle \mathtt{Nop}^i, \langle \varsigma[r := (\!|e|\!)_\varsigma], \sigma, \Sigma \rangle \rangle$$

$$\frac{i \in I}{\langle r = \mathtt{LD}^i\ x, \langle \varsigma, \sigma, \Sigma \rangle \rangle \xrightarrow{c} \langle \mathtt{Nop}^i, \langle \varsigma[r := \sigma^I[\Sigma^{i,I}](x)], \sigma, \Sigma \rangle \rangle}$$

$$\frac{i \in I}{\langle x = \mathtt{ST}^i\ e, \langle \varsigma, \sigma, \Sigma \rangle \rangle \xrightarrow{c} \langle \mathtt{Nop}^i, \langle \varsigma, \sigma, \Sigma[\{\Sigma^{i,I}.\mathtt{enqueue}(x, (\!|e|\!)_\varsigma) \mid I\}] \rangle \rangle}$$

$$\frac{i \in I \qquad \sigma^I[\Sigma^{i,I}](x) = (\!|e_0|\!)_\varsigma}{\begin{array}{c}\langle r = \mathtt{CAS}^i\ x\ e_0\ e_1, \langle \varsigma, \sigma, \Sigma \rangle \rangle \xrightarrow{c}\\[2pt] \langle \mathtt{Nop}^i, \langle \varsigma[r := 1], \sigma[\{\sigma^I[x := (\!|e_1|\!)_\varsigma] \mid I\}], \Sigma[\{\Sigma^{i,I}.\mathtt{empty}(x) \mid I\}] \rangle \rangle\end{array}}$$

$$\frac{i \in I \qquad \sigma^I[\Sigma^{i,I}](x) \neq (\!|e_0|\!)_\varsigma}{\langle r = \mathtt{CAS}^i\ x\ e_0\ e_1, \langle \varsigma, \sigma, \Sigma \rangle \rangle \xrightarrow{c} \langle \mathtt{Nop}^i, \langle \varsigma[r := 0], \sigma, \Sigma \rangle \rangle}$$

$$\frac{\langle P, \langle \varsigma, \sigma, \Sigma \rangle \rangle \xrightarrow{c} \langle \mathtt{Nop}, \langle \varsigma', \sigma', \Sigma' \rangle \rangle}{\langle P; Q, \langle \varsigma, \sigma, \Sigma \rangle \rangle \xrightarrow{c} \langle Q, \langle \varsigma', \sigma', \Sigma' \rangle \rangle} \qquad \frac{\langle P, \langle \varsigma, \sigma, \Sigma \rangle \rangle \xrightarrow{c} \langle P', \langle \varsigma', \sigma', \Sigma' \rangle \rangle}{\langle P; Q, \langle \varsigma, \sigma, \Sigma \rangle \rangle \xrightarrow{c} \langle P'; Q, \langle \varsigma', \sigma', \Sigma' \rangle \rangle}$$

$$\frac{\langle P, \langle \varsigma, \sigma, \Sigma \rangle \rangle \xrightarrow{c} \langle P', \langle \varsigma', \sigma', \Sigma' \rangle \rangle}{\langle P \parallel Q, \langle \varsigma, \sigma, \Sigma \rangle \rangle \xrightarrow{c} \langle P' \parallel Q, \langle \varsigma', \sigma', \Sigma' \rangle \rangle} \qquad \frac{\langle Q, \langle \varsigma, \sigma, \Sigma \rangle \rangle \xrightarrow{c} \langle Q', \langle \varsigma', \sigma', \Sigma' \rangle \rangle}{\langle P \parallel Q, \langle \varsigma, \sigma, \Sigma \rangle \rangle \xrightarrow{c} \langle P \parallel Q', \langle \varsigma', \sigma', \Sigma' \rangle \rangle}$$

$$\langle P, \langle \varsigma, \sigma, \Sigma \rangle \rangle \xrightarrow{e} \langle P, \langle \varsigma, \sigma[\sigma^I[x := v]], \Sigma[\Sigma^{i,I}.\mathtt{dequeue}(x, v)] \rangle \rangle$$

Fig. 7. Operational semantics

Specifically, $r = \mathtt{MV}^i\ e$ evaluates e at ς and updates ς, where $(\!|e|\!)_\varsigma$ represents the valuation of expression e as

$$(\!|v|\!)_\varsigma = v \qquad (\!|r|\!)_\varsigma = \varsigma(r) \qquad (\!|e_0 + e_1|\!)_\varsigma = (\!|e_0|\!)_\varsigma + (\!|e_1|\!)_\varsigma \qquad \cdots .$$

Instruction $r = \mathtt{LD}^i\ x$ evaluates x on $\Sigma^{i,I}$ if $\Sigma^{i,I}(x)$ is defined, and on σ^I otherwise, where $i \in I$, and updates ς. Instruction $x = \mathtt{ST}^i\ e$ evaluates e on ς and updates not σ^I but $\Sigma^{i,I}$ for any I. The effect of the store operation is buffered in $\Sigma^{i,I}$ for any I. Instruction $r = \mathtt{CAS}^i\ x\ e_0\ e_1$ atomically loads x, compares the evaluation of e_0, stores the evaluation of e_1 at x, and returns 1 to r if the values of x and e_0 are equal; it returns 0 otherwise. Sequential and parallel compositions follow standard methods. In this paper, parallel composition is defined as a non-commutative and non-associative operator because the indices of segments are sensitive to operational semantics.

Whereas a transition $\xrightarrow{c}$ invokes and consumes one instruction, a transition $\xrightarrow{e}$, which represents an effect that is reflected from a buffer to shared memory, does not invoke or consume any instructions.

5.3   Assertion Language

The assertion language is defined as

$$\varphi ::= e = e \mid e \leq e \mid \neg \varphi \mid \varphi \supset \varphi \mid \forall r . \varphi \; .$$

Relation $\varsigma \vDash \varphi$ is defined in a standard manner as

$$\varsigma \vDash e_0 = e_1 \iff (\!|e_0|\!)_\varsigma = (\!|e_1|\!)_\varsigma \qquad \varsigma \vDash e_0 \leq e_1 \iff (\!|e_0|\!)_\varsigma \leq (\!|e_1|\!)_\varsigma$$
$$\varsigma \vDash \neg \varphi \iff \varsigma \not\vDash \varphi \qquad \varsigma \vDash \varphi \supset \varphi' \iff \varsigma \vDash \varphi \text{ implies } \varsigma \vDash \varphi'$$
$$\varsigma \vDash \forall r . \varphi(r) \iff \varsigma \vDash \varphi(v) \text{ for any } v \; .$$

Relation $\langle P, \langle \varsigma, \sigma, \Sigma \rangle \rangle \vDash \varphi$, which indicates that the configuration satisfies the assertion, is defined as $\varsigma \vDash \varphi$. An assertion can be inserted anywhere in a program, while a system in which an assertion must be located at the end of a program cannot support divergent programs.

The assertion language has no shared variable. The satisfiability is defined by registers only. Consequently, the assertion language requires the loading of a shared variable to identify the value of the shared variable.

5.4   Local Data Race Freedom and Observable Equivalence

An objective of in this section is to define a relation $\sim$ between configurations satisfying:

1. if cfg_0 and cfg_1 are related by the memory sharing optimization, then $cfg_0 \sim cfg_1$ holds,
2. if $cfg_0 \sim cfg_1$ holds, then $cfg_0 \vDash \varphi$ coincides with $cfg_1 \vDash \varphi$ for any φ, and
3. the relation $\sim$ is preserved by transitions on operational semantics.

Claim 1 means that the relation $\sim$ contains a pair of configurations $\langle cfg_0, cfg_1 \rangle$ where cfg_0 and cfg_1 are related by the memory sharing optimization. Claim 2 means that satisfiability of an assertion on cfg_0 can be checked by checking satisfiability of the assertion on cfg_1 and vice versa. Claim 3 means that the relation $\sim$, in particular, the memory sharing optimization is robust to transition.

First, let us define a relation $\sim$ satisfying Claim 1. A set of sequential programs $\{S_0, \ldots, S_{n-1}\}$ is called *load-store race free* if $R(S_k) \cap W(S_l) = \varnothing$ for any $0 \leq k \neq l < n$, where

$$R(S) = \bigcup \{ R(C) \mid C \in S \} \qquad R(C) = \begin{cases} \{x\} & \text{if } C \text{ is } r = \mathsf{LD} \; x \text{ or } r = \mathsf{CAS} \; x \; e_0 \; e_1 \\ \varnothing & \text{otherwise.} \end{cases}$$

$$W(S) = \bigcup \{ W(C) \mid C \in S \} \qquad W(C) = \begin{cases} \{x\} & \text{if } C \text{ is } x = \mathsf{ST} \; e \text{ or } r = \mathsf{CAS} \; x \; e_0 \; e_1 \\ \varnothing & \text{otherwise.} \end{cases}$$

A concurrent program $P \equiv S^0 \parallel \cdots \parallel S^{N-1}$ is called *LDRF with respect to partition* $\{I_{(m)} \mid 0 \leq m < M\}$ *of* $\{0, \ldots, N-1\}$ if for any segment $I_{(m)}$

- $\{S^i \mid i \in I_{(m)}\}$ is load-store race free, and
- for any x and $i \neq j \in I_{(m)}$, if $x \in R(S^i) \cap R(S^j)$ then $x \notin W(S^k)$ for any $0 \leq k < N$.

By definition, every DRF program that consists of N threads is LDRF with respect to discrete partition $\{\{m\} \mid 0 \leq m < N\}$, although memory sharing optimization based on the discrete partition never improves model checking with non-multi-copy atomicity.

Let $\mathcal{R}$ be a relation. Relation $\mathcal{R}^+$ represents the transitive closure of $\mathcal{R}$. Relation $\mathcal{R}^*$ represents the reflexive and transitive closure of $\mathcal{R}$.

Let $\{I_{j,(m)} \mid 0 \leq m < M_j\}$ be a partition of $\{0, \ldots, N-1\}$ for any $j = 0, 1$. We define an *expansion relation* as $\langle P_0, \langle \varsigma, \sigma_0, \Sigma_0 \rangle \rangle \succsim \langle P_1, \langle \varsigma, \sigma_1, \Sigma_1 \rangle \rangle$ if

- for any $j = 0, 1$
  - $P_j \equiv S^0 \parallel \cdots \parallel S^{N-1}$,
  - $\langle \varsigma, \sigma_j, \Sigma_j \rangle$ is defined on $\{I_{j,(m)} \mid 0 \leq m < M_j\}$, and
  - P_j is LDRF with respect to partition $\{I_{j,(m)} \mid 0 \leq m < M_j\}$,
- $\{I_{0,(m)} \mid 0 \leq m < M_0\}$ is a refinement of $\{I_{1,(m)} \mid 0 \leq m < M_1\}$, that is, for any $0 \leq m_0 < M_0$, there exists $0 \leq m_1 < M_1$ such that $I_{0,(m_0)} \subseteq I_{1,(m_1)}$, and
- for any x and $0 \leq i < N$,
  - if $x \in R(S^i)$, then $\sigma_0{}^{I_0}[\Sigma_0{}^{i,I_0}](x) = \sigma_1{}^{I_1}[\Sigma_1{}^{i,I_1}](x)$,
  - if $\langle P_0, \langle \varsigma, \sigma_0, \Sigma_0 \rangle \rangle \xrightarrow{e}{}^+ \langle P_0, \langle \varsigma, \sigma_0', \Sigma_0' \rangle \rangle$, then there exist σ_1' and Σ_1' such that $\langle P_1, \langle \varsigma, \sigma_1, \Sigma_1 \rangle \rangle \xrightarrow{e}{}^* \langle P_1, \langle \varsigma, \sigma_1', \Sigma_1' \rangle \rangle$ and $\sigma_0'{}^{I_0}[\Sigma_0'{}^{i,I_0}](x) = \sigma_1'{}^{I_1}[\Sigma_1'{}^{i,I_1}](x)$, and
  - if $\langle P_1, \langle \varsigma, \sigma_1, \Sigma_1 \rangle \rangle \xrightarrow{e}{}^+ \langle P_1, \langle \varsigma, \sigma_1', \Sigma_1' \rangle \rangle$, then there exist σ_0' and Σ_0' such that $\langle P_0, \langle \varsigma, \sigma_0, \Sigma_0 \rangle \rangle \xrightarrow{e}{}^+ \langle P_0, \langle \varsigma, \sigma_0', \Sigma_0' \rangle \rangle$ and $\sigma_0'{}^{I_0}[\Sigma_0'{}^{i,I_0}](x) = \sigma_1'{}^{I_1}[\Sigma_1'{}^{i,I_1}](x)$,

where I_0 and I_1 denote the unique segments such that $i \in I_0$ and $i \in I_1$, respectively.

Intuitively, $\langle P_0, \langle \varsigma, \sigma_0, \Sigma_0 \rangle \rangle \succsim \langle P_1, \langle \varsigma, \sigma_1, \Sigma_1 \rangle \rangle$ means that $\langle P_1, \langle \varsigma, \sigma_1, \Sigma_1 \rangle \rangle$ is the application of the memory sharing optimization to $\langle P_0, \langle \varsigma, \sigma_0, \Sigma_0 \rangle \rangle$.

It is noteworthy that the third condition is satisfied by executing programs with $\texttt{initstate} \equiv \langle \{\_ \mapsto 0\}, \{\_ \mapsto \{\_ \mapsto 0\}\}, \{\_ \mapsto \varnothing\} \rangle$ because no effect can be reflected from the state.

We describe a basic property that expansion relation $\succsim$ is a contextual relation. This property is useful to check whether two configurations are related by $\succsim$, because this property ensures that two configurations which are partially related by $\succsim$ are totally related by $\succsim$.

Proposition 1. *If $\langle P_0, \langle \varsigma, \sigma_0 \restriction \mathcal{I}_0, \Sigma_0 \restriction (\mathcal{I}_0 \times \mathcal{I}_0) \rangle \rangle \succsim \langle P_1, \langle \varsigma, \sigma_1 \restriction \mathcal{I}_1, \Sigma_1 \restriction (\mathcal{I}_1 \times \mathcal{I}_1) \rangle \rangle$ holds, then $\langle P_0 \parallel S^{N-1}, \langle \varsigma, \sigma_0, \Sigma_0 \rangle \rangle \succsim \langle P_1 \parallel S^{N-1}, \langle \varsigma, \sigma_1, \Sigma_1 \rangle \rangle$ holds where*

- $\mathcal{I}_j = \{I_{j,(m)} \mid 0 \leq m < M_j\}$ *is a partition of* $\{0, \ldots, N-2\}$ *for any* $j = 0, 1$,
- $\mathcal{I} = \{N-1\}$,
- $\sigma_0 \restriction \mathcal{I} = \sigma_1 \restriction \mathcal{I}$,
- $\Sigma_0 \restriction (\mathcal{I} \times \mathcal{I}) = \Sigma_1 \restriction (\mathcal{I} \times \mathcal{I})$, *and*

– $\Sigma_0 \restriction (\mathcal{I}_0 \times \mathcal{I})$, $\Sigma_0 \restriction (\mathcal{I} \times \mathcal{I}_0)$, $\Sigma_1 \restriction (\mathcal{I}_1 \times \mathcal{I})$, and $\Sigma_1 \restriction (\mathcal{I} \times \mathcal{I}_1)$ are empty

where dom f is the domain of f, and $f \restriction A$ is the restriction of f on A for any $A \subseteq$ dom f.

Proof. It is routine to check the conditions of $\succsim$ according to the definitions of $\succsim$ and the operational semantics in Fig. 7. $\qquad\square$

Next, let us confirm that the relation $\sim$ satisfies Claim 2. Satisfiabilities of assertions on configurations are invariant to the memory sharing optimization, which is shown as follows:

Proposition 2. *If $cfg_0 \succsim cfg_1$, then for any φ, $cfg_0 \vDash \varphi$ coincides with $cfg_1 \vDash \varphi$.*

Proof. It is obvious because expansion relation $\succsim$ is defined between configurations that have the *same* register, and $\vDash$ is defined by the register and the assertion φ, which cannot refer to variables on memories and buffers. $\qquad\square$

We define *observable equivalence* $\sim$ as the reflexive, symmetric, and transitive closure of the expansion relation $\succsim$. Intuitively, $cfg_0 \sim cfg_1$ means that cfg_0 and cfg_1 are related by the memory sharing optimization.

Proposition 3. *If $cfg_0 \sim cfg_1$, then for any φ, $cfg_0 \vDash \varphi$ coincides with $cfg_1 \vDash \varphi$.*

Proof. It is immediate from the definition of observable equivalence $\sim$. $\qquad\square$

Finally, let us prove that the relation $\sim$ satisfies Claim 3. We define a property by which a relation is preserved by transitions on operational semantics. We designate $\mathcal{R}$ as a *bisimulation* if $cfg_0 \; \mathcal{R} \; cfg_1$ implies

– if $cfg_0 \xrightarrow{c} cfg_0{'}$, then $cfg_1{'}$ exists such that $cfg_1 \xrightarrow{c} cfg_1{'}$ and $cfg_0{'} \; \mathcal{R} \; cfg_1{'}$,
– if $cfg_1 \xrightarrow{c} cfg_1{'}$, then $cfg_0{'}$ exists such that $cfg_0 \xrightarrow{c} cfg_0{'}$ and $cfg_0{'} \; \mathcal{R} \; cfg_1{'}$,
– if $cfg_0 \xrightarrow{e} cfg_0$, then $cfg_1{'}$ exists such that $cfg_1 \xrightarrow{e}{}^{*} cfg_1{'}$ and $cfg_0{'} \; \mathcal{R} \; cfg_1{'}$, and
– if $cfg_1 \xrightarrow{e} cfg_1{'}$, then $cfg_0{'}$ exists such that $cfg_0 \xrightarrow{e}{}^{*} cfg_0{'}$ and $cfg_0{'} \; \mathcal{R} \; cfg_1{'}$.

Proposition 4. *Let $\mathcal{R}_0$ and $\mathcal{R}_1$ be bisimulations. The inverse of $\mathcal{R}_0$, that is, $\{\langle cfg_1, cfg_0 \rangle \mid \langle cfg_0, cfg_1 \rangle \in \mathcal{R}_0\}$, and the composition of $\mathcal{R}_0$ and $\mathcal{R}_1$, that is, $\{\langle cfg_0, cfg_2 \rangle \mid \langle cfg_0, cfg_1 \rangle \in \mathcal{R}_0, \langle cfg_1, cfg_2 \rangle \in \mathcal{R}_1 \text{ for some } cfg_1\}$, are bisimulations. Therefore, the reflexive, symmetric, and transitive closure of $\mathcal{R}_0$ is a bisimulation.*

Proof. It is obvious by the definition of bisimulation.

LDRF is necessary to define $\succsim$ as a bisimulation. For example, $\langle x = \mathrm{ST}^0 \, 1 \; \| \; r = \mathrm{LD}^1 \, x \; \| \; r' = \mathrm{LD}^2 \, x, \langle \{ \_ \mapsto 0 \}, \sigma_0, \Sigma_0 \rangle \rangle \not\succsim \langle x = \mathrm{ST}^0 \, 1 \; \| \; r = \mathrm{LD}^1 \, x \; \| \; r' = \mathrm{LD}^2 \, x, \langle \{ \_ \mapsto 0 \}, \sigma_1, \Sigma_1 \rangle \rangle$, where

$$\sigma_0 = \{\, \{0\} \mapsto \{\_ \mapsto 0\}, \{1\} \mapsto \{\_ \mapsto 0\}, \{2\} \mapsto \{\_ \mapsto 0\}\}$$
$$\Sigma_0 = \{\langle 0, \{0\}\rangle \mapsto \varnothing, \langle 0, \{1\}\rangle \mapsto \varnothing, \langle 0, \{2\}\rangle \mapsto \varnothing, \langle 1, \{0\}\rangle \mapsto \varnothing, \langle 1, \{1\}\rangle \mapsto \varnothing,$$
$$\langle 1, \{2\}\rangle \mapsto \varnothing, \langle 2, \{0\}\rangle \mapsto \varnothing, \langle 2, \{1\}\rangle \mapsto \varnothing, \langle 2, \{2\}\rangle \mapsto \varnothing\}$$
$$\sigma_1 = \{\, \{0\} \mapsto \{\_ \mapsto 0\}, \{1, 2\} \mapsto \{\_ \mapsto 0\}\}$$
$$\Sigma_1 = \{\langle 0, \{0\}\rangle \mapsto \varnothing, \langle 0, \{1, 2\}\rangle \mapsto \varnothing, \langle 1, \{0\}\rangle \mapsto \varnothing, \langle 1, \{1, 2\}\rangle \mapsto \varnothing,$$
$$\langle 2, \{0\}\rangle \mapsto \varnothing, \langle 2, \{1, 2\}\rangle \mapsto \varnothing\}$$

because $\langle r = \mathsf{LD}^1\, x \parallel r' = \mathsf{LD}^2\, x, \langle\{\_ \mapsto 0\}, \sigma_0', \Sigma_0'\rangle\rangle \not\precsim \langle r = \mathsf{LD}^1\, x \parallel r' = \mathsf{LD}^2\, x, \langle\{\_ \mapsto 0\}, \sigma_1', \Sigma_1'\rangle\rangle$, where

$$\sigma_0' = \{\, \{0\} \mapsto \{x \mapsto 1, \_ \mapsto 0\}, \{1\} \mapsto \{x \mapsto 1, \_ \mapsto 0\}, \{2\} \mapsto \{\_ \mapsto 0\}\}$$
$$\Sigma_0' = \{\langle 0, \{0\}\rangle \mapsto \varnothing, \langle 0, \{1\}\rangle \mapsto \varnothing, \langle 0, \{2\}\rangle \mapsto x = 1, \langle 1, \{0\}\rangle \mapsto \varnothing, \langle 1, \{1\}\rangle \mapsto \varnothing,$$
$$\langle 1, \{2\}\rangle \mapsto \varnothing, \langle 2, \{0\}\rangle \mapsto \varnothing, \langle 2, \{1\}\rangle \mapsto \varnothing, \langle 2, \{2\}\rangle \mapsto \varnothing\}$$
$$\sigma_1' = \{\, \{0\} \mapsto \{x \mapsto 1, \_ \mapsto 0\}, \{1, 2\} \mapsto \{x \mapsto 1, \_ \mapsto 0\}\}$$

after $x = \mathsf{ST}^0\, 1$ is invoked.

Lemma 5. *Expansion relation $\succsim$ is a bisimulation.*

Proof. Each shared variable has its own queue. Therefore, any pair of e-transitions related to distinct shared variables can be reordered.

Let $\langle P_0, \langle \varsigma_0, \sigma_0, \Sigma_0\rangle\rangle \succsim \langle P_1, \langle \varsigma_1, \sigma_1, \Sigma_1\rangle\rangle$. Assume that S^j belongs to a common segment with S^i on $\langle P_1, \langle \varsigma_1, \sigma_1, \Sigma_1\rangle\rangle$. If $R(S^i) \cap R(S^j) = \varnothing$ holds, then the first item of the third condition of $\succsim$ does not matter. If $x \in R(S^i) \cap R(S^j)$, then there exists no $x = \mathsf{ST}^k\, e$ according to LDRF; the first item of the third condition of $\succsim$ also does not matter.

Otherwise, the queues of S^i and S^j are separated; any $\xrightarrow{\text{e}}$ on P_0 can be simulated by $\xrightarrow{\text{e}}^*$ on P_1. The second and third items of the third condition of $\succsim$ can be checked easily because it is sufficient to consider effects except those by invoking the $x = \mathsf{ST}^i\, e$ instruction.

The case of CAS is similar. The other cases related to the c-transition are routine because Σ remains unchanged. The c-transition of P_1 is similar. The cases of e-transitions are readily apparent by definition. $\qquad\square$

Theorem 6. *Observable equivalence $\sim$ is a bisimulation.*

Proof. It is immediate from Proposition 4 and Lemma 5. $\qquad\square$

Thus, the objective has been accomplished because Claim 1 is satisfied by the definition of observable equivalence, Claim 2 is satisfied by Proposition 3 and Claim 3 is satisfied by Theorem 6.

6 Implementation of Memory Sharing Optimization

In this section, we explain the implementation of memory sharing optimization.

We implemented memory sharing optimization on a stateful model checker VeriDAG, which performs model checking not only with multi-copy atomicity, but also non-multi-copy atomicity [2]. VeriDAG takes a concurrent program written in the C programming language (or a sequence of LLVM-IRs) and an MCM as inputs, and generates a directed acyclic graph called a *program graph* as an intermediate representation, which was introduced in [4]. Program graphs are defined to support various MCMs, such as relaxed memory ordering (RMO) [5] that allows load-load reordering. Furthermore, the definition of program graphs was extended to support non-multi-copy atomicity [2]. Operational semantics for program graphs can simulate the general machine introduced in Sect. 3, and the formal discussion in Sect. 5 can be applied to program graphs and its operational semantics.

A node of a program graph corresponds to an instruction or an effect of an instruction from thread i to a set of threads I written as $x = \mathrm{E}^{i,I} v$, which makes the execution of the instruction visible to the other threads. For example, an effect means a reflect from the store buffer on thread i to shared memory under x86-TSO. An effect also means a reflect from the memory on thread i to the other memories on threads I under the POWER MCM.

Figures 8(a) and (b) depict program graphs that consist of $x = \mathrm{ST}^1\, 3$ and its effects on three threads under multi-copy atomicity and non-multi-copy atomicity, respectively. The edges of the program graph denote dependencies. In the figures, $x = \mathrm{E}^{1,\{0,1,2\}}\, 3$, $x = \mathrm{E}^{1,\{0\}}\, 3$, $x = \mathrm{E}^{1,\{1\}}\, 3$, and $x = \mathrm{E}^{1,\{2\}}\, 3$ are necessarily invoked after $x = \mathrm{ST}^1\, 3$ is invoked.

One method to implement memory sharing optimization is as follows: We introduced a partition of threads that corresponded to memory sharing by extending E to take not only the set of threads that corresponded to multi-copy atomicity or a singleton that corresponded to non-multi-copy atomicity, but also *any segment* of the partition. For example, $x = \mathrm{ST}^1\, 3$ on an LDRF program that consists of three threads was represented as shown in Fig. 8(c), where the two threads share one memory. Another method is to abandon unnecessary effects, although it was not adopted in this work. Because VeriDAG was well-designed to address reflected stores partially, the implementation of memory sharing optimization was straightforward.

Program graphs on VeriDAG have been modified from the original ones described in a previous paper [4], for performance improvement. An *atomic edge*, denoted by $\Longrightarrow$, means that if its source node is consumed, then its target node is preferably chosen at one of the roots of the updated program graph in the next step; that is, a pair of instructions related by an atomic edge is invoked instantaneously. Atomic edges are carefully implemented to not disturb the so-called partial order reduction based on the notion of *ample sets* [21] using invisibility that is already implemented in VeriDAG.

The previous program graphs in Fig. 8 were modified, as shown in Fig. 9. The validity of the optimization was ensured because there was no necessity to

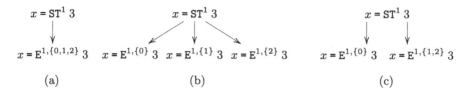

Fig. 8. Program graphs with multi-copy atomicity, non-multi-copy atomicity, and memory sharing optimization

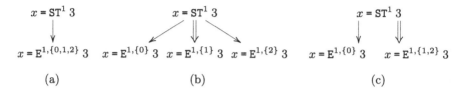

Fig. 9. Program graphs with atomic edges

consider interleavings between these nodes because every thread i used its own σ^I, and every σ^I was always used via $\Sigma^{i,I}$ in the form of $\sigma^I[\Sigma^{i,I}]$, where $i \in I$. Note that thread 2 did not read x in the last program graph according to the LDRF condition. Additionally, note that the first program graph had no atomic edge because the graph was generated with multi-copy atomicity.

7   Experiments

In this section, we demonstrate the effectiveness of memory sharing optimization by conducting model checking of the IRIW program and CCGC algorithms. We used VeriDAG, on which memory sharing optimization was implemented, as explained in Sect. 6. MCMs were RMO with and without multi-copy-atomicity. RMO with multi-copy-atomicity corresponds to the SPARC RMO MCM. RMO with non-multi-copy-atomicity corresponds to the POWER MCM. The experimental environment was as follows: the CPU was Intel Xeon E5-1620 v4 3.50 GHz, the memory was DDR4-2400 256 GB, the OS was Ubuntu 17.10, and VeriDAG was compiled using Glasgow Haskell Compiler 8.0.2.

7.1   Independent Reads Independent Writes Program

The IRIW program is (r0=y; r1=x) ∥ (r2=x; r3=y) ∥ x=1 ∥ y=1, and an assertion to observe curious behaviors under non-multi-copy atomicity is (r0==1 && r2==1) -> (r1==1 ∥ r3==1), as explained in Sect. 3. We used *acquire loads* in the IRIW program, which prohibit load-load reordering because the IRIW program has curious behaviors with non-multi-copy atomicity even if load-load reordering is prohibited.

We increase the number of writer threads in the IRIW because memory optimization should be more effective when the number of threads whose buffers

Table 1. Experimental results of the IRIW programs

# of Ws	Multi-copy atomicity			Non-multi-copy atomicity			Memory sharing optimiz.		
	States (K)	Memory (MB)	Time (s)	States (K)	Memory (MB)	Time (s)	States (K)	Memory (MB)	Time (s)
2	1	2	0.02	2	3	0.08	1	2	0.05
3	3	3	0.16	35	9	2.06	10	4	0.54
4	17	5	1.15	718	142	63.91	79	17	5.83
5	92	20	12.14	16650	3339	2526.31	666	125	84.07
6	463	87	71.00	407439	80912	88382.43	5100	941	847.56

are shared is larger. The number of writer threads in the original IRIW program is two. Additionally, we conducted model checking with the IRIW programs with three to six writer threads. The additional writer threads wrote integer 1 to additional shared variables. The two reader threads read additional values from the shared variables. For example, in a case that the number of writer threads is 3, the program is (r0=z; r1=y; r2=x) || (r3=x; r4=y; r5=z) || x=1 || y=1 || z=1. The number of interleavings should have increased drastically.

Table 1 presents the experimentally obtained results for the IRIW programs. The first column shows the number of writer threads (denoted by Ws). The second, third, and fourth columns refer to multi-copy atomicity. Model checking with multi-copy atomicity was conducted to represent the difficulty of model checking with non-multi-copy atomicity. Of course, model checking with multi-copy atomicity does not ensure the correctness of programs with non-multi-copy atomicity. There might exist a counterexample with non-multi-copy atomicity even if model checking with multi-copy atomicity detects no counterexample.

The second, third, and fourth columns list the numbers of states visited, memory consumed, and time elapsed, respectively. Even if a counterexample was detected, model checking continued until an exhaustive search was complete. The command-line option of VeriDAG includes -c0, which denotes that an exhaustive search is complete even if a counterexample is detected and printed out, whereas the default is -c1, which denotes that if a counterexample is detected, model checking stops and returns the counterexample. Similarly, the fifth, sixth, and seventh columns refer to non-multi-copy atomicity, and the eighth, ninth, and tenth columns refer to memory sharing optimization.

Model checking with multi-copy atomicity was completed more rapidly than the others with non-multi-copy atomicity and memory sharing optimization. However, they printed out no counterexamples because the assertion (r0==1 && r1==1) -> (r2==1 || r3==1) holds with multi-copy atomicity when the IRIW program (r0=y; r1=x) || (r2=x; r3=y) || x=1 || y=1 is complete. They are just experiments to compare model checking with multi-copy atomicity with model checking with non-multi-copy atomicity.

The numbers of states increased drastically during model checking with non-multi-copy atomicity. Accordingly, the consumed memories and elapsed times

Table 2. Experimental results of the CCGC algorithms

CCGC algorithm	Non-multi-copy atomicity			Memory sharing optimization		
	States (K)	Memory (MB)	Time (s)	States (K)	Memory (MB)	Time (s)
Schism	1744	320	205.17	1131	210	128.80
Sapphire	159052	28576	22312.51	41926	7589	5503.61

increased. Memory sharing optimization mitigated the state explosion problem. The greater the number of writer threads, that is, the larger the shared buffer, the more effective it is because of the combinatorial explosion.

Memory sharing optimization mitigated the state explosion problem. When the number of writer threads was two, memory sharing optimization improved performance approximately twice. When the number of writer threads was six, memory sharing optimization improved performance by 79–105 times. Thus, we confirmed that memory sharing optimization was more effective when the number of threads whose memories were shared was larger.

7.2   Concurrent Copying Garbage Collection Algorithms

Some CCGC algorithms are typical LDRF programs. CCGCs consist of mutators, which correspond to threads in user programs, and a collector. We can assume that there exists no load-store race in any period between synchronization points because threads in user programs that do not exist at the garbage collection layer must be DRF in programming languages with MCMs that require DRF. However, it may be the case that mutators share variables because a collector communicates with mutators when collecting objects that have not been used.

We conducted model checking of popular CCGC algorithms [15] that were modeled in the paper [27]. We extended the models to those whose mutators consisted of two threads, whereas the number of mutators in the original models was one. The original models have restrictions that their behaviors are fixed to read-write or write-read flows. Details of the restrictions are in the paper [27]. We modified the models to include both the flows by adding non-deterministic choice statements to the models. The modified models are more realistic than the original models. Table 2 presents the experimentally obtained results of the CCGC algorithms. The first column shows the names of the CCGC algorithms. The remaining columns are similar to those in Table 1.

Table 2 shows that the experimental results for Schism [22] and Sapphire [24], even those that were real applications, had a similar feature to that for the IRIW program, which is a litmus test for multi-copy-atomicity. The experiment for the other larger CCGCs was not complete in half a day (= 43, 200 s).

8   Conclusion, Discussion, and Future Work

In this paper, we provided small-step operational semantics for relaxed memory consistency models with store buffers, defined observable equivalence on the semantics, and proposed LDRF, a local property of concurrent programs, which runs on non-multi-copy atomic MCMs. LDRF includes the IRIW programs that DRF cannot include. We also introduced memory sharing optimization on model checking of LDRF programs, and demonstrated that memory sharing optimization mitigates state explosion problems with non-multi-copy atomic MCMs.

Multi-copy atomicity, also known as remote write atomicity, has been studied [6,13]. Although ARM adopted non-multi-copy atomicity until ARMv8 [7], Pulte et al. reported that ARMv8 will be revised to prohibit non-multi-copy atomicity because they claim that the complexity derived from non-multi-copy atomicity has a cost, particularly for architectures implemented by multiple vendors [23]. In contrast, Vafeiadis argued that multi-copy atomicity did not seem relevant because its enforcement of global orders between instructions prevents scalability of verification [28]. Thus, multi-copy atomicity is a topic of debate. We hope that the present paper helps to elucidate non-multi-copy atomicity, and therefore contributes to decisions to adopt various multi-copy atomicities.

The experimental results demonstrated that the performance of VeriDAG with the memory sharing optimization was not substantially high. This is because VeriDAG is a stateful model checker that adopts classical partial order reduction optimization [21], differently from Nidhugg [1] with the POWER MCM [12] and RCMC [16] with the repaired version of C/C++11 MCM [14] which adopt dynamic partial order reduction [10]. However, this is independent of the goal of demonstrating the effectiveness of memory sharing optimization.

Because TRF and LDRF are variants of DRF in different directions, it might be expected that a novel property can be defined by combining the two properties. However, this appears to be difficult because TRF is strongly specific to x86-TSO, which preserves the order of stores of different shared variables, whereas LDRF requires that store buffers consist of multiple queues.

This work has a few limitations. LDRF is syntactically and conservatively defined while DRF is defined by observing execution traces, because local data race detection has not been implemented yet.

It seems reasonable that LDRF should be defined as a pair-wise property because the locality may be a pair-wise property. For example, let us consider a case that threads 0 and 1 do not race, threads 0 and 2 do not race, but threads 1 and 2 do. However, LDRF in this paper cannot capture the case since LDRF is defined as a property for a partition of the set of threads.

The memory sharing optimization that mitigates the state explosion problem is not a scalable method for increasing the number of threads. We would like to revise LDRF as a pair-wise property, find any better characterization for scalability, and provide local data race detection.

214   T. Abe

Acknowledgments. The author thanks Toshiyuki Maeda and Tomoharu Ugawa. The motivation of this work was fostered through discussions with them. The author also thanks the anonymous reviewers for several comments to improve the paper. This work was supported by JSPS KAKENHI Grant Number 16K21335.

References

1. Abdulla, P.A., Atig, M.F., Jonsson, B., Leonardsson, C.: Stateless model checking for POWER. In: Chaudhuri, S., Farzan, A. (eds.) CAV 2016, Part II. LNCS, vol. 9780, pp. 134–156. Springer, Cham (2016). https://doi.org/10.1007/978-3-319-41540-6_8
2. Abe, T.: A verifier of directed acyclic graphs for model checking with memory consistency models. Hardware and Software: Verification and Testing. LNCS, vol. 10629, pp. 51–66. Springer, Cham (2017). https://doi.org/10.1007/978-3-319-70389-3_4
3. Abe, T., Maeda, T.: Observation-based concurrent program logic for relaxed memory consistency models. In: Igarashi, A. (ed.) APLAS 2016. LNCS, vol. 10017, pp. 63–84. Springer, Cham (2016). https://doi.org/10.1007/978-3-319-47958-3_4
4. Abe, T., Maeda, T.: Concurrent program logic for relaxed memory consistency models with dependencies across loop iterations. J. Inf. Process. **25**, 244–255 (2017)
5. Adve, S.V., Gharachorloo, K.: Shared memory consistency models: a tutorial. Computer **29**(12), 66–76 (1996)
6. ARM Limited: ARM Architecture Reference Manual (ARMv7-A and ARMv7-R edition) (2012)
7. ARM Limited: ARM Architecture Reference Manual (ARMv8, for ARMv8-A architecture profile) (2017)
8. Basten, T., Bošnački, D., Geilen, M.: Cluster-based partial-order reduction. Autom. Softw. Eng. **11**(4), 365–402 (2004)
9. Dolan, S., Sivaramakrishnan, K., Madhavapeddy, A.: Bounding data races in space and time. In: Proceedings of PLDI (2018, to appear)
10. Flanagan, C., Godefroid, P.: Dynamic partial-order reduction for model checking software. In: Proceedings of POPL, pp. 110–121 (2005)
11. Gao, G.R., Sarkar, V.: Location consistency-a new memory model and cache consistency protocol. IEEE Trans. Comput. **49**(8), 798–813 (2000)
12. IBM Corporation: Power ISA Version 3.0 (2015)
13. Intel Corporation: A Formal Specification of Intel Itanium Processor Family Memory Ordering (2002)
14. ISO/IEC 14882:2011: Programming Language C++ (2011)
15. Jones, R., Hosking, A., Moss, E.: The Garbage Collection Handbook. CRC Press, Boca Rotan (2012)
16. Kokologiannakis, M., Lahav, O., Sagonas, K., Vafeiadis, V.: Effective stateless model checking for C/C++ concurrency. Proc. ACM Program. Lang. **2**(POPL:17), 1–32 (2018)
17. Lamport, L.: How to make a multiprocessor computer that correctly executes multiprocess programs. IEEE Trans. Comput. **c-28**(9), 690–691 (1979)
18. O'Hearn, P.W.: Resources, concurrency, and local reasoning. Theor. Comput. Sci. **375**(1–3), 271–307 (2007)
19. Owens, S.: Reasoning about the implementation of concurrency abstractions on x86-TSO. In: D'Hondt, T. (ed.) ECOOP 2010. LNCS, vol. 6183, pp. 478–503. Springer, Heidelberg (2010). https://doi.org/10.1007/978-3-642-14107-2_23

20. Owens, S., Sarkar, S., Sewell, P.: A better x86 memory model: x86-TSO. In: Berghofer, S., Nipkow, T., Urban, C., Wenzel, M. (eds.) TPHOLs 2009. LNCS, vol. 5674, pp. 391–407. Springer, Heidelberg (2009). https://doi.org/10.1007/978-3-642-03359-9_27

21. Peled, D.: All from one, one for all: on model checking using representatives. In: Courcoubetis, C. (ed.) CAV 1993. LNCS, vol. 697, pp. 409–423. Springer, Heidelberg (1993). https://doi.org/10.1007/3-540-56922-7_34

22. Pizlo, F., Ziarek, L., Maj, P., Hosking, A.L., Blanton, E., Vitek, J.: Schism: fragmentation-tolerant real-time garbage collection. In: Proceedings of PLDI, pp. 146–159 (2010)

23. Pulte, C., Flur, S., Deacon, W., French, J., Sarkar, S., Sewell, P.: Simplifying ARM concurrency: multicopy-atomic axiomatic and operational models for ARMv8. Proc. ACM Program. Lang. 2(POPL:19), 1–29 (2018)

24. Ritson, C.G., Ugawa, T., Jones, R.: Exploring garbage collection with Haswell hardware transactional memory. In: Proceedings of ISMM, pp. 105–115 (2014)

25. Saraswat, V., Jagadeesan, R., Michael, M., von Praun, C.: A theory of memory models. In: Proceedings of PPoPP, pp. 161–172 (2007)

26. Sarkar, S., Sewell, P., Alglave, J., Maranget, L., Williams, D.: Understanding POWER multiprocessors. In: Proceedings of PLDI, pp. 175–186 (2011)

27. Ugawa, T., Abe, T., Maeda, T.: Model checking copy phases of concurrent copying garbage collection with various memory models. Proc. ACM Program. Lang. 1(OOPSLA:53), 1–26 (2017)

28. Vafeiadis, V.: Sequential consistency considered harmful. In: New Challenges in Parallelism (Report from Dagstuhl Seminar 17451), p. 21 (2018)

A Comparative Study of Decision Diagrams for Real-Time Model Checking

Omar Al-Bataineh[1], Mark Reynolds[2]($\boxtimes$), and David Rosenblum[1]

[1] National University of Singapore, Singapore, Singapore
[2] University of Western Australia, Perth, Australia
mark.reynolds@uwa.edu.au

Abstract. The timed automata model, introduced by Alur and Dill, provides a powerful formalism for describing real-time systems. Over the last two decades, several dense-time model checking tools have been developed based on that model. This paper considers the verification of a set of interesting real-time distributed protocols using dense-time model checking technology. More precisely, we model and verify the distributed timed two phase commit protocol, and two well-known benchmarks, the Token-Ring-FDDI protocol, and the CSMA/CD protocol, in three different state-of-the-art real-time model checkers: UPPAAL, RED, and Rabbit. We illustrate the use of these tools using one of the case studies. Finally, several interesting conclusions have been drawn about the performance, usability, and the capability of each tool.

1 Introduction

Real-time systems are systems that are designed to run applications and programs with very precise timing and a high degree of reliability. These systems can be said to be failed if they can not guarantee response within strict time constraints. Ensuring the correctness of real-time systems is a challenging task. This is mainly because the correctness of real-time systems depends on the actual times at which events occur. Hence, real-time systems need to be rigorously modeled and verified in order to have confidence in their correctness with respect to the desired properties.

Because of time constraints in real-time systems, traditional model checking approaches based on finite state automata and temporal logic are not sufficient. Since they can not capture the time requirements of real-time systems upon which the correctness of these systems relies. Several researchers have proposed different modeling formalisms for describing real-time systems such as timed transition systems [21], timed I/O automata [20], and timed automata model [4]. Although a number of formalisms have been proposed, the *timed automata model* of Alur, Courcoubetis, and Dill [4] has become the standard.

In this contribution, we conduct a comparative study of a number of model checking tools, based on a variety of approaches to representing real-time systems. We have selected three real-time protocols, the *timed two phase commit*

© Springer International Publishing AG, part of Springer Nature 2018
M. M. Gallardo and P. Merino (Eds.): SPIN 2018, LNCS 10869, pp. 216–234, 2018.
https://doi.org/10.1007/978-3-319-94111-0_13

protocol (T2PC) [16], the *Token-Ring-FDDI protocol* [19], and the *CSMA/CD protocol* [27], implemented them in quite different 'dense' timed model checkers, and verified their relevant properties. Specifically, we consider the model checkers UPPAAL [7], Rabbit [12] and RED [26]. We focus more on the particular T2PC protocol since the protocol has not been model checked before and we use it to illustrate how one can use the three tools to model real-time systems. The tools use different decision diagrams to model and verify real-time systems. UPPAAL deals with the logic of TCTL [2] using an algorithm based on DBMs (Difference Bound Matrices) [17]. Rabbit is a model checker based on timed automata extended with concepts for modular modeling and performs reachability analysis using BDD (Binary Decision Diagrams) [15]. RED is a model checker with dense-time models based on CRD (Clock-Restriction Diagrams) [26]. Comparing model-checking tools is challenging because it requires mastering various modelling formalisms to model the same concepts in different paradigms and intimate knowledge of tools' usage.

We compare the three tools from four different perspectives: (a) their modeling power, (b) their verification and specification capabilities, (c) their theoretical (algorithmic) foundation, and (d) their efficiency and performance. RED outperformed both UPPAAL and Rabbit in two of the case studies (T2PC and FDDI) in terms of scalability, and expressivity of its specification language. On the other hand, Rabbit outperformed both RED and UPPAAL on the CSMA/CD case study. However, UPPAAL was a lot faster than both tools in cases where it gave a result, but it is less scalable than RED.

The CRD-based data structure implemented in RED turns out to be an efficient data structure for handling case studies with huge number of clocks since it scales better with respect to number of clocks. The data structure BDD turns out to be efficient for handling case studies with huge number of discrete variables but it is very sensitive to the scale of clock constants in the model. The DBM-based data structure implemented in UPPAAL handles the complexity of timing constant magnitude very well, but when the number of clocks increases its performance degrades rapidly. It is interesting to mention also that the three tools agreed on the results of all the experiments that we conducted.

Related Work. Some work has already been done on the verification of commitment protocols using formal techniques. In particular, the basic 2PC protocol has frequently been the focus of studies of verification of distributed computing [6,22,24], but it is just one of several variants discussed in the literature. One of the interesting variants of the protocol is the T2PC protocol that has complex timing constraints. In this work we have shown how the T2PC protocol can be analyzed with three various tools: UPPAAL, Rabbit, and RED. To the best of our knowledge the T2PC protocol has not been model checked before.

The literature of timed automata theory is a rich literature since it was introduced by Alur and Dill in 1990. In [3] Alur et al. showed that the TCTL is in PSPACE-complexity and gave a model checking algorithm of TCTL. In [18] Henzinger et al. proposed an efficient algorithm for model checking TCTL. Alur and Madhusudan [5] present a full survey of known results for decidability problems in timed automata theory. Ober et al. [23] proposed a timed unified modeling language (UML) for real-time systems and showed how to translate timed UML into timed automata that can be used for formal analysis. Tripakis [25] gives algorithms and techniques to verify timed systems using TCTL logic and Timed Buchi Automata. which have implemented in KRONOS model checking tool. KRONOS is a full DBM-based model checker that supports both forward and backward TCTL model checking. One of the limitations of KRONOS is that its input language supports a very restricted data types that allow only the declaration of clock variables. For this reason we have not included KRONOS in our comparative study since the case study that we consider requires much richer modeling language.

The BDD-like data structures have been also used in the verification of timed systems. The model checkers Rabbit and RED have been developed based on BDD-like technology. Empirical results given in [12,26] have shown that RED and Rabbit outperformed UPPAAL in some particular examples such as Fisher mutual exclusion and FDDI Token Ring protocol. However, the empirical results presented in these works were reported using an old version of UPPAAL (v3.2.4), which lack many of the optimisations that are used in the current version of the tool (v4.1.13). In [13] Beyer shows that the size of the BDD and the CRD representation of the reachability set depends on two properties of the models: the number of automata and the magnitude of the clock values. In [26] Wang shows that CRDs outperform DBMs when verifying specifications that contain large number of clocks. However, he pointed out that CRDs consume much space (memory) in handling intermediate data structures, and therefore require intensive use of garbage collection.

2   Preliminaries

In this section, we introduce the basics of the timed two phase commit protocol, which is the main case study considered in this. We then give a brief review of the syntax and semantics of timed automata model, real-time temporal logic, and the zone abstraction which is an abstraction for representing the timing information in the timed models.

2.1   Timed Two Phase Commit Protocol (T2PC)

The T2PC protocol aims to maintain data consistency of all distributed database systems as well as having to satisfy the time constraints of the transaction under processing. The protocol is mainly based on the well-known two phase commit (2PC) protocol, but it incorporates several intermediate deadlines in order to be able to handle real-time transactions. We describe first the basic 2PC protocol (without deadlines) and then discuss how it can be modified to be used for real-time transactions. The 2PC protocol can be summarised as follows [11].

A set of processes $\{p_1, .., p_n\}$ prepare to involve in a distributed transaction. Each process has been given its own subtransaction. One of the processes will act as a coordinator and all other processes are participants. The protocol proceeds into two phases. In the first phase (voting phase), the coordinator broadcasts a start message to all the participants, and then waits to receive vote messages from the participants. The participant will vote to commit the transaction if all its local computations regarding the transaction have been completed successfully; otherwise, it will vote to abort. In the second phase (commit phase), if the coordinator received the votes of all the participants, it decides and broadcasts the decision. If all the votes are 'yes' then the coordinator will commit the transaction. However, if one process voted 'no', then the coordinator will decide to abort the transaction. After sending the decision, the coordinator waits to receive a COMPLETION messages from all the participants.

Three intermediate deadlines have been added to the basic 2PC protocol in order to handle real-time transactions [16]: the deadline V which is a deadline for a participant to send its vote, DEC the deadline for the coordinator to broadcast the decision, and D_p the deadline for a participant to send a COMPLETION message to the coordinator. Note that the correctness of the T2PC protocol depends mainly on the way we select the values of the above timing parameters. In particular, the coordinator should choose the value of D to be sufficiently long to allow the participants to receive the start message and return the completion message in time for the coordinator to determine the result. The correctness of the protocol depends also on a condition that a fair scheduling policy is imposed, this condition is necessary in order to avoid situations in which some participants may miss the deadline if they schedule to execute until after the deadline D. Note also that the protocol can only guarantee correctness in the absence of failures both node failures and link failures, since a failure if happens might delay the execution of some processes until after the deadline expires, which therefore cause the protocol to fail.

2.2 The Timed Automata Model and Real-Time Temporal Logic

Timed automata are an extension of the classical finite state automata with clock variables to model timing aspects [4]. Let X be a set of clock variables, then the set $\Phi(X)$ of clock constraints ϕ is defined by the following grammar

$$\phi ::= t \sim c \mid \phi_1 \wedge \phi_2$$

where $t \in X$, $c \in \mathbb{N}$, and $\sim \in \{<, \leq, =, >, \geq\}$. A clock interpretation v for a set X is a mapping from X to $\mathbb{R}^+$ where $\mathbb{R}^+$ denotes the set of nonnegative real numbers.

Definition 1. *A timed automaton A is a tuple $(\Sigma, L, L_0, X, E, \mathcal{L})$, where*

- *Σ is a finite set of actions.*
- *L is a finite set of locations.*
- *L_0 is a finite set of initial locations.*
- *X is a finite set of clocks.*

- $E \subseteq L \times L \times \Sigma \times 2^X \times \Phi(X)$ *is a finite set of transitions. An edge* $(l, l', a, \lambda, \sigma)$ *represents a transition from location* l *to location* l' *after performing action* a. *The set* $\lambda \subseteq X$ *gives the clocks to be reset with this transition, and* σ *is a clock constraint over* X.
- $\mathcal{L} : L \to 2^{AP}$ *is a labeling function mapping each location to a set of atomic propositions.*

The semantics of a timed automaton $(\Sigma, L, L_0, X, E, \mathcal{L})$ can be defined by associating a transition system with it. With each transition a clock constraint is associated. The transition can be taken only if the clock constraint on the transition is satisfied. There are two basic types of transitions:

1. delay transitions that model the elapse of time while staying at some location,
2. action transitions that execute an edge of the automata.

A state $s = (l, v)$ consists of the current location and the set of clock valuations at that location. The initial state is (l_0, v_0) where the valuation $v_0(x) = 0$ for all $x \in X$. A timed action is a pair (t, a) where $a \in \Sigma$ is an action performed by an automaton $\mathcal{A}$ after $t \in \mathbb{R}^+$ time units since $\mathcal{A}$ has been started.

Definition 2. *An execution of a timed automaton* $\mathcal{A} = (\Sigma, L, L_0, X, E, \mathcal{L})$ *with an initial state* (l_0, v_0) *over a timed trace* $\zeta = (t_1, a_1), (t_2, a_2), (t_3, a_3), ..$ *is a sequence of transitions of the form.*

$$\langle l_0, v_0 \rangle \xrightarrow{d1 \ a1} \langle l_1, v_1 \rangle \xrightarrow{d2 \ a2} \langle l_2, v_2 \rangle \xrightarrow{d3 \ a3} \langle l_3, v_3 \rangle ...$$

satisfying the condition $t_i = t_{i-1} + d_i$ *for all* $i \geq 1$. □

In order to allow the verification of dense-time properties we need to add bounds in the classical CTL temporal operators. The extended logic is called TCTL. We now give the syntax and the semantics of the TCTL logic.

$$\mathbf{TCTL} \ni \varphi ::= p \mid \neg\varphi \mid \varphi_1 \vee \varphi_2 \mid E\varphi_1 U_I \varphi_2 \mid A\varphi_1 U_I \varphi_2$$

where I is an interval of $\mathbb{R}^+$ that can be either bounded or unbounded. The basic TCTL modality in the above definition is the U-modality which can be used to define the time interval in which the property should be true. Given a formula φ and a state (ℓ, v) of a timed automata $\mathcal{A}$, the satisfaction relation $(\ell, v) \models \varphi$ is defined inductively on the syntax of φ as follows.

- $(\ell, v) \models p$ iff $p \in \mathcal{L}(\ell)$
- $(\ell, v) \models \neg\varphi$ iff $(\ell, v) \nvDash \varphi$
- $(\ell, v) \models \varphi \vee \psi$ iff $(\ell, v) \models \varphi$ or $(\ell, v) \models \psi$
- $(\ell, v) \models E\varphi U_I \psi$ iff there is a run ζ in $\mathcal{A}$ from (ℓ, v) such that $\zeta \models \varphi U_I \psi$.
- $(\ell, v) \models A\varphi U_I \psi$ iff for any run ζ in $\mathcal{A}$ from (ℓ, v) such that $\zeta \models \varphi U_I \psi$.
- $(\ell, v) \models \varphi U_I \psi$ iff there exists a position $\pi > 0$ along a run ζ such that $\zeta[\pi] \models \psi$, for every position $0 < \pi' < \pi$, $\zeta[\pi'] \models \varphi$, and duration $(\zeta_{\leq \pi}) \in I$.

2.3   The Zone-Based Abstraction Technique

In the original work of Alur and Dill [4], they presented an abstraction technique by which an infinite timed transition system (i.e., timed automata) can be converted into an equivalent finitely symbolic transition system called region graph where reachability is decidable. However, it has been shown that the region automaton is highly inefficient to be used for implementing practical tools. Instead, most real-time model checking tools like UPPAAL, Kronos and RED apply abstractions based on so-called zones, which is much more practical and efficient for model checking real-time systems.

In a zone graph [17], zones are used to denote symbolic states. A zone is a pair (ℓ, Z), where l is a location in the TA model and Z is a clock zone that represents sets of clock valuations at l. Formally a clock zone is a conjunction of inequalities that compare either a clock value or the difference between two clock values to an integer. In order to have a unified form for clock zones we introduce a reference clock x_0 to the set of clocks X in the analyzed model that is always zero. The general form of a clock zone can be described by the following formula

$$(x_0 = 0) \wedge \bigwedge_{0 \leq i \neq j \leq n} ((x_i - x_j) \sim c_{i,j})$$

where $x_i, x_j \in X$, $c_{i,j}$ represents the difference between them, and $\sim \in \{\leq, <\}$. Considering a timed automaton $\mathcal{A} = (\Sigma, L, L_0, X, E, \mathcal{L})$, with a transition $e = (\ell, a, \psi, \lambda, \ell')$ in E we can construct an abstract zone graph $\mathcal{Z}(\mathcal{A})$ such that states of $\mathcal{Z}(\mathcal{A})$ are zones of $\mathcal{A}$. The clock zone $succ(Z, e)$ will denote the set of clock valuations Z' for which the state (ℓ', Z') can be reached from the state (ℓ, Z) by letting time elapse and by executing the transition e. The pair $(\ell', succ(Z, e))$ will represent the set of successors of (ℓ, Z) under the transition e. Since every constraint used in the invariant of an automaton location or in the guard of a transition is a clock zone, we can use zones for various state reachability analysis algorithms for timed automata.

It is interesting to note that without further abstractions ("extrapolation"), the zone graph can be infinite. To obtain a finite zone graph most model checkers use some kind of extrapolation of zones. In the last two decades, there has been a considerable development in the extrapolation procedure for TA for the purpose of providing coarser abstractions of TA [8,10,14]. We refer the reader to [1] for more details about different kinds of extrapolation techniques.

2.4   Data Structures for Representing Zone Graphs

In this section we review briefly the three data structures DBM, BDD, and CRD which have been used respectively to represent clock zones in the tools UPPAAL, Rabbit, and RED.

Difference Bound Matrices (DBMs). [17] are two-dimensional matrices that record the difference upper bounds between clock pairs up to a certain constant. Each row in the matrix represents the bound difference between the value of the clock x_i and all the other clocks in the zone, thus a zone can be represented by at most $|X|^2$ atomic constraints. The element $D_{i,j}$ in DBM is on the form $(n, \sim)$ where $x_i, x_j \in X$, n represents the difference between them, and $\sim \in \{\leq, <\}$. DBM-technology generally handles the complexity of timing constant magnitude very well. But when the number of clocks increases, its performance degrades rapidly. The DBM-based technology has been implemented in the tool UPPAAL.

Binary Decision Diagrams (BDDs). [15] are propositional directed acyclic graphs. The BDD graph consists of a set of decision nodes and has two terminal nodes TRUE-terminal and FALSE-terminal. Each decision node is labeled by a Boolean variable and has two child nodes called low child and high child. A path from the root node to the TRUE-terminal represents a variable assignment for which the represented Boolean function is true. As the path descends to a low child (high child) from a node, then that node's variable is assigned to FALSE (TRUE). For untimed system veification, BDD has shown great success. But for timed system verification, so far, all BDD-like structures have not performed as well as the popular DBM. The BDD data structure is used in the tool Rabbit.

Clock Restriction Diagrams (CRDs). [26] is a BDD-like data structure for representation of sets of zones, with related set-oriented operations for fully symbolic verification of real-time systems. It has similar structure as BDD without FALSE terminal. Unlike BDD, CRD is not a decision diagram for state space membership. It acts like a database for zones and is appropriate for manipulation of sets of clock difference constraints. It has been claimed that CRDs provide more efficient space representation of timed automata than DBMs data structure [26]. The CRD technology is used in the current version of the tool RED. It is worth mentioning here that the CRD data structure of RED is very similar to the CDD data-structure (clock difference diagram) [9].

3   Modeling the Protocol in the Three Tools

In this section we describe how we formalize the T2PC protocol in the tools UPPAAL, RED, and Rabbit. The reason for choosing these tools in the comparison is due to the fact that the tools have been mainly developed for real-time model checking based on TA formalism (or some of its variants). The other reason is that the specification languages of the tools allow one to express common properties of real-time systems in a very natural and easy way (specially the tools UPPAAL and RED). The availability of the user guide of the tools which describes the different options of the tools is another reason for choosing them in this comparison. It is interesting to mention that the protocol has been verified while considering the different available verification options of each tool including the research order, state space representation, and extrapolation technique.

3.1 UPPAAL Model Checker

UPPAAL [7] is a model checker for real-time systems developed in conjunction by Uppsala University, Sweden, and Aalborg University, Denmark. It extends the basic timed automata with features for concurrency, communication, data variables, and priority. UPPAAL uses a client-server architecture which splits the tool into a graphical user interface (client) and a model checking engine (server). The user interface consists of three main sections: system editor, simulator, and verifier. The editor allows the user to model the system as a network of timed automata. The simulator gives the user the capability to interactively run the system to check if there are some trivial errors in the system design. The verifier allows the user to enter the properties to be verified in a sub-language of TCTL. UPPAAL can verify safety, bounded liveness, and reachability properties. UPPAAL uses fragment of TCTL language and it does not support the direct verification of bounded response properties.

The T2PC Protocol in UPPAAL. The coordinator template is depicted in Fig. 1. Initially, the coordinator attempts to reserve a CPU time slot via sending a reservation request signal to the CPU resource manager (see Fig. 3) using the channel reserve[rsc_id] indexed with the resource to be allocated. If the CPU is busy in executing other tasks, the manager will add the coordinator process to the waiting queue. Otherwise, it will send immediately the process to the CPU for processing. When the manager receives a finished signal from the CPU indicating that the CPU has finished processing the current process and it is currently in an idle state, the manager will send the process at the front of the queue (if any) to the CPU for processing. The abstract model of the CPU (see Fig. 4) has two locations idle and InUse which reflects the status of the CPU. When it receives a ready[pid] signal from process pid, it moves from idle to InUse, and then returns from InUse to idle after the determined execution time is completed. If the resource (CPU) is granted (rsc_granted ==true), the coordinator initiates the protocol via broadcasting a start message to all the participants. The coordinator then waits to receive the votes of the participants. If V time units passed before receiving all the votes, the coordinator decides to abort and then terminate. Otherwise, it will move to location $m2$ at which it decides and broadcast the decision.

A function result(part_vote) returns the result of the transaction based on the values of the received votes. The coordinator broadcasts this result using the broadcast channel fin_result and the global variable outcome. The coordinator then moves to location $m3$ at which it waits to receive the completion messages of the participants. If D_p time units passed before receiving all completion messages, it decides to abort and then terminate. The protocol ends at location finished at which the coordinator updates its database server.

The template of the participants is depicted in Fig. 2. All the participants start their execution at location idle where they wait to receive a start signal from the coordinator. Once they receive that signal, each participant i will try to reserve t_i time units via signalling the resource manager component. If the CPU is busy at that time, it will join the waiting queue until it gets executed. If the deadline V expired before sending their votes to the coordinator they decide to abort and then terminate. Each participant then moves to location $r2$ at which it waits to receive the decision of the coordinator. If it does not receive it within DEC time units, it decides to abort the transaction and terminate. Otherwise, it sets its comp variable to true and moves to location $r4$ where it updates its database server and terminates.

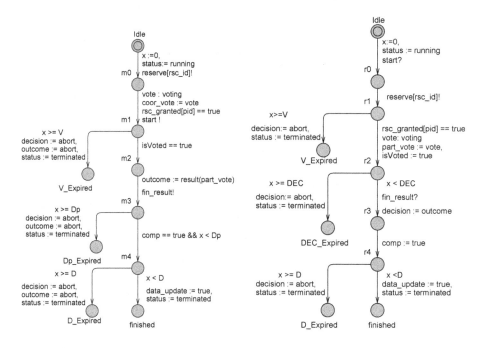

Fig. 1. The coordinator template   **Fig. 2.** The participant template

3.2 Rabbit Model Checker

Rabbit [12] is a model checking tool for real-time systems. The theoretical foundation of the tool is mainly based on timed automata extended with concepts for modular modeling. We give an informal description of the formalism of Cottbus Timed Automata (CTA), which is used in the modeling language of Rabbit.

A CTA system consists of a set of modules that can be defined in a hierarchical way. Each module in the system model should have the following components:

– An *identifier*. Identifiers are used to name the modules within the system description. Using identifiers we can create several instances of the modules associated with these identifiers.

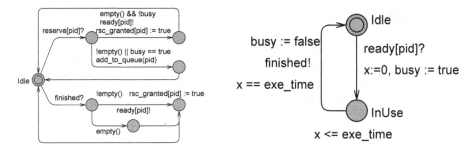

Fig. 3. The resource manager template   **Fig. 4.** The CPU template

- An *Interface.* The interface of a module contains the declarations of the variables that are used in that module. In a CTA module, we can declare clock variables, discrete variables, and synchronisation labels.
  - *Synchronisation labels.* Sometimes called signals which are used to synchronise timed automata that exist in different modules in the system. The concept of synchronisation labels in modules is very similar to the concept of events in CSP.
  - *Variables.* Rabbit allows us to declare both continuous (clock) variables and discrete variables. The values of these variables can be updated using assignment statements in the transition rules of the automaton.
- A *timed automaton.* Each module contains a timed automaton. The automaton consists of a finite set of states, a finite set of transitions, and a set of synchronisation labels. In the CTA language, a process transition is declared as a transition rule which starts with the keyword **TRANS**, while the locations of the automaton are declared using the keyword **STATE**.
- *Initial condition.* This is a formula over the module variables and the states of the module's automaton, which specifies the initial state of the module.
- *Instances.* In the CTA model, a module can contain instances of the other defined modules in the model.

Due to space reasons, we do not present the full model of the T2PC protocol in Rabbit here, and we refer the reader to Appendix A of the longer version of the paper at http://arxiv.org/abs/1201.3416. However, we pick some statements in the Rabbit model of the T2PC protocol in order to explain how to declare the model behaviour structure with Rabbit. The declaration is a sequence of **STATE** declarations. The statements declare a state whose name is **InUse** and whose invariance condition is "x<= exe_time". Inside the transition **TRANS** we have a synchroniser **finished**, a triggering condition "x == exe_time", and two actions "DO busy' = 0;" and "GOTO Idle;".

```
AUTOMATON CPU
{
  STATE InUse{ INV  x<= exe_time;
               TRANS  {GUARD x = exe_time; SYNC ! finished;
               DO busy' = 0; GOTO Idle;} }
  STATE Idle{  TRANS  {SYNC ? ready; DO x' =0 AND
               busy' =1; GOTO InUse;} }
}
```

3.3 RED Model Checker

RED [26] stands for (Region-Encoding Diagrams) is a TCTL model checker for real-time systems. An interesting feature of the RED model checker is that it is totally based on symbolic technology with BDD-like diagrams.

In RED, systems are described as parametrized communicating timed automata, where processes can be model processes, specification processes, or environment processes. In a system with n processes, the user invokes the RED model checker via telling it which processes are for the model, and which for the specification. The remaining processes will be for the environment. Since the automata in RED are parametrised automata then we can declare many process automata with the same automaton template and identify each process automaton with a process index. RED supports both forward and backward analyses, deadlock detection, and counter-example generation. In RED, users can declare global and local variables of type boolean, discrete, clock-restriction variable, and hybrid-restriction variable. Due to space reasons, we don't present here the full model of the T2PC protocol in RED, and we refer the reader to Appendix B of the longer version of the paper at http://arxiv.org/abs/1201.3416. The statements declare a mode whose name is InUse and whose invariance condition "x<= exe_time". Inside the transition rule when we have a synchronizer finished, a triggering condition "x == exe_time", and the two actions "busy = 0" and "goto idle".

```
    mode InUse (x<= exe_time)
    {
     when !finished (x == exe_time) may busy = 0; goto Idle;
    }
     mode Idle (true)
    {
     when ? ready (true) may busy = 1; x =0; goto InUse;
    }
```

4   Correctness Conditions of the T2PC Protocol

The first formula of interest is global atomicity (i.e. all processes must agree on the final decision: all must abort or all must commit.)

Specification 1: The global atomicity is always guaranteed.

$$\mathbf{AG} \left(\bigwedge_{i \neq j} \neg(i.\mathtt{decision} = abort \wedge j.\mathtt{decision} = commit) \right)$$

Note that the variable `decision` can take one of the following values {*undecided, abort, commit*}. Initially, all agents are *undecided*. Recall that the goal of the protocol is to preserve data consistency as well as to satisfy all designated intermediate deadlines D_p, DEC, and V. If any of these deadlines expired during the execution of the transaction, all processes will decide to abort. Note that the execution of the transaction may be delayed due to queuing delay or due to a communication delay which might cause the protocol to miss its deadlines. The following specifications verify whether the protocol can satisfy these deadlines.

Specification 2: If the coordinator sent successfully a commit request message, then it is guaranteed to receive all participants' votes within V time units.

$$\mathbf{AG} \left((\mathtt{C.request\_sent}) \Rightarrow \mathbf{AF}_{\leq V} \left(\bigwedge_{i=1..n} (\mathtt{C.vote\_rcvd[i]}) \right) \right)$$

Specification 3: If the coordinator received all the votes successfully, then all the participants can receive the decision within DEC time units.

$$\mathbf{AG} \left(\left(\bigwedge_{i=1..n}(\mathtt{C.vote\_rcvd[i]}) \right) \Rightarrow \mathbf{AF}_{\leq DEC} \left(\bigwedge_{i=1..n}(i.\mathtt{dec\_rcvd}) \right) \right)$$

Specification 4: If the coordinator announced the decision successfully, it can receive acknowledgement signals within D_p time units.

$$\mathbf{AG} \left((\mathtt{C.dec\_sent}) \Rightarrow \mathbf{AF}_{\leq D_p} \left(\bigwedge_{i=1..n} (\mathtt{C.ack[i]}) \right) \right)$$

We discuss now how we specify the properties of the protocol in the input language of each model checker. UPPAAL uses fragment of TCTL logic, RED uses full TCTL logic, while on other hand, TCTL is not available in Rabbit and it uses techniques based on reachability analysis to verify systems properties. Due to space limitation, we consider here only specification 1. For more details about how we specify the whole protocol's properties in each tool we refer the reader to the full version of this paper (http://arxiv.org/abs/1201.3416).

In UPPAAL, we can capture specification 1 as follows.

```
A[] not (coor.decision == commit and part.decision == abort)
```

Since Rabbit does not support the TCTL language, it alternatively provides an analysis command language to write a simple segment of code for verifying properties based on reachability analysis. Using this language, we declare a set of variables that are used to represent a set of states, called regions, followed by a set of iterative command statements. We then check whether the model can reach a region where the formula can be violated.

```
REACHABILITY CHECK T2PC {
1   VAR  initial, error, reached : REGION;
2   COMMANDS
3   initial:= INITIALREGION;
4   error := ((coor.decision == 1) AND (part.decision ==2));
5   reached := REACH FROM initial FORWARD;
6   IF (EMPTY(error INTERSECT reached)){
7     PRINT "Specification 1 satisfied.";}
8   ELSE  { PRINT " Specification 1 violated.";}  }
```

The first line declares three regions. Region `initial` represents the set of initial states from the Rabbit's modules. Lines 4 characterizes the set of states that violate specification 1 of the protocol: some process decided to abort while some other process decided to commit. Line 5 assigns to `reached` the set of states reachable from the initial state. The specification is satisfied if the intersection between the `reached` region and the `error` region is empty. However, in RED we can express specification 1 as follows.

```
forall always not (decision[1]  ==  1 && decision[2]  ==  2)
```

5   Comparing the Performance of the Three Tools

In this section, we present the model checking runtimes obtained in testing the tools, with version 4.1.13 for UPPAAL, 2.1 for Rabbit, and 5.0 for RED. All experiments are conducted on a PC with 32-bit Redhat Linux 7.3 with Intel (R) core CPU at 2.66 GHz and with 4 GB RAM. The specifications of the T2PC protocol were checked with backward and forward analysis in Rabbit and RED, and using the on the fly approach for UPPAAL. In the tables below we show the CPU time used by the system on behalf of the calling process (system time). An entry of "x" indicates that the model checker ran out of memory on that specification. As shown in Sect. 4 some properties of the T2PC protocol require us to use a full TCTL language and to verify formulas with nested temporal modalities which are not allowed in Rabbit. Moreover, Rabbit does not allow the direct verification of bounded liveness properties of the form $\mathbf{AG}(\phi \Rightarrow \mathbf{AF}_{\leq p}\ \psi)$ which are necessary for the verification of the T2PC protocol. We therefore reduce the bounded liveness properties of the protocol into reachability properties and then add extra monitor automata which interact with the actual model of the protocol in order to capture correctly the required properties. This in fact represents an extra unnecessary overhead and a big disadvantage for the tool Rabbit. In RED we can verify such properties directly. However, UPPAAL supports this special case of nested properties by offering leads-to operator $\rightarrow$ and thus the property $\mathbf{AG}(\phi \Rightarrow \mathbf{AF}_{\leq p}\ \psi)$ can be expressed by: $(\phi \rightarrow (x \wedge c \leq p)\ \psi)$, where x is a clock and c is reset upon ϕ.

We scaled the model of the protocol until the tools could not verify the protocol properties, due to the state space problem. Note that the T2PC protocol uses a huge number of discrete variables and huge number of clocks which increases

Table 1. Model checking runtimes (seconds) for T2PC protocol using Rabbit and RED backward analysis

Backward analysis					
Number of processes	Model checker	Specification			
		1	2	3	4
6	Rabbit	1.22	1.21	1.37	1.5
6	RED	10.88	12.9	11.26	9.57
9	Rabbit	x	x	x	x
9	RED	554	249	734	981
12	Rabbit	x	x	x	x
12	RED	2667	6135	6283	4339

Table 2. Model checking runtimes (seconds) for T2PC protocol using Rabbit and RED forward analysis approach

Forward analysis					
Number of processes	Model checker	Specification			
		1	2	3	4
6	Rabbit	160	160	161	163
6	RED	2.58	1.19	1.36	1.52
9	Rabbit	x	x	x	x
9	RED	69.7	26.9	29.5	31
12	Rabbit	x	x	x	x
12	RED	3088	884	939	943

as we increase the number of processes in the model. In Table 1 we give the runtimes obtained in checking the protocol using Rabbit backward reachability analysis and RED backward TCTL model-checking. RED could verify successfully the protocol up to 12 processes with 8 clocks, while Rabbit could verify only the simplest cases of the protocol. In Table 2 we report the runtimes obtained in testing the tools Rabbit and RED using forward reachability analysis. Optimizations used in RED make it more scalable than Rabbit by several order of magnitude.

In Table 3 we give the model-checking runtimes of the protocol using UPPAAL's on the-fly approach. UPPAAL could verify successfully the protocol up to 9 processes with 6 clocks. However, UPPAAL was a lot faster in cases where it gave a result, but it is less scalable than RED. As we can see, the DBM-based tool UPPAAL outperforms the CRD-based tool RED when considering small instances of the protocol with small number of clocks. However, when considering instances involving larger numbers of processes and larger numbers of clocks we find that RED outperforms UPPAAL where we could analyze the protocol up to 12 processes in RED while we fail to do so in UPPAAL.

Table 3. Model checking runtimes (seconds) for T2PC protocol using UPPAAL on the fly approach

On the fly approach				
Number of processes	Specification			
	1	2	3	4
6	0.01	0.001	0.002	0.003
9	4.4	5.5	10.3	8.84
12	x	x	x	x

In Table 4 we summarize information about the time taken to do the modeling and verification in each tool, the number of code line, the number of automata used to model and verify the basic case of the T2PC protocol, and the available verification options in each tool. Note that the time spent to learn the language of UPPAAL and then to verify the protocol is significantly shorter than the time spent to learn and model the protocol in both RED and Rabbit since UPPAAL is a very user-friendly tool. It is interesting to mention that the experience level of the authors about the three tools before conducting the experiments was initially the same. It is worth mentioning also that in Rabbit we use 9 automata: 6 automata to model the processes of the protocol and 3 extra monitor automata to capture bounded liveness properties (see specifications 2–4 in Sect. 4). On the other hand, we use only 6 automata to model and verify the protocol in RED and UPPAAL since they allow us to verify directly bounded liveness properties. In interesting to mention that in addition to the GUI automata used in the UPPAAL's model, we use also some extra simple functions as shown in Figs. 1, 2 and 3, namely add_queue(pid), rsc_granted(pid), and result(part_vote). The implementation and of these functions are very straightforward which requires only a few lines of code (about 35 lines).

Table 4. Modeling time and effort for the T2PC protocol in the Three tools

Tool	Time spent	# of code line	# of automata	Verification options
UPPAAL	≈ 18 h	GUI automata plus 35 lines	6	Breadth, Depth, random On-the-fly
RED	≈ 45 h	85	6	Backward/Forward TCTL
Rabbit	≈ 52 h	110	9	Backward/Forward reachability

Now we turn to discuss the model checking runtimes obtained in testing the three tools on the following two benchmarks. The models of the benchmarks have been taken from the distributed installation package of each tool.

Token-Ring-FDDI Protocol. Fiber Distributed Data Interface (FDDI) [19] is a high speed protocol for local networks based on token ring technology. We use a simplified model of N-processes. One process models the ring, that hands the token in one direction to $N - 1$ symmetric processes, that may hand back the token in a synchronous (high-speed) fashion. The ring process owns a local clock and every station owns three local clocks. This case study uses a huge number of clocks and a huge number of synchronisation labels. Here again RED outperformed both UPPAAL and Rabbit since RED is the only tool that succeeded to verify the protocol up to 16 senders. In fact the number of reachable locations in the RED model does not explode with growing number of senders. This proves again that the CRD-technology scales better with respect to number of clocks.

Table 5. Time for the computation of the reachability set of FDDI protocol

No. of senders	2	4	6	8	10	12	14	16
UPPAAL	0.01	0.03	0.16	1.42	18.2	280	4535	x
RED	0.02	0.09	0.26	0.61	1.18	3.8	3.6	8.9
Rabbit	0.04	0.25	0.99	4.20	11.7	29.9	x	x

CSMA/CD Protocol. Carrier Sense Multiple Access with Collision Detection (CSMS/CD) [27] is a protocol for communication on a broadcast network with a multiple access medium. This case study uses a huge number of synchronisation labels and discrete variables and small number of clocks. For this case study, Rabbit outperformed both RED and UPPAAL since the BDD-based tool Rabbit handles case studies with huge discrete variable much better than the CRD-based tool RED and the DBM-based tool UPPAAL (Tables 5 and 6).

Table 6. Time for the computation of the reachability set of CSMA/CD protocol

No. of processes	2	4	6	8	10	12	14	16	32
UPPAAL	0.01	0.04	7.1	9.5	x	x	x	x	x
RED	0.05	0.27	1.25	7.88	51.2	518	x	x	x
Rabbit	0.02	0.08	0.25	0.79	1.5	2.8	14.6	65.8	3260

Several conclusions can be drawn from the above reported results. RED is able to verify properties that are not expressible in UPPAAL and Rabbit and it supports full TCTL language with fairness assumptions. RED also allows verifying bounded liveness formulas that contain nested temporal modalities. On the other hand, UPPAAL's specification language supports fragment of TCTL and Rabbit specification language is restricted to reachability formulas. We believe that this limitation of the specification language of Rabbit is something that can lift the usability of the tool in particular when considering systems with timing constraints of the form $\mathbf{AG}(\phi \Rightarrow \mathbf{AF}_{\leq p} \psi)$.

Unlike UPPAAL, RED and Rabbit provide no graphical interface or simulation facilities. Moreover, UPPAAL allows a very natural formalization of systems this is not, or less, possible in Rabbit or RED. In case the specification fails, UPPAAL provides a counterexample and allows one to trace (simulate) the counterexample state by state in a very intuitive way. RED also provides this facility (it generates a counterexample when a specification fails) but in a less intuitive way than UPPAAL. The CRD-based data structure implemented in RED turns out to be an efficient data structure for handling case studies with huge number of clocks since it scales better with respect to number of clocks. The data structure BDD turns out to be efficient for handling case studies with huge number of discrete variables but it is very sensitive to the scale of clock constants in the model. While the DBM-based data structure implemented in UPPAAL handles the complexity of timing constant magnitude very well, its performance degrades rapidly when the number of clocks increases.

6   Conclusion

We have verified three timed distributed protocols (T2PC, FDDI, and CSMA/CD) in the model checkers UPPAAL, Rabbit, and RED. The three model checkers vary in how easy, or difficult, it is to formalise the protocol and its properties in the language of each model checker. In summary, to model and verify real-time systems that have complex timing requirements, we recommend using the tool RED as it supports a full TCTL language which allows to express a wide variety of timed properties. For timed systems with complex modeling details, we recommend using the tool UPPAAL as it has richer expressiveness in modeling systems than Rabbit and RED. Since Rabbit supports modular modelling that allows one to represent systems components in a hierarchical way, we recommend using it when the system has components with different levels of hierarchy.

References

1. Al-Bataineh, O.I., Reynolds, M., French, T.: Finding minimum and maximum termination time of timed automata models with cyclic behaviour. Theor. Comput. Sci. **665**, 87–104 (2017)
2. Alur, R., Courcoubetis, C., Dill, D.: Model-checking in dense real-time. Inf. Comput. **104**, 2–34 (1993)
3. Alur, R., Courcoubetis, C., Dill, D.L.: Model-checking for real-time systems. In: Proceedings of the 5th Annual Symposium on Logic in Computer Science, pp. 414–425 (1990)
4. Alur, R., Dill, D.: A theory of timed automata. TCS **126**, 183–235 (1994)
5. Alur, R., Madhusudan, P.: Decision problems for timed automata: a survey. In: International School on Formal Methods for the Design of Computer, Communication and Software Systems, SFM-RT 2004, pp. 200–236 (2004)
6. Atif, M.: Analysis and verification of two-phase commit and three-phase commit protocols. In: Emerging Technologies ICET 2009, pp. 326–331 (2009)

7. Behrmann, G., David, A., Larsen, K.G.: A tutorial on UPPAAL. In: Bernardo, M., Corradini, F. (eds.) SFM-RT 2004. LNCS, vol. 3185, pp. 200–236. Springer, Heidelberg (2004). https://doi.org/10.1007/978-3-540-30080-9_7

8. Behrmann, G., Bouyer, P., Larsen, K.G., Radek, P.: Lower and upper bounds in zone-based abstractions of timed automata. Int. J. Softw. Tools Technol. Transf. **8**, 204–215 (2006)

9. Behrmann, G., Larsen, K.G., Pearson, J., Weise, C., Yi, W.: Efficient timed reachability analysis using clock difference diagrams. In: Halbwachs, N., Peled, D. (eds.) CAV 1999. LNCS, vol. 1633, pp. 341–353. Springer, Heidelberg (1999). https://doi.org/10.1007/3-540-48683-6_30

10. Bengtsson, J., Yi, W.: Timed automata: semantics, algorithms and tools. In: Desel, J., Reisig, W., Rozenberg, G. (eds.) ACPN 2003. LNCS, vol. 3098, pp. 87–124. Springer, Heidelberg (2004). https://doi.org/10.1007/978-3-540-27755-2_3

11. Bernstein, P.A., Hadzilacos, V., Goodman, N.: Concurrency Control and Recovery in Database Systems. Addison-Wesley, Reading (1987)

12. Beyer, D., Lewerentz, C., Noack, A.: Rabbit: a tool for BDD-based verification of real-time systems. In: Hunt, W.A., Somenzi, F. (eds.) CAV 2003. LNCS, vol. 2725, pp. 122–125. Springer, Heidelberg (2003). https://doi.org/10.1007/978-3-540-45069-6_13

13. Beyer, D., Noack, A.: Can decision diagrams overcome state space explosion in real-time verification? In: König, H., Heiner, M., Wolisz, A. (eds.) FORTE 2003. LNCS, vol. 2767, pp. 193–208. Springer, Heidelberg (2003). https://doi.org/10.1007/978-3-540-39979-7_13

14. Bouyer, P.: Forward analysis of updatable timed automata. Formal Meth. Syst. Des. **24**, 281–320 (2004)

15. Bryant, R.E.: Graph-based algorithms for Boolean function manipulation. IEEE Trans. Comput. **35**, 677–691 (1986)

16. Davidson, S., Lee, I., Wolfe, V.: A protocol for times atomic commitment. In: Proceedings of 9th International Conference on Distributed Computing System (1989)

17. Dill, D.L.: Timing assumptions and verification of finite-state concurrent systems. In: Sifakis, J. (ed.) CAV 1989. LNCS, vol. 407, pp. 197–212. Springer, Heidelberg (1990). https://doi.org/10.1007/3-540-52148-8_17

18. Henzinger, T.A., Nicollin, X., Sifakis, J., Yovine, S.: Symbolic model checking for real-time systems. Inf. Comput. **111**, 394–406 (1992)

19. Jain, R.: FDDI Handbook: High-Speed Networking Using Fiber and Other Media. Addison-Wesley Longman Publishing Co. Inc., Boston (1994)

20. Kaynar, D., Lynch, N., Segala, R., Vaandrager, F.: Timed I/O automata: a mathematical framework for modelling and analyzing real-time systems. In: Proceedings of 24th IEEE International Real-Time Systems Symposium (RTSS 2003), pp. 166–177 (2003)

21. Larsen, K., Larsson, F., Pettersson, P., Yi, W.: Efficient verification of real-time systems: compact data structures and state-space reduction. In: Proceedings of the 18th IEEE Real-Time Systems Symposium, pp. 14–24 (1997)

22. Magee, J.: Analyzing synchronous distributed algorithms (2003)

23. Ober, I., Graf, S., Ober, I.: Validation of UML models via a mapping to communicating extended timed automata. In: Graf, S., Mounier, L. (eds.) SPIN 2004. LNCS, vol. 2989, pp. 127–145. Springer, Heidelberg (2004). https://doi.org/10.1007/978-3-540-24732-6_9

24. Ölveczky, P.C.: Formal modeling and analysis of a distributed database protocol in Maude. In: Proceedings of the 2008 11th IEEE International Conference on Computational Science and Engineering - Workshops, pp. 37–44 (2008)
25. Tripakis, S.: The analysis of timed systems in practice. Ph.D. thesis, Universite Joseph Fourier, Grenoble, France (1998)
26. Wang, F.: Symbolic verification of complex real-time systems with clock-restriction diagram. In: Proceedings of the IFIP TC6/WG6.1, pp. 235–250. Kluwer, B.V. (2001)
27. Yovine, S.: Kronos: a verification tool for real-time systems. Int. J. Softw. Tools Technol. Transfer 1, 123–133 (1997)

Lazy Reachability Checking for Timed Automata with Discrete Variables

Tamás Tóth$^{(\boxtimes)}$ ⓘ and István Majzik ⓘ

Department of Measurement and Information Systems,
Budapest University of Technology and Economics, Budapest, Hungary
{totht,majzik}@mit.bme.hu

Abstract. Systems and software with time dependent behavior are often formally specified using timed automata. For practical real-time systems, these specifications typically contain discrete data variables with nontrivial data flow besides real-valued clock variables. In this paper, we propose a lazy abstraction method for the location reachability problem of timed automata that can be used to efficiently control the visibility of discrete variables occurring in such specifications, this way alleviating state space explosion. The proposed abstraction refinement strategy is based on interpolation for variable assignments and symbolic backward search. We combine in a single algorithm our abstraction method with known efficient lazy abstraction algorithms for the handling of clock variables. Our experiments show that the proposed method performs favorably when compared to other lazy methods, and is suitable to significantly reduce the number of states generated during state space exploration.

Keywords: Timed automata · Model checking
Reachability checking · Lazy abstraction
Visible variables abstraction · Zone abstraction · Interpolation

1 Introduction

Timed automata [1] is a widely used formalism for the modeling and verification of systems and software with time-dependent behavior. In timed automata models, erroneous or unsafe behavior (that is to be avoided during operation) is often modeled by error locations. The location reachability problem deals with the question whether a given error location is reachable from an initial state along the transitions of the automaton.

As timed automata contain real-valued clock variables, to ensure performance and termination, model checkers for timed automata apply abstraction over clock variables. The standard solution involves performing a forward exploration in the zone abstract domain [7], combined with extrapolation [3] parametrized by

---

T. Tóth—This work was partially supported by Gedeon Richter's Talentum Foundation (Gyömrői út 19-21, 1103 Budapest, Hungary).

© Springer International Publishing AG, part of Springer Nature 2018
M. M. Gallardo and P. Merino (Eds.): SPIN 2018, LNCS 10869, pp. 235–254, 2018.
https://doi.org/10.1007/978-3-319-94111-0_14

bounds appearing in guards, extracted by static analysis [2]. Other zone-based methods propagate bounds lazily for all transitions [11] or along an infeasible path [10], and perform efficient inclusion checking with respect to a non-convex abstraction induced by the bounds [12]. Alternatively, some methods perform lazy abstraction directly over the zone abstract domain [19,20]. However, in the context of timed automata, methods rarely address the problem of *abstraction for discrete data variables* that often appear in specifications for practical real-time systems, or do so by applying a fully SMT based approach, relying on the efficiency of underlying decision procedures for the abstraction of both continuous and discrete variables.

In our work, we address the location reachability problem of timed automata with discrete variables by proposing an abstraction method that can be used to *lazily control the visibility of discrete variables* occurring in such specifications. If the abstraction is too coarse to disable an infeasible transition, then we propagate the pre-image of the transition backward using weakest precondition computation, and use interpolation (defined for variable assignments) to extract a set of variables that are sufficient to block the transition from the abstract state. We use interpolation in a similar fashion to attempt to enforce coverage of a newly discovered state with an already visited state when possible, this way effectively pruning the search space. Our method does not rely on an interpolating SMT solver, and can be freely combined with zone-based forward search (eager or lazy) methods for efficient handling of clock variables.

We evaluated the proposed abstraction method by combining it with lazy refinement techniques for continuous variables. Results show that in terms of execution time our method performs similarly to lazy methods without abstraction of discrete variables, but generates a smaller (in cases significantly smaller) state space.

Comparison to Related Work. Lazy abstraction [9], a form of counterexample-guided abstraction refinement [6], is an approach widely used for reachability checking, and in particular for model checking software. It consists of building an abstract reachability graph on-the fly, representing an abstraction of the system, and refining a part of the tree in case a spurious counterexample is found. For timed automata, a lazy abstraction approach based on non-convex LU-abstraction and on-the-fly propagation of bounds has been proposed [10]. A significant difference of this algorithm compared to usual lazy abstraction algorithms is that it builds an abstract reachability graph that preserves exact reachability information (a so-called adaptive simulation graph or ASG). As a consequence it is able to apply refinement as soon as the abstraction admits a transition disabled in the concrete system. Similar abstraction techniques based on building an ASG include difference bound constraint abstraction [20] and the zone interpolation-based technique of [19]. In our work, we follow the same approach, but for discrete variables instead of clock variables. The proposed abstraction method is orthogonal to the aforementioned techniques and can be freely combined with any of them.

Symbolic handling of integer variables for timed automata is often supported by unbounded fully symbolic SMT-based approaches. Symbolic backward search techniques like [5,17] are based on the computation and satisfiability checking of pre-images. In [13], reachability checking for timed automata is addressed by solving Horn clauses. In the IC3-based technique of [15], the problem of discrete variables is not addressed directly, but the possibility of generalization over discrete variables is (to some extent) inherent to the technique. In [14], also based on IC3, generalization of counterexamples to induction is addressed for both discrete and clock variables by zone-based pre-image computation. In our work, we propose an abstraction method over discrete variables that is completely theory agnostic, and does not rely on an SMT-solver.

In [8], an abstraction refinement algorithm is proposed for timed automata that handles clock and discrete variables in a uniform way. There, given a set of visible variables, an abstracted timed automaton is derived from the original by removing all assignments to abstracted variables, and by replacing all constraints by the strongest constraint that is implied and that does not contain abstracted variables. In case the model checker finds an abstract counterexample, a linear test automaton is constructed for the path, which is then composed with the original system to check whether the counterexample is spurious. If the final location of the test automaton is unreachable, a set of relevant variables is extracted from the disabled transition that will be included in the next iteration of the abstraction refinement loop. In our work, we use a similar approach, but instead of building abstractions globally on the system level and then calling to a model checker for both model checking and counterexample analysis, we use a more integrated, lazy abstraction method, where the abstraction is built on-the-fly, and refinement is performed locally in the state space where more precision is necessary.

Interpolation for variable assignments was first described in [4]. There, the interpolant is computed for a prefix and a suffix of a constraint sequence, and an inductive sequence of interpolants is computed by propagating interpolants forward using the abstract post-image operator. In our work, we define interpolation for a variable assignment and a formula, and compute inductive sequences of interpolants by propagating interpolants backward using weakest precondition computation. In our context, this enables us to consider a suffix of an infeasible path, instead of the whole path, for computing inductive sequences of interpolants.

Organization of the Paper. The rest of the paper is organized as follows. In Sect. 2, we define the notations used throughout the paper, and present the theoretical background of our work. In Sect. 3 we propose a lazy reachability checking algorithm based on the visibility of discrete variables for timed automata. Section 4 describes experiments performed on the proposed algorithm. Finally, conclusions are given in Sect. 5.

2   Background and Notations

Let V be a set of *data variables* over $\mathbb{Z}$, and X a set of *clock variables* over $\mathbb{R}_{\geq 0}$. A *data constraint* over V is a well-formed formula $\varphi \in DC(V)$ built from variables in V and arbitrary function and predicate symbols interpreted over $\mathbb{Z}$. A *clock constraint* over X is a formula $\varphi \in CC(X)$ that is a conjunction of atoms of the form $x \prec c$ and $x_i - x_j \prec c$ where $x, x_i, x_j \in X$, $c \in \mathbb{Z}$ and $\prec \in \{<, \leq\}$. A *data update* over V is an assignment $u \in DU(V)$ of the form $v := t$ where $v \in V$ and t is a term built from variables in V and function symbols interpreted over $\mathbb{Z}$. A *clock update* (clock reset) over X is an assignment $u \in CU(X)$ of the form $x := n$ where $x \in X$ and $n \in \mathbb{Z}$. The set of variables appearing in a formula φ is denoted by $\mathsf{vars}(\varphi)$.

A *valuation* over a finite set of variables is a function that maps variables to their respective domains. A *data valuation* is a valuation over a set of data variables V, that is, a function $\nu : V \to \mathbb{Z}$. Similarly, a *clock valuation* is a valuation over a set of clock variables X, that is, a function $\eta : X \to \mathbb{R}_{\geq 0}$. We will denote by $Eval(Q)$ the set of valuations over a set of variables Q.

Throughout the paper we will allow partial functions as valuations. We extend valuations to range over terms and formulas the usual way, with the possibility that the value of a term is undefined over a valuation. We will denote by $\sigma \models \varphi$ iff formula φ is satisfied under valuation σ. Note that in the context of partial valuations $\sigma \models \neg\varphi$ is a strictly stronger statement than $\sigma \not\models \varphi$ (e.g. $\{x \hookleftarrow 1\} \not\models y \doteq 1$ but it is not the case that $\{x \hookleftarrow 1\} \models y \not\doteq 1$).

We will denote by $\mathsf{def}(\sigma)$ the domain of definition of a valuation, that is, $\mathsf{def}(\sigma) = \{q \mid \sigma(q) \neq \bot\}$, and by $\mathsf{form}(\sigma)$ the formula characterizing the valuation, that is, $\mathsf{form}(\sigma) = \bigwedge_{q \in \mathsf{def}(\sigma)} q \doteq \sigma(q)$. Valuation $\top$ is the unique valuation such that $\mathsf{def}(\top) = \emptyset$. We denote by $\sigma \sqsubseteq \sigma'$ iff $\sigma(q) = \sigma'(q)$ for all $q \in \mathsf{def}(\sigma')$. Note that $\sqsubseteq$ is a partial order, as expected. Moreover if $\sigma \sqsubseteq \sigma'$ and $\sigma' \models \varphi$ then $\sigma \models \varphi$, and $\sigma \sqsubseteq \sigma'$ iff $\sigma \models \mathsf{form}(\sigma')$.

We will denote by $\otimes$ the partial function over valuations that is defined as

$$(\sigma \otimes \sigma')(q) = \begin{cases} \sigma(q) & \text{if } q \in \mathsf{def}(\sigma) \\ \sigma'(q) & \text{if } q \in \mathsf{def}(\sigma') \\ \bot & \text{otherwise} \end{cases}$$

if $\sigma(q) = \sigma'(q)$ for all $q \in \mathsf{def}(\sigma) \cap \mathsf{def}(\sigma')$, and is undefined otherwise.

Given a valuation $\sigma \in Eval(Q)$ and an assignment $q := t$, we denote by $\sigma\{q := t\}$ the valuation $\sigma' \in Eval(Q \cup \{q\})$ such that $\sigma'(q) = \sigma(t)$ and $\sigma'(q') = \sigma(q')$ for all $q' \neq q$. For a sequence of updates μ and a set of updates U we define

$$\sigma\{\mu\}_U = \begin{cases} \sigma & \text{if } \mu = \epsilon \\ \sigma\{u\}\{\mu'\}_U & \text{if } \mu = u \cdot \mu' \text{ and } u \in U \\ \sigma\{\mu'\}_U & \text{if } \mu = u \cdot \mu' \text{ and } u \notin U \end{cases}$$

2.1   Timed Automata

In the area of real-time verification, timed automata [1] is the most prominent formalism. To make the specification of practical systems more convenient, the traditional formalism is often extended with various syntactic and semantic constructs, in particular with the handling of discrete variables. In the following, we describe such an extension.

Definition 1 (Syntax). *Syntactically, a timed automaton with discrete variables is a tuple $\mathcal{A} = (L, V, X, T, \ell_0)$ where*

- *L is a finite set of locations,*
- *V is a finite set of data variables of integer type,*
- *X is a finite set of clock variables,*
- *$T \subseteq L \times \mathcal{P}(C) \times U^* \times L$ is a finite set of transitions with sets C and U defined as $C = DC(V) \cup CC(X)$ and $U = DU(V) \cup CU(X)$, where for a transition (ℓ, G, μ, ℓ'), the set $G \subseteq C$ is a set of guards and $\mu \in U^*$ is a sequence of updates,*
- *$\ell_0 \in L$ is the initial location.*

Throughout the paper, we will refer to a timed automaton with discrete variables simply as a timed automaton.

A state of $\mathcal{A}$ is a triple (ℓ, ν, η) where $\ell \in L$, $\nu \in Eval(V)$ and $\eta \in Eval(X)$. We will denote by ν_0 the unique total function $\nu_0 : V \to \{0\}$ and by η_0 the unique total function $\eta_0 : X \to \{0\}$.

Definition 2 (Semantics). *The operational semantics of a timed automaton is given by a labeled transition system with initial state (ℓ_0, ν_0, η_0) and two kinds of transitions:*

- *Delay: $(\ell, \nu, \eta) \xrightarrow{\delta} (\ell, \nu, \eta')$ for some real number $\delta \geq 0$ where $\eta' = \eta + \delta$ with $(\eta + \delta)(x) = \eta(x) + \delta$ for all $x \in X$;*
- *Action: $(\ell, \nu, \eta) \xrightarrow{t} (\ell', \nu', \eta')$ for some transition $t = (\ell, G, \mu, \ell')$ where we have $\nu' = \mathsf{dpost}_t(\nu)$ and $\eta' = \mathsf{cpost}_t(\eta)$ with partial functions*

$$\mathsf{dpost}_t(\nu) = \begin{cases} \bot & \text{if } \nu \models \neg g \text{ for some } g \in G \cap DC(V) \\ \nu\{\mu\}_{DU(V)} & \text{otherwise} \end{cases}$$

$$\mathsf{cpost}_t(\eta) = \begin{cases} \bot & \text{if } \eta \models \neg g \text{ for some } g \in G \cap CC(X) \\ \eta\{\mu\}_{CU(X)} & \text{otherwise} \end{cases}$$

Here, $\mathsf{dpost}_t(\nu)$ denotes the strongest (discrete) postcondition of ν with respect to transition t. Note that for any $t \in T$, function dpost_t is monotonic with respect to $\sqsubseteq$, as expected. Moreover, we define the weakest (discrete) precondition $\mathsf{wp}_t(\varphi)$ as the formula such that $\nu \models \mathsf{wp}_t(\varphi)$ iff $\mathsf{dpost}_t(\nu) \models \varphi$ for all ν and φ, with respect to t.

A *run* of a timed automaton is a sequence of states from the initial state along the transition relation

$$(\ell_0, \nu_0, \eta_0) \xrightarrow{\alpha_1} (\ell_1, \nu_1, \eta_1) \xrightarrow{\alpha_2} \dots \xrightarrow{\alpha_n} (\ell_n, \nu_n, \eta_n)$$

where $\alpha_i \in T \cup \mathbb{R}_{\geq 0}$ for all $0 \leq i \leq n$. A location $\ell \in L$ is *reachable* iff there exists a run such that $\ell_n = \ell$.

2.2 Symbolic Semantics

As the concrete semantics of a timed automaton is infinite due to real valued clock variables, model checkers are often based on a symbolic semantics defined in terms of zones. A zone is the solution set of a clock constraint $\varphi \in CC(X)$. For sets of clock valuations Z and Z', we will denote by $Z \sqsubseteq Z'$ iff $Z \subseteq Z'$. Moreover, if Z is a zone and $t \in T$, then

- $\perp = \emptyset$,
- $Z_0 = \{\eta \mid \eta = \eta_0 + \delta \text{ for some } \delta \geq 0\}$ and
- $\mathsf{zpost}_t(Z) = \left\{\eta' \mid (\cdot, \cdot, \eta) \xrightarrow{t} s \xrightarrow{\delta} (\cdot, \cdot, \eta') \text{ for some } \eta \in Z \text{ and } \delta \geq 0\right\}$

are also zones. Here, $\mathsf{zpost}_t(Z)$ represents the strongest postcondition of Z with respect to a transition t of a timed automaton. As defined above, function zpost_t is monotonic with respect to $\sqsubseteq$ for any $t \in T$.

Definition 3 (Symbolic semantics). *The symbolic semantics of a timed automaton is given by a labeled transition system with states of the form (ℓ, ν, Z), with initial state (ℓ_0, ν_0, Z_0), and for $t = (\ell, \cdot, \cdot, \ell')$ with transitions of the form $(\ell, \nu, Z) \xRightarrow{t} (\ell', \mathsf{dpost}_t(\nu), \mathsf{zpost}_t(Z))$.*

We will say that a transition t is enabled from a symbolic state (ℓ, ν, Z) iff $(\ell, \nu, Z) \xRightarrow{t} (\ell', \nu', Z')$ for some ℓ', ν' and $Z' \neq \perp$, otherwise it is disabled. Note that a transition $t = (\ell, \cdot, \cdot, \cdot)$ is disabled from a symbolic state (ℓ, ν, Z) iff $\mathsf{dpost}_t(\nu) = \perp$ or $\mathsf{zpost}_t(Z) = \perp$.

Definition 4 (Symbolic run). *A symbolic run of a timed automaton is a sequence $(\ell_0, \nu_0, Z_0) \xRightarrow{t_1} (\ell_1, \nu_1, Z_1) \xRightarrow{t_2} \dots \xRightarrow{t_n} (\ell_n, \nu_n, Z_n)$ where $Z_n \neq \perp$.*

Proposition 1. *For a timed automaton, a location $\ell \in L$ is reachable iff there exists a symbolic run with $\ell_n = \ell$.*

3   Algorithm for Lazy Reachability Checking

In this section, we present our algorithm for lazy reachability checking of timed automata with discrete variables. During the description, we will focus on the handling of discrete variables, but formulate the algorithm so that it is straightforward to combine the method with a corresponding (eager or lazy) method for the handling of clock variables.

3.1 Adaptive Simulation Graph

The central structure of the algorithm is an abstract simulation graph. The presented formulation is a generalization of the definition presented in [19] for the handling of discrete variables and the possibility of using various methods for the handling of clock variables.

Definition 5 (Unwinding). *An unwinding of a timed automaton (L, V, X, T, ℓ_0) is a tuple $U = (N, E, n_0, M_n, M_e, \triangleright)$ where*

- (N, E) *is a directed tree rooted at node $n_0 \in N$,*
- $M_n : N \to L$ *is the node labeling,*
- $M_e : E \to T$ *is the edge labeling and*
- $\triangleright \subseteq N \times N$ *is the covering relation.*

For an unwinding we require that the following properties hold:

- $M_n(n_0) = \ell_0$,
- *for each edge $(n, n') \in E$ the transition $M_e(n, n') = (\ell, \cdot, \cdot, \ell')$ is such that $M_n(n) = \ell$ and $M_n(n') = \ell'$,*
- *for all nodes n and n' such that $n \triangleright n'$ it holds that $M_n(n) = M_n(n')$.*

The purpose of the covering relation $\triangleright$ is to mark that a node of the search tree has been pruned due to another node that admits all runs that are possible from the covered node. We define the following shorthand notations for convenience: $\ell_n = M_n(n)$ and $t_{n,n'} = M_e(n, n')$.

Definition 6 (Adaptive simulation graph). *An adaptive simulation graph (ASG) for a timed automaton $\mathcal{A}$ is a tuple $\mathcal{G} = (U, \psi_\nu, \psi_{\hat{\nu}}, \psi_Z, \psi_{\hat{Z}})$ where*

- U *is an unwinding of $\mathcal{A}$,*
- $\psi_\nu, \psi_{\hat{\nu}} : N \to Eval(V)$ *are labelings of nodes by data valuations and*
- $\psi_Z, \psi_{\hat{Z}} : N \to \mathcal{P}(Eval(X))$ *are labelings of nodes by sets of clock valuations.*

We will use the following shorthand notations: $\nu_n = \psi_\nu(n)$, $\hat{\nu}_n = \psi_{\hat{\nu}}(n)$, $Z_n = \psi_Z(n)$ and $\hat{Z}_n = \psi_{\hat{Z}}(n)$.

A node n is *expanded* iff for all transitions $t \in T$ such that $t = (\ell, \cdot, \cdot, \cdot)$ and $\ell_n = \ell$, either t is disabled from (ℓ_n, ν_n, Z_n), or n has a successor for t. A node n is *covered* iff $n \triangleright n'$ for some node n'. It is *excluded* iff it is covered or it has an excluded parent. A node is *complete* iff it is either expanded or excluded. A node n is ℓ-safe iff $\ell_n \neq \ell$.

For an ASG to be useful for reachability checking, we have to introduce restrictions on the labeling. Therefore while building the ASG we will ensure that (ℓ_n, ν_n, Z_n) represents an exact set of reachable states for n (thus with Z_n being a zone), and that $\nu_n \sqsubseteq \hat{\nu}_n$ and $Z_n \sqsubseteq \hat{Z}_n$. We formalize this notion in the next definition.

Definition 7 (Well-labeled node). *A node n of an ASG $\mathcal{G}$ for a timed automaton $\mathcal{A}$ is well-labeled iff the following conditions hold:*

- *(initiation)* if $n = n_0$, then
  (a) $\nu_n = \nu_0$ and $Z_n = Z_0$
  (b) $\nu_0 \sqsubseteq \hat{\nu}_n$ and $Z_0 \sqsubseteq \hat{Z}_n$
- *(consecution)* if $n \neq n_0$, then for its parent m and the transition $t = t_{m,n}$
  (a) $\nu_n = \mathsf{dpost}_t(\nu_m)$ and $Z_n = \mathsf{zpost}_t(Z_m)$
  (b) $\mathsf{dpost}_t(\hat{\nu}_m) \sqsubseteq \hat{\nu}_n$ and $\mathsf{zpost}_t(\hat{Z}_m) \sqsubseteq \hat{Z}_n$
- *(coverage)* if $n \rhd n'$ for some node n', then $\hat{\nu}_n \sqsubseteq \hat{\nu}_{n'}$ and $\hat{Z}_n \sqsubseteq \hat{Z}_{n'}$ and n' is not excluded
- *(simulation)* if n is expanded, then any transition disabled from (ℓ_n, ν_n, Z_n) is also disabled from $(\ell_n, \hat{\nu}_n, \hat{Z}_n)$.

The above definitions for nodes can be extended to ASGs. An ASG is complete, ℓ-safe or well-labeled iff all its nodes are complete, ℓ-safe or well-labeled, respectively. The main challenge for the construction of a well-labeled ASG as defined above is how the labelings $\psi_{\hat{\nu}}$ and $\psi_{\hat{Z}}$ are computed. A well-labeled ASG preserves reachability information, which is expressed by the following proposition.

Proposition 2. *Let $\mathcal{G}$ be a complete, well-labeled ASG for a timed automaton $\mathcal{A}$. Then $\mathcal{A}$ has a symbolic run $(\ell_0, \nu_0, Z_0) \overset{t_1}{\Rightarrow} (\ell_1, \nu_1, Z_1) \overset{t_2}{\Rightarrow} \ldots \overset{t_k}{\Rightarrow} (\ell_k, \nu_k, Z_k)$ iff $\mathcal{G}$ has a non-excluded node n such that $\ell_k = \ell_n$.*

Proof. The right-to-left direction is a consequence of the subsequent Lemma 1. and the converse follows from Lemma 2.   □

Lemma 1. *Let $\mathcal{G}$ be a well-labeled ASG for a timed automaton $\mathcal{A}$. If $\mathcal{G}$ has a node n then $\mathcal{A}$ has a symbolic run $(\ell_0, \nu_0, Z_0) \overset{t_1}{\Rightarrow} (\ell_1, \nu_1, Z_1) \overset{t_2}{\Rightarrow} \ldots \overset{t_k}{\Rightarrow} (\ell_k, \nu_k, Z_k)$ such that $\ell_k = \ell_n$.*

Proof. The statement is a direct consequence of conditions *initiation(a)* and *consecution(a)*.   □

Lemma 2. *Let $\mathcal{G}$ be a complete, well-labeled ASG for a timed automaton $\mathcal{A}$. If $\mathcal{A}$ has a symbolic run $(\ell_0, \nu_0, Z_0) \overset{t_1}{\Rightarrow} (\ell_1, \nu_1, Z_1) \overset{t_2}{\Rightarrow} \ldots \overset{t_k}{\Rightarrow} (\ell_k, \nu_k, Z_k)$ then $\mathcal{G}$ has a non-excluded node n such that $\ell_k = \ell_n$ and $\nu_k \sqsubseteq \hat{\nu}_n$ and $Z_k \sqsubseteq \hat{Z}_n$.*

Proof. We prove the statement by induction on the length k of the symbolic run. If $k = 0$, then $\ell = \ell_0$ and $\nu = \nu_0$ and $Z = Z_0$, thus n_0 is a suitable witness by condition *initiation(b)*. Suppose the statement holds for runs of length at most $k - 1$. Hence there exists a non-excluded node m such that $\ell_{k-1} = \ell_m$ and $\nu_{k-1} \sqsubseteq \hat{\nu}_m$ and $Z_{k-1} \sqsubseteq \hat{Z}_m$.

Clearly the transition t_k is not disabled from $(\ell_m, \hat{\nu}_m, \hat{Z}_m)$, as then by condition *simulation* it would be also disabled from $(\ell_{k-1}, \nu_{k-1}, Z_{k-1})$, which contradicts our assumption. As m is complete and not excluded, it is expanded, and thus has a successor n for transition t_k with $\ell_n = \ell_k$. By condition *consecution(b)*, we have $\mathsf{dpost}_{t_k}(\hat{\nu}_m) \sqsubseteq \hat{\nu}_n$. As $\nu_{k-1} \sqsubseteq \hat{\nu}_m$ and dpost_t is monotonic w.r.t. $\sqsubseteq$, we have $\nu_k \sqsubseteq \hat{\nu}_n$. We can obtain $Z_k \sqsubseteq \hat{Z}_n$ symmetrically.

Thus if n is not covered, then it is a suitable witness for the statement. Otherwise there exists a node n' such that $n \triangleright n'$. By condition *coverage*, we know that $\hat{\nu}_n \sqsubseteq \hat{\nu}_{n'}$ and $\hat{Z}_n \sqsubseteq \hat{Z}_{n'}$ and n' is not excluded, thus n' is a suitable witness.

$\square$

3.2   Reachability Algorithm

The pseudocode of the algorithm is shown in Algorithm 1. The algorithm gets as input a timed automaton $\mathcal{A}$ and a distinguished error location $\ell_e \in L$. The goal of the algorithm is to decide whether ℓ_e is reachable for $\mathcal{A}$. To this end the algorithm gradually builds an ASG for $\mathcal{A}$ and continually maintains its well-labeledness. Upon termination, it either witnesses reachability of ℓ_e by a node n such that $\ell_n = \ell_e$, which by Lemma 1 corresponds to a symbolic run of $\mathcal{A}$ to ℓ_e, or produces a closed, well-labeled, ℓ_e-safe ASG that proves unreachability of ℓ_e by Lemma 2.

The main data structures of the algorithm are the ASG $\mathcal{G}$ and sets *passed* and *waiting*. The set *passed* is used to store nodes that are expanded and *waiting* stores nodes that are incomplete. The algorithm consists of subprocedures CLOSE, EXPAND and REFINE, and of procedures ZCOVER and ZBLOCK. Procedure ZCOVER and ZBLOCK serve for abstraction refinement over clock variables. These procedures can be soundly implemented in various ways [3,10–12,19,20], and we assume such an implementation. Procedure CLOSE attempts to cover a node by some other node. Procedure EXPAND expands a node by creating the successors of a node for all non-blocked transitions for the given location. Procedure REFINE (see in Sect. 3.3) can be used to ensure for a node n and some formula φ that if $\nu_n \models \varphi$ then $\hat{\nu}_n \models \varphi$ as well. Both CLOSE and EXPAND maintain well-labeledness by calls to REFINE. In particular, CLOSE calls to REFINE in order to enforce condition *coverage*, and EXPAND calls to REFINE to establish condition *simulation*.

The algorithm consists of a single loop in line 8 that employs the following strategy. The loop consumes nodes from *waiting* one by one. If *waiting* becomes empty, then $\mathcal{A}$ is deemed safe. Otherwise, a node n is removed from *waiting*. If the node represents an error location, then $\mathcal{A}$ is deemed unsafe. Otherwise, in order to avoid unnecessary expansion of the node, the algorithm tries to cover it by a call to CLOSE. If there are no suitable candidates for coverage, then the algorithm establishes completeness of the node by expanding it using EXPAND, which puts it in *passed* and puts all its successors in *waiting*.

We show that EXPLORE is correct with respect to the annotations (procedure contracts) in Algorithm 1. As, given a suitable refinement method for clock variables, termination of the algorithm is trivial, we focus on partial correctness.

Proposition 3. *Procedure* EXPLORE *is partially correct: if* EXPLORE$(\mathcal{A}, \ell_e)$ *terminates, then the result is* SAFE *iff* ℓ_e *is unreachable for* $\mathcal{A}$.

Algorithm 1. Reachability algorithm for timed automata with discrete variables

1: **ensure** $\rho = \text{SAFE}$ iff ℓ_e is unreachable for $\mathcal{A}$
2: **function** EXPLORE($\mathcal{A}, \ell_e$) **returns** $\rho \in \{\text{SAFE}, \text{UNSAFE}\}$
3:     **let** n_0 be a node with $\ell_{n_0} = \ell_0$, $\nu_{n_0} = \nu_0$, $\hat{\nu}_{n_0} = \top$, $Z_{n_0} = Z_0$ and $\hat{Z}_{n_0} = \top$
4:     $N \leftarrow \{n_0\}$, $E \leftarrow \emptyset$, $\rhd \leftarrow \emptyset$
5:     **let** $\mathcal{G}$ be an ASG for $\mathcal{A}$ over N, E and $\rhd$
6:
7:     $passed \leftarrow \emptyset$, $waiting \leftarrow \{n_0\}$
8:     **while** $n \in waiting$ for some n **do**
9:         $waiting \leftarrow waiting \setminus \{n\}$
10:        **if** $\ell_n = \ell_e$ **then**
11:            **return** UNSAFE
12:        **else**
13:            CLOSE(n)
14:            **if** n is not covered **then**
15:                EXPAND(n)
16:        **return** SAFE

17: **procedure** CLOSE(n)
18:     **for all** $n' \in passed$ such that $\ell_n = \ell_{n'}$ and $\nu_n \sqsubseteq \hat{\nu}_{n'}$ and $Z_n \sqsubseteq \hat{Z}_{n'}$ **do**
19:         REFINE($n, \text{form}(\hat{\nu}_{n'})$)
20:         ZCOVER(n, n')
21:         **if** $\hat{\nu}_n \sqsubseteq \hat{\nu}_{n'}$ and $\hat{Z}_n \sqsubseteq \hat{Z}_{n'}$ **then**
22:             $\rhd \leftarrow \rhd \cup \{(n, n')\}$
23:             **return**

24: **ensure** n is expanded
25: **procedure** EXPAND(n)
26:     **for all** $t \in T$ such that $t = (\ell, \cdot, \cdot, \ell')$ with $\ell = \ell_n$ **do**
27:         **let** $\nu' = \text{dpost}_t(\nu_n)$
28:         **let** $Z' = \text{zpost}_t(Z_n)$
29:         **if** $\nu' = \bot$ **then**
30:             REFINE($n, \text{wp}_t(\bot)$)
31:         **else if** $Z' = \bot$ **then**
32:             ZBLOCK(n, t)
33:         **else**
34:             **let** n' be a new node with $\ell_{n'} = \ell'$, $\nu_{n'} = \nu'$, $Z_{n'} = Z'$, $\hat{\nu}_{n'} = \top$, $\hat{Z}_{n'} = \top$
35:             **let** (n, n') be a new edge with $t_{n,n'} = t$
36:             $N \leftarrow N \cup \{n'\}$, $E \leftarrow E \cup \{(n, n')\}$
37:             $waiting \leftarrow waiting \cup \{n'\}$
38:     $passed \leftarrow passed \cup \{n\}$

39: **require** $\nu_n \models \varphi$
40: **ensure** $\hat{\nu}_n \models \varphi$
41: **procedure** REFINE(n, φ)

42: **require** $Z_n \sqsubseteq \hat{Z}_{n'}$ 45: **require** $\text{zpost}_t(Z) = \bot$
43: **ensure** $\hat{Z}_n \sqsubseteq \text{old}(\hat{Z}_{n'})$ 46: **ensure** $\text{zpost}_t(\hat{Z}) = \bot$
44: **procedure** ZCOVER(n, n')   47: **procedure** ZBLOCK(n, t)

Proof (sketch). Let *covered* = $\{n \in N \mid n \text{ is covered}\}$. It is easy to verify that the algorithm maintains the following invariants:

- $N = passed \cup waiting \cup covered$,
- *passed* is a set of non-excluded, expanded, ℓ_e-safe nodes,
- *waiting* is a set of non-excluded, non-expanded nodes,
- *covered* is a set of covered, non-expanded, ℓ_e-safe nodes.

It is easy to see that under the above assumptions sets *passed*, *waiting* and *covered* form a partition of N. Assuming that $\mathcal{G}$ is well-labeled, partial correctness of the algorithm is then a direct consequence. At line 11 a node is encountered that is not ℓ_e-safe, thus by Lemma 1 there is a symbolic run of $\mathcal{A}$ to ℓ_e. Conversely, at line 16 the set *waiting* is empty, so $\mathcal{G}$ is complete and ℓ_e-safe, and as a consequence of Lemma 2 the location ℓ_e is indeed unreachable for $\mathcal{A}$.

What remains to show is that the algorithm maintains well-labeledness. We assume that procedures ZCOVER and ZBLOCK and procedure REFINE maintain well-labeledness (this later statement we prove to hold in Sect. 3.3). Initially node n_0 is well-labeled as it satisfies *initiation*. Procedure CLOSE trivially maintains well-labeledness, as it just possibly adds a covering edge for two nodes such that condition *coverage* is not violated. For procedure EXPAND, if a given transition t is enabled, then a node is created that satisfies *consecution*. Otherwise the corresponding refinement procedure is called, ensuring that *simulation* holds for the given transition. In particular, if t is blocked due to $\mathsf{dpost}_t(\nu_n) = \bot$, we have $\nu_n \models \mathsf{wp}_t(\bot)$, and thus can call REFINE to update $\hat{\nu}_n$ so that $\hat{\nu}_n \models \mathsf{wp}_t(\bot)$, ensuring $\mathsf{dpost}_t(\hat{\nu}_n) \models \bot$ and effectively disabling t from $(\cdot, \hat{\nu}_n, \cdot)$. □

3.3 Abstraction Refinement

To maintain well-labeledness, the algorithm relies on procedure REFINE that performs abstraction refinement by safely adjusting abstract data valuations labeling nodes of the ASG. The pseudocode of the refinement algorithm is shown in Algorithm 2.

Informally, REFINE works as follows. Given a node n and a formula φ such that $\nu_n \models \varphi$ holds, a weakening ν_I of ν_n is computed such that $\nu_I \models \varphi$ by calling to procedure INTERPOLATE, which simply removes variables from the domain of definition that are not necessary for satisfying the formula. Then all covering edges are dropped that would violate condition *coverage* after strengthening. To maintain condition *consecution(b)*, procedure REFINE is then recursively called for the predecessor m of n. The computed interpolant is then used to strengthen the current labeling by including variables occurring in the interpolant in the current abstraction. We show that REFINE maintains well-labeledness and is correct with respect to the annotations in Algorithm 2.

Proposition 4. *Procedure* REFINE *is totally correct: if* $\nu_n \models \varphi$, *then* REFINE(n, φ) *terminates and ensures* $\hat{\nu}_n \models \varphi$. *Moreover, it maintains well-labeledness.*

Algorithm 2. Refinement of visible variables

1: **require** $\nu_n \models \varphi$
2: **ensure** $\hat{\nu}_n \models \varphi$
3: **procedure** REFINE(n, φ)
4:     **if** $\hat{\nu}_n \models \varphi$ **then**
5:         **return**
6:     **else**
7:         **let** $\nu_I = $ INTERPOLATE(ν_n, φ)
8:         **for all** m such that $m \triangleright n$ and $\hat{\nu}_m \not\sqsubseteq \nu_I$ **do**
9:             $\triangleright \leftarrow \triangleright \setminus (m, n)$
10:             $waiting \leftarrow waiting \cup \{m\}$
11:             **if** $(m, n) \in E$ for some m **then**
12:                 **let** $t = t_{m,n}$
13:                 REFINE$(m, \mathsf{wp}_t(\mathsf{form}(\nu_I)))$
14:         $\hat{\nu}_n \leftarrow \hat{\nu}_n \otimes \nu_I$

15:
16: **require** $\nu_A \models \varphi_B$
17: **ensure** $\nu_A \sqsubseteq \nu_I$
18: **ensure** $\nu_I \models \varphi_B$
19: **ensure** $\mathsf{def}(\nu_I) \subseteq \mathsf{def}(\nu_A) \cap \mathsf{vars}(\varphi_B)$
20: **function** INTERPOLATE(ν_A, φ_B) **returns** ν_I
21:     $\nu_I \leftarrow \nu_A|_{\mathsf{vars}(\varphi_B)}$
22:     **let** $Q = \mathsf{def}(\nu_A) \cap \mathsf{vars}(\varphi_B)$
23:     **for all** $v \in Q$ **do**
24:         **let** $\nu'_I = \nu_I|_{\mathsf{def}(\nu_I) \setminus \{v\}}$
25:         **if** $\nu'_I \models \varphi_B$ **then**
26:             $\nu_I \leftarrow \nu'_I$
27:     **return** ν_I

Proof. Termination of the procedure is trivial, so we focus on partial correctness and the preservation of well-labeledness.

Function INTERPOLATE has no side effect, it thus trivially maintains well-labeledness. Moreover, it is easy to see that it satisfies its contract, as it simply drops variables not necessary to ensure satisfiability of φ_B from the domain of definition of ν_A.

In procedure REFINE, if $\hat{\nu}_n \models \varphi$ then no refinement is needed, and the contract is trivially satisfied. Otherwise, the interpolant ν_I is computed by function INTERPOLATE. As $\nu_n \sqsubseteq \hat{\nu}_n$ by well-labeledness and $\nu_n \sqsubseteq \nu_I$ by the precondition, we know that $\hat{\nu}_n \otimes \nu_I$, and thus the new value of $\hat{\nu}_n$, is defined. As $\hat{\nu}_n \otimes \nu_I \sqsubseteq \nu_I$ and $\nu_I \models \varphi$, we have $\hat{\nu}_n \otimes \nu_I \models \varphi$, which ensures the postcondition.

Next we show that well-labeledness is maintained. Condition *simulation* is trivially ensured, as if $\hat{\nu}_n \models \neg g$ for some guard g, then $\hat{\nu}_n \otimes \nu_I \models \neg g$ as well. After the loop we have $\hat{\nu}_m \sqsubseteq \nu_I$ for all m such that $m \triangleright n$. Moreover, $\hat{\nu}_m \sqsubseteq \hat{\nu}_n$ by well-labeledness. Thus $\hat{\nu}_m \sqsubseteq \hat{\nu}_n \otimes \nu_I$, which ensures condition *coverage*. If n has no parent then condition *initiation(b)* is trivially maintained. Otherwise we have $\nu_n \sqsubseteq \nu_I$, thus $\mathsf{dpost}_t(\nu_m) \models \mathsf{form}(\nu_I)$, from which $\nu_m \models \mathsf{wp}_t(\mathsf{form}(\nu_I))$

follows. Hence REFINE can be called to ensure $\hat{\nu}_m \models \mathsf{wp}_t(\mathsf{form}(\nu_I))$, and thus $\mathsf{dpost}_t(\hat{\nu}_m) \sqsubseteq \nu_I$. Moreover, $\mathsf{dpost}_t(\hat{\nu}_m) \sqsubseteq \hat{\nu}_n$ by well-labeledness. It follows that $\mathsf{dpost}_t(\hat{\nu}_m) \sqsubseteq \hat{\nu}_n \otimes \nu_I$, which ensures condition *consecution(b)*.   □

3.4   Example

In this subsection, we give an example that demonstrates how the algorithm described above lazily controls the visibility of discrete variables of the system during construction of the abstraction.

Figure 1 shows automaton $\mathcal{A}_k$, a modified version of the examples given in [10,16] where clock variables are replaced by discrete variables and a component is added that nondeterministically increments all variables. The resulting automaton is the parallel composition of four components, and has $2k$ discrete variables, namely $a_1, a_2, \ldots, a_k$ and $b_1, b_2, \ldots, b_k$.

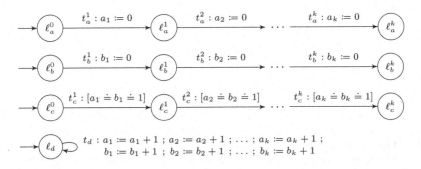

Fig. 1. Automaton $\mathcal{A}_k$

As an example, we are going to consider $\mathcal{A}_1$, the simplest version of the automaton. For simplicity, we are going to omit the indexes in names whenever possible. Figure 2 shows part of the ASG produced by the algorithm. Here, normal edges represent edges of the unwinding (elements of the relation E), dashed edges represent covering edges (elements of the relation $\triangleright$), and dotted edges represent edges of the unwinding that lead to subtrees omitted from the figure. For each node n, the set of visible variables $\mathsf{def}(\hat{\nu}_n)$ is shown.

The algorithm starts by instantiating the root node n_0 with $\hat{\nu}_{n_0} = \top$. As transition t_c is disabled from ν_{n_0} but not from $\hat{\nu}_{n_0}$, the set of visible variables has to be refined in n_0. Hence during refinement, a will be included in the set of visible variables, ensuring $\hat{\nu}_{n_0} = \{a \hookleftarrow 0\} \models (a \neq 1 \vee b \neq 1) = \mathsf{wp}_{t_c}(\bot)$. For the same reason, a will become visible when expanding n_1 and n_2. For any other node n however, t_c is either not an outgoing transition of location ℓ_n, or is enabled from ν_n, thus no refinement will be triggered during expansion, resulting in abstraction $\hat{\nu}_n = \top$. This enables coverage between nodes that assign different concrete values to the variables. E.g. covering edges (n_5, n_4) and (n_{10}, n_9) are only possible because b is not visible in either nodes (as $\nu_{n_4} = \nu_{n_9} = \{a \hookleftarrow 1, b \hookleftarrow 1\}$

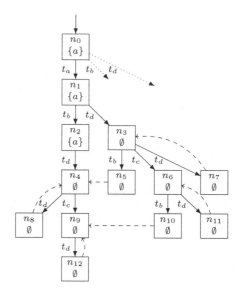

Fig. 2. ASG of $\mathcal{A}_1$

and $\nu_{n_5} = \nu_{n_{10}} = \{a \hookleftarrow 1, b \hookleftarrow 0\}$). More importantly, the algorithm is able to quickly cover nodes that result from the second firing of t_d along a path, thus the resulting ASG remains finite. Even if the number of times t_d can be taken is bounded by some number N, an algorithm that handles discrete variables explicitly would generate a significantly larger state space depending on N. Similarly, as k increases, the advantage of the abstraction based method compared to the explicit handling of variables becomes increasingly notable.

4   Evaluation

We implemented a prototype version of our algorithm in the open source model checking framework THETA [18]. In order to enable abstraction refinement for clock variables, we implemented a variant of the lazy abstraction method of [10] based on LU-bounds, and the method described in [19] based on interpolation for zones (with refinement strategy SEQ). These strategies are then combined both with the explicit handling of discrete variables, resulting in algorithms similar to that of the original papers [10,19], and with the abstraction and refinement method proposed in this paper. The algorithms are evaluated for both breadth-first and depth-first search orders. This results in 8 algorithm configurations by combining the above mentioned alternatives:

- explicit (E) or abstraction-based (A) handling of discrete variables,
- lazy $\mathbf{a}_{\preceq LU}$ abstraction (L) or interpolation (I) for clock variables and
- breadth-first (B) or depth-first (D) search order.

For the configurations that handle discrete variables explicitly, we partitioned the set of nodes based on the value of the data valuation, this way saving the $\mathcal{O}(n)$ cost of checking inclusion for valuations. This optimization also significantly reduces the number of nodes for which coverage is checked and attempted during CLOSE. Apart from this and the difference in refinement strategies, the implementation of the configurations is shared.

As inputs we considered 15 timed automata models in UPPAAL 4.0 XTA format that contain integer variables. For each model, the number of discrete variables/number of clock variables is given in parentheses.

- bocdp (26/3), bocdpf (26/3): models of the Bang & Olufsen Collision Detection Protocol obtained from the UPPAAL[1] benchmark set
- brp (9/7): a model of the Bounded Retransmission Protocol
- c1 (12/3), c2 (14/3), c3 (15/3), c4 (17/3): models of a real-time mutual exclusion protocol obtained from the MCTA[2] benchmark set
- m1 (11/4), m2 (13/4), m3 (13/4), m4 (15/4), n1 (11/7), n2 (13/7), n3 (13/7), n4 (15/7): industrial cases studies obtained from the MCTA benchmark set

We performed our measurements on a machine running Windows 10 with a 2.6 GHz dual core CPU and 8 GB of RAM. We evaluated the algorithm configurations for both execution time (Table 1) and the number of nodes in the resulting ASG (Table 2). The timeout (denoted by "—" in the tables) was set to 120 s. In the tables the best values among both the explicit and abstraction based configurations are emphasized with bold font for each model. The execution time is the average of 10 runs, obtained from 12 deterministic runs by removing the slowest and the fastest one.

As can be seen in Table 1, in general, the performance of the fastest configurations of the two categories (explicit and abstraction based configurations) with respect to execution time is balanced (there are no more difference than 100%). For models c1–3, the explicit configuration was faster, but the absolute difference in execution time is not significant. For the other MCTA models, the fastest configurations perform similarly with respect to execution time. For model bocdpf the abstraction-based variant was almost twice as fast, whereas the opposite is true for models bocdp and brp. In total, the abstraction based variant is faster than the corresponding configuration without abstraction in one fourth of the cases, and configuration AID is faster than a given configuration without abstraction in two thirds of the cases.

When comparing the methods based on the number of ASG nodes generated, the difference is more significant, as it can be seen in Table 2. As expected, the abstraction-based method produces a smaller ASG than the corresponding configuration without abstraction in most (97%) of the cases, and the state space generated by configuration AID is smaller in all cases. On average, the reduction in size in favor of the abstraction based handling of discrete variables is around 50%. In the worst case (model c1), the reduced size is around 80%,

---

[1] https://www.it.uu.se/research/group/darts/uppaal/benchmarks.
[2] http://gki.informatik.uni-freiburg.de/tools/mcta.

Table 1. Execution time in seconds per model and configuration

	EIB	ELB	EID	ELD	AIB	ALB	AID	ALD
bocdp	11.2	**4.8**	8.7	7.0	11.7	11.1	8.7	**7.9**
bocdpf	23.7	**14.3**	20.0	16.4	14.9	13.4	7.7	**7.5**
brp	12.0	**5.4**	20.9	9.2	12.2	**9.5**	14.3	16.3
c1	2.0	**1.3**	1.6	1.8	3.6	4.0	**2.9**	3.2
c2	5.3	**3.2**	3.9	4.7	7.1	8.5	**5.0**	6.8
c3	6.2	**4.5**	5.0	4.9	8.5	9.1	**6.9**	7.6
c4	71.5	53.9	**43.2**	52.4	59.8	77.2	**41.0**	49.6
m1	2.0	1.8	**0.9**	1.5	2.5	4.6	**1.1**	1.7
m2	4.6	4.7	**2.3**	4.3	6.5	12.4	**2.1**	4.2
m3	5.2	4.7	**2.4**	4.6	7.2	13.0	**2.6**	4.7
m4	17.4	23.1	**6.3**	16.0	27.4	68.5	**6.1**	—
n1	2.4	2.2	**1.2**	1.6	2.8	4.4	**1.2**	1.6
n2	6.2	5.9	**3.0**	4.3	7.0	13.9	**2.6**	4.7
n3	6.1	6.0	**3.4**	4.9	7.7	14.5	**2.8**	4.8
n4	23.9	31.5	**7.5**	27.8	30.5	78.6	**5.6**	18.0

Table 2. Number of nodes in the ASG per model and configuration

	EIB	ELB	EID	ELD	AIB	ALB	AID	ALD
bocdp	94801	**74052**	84136	96133	32639	34107	**29846**	32520
bocdpf	212225	**172865**	182085	196003	38492	39801	**26544**	29491
brp	**72117**	96624	114198	159249	**39702**	68979	52049	104552
c1	20967	**18590**	18612	23030	17155	20825	**14973**	18155
c2	67433	67325	**57260**	70198	44711	58351	**39644**	47725
c3	86285	85695	**76122**	94887	50617	62215	**46594**	55473
c4	876266	866890	**737271**	917527	339560	418619	**318470**	384214
m1	8541	19217	**3650**	14720	4394	13078	**1941**	4868
m2	31932	73667	**15610**	62879	16246	39773	**5728**	15797
m3	38128	74514	**15966**	73879	18463	42574	**6707**	17783
m4	145378	297343	**63523**	250221	66406	146804	**20519**	—
n1	7510	18660	**3915**	13132	4222	11802	**1942**	4222
n2	32038	79741	**15534**	54954	15819	42937	**5932**	17695
n3	32799	83982	**16602**	68010	17014	44741	**6547**	17903
n4	142053	325485	**60120**	342408	64934	155729	**17568**	70762

and in the best case (model **bocdpf**) it is 15%, i.e. the introduction of abstraction has significant gain.

To characterize the fastest configurations, Fig. 3 depicts the execution time (first column in blue) and number of nodes generated (second column in red) for the fastest configuration with abstraction relative to the performance of the fastest configuration without abstraction. Similarly, Fig. 4 depicts the relative performance when considering the configurations generating the least number of nodes. According to Fig. 3, if the configuration with abstraction performs well in execution time, then it also performs well in the number of nodes generated. Conversely, according to Fig. 4, if significant reduction is achieved in the size of the state space, then the algorithm with abstraction also tends to perform well in terms of execution time (except for model **bocdp**). Moreover, as can be seen on both charts, within a group of models (c, m and n), the relative performance of the abstraction method tends to increase with increasing model complexity.

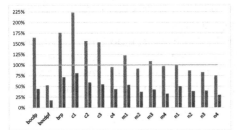

Fig. 3. Relative execution time and number of nodes generated of fastest configurations (Color figure online)

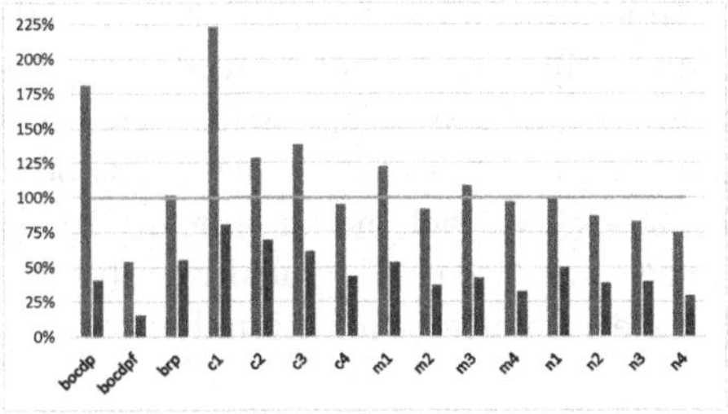

Fig. 4. Relative execution time and number of nodes generated of configurations with the smallest ASG

Moreover, for the models considered, configuration **AID** (Abstraction of discrete variables, Interpolation-based abstraction of clock variables, Depth-first search order) approximates the best configuration well for both execution time and ASG size, as this configuration tends to have a good performance on the more complex models. This is depicted on Figs. 5 and 6, where we compared configuration **AID** with the E-configurations in terms of execution time and size of the generated state space, respectively. In Fig. 5, we denote by **BEST** the virtual best configuration, calculated from the best results of all other configurations. This data is omitted in Fig. 6, as **BEST** greatly overlaps with configuration **AID** in terms of states generated. Moreover, to focus on the significant differences, we only depicted data for the hardest six models (denoted as 10 . . . 15 on the horizontal axis) for each configuration.

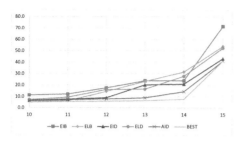 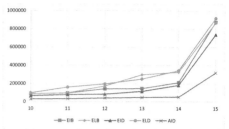

Fig. 5. Time to solve the hardest model instances (seconds)

Fig. 6. Number of nodes generated for the hardest model instances

5   Conclusions

In this paper we proposed a lazy algorithm for the location reachability problem of timed automata with discrete variables. The method is based on controlling the visibility of discrete variables by using interpolation for valuations of variables. We demonstrated with experiments that our abstraction and refinement strategy, combined with lazy methods for the abstraction of continuous clock variables, can achieve significant reduction in the size of the generated state space during search, typically with low or no overhead in execution time, and in cases even with an additional speedup.

Future Work. According to the method described in this paper, refinement is triggered upon encountering a disabled transition. In the future, we intend to experiment with counterexample-guided refinement for both the abstraction of discrete and continuous variables. In addition, we plan to experiment with different abstract domains (e.g. intervals), and investigate alternative refinement strategies for the discrete variables of timed systems. In particular we are interested in the performance for timed automata of the forward interpolation technique described in [4]. Moreover, we plan to explore more sophisticated strategies for finding covering states, as this can potentially yield considerable speedups for our method. Furthermore, although we evaluated our abstraction method in the context of timed systems, the technique itself can be applied in a more general context, and we plan to investigate its uses for model checking imperative programs.

References

1. Alur, R., Dill, D.L.: A theory of timed automata. Theoret. Comput. Sci. **126**(2), 183–235 (1994). https://doi.org/10.1016/0304-3975(94)90010-8
2. Behrmann, G., Bouyer, P., Fleury, E., Larsen, K.G.: Static guard analysis in timed automata verification. In: Garavel, H., Hatcliff, J. (eds.) TACAS 2003. LNCS, vol. 2619, pp. 254–270. Springer, Heidelberg (2003). https://doi.org/10.1007/3-540-36577-X_18

3. Behrmann, G., Bouyer, P., Larsen, K.G., Pelánek, R.: Lower and upper bounds in zone based abstractions of timed automata. In: Jensen, K., Podelski, A. (eds.) TACAS 2004. LNCS, vol. 2988, pp. 312–326. Springer, Heidelberg (2004). https://doi.org/10.1007/978-3-540-24730-2_25

4. Beyer, D., Löwe, S.: Explicit-state software model checking based on CEGAR and interpolation. In: Cortellessa, V., Varró, D. (eds.) FASE 2013. LNCS, vol. 7793, pp. 146–162. Springer, Heidelberg (2013). https://doi.org/10.1007/978-3-642-37057-1_11

5. Carioni, A., Ghilardi, S., Ranise, S.: MCMT in the land of parametrized timed automata. In: 6th International Verification Workshop (VERIFY-2010), pp. 47–64 (2010)

6. Clarke, E., Grumberg, O., Jha, S., Lu, Y., Veith, H.: Counterexample-guided abstraction refinement for symbolic model checking. J. ACM **50**(5), 752–794 (2003). https://doi.org/10.1145/876638.876643

7. Daws, C., Tripakis, S.: Model checking of real-time reachability properties using abstractions. In: Steffen, B. (ed.) TACAS 1998. LNCS, vol. 1384, pp. 313–329. Springer, Heidelberg (1998). https://doi.org/10.1007/BFb0054180

8. Dierks, H., Kupferschmid, S., Larsen, K.G.: Automatic abstraction refinement for timed automata. In: Raskin, J.-F., Thiagarajan, P.S. (eds.) FORMATS 2007. LNCS, vol. 4763, pp. 114–129. Springer, Heidelberg (2007). https://doi.org/10.1007/978-3-540-75454-1_10

9. Henzinger, T.A., Jhala, R., Majumdar, R., Sutre, G.: Lazy abstraction. In: Principles of Programming Languages, pp. 58–70. ACM (2002). https://doi.org/10.1145/503272.503279

10. Herbreteau, F., Srivathsan, B., Walukiewicz, I.: Lazy abstractions for timed automata. In: Sharygina, N., Veith, H. (eds.) CAV 2013. LNCS, vol. 8044, pp. 990–1005. Springer, Heidelberg (2013). https://doi.org/10.1007/978-3-642-39799-8_71

11. Herbreteau, F., Kini, D., Srivathsan, B., Walukiewicz, I.: Using non-convex approximations for efficient analysis of timed automata. In: Foundations of Software Technology and Theoretical Computer Science. LIPIcs, vol. 13, pp. 78–89 (2011). https://doi.org/10.4230/LIPIcs.FSTTCS.2011.78

12. Herbreteau, F., Srivathsan, B., Walukiewicz, I.: Better abstractions for timed automata. In: Logic in Computer Science, pp. 375–384. IEEE (2012). https://doi.org/10.1109/LICS.2012.48

13. Hojjat, H., Rümmer, P., Subotic, P., Yi, W.: Horn clauses for communicating timed systems. In: Horn Clauses for Verification and Synthesis. EPTCS, vol. 169, pp. 39–52. Open Publishing Association (2014). https://doi.org/10.4204/EPTCS.169.6

14. Isenberg, T., Wehrheim, H.: Timed automata verification via IC3 with zones. In: Merz, S., Pang, J. (eds.) ICFEM 2014. LNCS, vol. 8829, pp. 203–218. Springer, Cham (2014). https://doi.org/10.1007/978-3-319-11737-9_14

15. Kindermann, R., Junttila, T., Niemelä, I.: SMT-based induction methods for timed systems. In: Jurdziński, M., Ničković, D. (eds.) FORMATS 2012. LNCS, vol. 7595, pp. 171–187. Springer, Heidelberg (2012). https://doi.org/10.1007/978-3-642-33365-1_13

16. Lugiez, D., Niebert, P., Zennou, S.: A partial order semantics approach to the clock explosion problem of timed automata. In: Jensen, K., Podelski, A. (eds.) TACAS 2004. LNCS, vol. 2988, pp. 296–311. Springer, Heidelberg (2004). https://doi.org/10.1007/978-3-540-24730-2_24

17. Morbé, G., Pigorsch, F., Scholl, C.: Fully symbolic model checking for timed automata. In: Gopalakrishnan, G., Qadeer, S. (eds.) CAV 2011. LNCS, vol. 6806, pp. 616–632. Springer, Heidelberg (2011). https://doi.org/10.1007/978-3-642-22110-1_50

18. Tóth, T., Hajdu, Á., Vörös, A., Micskei, Z., Majzik, I.: Theta: a framework for abstraction refinement-based model checking. In: Formal Methods in Computer Aided Design, pp. 176–179. FMCAD Inc. (2017). https://doi.org/10.23919/FMCAD.2017.8102257

19. Tóth, T., Majzik, I.: Lazy reachability checking for timed automata using interpolants. In: Abate, A., Geeraerts, G. (eds.) FORMATS 2017. LNCS, vol. 10419, pp. 264–280. Springer, Cham (2017). https://doi.org/10.1007/978-3-319-65765-3_15

20. Wang, W., Jiao, L.: Difference bound constraint abstraction for timed automata reachability checking. In: Graf, S., Viswanathan, M. (eds.) FORTE 2015. LNCS, vol. 9039, pp. 146–160. Springer, Cham (2015). https://doi.org/10.1007/978-3-319-19195-9_10

From SysML to Model Checkers via Model Transformation

Martin Kölbl$^{(\boxtimes)}$, Stefan Leue$^{(\boxtimes)}$, and Hargurbir Singh

University of Konstanz, Konstanz, Germany
{martin.koelbl,stefan.leue,Hargurbir.Singh}@uni.kn

Abstract. In this paper we present an automated translation from the systems engineering modeling language SysML into the input languages of the NuSMV, Prism and Spin model checkers. A special focus of this work is the semantics of the communication mechanisms used in a syntactic fragment of SysML, in particular synchronous and asynchronous, broadcast and buffered communication. In order to achieve generality of our approach, which supports establishing the consistency of the translation as well as enabling easy adaption between different source and target languages, we use a model based transformation approach. In particular, we use the ATLAS Transformation Language (ATL) framework that is nicely integrated in the Eclipse Modeling Framework (EMF) and in the Meta-Object Facility. We illustrate the application of this model transformation approach using an airbag system as a case study.

1 Introduction

The use of model-based software and systems engineering in the design of critical systems implies the need to prove high dependability properties, including correctness, of these designs since human life or substantial damage to the environment is at stake. While a vast array of formal analysis techniques, such as model and causality checking [1,2], have been developed to analyze model based designs for compliance with these properties, there is a substantial gap between the syntax and the semantics of model-based engineering languages and the input formats that the formal analysis tools accept. In particular, each model checking tool typically provides its own input language, designed to provide optimal abstractions enabling efficient model checking. Even if some model checking tools aim to provide open interfaces, e.g., LTSmin [3], there is no commonly accepted input format for models that would be processed by a large number of model checking tools. Also, none of the available model checkers can directly process the OMG System Modelling Language (SysML) [4,5] which is widely used in industrial practice to model system architectures. SysML is supported by a large number of commercial and open source modeling tools (e.g., Rhapsody [6], Enterprise Architect [7], Papyrus [8].) SysML allows for modeling the structure and behavior of systems, including inter-object communication. If used in a design process, the architecture models need to be manually transformed

© Springer International Publishing AG, part of Springer Nature 2018
M. M. Gallardo and P. Merino (Eds.): SPIN 2018, LNCS 10869, pp. 255–274, 2018.
https://doi.org/10.1007/978-3-319-94111-0_15

into the input language of the chosen model checker. This is human intensive, and therefore extremely expensive, and furthermore an error prone activity. With an automated transformation from SysML towards different model checkers, a system can easily be checked for faults. When a model checking algorithm detects a fault in a model, it returns a trace to the faulty state in the form of a counterexample. Each model checking tool, however, returns a counterexample using a different syntax. Interpreting the counterexample in order to correct the fault in the model requires intimate knowledge of this syntax.

We propose an automated, rule-based approach to transforming SysML models to models specified in the input languages of various model checking tools that we consider. In particular, we will define transformations for the Spin [9], Prism [10] and NuSMV2 [11] model checkers. Spin is an explicit-state temporal logic model checker frequently used in the analysis of concurrent software systems. Prism is a model checker used for the analysis of probabilistic systems. NuSMV2 is a symbolic temporal logic model checker frequently applied to hardware systems analysis. Automated model transformation facilitates maintaining consistency by following defined transformation mappings. Notice that since the input languages of model checkers typically have very specific semantics, only subsets of the SysML language will be transformed in our approach. We base our translation on the following precursory research.

- The safety analysis of SysML models implemented in the QuantUM [12] approach and tool includes a transformation of SysML models to the input languages of the Prism and Spin model checkers. Using causality checking, QuantUM computes causes for faults of a system and presents the computed causes by fault trees to the user.
- In [13], an approach is described which transforms SysML to NuSMV2. The transformation is based on an object-oriented view and first transforms the SysML model to a general model checker model using the support of JDOM [14]. Afterwards, the general model is translated to NuSMV2 code using a non-rule based approach.

We exploit, extend and generalize these ideas as follows.

- First, our approach reuses the idea of an object-oriented meta-model and generalizes it by using model-to-model transformation (MMT) technology. The previous translation approaches implemented model transformation by using JDOM or by direct Java programming. A concern with these non rule based translation approaches is that it is difficult to ensure consistency of the translation. They also lack flexibility and concept reuse when changing from one target modeling language to another. We propose to use an MMT approach, which ensures consistency of the input, output and transformation model against meta-models during the model transformation, and allows for flexible re-definition of translation rules when considering a different target modeling language. As an MMT framework we use the Atlas Transformation Language (ATL) [15], and the Xpand framework [16] for the model-to-code transformation, both integrated into the Eclipse Modeling Framework (EMF) [17].

- Second, the works cited above transform states, transitions and nested states along with guards, actions and asynchronous communication. Our approach extends the forms of communication that the previous approaches support by also considering SysML synchronous and asynchronous point-to-point communication, asynchronous broadcast, and buffered communication. Although asynchronous communication can be used to emulate synchronous communication and broadcasting, we want to take advantage of the expressiveness of different communication paradigms provided by SysML and enable the user to model the system using the envisioned logical syntax. The usage of different communication mechanisms also helps us produce more efficient code in the target model checker input languages, contributing to addressing the state space explosion problem [1].
- Finally, our approach enables a user to understand a given counterexample by a transformation from the counterexample syntax of the used model checker to a SysML sequence diagram.

We illustrate the application of our approach by a case study that applies the proposed transformation to an airbag model used in previous transformations [13].

Structure of the Paper. In Sect. 2 we provide a brief overview of SysML, the considered model checking input languages, ATL and Xpand. In Sect. 3 we describe our transformation approach, in particular the necessary transformation steps from SysML to the model checker input languages, and from counterexamples to Sequence Diagrams. In Sect. 4 we illustrate the transformations by a case study. We conclude in Sect. 5.

Related Work. A number of publications related to the transformation of SysML to different analysis tools are available in the literature. For an overview we refer to [13]. In [18] a transformation is presented which transforms SysML to a hardware description language using MMT. Similar to our work, that work uses ATL and meta models, but the target model is fundamentally different from our target model. We are not aware of any work that translates SysML using automated model transformation technology into any of the input languages of the model checkers that we consider.

2   Preliminaries

SysML Model Elements. The purpose of the SysML standard is to define a general modeling language for system engineering [4]. SysML uses a subset of the Unified Modeling Language (UML) [19], but also adds diagrams to the UML. In the remainder of the paper we will only refer to SysML in the understanding that many of the syntax and semantics definitions can be found in the UML specification. In the current paper, we transform only a syntactic subset of the full SysML language. In SysML, a system model is given by block definition

diagrams (bdd), depicting the structure of the architecture, internal block definition diagrams (ibd), representing the internal structure of blocks, and state
chart diagrams (stm), specifying the behavior of the respective block they are
associated with. A bdd describes the overall structure of a system. It comprises
blocks which represent classes, with associations between blocks depicted by
straight lines. An ibd is a refinement of a bdd and encompasses the same structural elements as a bdd. A block that possesses a behavior description is called
an active block. Using an stm, the behavior of a block is described by states
and transitions. States represent a location of control, and transitions between
states representing state changing activities in the system. In particular, a state
transition may be labeled by a trigger, indicating a wait condition for an event
to occur, a guard controlling the activation of the transition, and effects which
are being executed when the transition is taken. In the context of this paper,
we only consider activities and opaque behavior as transition effects. An opaque
behavior is defined as an arbitrary text that is not specified in terms of its syntax
and semantics in the SysML standard. In SysML, an activity is defined as being
represented by a complex activity diagram. In this paper we only consider activities that consist of a single send action. The stms of all blocks in the system
are executed concurrently. Stms of one block can interact with stms of other
blocks using shared variable as well as message passing based communication.
Stms follow the hierarchical state machine idea and can contain substates that
represent other hierarchical state machines. We call such states composite states.

Execution of SysML Models. When interpreting the behavior of an SysML model
operationally, for instance by a model checker, we need to comply with the
run-to-completion principle in the semantics of executing stms. As we now
illustrate, this principle leads to ambiguous interpretations of SysML model
behavior. In an SysML model, a state can be active, which means that the
current location of control is in this state. If a composite state is active, this
means that control rests in one of its sub states as well as in the composite state
itself, which means that a set of states can be active at any given point in time.
The set of active states is called a state configuration. A state may be labeled by
entry and exit behaviors which are executed when the state is entered or exited,
respectively, as well as by behavior executed while the system is in that state.
The stm maintains an event pool that contains events that are available to trigger transitions. A state configuration is called stable if all entry behaviors of the
current state configuration are completed and no more transitions are enabled.
The SysML specification defines an execution environment that selects an event
to be processed from the event pool. The precise mechanism how this selection is
performed is not specified. The run-to-completion principle means that when
an stm is in a stable state configuration, the execution environment of the SysML
model selects an event to trigger a transition, the effects of the selected transition will be executed and the system returns to a stable state. Applying this
principle to a loop in an stm that consists exclusively of transitions that have
enabled guards but no triggers implies that the stm enters a livelock and never
reaches a stable state configuration again. This is not consistent with a further

specification in the SysML standard which states that once the execution of an stm reaches a state, the stm remains in the state until a transition is triggered by an event from the event pool, or an external asynchronous message terminates the execution. In order to resolve this inconsistency, we assume that in the context of this paper each transition without an explicitly specified trigger will find an implicitly defined trigger event in the event pool that allows it to perform the next transition. Under this assumption a cycle of transitions reaches a stable configuration in each state of the cycle.

Communication in SysML. The SysML standard defines a large number of types of communication, including messages. In this paper we only consider communication between the stms by messages without parameters and return values. We use the syntax options of SysML to express different forms of communication. A message event in SysML can be instantiated as a call or a signal event. The behavior implied by a message event depends on this instantiation. If the message event is of type signal event, then the communication is asynchronous and the stm continues after sending a message without blocking. If the message event is of the type of a synchronous call event, then the communication is synchronous and the stm waits until the called operation has finished. Notice that in accordance with the SysML specification, a transition with a synchronous call only completes the current execution step when the called operation has completed. In this paper we do not consider asynchronous call events for which the invoking stm only waits until the operation is called. The type of a send action depends on the kind of message event that is to be sent. A send signal action sends a signal event. A call operation action sends a call event. A send action sends a message to a reception if both refer to the same message event. In the models we consider in this paper the sending stm is assumed always to be different from the receiving stm. Signal events and call events are received when executing a trigger in a transition. If several triggers can receive an event, then the SysML standard suggests that the trigger from an active substate has priority in execution over the trigger of the composite state. If several transitions have the same priority, then the transition to be executed is selected non-deterministically.

Special forms of asynchronous communication are broadcast and buffered communication:

- SysML provides *broadcast communication* using a send action of type broadcast signal action. SysML defines the receivers of a broadcast as all potentially available targets and mentions that the exact set of targets is not defined. To represent broadcast in this paper we assume that the broadcast is directed to every block that has an stm with a matching receiving trigger on one of its transitions.
- SysML supports the modeling of *buffered communication* by adding First-In-First-Out (FIFO) queues to the sending actions. Since the target of our work is the use of finite state verification technology to analyze SysML models we restrict the capacity of the queues to be finite. If no queue length is specified in the SysML model we assume a default queue size of one message. According

to SysML specification, in case of a full queue the message sent by a send signal action will be lost. This is a consequence of the fact that a send signal action just sends a message but does not consider any reception of the signal event.

Properties in SysML. Since the objective of this paper is to use model checking technology to verify properties against SysML models we need to consider how to specify the desired type of properties in SysML. We express a specification in SysML by using invariants. An invariant is an expression that before and after each execution step has to evaluate to true and consists of a composition of Boolean condition about states and variable values inside of a block. Invariants can be specified using the Object Constraint Language (OCL) [20] which is a higher order logic formalism defined to specify logical constraints on the SysML. As a property specification we add an OCL invariant to a model by adding an OCL formula expressing the property to the topmost element of the model, called the root. An invariant can refer to other invariants in the other blocks of the model and use those in order to check a combination of states or variable values belonging to different blocks. We restrict the OCL formula representing the desired property to be a propositional formula ϕ, where the propositions in ϕ refer to variable values and states being active or not. The model checkers NuSMV2, Prism and Spin are capable of verifying such invariant properties, for instance by translating them to the Linear Time Temporal Logic (LTL) [21] formula $\Box\phi$ and performing LTL model checking using this property on the model.

SysML Sequence Diagrams. A SysML sequence diagram [4] is an interaction diagram and depicts the message flow between actors and blocks of the system. The diagram consists of several **Lifelines** which model concurrent processes. Behaviors like activities and send actions of a process can be added to a lifeline by a behavior execution specification. A behavior execution specification is depicted by a rectangle on the lifeline of the executing process. **Lifelines** are arranged next to each other and along each line, the order of the events in each of the depicted actors and blocks is from top to bottom. A message is depicted by arrows from a sender to a receiver process. Asynchronous message are depicted with an arrow and synchronous messages are depicted with a filled arrow.

The NuSMV2 Modeling Language. NuSMV2 is a symbolic model checker which is used for the verification of synchronous and asynchronous finite state systems [11]. NuSMV2 can perform finite state model checking for LTL specifications. In this section, we introduce the parts of the NuSMV2 input language which are relevant for our approach. A short example of NuSMV2 code is given in Listing 1.1.

```
MODULE main(events)
  VAR
        state: {run, undetected};
  ASSIGN
    init(state) :=        run;
    next(state) :=
      case
        state = run & events != ECU_error: undetected;
        TRUE: state;
      esac;
```

Listing 1.1. NuSMV2 Example

An asynchronous model consists of several concurrent processes. In NuSMV2, each concurrent process is defined by the keyword **MODULE**. Each MODULE consists of two sections. In the section **VAR** the variables are declared. Section **ASSIGN** contains variable assignments. The keyword **init** declares the initial value of a variable. The NuSMV2 model specifies a transition system. Variable values can be changed in the **next** clauses which describe how the value of a variable changes in the course of a state transition. In the example, the statement **next(state)** changes to the value of the variable **undetected** if the guards **state = run** and **events != ECU_error** evaluate to true. The **TRUE:state** clause is executed if the guards are false, which means that the state remains unchanged. All possible variable changes of a single process are done at once, but only one process at a time. NuSMV2 allows the declaration of variables as an enumeration of non reserved strings as value range. The MODULE called **main** can define global variables and other MODULES. NuSMV2 has no special syntax or semantic definition for the declaration of communication channels.

The Promela Modeling Language. Promela is the input language of the explicit state model checker Spin. It combines a fragment of the syntax of the C programming language with guarded commands and specific communication primitives [9].

```
int process1_states = 0;
chan channel1 = [0] of { bool };
chan channel2 = [1] of { bool };
proctype process1 {
  do
  :: process1_states == 0 -> process1_states = 1; channel1!true;
  :: process1_states == 1 -> channel2?true; process1_states = 0;
  od;
```

Listing 1.2. Promela example

Concurrent processes in Promela are defined as **proctypes**, as illustrated in Listing 1.2. Variables are declared with a type and can either be defined locally inside a proctype, or globally. Computation steps from different proctypes are arbitrarily interleaved. Sequences of Promela statements included in an **atomic** statement will not be interleaved by statements in concurrent proctypes. Promela provides keywords for the definition of channels as well as the sending and receiving of messages. As shown in the example, if the process1 is in state 0 then it can send a message to channel1 and if the process is in state 1 it can receive a message from channel2. Channels are defined with the keyword chan, indicating a type and a capacity of the channel. A channel is defined as synchronous if the size is zero as in the example with channel1, or asynchronous with a non-zero positive size as with channel2. A synchronous message can only be sent by a sender if another process is ready to receive the message. The synchronization statement of a channel breaks the atomicity of an atomic statement at the point of sending the message and goes on with the receiving statement. For asynchronous communication in SysML we use a asynchronous First-In-First-Out (FIFO) channel of Spin. If the channel is full we instruct Spin to lose the message and proceed.

The Prism Modeling Language. The model checker Prism allows for the model checking of a probabilistic timed variant of CTL relative to discrete or continuous time finite state Markov chain models. SysML has language elements that allow to add probabilities and stochastic rates to the model. We currently do not interpret these SysML elements and assume all probabilities to have a rate of 1.

A Prism code sample is presented in Listing 1.3. Concurrent processes in Prism are defined by the keyword module. Variables can be defined locally by a name, type, initial value and range. Transitions can have a synchronization event name inside of the brackets [...], a guard, a probability and several actions. If different processes have a transition labeled with the same synchronization event, then these transitions can only be executed synchronously. All other transitions are taken sequentially in an arbitrary sequence. The update of a variable is indicated using the frequently encountered "prime" notation. For instance, in the course of the transition1 transition in Listing 1.3 the variable done is assigned the new value true. There is no explicit syntax in Prism to define a communication channel.

```
module process1
   states : [0..1] init 0;
   done : bool init false;
   [transition1] (done = false) -> 0.01 : (done'=true);
endmodule
```

Listing 1.3. Prism example

The Atlas Transformation Language (ATL). ATL is a domain specific transformation language and provides a framework for the rule-based model-to-model transformation of XMI [22] based models. ATL addresses two important issues in model transformation. First, it checks the syntactic correctness of the input model and hence avoids an ill formed input model to lead to an ill formed output model. Second, it supports the assurance of correctness and unambiguity of the transformation rules for complex model transformations. ATL addresses these problems by exploiting the idea of meta-models for the purpose of model transformation. A meta-model is a special model representing the model elements of the modeling language used [23]. For instance, it specifies rules that determine what the correct structure of a SysML model is, and what its admissible elements are. ATL allows a declarative description of transformation rules by the use of meta-models. Transformation rules can refer to the elements in the source and target model. This leads to a more dependable model transformation than a non MMT based approach since the complexities entailed by the selection of source elements and the application of rules is handled automatically by ATL [15].

The structure of an ATL transformation process is depicted in Fig. 1. ATL parses a source model MA in accordance with a source meta-model MMA and ensures that a source model conforms to its source meta-model or recognizes the source model as ill defined input model. Then the ATL code mma2mmb.atl describes how a source model is converted to a target model which conforms to a target meta-model MMB. The ATL code itself has to conform to the ATL meta-model ATL. To ensure correctness of the transformation, all meta-models have to conform to the standard meta-meta-model *Meta Object Facility* (MOF) [15] proposed by the OMG. ATL has its own syntax, but also inherits a subset of Java and OCL syntax. OCL operations provide a common way to work with collections, for instance the forall operator that can be used to iterate over a collection. Transformation rules are described in the ATL code as a set of mappings between source and target patterns with imperative operations performed on the source elements. Each element of the source model matches at most to one transformation rule.

An example for an ATL rule E2E is given in Listing 1.4. The rule refers to elements of the meta-models MMa and MMb. In the rule, we describe the transformation from a source element of type EnumerationLiteral to a target element of type StringEnumeration where the rule transfers the information from the attributes name and id. The source pattern contains a conditional statement which restricts the matching to source elements whose name starts with an A.

```
rule E2E{from s: MMa! EnumerationLiteral (s.name.startsWith("A"))
         to t: MMb! StringEnumeration (name <- s.name, ID <- s.ID)}
```

Listing 1.4. ATL example

There are three types of ATL rules:

1. *Matched rules.* These are the basic rules which will be matched against the source elements. The rule name must be unique and contain a source and a target pattern. The example in Listing 1.4 is a matched rule.
2. *Lazy rules.* This type of rule is only called through other rules. It is usually used to create child elements and helps in traversing the XMI model.
3. *Called rules.* These rules behaves similar to lazy rules but don't contain any source pattern. They can be called at the entry and exit of the transformation execution. Called rules are used to create new elements in the output model for which no source elements exist.

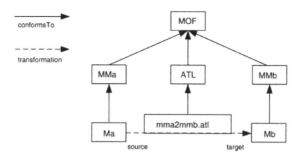

Fig. 1. Overview of ATL transformation [15]

Xpand is a framework supporting the model-to-text transformation for the generation of text files for domain specific languages (DSLs). We use Xpand here to generate code of the model checker input languages based on the XMI produced by the ATL model transformation. To do so, we need a source model, a source meta-model and the Xpand code which is executed to create the output text file, representing the model checker input code. For the source meta-model in Xpand, we reuse the target meta-model of ATL. The Xpand code for a transformation is called a template, for an example see Listing 1.5. In a template, we define the structure of the target text file. Xpand specific code is written between the signs « and ». Any text outside of these characters is considered part of the target output file syntax and is written directly to the target file.

```
«IMPORT MMb»
«DEFINE main FOR Model−»
«FILE filename +".txt"−»
states = {«EXPAND substate FOREACH this.states SEPARATOR ',' −»}
«DEFINE substate FOR State−»«this.name−»«ENDDEFINE»
«ENDFILE»
«ENDDEFINE»
```

Listing 1.5. XPAND example

The Xpand code example in Listing 1.5 first checks whether the input model conforms to a meta-model MMb. The Xpand code starts inside the «DEFINE» statement **main** by creating a file and writing the text "states =" to the file. Afterwards the «EXPAND» statement **substates** iterates over a comma separated list **states** of states. For each state of the list the «DEFINE» statement with the same name as the EXPAND statement is called with a element of type **State**. The called «DEFINE» statement writes the name of the current state into the file.

3   Model Transformation

Model Transformation Approach. Our approach consists of two transformations. First, we transform a SysML model into the input language of the considered model checkers. Second, if a model checker identifies a counterexample to the

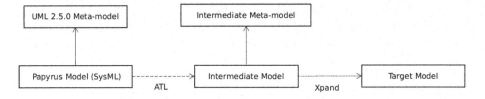

Fig. 2. Structure of the transformation

property that we are interested in, we translate this counterexample into a SysML sequence diagram. The SysML models that we wish to analyze are edited using the Papyrus editor and saved in XMI format. We then use ATL to parse the XMI model of Papyrus and transform the model to an `Intermediate Model`, and finally transform this model to the different model checking languages using Xpand. An overview of the model transformation approach is depicted in Fig. 2. ATL parses the input `Papyrus Model` and checks if the contained model conforms to the UML 2.5.0 meta-model of Eclipse. Afterwards, ATL transforms the model into an `Intermediate Model`. As a target meta-model we use the one defined as `intermediate meta-model` in [13]. We use the intermediate meta-model in order to ensure that the intermediate model contains all necessary information, for example stms, states, transitions, guard, etc. After the generation of the intermediate model and using the specific templates of the model checkers, Xpand translates the elements of the intermediate model into the `Target Model`. The `Target Model` contains the model and the property in the syntax of the currently considered model checker. The support for further model checkers can be added by using additional Xpand templates.

Property Generation Rules. As explained before, we transform a property defined as a state invariant in SysML to an LTL expression in the syntax of the considered model checker. ATL parses the state invariant included in the SysML model and adds it to the Intermediate Model. Xpand then transforms the property from the Intermediate Model to the property used by the currently considered model checker. While the transformation of the SysML model is independent of the property we wish to check, we currently only support the transformation of OCL specified invariant properties.

State and Transition Transformation Rules. We shortly sum the basic transformation rules from SysML to a model checker model that we adopt from our precursory work, [12,13]. We only support nested states in stm diagrams and not referenced stms. Each stm defines a concurrent process in the respective model checking input language. We flatten nested states by encoding each state in the model by a unique name. The unique name is the combination of the names of all nesting states of the current state and the name of the state itself. Spin directly uses state names and can change the current state by a `goto` statement to the next state. In NuSMV2 and Prism, the current state of an stm is stored by a variable with a name of the stm extended with "_states" for Prism and in the variable named state in NuSMV2. In NuSMV, the variable is of type enumeration and stores the current state name. In Prism, the state variable stores a unique number for each state of a block. A model transition can change the current state by changing the value of the state variable. A model transition is only enabled if the source state is the current state of the stm. We add an extra guard, which enables a transition if the current state of the stm is the source state of the transition, to each transition. If the current state is a substate and has a composite state, then the transitions of the composite state are also enabled. Our transformation flattens the state hierarchy and hence, a transition that was enabled in the composite state is no longer enabled when entering a substate. As a consequence we enable all those disabled transitions in the composite state again by copying them to the substate. The translation of guards and effects of transitions is straightforward. Entry and exit behavior of a model state are added during the model transformation as effects to the corresponding transition in the intermediate model. An effect of a transition can be an activity or opaque behavior. We use an activity with a single action to represent the sending of a message event, and an opaque behavior in OCL format to characterize the update of a variable using a logical formula. In the context of this paper, we only allow a single effect for each transition. This ensures consistency of the generated model checking input code among the different model checkers that we support since it avoids problems ensued by the different execution order semantics that these model checkers assume. In particular, just like SysML, Spin executes effects of a transition one after another in a sequential sequence while the Prism and NuSMV models that we generate execute all effects of taken transitions in one atomic step. With only one effect on a transition the model checkers do not deviate from the restricted SysML behavior.

Messages in Promela. Synchronous and asynchronous point-to-point communication messages are first class citizens in the Promela language. They are introduced in the language by declaring synchronous or asynchronous channels, and listing certain message names as being valid message names along these channels. We use the language constructs that Promela provides in order to define synchronous and asynchronous buffered communication. A transition with a synchronous call is executed at once or not at all since we clasp the guard and effects of a transition in Promela by an atomic statement. Sequences of Promela statements inside an atomic statement are not interleaved by other concurrent statements. However, with a synchronous message, the atomic statement of the sender will break and execute the atomic statement of the receiver. Since in our modeling the sending transition can have only one action as an effect, all effects in the synchronization are executed in the correct sequence. In order to emulate asynchronous broadcast, we create an asynchronous channel for each receiver and send a message to each one of them. Since we need to send all messages at once, we enclose the sending actions to these channels by an atomic statement.

Messages in NuSMV2. There is no native syntax for messages in NuSMV2. In order to emulate *synchronous communication* we add the guard conditions for the receive transition in the receiving process to the guard condition of the send transition in the sender, thus ensuring that the sending can only be executed when the receiver is ready to receive. Furthermore, in order to ensure that in the course of one transition in the NuSMV2 model only one synchronous communication occurs the sending process sets a global variable to a value that is unique for this communication. This variable deactivates all transitions except the receiving transition. When executing the receiving of the message, the receiver resets the global variable. In order to emulate an *asynchronous broadcast* communication we create an array with one element corresponding to one receiving stm, for every receiving stm. When broadcasting the message, each entry of the array is set to true at once. Since the semantics of this broadcast is asynchronous in nature, there is no requirement to suspend the execution of any of the other modules. To emulate *buffered communication*, we use an array of variables that behaves like a FIFO queue. The length of the array is equal to the capacity of the sender queue as defined in the SySML model. Each entry of the array represents a position in the queue. As a consequence, multiple sending of messages are stored in the queue until the queue is full and then the extra messages are discarded. This persists until the receiver processes previously sent messages.

Messages in Prism. There is no native syntax for messages in the Prism input language either. Similar to the case of NuSMV2, we emulate the channels by using variables, but with slight differences. In order to emulate *synchronous communication* we take advantage of the implicit synchronization that Prism performs for several transitions synchronization event names, for which we use the name of the call event and the sender process. With this name encoding, we distinguish between several possible senders sending the same call event to the same receiver. In order to emulate *asynchronous communication*, like for NuSMV2 we create a variable. Prism does not permit the use of global variables together with label based transition synchronization. We therefore use a local variable inside the sending stm in order to coordinate the asynchronous sending and receiving. When sending the message, this variable is set to true. Since the variable is local, it can only be reset in the sending process. We generate an auxiliary transition in the sender which is independent of the remaining behavior of the sender. It is synchronized with the receive transition in the receiving process via a transition label and resets the local variable. *Broadcasting* and *buffered communication* are emulated similarly as in the case of NuSMV2. A minor difference is that Prism has no syntax for arrays. We therefore create an individual variable for each entry of the array. In buffered communication, when the first element of the fifo queue is read, the value of each entry of the queue is copied to the entry ahead of it.

Counterexample to SysML Sequence Diagram Transformation. We propose the following steps to transform the counterexample that one of the considered model checkers produces into a Sequence Diagram. We interpret the counterexample, for which every one of the considered model checkers uses a different syntax, as a model and apply ATL based model transformation to this syntax in order to obtain a sequence diagram representation in XMI format.

1. *Parsing the Counterexample.* For an ATL transformation, we first need to parse the counterexamples which are stored in different textual formats depending on the model checker that was used. In order to accomplish this we need extra information from the original model, for instance regarding the names of the blocks that exchange messages, the events occurring along a state sequence, etc., since not all of this information is included in the state name sequences that the model checkers generate as counterexamples. We obtain this information by parsing the original SysML model.

2. *Transformation into a Sequence Diagram.* We next transform the parsed counterexample to a sequence diagram using an ATL transformation. For each process in the input model of the model checker we create a `Lifeline` in the sequence diagram, representing a concurrent thread of execution. A counterexample consists of a sequence of state and transition whereas a sequence diagram depicts the control flow of the system by a sequence of message send and receive events. Transitions of a stm without messages are depicted by a behavior execution specification. The behavior execution specification has as a name the current state name and contains the name and values of any changed variable. When a message is sent to another stm, then the message points from the sending to the receiving stm and the message name is set to the name of the sender, the current state name of the sender and the message event name corresponding to the message sending. A possible variable change of the reiving transition is added as an invisible attribute to the message arrow.

3. *Generation of Graphical View.* Using another ATL transformation step we generate a graphical view for the Papyrus IDE from the sequence diagram.

4   Case Study

The Airbag Model. We illustrate our approach by applying it to a real world model of an airbag system adopted from [24]. The SysML model of this system was edited using the Papyrus tool and is an extension of on the SysML model of the same system used in [13]. In particular, we added different inter process communication mechanisms in order to be able to experiment with the model translation rules for these mechanisms that we defined above. An overview of the airbag SysML model is given as a bdd in Fig. 3. The dashed arrows represent communication from a sender to a receiver block. The most important block in the airbag model is the `MicroController`. It continuously evaluates whether the two sensors represented by the block `MainSensor` and the block `SafetySensor` detect a critical accident of the vehicle, represented by the block `Car`. When this is the case, the deployment procedure for the airbag will be activated.

There are two meaningful properties to check for an airbag system. The first is to ensure proper functioning, i.e., to ensure that the airbag can be deployed.

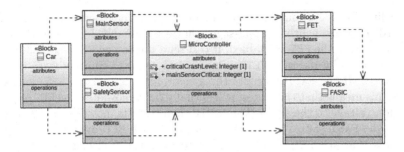

Fig. 3. bdd of the Airbag model

The second property is the absence of an inadvertent deployment of the airbag when no accident has occurred. From a system safety point of view this is the more significant property to check, and we have focussed on it in some of our previous work on this model, e.g., in [24]. However, the counterexamples to inadvertent deployment are relatively short. We focus on the proper functioning property in this paper since it returns longer counterexamples and is hence better suited to illustrate the application of our approach.

In order to understand the behavior of the Airbag model, an understanding of the two safety mechanisms designed to avoid an inadvertent deployment is essential. First, the Field Effect Transistor (FET) controls the power supply of the airbag squib. Only if the MicroController enables the FET, the airbag squib has enough power to deploy the airbag by igniting the explosive. Second, the Firing Application Specific Integrated Circuit (FASIC) only ignites the airbag squib if it first receives an armFASIC message and then a fireFASIC message from the MicroController.

Communication in the Airbag System. We use different forms of communication to forward information in the airbag system. In case of an accident the block Car broadcasts a message crashHappened to both sensors. The two sensors receive the broadcast message and start to repeatedly forward the information regarding the accident by buffered communication. The block MainSensor sends a mess-sage mainSensorCrashDetection and the block SafetySensor sends a message safetySensorCrashDetection. The repetition of the message ensures, that not a single wrong message can deploy the airbag. The microcontroller receives the messages of both sensors and starts the airbag deployment process after receiv-ing the accident notification of each sensor two times. In order to start the deployment process the block MicroController sends the following three asyn-chronous messages. A message armFASIC is sent to the block FASIC and causes the fasic to go into state arm. A message FETPoweredOn is sent to the block FET which enables the power supply when received. A message fireFASIC is sent to the block FASIC which causes the fasic to transit from state arm into state fire. It is now important to ensure that the squib will only explode and deploy the airbag if the power supply is enabled at the time of firing the squib. We model the coordination regarding the deployment of the airbag between the FET and the FASIC by two synchronous messages that are exchanged between these two processes. In case the FET is enabled, it can send a message FETPoweredOn, otherwise it can send a message FETPoweredOff in order to communicate its state to the FASIC. If the FASIC accepts the synchronization via the FETPoweredOn message this means that the airbag will actually be deployed by the FET applying an ignition voltage to the squib. The FASIC then transits into the state fired. If, however, the FASIC and the FET synchronize via the FETPoweredOff message, this means that the FET is not prepared to deploy the airbag and the FASIC transits into its initial state.

Property Specification. We specify the proper functioning property of the airbag system using an invariant. The invariant expresses that it is always not the case that the airbag is deployed and the car has an accident. If a model checker finds a counterexample for this invariant then the counterexample contains a sequence of states and transitions that starts with a car accident and terminates with the deployment of the airbag.

Analysis of the Airbag Model. We model check the models that we obtain from the above described translation into the target languages of the NuSMV2, Spin and Prism model checkers for the proper functioning property. Each model checker results in a counterexample to the property. We automatically transform the resulting counterexample of NuSMV2 to a SysML sequence diagram, depicted in Fig. 4. A similar translation of the counterexamples for the other two model checkers is easily possible, but currently not implemented. Note that the change of the variable values is not visible in the figure, but it is viewable when browsing the diagram in the Papyrus IDE. The model transformations were performed on a computer with an i7-4820K CPU (3.7 GHz), 32 GB of RAM and a 64 bit Linux operation system. In Table 1 we show the memory usage and time necessary to transform SysML models to the different model checker input models, to verify the airbag model in the different model checkers, and for the NuSMV2 case to transform a counterexample to a sequence diagram. Additionally, we depict the count of states searched by each model checker. For the verification of the airbag model, Spin uses with 128.3 MB an order of magnitude more memory than the other model checkers. The higher memory consumption of Spin is due to the use of a hash table which has at least a size of 128 MB.

Table 1. Computational effort

	Model transformation		Model checking			Sequence diagram generation	
	Memory	Time	Memory	Time	States	Memory	Time
NuSMV2	9.6 MB	37 ms	10.0 MB	0.092 s	3279	9.6 MB	75 ms
Spin	9.6 MB	35 ms	128.3 MB	<1 s	1432		
Prism	9.6 MB	34 ms	8.5 MB	0.023 s	984		

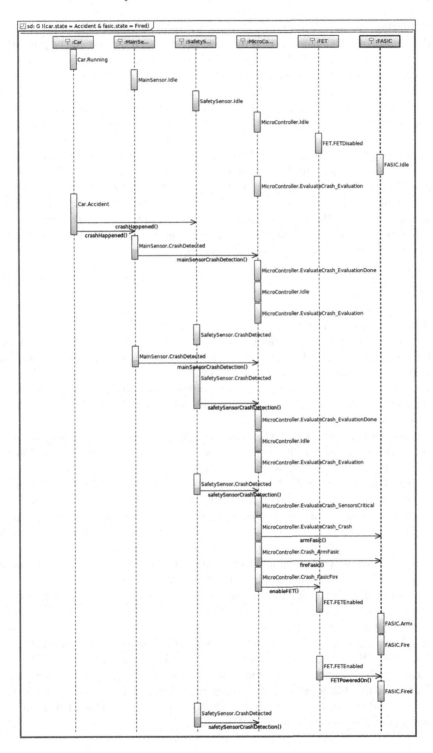

Fig. 4. Sequence diagram depicting the NuSMV2 counterexample, rendered by Papyrus

Result Interpretation. The sequence diagram representing the counterexample produced by NuSMV2 consists of 6 lifelines, one for each module in the NuSMV2 code of the airbag model. The sequence diagram depicts ordered sequences of local module events, corresponding to local steps in the Airbag SysML model, as well as synchronous and asynchronous message passing events that lead up to the firing of the airbag, indicated by the FASIC entering the fired state.

The counterexamples produced by all three model checkers are similar. Each counterexample contains the necessary transitions to get from a car accident to a deployment of the airbag. The counterexamples mainly only differ in the order in which the transitions in the model are executed, but all contain the same set of transitions. NuSMV2 performs a short loop that the other model checkers do not include in the counterexample. For example with the deployment of the airbag, in NuSMV2 the messages armFasic, fireFasic and enableFet are all send before any of the messages is received, but in Prism and Promela each message is received before the next one is triggered.

5   Conclusion

We have presented an approach to automatically translating SysML models to the input languages of the model checkers NuSMV2, Spin and Prism, using the ATL framework for model to model transformation. We also propose to use ATL in order to translate the counterexamples for reachability properties to SysML sequence diagrams, thus facilitating error interpretation and debugging. We have illustrated the application of this approach using an industrially relevant case study.

In spite of the fact that at the time of writing only the SysML to NuSMV2 model transformation is fully automated we anticipate that the proposed automated model transformation approach is a lot more flexible in adapting to the target languages of other model checkers, compared to a manual encoding approach. We also foresee that the implicit consistency of the generated target models with meta models of the used modeling and target languages will support syntactic and semantic correctness of the generated target models. This will greatly help to bridge the syntactic and semantic gaps between domain specific modeling languages, such as SysML, and the somewhat idiosyncratic input languages of various model checking and other verification tools.

Currently, the flexibility of the approach is somewhat limited by requiring substantial specific, manual coding effort in the Xpand framework when generating the target models. We plan to devise meta models for each of the considered model checker input languages and transform to them from the general meta model. This will allow to greatly reduce the Xpand related coding effort. We also plan to establish semantic correctness properties of the model to model transformation using this more refined model transformation approach. We finally plan to extend the approach to handling liveness properties, which brings up the question how to specify them in SysML/OCL.

References

1. Baier, C., Katoen, J.: Principles of Model Checking. MIT Press, Cambridge (2008)
2. Leitner-Fischer, F., Leue, S.: Causality checking for complex system models. In: Giacobazzi, R., Berdine, J., Mastroeni, I. (eds.) VMCAI 2013. LNCS, vol. 7737, pp. 248–267. Springer, Heidelberg (2013). https://doi.org/10.1007/978-3-642-35873-9_16
3. Blom, S., van de Pol, J., Weber, M.: LTSMIN: distributed and symbolic reachability. In: Touili, T., Cook, B., Jackson, P. (eds.) CAV 2010. LNCS, vol. 6174, pp. 354–359. Springer, Heidelberg (2010). https://doi.org/10.1007/978-3-642-14295-6_31
4. Object Management Group: OMG Systems Modeling Language, Specification 1.5 (2017). http://www.omg.org/spec/SysML
5. Friedenthal, S., Moore, A., Steiner, R.: A Practical Guide to SysML, 3rd edn. Morgan Kaufmann, San Francisco (2014)
6. IBM Corporation: Rational Rhapsody (2017). https://www.ibm.com/us-en/marketplace/rational-rhapsody
7. Sparx Systems: Enterprise Architect (2017). http://www.sparxsystems.com/products/ea/
8. Eclipse Foundation: Papyrus IDE (2015). https://www.eclipse.org/papyrus/index.php
9. Holzmann, G.J.: The SPIN Model Checker - Primer and Reference Manual. Addison-Wesley, Boston (2004)
10. Kwiatkowska, M., Norman, G., Parker, D.: PRISM 4.0: verification of probabilistic real-time systems. In: Gopalakrishnan, G., Qadeer, S. (eds.) CAV 2011. LNCS, vol. 6806, pp. 585–591. Springer, Heidelberg (2011). https://doi.org/10.1007/978-3-642-22110-1_47
11. Cavada, R., Cimatti, A., Jochim, C.A., Keighren, G., Olivetti, E., Pistore, M., Roveri, M., Tchaltsev, A.: NuSMV 2.6 user manual (1998). http://nusmv.fbk.eu/NuSMV/userman/v26/nusmv.pdf
12. Leitner-Fischer, F., Leue, S.: Quantum: quantitative safety analysis of UML models. In: QAPL. EPTCS **57**, 16–30 (2011)
13. Caltais, G., Leitner-Fischer, F., Leue, S., Weiser, J.: SysML to NuSMV model transformation via object-orientation. In: Berger, C., Mousavi, M.R., Wisniewski, R. (eds.) CyPhy 2016. LNCS, vol. 10107, pp. 31–45. Springer, Cham (2017). https://doi.org/10.1007/978-3-319-51738-4_3
14. Hunter, J., Lear, R.: Java Data Object Model (2015). http://www.jdom.org/index.html
15. Jouault, F., Allilaire, F., Bézivin, J., Kurtev, I.: ATL: a model transformation tool. Sci. Comput. Program. **72**(1–2), 31–39 (2008)
16. Eclipse Foundation: Xpand (2007). https://www.eclipse.org/modeling/m2t/?project=xpand
17. Eclipse Foundation: Eclipse Modeling Framework (2017). https://www.eclipse.org/modeling/emf/
18. Gauthier, J., Bouquet, F., Hammad, A., Peureux, F.: Verification and validation of meta-model based transformation from SysML to VHDL-AMS. In: MODEL-SWARD, pp. 123–128. SciTePress (2013)
19. Object Management Group: Unified Modelling Language, Specification 2.5.1 (2017). http://www.omg.org/spec/UML
20. Object Management Group: OMG Object Constraint Language, Specification 2.4 (2014). http://www.omg.org/spec/OCL

21. Manna, Z., Pnueli, A.: The Temporal Logic of Reactive and Concurrent Systems - Specification. Springer, New York (1992). https://doi.org/10.1007/978-1-4612-0931-7
22. Object Management Group: XML Metadata Interchange, Specification 2.5.1 (2015). http://www.omg.org/spec/XMI/
23. Object Management Group: OMG Meta Object Facility (MOF) Core Specification, Specification 2.0 (2016). http://www.omg.org/spec/MOF
24. Aljazzar, H., Fischer, M., Grunske, L. Kuntz, M., Leitner-Fischer, F., Leue, S.: Safety analysis of an airbag system using probabilistic FMEA and probabilistic counterexamples. In: QEST, pp. 299–308. IEEE Computer Society (2009)

Genetic Synthesis of Concurrent Code Using Model Checking and Statistical Model Checking

Lei Bu[1], Doron Peled[2(✉)], Dachuan Shen[1], and Yuan Zhuang[1]

[1] State Key Laboratory for Novel Software Technology, Nanjing University,
Nanjing, China
[2] Department of Computer Science, Bar Ilan University, Ramat Gan, Israel
doron.peled@gmail.com

Abstract. Genetic programming (GP) is a heuristic method for automatically generating code. It applies probabilistic-based generation and mutation of code, combined with "natural selection" principles, using a fitness function. Often, the fitness is calculated based on a large test suite. Recently, GP was applied for synthesizing correct-by-design concurrent code from temporal specification, where model checking was used for calculating the fitness function. A deficiency of this approach is that it uses a limited number of fitness values, based on a small number of modes for each verified specification property (e.g., satisfies, does not satisfy a given property). Furthermore, the need to apply model checking on many candidate solutions using the genetic process makes using an off-the-shelf model checker such as Spin prohibitively expensive. The repeated invocation of such a tool, compiling the code for a new candidate solution and running it, can render the performance of this approach several orders of magnitude slower than using an internal model checking. To tackle this problem, we describe here the use of a combination of statistical model checking, and a light use of model checking, for calculating the fitness required by GP.

1 Introduction

The classical approach for synthesis of interactive systems from temporal specification uses automata and game theory [25]. Synthesis of distributed or concurrent programs from temporal specifications is in general undecidable [26]. This calls for the use of heuristic methods. In particular, genetic programming based on model checking [15] employs a powerful heuristic search in the state space of candidate programs, which can be controlled and adjusted by an intelligent user.

The research in this paper was partially funded by an ISF-NSFC grant "Runtime Measuring and Checking of Cyber Physical Systems" (ISF award 2239/15, NSFC No. 61561146394). The authors from Nanjing Univeristy were also partially funded by a National Natural Science Foundation of China grant No. 61690204 and No. 61572249.

Genetic programming (GP) is an automatic method for generating code. It is based on beam search, i.e., a search that maintains in each generation a set of objects, rather than a *single* object. The search attempts to improve the quality of candidates from one generation to another, with mutual influence between candidates. Candidates propagate from one generation to the next one with probability based on their *fitness* value, which is an estimation on how close the candidate is from a correct solution. In addition, it uses the genetic operations of *mutation*, i.e., making small random changes to a candidate, and *crossover*, i.e., combining elements of two candidates. Since GP does not use backtracking, the only possibilities to deal with a failed search is to start with a new random seed or to try searching with a different fitness function.

Classical genetic programming is based on calculating the fitness function with respect to a large training set of test cases. Recently, using model checking for calculating the fitness function was studied in [14–18]. Model checking is a comprehensive approach for checking correctness, hence its use provides a greater assurance of the correctness of the code than testing. On the other hand, the number of correctness properties are typically not large, which results in a small set of fitness values. Additional fitness levels can be provided, e.g., "some executions satisfy a property". However, even then, the fitness landscape is far from being smooth [8], which may sometimes limit the ability of the genetic search to converge.

Model checking based GP requires performing model checking for all the candidate programs generated during the process. Hence, it benefits greatly from having a dedicated model checker that is implemented within the genetic programming tool. Without it, the use of an off-the-shelf model checking tool like Spin [12] would be several orders of magnitude slower. This motivates using alternative ways of checking the fitness of candidates such as randomized testing and statistical model checking. However, these methods only provide a limited assurance about the correctness of the generated code.

In this work, we suggest to use statistical model checking (SMC) [20,27] to replace part of the work that is done by model checking. SMC is a simulation-based solution, which is less time and memory intensive than classical model checking. The goal of SMC is to check sample execution paths of the system and use methods like statistical hypothesis testing to calculate the probabilities of the system to satisfy a given property within a given statistical error. Compared with the model checking verdicts, probability measurement can provide smoother indication about how much the model satisfies a given property, which can assist in the convergence of the genetic process. Typical tools for SMC include Plasma [21] and Uppaal [3].

Applying SMC, which is based on finite executions, we immediately experience several inherent obstacles. The statistical sampling of the executions is limited to finite length, hence, the correctness of the generated programs is not guaranteed by the statistical evaluation. In particular, some properties may fail in very few executions (rare events), which may be missed in the statistical evaluation. Conversely, properties that hold for long or infinite execution sequences may not be manifested during some of the finite executions that are checked. This suggests using a combination of SMC and model checking to achieve the best of both wofair scheds. Our approach combines SMC with light use of model checking, based on the Spin model checker, performed at the later stages of the genetic process.

2   Genetic Programming

During the 1970s, Holland [11] established the field known as *Genetic Algorithms* (GA). Individual candidate solutions are represented as fixed length strings of bits, corresponding to chromosomes in biological systems. Candidates are evaluated using a *fitness* function. The fitness approximates the distance of the candidate from a desired solution. Genetic algorithms evolves a *set of candidates* into a successor set. Each such set forms a *generation*, and there is no backtracking. Candidates are usually represented as fixed length strings. They progress from one generation to the next one according to one of the following cases:

- *Reproduction.* Part of the candidates are selected to propagate from one generation to the subsequent one. The reproduction is done at random, with probability relative to the relation between the fitness of the individual candidate and the average of fitness values in the current generation.
- *Crossover.* Some pairs of the candidates selected at random for reproduction are combined using the crossover operation. This operation takes parts of bitstrings from two parent solutions and combines them into two new solutions, which potentially inherit useful attributes from their parents.
- *Mutation.* This operation randomly alters the content of a small number of bits from candidates selected for reproduction (this can also be done after the crossover). One can decide on mutating each bit separately with some probability.

Unlike traditional point-by point search such as depth-first search or breadth-first search, the different candidates in a single generation have a combined effect on the search; progress tends to promote, improve and combine candidates that are better than others in the same generation. The process of selecting candidates from the previous generation and deciding whether to apply crossover or mutation continues until we complete a new generation. All generations are of some predefined fixed size N. This can be, typically, a number between 50 and 500. Genetic algorithms thus perform the following steps:

1. Randomly generate N initial candidates.
2. Evaluate the fitness of the candidates.
3. If a satisfactory solution is found, or the number of generations created exceeds a predefined limit (say hundreds or a few thousands), terminate.
4. Otherwise, select candidates for reproduction using randomization, proportional to the fitness values and apply crossover or mutation on some of them, again using randomization, until N candidates are obtained.
5. Go to step 2.

If the algorithm terminates unsuccessfully, we can restart it with a new random seed, or change the way we calculate the fitness function.

Genetic programming, suggested by Koza [19], is a direct successor of genetic algorithms. In GP, each individual organism represents a computer program. Programs are represented by variable length structures, such as trees (see Fig. 1) or a sequences of instructions. It is quite easy to transfer between a program and a syntax tree and vice versa. These trees are well typed. Each node is classified as *code, Boolean, condition* or *expression*. Leaf nodes are variables or constants, and other nodes have successors according to their type. For example, a while node (of type *code*) has one successor of type *Boolean* or *condition* and one successor of type *code* (for the loop body); a *Boolean* node and has two successors that can be of type *Boolean* or *condition*, and a *condition* node < has two successors of type *expression*. The genetic operations need to respect these (and possibly further) types, e.g., *expressions* cannot be exchanged with *Booleans*.

Crossover is performed by selecting subtrees on each of the parents, and then swapping between them. This forms two new syntax trees, having parts from both of their parents. There are several kinds of mutation operations. In *replacement* mutation, one picks at random a node in the tree, which is the root of a subtree. Then one throws away this subtree and replace it with a subtree of the same type, generated at random. In Fig. 1, the rightmost leaf node was chosen, which is marked with double ellipse. The subtree consists of this single node, representing the constant 1. Thus, it needs to be replaced with another expression, built at random. A new subtree was randomly generated, consisting of two nodes, representing the expression $a[0]$. In *insertion* mutation, a new node of the same type as the selected subtree is generated and is inserted just above it (type permitting); then one may need to complete the tree by constructing another descendant of the newly inserted node. For example, if we select an expression and insert above it a node that corresponds to addition $+$, it can be made one of the descendants to be summed up, say the left, but we need to complete the tree with a new right descendant. The *reduction* mutation has the opposite effect of *insertion*: the selected node is replaced with one of its offsprings (type permitting). In *deletion* mutation we remove the selected subtree, and recursively update the ancestors to make the program syntactically correct.

Syntax trees are not limited to a fixed size. Therefore the candidates can shrink or grow after mutation and crossover. In GP, there is actually a tendency of candidates to *bloat* with unnecessary code, for example, an assignment such as $a[1] := a[1]$. The countermeasure for this, called *parsimony pressure*, is to include a (small) negative value in the fitness function, corresponding to the length of the code. As a consequence, the resulting solutions are not expected to have a perfect fitness value, but instead they need to pass all the tests/verifications performed.

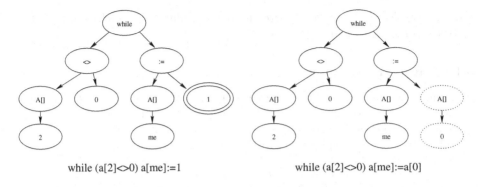

while (a[2]<>0) a[me]:=1   while (a[2]<>0) a[me]:=a[0]

Fig. 1. Mutation on a syntax tree

3 GP Based on Model Checking and Statistical Model Checking

We want to employ GP to synthesize concurrent programs from given a temporal specification. We use linear temporal logic, LTL syntax [24]. The input includes, besides the temporal specification, also a *configuration*, which restricts the parameters of the desired solution. The configuration can restrict the depth of the generated syntax trees, the variable used, the allowed arithmetic and Boolean operators, and the number of processes. It can also contain a template that restricts the code, e.g., dictates that the code is embedded within a fixed loop or contains some fixed parts of code. The template has several uses:

– Using the template we can guarantee part of the behavior of the targeted code, simplifying the specification.
– We use as specification formalism LTL, which is limited to assert on *all* the executions of the code. On top of that, we can use the template to force checking different cases, providing some expressive power of branching temporal logic such as CTL [2]. Furthermore, templates also provide a testbed environment with *uncontrolled* actions, where the code needs to behave under all the interactions with it. This provides some expressive power of game logics [5].
– The template can be used to limit the state space of the search, e.g., suggesting that a solution will start with an assignment, or that it is embedded in a main loop. This can reduce the complexity of the genetic search and improve the chance and speed of coverage.

In [14–18], GP based on model checking was described and experimented with. The fitness function was solely calculated based on model checking results. Using model checking instead of testing to calculate the fitness function for GP allows a more reliable evidence of the correctness of the code. On the other hand, model checking is computationally expensive. In [15–18], it was observed that the number of specification properties is rather small, which creates a small number of fitness values. Therefore, a few intermediate levels were added on top of the obvious *satisfies/does not satisfy* verdicts; in particular, levels such as *sometimes satisfies* and *satisfies with probability 1*.

3.1   A Running Example

As a running example, we look at synthesizing a solution for the well known *mutual exclusion* problem. Solutions for this problem from temporal specifications were synthesized using GP, where the fitness function is based on model checking [15,16]. The configuration provided dictates the following structure:

```
p1: While W1 do          p2: While W2 do
    nonCrit1:no-op           nonCrit2:no-op
    preCS1                   preCS2
    CS1:no-op               CS2:no-op
    postCS1                 postCS2
end while                end while
```

The labels nonCrit*i* represent the actions of the process p*i* outside the critical section. The labels CS*i* represent the critical section, which both processes want to enter a finite or unbounded number of times. These segments are not part of the synthesis task, and can be represented by trivial code no-op. The critical section is controlled by the code that will be synthesized for preCS*i* and postCS*i*. We require the following LTL properties:

Safety: $\Box\neg$(p1 *in* CS1 $\wedge$ p1 *in* CS2), i.e., there is no state where the program counters of both processes are in the critical section simultaneously.

Liveness: $\Box$(p*i* *in* preCS*i* $\rightarrow$ $\Diamond$p*i* *in* CS*i*), i.e., if a process wants to enter the critical section, then it will eventually succeed in doing so.

A solution that necessarily alternate between the process in entering their critical sections would also satisfy these conditions. Then, if one of them ceases to try entering its critical section, the other one can get blocked. To eliminate this problem, the variables W*i* in the configuration are used to control whether processes want to keep entering the critical section. We can set different values to W1 and W2 to control the program behavior in different scenarios, including both processes want to enter the critical section, or only one wants to enter the critical section. This part of the code is fixed and not subject to synthesis.

Note that the configuration assures that the duration of the critical sections CS*i* are finite. Hence there is no need to require that $\neg\Diamond\Box$p*i* *in* CS*i*. We assume no (goto) statements are allowed, hence the synthesized parts are executed to completion each time they are entered.

3.2   Replacing Model Checking with Statistical Model Checking

Due to the two deficiencies of the use of model checking in genetic programming mentioned, complexity and lack of smoothness of the fitness value, we were motivated to replace part of its use by statistical model checking. In particular, we generate for each GP candidate solution a large set of pseudo random executions; we check if these executions satisfy related specification properties.

The fitness function used in GP needs to be rather smooth in order to provide good convergence, and the statistical evaluation can provide multiple levels. Statistical evaluation may also be more affordable for some intricate synthesis problems. The simplicity of statistical methods is even further apparent for real time or cyber-physical systems. Another advantage that statistical model checking has over model checking is that it can be used for parametric systems and systems with infinite state space, where model checking has limited use for these applications.

For using statistical model checking over *finite* prefixes, we form a set of bounded temporal properties over *finite* prefixes of executions that are related to the original LTL properties over infinite sequences. Safety properties can be migrated directly to finite prefixes (A safety property is violated when there is a finite prefix that does so [1]). We use an additional temporal operator ♦, where ♦φ holds in a sequence when φ holds at its last state. A finite prefix may present only partial information, and the property may be violated or satisfied only in a longer prefix. The properties over finite prefixes that correspond to the original properties *provide support* to the case that the original properties hold for the infinite sequences, but do not always guarantee them. For example, instead of the liveness property, we use a property that a process enters its critical section some fixed amount of times. The larger this number is, the more we are convinced that the liveness property holds. However, a large number will only be manifested in a long prefix. We pick up these related properties over finite prefixes according to our intuition (we may fine tune them if the genetic process fails).

At the moment we do not have a way of obtaining these related properties *automatically* from the original LTL properties, and this can be the subject of further research (e.g., using genetic co-evolution [19] or learning). Nevertheless, we do not expect the synthesis of concurrent programs to be completely automatic, as it was shown to be undecidable [26].

We illustrate the choice of related properties over finite prefixes for the running example. Suppose that we decide to check n executions, each one of them is limited to a length of k. We can fine tune the parameters n and k on several test runs to see what works. We can also try to estimate the size (number of states) of the desired solution to provide such parameters where errors will be found with high probability [10].

We split the original liveness property into several bounded properties. The predicates $enter_i$ represent the total number of times process pi entered its critical section in the current prefix.

- B. The case that both processes want to enter the critical section. We enforce that by setting (W1∧W2). We add two counters $enter_1$ and $enter_2$ to indicate the times that each process enters the critical section. Out of which we have:
  - B_1. Both processes succeed entering the critical section multiple times:
    $\rho_{B_1} = ♦(enter_1 > 1 \land enter_2 > 1)$.

- B_2. One process enters the critical section multiple times and the other only once: $\rho_{B_2} = \blacklozenge((enter_1 > 1 \wedge enter_2 = 1) \vee (enter_1 = 1 \wedge enter_2 > 1))$.
- B_3, Only one process succeeds in entering, or both enter exactly once: $\rho_{B_3} = \blacklozenge(enter_1 + enter_2 \geq 1 \wedge 0 \leq enter_1 \times enter_2 \leq 1)$.
- B_4. Both processes do not succeed in entering their critical section $\rho_{B_4} = \blacklozenge(enter_1 + enter_2 = 0)$.
- O. Only one process p_1 wants to enter, when forcing (W1 $\wedge$ ¬W2). Out of which we have:
  - O_1. The process p_1 succeeds entering its critical section multiple times: $\rho_{O_1} = \blacklozenge(enter_1 > 1)$
  - O_2. The process p_1 succeeds entering its critical section only once: $\rho_{O_2} = \blacklozenge(enter_1 = 1)$
  - O_3, The process p_1 does not succeed entering its critical section: $\rho_{O_3} = \blacklozenge(enter_1 = 0)$

We mark the SMC probabilities (as estimated by an SMC tool, or just the portions of executions satisfying each property among the randomly generated test cases) of the model satisfying these given properties by P_{B_1}, P_{B_2}, P_{B_3}, P_{B_4}, P_{O_1}, P_{O_2} and P_{O_3} respectively and the safety property by P_M. The fitness function is based on the above parameters.

We have the following coefficients, which can be assigned various values between 0 and 1:

- α multiplies P_M, the probability that the model satisfies the safety property.
- $\beta_1, \beta_2, \beta_3$ multiply P_{B_1}, P_{B_2}, P_{B_3}, the probability that the model satisfies ρ_{B_1}, ρ_{B_2} and ρ_{B_3}, respectively.
- γ_1, γ_2 multiply P_{O_1}, P_{O_2} the probability that the model satisfies ρ_{O_1}, and ρ_{O_2}, respectively[1].

We enforce that $\beta_3 < \beta_2 < \beta_1$, $\gamma_2 < \gamma_1$. A possible fitness function is

$$(\alpha \times P_M + \beta_1 \times P_{B_1} + \beta_2 \times P_{B_2} + \beta_3 \times P_{B_3} + \gamma_1 \times P_{O_1} + \gamma_2 \times P_{O_2}) \times 100$$

We normalize fitness to be between 0 and 100 by requiring that $\alpha + \beta_1 + \gamma_1 = 1$.

3.3   Problems and Solutions in Using SMC for Fitness Function

We need to pay attention to some issues in transforming SMC probabilities into fitness results. We will first list the difficulties, and then suggest some solutions.

Limited Distinction of the Probabilistic Approach. Although providing a smooth fitness value range, SMC based fitness function is only a rough estimate. In particular, it is hardly reasonable to assume that a solution that has 75% of its sampled prefixes satisfy some properties is uniformly worse than one in which 85% of the sampled prefixes satisfy them. However, the use of stochastic

---

[1] The coefficients for P_{B_4} and P_{O_3} are both 0, as these cases correspond to an inept solution.

selection of candidates for propagation by the genetic programming algorithm, where the given fitness only affects the *probability* of selecting the candidate, rather than directly selecting the best fitted ones, somewhat smoothens out the difference between such similar cases.

False Positives: Failure of Properties that Appear as Rare Events. The executions where an error is demonstrated may be rare; in which case one may need a lot of experiments and would, by chance, not catch the bad executions. For mutual exclusion, the processes *may* enter the critical section simultaneously, but on many executions they just independently enter and then exit, where the simultaneous stay within the critical section is not manifested on the selected random prefixes.

False Negatives: Negative Bias Due to Scheduling. Another problematic situation is where some liveness properties would not show up on a substantial number of prefixes due to scheduling. In a particular finite execution, a process may fail to enter the critical section since the other process is scheduled more frequently, although it could do so in a longer prefix or under a different scheduling.

Fairness. Many solutions of the mutual exclusion are based on some fairness assumption [23]; there, without allowing both processes ample opportunities to progress, the liveness will not hold. In particular, this is the case for the classical *Dekker* solution for mutual exclusion, presented by Dijkstra [4]. However, fairness is defined over infinite executions, and SMC checks only finite ones.

In order to tackle the above issues, wcich stem from the randomness and finiteness of the checked prefixes, we used a combination of the following ideas.

Extending the Measurements. Depending on the checked property, we may want to extend the measurements. For example, for the safety property, we can check more executions to increase the probability that we find the violation. For the liveness property, we may want to use longer executions to diminish the effect of unfair scheduling. These parameters are adjusted after some initial failures to synthesize correct solutions.

Using Combination of Cases. Because we cannot rely on fairness, and our tested sequences are finite, we should learn about the satisfaction of a property from observing the *combination* of the random checks. Take for example the case where we want to check that a process is not prohibited from entering the critical section. There may exist some prefixes where it fails to do so. However, if in a large percentage of the executions, it succeeds in entering the critical section, this can be used as evidence that the failure in the minority of the executions is due to unfavored scheduling. Then, given a certain threshold, we may apply "majority rules" to conclude that the liveness property holds. Accordingly, we may decide that when at least, say, 70% of the executions are satisfy ρ_{B_1}, the fitness treats all the executions in B as if they all satisfy ρ_{B_1}. Accordingly, in that case we use a simpler fitness function $(\alpha \times P_M + \beta_1 \times (P_{B_1} + P_{B_2} + P_{B_3}) + \gamma_1 \times P_{O_1} + \gamma_2 \times P_{O_2}) \times 100$.

However, this is not the only possible conclusion for this measurement: it may not be the discrimination of the scheduling that makes a process fail to enter its critical section, but rather some scheduling that subsequently prevents the entrance to the critical section. Such a situation of multiple possible conclusions from the same statistical experiments can be resolved by the combined use of both majority rules *and* the light use of model checking (see below); model checking will catch such rare event errors that may otherwise not affect the fitness function.

Biasing the Probabilistic Selection. If we identify cases that may happen rarely, we can use biasing of the different choices in order to inspect them closer. For example, since catching violation of the safety property may be rare, we can reduce the probability of transitions that *exit* the critical section in favor of transitions of the other process that is outside the critical section. In essence, we are "waiting" for the other process to enter the critical section. For promoting liveness and providing more "fair" scheduling, we can decrease the probability of a transition of some process to be selected relative to the number of states where the other process has been waiting. A related technique for handling rare events, in the context of statistical model checking, is *importance splitting* [13], which split the test sequences into cases. Then one can zoom into checking cases where the rare events are believed to appear more frequently. This can also be a potential technique to handle the rare events problem.

Light Use of Model Checking as Certification or as Part of the Fitness. When candidates that receive very high fitness values are produced, in late generations, model checking can be used to certify that they indeed satisfy the desired properties. One can apply model checking sparingly, late on the genetic process, on candidates with already very high fitness value. We then may integrate the result of the model checking into the fitness and allow it to participate in additional generations.

Checking Ultimately Periodic Executions. We can replace checking finite executions by ultimately periodic ones. This can be done as in [7]. However, checking ultimately periodic sequences is more expensive than checking finite prefixes, as states on a sequence need to be hashed in order to detect cycles. This part was not implemented in our prototype.

4   Experiments

For each of the synthesis problems described above we performed experiments with SMC using Plasma [21]. Plasma uses Approximate Probabilistic Model Checking (APMC) [9] to provide a controlled accuracy on the statistical results[2]. For accelerating the performance, we have also implemented an ad-hoc statistical evaluation algorithm which shares some of the merits of SMC. This implementation selects a given number of finite execution sequences and calculates the

---

[2] The configuration of running Plasma in our experiment includes the approximation threshold $\epsilon = 0.05$, and the confidence threshold $\delta = 0.01$. Please refer to [9] for detailed explanation of these parameters.

ratio of executions that satisfy a given property. However, it does not provide a *significance level* [6] for the measurement result.

The model checking is performed by Spin. Spin works here as separate software interfacing with ours, which needs to prepare its own (multiple) files and performs compilation on each candidate it checks, in order to make the verification; each activation of Spin by our code is slower than the statistical evaluations we make per candidate, hence we applied it sparingly. The Spin model checker was invoked when the fitness value reaches some threshold, which we set as 98. If model checking fails, we continue the genetic process, since the failed candidate solutions may still contain good "genetic material" so we can proceed from this point based on the SMC fitness calculations.

4.1 Synthesis of Solutions for Mutual Exclusion

The first set of experiments we conducted is to use GP to synthesize solutions of mutual exclusion. Without using Spin in the last stage to do the certification, our implementation can generate dozens of solutions that reach the highest fitness value easily. For example, three representative solutions (a), (b) and (c) are shown below. The processes are symmetric. The variables *me* and *other* can be concretized to i and $(i+1)\ mod\ 2$ for process p_i $(1 \leq i \leq 2)$ respectively.

```
While W1 do              While W1 do              While W1 do
  v[me]=1                  v[me]=1                  v[me]=1
  While (v[2]!=me) do      While (v[2]==other) do   While (v[other]!=0) do
    v[2]=0                   v[2]=1                   While (v[other]==other) do
    if(v[other]!=me)        if(v[other]!=other)        v[me]=0
      v[2]=1                  v[2]=0                   end while
  end while               end while                 v[me]=1
  CS                       CS                       end while
  v[2]=other               v[2]=other               CS
end while                 end while                 v[me]=0
    (a)                       (b)                    end while
                                                       (c)
```

In the random simulations, both the processes show no violation of the mutual exclusion, starvation or deadlock. However, if we investigate the two solutions (a) and (b), we can find that they fail to satisfy the safety requirement. In some execution sequences, two processes can enter the critical section at the same time. Actually, for solution (a), among 10000 simulations, we could observe only 139 failures to satisfy the safety requirement. The unsafe scenario happened even fewer times in scenario (b): 4 times in 100000 simulations.

Solution (c) does not satisfy the liveness property. Actually, this solution represents the scenario where only if both processes want to enter the critical section indefinitely, then the liveness is satisfied; however, if one process decides to stop, then the other process will eventually be blocked forever. These examples demonstrate the problems raised in Sect. 3.3, where one may need a lot of experiments and may, by chance, not catch the bad rare events. This leads us to the next experiment, where we used model checking as certification in the last generation of the genetic process.

For candidates that received fitness value of at least 98, we used the model checker Spin [12] to certify whether the desired properties are satisfied. To do that, we implemented an automatic generator to translate the solution generated by GP into the modeling language PROMELA of Spin. If the model checking confirmed correctness, the procedure was stopped. Otherwise, we continued the GP process (until the limit on the number of generations has been reached).

After integrating Spin to the GP process, we started to obtain correct solutions. One such solution is (d) below. This is a perfect solution that shares a similar structure with Dekker's algorithm. Another representative solution, (e), is similar to Peterson's algorithm. The difference between (e) and (d) is that (e) allows Boolean operators *and* and *or* in the conditions.

```
While W1 do
    v[me]=1
    While (v[other]==1) do
        While (v[2]!=other) do
            v[me]=0
        end while
        v[me]=1
    end while
    CS
    v[me]=0
    v[2]=me
end while
    (d)
```

```
While W1 do
    v[me]=1
    v[2]=me
    While((v[other]!=0) && (v[2]==me)) do
    end while
    CS
    v[2]=other
    v[me]=0
end while
    (e)
```

4.2   Synthesizing Solutions for Round Robin Scheduling

In this example, there are three processes p_0, p_1 and p_2, each with a critical section. The processes need to enter their critical sections in round robin order. That is, p_0 before p_1, then p_2, and repeating that order with p_0, etc. The processes always want to enter the critical section (there is no flag Wi that restricts a process from wishing to enter). A trivial solution is that the processes would use a turn variable with three values, 0, 1 and 2, and each process will enter only when turn points to it and then increment it modulo 3. However, to make things less trivial, we require that we use only Boolean variables.

We allow solutions that are asymmetric in the sense that different values will be assigned in different processes. To allow that but still generate one candidate that will be concretized into three processes, we introduced to the generated process template as a syntactic construct an assignment statement of the form "v[i]=$b_0 b_1 b_2$", where $b_i \in \{0,1\}, 0 \leq i \leq 3$. This dictates that for the actual process p_i, the concretized statement will be v[i]=b_i. The variables which can show up in the solution are v[0] to v[3], and also v[me], v[other1], and v[other2].

For each process p_i, me is concretized to i, other1 is concretized as $(i+1) \bmod 3$, and other2 is concretized to $(i+2) \bmod 3$.

Our GP based synthesizer generated several solutions similar to the following solution (f).

While true do
  v[3]=010
  While(v[me]==001) do
    v[3]=101
    v[3]=010
  end while
  CS
  v[me]=001
  v[other1]=101
end while
    (f)

While true do
  While(v[me]==001) do
  end while
  CS
  v[me]=001
  v[other1]=101
end while
    (g)

We can see that each process in solution (f) refers to v[me] and v[other1]. There are also assignments to v[3] among the statements. However, as v[3] is not used in any conditions at all, such statements can be safely removed. This is done here manually to demonstrate the solution, resulting in solution (g), and we did not implement parsimony pressure.

Let us concretize the solution of the three process p_0, p_1, and p_2 to (g_0), (g_1), and (g_2) respectively. Observe that only three variables are used in the solution, which makes this solution simple and elegant.

While true do
  While(v[0]==0) do
  end while
  CS
  v[0]=0
  v[1]=1
end while
  (g_0)

While true do
  While(v[1]==0) do
  end while
  CS
  v[1]=0
  v[2]=0
end while
  (g_1)

While true do
  While(v[2]==1) do
  end while
  CS
  v[2]=1
  v[0]=1
end while
  (g_2)

4.3 Synthesizing Solutions for Dining Philosopher

This synthesis problem involves several philosophers sit around a table; a philosopher can take the fork on his right or the one on his left as they become available. If a philosopher wants to eat, she must have both left and right forks and if he finishes eating, she needs to put the forks back and these forks will be available again. The problem is to design a concurrent algorithm with no deadlock and, under fair scheduling [22], no philosopher will starve.

To support this problem, we extend the basic variable library with semaphore variables, and also add semaphore-related operations such as *wait* and *signal* into the expression library. Two representative solutions generated by our method are shown below in (h) and (i). It is interesting to see that although the GP synthesis processes allowed different kinds of programming constructs, including *while* loop, *if* condition and variable assignments in the expression library, the generated solutions are composed by only manipulation of semaphores. In these solutions, each philosopher (process) waits for the semaphore "mutex" to be free. Then she takes both the forks by capturing the semaphores "left" and "right"; these semaphores are be translated to $i \bmod m$ and $i + 1 \bmod m$, for the ith philosopher. After finishes eating, a philosopher frees the semaphores she captured.

Both solutions (h) and (i) can pass the verification of Spin. In (h), when one philosopher is eating, all the other philosophers are blocked. Solution (i) permits more concurrency, as only philosophers that share forks with the dining ones will be blocked.

```
While true do              While true do
    think                      think
    wait(mutex)                wait(mutex)
    wait(right)                wait(right)
    wait(left)                 wait(left)
    eat                        signal(mutex)
    signal(left)               eat
    signal(right)              signal(right)
    signal(mutex)              signal(left)
end while                  end while
     (h)                        (i)
```

4.4   Performance Evaluation

We run the experiments on the SMC guided GP synthesis using Plasma, and using our own implementation of statistical evaluation. The corresponding data are marked with SMC and SE, respectively. The data for mutual exclusion, round robin and dining philosopher problems are marked as ME, RR, and DP, respectively.

In the experiment, we have 100 seeds for each generation, and if the GP does not generate a correct solution in 2000 generations, we abandon the current GP search. As the GP process involves randomness, we repeated the experiments for each problem 100 times. We record the average time each execution takes, the number of successful executions which generate perfect solution, the average number that the GP calls model checker per execution, and the average number of generations per execution. The performance data is given below in Table 1.

The built-in statistical evaluation (SE) algorithm basically implements a simplified method of SMC. We can see the success ratio of SE for each problem aligns with SMC, but performs almost two orders of magnitude faster. However, our built-in SE diminished the effect of having most of the overhead due to the invocation and repeated use of the tool. In fact, given that Plasma was used in this mode, its use should be considered very efficient. Moreover, the light need to

Table 1. Performance data

Problem	Method	Total executions	Average time	Success executions	Success rate	Average Spin call	Average generations
ME	SMC	21	7 h 53 m	0	0	280	2000
	SE	100	341.4 s	15	15%	378.3	1754
RR	SMC	22	7 h 25 m	8	36.4%	502	1751
	SE	100	479.4 s	41	41%	436.3	1389
DP	SMC	11	15 h 23 m	9	81.8%	1178	687
	SE	100	34 m 6 s	65	65%	1287	116

invoke Spin (in both modes), also as an external tool, did not make the entire synthesis process prohibitively expensive.

This experiments seem to support that our proposed SMC guided genetic synthesis method can be applicable and efficient in concurrent code synthesis with the help of a built-in implementation of SMC and model checking procedures. It can generate a correct solution with high success ratio within reasonable time overhead. Moreover, allowing SMC tools such as Plasma or Uppaal [3], and model checking tools such as Spin, to be integrated into a GP tool would make the genetic synthesis both efficient and powerful.

We do not compare our experiments directly to the results in [15–18] since there, an internal tool for performing model checking was used, which was tailored to provide additional levels besides the yes/no (+counterexample) that standard model checkers provide. But a powerful internal model checking is hard to implement, and can hardly compete with the breadth of a tool like Spin. Moreover, even with the additional model checking levels, the fitness function may not be smooth enough in some cases.

5 Conclusions

We described here the use of genetic programming based on statistical model checking for synthesizing concurrent code from its temporal specifications. Using statistical model checking for defining the fitness function has several advantages over using model checking. In particular, it can be more efficient, can be used in domains where model checking is not applicable, and can provide a smoother function, which helps to converge. We presented different ideas and parameters for defining statistical based fitness function.

We implemented these ideas and conducted experiments of synthesizing concurrent code. One of the main lessons we learned is that some common properties, such as mutual exclusion or eventual progress, may happen to be quite elusive in a model. This makes the tradeoff between efficiency and reliability. This also calls for using model checking to verify the generated solutions.

We used a hybrid approach, where we used statistical model checking for most of the duration of the genetic process, but involved model checking at the later part of the genetic process to certify the potential solution.

Our research on the combination of genetic programming, synthesis, statistical model checking and model checking already shows some encouraging results, but also calls for several follow ups. Besides improving our implementation (in particular, using built-in verification, as the connection with Spin and Plasma is quite time consuming) there are some interesting theoretical/practical directions. One direction is the use of biasing of the randomized experiments. Finally, we intend to make more experiments in synthesizing code, in particular of timed, probabilistic and cyber physical systems, where statistical approaches, such as statistical model checking, are found to be quite efficient.

References

1. Alpern, B., Schneider, F.B.: Recognizing safety and liveness. Distrib. Comput. **2**(3), 117–126 (1987)
2. Clarke, E.M., Emerson, E.A.: Design and synthesis of synchronization skeletons using branching time temporal logic. In: Kozen, D. (ed.) Logic of Programs 1981. LNCS, vol. 131, pp. 52–71. Springer, Heidelberg (1982). https://doi.org/10.1007/BFb0025774
3. David, A., Larsen, K.G., Legay, A., Mikucionis, M., Poulsen, D.B.: Uppaal SMC tutorial. STTT **17**(4), 397–415 (2015)
4. Dijkstra, E.W.: Cooperating sequential processes. In: Hansen, P.B. (ed.) The Origin of Concurrent Programming, pp. 65–138. Springer, New York (1968). https://doi.org/10.1007/978-1-4757-3472-0_2
5. Finkbeiner, B., Schewe, S.: Coordination logic. In: Dawar, A., Veith, H. (eds.) CSL 2010. LNCS, vol. 6247, pp. 305–319. Springer, Heidelberg (2010). https://doi.org/10.1007/978-3-642-15205-4_25
6. Fisher, R.: Statistical Methods for Research Workers. Oliver and Boyd, Edinburgh (1925)
7. Grosu, R., Smolka, S.A.: Monte carlo model checking. In: Halbwachs, N., Zuck, L.D. (eds.) TACAS 2005. LNCS, vol. 3440, pp. 271–286. Springer, Heidelberg (2005). https://doi.org/10.1007/978-3-540-31980-1_18
8. Harman, M., Mansouri, S.A., Zhang, Y.: Search-based software engineering: trends, techniques and applications. ACM Comput. Surv. **45**(1), 11:1–11:61 (2012)
9. Hérault, T., Lassaigne, R., Magniette, F., Peyronnet, S.: Approximate probabilistic model checking. In: Steffen, B., Levi, G. (eds.) VMCAI 2004. LNCS, vol. 2937, pp. 73–84. Springer, Heidelberg (2004). https://doi.org/10.1007/978-3-540-24622-0_8
10. Hoeffding, W.: Probability inequalities for sums of bounded random variables. J. Am. Stat. Assoc. **58**(301), 13–30 (1963)
11. Holland, J.H.: Adaptation in Natural and Artificial Systems: An Introductory Analysis with Applications to Biology, Control and Artificial Intelligence. MIT Press, Cambridge (1992)
12. Holzmann, G.J.: The SPIN Model Checker. Pearson Education, Boston (2003)
13. Jegourel, C., Legay, A., Sedwards, S.: An effective heuristic for adaptive importance splitting in statistical model checking. In: Margaria, T., Steffen, B. (eds.) ISoLA 2014. LNCS, vol. 8803, pp. 143–159. Springer, Heidelberg (2014). https://doi.org/10.1007/978-3-662-45231-8_11
14. Johnson, C.G.: Genetic programming with fitness based on model checking. In: Ebner, M., O'Neill, M., Ekárt, A., Vanneschi, L., Esparcia-Alcázar, A.I. (eds.) EuroGP 2007. LNCS, vol. 4445, pp. 114–124. Springer, Heidelberg (2007). https://doi.org/10.1007/978-3-540-71605-1_11

15. Katz, G., Peled, D.: Genetic programming and model checking: synthesizing new mutual exclusion algorithms. In: Cha, S.S., Choi, J.-Y., Kim, M., Lee, I., Viswanathan, M. (eds.) ATVA 2008. LNCS, vol. 5311, pp. 33–47. Springer, Heidelberg (2008). https://doi.org/10.1007/978-3-540-88387-6_5
16. Katz, G., Peled, D.: Model checking-based genetic programming with an application to mutual exclusion. In: Ramakrishnan, C.R., Rehof, J. (eds.) TACAS 2008. LNCS, vol. 4963, pp. 141–156. Springer, Heidelberg (2008). https://doi.org/10.1007/978-3-540-78800-3_11
17. Katz, G., Peled, D.: Synthesizing solutions to the leader election problem using model checking and genetic programming. In: Namjoshi, K., Zeller, A., Ziv, A. (eds.) HVC 2009. LNCS, vol. 6405, pp. 117–132. Springer, Heidelberg (2011). https://doi.org/10.1007/978-3-642-19237-1_13
18. Katz, G., Peled, D.: Code mutation in verification and automatic code correction. In: Esparza, J., Majumdar, R. (eds.) TACAS 2010. LNCS, vol. 6015, pp. 435–450. Springer, Heidelberg (2010). https://doi.org/10.1007/978-3-642-12002-2_36
19. Koza, J.R.: Genetic Programming: On the Programming of Computers by Means of Natural Selection. MIT Press, Cambridge (1992)
20. Legay, A., Delahaye, B., Bensalem, S.: Statistical model checking: an overview. In: Barringer, H., Falcone, Y., Finkbeiner, B., Havelund, K., Lee, I., Pace, G., Roşu, G., Sokolsky, O., Tillmann, N. (eds.) RV 2010. LNCS, vol. 6418, pp. 122–135. Springer, Heidelberg (2010). https://doi.org/10.1007/978-3-642-16612-9_11
21. Legay, A., Traonouez, L.-M.: Statistical model checking of simulink models with plasma lab. In: Artho, C., Ölveczky, P.C. (eds.) FTSCS 2015. CCIS, vol. 596, pp. 259–264. Springer, Cham (2016). https://doi.org/10.1007/978-3-319-29510-7_15
22. Lehmann, D.J., Rabin, M.O.: On the advantages of free choice: a symmetric and fully distributed solution to the dining philosophers problem. In: Conference Record of the Eighth Annual ACM Symposium on Principles of Programming Languages, Williamsburg, Virginia, USA, January 1981, pp. 133–138 (1981)
23. Manna, Z., Pnueli, A.: How to cook a temporal proof system for your pet language. In: Conference Record of the Tenth Annual ACM Symposium on Principles of Programming Languages, Austin, Texas, USA, January 1983, pp. 141–154 (1983)
24. Pnueli, A.: The temporal logic of programs. In: 18th Annual Symposium on Foundations of Computer Science, Providence, Rhode Island, USA, 31 October–1 November 1977, pp. 46–57 (1977)
25. Pnueli, A., Rosner, R.: On the synthesis of a reactive module. In: Conference Record of the Sixteenth Annual ACM Symposium on Principles of Programming Languages, Austin, Texas, USA, 11–13 January 1989, pp. 179–190 (1989)
26. Pnueli, A., Rosner, R.: Distributed reactive systems are hard to synthesize. In: 31st Annual Symposium on Foundations of Computer Science, St. Louis, Missouri, USA, 22–24 October 1990, vol. II, pp. 746–757 (1990)
27. Younes, H.L.S., Simmons, R.G.: Probabilistic verification of discrete event systems using acceptance sampling. In: Brinksma, E., Larsen, K.G. (eds.) CAV 2002. LNCS, vol. 2404, pp. 223–235. Springer, Heidelberg (2002). https://doi.org/10.1007/3-540-45657-0_17

Quantitative Model Checking for a Controller Design

YoungMin Kwon[1(✉)] and Eunhee Kim[2]

[1] Department of Computer Science, The State University of New York, Korea,
119 Songdo Moonhwa-Ro, Yeonsu-Gu, Incheon 21985, Korea
youngmin.kwon@sunykorea.ac.kr
[2] 2e Consulting Corporation, 1710 KnK Digital Tower, 220 Yeongsin-Ro, Yeongdeungpo-gu,
Seoul 07288, Korea
keh@2e.co.kr

Abstract. A controller design method based on a quantitative model checking technique is proposed. Controllers have been designed to shape the closed-loop system's responses to meet certain requirements. We use *Linear Temporal Logic for Control* (LTLC) [16] to formally describe complex requirements and design a controller to meet the requirements with guidance from model checking results. The technique can help design a controller robust against errors systematically hampering the controller's efforts. To demonstrate the usefulness of the proposed technique, we exercised several controller design examples with different types of errors.

1 Introduction

In a Cyber-Physical System (CPS), computers not only perform computations on their memory, but interact with the physical world as well. With the advances in sensor and actuator technologies, CPS can be found in many places such as autonomous cars, smart home appliances, automated farms, and so on. Automatic controllers, right at the border between cyber systems and physical systems, are interfacing the two systems. As cyber systems are becoming more and more complex, it is crucial to be able to formally specify certain requirements about the physical systems and design controllers to guarantee them.

Automatic controllers have been designed to meet certain global properties of a system. For instance, Nyquist plots are drawn for the stability of a system, Bode plots are used to shape overall frequency responses [6]. Even though controllers are designed with some margin of errors, these design practices do not guarantee the non-existence of events that can violate certain properties. In other words, the system cannot guarantee the requirements when events are systematically hampering the system. Formally describing such requirements and designing a controller to meet the requirements will be crucial especially for mission critical or safety critical systems.

We propose a quantitative model checking technique to specify the requirements and to design a controller. Requirements about a closed-loop system are written in a quantitative temporal logic called *Linear Temporal Logic for Control* (LTLC) [1, 15, 16]

© Springer International Publishing AG, part of Springer Nature 2018
M. M. Gallardo and P. Merino (Eds.): SPIN 2018, LNCS 10869, pp. 292–307, 2018.
https://doi.org/10.1007/978-3-319-94111-0_17

and controller parameters are searched while guided by the model checking results. In this paper, we designed a Pole-placement controller whose pole locations are chosen by model checking results. Furthermore, we considered two types of measurement errors: simply bounded errors and an effect of buffering in sensors.

LTLC is expressive enough to specify nontrivial properties about the system. LTLC has the logical and temporal operators of *Linear Temporal Logic* (LTL) that make the specification concise and easy to understand [5, 12]. Its atomic propositions are linear (in)equalities about the input, output, and state variables of a hybrid system. Regarding the expressiveness of LTLC, an (in)equality specifies a hyperplane or a half space in the state space; their conjunctions can express a polytope in the space; and the disjunctions of the polytopes can form non-convex regions. Using the temporal operators, one can specify how such regions should change over time in the state space.

There have been model checking techniques for *infinite* state space. One of the first approaches is Timed Automata where clocks with a constant rate comprise the continuous state space [2]. A more expressive model is hybrid automata, where properties on the trajectories of continuous variables governed by differential equations can be specified [10], but its model checker implementations such as HyTech and UPPAAL handle simplified dynamics like clocks [11, 18]. HySAT, SpaceEX, and BACH are reachability checkers for hybrid automata [4, 7, 8]. Unlike model checkers, reachability checkers do not check whether a system satisfies a given specification usually written in a temporal logic, but check whether certain states can be reached. When considering computation paths only up to a certain finite length, the finite automaton for an LTLC formula might be checked by the reachability checkers. However, arguably, specifications expressed in a logic would be easier to manage than those described in an automaton.

In this paper, the LTLC model checking technique is introduced to check if a controller design can satisfy requirements. Another direction of utilizing the technique is to embed the model checking algorithm into the controller to generate a control input directly [17]. In particular, a goal is described in LTLC and its negation is model-checked within the controller. Because a counterexample contains a control input that can be applied to the system to achieve the original goal, LTLC model checking technique can be employed in the feedback control loop [16]. Model checking techniques have been used in the automatic control systems to find control strategies to satisfy high-level goals [9, 13, 14, 19, 23]. They are based on finite abstraction of state spaces, where a state space is partitioned into finite polytopes and a transition system is built on the equivalent sets of states. A control strategy is computed such that the transition system can satisfy the goals. One of the advantages the LTLC based technique has over the finite abstraction based approaches is that it does not need to pre-partition the whole state space which usually takes a long time.

2   Hybrid System Model

A hybrid system is a mixed system with a continuous system described by differential equations and a discrete system governed by discrete events. For example, changing the transmission gears of a car is a discrete event and the responses of the car at a certain gear position follow a differential equation. We will design a controller for a *Linear*

Time Invariant (LTI) system. Furthermore, to capture the effect of system dynamics changes, a hybrid system model is introduced. In this section, we formally define an LTI system, a hybrid system, and a computation path.

A *Linear System* is a system where the superposition principle holds. A *Linear Time Invariant System* is a linear system whose dynamics do not change over time. In this paper, we consider a discrete-time LTI system that can be obtained by periodically sampling its continuous-time counterpart.

Definition 1. *A discrete-time* Linear Time Invariant (LTI) system[1] *is a seven tuple* $L = \langle U, Y, X, A, B, C, D \rangle$, *where* $U = \{u_1, \ldots, u_{nu}\}$, $Y = \{y_1, \ldots, y_{ny}\}$, $X = \{x_1, \ldots, x_{nx}\}$ *are the set of input, output, and state variables respectively,* $A \in \mathbb{R}^{nx \times nx}$, $B \in \mathbb{R}^{nx \times nu}$, $C \in \mathbb{R}^{ny \times nx}$, *and* $D \in \mathbb{R}^{ny \times nu}$ *are system matrices.*   □

The relation between the input, output, and state variables of an LTI system satisfy the dynamics equations below.

$$\mathbf{x}(t + 1) = A \cdot \mathbf{x}(t) + B \cdot \mathbf{u}(t), \quad \mathbf{y}(t) = C \cdot \mathbf{x}(t) + D \cdot \mathbf{u}(t), \tag{1}$$

where $\mathbf{u} : \mathbb{N} \rightarrow \mathbb{R}^{nu}$, $\mathbf{y} : \mathbb{N} \rightarrow \mathbb{R}^{ny}$, and $\mathbf{x} : \mathbb{N} \rightarrow \mathbb{R}^{nx}$ are trajectories of the input, output, and state variables respectively. That is, $\mathbf{u}(t)_i = u_i$ at time t for $i = 1, \ldots, nu$, $\mathbf{y}(t)_i = y_i$ at time t for $i = 1, \ldots, ny$, and $\mathbf{x}(t)_i = x_i$ at time t for $i = 1, \ldots, nx$.

A hybrid system is a graph of LTI systems, called *modes*, such that the system can change its dynamics from the set of modes.

Definition 2. *A* Hybrid system *is a quintuple* $H = \langle U, Y, X, M, E \rangle$, *where* $U = \{u_1, \ldots, u_{nu}\}$, $Y = \{y_1, \ldots, y_{ny}\}$, $X = \{x_1, \ldots, x_{nx}\}$ *are the set of input, output, and state variables respectively,* $M = \{m_1, \ldots, m_{nm}\}$ *is a set of LTI systems called* modes, *and* $E = \{e_1, \ldots, e_{ne}\}$ *is a set of labeled directed edges between the modes.*   □

All modes of a hybrid system share the same set of input, output, and state variables. Therefore, a mode m_i of Definition 2 is in the form $m_i = \langle U, Y, X, A_i, B_i, C_i, D_i \rangle$ for $i = 1, \ldots, nm$. A labeled directed edge $e = (m_i, m_j, \psi)$ defines a mode-switch condition from m_i to m_j, where the label ψ is a propositional formula defining its enabling condition. When more than one edge are enabled at a time, the mode transition can nondeterministically occur along any of the enabled edges. For simplicity, we write $m_i \xrightarrow{\psi} m_j$ for (m_i, m_j, ψ) and $m_i \longrightarrow m_j$ for (m_i, m_j, T).

The syntax of the propositional formula[2] ψ is

$$\psi ::= \mathrm{T} \mid \mathrm{F} \mid AP \mid (\psi) \mid \neg\psi \mid \psi \wedge \psi \mid \psi \vee \psi \mid \psi \rightarrow \psi \mid \psi \leftrightarrow \psi,$$
$$AP ::= c_1 \cdot v_1 + \cdots + c_n \cdot v_n \bowtie d,$$

where $c_i, d \in \mathbb{R}$ for $i = 1, \ldots, n$, $v_i \in U \cup Y \cup X$ for $i = 1, \ldots, n$, and $\bowtie \in \{\leq, <, =, \neq, >, \geq\}$. The operators of ψ have their usual meanings and the truth value of AP

---

[1] We use the term LTI systems for both continuous-time LTI systems and discrete-time LTI systems when the usage is clear from the context.

[2] We use the term propositional formula because the semantics of LTLC is interpreted over each computation path where all the variables are assigned with a value.

depends on the system state. Let a state of a hybrid system $s \in M \times \mathbb{R}^{nu} \times \mathbb{R}^{ny} \times \mathbb{R}^{nx}$ be $s = (m, \mathbf{u}(t), \mathbf{y}(t), \mathbf{x}(t))$ and let an assignment function $\theta_s : U \cup Y \cup X \to \mathbb{R}$ be $\theta_s(v) = \mathbf{u}(t)_i$ if $v = u_i$ for some $i \in [1, nu]$, $\theta_s(v) = \mathbf{y}(t)_i$ if $v = y_i$ for some $i \in [1, ny]$, and $\theta_s(v) = \mathbf{x}(t)_i$ if $v = x_i$ for some $i \in [1, nx]$. Then, $c_1 \cdot v_1 + \cdots + c_n \cdot v_n \bowtie d$ is true in s iff $c_1 \cdot \theta_s(v_1) + \cdots + c_n \cdot \theta_s(v_n) \bowtie d$.

Let $\mu : \mathbb{N} \to M$ be a function that returns the mode at time t and by overloading the notations let $A : \mathbb{N} \to \mathbb{R}^{nx \times nx}$, $B : \mathbb{N} \to \mathbb{R}^{nx \times nu}$, $C : \mathbb{N} \to \mathbb{R}^{ny \times nx}$, and $D : \mathbb{N} \to \mathbb{R}^{ny \times nu}$ be the functions that return the system matrices A, B, C and D of the mode $\mu(t)$. Then the system variables satisfy the dynamics equations below.

$$\mathbf{x}(t+1) = A(t) \cdot \mathbf{x}(t) + B(t) \cdot \mathbf{u}(t), \quad \mathbf{y}(t) = C(t) \cdot \mathbf{x}(t) + D(t) \cdot \mathbf{u}(t). \tag{2}$$

Solving $\mathbf{x}(t)$ and $\mathbf{y}(t)$ in Eq. (2) in terms of $\mathbf{x}(0)$, $\mathbf{u}(\tau)$, $A(\tau)$, $B(\tau)$, $C(\tau)$ and $D(\tau)$ for $0 \le \tau \le t$,

$$\mathbf{x}(t) = \left(\prod_{i=0}^{t} A(i) \right) \cdot \mathbf{x}(0) + \sum_{i=0}^{t-1} \left(\prod_{j=i+1}^{t-1} A(j) \right) \cdot B(i) \cdot \mathbf{u}(i),$$
$$\mathbf{y}(t) = C(t) \cdot \mathbf{x}(t) + D(t) \cdot \mathbf{u}(t), \tag{3}$$

where $\prod_{i=0}^{t} A_i = A_t \cdot A_{t-1} \cdots A_1 \cdot A_0$.

Definition 3. *A computation path of a hybrid system $H = \langle U, Y, X, M, E \rangle$ is a function $\pi : \mathbb{N} \to M \times \mathbb{R}^{nu} \times \mathbb{R}^{ny} \times \mathbb{R}^{nx}$ such that $\pi(t) = (\mu(t), u(t), y(t), \mathbf{x}(t))$. The input, output, and state trajectories u, y, and $\mathbf{x}$ satisfy Eq. (2), and for all $t \ge 0$, there is a ψ such that $\mu(t) \xrightarrow{\psi} \mu(t+1) \in E$ and ψ is true in $\pi(t)$.* $\square$

3 Specifications on Hybrid System Models

Given a hybrid system, we need a way to write some desirable or undesirable properties about the system. We developed a quantitative temporal logic called *Linear Temporal Logic for Control* (LTLC) [16] to formally specify those properties. In this section, we describe the syntax and semantics of LTLC.

LTLC has the logical and temporal operators of LTL. However, to specify properties of the infinite states of hybrid systems, its atomic propositions are linear (in)equalities about the system states.

Definition 4. *The syntax of LTLC is*

$$\phi ::= \text{T} \mid \text{F} \mid AP \mid (\phi) \mid \neg\phi \mid \phi \wedge \varphi \mid \phi \vee \varphi \mid \phi \to \varphi \mid \phi \leftrightarrow \varphi \mid$$
$$\text{X}\,\phi \mid \Diamond\,\phi \mid \Box\,\phi \mid \phi\,\text{U}\,\varphi \mid \phi\,\text{R}\,\varphi,$$
$$AP ::= c_1 \cdot v_1 + \cdots + c_n \cdot v_n \bowtie d \mid H@m,$$

where $c_i, d \in \mathbb{R}$ for $i = 1, \ldots, n$, $v_i \in U \cup Y \cup X$ for $i = 1, \ldots, n$, $\bowtie \in \{\le, <, =, \neq, >, \ge\}$, and m is a mode of a hybrid system H. $\square$

$\pi, t \models \mathsf{T},$	$\pi, t \models_b \mathsf{T},$
$\pi, t \not\models \mathsf{F},$	$\pi, t \not\models_b \mathsf{F},$
$\pi, t \models c_1 \cdot v_1 + \cdots + c_n \cdot v_n \bowtie d$	$\pi, t \models_b c_1 \cdot v_1 + \cdots + c_n \cdot v_n \bowtie d$
$\quad \Leftrightarrow \sum_{i=1}^{n} c_i \cdot \theta_{\pi(t)}(v_i) \bowtie d,$	$\quad \Leftrightarrow \sum_{i=1}^{n} c_i \cdot \theta_{\pi(t)}(v_i) \bowtie d,$
$\pi, t \models H@m \Leftrightarrow \mu(t) = m,$	$\pi, t \models_b H@m \Leftrightarrow \mu(t) = m,$
$\pi, t \models \neg \phi \quad \Leftrightarrow \pi, t \not\models \phi,$	$\pi, t \models_b \neg \phi \quad \Leftrightarrow \pi, t \not\models_b \phi,$
$\pi, t \models \phi \wedge \varphi \Leftrightarrow \pi, t \models \phi$ and $\pi, t \models \varphi,$	$\pi, t \models_b \phi \wedge \varphi \Leftrightarrow \pi, t \models_b \phi$ and $\pi, t \models_b \varphi,$
$\pi, t \models \phi \vee \varphi \Leftrightarrow \pi, t \models \phi$ or $\pi, t \models \varphi,$	$\pi, t \models_b \phi \vee \varphi \Leftrightarrow \pi, t \models_b \phi$ or $\pi, t \models_b \varphi,$
$\pi, t \models \mathsf{X}\phi \quad \Leftrightarrow \pi, t+1 \models \phi,$	$\pi, t \models_b \mathsf{X}\phi \quad \Leftrightarrow t < b$ and $\pi, t+1 \models_b \phi,$
$\pi, t \models \phi \mathsf{U} \varphi \Leftrightarrow \pi, i \models \varphi$ for some $i \geq t$ and	$\pi, t \models_b \phi \mathsf{U} \varphi \Leftrightarrow \pi, i \models_b \varphi$ for some $t \leq i \leq b$ and
$\quad \pi, j \models \phi$ for all $t \leq j < i,$	$\quad \pi, j \models_b \phi$ for all $t \leq j < i,$
$\pi, t \models \phi \mathsf{R} \varphi \Leftrightarrow \pi, t \models \varphi$ and for $i > t,\ \pi, i \models \varphi$	$\pi, t \models_b \phi \mathsf{R} \varphi \Leftrightarrow \pi, i \models_b \phi$ for some $t \leq i \leq b$ and
$\quad$ if $\pi, j \not\models \phi$ for all $t \leq j < i.$	$\quad \pi, j \models_b \varphi$ for all $t \leq j \leq i.$
(a)	(b)

Fig. 1. (a) ternary satisfaction relation $\models$ and (b) bounded ternary satisfaction relation $\models_b$.

An implicit meaning of LTLC formulas is as follows. An *atomic proposition* $c_1 \cdot v_1 + \cdots + c_n \cdot v_n \bowtie d$ at time t is true iff the (in)equality is true when the variables are assigned with their corresponding values at the state $\pi(t)$. That is, $c_1 \cdot v_1 + \cdots + c_n \cdot v_n \bowtie d \Leftrightarrow c_1 \cdot \theta_{\pi(t)}(v_1) + \cdots + c_n \cdot \theta_{\pi(t)}(v_n) \bowtie d$. $H@m$ is true at time t iff the system is in mode m at the state $\pi(t)$. In other words, $H@m \Leftrightarrow \mu(t)$ is m.

The *logical operators* have their usual meanings. $\neg \phi$ is true at t iff ϕ is false at t; $\phi \wedge \varphi$ is true at t iff both ϕ and φ are true at t; $\phi \vee \varphi$ is true at t iff ϕ is true at t or φ is true at t. $\phi \rightarrow \varphi$ is equivalent to $\neg \phi \vee \varphi$ and $\phi \leftrightarrow \varphi$ is equivalent to $(\phi \rightarrow \varphi) \wedge (\varphi \rightarrow \phi)$.

The *temporal operators* have the following meanings. $\mathsf{X}\phi$ is true at t iff ϕ is true at $t + 1$; $\Box \phi$ is true at t iff ϕ is always true from t; $\Diamond \phi$ is true at t iff ϕ eventually becomes true at some $t' \geq t$. $\phi \mathsf{U} \varphi$ is true at t iff ϕ is true until φ eventually becomes true. To be more specific, $\phi \mathsf{U} \varphi$ is true iff there is a time $t' \geq t$ when φ becomes true and ϕ is true for all $\tau \in [t, t')$. $\phi \mathsf{R} \varphi$ is equivalent to $\varphi \mathsf{U} (\phi \wedge \varphi)$ except that ϕ is not required to hold eventually. Between U and R operators, the following equivalence holds $\neg(\neg \phi \mathsf{U} \neg \varphi) \equiv \phi \mathsf{R} \varphi$.

Formally, the semantics of LTLC can be defined by the ternary satisfaction relation $\models \subset \Pi \times \mathbb{N} \times \Phi$ and the binary satisfaction relation $\models \subset \mathcal{H} \times \Phi$, where Π is the set of computation paths, Φ is the set of LTLC formulas, and $\mathcal{H}$ is the set of hybrid system models. For simplicity, we write $\pi, t \models \phi$ for $(\pi, t, \phi) \in \models$ and $H \models \phi$ for $(H, \phi) \in \models$.

Definition 5. *The* ternary satisfaction relation $\models \subset \Pi \times \mathbb{N} \times \Phi$ *is defined in Fig. 1(a). Using the ternary relation, the* binary satisfaction relation $\models \subset \mathcal{H} \times \Phi$ *is*

$$H \models \phi \Leftrightarrow \phi, 0 \models \phi \text{ for all computation paths } \pi \text{ of } H.$$

$\square$

The missing operators have the following equivalence relations. $\Box \phi \equiv \mathsf{F} \mathsf{R} \phi$, and $\Diamond \phi \equiv \mathsf{T} \mathsf{U} \phi$. In addition, $\phi \mathsf{U} \varphi \equiv \varphi \vee (\phi \wedge \mathsf{X}(\phi \mathsf{U} \varphi))$ and $\phi \mathsf{R} \varphi \equiv (\phi \wedge \varphi) \vee (\varphi \wedge \mathsf{X}(\phi \mathsf{R} \varphi))$ are commonly used equivalence relations in the model checking process.

The satisfaction relation $\models$ of Definition 5 is about computation paths of the infinite length. However, in practice, it is difficult to track system trajectories unboundedly. Hence, we developed a bounded model checking algorithm, where infinite paths ending with a loop before the bound or paths whose satisfiability can be decided before the bound are considered [3].

To define the bounded satisfaction relation $\models_b$, let us define a helper function $\tau_{s,p} : \mathbb{N} \to [0, s + p)$ first. $\tau_{s,p}$ maps a time step to an index into a loop-ending computation path such that $\tau_{s,p}(t) = t$ if $t < s + p$; otherwise, $\tau_{s,p}(t) = s + (t - s) \bmod p$. A simple example of this helper is: $\tau_{1,2}(t) = 0, 1, 2, 1, 2, \ldots$ when $t = 0, 1, 2, 3, 4, \ldots$. A computation path ending with a loop of a period p starting from time s satisfies $\pi(t) = \pi(\tau_{s,p}(t))$ for $t \geq 0$.

Definition 6. *The* ternary bounded satisfaction relation $\models_b \subset \Pi \times \mathbb{N} \times \Phi$ *is defined in Fig. 1(b). Using the ternary relation, the* bounded binary satisfaction relation $\models_b \subset \mathcal{H} \times \Phi$ *is*

$$H \models_b \phi \Leftrightarrow \begin{cases} \pi, \ 0 \models \phi & if \ \pi(t) = \pi(\tau_{s,p}(t)) \ for \ t \geq 0 \ and \ s + p \leq b \\ \pi, \ 0 \models_b \phi & otherwise. \end{cases}$$

$\square$

Finally, to bring some intuitions about LTLC model checking algorithm, let us explain an example. LTLC model checking algorithm converts model checking problems to a series of *Linear Programming* (LP) [20] problems.

Example 1. Let $H = \langle \{u\}, \{y\}, \{x\}, \{M, N\}, \{M \to N, N \to N\} \rangle$ be a hybrid system, where $M = \langle \{u\}, \{y\}, \{x\}, 1, 2, 5, 0 \rangle$ and $N = \langle \{u\}, \{y\}, \{x\}, 3, -1, 7, 0 \rangle$ are its modes; a specification φ be $\varphi = \neg\phi$, where $\phi = (H @ M \wedge y \leq 1) \wedge X (y \leq 1) \wedge X X (y \leq 1)$; and the model checking problem be $H \models_2 \varphi$.

In the model checking process, we are looking for a counterexample that would violate the specification φ. Hence, we are searching for a computation path π, such that $\pi, 0 \models_2 \phi$. Based on the ternary satisfaction relation of Fig. 1(b), π should satisfy

$$\pi, 0 \models_2 H @ M \ \text{and} \ \pi, 0 \models_2 y \leq 1 \ \text{and} \ \pi, 1 \models_2 y \leq 1 \ \text{and} \ \pi, 2 \models_2 y \leq 1.$$

Let $\mu : \mathbb{N} \to \{M, N\}$ be a mode function, $\mathbf{u} : \mathbb{N} \to \mathbb{R}$, $\mathbf{y} : \mathbb{N} \to \mathbb{R}$, and $\mathbf{x} : \mathbb{N} \to \mathbb{R}$ be the input, output, and state trajectories of H. Observe that depending on the mode $\mu(t)$ at time t, $\mathbf{u}$, $\mathbf{y}$, and $\mathbf{x}$ conform either to the dynamics equations of M or to those of N. The variable assignment at time t is $\theta_{\pi(t)}(u) = \mathbf{u}(t)$, $\theta_{\pi(t)}(y) = \mathbf{y}(t)$, and $\theta_{\pi(t)}(x) = \mathbf{x}(t)$.

Let us check the conditions about the modes first. Based on the edges of H, μ can be either $MNNN \cdots$ or $NNN \cdots$. Because $H @ M$ in ϕ is enforced at $t = 0$, μ should be $MNNN \cdots$.

The other inequality conditions can be written as

$$\mathbf{y}(0) \leq 1 \ \text{and} \ \mathbf{y}(1) \leq 1 \ \text{and} \ \mathbf{y}(2) \leq 1.$$

We rewrite the conditions in term of $\mathbf{x}(0)$ and $\mathbf{u}$. Let a vector of variables $\mathbf{v}$ be $\mathbf{v} = [\mathbf{x}(0), \mathbf{u}(0), \mathbf{u}(1)]^T$, then because $\mu = MNNN \cdots$, the following holds.

$$\begin{aligned} \mathbf{y}(0) &= 5 \cdot \mathbf{x}(0) & &= [5, 0, 0] \cdot \mathbf{v}, \\ \mathbf{y}(1) &= 7 \cdot (\mathbf{x}(0) + 2 \cdot \mathbf{u}(0)) & &= [7, 14, 0] \cdot \mathbf{v}, \\ \mathbf{y}(2) &= 7 \cdot (3 \cdot (\mathbf{x}(0) + 2 \cdot \mathbf{u}(0)) - \mathbf{u}(1)) &= [21, 42, -7] \cdot \mathbf{v}. \end{aligned}$$

Now, the model checking problem can be converted to a feasibility checking problem as below.

$$\pi, \ 0 \not\models_2 \phi \Leftrightarrow \{\mathbf{v} : [5, 0, 0] \cdot \mathbf{v} \leq 1, \ [7, 14, 0] \cdot \mathbf{v} \leq 1, \ [21, 42, -7] \cdot \mathbf{v} \leq 1\} \neq \emptyset.$$

The feasibility of the set of inequality constraints can be checked by solving an LP problem [20]. There are feasible solutions that satisfy all inequalities. For example $\mathbf{v} = 0$ is a feasible solution. Hence, any computation path with $\mu(0) = N, \mu(t) = M$ for $t \geq 1$, $\mathbf{x}(0) = 0$, $\mathbf{u}(0) = 0$, and $\mathbf{u}(1) = 0$ violates the original specification φ. □

4   Pole-Placement Control

Automatic control is a process of shaping the system responses to a desirable one and making the system output follow a *reference value*. In a feedback control system the output of a system is fed back to a controller such that a *control input* to the system can be generated based on the value. The whole system is called a *closed-loop system*.

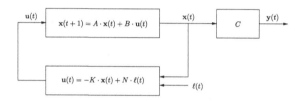

Fig. 2. Pole-placement control: $\mathbf{u}(t) = -K \cdot \mathbf{x}(t) + N \cdot \ell(t)$ is the control law.

The *transfer function* of a system is a mapping from the Laplace transform of an input to the Laplace transform of the output [6]. The roots of the numerator of the transfer function are called *zeros* and the roots of the denominator of the transfer function are called *poles*. The responses of the system are determined by the locations of the poles and zeros called *pole-zero constellation*.

Pole-placement control is a state space control method that shapes the closed-loop system responses by placing the poles of the system at predetermined locations [6]. Figure 2 shows a block diagram of a closed-loop system using the Pole-placement control. The target system, the upper-left-side block of Fig. 2, has the dynamics equations of Eq. (1). Let the *control law* be a feedback of a linear combination of the state variables.

$$\mathbf{u}(t) = -K \cdot \mathbf{x}(t),$$

where $K \in \mathbb{R}^{nu \times nx}$ is a design parameter that we need to decide. Substituting this equation into Eq. (1), the characteristic equation of the closed-loop system is

$$\det(p \cdot I - A + B \cdot K) = 0.$$

The poles of the closed-loop system are the roots of this polynomial and K can be computed once the desired locations of the poles are decided.

The control law above decides the transient responses of the system, but we still need to make the system follow a reference value. Considering the reference input $\ell(t)$ the control law has the following form.

$$\mathbf{u}(t) = -K \cdot \mathbf{x}(t) + N \cdot \ell(t), \tag{4}$$

where the value of $N \in \mathbb{R}^{nu \times ny}$ can be computed from A, B, C, D, and K matrices [6]. Equation (4) is the control law of Pole-placement control, represented by the lower block of Fig. 2.

In this paper, we employed the LTLC model checking technique to decide the locations of the poles. Specifically, the desirable responses of the closed-loop system were described in LTLC and the locations of the poles were iteratively searched while guided by the model checking results.

Model checking an uncontrolled system is straightforward: in a model checking problem $H \models \phi$, the system dynamics of Eq. (2) can be easily described in H. However, model checking a closed-loop system is a little trickier unless the dynamics of the closed-loop system are computed separately. To avoid this additional step and to make the proposed method readily applicable to many situations, we embedded the control law in the specification ϕ. Particularly, the control law was brought in as an always enforced equality constraint between the input $\mathbf{u}(t)$ of Eq. (2) and the RHS of the control law of Eq. (4). To restrict the computation paths to only those that respect the control law, we added ϕ_c below to a specification as a precondition.

$$\phi_c = \square\,(\mathbf{u} = -K \cdot \mathbf{x} + N \cdot \ell).$$

Observe that the equality sign between $\mathbf{u}$ and $-K \cdot \mathbf{x} + N \cdot \ell$ is not the assignment but the equality constraint.

5   Controller Design Guided by LTLC Model Checking

To demonstrate the proposed method, we design a helicopter velocity control system [6]. We will express properties such as the settling time, the maximum overshoot, etc. in LTLC and evaluate the effects of measurement errors through model checking. Guided by model checking results, we will design a Pole-placement controller and make it robust against the errors.

5.1   Pole-Placement Controller Design

Figure 3 shows a third-order continuous-time dynamics model of the longitudinal motion of a helicopter. By sampling the continuous-time model at $T = 100\,\text{ms}$ period, we acquired its discrete-time dynamics equations. Let $w(t)$ be a wall clock and $\ell(t)$ be a constant input of one that will be used for a clock duration and for a reference input

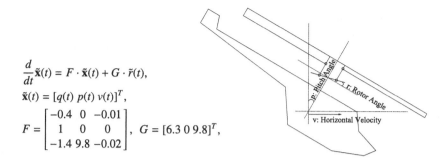

$$\frac{d}{dt}\tilde{\mathbf{x}}(t) = F \cdot \tilde{\mathbf{x}}(t) + G \cdot \tilde{r}(t),$$

$$\tilde{\mathbf{x}}(t) = [q(t)\ p(t)\ v(t)]^T,$$

$$F = \begin{bmatrix} -0.4 & 0 & -0.01 \\ 1 & 0 & 0 \\ -1.4 & 9.8 & -0.02 \end{bmatrix}, \quad G = [6.3\ 0\ 9.8]^T,$$

Fig. 3. A helicopter model. In the dynamics equations, q and p are the pitch rate and the pitch angle of the fuselage respectively, v is the horizontal velocity, and r is the rotor angle.

value. Let $\mathbf{x}(t)$ be $[q(t), p(t), v(t), w(t)]^T$ and $\mathbf{u}(t)$ be $[r(t), \ell(t)]^T$, then the discrete-time model obtained by the *Zero Order Hold* (ZOH) method [21] with 100 ms sampling interval is

$$\mathbf{x}(t+1) = A \cdot \mathbf{x}(t) + B \cdot \mathbf{u}(t), \tag{5}$$

where the matrices A and B are in the mode n of Fig. 4.

The hybrid system model with this single mode is

$$H = \langle U, Y, X, \{n\}, \{n \longrightarrow n\}\rangle, \quad n = \langle U, Y, X, A, B, 0, 0\rangle,$$

where $U = \{r, \ell\}$ is the set of input variables, $Y = \{\}$ is the empty set for the output variables, $X = \{q, p, v, w\}$ is the set of state variables, and n is the LTI system model.

From Eq. (4), the control law is in the form

$$r(t) = N \cdot \ell(t) - Kq \cdot q(t) - Kp \cdot p(t) - Kv \cdot v(t).$$

Suppose that we want to place the poles of the closed-loop system at 0.7, $0.7 \cdot e^{\frac{\pi}{12}i}$ and $0.7 \cdot e^{-\frac{\pi}{12}i}$, then $N = 0.6833$, $Kq = 0.1644$, $Kp = 5.2374$, and $Kv = 0.6793$.

This control law can be described in LTLC as

$$\phi'_c = \Box\,(\phi_c), \quad \text{where} \quad \phi_c = (r = N \cdot \ell - Kq \cdot q - Kp \cdot p - Kv \cdot v),$$
$$\phi'_\ell = \Box\,(\phi_\ell), \quad \text{where} \quad \phi_\ell = (\ell = 1).$$

The desired properties about the closed-loop system can be specified in LTLC as well. (1) we want to limit the maximum *overshoot* to 0.1 m/s when the reference input is 1 m/s. Because the output variable for the velocity is v, using the *always* operator, this condition can be written as below.

$$\phi'_o = \Box\,(\phi_o), \quad \text{where} \quad \phi_o = (v \le 1.1).$$

(2) we want to keep the maximum *pitch-angle* not larger than 0.13 radian. Similarly to the previous condition, we can make an always formula about the output variable p.

$$\phi'_a = \Box\,(\phi_a), \quad \text{where} \quad \phi_a = (p \le 0.13).$$

(3) with regard to the *settling-time*, we want to maintain the velocity of helicopter within the interval $[0.9, 1.1]$ m/s from 1.5 s onwards. In general, the time step t used in LTL model checking processes is not exposed to the specification. However, we can define a clock like $w(t + 1) = w(t) + T \cdot \ell(t)$ and explicitly use it in the specification. To specify that this settling-time condition is enforced only after 1.5 s, we used the precondition $w(t) \geq 1.5$ in the always formula as below.

$$\phi'_s = \square\,(\phi_s), \quad \text{where } \phi_s = (w \geq 1.5 \rightarrow (0.9 \leq v \wedge v \leq 1.1)).$$

(4) finally, the initial condition that the system is in the relaxed state can be expressed as below.

$$\phi_i = (q = 0 \wedge p = 0 \wedge v = 0 \wedge w = 0).$$

Combining them, the overall specification ϕ can be constructed as below.

$$\phi = (\phi_i \wedge \square\,\phi_c \wedge \square\,\phi_\ell) \rightarrow (\square\,\phi_o \wedge \square\,\phi_a \wedge \square\,\phi_s).$$

One of the practical concerns is that we will need to check the specification over and over again while searching for the location of poles. Hence, any speed up in the model checking process will greatly improve the whole design process. An immediate improvement is to combine the *always* operators together as below so that the Büchi automaton $\mathcal{B}_\phi$ for the specification ϕ has a smaller number of nodes.

$$\phi = (\phi_i \wedge \square\,(\phi_c \wedge \phi_\ell)) \rightarrow \square\,(\phi_o \wedge \phi_a \wedge \phi_s).$$

A more significant improvement came from removing the *always* operators all together. Checking the bounded satisfaction relation $\models_b$ of Fig. 1(b) is usually faster than its unbounded counterpart $\models$ of Fig. 1(a).[3] Observe that, based on Fig. 1(b), *always* formula does not satisfy $\models_b$. If we relax the validation to a finite horizon, then we can reformulate the specification that can be checked by the efficient $\models_b$.

It might be easier to understand the formula to build by examining its counterexample. All counterexamples violate any of ϕ_o, ϕ_a, or ϕ_s conditions at some time. On the other hand, the computation paths that do not satisfy ϕ_c and ϕ_ℓ before any of ϕ_o, ϕ_a, or ϕ_s are violated cannot be a counterexample. Likewise, computation paths that do not satisfy the precondition ϕ_i initially should be disregarded as well. To recap, a counterexample is a computation path that satisfies ϕ_i initially and satisfies ϕ_c and ϕ_ℓ until any of ϕ_o, ϕ_a, or ϕ_s are violated. Hence, the reformulated specification to check is

$$\phi = \phi_i \rightarrow \neg(\,(\phi_c \wedge \phi_\ell)\,\mathsf{U}\,\neg(\phi_o \wedge \phi_a \wedge \phi_s)\,).$$

Note that counterexamples satisfy $\phi_i \wedge (\,(\phi_c \wedge \phi_\ell)\,\mathsf{U}\,\neg(\phi_o \wedge \phi_a \wedge \phi_s)\,)$.

For a bound of 18, the model checking problem we want to examine is

$$H \models_{18} \phi.$$

---

[3] To check the ternary satisfaction relation $\models$, LTLC model checker has to find accepting runs ending with a loop and examine the feasibility of the runs generated by the Cartesian product of the accepting runs and computation paths ending with a loop of all possible periods.

```
model:                                   edge
 const                                    Enn = n -> n, Ens = n -> s,
  ### controller params & err bound       Esn = s -> n, Ess = s -> s;
  Kq=0.1644,Kp=5.2374,Kv=0.6793,N=0.6833  system
  EB=0.0005;                              ### ex1, ex2
 var                                       sys = ( {n}, {Enn} );
  ### pitch rate, pitch angle, velocity   ### ex3
  q: state, p: state, v: state,           # sys = ( {n, s}, {Enn, Ens, Esn, Ess} );
  ### errors in q, p, v
  eq: input, ep: input, ev: input,
  ### measured q, p, v                    specification:
  mq: output, mp: output, mv: output,     condition
  ### rotor angle, constant one            init = (q=0 /\ p=0 /\ v=0 /\ w=0 /\ rr=0),
  r: input, l: input,                      overshoot = (v <= 1.1),
  ### wall-clock, last rotor angle         settling_time = (w >= 1.5 ->
  w: state, rr: state;                                     (0.9 <= v /\ v <= 1.1)),
 mode                                      pitch_angle = (p <= 0.13),
  ### sampled at 100 msec interval         ebound = ( -EB < eq /\ eq < EB /\
  n = {                                               -EB < ep /\ ep < EB /\
   q = 0.9608*q-0.0005*p-0.0010*v+0.6171*r,           -EB < ev /\ ev < EB ),
   p = 0.0980*q+1.0000*p         +0.0311*r, precond = (ctrl_law /\ l = 1 /\ ebound),
   v =-0.0888*q+0.9790*p+0.9981*v+0.9457*r, ### ex1
   mq = q, mp = p, mv = v, rr = r,         ctrl_law = (r = N*l - Kq*q  - Kp*p  - Kv*v),
   w = w + 0.1*l },                        ### ex2
  ### sampled at 90 msec interval          # ctrl_law = (r = N*l - Kq*q  - Kp*p  - Kv*v
  s = {                                    #                    - Kq*eq - Kp*ep - Kv*ev),
   q = 0.9608*q-0.0005*p-0.0010*v+0.6171*r, ### ex3
   p = 0.0980*q+1.0000*p         +0.0311*r, # ctrl_law = (r = N*l - Kq*mq - Kp*mp - Kv*mv),
   v =-0.0888*q+0.9790*p+0.9981*v+0.9457*r, spec = (init -> ~(precond U ~(overshoot /\
   mq= 1.0040*q         +0.0001*v-0.0631*rr,                              settling_time /\
   mp=-0.0100*q+1.0000*p         +0.0003*rr,                              pitch_angle)));
   mv= 0.0145*q-0.0980*p+1.0002*v-0.0985*rr,
   rr= r,                                  check
   w = w + 0.1*l };                        sys |= spec in 18;
```

Fig. 4. LTLC description for the hybrid system model and the specification.

Figure 4 shows an LTLC-Checker description for the model checking problem. In the description, contents from the # mark to the end of the line are comments. The description has two main sections: model section for a hybrid model definition and specification section for describing a model checking problem. Input, output, and state variables are defined after var tag with their corresponding types suffixed. Using the variables, LTI systems and edges are defined after mode and edge tags respectively. A hybrid system comprising the modes and edges is defined after system tag. Regarding the checker description for the operators of LTLC, the logical operators $\land$, $\lor$, $\neg$, $\rightarrow$, and $\leftrightarrow$ are /\, \/, ~, ->, and <-> respectively. The temporal operators X, U, R, $\Diamond$, and $\Box$ are X, U, R, <>, and [] respectively. Finally, sys |= spec in 18 after check tag describes the model checking problem $H \models_{18} \phi$.

To simplify the example, we restricted the locations of poles to $\{r, r \cdot e^{\frac{\pi}{12}i}, r \cdot e^{-\frac{\pi}{12}i}\}$ and looked for the range of r that would make the closed-loop system satisfy the requirements. While model checking the description of Fig. 4 with the controller parameters Kq, Kp, Kv, and N computed from the locations of poles, we found that if r is in the range of $0.700 \leq r \leq 0.716$, the controller satisfies the requirements. The responses of a controller when $r = 0.715$ are in Fig. 5(a) and (b) although their trajectories are disturbed by errors.

5.2   Controller Design with Measurement Errors

Practically all measurements about a system have errors coming from various sources like device errors, environmental noise, and so on. Here, we design a controller that can satisfy the requirements despite the presence of measurement errors. We do not assume that the errors are governed by any dynamics equations or they have any statistical behaviors. Instead, they can take any values in a range and trying to drive the closed-loop system to violate the requirements. One can regard the model checking process a two player game: the errors are trying to attack the system to violate the requirements, whereas the controller is trying to make the system comply with them.

We consider a case where additive errors are disturbing some or all of state variables directly. The measurement errors do not alter the underlying system state, but they feed incorrect state information to the controller and have effects on the computation of the next control input. The control law is reformulated as below.

$$\mathbf{u}(t) = -K \cdot (\mathbf{x}(t) + \mathbf{e}(t)) + N \cdot \ell(t),$$

where $\mathbf{e} : \mathbb{N} \to \mathbb{R}^{nx}$ is the measurement error function. The state trajectory of the closed-loop system deviates from the ideal one from the next step onward.

For the helicopter example, let $eq(t)$, $ep(t)$, and $ev(t)$ be the measurement errors in the pitch rate, pitch angle, and velocity. Including these errors, the control law is rewritten as below.

$$r(t) = N \cdot \ell(t) - Kq \cdot (q(t) + eq(t)) - Kp \cdot (p(t) + ep(t)) - Kv \cdot (v(t) + ev(t)).$$

To describe the new control law in LTLC, we added three input variables eq, ep, and ev respectively for the errors in the pitch rate, pitch angle, and velocity. These variables are added to the state variables q, p, and v in the control law and disturb the computation of the next control input value. The control law in LTLC is

$$\phi'_c = \square \, (\phi_c), \quad \text{where} \quad \phi_c = (r = N \cdot \ell - Kq \cdot (q + eq) - Kp \cdot (p + ep) - Kv \cdot (v + ev)).$$

Observe that the additive measurement errors do not touch the system dynamics directly, but disturb the control law and change the state trajectories of the closed-loop system. During the LTLC model checking process, the checker will try to find error functions $eq(t)$, $ep(t)$, and $ev(t)$ that can violate the requirements.

For these measurement errors, we assume that they are always within $(\underline{e}, \bar{e})$ range, where $\underline{e} = -0.0005$ and $\bar{e} = 0.0005$. This *error bound* condition can be expressed in LTLC as follows

$$\phi'_e = \square \, (\phi_e), \quad \text{where} \quad \phi_e = \underline{e} < eq \wedge eq < \bar{e} \ \wedge \ \underline{e} < ep \wedge ep < \bar{e} \ \wedge \ \underline{e} < ev \wedge ev < \bar{e}.$$

With the reformulated control law ϕ_c and the error bound condition ϕ_e, the combined formula ϕ to check is as below.

$$\phi = \phi_i \to \neg(\, (\phi_c \wedge \phi_\ell \wedge \phi_e) \, \mathbf{U} \, \neg(\phi_o \wedge \phi_a \wedge \phi_s) \,).$$

When the locations of the poles are $\{r, \ r \cdot e^{\frac{\pi}{12}i}, \ r \cdot e^{-\frac{\pi}{12}i}\}$, the closed-loop system satisfies the requirements if $0.703 \le r \le 0.707$.

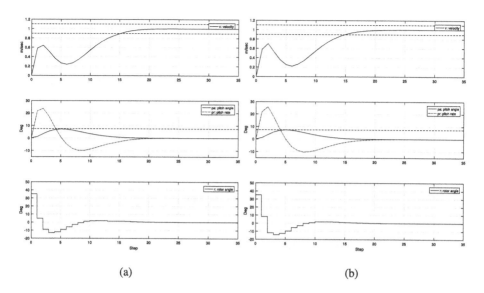

Fig. 5. Helicopter responses of the Pole-placement control. (a) System responses with measurement errors of Sect. 5.2 and (b) System responses with mode switches of Sect. 5.3 in every step.

Figure 5(a) shows the responses of the system when $r = 0.715$. Because r is not in the safe range of $[0.703, 0.707]$, the model checker reported a sequence of measurement errors $eq(t)$, $ep(t)$, and $ev(t)$ in the counterexample. Figure 5(a) is plotted when these error values were added to the states in the control law. Observe that at time 15, the velocity is slightly below 0.9 and the requirement is violated.

5.3   Controller Design with Nondeterministic Dynamics Changes

Unexpected system dynamics change poses a nontrivial challenge to a controller design. Some examples of such systems are: an airplane flying at different altitudes shows different aerodynamics, a car changes its dynamics after shifting the transmission gear, the ADME process of a drug shows different drug kinetics when the drug molecules outnumber the enzymes, and so on. It is desirable or even critical to design a controller that can maintain its required properties regardless of the system dynamics changes. In this section, we will demonstrate how LTLC model checking can help design a controller that is robust against the dynamics changes.

Some smart sensors perform measurements at a specific interval and keep the results in a buffer. On data request, they return the buffered value without making a new measurement. Suppose that the sensors of the helicopter example sample 10 times during a 100 ms discretization interval. Then, depending on when the last measurement is buffered and when the data request is made, the data can be as much as 10 ms old. Furthermore, if the data requests and the data measurements are closely aligned, the readings can be either without any delay or 10 ms stale. To the controller, this buffering effect may look like a system dynamics change. We model this dynamics change by a hybrid system with two modes: one for the normal sampling and one for the 10 ms hasty sampling.

Discrete-time system dynamics are obtained from their continuous-time counterparts by the ZOH sampling. Let $\tilde{u} : \mathbb{R} \to \mathbb{R}^{nu}$ and $\tilde{x} : \mathbb{R} \to \mathbb{R}^{nx}$ be continuous-time trajectories for the input and state variables respectively, $u' : \mathbb{N} \to \mathbb{R}^{nu}$ and $x' : \mathbb{N} \to \mathbb{R}^{nx}$ be their discrete-time counterparts, and let the continuous-time dynamics equations of an LTI system be

$$\frac{d}{dt}\tilde{x}(t) = F \cdot \tilde{x}(t) + G \cdot \tilde{u}(t).$$

Let δ be a buffering delay, T be the discretization interval, and $T' = T - \delta$, then the discrete-time model has the following dynamics equations.

$$\tilde{x}((t + 1) \cdot T') = e^{F \cdot T'} \cdot \tilde{x}(t \cdot T') + \left(e^{F \cdot T'} \cdot \int_0^{T'} e^{-F \cdot \tau} d\tau \cdot G \right) \cdot \tilde{u}(t \cdot T')$$

$$= A' \cdot \tilde{x}(t \cdot T') + B' \cdot \tilde{u}(t \cdot T'),$$

$$x'(t + 1) = A' \cdot x'(t) + B' \cdot u'(t).$$

However, because the actual state trajectory is still governed by Eq. (5), and the buffered measurement is from the actual state $x(t)$,

$$x'(t + 1) = A' \cdot x(t) + B' \cdot u(t). \tag{6}$$

That is, we need both x' and x state vectors in the model checking. Because doubling the state space significantly slows down the model checking process (it quadruples A matrix and doubles B and C matrices), we reformulated Eq. (6) to make x' an output vector as below.

$$\begin{bmatrix} x'(t+1) \\ u(t) \end{bmatrix} = \begin{bmatrix} A' & B' \\ 0 & 1 \end{bmatrix} \cdot \begin{bmatrix} x(t) \\ u(t) \end{bmatrix} = \begin{bmatrix} A' & B' \\ 0 & 1 \end{bmatrix} \cdot \begin{bmatrix} A & B \\ 0 & 1 \end{bmatrix}^{-1} \cdot \begin{bmatrix} A & B \\ 0 & 1 \end{bmatrix} \cdot \begin{bmatrix} x(t) \\ u(t) \end{bmatrix}$$

$$= \begin{bmatrix} A' & B' \\ 0 & 1 \end{bmatrix} \cdot \begin{bmatrix} A & B \\ 0 & 1 \end{bmatrix}^{-1} \cdot \begin{bmatrix} x(t+1) \\ u(t) \end{bmatrix} = C' \cdot \begin{bmatrix} x(t+1) \\ u(t) \end{bmatrix},$$

where $0 \in \mathbb{R}^{2 \times 3}$ is a matrix of zeros and $1 \in \mathbb{R}^{2 \times 2}$ is the identity matrix. C' exist if the system is *controllable*. Let an extended state vector be $x(t) = [q(t), p(t), v(t), w(t), r'(t)]$, and an output vector be $y(t) = [q'(t), p'(t), v'(t)]$, where $r'(t)$ is the previous value of $r(t)$, and $q'(t)$, $p'(t)$, and $v'(t)$ are the measured pitch rate, pitch angle, and velocity respectively. Then, the dynamics equations are

$$x(t + 1) = A \cdot x(t) + B \cdot u(t), \quad y(t) = C \cdot x(t), \tag{7}$$

where A and B are extended from Eq. (5) to accommodate the new state variable r' with the dynamics $r'(t + 1) = r(t)$, and C is the first 3 rows of C'. The elements of C matrix are in the mode s of Fig. 4.

A hybrid system model can be built as below using the two modes (a normal mode n and a hasty mode s).

$$H = \langle U, Y, X, \{n, s\}, \{n \longrightarrow n, n \longrightarrow s, s \longrightarrow n, s \longrightarrow s\} \rangle,$$

$$n = \langle U, Y, X, A, B, I, 0 \rangle, \quad s = \langle U, Y, X, A, B, C, 0 \rangle,$$

where $U = \{r, \ell\}$, $Y = \{q', p', v'\}$, and $X = \{q, p, v, w, r'\}$. Observe that from mode n, H can switch its mode to s or remain in n nondeterministically. Similarly, from mode s, H can move to n or stay in s nondeterministically.

The LTLC specification for the control law is

$$\phi_c' = \Box (\phi_c), \quad \text{where} \ \phi_c = (r = N \cdot \ell - Kq \cdot q' - Kp \cdot p' - Kv \cdot v').$$

Using the new control law ϕ_c, the LTLC formula to check is

$$\phi = \phi_i \rightarrow \neg((\phi_c \wedge \phi_\ell) \cup \neg(\phi_o \wedge \phi_a \wedge \phi_s)).$$

Like the previous examples, when the locations of the poles are $\{r, r \cdot e^{\frac{\pi}{12}i}, r \cdot e^{-\frac{\pi}{12}i}\}$, the closed-loop system satisfies the requirements if $0.700 \le r \le 0.715$. Figure 5(b) shows the trajectories of input, output, and state variables when $r = 0.715$ and the system mode switches between n and s at every step. The figure shows that the closed-loop system satisfies the requirements despite the mode switches.

6   Conclusion

Using the LTLC model checking technique, required properties about a control system can be formally specified and the controller can be designed to satisfy the requirements. We proposed a controller design method guided by LTLC model checking results and showed that the resulting closed-loop system is robust against errors not just stochastically disturbing the system but also systematically hampering it as well.

One of the missing elements in the proposed technique is the state observer. Instead of adding measurement noise directly to the state variables, we are working on extending the model checking technique to incorporate state observers like a Kalman filter [22]. We are expecting a more efficient controller design using the probability distributions of errors.

With the advances in CPS and IoT technologies, computer systems will interact more tightly with physical systems. Because the behaviors of physical systems are commonly modeled by differential equations, a natural way to interface cyber systems and physical systems is a logic that can handle quantitative values. We believe many quantitative techniques, including the proposed LTLC model checking technique, will produce many fruitful results.

Acknowledgement. The authors thank the anonymous referees for their helpful comments. This work was supported by MSIP, Korea under the ICTCCP program (IITP-2017-R0346-16-1007) and by KEIT under the GATC program (10077300).

References

1. LTLC-Checker. https://sites.google.com/site/youngminkwon
2. Alur, R., Dill, D.L.: A theory of timed automata. Theor. Comput. Sci. **126**, 183–235 (1994)
3. Biere, A., Cimatti, A., Clarke, E., Zhu, Y.: Symbolic model checking without BDDs. In: Cleaveland, W.R. (ed.) TACAS 1999. LNCS, vol. 1579, pp. 193–207. Springer, Heidelberg (1999). https://doi.org/10.1007/3-540-49059-0_14

4. Bu, L., Li, Y., Wang, L., Li, X.: BACH: bounded reachability checker for linear hybrid automata. In: Formal Methods in Computer Aided Design, pp. 65–68. IEEE Computer Society (2008)
5. Clarke, E., Grumberg, O., Peled, D.: Model Checking. MIT Press, Cambridge (2000)
6. Franklin, G.F., Powell, J.D., Emami-Naeini, A.: Feedback Control of Dynamic Systems, 3rd edn. Addison Wesley, Reading (1994)
7. Fränzle, M., Herde, C.: HySAT: an efficient proof engine for bounded model checking of hybrid systems. Formal Methods Syst. Des. **30**, 179–198 (2007)
8. Frehse, G., Le Guernic, C., Donzé, A., Cotton, S., Ray, R., Lebeltel, O., Ripado, R., Girard, A., Dang, T., Maler, O.: SpaceEx: scalable verification of hybrid systems. In: Gopalakrishnan, G., Qadeer, S. (eds.) CAV 2011. LNCS, vol. 6806, pp. 379–395. Springer, Heidelberg (2011). https://doi.org/10.1007/978-3-642-22110-1_30
9. Girard, A., Pola, G., Tabuada, P.: Approximately bisimilar symbolic models for incrementally stable switched systems. Trans. Autom. Control **55**, 116–126 (2010)
10. Henzinger, T.A.: The theory of hybrid automata. In: Annual Symposium on Logic in Computer Science, pp. 278–292. IEEE Computer Society (1996)
11. Henzinger, T.A., Ho, P.-H., Wong-Toi, H.: HyTech: a model checker for hybrid systems. In: Grumberg, O. (ed.) CAV 1997. LNCS, vol. 1254, pp. 460–463. Springer, Heidelberg (1997). https://doi.org/10.1007/3-540-63166-6_48
12. Holzmann, G.J.: The model checker spin. IEEE Trans. Softw. Eng. **23**, 279–295 (1997)
13. Kloetzer, M., Belta, C.: A fully automated framework for control of linear systems from temporal logic specifications. Trans. Autom. Control **53**, 287–297 (2008)
14. Kress-Gazit, H., Fainekos, G.E., Pappas, G.J.: Temporal-logic-based reactive mission and motion planning. Trans. Robot. **25**, 1370–1381 (2009)
15. Kwon, Y.M., Agha, G.: LTLC: linear temporal logic for control. In: Egerstedt, M., Mishra, B. (eds.) HSCC 2008. LNCS, vol. 4981, pp. 316–329. Springer, Heidelberg (2008). https://doi.org/10.1007/978-3-540-78929-1_23
16. Kwon, Y., Kim, E.: Bounded model checking of hybrid systems for control. IEEE Trans. Autom. Control **60**, 2961–2976 (2015)
17. Kwon, Y., Kim, E., Jeong, S., Lee, A.: Quantitative model checking for a smart grid pricing. In: International Conference on the Quantitative Evaluation of Systems (QEST), pp. 55–71. IEEE (2017)
18. Larsen, K.G., Pettersson, P., Yi, W.: UPPAAL in a nutshell. Int. J. Softw. Tools Technol. Transf. **1**, 134–152 (1997)
19. Liu, J., Ozay, N., Topcu, U., Murray, R.M.: Synthesis of reactive switching protocols from temporal logic specifications. IEEE Trans. Autom. Control **58**, 1771–1785 (2013)
20. Luenberger, D.G.: Linear and Nonlinear Programming, 2nd edn. Addison Wesley, Reading (1989)
21. Oppenheim, A.V., Willsky, A.S.: Signals and Systems. Prentice-Hall, Englewood Cliffs (1983)
22. Start, H., Woods, J.W.: Probability and Random Processes with Applications to Signal Processing, 3rd edn. Prentice-Hall, Upper Saddle River (2002)
23. Tabuada, P., Pappas, G.J.: Linear time logic control of discrete-time linear systems. Trans. Autom. Control **51**, 1862–1877 (2006)

Modelling Without a Modelling Language

Antti Valmari[✉] and Vesa Lappalainen

University of Jyväskylä, Jyväskylä, Finland
{antti.valmari,vesa.t.lappalainen}@jyu.fi

Abstract. Developments in computer hardware and programming languages, in this case C++, have made it feasible to write models of concurrent systems under verification in the programming language, instead of some established modelling language such as Promela. While this does not reduce the usefulness of modelling languages, it offers new possibilities that may be advantageous, for instance, when teaching state space ideas to newcomers or when experimenting with new scientific ideas. In earlier work, we were able to express everything else fairly naturally in C++, except the set of transitions. The present study uses C++ lambda functions to represent naturally transitions that consist of a tail state, guard, body, and head state. We discuss two implementations, a simple one and a faster one. We present measurements demonstrating that the loss of performance compared to the earlier approach is not big. Starting to use our approach is easy, because one only needs to have a C++ compiler and download (not install) one C++ file.

Keywords: Explicit state spaces · Modelling languages
Implementation issues

1 Introduction

In this publication, our focus is on concurrency aspects of systems. Therefore, by a *modelling language* we mean a language that has been designed for model checking concurrency aspects. Often, but not always, the model is an abstraction that, for instance, replaces the computation of a checksum by a nondeterministic choice between two values "correct checksum" and "incorrect checksum". A *programming language*, on the other hand, is a language meant for implementing systems. It need not support concurrency. In an implementation, abstractions of the kind mentioned above are not made.

Even when focusing on concurrency aspects, and therefore abstracting away from many details such as the computation of checksums, a model may have to contain some sequential computation. For instance, in a telecommunication protocol, the number of retransmission attempts may be counted and compared against a pre-defined constant maximum value. Therefore, many modelling languages contain at least some machinery for expressing sequential or functional computation.

© Springer International Publishing AG, part of Springer Nature 2018
M. M. Gallardo and P. Merino (Eds.): SPIN 2018, LNCS 10869, pp. 308–327, 2018.
https://doi.org/10.1007/978-3-319-94111-0_18

If the machinery is powerful enough, then it may be possible to express the system, instead of just an abstraction, in the modelling language. There may be a compiler that can compile the model into one or more executables that can be installed in the hardware components of the system. In this case, the model is actually a program and the modelling language is a programming language. That is, a language may be both a modelling and a programming language.

Because of the computational complexity of model checking, it is often the case (at least with current state of the art) that the system cannot be verified but its abstraction that focuses on concurrency aspects can. Therefore, although the distinction between modelling and programming languages is not sharp, we feel it important to maintain a distinction between modelling and programming. Modelling is the act of writing something for the purpose of model checking, and programming is the act of writing something for implementation purpose.

There are tools that can model check systems expressed in ordinary programming languages, such as Java PathFinder [21], Bandera (another toolset for Java) [2], and CBMC (C/C++ bounded model checker) [1]. When they succeed, they make it possible to forget about the distinction between programming and modelling. Because of the complexity of verification, they often fail.

A well-designed modelling language, such as Promela [6], FDR-CSP [11], or CPN ML [7,9], has many advantages. It supports some modelling paradigm very well. It facilitates efficient model checking. If it has many users, it serves as a widely known medium for sharing models. If it is powerful and flexible, it can also be used, albeit perhaps clumsily, for model checking tasks that arise from other domains than what it was designed for. For instance, encoding place/transition Petri nets [10] in Promela would be unnatural but certainly possible. The same can be said about the wolf, goat, cabbage and farmer puzzle, or the knight's tour.

On the other hand, learning a modelling language is a non-trivial task, in particular for a newcomer to model checking of concurrent systems. In addition to learning mundane details of the language, such as how loops and **if**-statements are written, the newcomer must grasp the fundamental ideas of concurrent execution and nondeterministic choice between alternative atomic actions, and various concepts for expressing properties that should be checked on the model. These ideas are radically different from everything that many students and software engineers have encountered before. To avoid state explosion, the newcomer must also learn to use so little memory in the model that it seems ridiculous from ordinary programming point of view. Furthermore, installing SPIN, FDR, or CPN Tools is not absolutely trivial.[1]

In the case of Java PathFinder, Bandera, and CBMC, the students need not learn a new low-level syntax. On the other hand, the use of Java or C/C++ as such makes the above-mentioned fundamental ideas of concurrency and nondeterminism somewhat implicit, making it harder to learn them. In many (albeit not all)

---

[1] The first author tried to install SPIN to Ubuntu 16.04 LTS according to the instructions at [12]. It failed because of the absence of yacc in the system, but succeeded after installing yacc. He also tried both of the Linux precompiled executables at http://spinroot.com/spin/Bin/ in vain.

algorithm textbooks such as [3], algorithms are expressed in pseudocode, to avoid hiding the essence behind low-level implementation issues. We believe that for the same reason, when introducing model checking to newcomers, it is advantageous to use a notation that brings concurrency and nondeterminism forward.

From the research point of view, to experiment with an idea, it may be necessary to make modifications to the input language or other features of the verification tool in use. SPIN is distributed freely in source form, so making such modifications is possible. However, because SPIN is a big program, making modifications to it is far from trivial.

It is often possible to express the state space construction problem in terms of guarded transitions that act on shared variables. That is, there is a set of variables, called *state variables*, and a set of transitions. A transition consists of a Boolean function on the state variables and of a (possibly complicated) piece of code that makes assignments to the state variables. The value of the former tells whether or not the transition is *enabled*. If the transition is enabled, then the latter may be executed, assigning new values to zero or more state variables, based on the earlier values of the state variables. This approach makes concurrency and nondeterminism explicit.

Petri nets are clearly an instance of this idea. The processes of Promela can be interpreted in these terms by treating the location of control of each process as an extra state variable. On-the-fly process creation goes beyond the basic version of this model. However, it need not be among the first topics that are taught to a newcomer in model checking.

It is the opinion, and to some extent also the experience, of the first author that it is easier for newcomers to learn the fundamentals of state spaces with guarded transitions on state variables, because they are so different from ordinary programming languages that the learner is not misguided by earlier intuition on sequential programs. For instance, it is sometimes hard for a newcomer to accept that a process may choose the second nondeterministic alternative (e.g., timeout) even if also the first (e.g., inputting a message) is enabled. It becomes less hard, if the alternatives do not look like an ordinary **if**-statement with **else** replaced by : :. Guarded transitions on state variables are also sometimes a very good formalism for experimenting with new model checking algorithms.

Of course, this does not mean that one should reject established modelling languages and switch to guarded transitions on state variables. It only means that sometimes there are valid reasons for using something else than an established modelling language.

The research that led to the present study started in autumn 2014 as an attempt to give students a small quickly written tool with which they could play with state space ideas, without having to install any program or learn any new syntax. The students had strong background in C++ [13] and sequential programming, varied but mostly rather weak background in theoretical aspects of software and computer science, and little background in concurrency. The idea was that students write the guards and assignment parts of guarded transitions in C++ (where the assignment parts are not restricted to just assignments, but may contain loops, etc.), and the file containing them is `#included` to a program written by the first author which constructs the state space. The students also write C++ functions that specify some correctness properties, the simplest example being a function that checks a state and either deems it good or returns an error message in the form of a character string chosen by the student.

This use of a programming language is fundamentally different from how Java or C/C++ is used with Java PathFinder, Bandera, or CBMC. The latter aim at model checking implementations. Therefore, they use the semantics of the programming language as such. Our approach aims at expressing and model checking abstractions (in the sense discussed above). The semantics of concurrency and nondeterminism are not picked from the native semantics of C++, but defined outside the definition of C++ and implemented as classes and other C++ mechanisms. The main goal was not to build a heavy-duty verification tool. Instead, it was to make it as easy as possible for newcomers to learn essential ideas behind model checking. Even so, the resulting tool is actually fast.

The first version of the tool suffered from serious weaknesses. Most importantly, the global state was represented as a single unsigned integer, forcing the students to represent state variables as bit segments within it. Despite this, the tool was pedagogically successful. Almost all students understood the idea of exhaustive search and became able to model such systems as the knight's tour, and most students succeeded in modelling a non-trivial concurrent system such as a token ring protocol. At the same time, the first author wanted to experiment with a new way [17, 18] of applying stubborn set/partial order methods, to solve the so-called ignoring problem [4, 14] much better than before. The tool proved suitable for this purpose.

To let the modeller use more than the 32 (or 64) bits of a single unsigned integer to represent the global state, a C++ class `state_var` was written that looks like an ordinary variable to the modeller but behind the scenes operates on the data structure that stores the so far constructed states. As a consequence, all but one aspects of the modelling of concurrent systems and their correctness properties as systems of guarded transitions on state variables became simple and intuitive. The remaining problem was that often the transitions had to be modelled as complicated collections of `switch`- and `if`-statements. At that stage, the tool was given the name ASSET (A State Space Exploration Tool) and published [16].

Then it turned out that the complicated `switch`-statements can be avoided by representing the transitions with the aid of C++ lambda functions. The present study focuses on this idea.

Section 2 introduces the example system used in this study. In Sect. 3, it is modelled for ASSET. Natural modelling of transitions relies on two C++ classes written for this purpose. A straightforward version of them is shown in Sect. 4, and a faster but more complicated version is discussed in Sect. 5. Section 6 presents some measurements comparing the two implementations to each other and to a model based on the use of `switch` and `if` statements. There also is a tiny comparison to SPIN. The study is concluded in Sect. 7.

2   A Demand-Driven Token Ring

In this section we present the system that is used as the main example in this publication. It is from [15,16], but we model it in a different fashion.

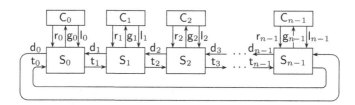

Fig. 1. Overall structure of the demand-driven token ring

Figure 1 shows its architecture. It is a demand-driven token ring consisting of n *clients* $C_0, \ldots, C_{n-1}$ and n *servers* $S_0, \ldots, S_{n-1}$. There is precisely one *token* in the ring. Each client has a region in its code that is called *critical section*. The purpose of the system is to ensure *mutual exclusion* between the clients, that is, two clients must never be simultaneously in their critical sections. Client i requests for access to its critical section by executing the action r_i. If server i does not have the token, it obtains it as is described below. When it has the token, it grants client i the permission by executing g_i. Now client i is in its critical section. When client i leaves its critical section, it executes l_i to inform the server that it may now give the token to the next server.

When necessary, server i demands the token from the previous server by executing d_i. The demand progresses in the ring until it reaches the server in possession of the token. Let that server be number j. When server j no longer needs the token, it gives it to the next server by executing $t_{j\oplus 1}$, where $j \oplus 1 = 0$ if $j = n-1$ and $j \oplus 1 = j+1$ if $0 \le j < n-1$. The token travels in the ring to server i. The servers through which it travels may serve their own clients before passing the token to the next server.

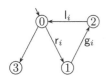

0: **wait until** C_i has requested or $S_{i\oplus 1}$ needs the token
   goto 1
1: **wait** until I have the token
   if C_i has requested **then** grant it permission; **goto** 2
   else give the token to $S_{i\oplus 1}$; **goto** 0
2: **wait until** C_i has left its critical section
   give the token to $S_{i\oplus 1}$; **goto** 0

Fig. 2. The clients as labelled transition systems (left) and servers in pseudocode (right)

The clients can be easily described precisely. Figure 2 left shows them as labelled transition systems. Each client has a terminal state (state 3) and a transition to it, to model the fact that a client need not request for access to its critical section if it does not want to. We will now discuss this detail a bit.

The termination branch (or some other modelling trick) is necessary to avoid a modelling trap. Assume that after getting the token, each server always waits until its client makes a request, then serves the client, and only then passes the token forward. This is unacceptable, because it may take a long time before the client makes the request, forcing other clients to wait unnecessarily. What is worse, if the server's own client never requests, then other clients that have requested are never served. However, if a client consists of just an r_i-g_i-l_i-cycle, then this error is not caught. This is because then the model lacks the possibility of the server's own client not requesting in the described situation. The request transition is then enabled, and will therefore occur, if nothing else can happen in the system. The termination branch makes it possible for the request transition to not occur, resulting in a deadlock and thus revealing the error.

The typical way of solving the above-mentioned problem is the use of so-called weak fairness assumptions as described in [8]. However, the termination branch is also valid, and has certain advantages. It tends to make non-progress errors manifest themselves as illegal deadlocks instead of unfair cycles, making them technically easy to detect. It is also better compatible with so-called partial order/stubborn set methods that help keep the size of the state space manageable. It has a solid theoretical justification via the notion of stable failures in process algebras. Further discussion can be found in [19] or in Sect. 3 of [17,18].

The labelled transition systems that represent the servers are too big and unintuitive to be shown here. (Please see [15] for a slight variant.) This is because the behaviour of a server depends on the presence or absence of a request by its client, the presence or absence of a demand for the token by the next server, whether the server itself has expressed such a demand, and whether it has the token. Figure 2 right describes the servers via a mixture of a state machine and natural language. In the next section we will see a more precise description in the form of guarded transitions on state variables.

3   An ASSET Model of the Example System

In this section we illustrate that, using C++ lambda functions, our example system can be expressed as a guarded transition model, in a readable fashion.

In many modern programming languages, libraries constitute an intermediate layer between a program and the core language. When a program uses, say, a sorting subroutine that is picked from a library, it gets a significant piece of code that is usually not counted as a part of the program, although it is not part of the core language either. If a better sorting subroutine becomes available, the program may be easily modified to use it.

Similarly, the model in this section relies on some facilities, one version of which will be developed in Sect. 4 and an alternative version in Sect. 5. We do not consider these facilities as part of the model proper, since they play a similar role as subroutines picked from a library. (We do admit, however, that we have not yet implemented them in the form of a library, nor made them as generic as they could be.) To verify the model, one only needs to have a C++ compiler, download the program `asset.cc`,[2] copy the model with the supporting facilities to the file `asset.model`, compile `asset.cc`, and run the result.[3]

To model the system for ASSET, we first specify the size of the system. The simplest way to do this would be

```
const unsigned n = 6;
```

However, to make it easier to experiment with systems of different sizes, we exploit C++ macros as follows:

```
#ifdef size_par
  const unsigned n = size_par;
#else
  const unsigned n = 6;
#endif
```

This means that if the compilation command specifies a value for `size_par`, then it is used as the size of the system; and otherwise the size is 6. With the g++ compiler, the value is given with the option `-Dsize_par=10` (with any natural number in the place of 10).

Next we introduce the state variables. Each client has four states: $0 =$ idle, $1 =$ requested, $2 =$ critical, and $3 =$ terminated. There are n clients. We model them with `C[n]`, that is, an array named `C` whose indices run from 0 to $n - 1$. The tokens are modelled with an array `T[n]` such that `T[i] == true` if and only if server i has the token. If we let the transitions of the server read the state of the client directly, then the server need not store the piece of information whether the client has requested or not. The same idea can be applied to the demand. These simplify the server so much that three states suffice: $0 =$ initial, $1 =$ waiting for the token, $2 =$ waiting for the client to leave its critical section. These states match Fig. 2 right. The following is written to the model:

```
enum { idle, requested, critical, terminated };
enum { initial, wait_token, wait_client };
state_var C[n], S[n];
state_bit T[n];
```

The only things above that are not readily available in C++ are `state_var` and `state_bit`. They are classes that have been defined in `asset.cc`. From the point of view of the modeller, variables of their types look like ordinary 8-bit and 1-bit unsigned integer variables.

However, as was explained in [16], behind the scenes `state_var` takes care of the memory management needed to store a state into the state space. The class `state_bit` was added to ASSET when writing the present study. It is important

---

[2] http://users.jyu.fi/%7eava/ASSET/asset.cc.
[3] http://users.jyu.fi/%7eava/ASSET/run.

to realize that from the point of view of ASSET, variables of these types do not store state information. Instead, all global states are stored in a C++ vector of unsigned integers. (C++ vector is an array with some special services. Most importantly, it can be extended on-the-fly.)

An individual global state occupies some constant number of successive slots of the vector. A variable of these types only contains the information needed to access the value (as seen by the modeller) of the state variable from within the unsigned integers that represent a single global state. When the model uses a state variable, its value (as seen by the modeller) is accessed from one or another global state depending on the value of a variable that contains the index of the current global state. This variable is part of ASSET and not part of the model.

To fire a transition on a global state, ASSET (not always, see below) copies the state (as a sequence of unsigned integers) to a free sequence of slots, makes the latter be the current global state, and asks the model to fire the transition. If the transition is enabled, the model executes its body, potentially modifying the global state. ASSET checks whether the resulting state has been encountered before. If not, it is made an official state of the state space, the sequence of slots is permanently reserved for it, and a new free sequence of slots is acquired by extending the vector. If the model replies that the transition is disabled, ASSET tries the next transition without copying the state, because it has not changed, because the previous transition did not fire. This speeds up the processing of disabled transitions. We will see later that the processing speed of disabled transitions is important.

By default, all state variables hold initially the value 0, also known as `false`. However, there must initially be one token in the ring. Therefore, we write

```
void initialize(){ T[0] = true; }
```

How to write transitions nicely depends on the modelling paradigm and perhaps also on the system. Classes, macros, or other means may have to be defined. In this section we show the transitions of our example system. The first version of the classes and macros that we used is shown in Sect. 4. To illustrate experimentation with implementation ideas, in Sect. 5 we describe another, more complicated version of the classes that uses precisely the same representation of the transitions, but speeds up the construction of the state space. We also describe a small modification to the representation of the transitions that yields further speed-up.

The transitions of the clients are copied almost trivially from Fig. 2 left using the names of states. All transitions of the client except the termination transition are joint with the server. However, each of them has a natural direction of the signal, as shown by arrowheads in Fig. 1. Each transition is modelled at the tail of the arrow, that is, at the sender of the signal. Therefore, the transition that moves the client from `requested` to `critical` is modelled as a server transition.

```
client_tr clients[] = {
  client_tr( idle, terminated ),  // termination transition
  client_tr( idle, requested ),   // request access
```

```
      client_tr( critical, idle )        // leave critical
   };
```

The transitions of the servers are less trivial. We first need a simple helper function that, given the index of a server, yields the index of the next server.

```
inline unsigned next( unsigned i ){ return ( i+1 ) % n; }
```

The transitions of the servers are shown in Fig. 3. Each of them consists of four components: tail state, guard, body, and head state. A transition is enabled if and only if the control of the server is at the tail state and the guard evaluates to true. When the transition occurs, it executes the body and moves the control of the server to the head state.

```
server_tr servers[] = {
  server_tr(
    initial,
    GUARD( C[i] == requested || S[ next(i) ] == wait_token ),
    BODY(),
    wait_token
  ),
  server_tr(
    wait_token,
    GUARD( T[i] && C[i] == requested ),
    BODY( C[i] = critical; ),
    wait_client
  ),
  server_tr(
    wait_token,
    GUARD( T[i] && C[i] != requested && S[ next(i) ] == wait_token ),
    BODY( T[i] = false; T[ next(i) ] = true; ),
    initial
  ),
  server_tr(
    wait_client,
    GUARD( C[i] != critical ),
    BODY( T[i] = false; T[ next(i) ] = true; ),
    initial
  )
};
```

Fig. 3. The transitions of the servers

The first transition moves the server from initial to wait_token when there is a reason for that, that is, its own client has requested or the next server needs the token. When the token is available, the second transition moves the client to its critical section, provided that it has requested for access. If it has not requested for access but the next server needs the token, and the current server has it, then the current server gives the token to the next server and returns to its initial state. The fourth transition is enabled when the server is waiting for the client to leave its critical section, and the client has done so. When it occurs, the server gives the token to the next server and returns to its initial state.

After serving its client, the server pushes the token to the next server even if the latter has not demanded. This prevents the system from executing an infinite cycle, where a client requests and its server serves it again and again, while some other client has requested but is never served. In the system as it is in Fig. 3, after a client is served, the token must circulate the ring before the same client may be served again. This guarantees that the other clients will be served if they want.

The verification tool must also be given some properties to check. We first describe mutual exclusion via a feature that makes ASSET check every state that it has constructed. The #define switches this feature on. The function counts the number of clients that are in their critical sections, and returns an error message, if and only if that number is at least two.

```
#define chk_state
const char *check_state(){
  unsigned cnt = 0;
  for( unsigned i = 0; i < n; ++i ){ if( C[i] == critical ){ ++cnt; } }
  if( cnt >= 2 ){ return "Mutual exclusion violated"; }
  return 0;
}
```

To see that this function works, we temporarily changed the initialization function so that it puts two tokens to the system: T[n/2] = T[0] = true;. As a consequence, ASSET reported !!! Safety error: Mutual exclusion violated and printed the sequence of states of an execution that led to the error. ASSET prints each state using a function provided by the modeller. So the modeller has full control on how each state is printed. Because the sequences leading to errors may be long, it is often a good idea to print states so densely that one line suffices. In our experiments we used the following function that encodes the local states of clients and servers as characters.

```
const char Cchr[] = { '-', 'R', 'C', ' ' }, Schr[] = { 'i', 't', 'c' };
void print_state(){
  for( unsigned i = 0; i < n; ++i ){
    std::cout << Cchr[ C[i] ] << Schr[ S[i] ];
    if( T[i] ){ std::cout << '*'; }else{ std::cout << ' '; }
  }
  std::cout << '\n';
}
```

With $n = 6$, the sequence of states mentioned above is as follows. The two tokens are shown as *. They are permanently at positions 0 and 3. We have added comments that describe what happened in each transition. "to CS" abbreviates "to its critical section".

```
-i*-i -i -i*-i -i   Initial state
-i*-i -i Ri*-i -i   Client 3 requested.
Ri*-i -i Ri*-i -i   Client 0 requested.
Ri*-i -i Rt*-i -i   Server 3 moved to wait_token.
Ri*-i -i Cc*-i -i   Server 3 moved to wait_client, taking client 3 to CS.
Rt*-i -i Cc*-i -i   Server 0 moved to wait_token.
Cc*-i -i Cc*-i -i   Server 0 moved to wait_client, taking client 0 to CS.
```

We also used a function that verifies that when the system has terminated, all clients have terminated on purpose instead of being blocked. If the initialization function is changed so that it puts no token to the system, then ASSET reports !!! Illegal deadlock: Client not terminated and shows a sequence of states where one by one, all clients move to requested.

```
#define chk_deadlock
const char *check_deadlock(){
  for( unsigned i = 0; i < n; ++i ){
    if( C[i] != terminated ){ return "Client not terminated"; }
  }
  return 0;
}
```

We mentioned earlier that after serving its client, the server pushes the token to the next server even if the latter has not demanded. To illustrate that this is important, we temporarily removed the latter T[i] = false; T[next(i)] = true; and permanently added the following checking function. It verifies that the system has no infinite execution where client 0 stays permanently in requested. This fails in the intentionally broken system, causing ASSET to report !!! Must-type non-progress error together with a long sequence of states that ends with a cycle where server 5 repeatedly serves client 5 while client 0 is in requested. The other clients have terminated and all servers other than 5 are waiting for the token.

```
#define chk_must_progress
bool is_must_progress(){ return C[0] != requested; }
```

An implementation of client_tr and server_tr will be described in the next section, and a faster, more complicated implementation in Sect. 5. The code fragments in this section together with either implementation constitute a complete model that ASSET can check. Our claim is that for a person who knows C++ and the basics of state spaces, the model in this section is reasonably easy to follow. It is also reasonably easy to make experiments by making modifications to the model. The classes in the next two sections are more difficult, but they can be re-used in other models.

4 Simple Transition Classes

In this section we describe a simple version of the generic facilities that the model in the previous section uses. The idea is that in the future, there would be a library from which these and other similar facilities could be picked. The next section discusses a more advanced alternative.

```
typedef bool (*guard_type)( unsigned );
typedef void (*body_type)( unsigned );
#define GUARD(x) { [](unsigned i) {return x;} }
#define BODY(x) { [](unsigned i) {x} }

class server_tr{
  unsigned tail, head; guard_type guard; body_type body;
public:
  static unsigned cnt;
  server_tr(
    unsigned tail, guard_type guard, body_type body, unsigned head
  ): tail( tail ), head( head ), guard( guard ), body( body ) { ++cnt; }
  bool operator()( unsigned i ) const {
    if( S[i] != tail || !guard( i ) ){ return false; }
    body( i ); S[i] = head; return true;
  }
};
unsigned server_tr::cnt = 0;
```

Fig. 4. The server transition facilities

The facilities needed by the transitions of the server are shown in Fig. 4. A guard is a function that takes the index of the server and returns a Boolean value, and a body is a function that takes the index of the server and returns nothing. First these two types of functions are given names. Then two macros are shown that facilitate intuitive syntax for the guards and bodies. Each guard and body is a C++ lambda function, that is, a C++ function that has no name. In the definition of a lambda function, [] (or something more complicated) appears in the place of the return type and name of the function.

Each server_tr object consists of four components: the tail state, the head state, the guard and the body. The execution of a server transition is defined by bool operator(). If the current local state of the server is not the same as the tail state of the transition, the execution terminates immediately returning false, indicating that the transition is not enabled. In the opposite case (that is, if these two states are the same), the guard is evaluated. If the guard returns false, then again the execution terminates returning false. In the opposite case, the transition is enabled. Then the body of the transition is executed, the head state is made the current local state of the server, and true is returned.

With the aid of cnt, the class counts the number of server transitions that
are created. (Being an array instead of a vector, servers has no size operator.)
The last line initializes cnt to 0. The three lines above bool operator() copy
the tail and so on from the command that creates a server transition, to the
corresponding fields of the object. They also increment cnt.

The class client_tr is simpler. It only contains tail, head, cnt, and the
operations that manipulate them.

We have described how the client and server transitions become stored in
the arrays clients[] and servers[]. We still have to explain how ASSET uses
these arrays when constructing the state space. Figure 5 shows the code that
implements this functionality.

```
unsigned nr_server_tr = 0;

unsigned nr_transitions(){
  initialize();
  nr_server_tr = server_tr::cnt * n;
  return nr_server_tr + client_tr::cnt * n;
}

bool fire_transition( unsigned i ){
  if( i < nr_server_tr ){
    return servers[ i % server_tr::cnt ]( i / server_tr::cnt );
  }
  i -= nr_server_tr;
  return clients[ i % client_tr::cnt ]( i / client_tr::cnt );
}
```

Fig. 5. The firing of transitions

Before starting to construct the state space, ASSET calls nr_transitions(),
to obtain the number of transitions in the model and to perform whatever initialization is needed. The function calls the initialization function discussed in
Sect. 3, computes the total number of transitions as seen by ASSET, and computes the total number of server transitions as seen by ASSET for a reason
that will be discussed soon. The number of client transitions that we wrote is in
client_tr::cnt, and similarly for the server. The total number of transitions
that we wrote is the sum of these. However, from the point of view of ASSET,
the transitions of each client and server are distinct from the transitions of any
other client or server, although we modelled them as parameterized transitions
that got the index of the client or server as the parameter. Therefore, for ASSET,
both numbers of transitions must be multiplied by the number of servers. Let
M denote the total number of transitions as seen by ASSET.

ASSET tries to fire a transition by calling fire_transition with the number of the transition as a parameter. If it returns false, then ASSET treats the

transition as disabled. If it returns **true**, then ASSET assumes that the transition was enabled and has been executed, changing the values of zero or more state variables. If this happens when ASSET is in the state space construction mode, then ASSET behaves like any state space construction tool, that is, checks whether the resulting state has been encountered before, and, if not, stores it in the state space. Then it either copies the original state to a fresh working area and tries the next transition on it or, if all transitions have been tried on the state, chooses the next state for processing.

For fast access, the total number of server transitions, as seen by ASSET, is stored in the global variable **nr_server_tr**. Let that number be denoted with m. Let s denote the number of server transitions that we wrote (that is, $s = 4$). So $m = ns$. Transition numbers from 0 to $m - 1$ correspond to the servers. Using the modulus operator and integer division, **fire_transition** splits the number to a number in the range from 0 to $s - 1$ and another in the range from 0 to $n - 1$. The former is used for picking a transition from the array **servers**, and the latter is given to the picked transition as a parameter. That is, the latter is the index of the server. The transition is executed by invoking the () operator, and the returned Boolean value is forwarded to ASSET as the return value of **fire_transition**.

Transition numbers from m to $M - 1$ correspond to the clients. The function **fire_transition** first subtracts m from them and then processes them similarly to the transition numbers that correspond to the servers.

The transition classes developed in this section can be thought of as a middle layer between the model and the ASSET tool. Further classes could be developed for different needs. For instance, there could be a non-parameterized class to model processes that, unlike our clients and servers, exist in only one copy. Writing a class may be non-trivial, but after it has been written, it may be easily usable in many different models. This is analogous to data structure and algorithm libraries.

5   Faster Transition Classes

In the design of the transition classes in the previous section, simplicity was preferred over performance. First, lambda functions are slower than the methods used in ASSET models until now. Before the present study, individual transitions were written as branches of **if** and **switch** statements that direct the control to the right transition on the basis of the number of the transition and the local states of the clients and servers. The statements were inside **fire_transition**. In the present study, the execution of an enabled server transition involves the invocations of two functions whose addresses are picked from an array. This introduces overhead.

Second, from the point of view of ASSET, the model in Sects. 3 and 4 contains $7n$ transitions, three for each client and four for each server. Because a server transition is disabled if its tail state is different from the current local state of the server, and because the guards of the second and third transition of the server are in contradiction, at most one of the four transitions of a server can be simultaneously enabled. For a similar reason, at most two transitions of a client can be simultaneously enabled. This means that during state space construction, numerous calls to `fire_transition` are made that yield `false` because of the local state of the client or server. In `switch`-based models, transitions with different tail states may share the transition number, reducing the number of unproductive calls to `fire_transition`.

To obtain information on the magnitude of these phenomena, we implemented four additional models. By Simple we refer to the model developed in the previous sections. Switch3 uses `if` and `switch` statements in the traditional, optimized manner. Also Switch7 uses `if` and `switch` statements, but it uses the same, non-optimal numbering of transitions as Simple. Lambda4 and Lambda3 exploit an improved way of using lambda functions that we will develop in this section. Lambda4 uses precisely the same transition specifications as Simple, but uses only $4n$ transition numbers. In Lambda3, the two transitions that start at `wait_token` have been merged. Like Switch3, it uses $3n$ transition numbers.[4]

The idea is to reduce the number of ASSET transition numbers and eliminate the tests on the tail states of transitions by sharing transition numbers between transitions with different tail states. The transitions (as seen by the modeller) of a server are partitioned to *levels*. The transitions on the same level share an ASSET transition number. Each level contains precisely one transition for each local state of the server, but this transition may be a special transition $\wp$ that is never enabled.

Consider the introduction of a new transition whose tail state is t. Location t on level 0 is checked, then on level 1 and so on, until a location containing $\wp$ is found or the levels are exhausted. In the latter case, a new level is introduced and all its locations are initialized with $\wp$. In both cases, then the new transition is stored on location t on the level.

When ASSET tries to fire transition number k where k is in the range for the server transitions, the index i of the server and the level ℓ are computed using integer division and modulus by the number of the levels. Then the current local state of the server (that is, `S[i]`) is used to pick the right transition on the chosen level. This takes place by using $s\ell + $ `S[i]` to index an array, where s is the number of local states of the server, that is, $s = 3$. So this is a constant time operation. Next the guard of the transition is evaluated. If it yields `true`, the head state of the transition is assigned as the current local state of the server, and the body of the transition is executed. These two actions are executed in this order to make it possible for the body to override the default head state. This feature is needed in merging the two server transitions whose tail state is `wait_token`.

Transitions of the clients are partitioned to levels in a similar fashion. Before sending an ASSET transition number to the firing function of `client_tr`, the total number of server transitions is subtracted from it, to make the range of numbers as seen by `client_tr` start from 0.

---

[4] http://users.jyu.fi/%7eava/ASSET/MWML/simple.cc, switch3.cc, and so on.

An idea of how complicated this optimized approach is can be obtained from the fact that Simple consists of 158 lines of code (including comments), Lambda4 of 208, and Lambda3 of 205.

The number of levels needed by a process is the maximum number of transitions of the process that may be simultaneously enabled. It can thus be thought of as the degree of nondeterminism of the process. This is not necessarily the same as the maximum outdegree of a local state of the process, because two transitions that share their tail state may have mutually exclusive guards. The two server transitions that start at wait_token are an example of this.

The degree of nondeterminism is typically small, often 1 or 2. On the other hand, with the simple technique of the previous section, the number of ASSET transition numbers used by a process is the same as the total number of transitions of the process. This number is 3 for our clients and 4 for our servers, but it is often bigger. For instance, the sender of the self-synchronizing alternating bit protocol in [20] has 22 transitions and its degree of nondeterminism is 2. Therefore, one might expect that the levelling technique of this section might yield significant savings with that protocol, but not necessarily with the example of the present study. The next section reports what happened in our measurements.

6   Measurements

Although our main motivation was pedagogical, it is important that the tool is not woefully slow. In this section we demonstrate experimentally that it is actually quite fast. On the other hand, the effect of the improvements in Sect. 5 over the implementation in Sect. 4 will turn out not big on our example.

We analysed the five models introduced in the previous sections with $n = 7$, $n = 8$, and $n = 9$, with various hash table sizes. (Hash table is the data structure from which ASSET checks whether a newly constructed state has been encountered before.) For each n, each of the models has the same number of reachable states and edges. These numbers are shown below. An observation that we will refer to in the sequel is that the number of edges is roughly $1.04n$ times the number of states.

n	7	8	9
States	2 939 328	20 155 392	136 048 896
Edges	21 500 640	167 588 352	1 267 270 272

Table 1 shows the times it took to construct and analyse the state spaces by ASSET on a machine with 3.60 GHz clock rate and 16 gibibytes of memory. The analysis algorithm tries to fire each transition twice on each reachable state: first to construct the set of reachable states as usual, and then as a part of an algorithm that checks the property specified by is_must_progress.

Table 1. Running times

n	Hash	Simple	Lambda4	Lambda3	Switch7	Switch3	Seconds
7	23	1.38	1.27	1.18	1.22	1.00	3.33
7	24	1.37	1.27	1.19	1.24	1.00	3.28
8	23	1.31	1.23	1.19	1.10	1.00	45.7
8	27	1.44	1.34	1.27	1.15	1.00	29.6
9	27	1.26	1.19	1.17	1.11	1.00	355
9	28	1.30	1.21	1.17	1.13	1.00	321

The rightmost column shows the analysis times of Switch3 in seconds, and the five preceding columns show the relation of the analysis time of each model to the analysis time of Switch3. Although we show two decimals, we point out that the information content of the latter decimal is limited, because the analysis times of identical runs on the same machine varied as much as 18 %. So the second decimal is unreliable. The second column shows the base-2 logarithm of the hash table size used in the experiments. For each n, the lower row uses the hash table size that yielded the fastest runs. To obtain information on the effect of the hash table size, the upper row presents the analysis times with a smaller hash table size, which is 23 in most cases but 27 with $n = 9$, because 23 took too much time. The compiler refused to compile when hash was 29.

The total number of transition numbers (as seen by ASSET) is $7n$ for Simple and Switch7, $4n$ for Lambda4 and $3n$ for Lambda3 and Switch3. Indeed, the analysis times of Switch7 are bigger than those of Switch3, and similarly with Simple, Lambda4, and Lambda3. We saw above that of these $7n$, $4n$, or $3n$ transitions, only about $1.04n$ were enabled on the average in each state. So in all models, most calls of `fire_transition` yield `false`. The processing time of such calls is thus important. Also, as one would expect, the `switch`-based models were faster to analyse than the models that use lambda functions.

However, the differences were at most only 44 %. The effect of the hash table size is of similar magnitude. So there is little point in spending human effort on optimizing analysis speed unless the analysis proves too slow. Even then the first thing is to set the hash table size. A good hash table size is at least roughly the number of reachable states, but not so big that the hash table uses too much of the available memory. In the absence of a better idea, the size of the available memory divided by 100 can be used as a rule of thumb. (An obvious idea for improving ASSET would be to make it choose the hash table size.)

During the development of the models, they were tested on a small 8 years old Linux mini-laptop with $n = 8$ and hash $= 23$. The analysis times were, of course, much bigger, because the computer was of much smaller performance. We feel that they are worth reporting, because there is an interesting difference. The following table shows the analysis times in seconds. They are user times measured with the `time` command, and they include also the roughly 4 s that it took to compile the model and `asset.cc`.

n	Hash	Simple	Lambda4	Lambda3	Switch7	Switch3	Sec
8	23	1.70	1.48	1.33	1.10	1.00	181

On that environment, the overhead of lambda functions is significant. We speculate that the overhead caused by indirect function calls may have become less significant over the years, thanks to developments in hardware (and compilers?). Clearly the measurements with a modern machine shown above do not suggest that lambda functions would be a serious performance problem.

We pointed out in Sect. 5 that the sender of the self-synchronizing alternating bit protocol has a high ratio of the number of transitions to the degree of nondeterminism. So we expected the levelling technique to yield much more dramatic improvement than it did in the demand-driven token ring example. We tested two different versions of the protocol on the old slow laptop. The improvement was small in both cases. It turned out that the manipulation of the fifo-channels of the protocol was so time consuming that it dominated the analysis time. Each time when a message is added to a fifo, the first empty location must be found to put it there, and each time when a message is removed, all contents of the fifo must be moved one step forward. Outside state space methods, the fifo could be made faster by implementing it as a ring buffer. However, in a verification model, such an implementation would cause state explosion by giving the same actual content many different representations.

We tried our approach also on the dining philosophers' model at [5]. Translation from Promela along the lines of Sect. 3 was straightforward. The framework of Sect. 4 was used, after removing everything related to clients as unnecessary. We tried up to 14 philosophers, with SPIN max search depth set to 18 000 000 (17 000 000 did not suffice) and no_show_cnt switched on in ASSET. ASSET always constructed one state and two edges less than SPIN. When $n \geq 12$, its running time was less than half of that of SPIN. When $n < 12$, ASSET terminated within one second. The machine was a modern laptop.

7   Conclusions

We illustrated how lambda functions can be used to write fairly natural and readable models of systems as guarded transitions on shared variables, with tail and head states. Lambda functions were added to C++ in the 2011 standard, so they are somewhat recent. Because in our application, the use of lambda functions involves calling functions picked from arrays, we expected it to add significant overhead. This proved to be so on an 8 year old mini-laptop, but not on modern machines. (We reported measurements on one modern machine but had tried also three others.) In our measurements, the overhead was so small that there is no point in spending human effort to avoid lambda functions unless the analysis speed has to be optimized to the extreme. Although we did not report them, we also made some experiments with virtual functions. Again, the result was that there is no strong need to avoid them.

We first presented simple classes that made it possible to write natural models using lambda functions. Then we developed more complicated, faster classes. However, in our experiments, the motivation for the faster classes was reduced by the fact that on modern machines, already the simple classes performed not much worse than highly optimized models relying on `switch` and `if` statements.

Our work is initial in that our classes are not universal. Instead, they were designed according to the needs of our example system. However, especially the simple classes are straightforward and can thus be mimicked as needed when modelling other systems. We also successfully re-used a class in another model. The work is initial also in that only three systems were modelled and experimented with. Because of the strong expressive power of C++, we are convinced that many further systems can be modelled, and more universal classes than ours can be developed.

References

1. Clarke, E., Kroening, D., Lerda, F.: A tool for checking ANSI-C programs. In: Jensen, K., Podelski, A. (eds.) TACAS 2004. LNCS, vol. 2988, pp. 168–176. Springer, Heidelberg (2004). https://doi.org/10.1007/978-3-540-24730-2_15
2. Corbett, J.C., Dwyer, M.B., Hatcliff, J., Laubach, S., Pasareanu, C.S., Robby, Zheng, H.: Bandera: extracting finite-state models from Java source code. In: Ghezzi, C., Jazayeri, M., Wolf, A.L. (eds.) Proceedings of the 22nd International Conference on Software Engineering, ICSE 2000, Limerick Ireland, 4–11 June 2000, pp. 439–448. ACM (2000). http://doi.acm.org/10.1145/337180.337234
3. Cormen, T.H., Leiserson, C.E., Rivest, R.L., Stein, C.: Introduction to Algorithms, 3rd edn. MIT Press, Cambridge (2009)
4. Evangelista, S., Pajault, C.: Solving the ignoring problem for partial order reduction. STTT **12**(2), 155–170 (2010). https://doi.org/10.1007/s10009-010-0137-y
5. Floinn, E.Ó.: Model of dining philosophers' problem in the Promela verification language (2016). https://github.com/oflynned/DiningPhilosophersPromela. Accessed 2 May 2018
6. Holzmann, G.J.: The SPIN Model Checker - Primer and Reference Manual. Addison-Wesley, Boston (2004)
7. Jensen, K., Kristensen, L.M.: Colored Petri nets: a graphical language for formal modeling and validation of concurrent systems. Commun. ACM **58**(6), 61–70 (2015). http://doi.acm.org/10.1145/2663340
8. Manna, Z., Pnueli, A.: The Temporal Logic of Reactive and Concurrent Systems - Specification. Springer, New York (1992). https://doi.org/10.1007/978-1-4612-0931-7
9. Milner, R., Tofte, M., Harper, R.: Definition of Standard ML. MIT Press, Cambridge (1990)
10. Reisig, W.: Petri Nets: An Introduction. Monographs in Theoretical Computer Science. An EATCS Series, vol. 4. Springer, Heidelberg (1985). https://doi.org/10.1007/978-3-642-69968-9
11. Roscoe, A.W.: Understanding Concurrent Systems. Texts in Computer Science. Springer, London (2010). https://doi.org/10.1007/978-1-84882-258-0
12. spinroot.com. SPIN Readme. http://spinroot.com/spin/Man/README.html. Accessed 1 May 2018

13. Stroustrup, B.: The C++ Programming Language, 3rd edn. Addison-Wesley Longman Publishing Co., Inc., Boston (1997)
14. Valmari, A.: Stubborn sets for reduced state space generation. In: Rozenberg, G. (ed.) ICATPN 1989. LNCS, vol. 483, pp. 491–515. Springer, Heidelberg (1991). https://doi.org/10.1007/3-540-53863-1_36
15. Valmari, A.: Composition and abstraction. In: Cassez, F., Jard, C., Rozoy, B., Ryan, M.D. (eds.) MOVEP 2000. LNCS, vol. 2067, pp. 58–98. Springer, Heidelberg (2001). https://doi.org/10.1007/3-540-45510-8_3
16. Valmari, A.: A state space tool for concurrent system models expressed in C++. In: Nummenmaa, J., Sievi-Korte, O., Mäkinen, E. (eds.) Proceedings of the 14th Symposium on Programming Languages and Software Tools (SPLST 2015), Tampere, Finland, 9–10 October 2015. CEUR Workshop Proceedings, vol. 1525, pp. 91–105. CEUR-WS.org (2015)
17. Valmari, A.: Stop it, and be stubborn! In: 15th International Conference on Application of Concurrency to System Design, ACSD 2015, Brussels, Belgium, 21–26 June 2015, pp. 10–19. IEEE Computer Society (2015). http://dx.doi.org/10.1109/ACSD.2015.14
18. Valmari, A.: Stop it, and be stubborn!. ACM Trans. Embed. Comput. Syst. 16(2), 46:1–46:26 (2017). http://doi.acm.org/10.1145/3012279
19. Valmari, A., Setälä, M.: Visual verification of safety and liveness. In: Gaudel, M.-C., Woodcock, J. (eds.) FME 1996. LNCS, vol. 1051, pp. 228–247. Springer, Heidelberg (1996). https://doi.org/10.1007/3-540-60973-3_90
20. Valmari, A., Vogler, W.: Int. J. Softw. Tools Technol. Transfer (2017). https://doi.org/10.1007/s10009-017-0481-2
21. Visser, W., Havelund, K., Brat, G.P., Park, S., Lerda, F.: Model checking programs. Autom. Softw. Eng. 10(2), 203–232 (2003). https://doi.org/10.1023/A:1022920129859

Context-Updates Analysis and Refinement in Chisel

Irina Măriuca Asăvoae[1], Mihail Asăvoae[2(✉)], and Adrián Riesco[3]

[1] Swansea University, Swansea, UK
I.M.Asavoae@swansea.ac.uk
[2] CEA LIST, Gif-sur-Yvette, France
mihail.asavoae@cea.fr
[3] Universidad Complutense de Madrid, Madrid, Spain
ariesco@fdi.ucm.es

Abstract. This paper presents the context-updates synthesis component of Chisel, a tool that synthesizes a program slicer directly from a given algebraic specification of a programming language operational semantics. By context-updates we understand programming language constructs that induce unconditional control-flow non-sequentiality, i.e., gotos or subroutine calls. The context-updates synthesis follows two directions: an over-approximation phase that extracts a set of potential context-update constructs and an under-approximation phase that refines the results of the first step by testing the behavior of the context-updates constructs produced at the previous phase. We use two experimental semantics that cover two types of language paradigms: high-level imperative languages and low-level assembly languages and we conduct the tests on standard benchmarks used in avionics.

Keywords: Generic slicing tool
Programming languages formal semantics · Maude · Synthesis

1 Introduction

Slicing is a program analysis technique that takes a program and a *slicing criterion* (i.e., a set of variables V) and produces a *program slice* (i.e., the program parts containing language construct units that may directly or indirectly change the value of the variables in V during execution). We refer to the language construct units, i.e., the syntactic components of the programming language, separated by sequencing operators, as *instructions*. In this paper, we focus on static slicing, i.e., when the slices are computed without executing the program, and we refer to it as simply *slicing*.

This research has been partially supported by the MINECO Spanish project *TRACES* (TIN2015-67522-C3-3-R) and by the Comunidad de Madrid project *N-Greens Software-CM* (S2013/ICE-2731).

M. M. Gallardo and P. Merino (Eds.): SPIN 2018, LNCS 10869, pp. 328–346, 2018.
https://doi.org/10.1007/978-3-319-94111-0_19

Program slicing relies on the evaluation of the data-flow equations over the control-flow graph of the program. Obviously, besides the data-flow, there is a need for additional techniques to deal with other language features. In [27] we find a comprehensive survey on the standard program slicing techniques applied over different programming language concepts such as standard imperative, pointers, unstructured control flow, and concurrency. Generally, these techniques use an augmented control-flow graph, e.g., the function calls are usually represented by edges [25] in a call graph.

Meanwhile, *the rewriting logic semantics project* [15] promotes the programming languages semantics are defined as rewriting systems using Maude [7], and it is followed by the work in the $\mathbb{K}$ framework [24]. Our work complements the rewriting logic semantics project by developing static analysis methods, in particular slicing, for programs written in languages with an already defined rewriting logic semantics in Maude. Our approach analyzes a given language semantics and synthesizes the necessary information for program slicing. We use these results to traverse the program term in order to obtain the program slice.

Our approach is implemented in Chisel,[1] a Maude tool for generic program slicing [21]. Chisel takes a programming language semantics, given as a Maude specification, breaks it into pieces of interest for slicing, and uses these pieces to augment the program and to produce the program model, which is then sliced. Chisel synthesizes these semantics to extract operators that produce certain update patterns in the underlying machine model. These operators are then used to produce necessary information for slicing, e.g., side-effect instructions. The final step of Chisel is the program slicing analysis that takes a program and produces its slice w.r.t. a slicing criterion. With Chisel we target sequential imperative code without dynamic allocation that is generated from synchronous designs—a class of applications used in real-time systems, e.g., avionics. We experiment for now two semantics: one for an imperative language with functions, WhileFun [3, 10], and one for the MIPS assembly language.

Chisel aims to evolve into a framework for *generic static slicing*. The progression in Chisel design and implementation is described in [3, 19, 20]. In [19] we present the methodology for performing intraprocedural slicing and in [3] we design and implement the interprocedural slicing. In [20] we introduce an algorithm for inferring the data-flow information to automatically detect how the language constructs work with the memory.

The contribution of this paper is presenting the context-updates synthesis component of Chisel, where by context-updates we understand programming language constructs that unconditionally produce non-sequential changes in the control-flow, such as goto instructions or function calls. The main motivation for our work is the fact that for the interprocedural slicing algorithm implemented in Chisel we need to identify the function calls in order to produce the appropriate control-flow. Until now we gave this information manually, as user input to the slicing component of Chisel. With the current work we improve the genericity of Chisel by automatic synthesis of context-updates.

---

[1] https://github.com/ariesco/chisel.

The context-updates synthesis follows two directions: an over-approximation phase when we analyze the language semantics specification to extract a set of potential context-update constructs and an under-approximation phase when we stress-test the semantics to refine the context-updates obtained at the first step. The under-approximation phase, introduced in this paper, is justified by the imprecision of the over-approximation phase for the context-updates. The imprecision is mostly due to the laxity of the automatic detection of stack-like memory operators.

1.1   Related Work

Program slicing [28] is a standard analysis technique used to compute program slices based on certain criteria for a given program input. Slicing without a program execution input is called static slicing and slicing based on execution of specific program inputs is called dynamic slicing.

Generic Slicing. Techniques of generic program slicing are proposed in [5,8]. The program slicing of [8] uses an algorithm that extracts slices from a common intermediate representation named PIM, however it requires a non-trivial language-dependent transformation between a particular language and PIM. The work in [8] is generic because it uses a notion of constraints slices to represent both static and dynamic slices and transforms various slicing methods into instances of a parametric slicing procedure. Chisel, extended with the proposed method of context-updates synthesis, considers only static slicing and addresses genericity from a different angle: it eliminates the need of a language-dependent translation by working directly on the formal language semantics. Generic program slicing is also the focus in [5]. The ORBS tool [5] proposes a technique for dynamic slicing based on statement deletion. A program slice is iteratively constructed by removing statements from the original program and then checking if the transformation is semantics-preserving w.r.t. the slicing criterion. Checking the semantics preservation relies on novel testing techniques [14]. The static slicing of Chisel complements the dynamic slicing of ORBS, as it computes static program slices based on in-depth investigation of the formal language semantics. And as in [14], Chisel, through the current work, integrates testing based on path-coverage to improve the precision of the context-updates synthesis, while it remains generic w.r.t. the language semantics.

Environments and Context-Updates. Functional programming proposes richer notions of contexts and context manipulation than what we consider in our framework. Briefly, the standard definition of a context as variables in scope is extended in functional languages in several directions. On the one hand, there are high-level constructs such as *call/cc* - call with current continuation - in the Scheme language [1], where snapshots of the current control states are manipulated as values (e.g., passed as arguments to function calls). On the other hand, there are extended notions of contexts to capture security properties, as in the SLam calculus [9] or parameters of execution platforms [17,26]. Such contexts are used to track how programs affect an execution environment (e.g., the effect systems [26]) or how programs depend on the execution environment (e.g., the coeffect systems [17]). In our work, the context is a first-order variable that could be explicitly or implicitly represented in a programming language semantics. We identify context changes (i.e., context-updates) in a generic manner, directly from a formal language semantics given as rewrite theories. Our context-updates synthesis is more general than the aforementioned work in functional programming, due to the genericity of our approach, i.e., we do not address a particular type of memory/environment representation as the one in functional programming. Nevertheless, the rich context representations from functional programming could be used to specialize our context-updates synthesis with the inference of types of variables updates during context changes.

Formal Semantics and Testing. The rewriting logic semantics project [15] advocates for specialized modeling and reasoning techniques based on formal semantics of programming languages. In this direction, the $\mathbb{K}$ framework [22] relies on a convenient notation to advance the development of formal language definitions and it argues that such language definitions should be used directly, as they are, in tool construction for program reasoning. Apart from its intrinsic specification strengths, the $\mathbb{K}$ framework proposes a verification environment called matching logic [23]. Matching logic uses patterns to specify properties over the program state space and employs symbolic execution and pattern matching to validate program properties. In this context, program verification with matching logic means to symbolically run the target program on the formal semantics, while the generic techniques behind Chisel allow for the symbolic analysis the formal semantics in order to synthesize the necessary semantic ingredients to address the program properties. The approach in [2] implements dynamic slicing for execution traces of Maude. The semantics is executed for an initial given state, then dependency relations are computed using a backward tracing mechanism. In comparison, our approach focuses on statically computing slices for programs and not for given traces (e.g., of model checker runs). The tool in [18] implements a technique of rule-coverage testing as it generates test cases from the formal semantics of programming languages given as rewrite theories. Specifically, the semantic rules are employed to instantiate the variables used by the given program based on a narrowing technique. The refinement phase of our context-updates synthesis uses path-coverage testing provided by PathCrawler [13], a specialized plugin of the Frama-C analyzer [12]. PathCrawler generates test sets for ANSI C code using a combination of symbolic execution and constraint solving capabilities to ensure complete path-coverage. The current work uses test-coverage with PathCrawler to refine the context-updates synthesis of Chisel as opposed to the aforementioned usage of rule-coverage, in [4] (which tests individual language constructs but it is agnostic w.r.t. the program semantics).

The rest of the paper is organized as follows: Sect. 2 overviews the Chisel system; Sect. 3 defines and characterizes the context-updates; Sects. 4 and 5 describe the context-updates synthesis and respectively context-updates refinement;

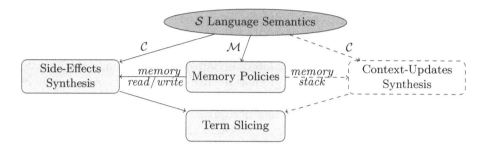

Fig. 1. Chisel components: the formal language semantics and the syntheses.

Sect. 6 presents the experimental evaluation on avionics benchmarks. Section 7 concludes and outlines future work directions.

2   The Chisel System

We briefly describe in this section the ideas underlying Chisel, which aims to synthesize slicers from programming language semantics specifications. An overview of Chisel is presented in [21]. Figure 1 summarizes the design structure of the tool. Namely, we denote by S the Chisel input, i.e., the semantics specification of a programming language defined in Maude. The memory policies work over M—the memory component of S, while the syntheses examine C—the language syntax component of S. Next we describe in Fig. 1 by levels, i.e., the structure of S, the syntheses that work over components of S, and the term slicing that synthesizes the slicer based on the results obtained from the above level.

2.1   Programming Language Semantics

The programming language semantics specification S is a Maude theory with the structure $C \implies \overrightarrow{M}$ where:

- C represents the context free grammar defining the language syntax;
- M defines the machine on which the programs are executed; M is formed by components such as static and dynamic memory where the program variables are assigned values directly or indirectly, program code section, and so on;
- $\implies$ is the set of rules $< C, M > \Rightarrow < C', M' >$ defining how the machine state $M \in M$ is changed into $M' \in M$ by the syntactic construct(s) $C \in C$, while $C' \in C$ represents the syntactic construct(s) that continue the computation;
- $\longrightarrow$ over the M component denote the machine operations, e.g., setting the value of a variable.

Note that the context free grammar production rules as $S \rightarrow S_1 t_1 \ldots S_n t_n$ are defined in Maude by operators op $t_{1-}...t_{n-} : S_1...S_n ->S$ where $t_i, 1 \leq i \leq n \in \mathbb{N}$ are terminal symbols and $S, S_i, \leq i \leq n$ are non-terminals defined by sorts/types in Maude. The sorts sequence $S_1...S_n$ is called the arity of the operator while S is the co-arity.

In S we assume that the syntax has a top non-terminal denoted by C that is the sort representing the co-arity of the language constructs. For example a branching instruction is defined as op If_Then_Else_ : $B \ C \ C$ -> C, where B is the top sort for Boolean expressions (note that the arity of this operator is $B \ C \ C$, while the co-arity is C). Hence, the language instructions are assumed to be defined in S by operators with the C co-arity. Consequently, the context free grammar denoted by C is equipped with a parser provided by Maude that transforms a program p into the associated parse tree t_p which in rewriting is called a *term* (of sort C). Also, an example of rules in $\Longrightarrow$ denoting the command of the branching instruction is:

```
crl [If1] : < If be Then C Else C', m > => < skip, m'' >
  if < be, m > => < T, m' > /\ < C, m' > => < skip, m'' > .
crl [If2] : < If be Then C Else C', m > => < skip, m'' >
  if < be, m > => < F, m' > /\ < C', m' > => < skip, m'' > .
```

where the rule labeled [If1] is executing the Then branch containing the code C if the condition be evaluates in the memory m to the true value T and the rule labeled [If2] is executing the Else branch containing the code C' if the condition be evaluates in the memory m to the false value F.

The machine representation in S is given by $\overrightarrow{M}$ where, for example, the static memory component is defined by an operator which lists elements of sort W representing pairs of the variables (of sort Var) with the values (of sort Val). Note that the pairs are defined by another operator of arity $Var \ Val$ and co-arity W. The changes in the machine are denoted by $\longrightarrow$ representing a set of operators and their associated equations or rewrite rules that specify how the machine internals are working. For example, a variable look-up in the static memory is defined by an operator op _[_] : $W \ Var$ -> Val defined by an equation or a rewrite rule that identifies the pair pr in the static memory $w : W$ containing the variable $v : Var$ as first element and returns the second element of pr that represents the value $n : Val$ associated to v in w.

2.2 Memory Policies and Syntheses

By a memory policy mp we understand a subset of memory operators $\mathcal{M}(mp) = \{o : w \to s \mid o \in \mathcal{M} \text{ s.t. } mp(\overrightarrow{o})\}$, where mp is a property of the arity and co-arity of o and of $\overrightarrow{o}$, i.e., the rules matching the operator o. Note that s denotes a sort while w denotes a list of sorts. Also, given a rewrite rule or equation $[r] : lhs \to rhs$ where r is the rule label, lhs, rhs are terms in $\mathcal{M}$ then $r \in \overrightarrow{o}$ iff the operator o is a subterm of lhs. For example, *memory-read* policy $\mathcal{M}(read)$ is the set of operators in $\mathcal{M}$ that contain in their arity the sort for variables Var and for static memory W and in their co-arity the sort for values Val. A *memory-write* operator $o_w \in \mathcal{M}(write)$ contains in its arity sorts for static memory W, variables Var, and values Val, and in its co-arity the static memory sort W.

Moreover, any $r \in \overrightarrow{o_w}$ replaces in rhs the value parameter of the operator o_w from lhs into the static memory pair containing the variable. The read/write memory policies are presented in [20].

The syntheses analyze $\Longrightarrow$, the semantics rules in $\mathcal{S}$, in order to identify the subset of instructions in $\mathcal{C}$ that induce a certain change pattern in the memory. The memory change pattern is defined by a combination of memory policies. The main assumption of the synthesis methodology is that rules $r_{\mathcal{C}}$ in $\Longrightarrow$ trigger rules $r_{\mathcal{M}}$ in $\overrightarrow{\mathcal{M}}$. If $r_{\mathcal{M}} \in \overrightarrow{\mathcal{M}}$ follows the assumed memory change pattern (i.e., the memory policies combination) then the instruction $i \in \mathcal{C}$ that matches the triggering rule $r_{\mathcal{C}} \in \Longrightarrow$ is selected by the synthesis. For example, in [19] we describe the side-effects synthesis defined as the set of instructions i that *may* trigger a memory write for some variable subterm in i, which we denote as destination variable, and memory reads for other subterms, which we denote as sources. In [20] we describe a follow-up methodology that identifies the source-destination subterms in i by following backwards the subterm dependencies between $r_{\mathcal{M}}$ and $r_{\mathcal{C}}$.

2.3 Term Analysis

Program slicing takes as input a program p and a *slicing criterion* S consisting of a set of program variables that are considered the initial side-effect destinations. In the *first step* all the instructions in p that have some element of S as a side-effect destination are added to the slice sp. Next, p is traversed with a fix-point algorithm that adds to S the side-effect sources in sp and repeats the first step until S is saturated. In Chisel we implement a state-of-the-art interprocedural slicing algorithm introduced in [11] that uses call graph information to produce a more precise slice sp. This part of Chisel is described in [3]. However, for preserving the genericity of the tool, the call graph had to be inferred from $\mathcal{S}$. Until now we assumed the call graph node patterns as given by the user where by *call graph node patterns* we understand the function call instructions that represent the source nodes in the call graph. In the current work we give the methodology for identifying call graph node patterns as context-updates.

3   Context-Updates Definition and Characterizations

In this section we give the definition of context-updates and present two (static and dynamic) characterizations for this notion. The static characterization analyzes $\mathcal{S}$ to extract the context-updates while the dynamic characterization executes the semantics $\mathcal{S}$ for the same purpose.

Definition 1. *A context-update is a ground term of $\mathcal{S}$ that instantiates an instruction which identifies an unconditional non-sequential control-flow in some program p in $\mathcal{S}$. The context-updates are the set of syntactic constructs that match a context-update in some program:*

$$CU := \{i \in \mathcal{C} \mid \exists p \in \mathcal{C} \text{ a ground term s.t. } \exists \theta \text{ a ground substitution s.t.} \\ \theta(i) \prec p \text{ and } \theta(i) \text{ is a context-update}\}$$

where a ground substitution replaces the non-terminals in the production rule of the context free grammar denoted by C with words in the language of C, while given two words w_1, w_2 we have $w_1 \prec w_2$ if $w_2 = w \ w_1 \ w'$.

Note that C is a part of S hence we use the complementary terminology terms instead of words while $\prec$ is the subterm relation.

The *static characterization* of CU relies on the observation that in imperative languages with local memory (i.e., the class of languages we consider) the function call instructions need to save the local context, i.e., a part of the static memory state. In a standard way, the local context is saved on a stack structure due to the fact that the rules $\implies$ behave as the transition rules in a pushdown system $\mathcal{P}$ where $\mathcal{M}$ represents the states in $\mathcal{P}$. Our assumptions regarding to the structure of the semantics S, i.e., the separation between the language syntax and the machine, induce the static characterization:

SC: The context-updates of the programming language specified by S is a subset of instructions in C that *must* trigger a memory stack change:

$$SC := \{i \in C \mid \forall r_C \in \implies$$
$$\text{if } i \ll lhs(r_C) \text{ then } \exists r_{\mathcal{M}} \in \mathcal{M}(stack) \text{ s.t. } r_C \text{ triggers } r_{\mathcal{M}}\}$$

where $t_1 \ll t_2$ defines the unification relation, i.e., a set of substitutions ϕ s.t. $\phi(t1)$ is a subterm of t_2 and $\mathcal{M}(stack)$ is the instantiation of $\mathcal{M}(mp)$ with a stack memory policy.

Note that **SC** produces an over-approximation of CU due to the abstract nature of the unification and the stack memory policy.

The *dynamic characterization* of CU relies on testing the semantics S by executing programs from a test set TP using certain testing technique(s) $TestTech$ to generate input states $In(p)$ for any $p \in TP$. Namely, given a set TP of test programs $p \in C$, $TestTech : TP \ S \to In(\mathcal{M})$ is a function that for each program $p \in TP$ provides a set of initial states that execute p in S, i.e., $In(p) = \{m_0 \in \mathcal{M} \mid \exists m \in \mathcal{M} :< p, m_0 >\stackrel{*}{\Rightarrow}< \emptyset, m >\}$. We denote by $\Pi_p = \{\pi_p \mid \exists m_0 \in In(p) \text{ s.t. } \pi_p =< p, m_0 >\stackrel{*}{\Rightarrow}< \emptyset, m >\}$ the executions traces of the program p from the initial states $In(p)$. Furthermore, we denote $L_p = [i_1 \ldots i_n]$ the list of instructions $i_k \in C, \forall 1 \leq k \leq n$ obtained by a preorder traversal of t_p–the tree term associated by parsing to the program p. The dynamic characterization exploits the fact that S is an *executable* formal semantics as follows:

DC: Assuming that for any execution trace $\pi \in \Pi_p$ (of length $|\pi|$) exists the segmentation $\pi \stackrel{L_p}{=} w_1 \ldots w_n$ such that w_i is a segment of L_p then the context-updates are the separator instructions:

$$DC := \{i \in C \mid \exists p \in TP, \forall \pi \in \Pi_p \text{ s.t. } \pi \stackrel{L_p}{=} w_1 \ldots w_n \text{ and } i \in \pi \text{ then}$$
$$\exists j : 1 \leq j \leq n, \exists a_j, b_j : 0 \leq a_j < b_j < |\pi| \text{ s.t.}$$
$$w_j = \pi(a_j)\pi(a_j + 1) \ldots \pi(b_j) \text{ and } i = \pi(b_j)\}$$

Hence, DC is the set of instructions that appear at the end of some segment w of L_p in every program execution π that contains them.

Note that **DC** produces an under-approximation of CU due to the fact that TP is a subset of all programs in $\mathcal{C}$ and $TestTech$ produces a subset of all possible program executions. In Sects. 4 and 5 we present details of **SC** and **DC**, respectively.

4   Context-Updates Synthesis

In this section we present our approach towards discovering context-updates based on their static characterization **SC**.

The methodology we propose for context-updates over-approximation follows the methodology described in the Sect. 2.2. Namely, we firstly apply sort-based patterns to define a memory policy that identifies stack structures/memory operators or, short, *memory-stacks*. Secondly, using the memory-stacks we construct a tree $\mathcal{T}$ based on $\Longrightarrow$ to discover the set $\mathcal{O}$ of language constructs that must use the memory-stacks. We call $\mathcal{T}$ a hyper-tree and we give in this section an example of such hyper-tree.

The stack memory policy determines $\mathcal{M}(stack)$ where $stack(\overrightarrow{o})$ property first requires that o is a non-commutative operator with the arity $S\ S$ and co-arity S, where S is a sort in $\mathcal{M}$. Moreover, we have two patterns we search for: explicit and implicit. The explicit memory-stack policy requires that all the rules in $\overrightarrow{o}$ either add or subtract one element. The implicit pattern uses the conditional rules over the language semantics to produce memory-stacks. The implicit pattern is produced by the Maude's evaluation semantics that uses a an evaluation stack for conditional rules. Namely, the evaluation of the conditional rule's body (i.e., the statement between the `crl` and `if` keywords) is postponed until the evaluation of the rule's condition (i.e., the statement after `if` keyword) is completed.

Example 1. We present in this example the memory specification for WhileFun–an imperative language with assignment, conditional, loops, local variables, an input/output buffer, and function calls [3,10]. Assuming we have defined the syntax for the language in a module `WHILE-SYNTAX` (which includes definitions for variables, Boolean values, and numeric values), the module `MEMORY` imports this module and defines the sorts `Env` for the environment, which maps variables to values, and `ESt` for a stack of environments, which will be used when a new context is required:

```
fmod MEMORY is
  pr WHILE-SYNTAX .
  sorts Env ESt .
  subsort Env < ESt .
  ...
```

where the `subsort` indicates that a single environment (of sort `Env`) represents a one element stack (of sort `ESt`), i.e., the environment type `Env` is a subtype of the environments' stack `ESt`. Constructors of these sorts are defined by using `op` and the attribute `ctor`. In this case, we define the empty environment (`mt`); a single assignment, which receives a variable and a value[2]; and the composition of environments (`__`), which is defined as commutative and associative and having `mt` as the identity element:

```
op mt : -> Env [ctor] .
op _=_ : Variable Value -> Env [ctor] .
op __ : Env Env -> Env [ctor comm assoc id: mt] .
```

Similarly, the stack is built by putting together stacks with the `_|_` operator:

```
op _|_ : ESt ESt -> ESt [ctor assoc] .
```

The operator `_|_` follows the explicit memory-stack policy and it will be used in the context-update synthesis, as described next in Example 2. The memory module also contains functions for variables' update, variables' look-up, and new variables allocation.

The synthesis of a set $\mathcal{O}$ of context-updates relies on the construction of a hyper-tree of rules and is similar to the side-effects synthesis described in [19]. The difference here is the fact that at the leaves level we now use a different memory policy (the memory-stack policy) to filter the paths leading to context-updates and we use a *must* strategy, i.e., *all* rules in $\Longrightarrow$ matching an instruction have to contain in their associated subtree a memory-stack.

The algorithm implementing this functionality in Chisel is defined by the operator `traverseHypertree` in Fig. 2. This operator takes as arguments (i) the module where the slicing process takes place; (ii) the set of statements contained in the hypernode that have not been traversed yet, represented as a set of rule labels; (iii) the list of terms already used to generate hypernodes, which are used to avoid non-termination by preventing matchings in the conditions; (iv) the side effects tuple, indicating the operators and rules that may generate side effects; and (v) an accumulator containing the current result of the hypernode, including the nodes in the olive and orange set. Using these elements, it computes the set of basic syntactic language constructs that *must* be context-updates by inspecting the conditions and the right-hand side of each rewrite rule in the set and updating the accumulator.

More specifically, the base case of the function returns the accumulator, while the recursive case works as follows. It first checks whether the current rule has been already traversed; in this case it is discarded and the next one is tried recursively. If it was not traversed and it provokes context updates then it is added in the orange. Otherwise, the children of the hypernode are computed with `traverseCond` and the label is added to the appropriate set depending of the color of the children.

The auxiliary function `traverseCond` just discards all conditions but rewrite conditions, that we assume are the ones in charge of defining the semantics. In this case we take the lefthand side of the condition and create a new term where all arguments has been substituted with fresh variables. We use this term to

---

[2] Please note that the underscore symbol _ represents a placeholder.

```
op traverseHypertree : Module QidSet TermList ContextUpdates
                HypertreeTraversalResult -> HypertreeTraversalResult .
eq traverseHypertree(M, none, TL, CU, HTR) = HTR .
ceq traverseHypertree(M, Q ; QS, TL, CU, HTR) =
    if traversed?(Q, HTR)
    then traverseHypertree(M, QS, TL, CU, HTR)
    else if Q in CU
        then traverseHypertree(M, QS, TL, CU, add2orange(Q, HTR))
        else if allOrange?(traverseCond(M, COND, (T, TL), CU,
                        setAllOrangeVar(true, HTR)))
                and not emptyHypernode(M, getCondition(M,Q),
                                (getLHS(M,Q), TL))
            then add2orange(Q, traverseCond(M, COND, (T, TL), CU,
                        setAllOrangeVar(true, HTR)))
            else add2olive(Q, traverseCond(M, COND, (T, TL), CU,
                        setAllOrangeVar(true, HTR)))
            fi
        fi
    fi .


op traverseCond : Module Condition TermList ContextUpdates
        HypertreeTraversalResult -> HypertreeTraversalResult .
eq traverseCond(M, nil, TL, CU, HTR) = setAllOrangeVar(false, HTR) .
eq traverseCond(M, T = T' /\ COND, TL, CU, HTR) =
                        traverseCond(M, COND, TL, CU, HTR) .
eq traverseCond(M, T := T' /\ COND, TL, CU, HTR) =
                        traverseCond(M, COND, TL, CU, HTR) .
eq traverseCond(M, T : S /\ COND, TL, CU, HTR) =
                        traverseCond(M, COND, TL, CU, HTR) .
eq traverseCond(M, T => T' /\ COND, TL, CU, HTR) =
    combineHypernodes(
      traverseHypertree(M,
                        getRulesUnifying(M, freshTerm(T),
                                getRls(M), TL),
                        TL, CU, HTR),
      traverseCond(M, COND, TL, CU, setAllOrangeVar(true, HTR')))
    ) .
```

Fig. 2. The traverseHypertree operator in Chisel.

find those rules whose lefthand side unifies with the term and use the function traverseHypertree to compute the corresponding hypernode.

In this way, traversalHypertree assigns each rule label Q to a particular set, either orange or olive, where these sets are defined as follows:

$$orangeSet := \{Q \in nodes(\mathcal{T}) \mid \exists Q' \in subtree(Q, \mathcal{T}) : Q' \in \text{ContextUpdates}\}$$
$$oliveSet := \{Q \in nodes(\mathcal{T}) \mid \forall Q' \in subtree(Q, \mathcal{T}) : Q' \notin \text{ContextUpdates}\}$$

The `orangeSet` contains Qs that are the root of a subtree containing context-updates while `oliveSet` is context-updates free. Assuming the given theory has a terminating algorithm for unification,[3] the termination of the algorithm in Fig. 2 is ensured by the fact that the specification S has a finite number of rules, and that any rule in T that was already added to either `orange` or `olive` set is not unfolded anymore. We give next an example that provides the intuition about the synthesis process.

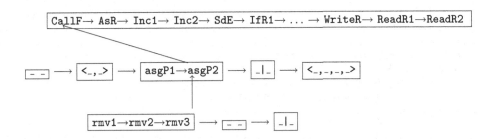

Fig. 3. The hyper-tree constructed for WhileFun.

Example 2. The first part of the hyper-tree T_{WhileFun}, constructed for WhileFun semantics, is depicted in Fig. 3. The memory-stack operator discovered here at the leaves level is $\_|\_$, which is obtained by the explicit memory-stack policy. The root of T_{WhileFun} contains the language constructs C where we show first `CallF` the rule label that specifies the semantics of a function call such as:

```
crl [CallF] :
  < Call fn(actPrms), st, rwb, fs > => < skip, st'', rwb', fs >
  if fn(Prms){ C } fs' := fs /\ < actPrms, st > => vals /\
     st' := assignPrms(actPrms, Prms, st | mt) /\
     < C, st', rwb, fs > => < skip, st'' | lenv', rwb', fs >  .
```

The first condition in the rule `CallF` extracts the function definition from the function set `fs` by means of a matching condition; the second condition evaluates the arguments passed to the function; the third condition uses the function `assignPrms` (listed below) to bind the parameters to the values previously obtained; and the fourth condition evaluates the body of the function in the new stack of environments.

---

[3] The current implementation of Maude provides a terminating unification algorithm [6] for theories without axioms and for combinations of operators with the axioms A, C, AC, ACU, CU, U, Ul, and Ur (where A stands for associativity, C for commutativity, U for identity or unit, Ul for left identity or unit, and Ur for right identity or unit). If the theory does not fulfill the requirements it would be possible to implement a mechanism in Chisel to give a warning; however, for the time being we just focus on the syntheses mechanisms.

```
op assignPrms : ExpL VarL ESt -> ESt .
eq [asgP1]   : assignPrms(nv, nv, ro) = ro .
eq [asgP2]   : assignPrms((N,EL), (X,VVs), mu | ro) =
                   assignPrms(EL, VVs, mu | remove(ro, X) (X = N)) .
```

The function `assignPrms` receives a list of expressions, a list of variables, and a stack of environments as arguments and traverses the lists removing the previous value associated to the variable at the top of the stack and binding it to the new one. Furthermore, the rules `rmv1` and `rmv2` for the `remove` operator used in `asgP2` to remove an element X from the commutative list `ro` are standardly specified as follows:

```
op remove : Env Variable -> Env .
eq [rmv1] : remove(mt, X) = mt .
eq [rmv2] : remove(X = V ro, X) = ro .
eq [rmv3] : remove(ro, X) = ro [owise] .
```

The first equation `rmv1` specifies the case when the we search X in the empty environment `mt`. The equation `rmv1` uses associative-commutative matching to identify X in the environment. Note that the associative-commutative matching could be applied for the environment variable of sort `Env` due to the `Env` constructor operator _ _ which is defined as associative, commutative, and with `mt` as unit element, i.e., op __ : Env Env -> Env [ctor comm assoc id: mt]. The equation `rmv3` is applied in the case when neither `rmv1` nor `rmv2` cannot be applied, via the [owise] option.

5   Context-Updates Refinement

This section describes how the dynamic characterization of context-updates is implemented and used for the refinement of the set $\mathcal{O}$ obtained by the context-updates synthesis.

First, similarly to the stack memory policy, we detect syntactic constructs that produce code sequencing. Namely, a sequencing syntactic construct is defined by a non-commutative operator with arity $\mathcal{C}\,\mathcal{C}$ and co-arity $\mathcal{C}$. For example, in WhileFun a sequencing operator is _; _.

We recall that the program p is parsed into a term tree t_p based on context free grammar defined by $\mathcal{C}$. We define the *code list* L_p as the flattening of p into a list of instructions (i.e., unit elements in $\mathcal{C}$) obtained by the preorder traversal of t_p's subtrees that represent the children of some sequencing operator in t_p. In Fig. 4 (i) and (ii) we give an example of a program p and the associated tree t_p, respectively, while (iii) describes the list L_p.

Also, we denote by $[L_p]_{fn}$ the set function definitions in p:

$$\{L_p(k)..L_p(k+n-1) \mid L_p(k) \in \mathcal{C}_{fn} \text{ and } (L_p(k+n) \in \mathcal{C}_{fn} \text{ or } L_p(k+n) = \epsilon)$$
$$\text{and } \forall i = k+1..k+n-1 : L_p(i) \notin \mathcal{C}_{fn}\}$$

where $L_p(i)$ represents the i-th element of the list L_p and $\mathcal{C}_{fn}$ is the set of program constructs representing function declarations.

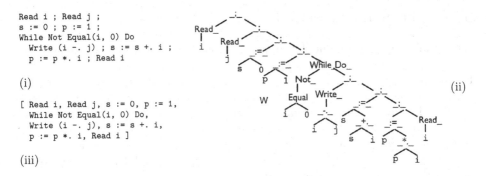

Fig. 4. The code list L_p (iii) for the program p (i) and parsed program term t_p (ii).

Second, given a set of execution traces Π_p of a program p, as defined in Sect. 3, we denote its elements by ϖ, i.e., an execution path of p w.r.t. $\mathcal{S}$. Furthermore, we denote by π the filtering of ϖ w.r.t. the application of the rules in $\Longrightarrow$. Namely, we only preserve in π the terms ϖ_i which match the *lhs* of a rule in $\Longrightarrow$. The executions traces ϖ and their filtering into π are obtained using the Maude debugger tool [18]. We use the standard notation for π, namely $|\pi|$ represents the length of the path, while $\pi_i, i \in \{0, \ldots, |\pi|\}$, represents the i-th element of the path. Note that π_0 is ϵ, the empty execution list.

Definition 2. *The property φ w.r.t. Π_p is defined as follows:*

$$\forall_\varsigma \in \mathcal{O}, \; \forall \varpi \in \Pi_p, \pi := filter_\mathcal{C}(\varpi), \; \forall i \in 1..|\pi| : \pi_i = \varsigma \implies$$
$$(\pi_{i-1}\pi_i \in L_p \implies \varsigma \in \mathcal{O}_r) \wedge$$
$$(\pi_{i-1}\pi_i \notin L_p \wedge (\pi_{i-1}, \pi_i) \in [L_p]_{fn} \implies \varsigma \in \mathcal{O}_g) \wedge$$
$$(\pi_{i-1}\pi_i \notin L_p \wedge (\pi_{i-1}, \pi_i) \notin [L_p]_{fn} \implies \varsigma \in \mathcal{O}_f)$$

Finally, based on **DC**, the dynamic characterization of context-updates, the definition of the property φ identifies separator instructions ς into the sets $\mathcal{O}_f$ (i.e., the separators that delimitate words pertaining to different functions in L_p) and $\mathcal{O}_g$ (i.e., the separators that delimitate words pertaining to the same function). The remaining operators are residual, part of $\mathcal{O}_r$, and are obtained in $\mathcal{O}$ due to the over-approximation character of the context-updates synthesis. Note that the residues $\mathcal{O}_r$ are constructs that may execute in programs' sequential order given by L_p; the gotos $\mathcal{O}_g$ and function calls $\mathcal{O}_f$ are constructs that break the sequential order for either jumping inside the current function body, or to another function, respectively. If the sets $\mathcal{O}_r$, $\mathcal{O}_g$, and $\mathcal{O}_f$ do not form a partition we use the remaining elements in $\mathcal{O}$ to signal counterexamples for the context-updates inference phase.

Next we describe the sets *TP* of benchmark tests, the function *TestTech* we used for the experimental semantics WhileFun and MIPS.

6   Experiments in Chisel

We evaluate our technique for dynamic characterization of context-updates on a set of programs TP provided by a real-time systems benchmark called PapaBench [16]. The *TestTech* function used to generate input test is based on a path coverage testing provided by the tool PathCrawler [13]. Next, we present the PapaBench benchmark forming the set TP, followed by the combined workflow of Chisel and PathCrawler where PathCrawler is used to generate the input states $In(p), \forall p \in TP$ and Chisel uses the Maude debugger to produce the execution traces $\Pi_p, \forall p \in TP$ which are later used with φ and L_p to refine the set of context-updates $\mathcal{O}$ obtained by **SC**.

PapaBench is extracted from a real-time design for an Unmanned Aerial Vehicle (UAV) application. The code presents the characteristics of an avionics application, and by extension, of a real-time design. First, it is *modular* at both structural and functional code levels; in this latter case there are several (exclusive) functional modes. Second, it contains a *global scheduling* to handle the high-level interleaving of the different functionalities. PapaBench has two communicating applications: a command management called fly_by_wire and a navigation management called autopilot. The functionalities are referred to as tasks and both these applications execute these tasks in control loops (i.e., the so-called *global schedulings*). The application fly_by_wire has the following five tasks: T1 - receive_radio_commands, T2 - send_data_to_autopilot, T3 - receive_data_from_autopilot, T4 - transmit_servos and T5 - check_failsafe. The application autopilot has the following eight tasks: T6 - manage_radio_commands, T7 - control_stabilization, T8 - send_data_to_fbw, T9 - receive_gps_data, T10 - control_navigation, T11 - control_altitude, T12 - control_climb and T13 - manage_reporting.

Semantically, PapaBench features two interacting functionality modes: manual and automatic. In the manual mode, the execution of the radio command task T1 triggers the task T2 responsible with data transmission to the autopilot application. In turn, autopilot analyzes this data and responds to the fly_by_wire application (i.e., task T8) the necessary information on the radio commands, task T6 and the flight stabilization, task T7 for processing and issuing commands, in tasks T3 and T4. The autopilot triggers the automatic mode when it receives GPS coordinates, task T9 and enables navigation, altitude and climb control, tasks T10, T11 and respectively T12. Finally, fly_by_wire handles failure checking with task T5 and autopilot uses a parameter report manager, as task T13.

We conduct our experiments on the following settings: we run Chisel with Maude (and Full-Maude) 2.7.1 on a MacBook Pro 2.5 GHz, 4 GB RAM, with PapaBench version 0.4 (for the WhileFun code) and the gcc 4.7.1 cross-compiler to obtain MIPS code (and with sufficient traceability to check the corresponding program slices at the high- and low-levels). The results of the context-updates synthesis in Chisel are refined with the path-coverage testing of PathCrawler. Briefly, the PathCrawler tool automatically generates test sets for a subset of C (and hence of our considered WhileFun language) with complete

Application fly_by_wire	LOC (WhileFun)	LOC (MIPS)	# Vars	# Test cases	#Total paths	Branch coverage
T1	119	534	19	54	75	95.45%
T2	59	329	21	11	14	100%
T3	82	501	26	37	40	92.86%
T4	50	235	15	60*	> 15*	>50%*
T5	66	453	16	27	27	92.86%
Application autopilot	LOC (WhileFun)	LOC (MIPS)	# Vars	# Test cases	#Total paths	Branch coverage
T6	306	1329	31	173	236	87.50%
T7	57	426	19	181	183	100%
T8	54	219	13	48	72	100%
T9	87	617	32	59	97	100%
T10	102	1002	25	60	90	95%
T11	15	90	10	11	11	100%
T12	49	363	23	78	102	100%
T13	240	1535	18	41	400	98.75%

Fig. 5. Refinement phase - testing coverage for PapaBench tasks using PathCrawler. *Test cases from multiple runs of PathCrawler.

coverage of all feasible execution paths. The path-coverage strategy uses propagation of symbolic values coupled with constraint solving support.

Our context-updates refinement with PathCrawler generates test sets for imperative code and uses gcc without optimizations to obtain test sets for the binary code. We report the path-coverage strategy using PathCrawler on PapaBench, in Fig. 5. Whereas code compilation without optimizations does not guarantee the exact preservation of the high-level test statements, in this paper we assume an one-to-one mapping of tests. The last two columns of Fig. 5 (i.e., Total paths and Branch coverage) show the PathCrawler results on the total number of covered paths and the branch coverage factor for the imperative code. Under the previously mentioned assumption, we consider the same statistics to the MIPS code. The columns Vars and Test cases present the test size and respectively the necessary number of test cases to report path coverage. We use PathCrawler to generate 840 test sets for the 13 tasks of autopilot and fly_by_wire, with significant branch coverage for all but task T4. In this case, PathCrawler guarantees at least a 50% branch coverage (i.e., certain variables consider restricted domain values) but it fails to return a result for a less constraint variable set. We vary the domain values for several variables and collect multiple instances of PathCrawler on T4 code.

The reduction factors obtained for the context-updates synthesis with path-coverage refinement are the same (and hence not reported again in Fig. 5) as in [4], whereas the path-coverage strategy is more powerful than the rule-coverage strategy. The first results [21] on PapaBench required manual annotation of the context-updates. In the current work and its previous draft [4] we automatically extract the context-updates set which is then refined with path-coverage and respectively rule-coverage testing. Because the formal language specifications are given as rewriting logic theories, we initially drafted, in [4], a testing methodology based on rule-coverage. As such, we randomly generated test cases in an attempt to cover a significant part of the program path (because the rule-coverage is agnostic to the program semantics). For particular programs and with carefully designed set of random test cases, it is possible to cover the exact set of language constructs, as we shown in [4]. But in general it is difficult to report coverage percentages in the rule-based testing. The current work with path-coverage testing reports, as for [4] the exact results for WhileFun while for MIPS the over-approximation at the synthesis phase is too large (the synthesized set of context-updates for MIPS includes most of the language instructions). Hence, the refinement phase, which is an under-approximation of the synthesized context-updates, is essential for context-updates synthesis in MIPS. As such, PathCrawler offers accurate path-coverage factors to exercise, in a systematic way, the most (if not all) context-updates constructs in the MIPS code.

7   Concluding Remarks and Future Work

In this paper we have presented a generic synthesis method for context-updates synthesis, directly from formal language semantics written in Maude. The synthesis strategy performs a context-updates over-approximation, followed by an under-approximation refinement based on a path-coverage strategy (provided by a specialized tool – PathCrawler). We integrated our method in Chisel, a Maude tool that can perform generic program slicing. We experimented with imperative and assembly language semantics on a standard avionics application.

As ongoing work we focus on a more complex strategy for the refinement step by using more evolved testing strategies. For future work, we plan to extend the language with pointers, hence supporting more complex memory policies based on a more refined memory model. Finally, our aim is to introduce concurrency in the framework so that we can cover and test out proposed methodology on a larger and significant class of programming languages.

Acknowledgements. The authors would like to thank the anonymous reviewers for their valuable comments to improve the quality of the paper.

References

1. Abelson, H., Sussman, G.J.: Structure and Interpretation of Computer Programs. MIT Press, Cambridge (1985)
2. Alpuente, M., Ballis, D., Frechina, F., Sapiña, J.: Combining runtime checking and slicing to improve Maude error diagnosis. In: Martí-Oliet, N., Ölveczky, P.C., Talcott, C. (eds.) Logic, Rewriting, and Concurrency. LNCS, vol. 9200, pp. 72–96. Springer, Cham (2015). https://doi.org/10.1007/978-3-319-23165-5_3

3. Asăvoae, I.M., Asăvoae, M., Riesco, A.: Towards a formal semantics-based technique for interprocedural slicing. In: Albert, E., Sekerinski, E. (eds.) IFM 2014. LNCS, vol. 8739, pp. 291–306. Springer, Cham (2014). https://doi.org/10.1007/978-3-319-10181-1_18
4. Asavoae, I.M., Asavoae, M., Riesco, A.: Context-updates analysis and refinement in Chisel. CoRR, abs/1709.06897 (2017)
5. Binkley, D., Gold, N., Harman, M., Islam, S., Krinke, J., Yoo, S.: ORBS: language-independent program slicing. In: FSE 2014, pp. 109–120 (2014)
6. Clavel, M., Durán, F., Eker, S., Escobar, S., Lincoln, P., Martí-Oliet, N., Meseguer, J., Talcott, C.: Maude manual (Version 2.7.1), July 2016. http://maude.cs.uiuc.edu/maude2-manual
7. Clavel, M., Duran, F., Eker, S., Lincoln, P., Marti-Oliet, N., Meseguer, J., Talcott, C.: All About Maude. LNCS, vol. 4350. Springer, Heidelberg (2007). https://doi.org/10.1007/978-3-540-71999-1
8. Field, J., Ramalingam, G., Tip, F.: Parametric program slicing. In: POPL, pp. 379–392. ACM Press (1995)
9. Heintze, N., Riecke, J.G.: The sLam calculus: programming with secrecy and integrity. In: POPL, pp. 365–377 (1998)
10. Hennessy, M.: The Semantics of Programming Languages: An Elementary Introduction Using Structural Operational Semantics. Wiley, New York (1990)
11. Horwitz, S., Reps, T., Binkley, D.: Interprocedural slicing using dependence graphs. In: PLDI, pp. 35–46 (1988)
12. Kirchner, F., Kosmatov, N., Prevosto, V., Signoles, J., Yakobowski, B.: Frama-C: a software analysis perspective. Formal Asp. Comput. **27**(3), 573–609 (2015)
13. Kosmatov, N., Williams, N., Botella, B., Roger, M., Chebaro, O.: A lesson on structural testing with pathcrawler-online.com. In: Brucker, A.D., Julliand, J. (eds.) TAP 2012. LNCS, vol. 7305, pp. 169–175. Springer, Heidelberg (2012). https://doi.org/10.1007/978-3-642-30473-6_15
14. Langdon, W.B., Yoo, S., Harman, M.: Inferring automatic test oracles. In: ICSE, pp. 5–6 (2017)
15. Meseguer, J., Rosu, G.: The rewriting logic semantics project. TCS **373**(3), 213–237 (2007)
16. Nemer, F., Casse, H., Sainrat, P., Bahsoun, J.P., Michiel, M.D.: Papabench: a free real-time benchmark. In: WCET (2006)
17. Petricek, T., Orchard, D.A., Mycroft, A.: Coeffects: a calculus of context-dependent computation. In: ICFP, pp. 123–135 (2014)
18. Riesco, A.: Using big-step and small-step semantics in Maude to perform declarative debugging. In: Codish, M., Sumii, E. (eds.) FLOPS 2014. LNCS, vol. 8475, pp. 52–68. Springer, Cham (2014). https://doi.org/10.1007/978-3-319-07151-0_4
19. Riesco, A., Asăvoae, I.M., Asăvoae, M.: A generic program slicing technique based on language definitions. In: Martí-Oliet, N., Palomino, M. (eds.) WADT 2012. LNCS, vol. 7841, pp. 248–264. Springer, Heidelberg (2013). https://doi.org/10.1007/978-3-642-37635-1_15
20. Riesco, A., Asavoae, I.M., Asavoae, M.: Memory policy analysis for semantics specifications in Maude. In: Falaschi, M. (ed.) LOPSTR 2015. LNCS, vol. 9527, pp. 293–310. Springer, Cham (2015). https://doi.org/10.1007/978-3-319-27436-2_18
21. Riesco, A., Asăvoae, I.M., Asăvoae, M.: Slicing from formal semantics: Chisel. In: Huisman, M., Rubin, J. (eds.) FASE 2017. LNCS, vol. 10202, pp. 374–378. Springer, Heidelberg (2017). https://doi.org/10.1007/978-3-662-54494-5_21
22. Rosu, G.: K - a semantic framework for programming languages and formal analysis tools. In: Dependable Software Systems Engineering. IOS Press (2017)

23. Rosu, G.: Matching logic. Logical Methods in Computer Science (2017, to appear)
24. Rosu, G., Serbanuta, T.F.: An overview of the K semantic framework. J. Logic Algebraic Program. **79**(6), 397–434 (2010)
25. Sharir, M., Pnueli, A.: Two approaches to interprocedural data flow analysis. New York University, Computer Science Department, New York, NY (1978)
26. Talpin, J., Jouvelot, P.: The type and effect discipline. In: LICS, pp. 162–173 (1992)
27. Tip, F.: A survey of program slicing techniques. J. Program. Lang. **3**(3), 121–189 (1995)
28. Weiser, M.: Program slicing. In: ICSE, pp. 439–449. IEEE Press (1981)

Author Index

Printed in the United States
By Bookmasters